June 15–17, 2011
Innsbruck, Austria

I0031386

**Association for
Computing Machinery**

Advancing Computing as a Science & Profession

SACMAT'11

Proceedings of the 16th ACM Symposium on
Access Control Models and Technologies

Sponsored by:
ACM SIGSAC

Supported by:
**University of Innsbruck, Arizona State University,
German Chapter of the ACM & Softnet Austria**

**Association for
Computing Machinery**

Advancing Computing as a Science & Profession

The Association for Computing Machinery
2 Penn Plaza, Suite 701
New York, New York 10121-0701

ISBN: 978-1-4503-0721-5 (Digital)

ISBN: 978-1-4503-1387-2 (Print)

Additional copies may be ordered prepaid from:

ACM Order Department
PO Box 30777
New York, NY 10087-0777, USA

Phone: 1-800-342-6626 (USA and Canada)
+1-212-626-0500 (Global)
Fax: +1-212-944-1318
E-mail: acmhelp@acm.org
Hours of Operation: 8:30 am – 4:30 pm ET

Printed in the USA

Foreword

It is our great pleasure to welcome you to the *16th ACM Symposium on Access Control Models and Technologies (SACMAT 2011)*. This year's symposium continues its tradition of being the premier forum for presentation of research results on leading edge issues of access control, including models, systems, applications, and theory.

The call for papers attracted 52 submissions from Asia, Canada, Europe, Africa, and the United States. The program committee accepted 16 papers that cover a variety of topics, including next generation access control models, engineering and analysis techniques for access control policies and models, and security administration. New this year in the program is a demo session with five demos covering topics such as security visualization, access control federation and social networks. In addition the program includes a panel on usability of access control models and systems from the perspective of the nonspecialist, and keynote talks by Professors David Basin and Jean-Pierre Seifert. We hope that these proceedings will serve as a valuable reference for security researchers and developers.

Putting together *SACMAT 2011* was a team effort. First of all, we would like to thank the authors for submitting to the symposium, the keynote speakers for graciously accepting our invitation, the demo presenters and panelists for contributing to the program. We are grateful to the program committee members and external reviewers for their efforts in reviewing the papers. Special thanks go to Lujo Bauer (Panels Chair), Andreas Schaad (Demonstrations Chair), Dongwan Shin (Webmaster), Mahesh Tripunitara (Publicity Chair) and Jaideep Vaidya (Proceedings Chair) for their help in organizing and publicizing the symposium. We are grateful to the Chair of the Steering Committee, Gail-Joon Ahn, for providing valuable advice. Many thanks also go to the local team at the University of Innsbruck, in particular Anja Niedworok and Thomas Schrettl.

We would like to thank our sponsor, ACM SIGSAC, for their continued support of this symposium. We would also like to acknowledge the valuable donations provided by University of Innsbruck, SOFTNET Austria and the German Chapter of the ACM.

We hope that you will find this program interesting and that the symposium will provide you with a valuable opportunity to share ideas with other researchers and practitioners from institutions around the world.

Ruth Breu
SACMAT'11
General Chair
University of Innsbruck, Austria

Jason Crampton
SACMAT'11
Co-Program Chair
Royal Holloway,
University of London, UK

Jorge Lobo
SACMAT'11
Co-Program Chair
IBM, USA

Table of Contents

Keynote Address
Session Chair: Jorge Lobo *(IBM)*

Session 1: Distributed Processing and Access Control
Session Chair: Murat Kantarcioglu *(University of Texas at Dallas)*

Session 2: Policy Languages
Session Chair: Mahesh Tripunitara *(University of Waterloo)*

Session 4: Data Flow and Access Control
Session Chair: Elisa Bertino *(Purdue University)*

Session 5: Applications
Session Chair: Philip Fong *(University of Calgary)*

System Demonstrations
Session Chair: Andreas Schaad *(SAP Labs)*

Panel
Session Chair: Robert W. Reeder *(Microsoft)*

Session 6: Policy Analysis and Obligations
Session Chair: Michael Huth *(Imperial College)*

Author Index

SACMAT 2011 Organization

General Chair: Ruth Breu *(University of Innsbruck, Austria)*

Program Chairs: Jason Crampton *(Royal Holloway, University of London, UK)*
Jorge Lobo *(IBM, USA)*

Panels Chair: Lujo Bauer *(Carnegie Mellon University, USA)*

Demonstrations Chair: Andreas Schaad *(SAP Labs, Germany)*

Proceedings Chair: Jaideep Vaidya *(Rutgers University, USA)*

Publicity Chair: Mahesh Tripunitara *(University of Waterloo, Canada)*

Webmaster: Dongwan Shin *(New Mexico Tech, USA)*

Steering Committee Chair: Gail-Joon Ahn *(Arizona State University, USA)*

Steering Committee: Axel Kern *(Beta Systems Software AG, Germany)*
Bhavani Thuraisingham *(University of Texas at Dallas, USA)*
Indrakshi Ray *(Colorado State University, USA)*
Ninghui Li *(Purdue University, USA)*
James Joshi *(University of Pittsburgh, USA)*

Program Committee: Gail-Joon Ahn *(Arizona State University, USA)*
Vijay Atluri *(Rutgers University, USA)*
Steve Barker *(King's College, London University, UK)*
David Basin *(ETH Zurich, Switzerland)*
Lujo Bauer *(Carnegie Mellon University, USA)*
Moritz Becker *(Microsoft Research, Cambridge, UK)*
Elisa Bertino *(Purdue University, USA)*
Konstantin Beznosov *(University of British Columbia, Canada)*
Barbara Carminati *(University of Insubria, Italy)*
Jason Crampton *(Royal Holloway, University of London, UK)*
David M. Eyers *(University of Cambridge, UK)*
David Ferraiolo *(National Institute of Standards and Technology, USA)*
Elena Ferrari *(University of Insubria, Italy)*
Philip Fong *(University of Calgary, Canada)*
Michael Huth *(Imperial College, UK)*
Trent Jaeger *(Pennsylvania State University, USA)*
James Joshi *(University of Pittsburgh, USA)*
Murat Kantarcioglu *(University of Texas at Dallas, USA)*
Adam Lee *(University of Pittsburgh, USA)*
Ninghui Li *(Purdue University, USA)*
Jorge Lobo *(IBM, USA)*

SACMAT 2011 Sponsor & Supporters

Sponsor:

Supporters:    University of Innsbruck

   Arizona State University

   German Chapter of the ACM

   Softnet Austria

A Decade of Model-Driven Security

David Basin
ETH Zurich
Switzerland
basin@inf.ethz.ch

Manuel Clavel
IMDEA Software Institute
Universidad Complutense
Madrid, Spain
manuel.clavel@imdea.org

Marina Egea
IMDEA Software Institute
Madrid, Spain
marina.egea@imdea.org

ABSTRACT

In model-driven development, system designs are specified using graphical modeling languages like UML and system artifacts such as code and configuration data are automatically generated from the models. Model-driven security is a specialization of this paradigm, where system designs are modeled together with their security requirements and security infrastructures are directly generated from the models.

Over the past decade, we have explored different facets of model-driven security. This research includes different modeling languages, code generators, model analysis tools, and even model transformations. For example, in multi-tier systems, we used model transformations to transform a security policy, formulated for a system's data model, to a security policy governing the behavior of the system's graphical user interface. In this paper, we survey progress made, tool support, and case studies, which attest to the flexibility and power of such a multi-faceted approach to building secure systems.

Categories and Subject Descriptors

D.2 [**Software Engineering**]: General

General Terms

Security, Languages, Design, Verification

Keywords

Model-driven security, model-driven development, model analysis, model transformation, code generation

1. INTRODUCTION

Model building is at the heart of system design. This is true in many engineering disciplines and is increasingly the case in software engineering. But model building is not an end in itself and certainly does not come for free: it takes time and knowledge to build good models and effort to keep

SACMAT'11, June 15–17, 2011, Innsbruck, Austria.
Copyright 2011 ACM 978-1-4503-0688-1/11/06 ...$10.00.

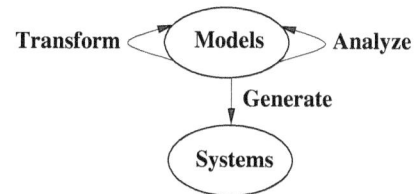

Figure 1: Use of Models in Model-Driven Security

them synchronized with end products. For this effort to be worthwhile, there must be added value.

In this paper, we examine some of the advantages over more traditional approaches to model building in the domain of security-critical systems. In particular, we survey our work [32, 9, 5, 6, 15, 7, 18] over the past decade on *model-driven security*. We show that models can be used for the following four activities in the development of secure systems:

A1. Precisely documenting security requirements together with design requirements.

A2. Analyzing security requirements.

A3. Model-based transformation, such as migrating security policies on application data to policies for other system layers or artifacts.

A4. Generating code, including complete, configured security infrastructures.

Figure 1 depicts these activities and their interrelationships. Designers specify security-design models that combine security and design requirements (A1). As our modeling languages have a well-defined semantics, we can formally analyze these designs (A2). When designing secure systems, security may be relevant at different system layers or views. Using model transformations, we can migrate a security policy from one model to other models (A3). Finally, we can use tools to automatically generate code and other system artifacts directly from the models (A4).

In the subsequent sections we explore these activities in more detail. In doing so, we highlight the central and multifaceted role that models can play in developing secure systems. We also explain the development of our ideas, advances in tool support, and applications.

Organization. In Section 2 we introduce security-design models and give examples. In Sections 3 and 4 we present different ways to analyze and transform such models. In

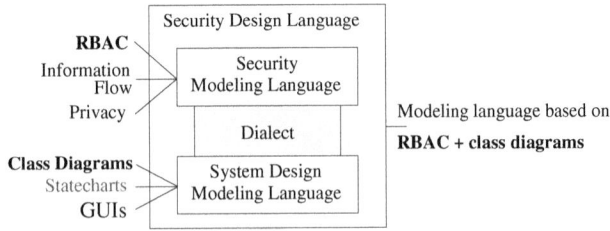

Figure 2: Model-languages and their Combination

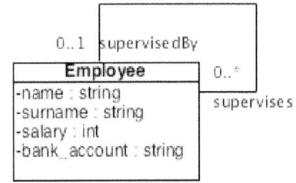

Figure 3: ComponentUML model for Employee.

Section 5 we describe SSG, a tool that supports the design, analysis, and transformation of security-design models for developing security-aware GUIs for data-centric applications. In Section 6 we report on our experience applying model-driven security in practice. Finally, we discuss related work in Section 7 and draw conclusions in Section 8.

2. MODELING

2.1 Languages

Model-driven security is a specialization of *model-driven development*, also called *model-driven architecture* [35], to the domain of security. The crucial part of this specialization concerns the modeling language. Instead of adopting a one-language-fits-all approach, we proposed a general schema for integrating security requirements into system design models. The main idea is to define security modeling languages that are general in that they leave open the nature of the protected resources, i.e., whether these resources are data, business objects, processes, controller states, etc. Figure 2 provides examples of different security notions which could be specified using a security modeling language (top-left) that one might integrate with different design modeling languages (bottom-left), resulting in a security-design modeling language (right side). For example, one might combine a modeling language for Role Base Access Control (RBAC) with Class Diagrams, as indicated in bold in the figure. This combination is made by defining a dialect (or "glue"), which identifies elements of the design language as the protected resources of the security language. In this way, we can flexibly define languages for formulating different kinds of system designs along with their security requirements.

In previous work, we defined a security modeling language called *SecureUML* for modeling authorization policies based on RBAC extended with constraints [9]. We initially combined SecureUML with a design modeling language based on class diagrams, called *ComponentUML*, and with a language based on state diagrams, called *ControllerUML*. We later [7] combined SecureUML with a language for modeling graphical user interfaces for data-centric applications, called *ActionGUI*.

2.2 Example

We introduce an example, which we use in this paper to illustrate the use of the modeling languages mentioned above, namely, ComponentUML, SecureUML+Component-UML, ActionGUI, and SecureUML+ActionGUI. In subsequent sections we use this example to illustrate model-based analysis and transformation techniques.

ComponentUML is a simple language for modeling component-based systems. Essentially, it provides a subset of UML class models: *entities* can be related by *associations* and may have *attributes* and *methods*.

In Figure 3 we use ComponentUML to model the data associated with a company's employees. In our example, an employee has a name, a surname, a salary, and a bank account. Also, an employee may possibly have a supervisor and may in turn supervise other employees. In the terminology of ComponentUML, `Employee` is an *entity*; name, surname, salary, and bank account are *attributes*, and supervisedBy and supervises are *association-ends*.

We can refine this model by adding constraints (also called *invariants*) to it. For example, we can specify that:

1. There is exactly one employee who has no supervisor.

2. Nobody is his (or her) own supervisor.

We use the Object Constraint Language (OCL) [36] to add constraints to ComponentUML models. For example, the above constraints can be formalized in OCL as follows:

(1) Employee.allInstances()
    ->one(e|e.supervisedBy->isEmpty())
(2) Employee.allInstances()
    ->forAll(e|e.supervisedBy->excludes(e))

SecureUML+ComponentUML is the combination of SecureUML with ComponentUML. As already mentioned, SecureUML extends RBAC with authorization constraints, which enable the specification of policies that depend on the system state. SecureUML leaves open what the protected resources are and which actions these resources offer to clients; both of these depend on the primitives for constructing models in the associated system-design modeling language. In the case of SecureUML+ComponentUML, the protected resources are the entities, as well as their attributes, methods, and association-ends. The actions that are offered to clients are to create or delete entities, update or read the entity's properties, and execute the entity's methods.

In Figure 4 we use SecureUML+ComponentUML to model the company's authorization policy for accessing the data associated with its employees, according to the employee data model in Figure 3. In this example, permissions are assigned to two non-disjoint sets of users: workers (any employee) and supervisors (any employee who supervises other employees). In the terminology of SecureUML, `Worker` and `Supervisor` are *roles*. Permissions in SecureUML are granted upon satisfaction of specific constraints, written in a simple extension of OCL.[1] Namely:

---

[1]The variables `self` and `caller` are interpreted as follows: `self` refers to the (root) resource being accessed and the variable `caller` refers to the user accessing the resource. In SecureUML+ComponentUML, the type of the variable `caller` must be an entity in the given model. In this ex-

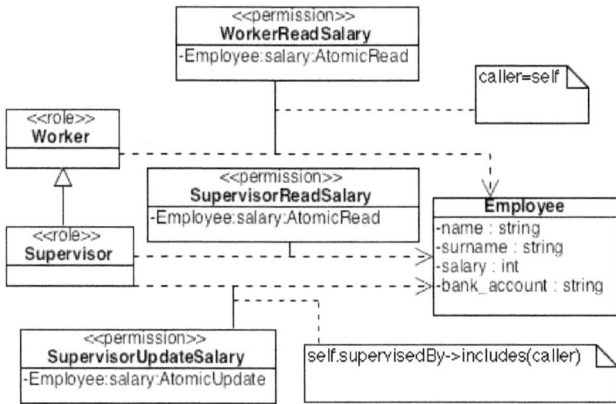

Figure 4: SecureUML+ComponentUML model for Employee.

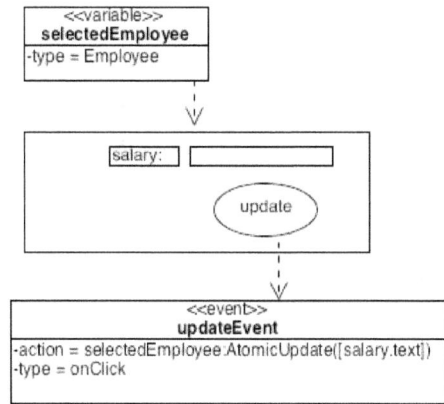

Figure 5: ActionGUI model for UpdateSalary window.

1. A worker is granted the permission to read an employee's salary (`Employee:salary:AtomicRead`), provided that it is its own salary (`caller=self`).

2. A supervisor is granted the permission to update an employee's salary (`Employee:salary:AtomicUpdate`), provided that he supervises this employee (`self.supervisedBy->includes(caller)`).

3. A supervisor is granted unrestricted permission to read any employee's salary (`Employee:salary:AtomicRead`), since no constraint is associated to this permission.

Finally, in our model, the role `Worker` generalizes the role `Supervisor`. This means that supervisors inherit all the permissions granted to workers, along with their associated authorization constraints.

Note that when modeling this authorization policy, our modeler probably has in mind the invariant (2) as a constraint on the data model: nobody can be his own supervisor. This prevents a (self-)supervisor from changing his own salary. We will return to this point in Section 3.

ActionGUI is a language for modeling graphical user interfaces (GUIs) for data-centric applications. In a nutshell, a GUI consists of *widgets*, which may be containers (e.g., windows, combo-boxes, or tables) or basic widgets (e.g., buttons, labels, or entries). A widget may have a set of associated *events* (e.g., entering or leaving a widget, creating a widget, or clicking on a widget.) Then, an event may trigger a set of (possibly conditional) *actions* on the widgets themselves (e.g., opening and closing a widget) or on the application data (e.g., reading or updating an attribute). Also, a widget may have associated *variables* which hold information to be used by the actions triggered by the events associated to the widget.

In Figure 5 we use ActionGUI to model a window for updating a (previously selected) employee's salary. The window has an entry labelled `salary`, and a button labelled `update`. In addition, it has a variable `selectedEmployee`, that holds a reference to an instance of the entity `Employee`; in this example, this is the employee whose salary will be updated. Within the window model, the modeler can refer

ample, the type of the variable `caller` is `Employee`, which means that the users accessing the resources will be employees, i.e., instances of the entity `Employee`.

to the string input by the user in the entry `salary` using the expression `salary.text` enclosed in square brackets. Notice that the button `update` supports an event `updateEvent`. In ActionGUI, each event has a type and, in our example, `updateEvent` has the type `onClick`. In this example, when the user clicks the `update` button, the salary of the `selectedEmployee` is updated (`selectedEmployee:salary:AtomicUpdate`) using as the parameter the string typed by the user in the entry `salary` (`[salary.text]`).

SecureUML+ActionGUI is the combination of SecureUML with ActionGUI. It provides a language for modeling security-aware GUIs. In the case of SecureUML+ActionGUI, the protected resources are the widgets, and the actions that are offered to clients are to execute the widgets's events.

In Figure 6 we use SecureUML+ActionGUI to model the authorization policy for executing the event `updateEvent` supported by the button `update` in the window modeled in Figure 5. In SecureUML+ActionGUI, authorization constraints are written using an extension of OCL where, as in the case of SecureUML+ComponentUML, the variable `caller` refers to the user who is accessing the resource (in this case, executing the event). In this model, only supervisors are granted permission to click on the `update` button (`update:onClick:AtomicExecute`) and, furthermore, they may only do this when they supervise the `selectedEmployee` (`selectedEmployee.supervisedBy->includes(caller)`).

The SecureUML+ActionGUI model in Figure 6 raises a number of "consistency" questions with respect to the SecureUML+ComponentUML model in Figure 4. For example, could a user who is not authorized to update the selected employee's salary still be permitted to click on the `update` button? Alternatively, could a user with this authorization fail to have permission to click on the `update` button? We will return to these questions in Section 3. On a more practical level, a question that also arises is whether it would be possible to automatically generate the model in Figure 6 from the models in Figures 4 and 5. We will explain how this can be done in Section 4.

3. ANALYSIS

Security-design models are formal objects and therefore one can reason about their properties. In our previous work, we have proposed formal techniques to answer questions

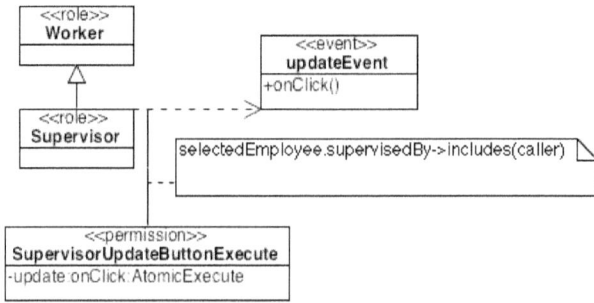

Figure 6: SecureUML+ActionGUI model for Up-dateSalary window.

about the meaning of security-design models at two different levels:

1. **The models themselves.** Here the questions are about the elements that are contained in a model and their relationships. For example, given a role, what are the actions that a user in this role can perform? Are there overlapping permissions for different roles? Are there two roles that have permission to perform the same set of actions?

2. **The models' instances.** Here the questions are about the scenarios that are consistent (or conformant) with the model, i.e., about all the valid instances of the model. For example, is there a scenario consistent with the model in which someone satisfying a property P_1 is allowed to perform an action on resources satisfying some other property P_2?

To answer questions about the models themselves in a semantically precise and meaningful way, we proposed in [6] a metamodel-based methodology consisting of: (i) formalizing these questions as queries in OCL, in the context of the metamodel combining SecureUML with the design language; and (ii) evaluating these OCL queries on the instance of the metamodel which corresponds to the model being analyzed. With respect to (i), [6] provides examples of non-trivial OCL queries about SecureUML+ComponentUML models. With respect to (ii), as reported in [13], current OCL evaluators can automatically answer complex queries about large collections (including up to a million objects) in less than 5 seconds. For example, in [6], an operation `allAtomics()` is defined in OCL that, given a role, returns the collection of atomic actions that a user in this role can perform upon the satisfaction of any associated constraints. Thus, by evaluating the expression `Supervisor.allAtomics()`, we can obtain all the atomic actions that supervisors are allowed to perform (again, upon satisfaction of the associated constraints) according to the model in Figure 4, namely, {`Employee:salary:AtomicRead`, `Employee:salary:AtomicUpdate`}. Recall that the expression `Supervisor.allAtomics()` is to be evaluated on the instance of the metamodel of SecureUML+ComponentUML corresponding to the model in Figure 4.

To answer questions about the model instances that are consistent with a given security-design model, we need to go beyond simple query evaluation and resort to theorem-proving techniques. Consider, for example, the access control policy model shown in Figure 4. Is the scenario in

which someone is allowed to change his own salary consistent with this model? First, by querying the model as explained above, we learn that only supervisors (i.e., users in the role `Supervisor`) can change employees' salaries (i.e., execute the action `Employee:salary:AtomicUpdate`). Second, by querying this model again, we see that supervisors can change employees' salaries only when these employees are under their supervision, as stated by the authorization constraint

    self.supervisedBy ->includes(caller)

which is associated to the permission `SupervisorUpdate-Salary`. Therefore, we can rephrase our initial query as: is there a scenario in which the following OCL expression evaluates to true?

```
(3) Employee.allInstances()->exists(self, caller|
    self.supervisedBy->includes(caller)
    and self=caller)
```

Recall that we intend to forbid self-supervision by imposing the invariant (2) on the employee data model. To answer our initial question (can someone change his own salary?) it is therefore sufficient to prove that for any scenario consistent with (2) then (3) must be false.

We currently answer such questions using a mapping from OCL to first-order logic that we introduced in [14]. Using this mapping, we can reformulate these questions as satisfiability problems in first-order logic and use theorem-proving tools (including SMT solvers, as reported in [14]) to automatically answer them. In Appendix A we give the satisfiability problem corresponding to this example, formulated in the syntax of the SMT solver Yices [19]. The answer automatically provided by Yices is **unsat**. Hence (2) and (3) cannot both be simultaneously true in any scenario of the model shown in Figure 3.

Another interesting question that can be answered using our mapping from OCL to first-order logic is the following: if an employee has no supervisor, is it possible at all to update his salary? This question can be rephrased as: is there a scenario in which the following expression evaluates to true?

```
(4) Employee.allInstances()->exists(self, caller|
    and self.supervisedBy->includes(caller)
    self.supervisedBy->isEmpty())
```

As before, the answer automatically provided by Yices is **unsat**. Thus (4) cannot be true in any scenario of the model shown in Figure 4.

4. TRANSFORMATION

In model-driven development, transformation is the way of using models to produce other development artifacts. The following types of transformations have been widely used in the model-driven development community.

Generation of Code and Execution Artifacts: Models may be mapped to code or other artifacts that affect the system's runtime behavior. When generating code, the transformation function amounts to a kind of translator or compiler. Examples of other artifacts generated are deployment and configuration data (e.g., for access control on an application server, database, firewall, operating system, etc.), which also affects the system's behavior.

Generation of Models: Models may be mapped to other models. In particular, when multiple models serve as input, one speaks of a many-models-to-model transformation. We will give an example of this shortly.

Generation of Test Cases: Test cases can be generated from models, e.g., to test an access control policy.

Below we elaborate on the first two possibilities, which we have pursued in model-driven security.

4.1 Code Generation

Originally [32, 8], we mainly used security-design models for generating code along with deployment and configuration data. We built translators that map models into access control infrastructures for distributed object-based systems. In particular, we built generators for systems conforming to the Enterprise JavaBeans (EJB) standard and Microsoft Enterprise Services for .NET. From models specifying secure components and secure controllers we generated access control infrastructures for multi-tier web applications. These ideas were integrated into several tools, both academic and commercial, e.g., the ArcStyler tool [28] of Interactive Objects GmbH.

We briefly describe the ideas behind code generation for security-design models in SecureUML+ComponentUML for an EJB platform. Given a model like that of Figure 4, our code generator produces Java code and access control configuration data stored in an XML configuration file (called a *deployment descriptor*). A class like `Employee`, which represents a persistent entity, is transformed to an EJB component of type *entity bean* with all necessary interfaces and an implementation class. Namely, each method in the class is transformed to a method declaration in the component interface of the respective entity bean and a method stub in the corresponding bean implementation class. Also, for each attribute, "getter" and "setter" access methods are generated for reading and writing the attribute value; association-ends are handled analogously.

The above describes routine code generation for the design part of a security-design model. For the security part, roles and permissions are mapped into an EJB security infrastructure based on RBAC. In particular, our translator maps the roles and permissions into XML formalizing which roles have access to which actions on which resources. Authorization constraints are translated to Java assertions that check these constraints at run time. For example, in Figure 4, we would generate the following RBAC configuration data for the permission `WorkerReadSalary`: anyone in the roles `Worker` or `Supervisor` can read the attribute `salary` in the `Employee` class, i.e., can execute the getter-method that reads the value of the attribute `salary`. Moreover, given the authorization constraint, we would generate an assertion, placed at the start of this getter method, that checks that the authenticated caller is the employee whose salary is being read, when the caller belongs to the role `Worker`.

4.2 Model Transformation

It is also possible to transform models into other models. Typically such transformations add details, specialize constructs, or change representations. An example of this is the specialization of platform-independent models to platform-specific models. In our work, we have explored a particular application of model transformation: how to consistently apply a security policy to multiple system layers. We see this as an important part of building effective security infrastructures, as we shall now explain.

Security is often built redundantly into systems. For example, in a web-application, access control may be enforced at all tiers: at the web server, in the back-end databases, and even in the GUI. There are good reasons for this. Redundant security controls is an example of defense in depth and is also necessary to prevent data access in unanticipated ways, for example, directly from the database thereby circumventing the web application server. Note that access control on the client is also important, but more from the usability rather than the security perspective. Namely, although client-side access control may be easy to circumvent, it enhances usability by presenting honest users an appropriate view of their options: unauthorized options can be suppressed and users can be prevented from entering states where they are unauthorized to perform any action, e.g., where their actions will result in security exceptions thrown by the application server or database.

This raises the following question: must one specify security policies separately for each of these tiers? The answer is "no" for many applications. Security can often be understood in terms of the criticality of data and an access control policy on data can be specified at the level of component (class) models, as discussed in Section 2. Afterwards, an access control policy modeled at the level of components may be lifted to other tiers. When the tiers are also modeled, this lifting can be accomplished using model transformation techniques and in a precise and meaningful way.

In our previous work [37, 7, 18] we have taken such a transformation-based approach to systematically lift security policies specified on data to policies governing graphical user interfaces. Under our proposal, the process of modeling a security-aware GUI has the following four parts.

1. Software engineers specify the application-data model.

2. Security engineers specify the security-design model.

3. GUI designers specify the application GUI model.

4. A many-models-to-model transformation automatically generates a security-aware GUI model from the security model and the GUI model.

We have implemented this transformation-based approach for generating security-aware GUIs using the Operational Query/View/Transformation (QVT) engine [20]. The many-models-to-model transformation at the core of this approach is ultimately defined in terms of *data actions*, since data actions are both controlled by the security policy and triggered by the events supported by the GUI.

Specifically, to generate a SecureUML+ActionGUI model, our model transformation proceeds in two steps.

Step 1: The model elements of the target model are created using the elements from the two source models. In particular, each role in the (source) SecureUML+ComponentUML model is copied, along with its generalization associations, to the (target) SecureUML+ActionGUI model. Afterwards, each widget in the (source) ActionGUI model is copied, along with its associated events and actions, to the (target) SecureUML+ActionGUI model.

Step 2: The permission assignments in the target model are created. Namely, for each role and each event in the (target) SecureUML+ActionGUI model, when the users in the role are allowed to perform all the data actions triggered by the event according to the (source) SecureUML+ComponentUML model, then a permission is created in the target model. This permission grants access to the role to execute the event, upon the satisfaction of the corresponding authorization constraints.[2]

Consider, for example, the security-design model and the GUI model shown in Figures 4 and 5. Using our many-models-to-model transformation, we automatically generate the security-aware GUI model shown in Figure 6. This model includes both the roles Worker and Supervisor, as well as the permission for the latter to execute the event of type onClick on the update button. Recall that this will trigger the action of updating the salary of the selectedEmployee. So, as expected, this permission is constrained by the following authorization: selectedEmployee.supervisedBy->includes(caller). Hence, to be authorized to click on the update button, the supervisor must be among the supervisors of the selectedEmployee.

In general, model transformations support problem decomposition during development where design aspects can be separated into different models which are later composed. As a methodology for designing security-aware GUIs, this approach supports the consistent propagation of a security policy from component models to GUI models and, via code generation, to GUI implementations. This decomposition also means that security engineers and GUI designers can independently model what they know best and maintain their models independently.

5. TOOL SUPPORT

As part of our work, we have developed a software-development environment, called SSG [18] for building security-aware graphical user interfaces for data-centric applications. SSG provides tool support for the four activities depicted in Figure 1: modeling, analysis, transformation, and generation.

SSG consists of a collection of plugins that have been developed for Eclipse. First, SSG contains three different editors for graphical modeling, which has been developed using the Eclipse Graphical Modeling Framework. These are (i) an editor for modeling application data using Component-UML; (ii) an editor for modeling the application's access control policy on data using SecureUML+ComponentUML; and (iii) an editor for modeling the application's graphical user interface using ActionGUI.

Second, SSG contains a plugin that allows modelers to use OCL to query their SecureUML+ComponentUML models, which corresponds to the first kind of model analysis described in Section 3. This plugin includes an OCL parser and an OCL evaluator [13], the latter serves to automatically answer queries about the elements (roles, permissions,

authorization constraints, actions, and resources) contained in models and their relationships. Moreover, a plugin is currently under construction to support the second kind of model analysis described in Section 3, namely, queries about the instances of SecureUML+ComponentUML models, using the mapping from OCL to first-order logic proposed in [14].

Third, SSG contains a QVT transformation that automatically performs the many-models-to-model transformation described in Section 4.2. It automatically transforms an ActionGUI model and a SecureUML+ComponentUML model (both sharing the same ComponentUML data model) into a SecureUML+ActionGUI model. The resulting model has the same behavioral properties as the one modeled by the given ActionGUI model, except that it is now security-aware with respect to the access control policy modeled by the SecureUML+ComponentUML model.

Finally, SSG includes a code generator, based on Java Emitter Templates (JET) [21], that automatically generates a full web application from a SecureUML+ActionGUI model. This application consists of a collection of PHP-web pages whose design and behavior implement those specified by the given model. In particular, windows are implemented as web pages. Thus, opening a window is implemented as loading the corresponding page and closing a window is implemented as loading the previously visited page. More interestingly, data actions (like creating or deleting entities and updating or reading their attributes) are implemented as MySQL statements on a data-base implementing the underlying ComponentUML data model. The code generator can also create this database for the user. Finally, permissions to execute events on widgets (like clicking a button or creating an entry or a text box) are implemented by conditional statements in the PHP-code responsible for interpreting those events. A key component of the SSG's code generator is a MySQL code generator [22, 17] for OCL, which translates into MySQL the OCL authorization constraints in the given SecureUML+ActionGUI model.

6. EXPERIENCE

In [15] we report on an industrial pilot project for assessing the benefits of model-driven security when applied to concrete software development projects. The project's goal was to enhance a test report configuration utility, developed in-house, with an access control policy. We used ComponentUML to model the functional requirements of the utility, and SecureUML+ComponentUML to model its access control policy. These requirements were provided to us in a five-page document listing fifty clauses in plain English. For example, users could choose from a pool of available test report configurations, which may include private, global, and default ones. Default configurations are in turn associated with individual test programs or with families of test programs. Since the permissions to create, edit, delete, or apply report configurations depended both on the user's role and on the properties (including the ownership) of the configurations, we extensively used OCL to formalize the corresponding authorization constraints.

Our experience in this project was very positive. Our security-design models helped us to understand (and discuss) the original requirements document by allowing us to independently model each clause based on its principal concern, whether functional or security-related. Their analysis

---

[2]Notice, however, that for these authorization constraints to be meaningful in the target model, they must also be transformed. Essentially, the variable self, which in the (source) SecureUML+ComponentUML refers to the data element being accessed by the user, must be replaced by the OCL expression that denotes, in the (source) ActionGUI model, the subject of the action triggered by the event.

prompted us to refine those requirements that were ambiguous, to eliminate those that were subsumed by others, and to discover those that were simply missing. Moreover, the models also provided a basis for refinement down to code. Overall, the use of security-design modeling languages provided the focal point for integrating security engineering into a model-driven software development process.

Another substantial case study was that of Lodderstedt [31], who used the model-driven security approach to construct secure web portals. As an extended example, he developed a secure version of the J2EE "Pet Store" application, which is a prototypical e-commerce application that demonstrates the use of the J2EE platform. The application features web front-ends for shopping, administration, and order processing. His application model consisted of 30 components and several front-end controllers. Lodderstedt extended this model with an access control policy formalizing the principle of least privilege, where a user is given only those access rights that are necessary to perform a job. The modeled policy comprised six roles and 60 permissions, 15 of which were restricted by authorization constraints. The corresponding infrastructure was generated automatically and consisted of roughly 5,000 lines of XML (overall application: 13,000) and 2,000 lines of Java source code (overall application: 20,000). This large expansion was due to the high level of abstraction provided by the security-design modeling languages used. Clearly, this much information cannot be managed practically at the source-code level.

7. RELATED WORK

Over the last decade, there has been substantial research on model-driven security. Here we report on related work in modeling, analysis, and transformation.

Modeling.

Numerous researchers have explored the use of UML-like languages for modeling role-based access control policies [1, 12, 11, 39, 3] and different kinds of security-design models [29, 16]. In the language UMLsec [29], for example, UML models are annotated with security requirements, such as confidentiality or secure information flow. Another prominent example is the Ponder specification language [16], which supports the rule-based formalization of authorization policies. As in the case of SecureUML [9], privileges may be organized similar to RBAC and rules can be restricted by conditions expressed in a subset of OCL. Ponder policies can be directly interpreted and enforced by a policy management platform. Model-driven security has also been employed for the development of secure XML databases [40, 24], secure databases, and data warehouses [23].

There has also been much work on integrating security requirements in process models and we mention several representative examples. In [8], we have combined SecureUML with a process design language to generate security architectures for distributed applications. SECTET [27, 4] is an extensible framework for designing and managing security-critical workflows based on web services. Finally, [43] describes a security policy and policy constraint modeling language that captures security requirements for business processes. In this work, security-annotated business processes can be translated into platform-specific target languages, such as XACML or AXIS2 security configurations.

Analysis.

There has been considerable work in analyzing the security of system designs within the Formal Methods communities, e.g., [41, 10, 30] to name a few examples. Usually traditional formal methods are used, based on model checking or theorem proving. Moreover, various groups have proposed approaches and associated tools for directly reasoning about access control policies [45, 46], including policies specified in standardized languages such as XACML [25].

With respect to the analysis of UML models, our use of OCL as a query language was inspired by [2] who used OCL to query RBAC policies; see also [38, 42]. One of the interesting challenges in our setting is that reasoning about security-design models involves different kinds of deduction problems as indicated in Section 3. This includes answering queries on models, which amounts to querying a potentially very large, but finite, scenario, and determining the existence of scenarios satisfying constraints, which calls for theorem proving or the use of constraint solvers. Model checkers or theorem provers are needed when reasoning about the combination of SecureUML with dynamic process-oriented models, such as those considered in [8].

Transformation.

Yie et al. [44] propose using model transformation-based techniques to integrate requirements, including security, in a model-driven software product line. In their setting, abstract design models of the application and of its security policy are built and refined using model transformation to obtain an implementation model with Java Platform, Enterprise Edition (JEE) security annotations. A related approach, using aspect-oriented programming, is outlined by Fox and Jürjens [26]. They propose to enrich a data model with a security policy by performing a model transformation using the bidirectional object-oriented transformation language (BOTL) [33, 34].

Finally, creating user interfaces is a common and time consuming task in application development. There have been numerous proposals and tools that aim to reduce the effort required to build effective, user-friendly graphical interfaces. Surprisingly, there has been no prior research on the systematic design of GUIs whose functionality should adhere to the security policy of the underlying application-data model.

8. PERSPECTIVE AND OUTLOOK

The ever-growing development and use of information and communication technologies is a constant source of security and reliability problems. Clearly we need better ways of developing software systems and approaching software engineering as a well-founded engineering discipline.

In model-driven development, models are the cornerstone of software and system development and can be used to abstract away irrelevant details, rigorously specify the interplay between security and functional requirements, and provide a basis for analysis and transformation. Proponents of model-driven development have in the past been guilty of making overambitious claims: positioning it as the Holy Grail of software engineering where modeling completely replaces programming in that systems are entirely generated from high-level models, each one specifying a different view of the same system. This vision is, of course, unrealizable in its entirety for simple complexity-theoretic reasons. If the modeling languages are sufficiently expressive then basic problems such as the consistency of the different models/views of a system becomes undecidable.

The original vision of model-driven security was to provide a way for software engineers to bridge the gap from security and design requirements to systems by taking a model-centric approach. This in turn necessitated bridging the gap between security modeling languages and design modeling languages, leading to the notion of security-design modeling languages, such as SecureUML+ComponentUML. Model-driven security has enormous potential not because it tackles the deep problem of synthesizing "business logic" but rather the shallow yet often extremely wide problem of generating security infrastructure. This infrastructure can be built from standard APIs and assertions and its complexity lies, essentially, in getting the deployment information right, despite the numerous details that must be considered. Security-design models provide a clear, declarative, high-level language for specifying these details. The strength of security-design models also lies in their well-defined semantics. This opens up a range of exploitation options and so far we have only scratched the surface of what is possible.

Our past work has focused primarily on access control. However, many systems have security requirements that go beyond access control, for example, obligations on how data must or must not be used once access is granted. We are currently working on handling usage control policies in the context of model-driven security. The challenge here is to define modeling languages that are expressive enough to capture these policies, support their formal analysis, and provide a basis for generating infrastructures to enforce or, at least, monitor these policies.

More generally, there are many challenging questions on the analysis side. Here, our goal is to be able to analyze the consistency of different system views. For example, suppose that access control is implemented at multiple tiers (or levels) of a system, e.g., at the middle tier implementing a controller for a web-based application and at the back-end persistence tier. If the policies for both of these tiers are formally modeled, we would like to answer questions like "will the controller ever enter a state in which the persistence tier throws a security exception?" Note that with advances in model transformations, perhaps such questions will some day not even need to be asked, as we can uniformly map a security policy across models of all tiers.

Ultimately we see model-driven security playing an important role in the construction and certification of critical systems. For example, certification under the Common Criteria requires models for the higher Evaluation Assurance Levels. Model-driven security provides many of the ingredients needed: models with a well-defined semantics, which can be rigorously analyzed and have a clear link to code. As the acceptance of model-driven development techniques spread, and as they become better integrated with well-established formal methods that support a detailed behavioral analysis, such applications should become a reality.

Acknowledgements

This work is partially supported by the EU FP7-ICT-2009.1.4 Project No. 256980, NESSoS: Network of Excellence on Engineering Secure Future Internet Software Services and Systems. We gratefully acknowledge our previous and current collaborators in this effort: Torsten Lodderstedt, Jürgen Doser, Michael Schläpfer, Miguel A. García de Dios, Carolina Dania, Javier Valdazo, and Gonzalo Ortiz.

9. REFERENCES

[1] G.-J. Ahn and M. E. Shin. UML-based representation of role-based access control. In *Proceedings of the 9th IEEE International Workshop on Enabling Technologies: Infrastructure for Collaborative Enterprises (WETICE'00)*, pages 195–200. IEEE Computer Society, June 2000.

[2] G. J. Ahn and M. E. Shin. Role-based authorization constraints specification using object constraint language. In *Proceedings of the 10th IEEE International Workshops on Enabling Technologies: Infrastructure for Collaborative Enterprises (WETICE'01)*, pages 157–162. IEEE Computer Society, 2001.

[3] M. Alam, M. Hafner, and R. Breu. Constraint based role based access control in the SECTET framework: A model-driven approach. *Journal of Computer Security*, 16(2):223–260, 2008.

[4] M. Alam, J. Seifert, and X. Zhang. A model-driven framework for trusted computing based systems. In *Proceedings of the 11th IEEE International Enterprise Distributed Object Computing Conference (EDOC'07)*, pages 75–87. IEEE Computer Society, 2007.

[5] D. Basin, M. Clavel, J. Doser, and M. Egea. A metamodel-based approach for analyzing security-design models. In G. Engels, B. Opdyke, D. Schmidt, and F. Weil, editors, *Proceedings of the 10th International Conference on Model Driven Engineering Languages and Systems (MODELS '07)*, volume 4735 of *LNCS*, pages 420–435. Springer-Verlag, 2007.

[6] D. Basin, M. Clavel, J. Doser, and M. Egea. Automated analysis of security-design models. *Information and Software Technology*, 51(5):815–831, 2009.

[7] D. Basin, M. Clavel, M. Egea, and M. Schläpfer. Automatic generation of smart, security-aware GUI models. In F. Massacci, D. S. Wallach, and N. Zannone, editors, *Proceedings of the 2nd International Symposium on Engineering Secure Software and Systems (ESSoS'10)*, volume 5965 of *LNCS*, pages 201–217, Pisa, Italy, 2010. Springer.

[8] D. Basin, J. Doser, and T. Lodderstedt. Model driven security for process-oriented systems. In *Proceedings of the 8th ACM Symposium on Access Control Models and Technologies (SACMAT '03)*, pages 100–109. ACM Press, 2003.

[9] D. Basin, J. Doser, and T. Lodderstedt. Model driven security: From UML models to access control infrastructures. *ACM Transactions on Software Engineering and Methodology*, 15(1):39–91, 2006.

[10] D. Basin, H. Kuruma, K. Miyazaki, K. Takaragi, and B. Wolff. Verifying a signature architecture: A comparative case study. *Formal Aspects of Computing*, 19(1):63–91, March 2007.

[11] R. Breu, G. Popp, and M. Alam. Model based development of access policies. *International Journal on Software Tools for Technology Transfer*, 5:457–470, 2007.

[12] C. Burt, B. Bryant, R. Raje, A. Olson, and M. Auguston. Model driven security: Unification of authorization models for fine-grain access control. In *Proceedings of the 7th International Enterprise Distributed Object Computing Conference (EDOC'03)*, pages 159–172. IEEE Computer Society, 2003.

[13] M. Clavel, M. Egea, and M. A. G. de Dios. Building an efficient component for OCL evaluation. *Electronic Communications of the EASST*, 15, 2008.

[14] M. Clavel, M. Egea, and M. A. G. de Dios. Checking unsatisfiability for OCL constraints. *Electronic Communications of the EASST*, 24, 2009.

[15] M. Clavel, V. Silva, C. Braga, and M. Egea. Model-driven security in practice: An industrial experience. In I. Schieferdecker and A. Hartman, editors, *Proceedings of 4th European Conference on Model Driven Architecture-Foundations and Applications (ECMDA-FA '08) - Industrial Track*, volume 5095 of *LNCS*, pages 327–338, Berlin-Germany, 2008. Springer-Verlag.

[16] N. Damianou, N. Dulay, E. Lupu, and M. Sloman. The Ponder policy specification language. In M. Sloman, J. Lobo, and E. C. Lupu, editors, *Policies for Distributed Systems and Networks (POLICY' 01)*, volume 1995 of *LNCS*, pages 18–38, Bristol-United Kingdom, 2001. Springer-Verlag.

[17] C. Dania and M. Egea. The MySQL4OCL code generator, 2010. http://www.bm1software.com/mysql-ocl/.

[18] M. A. G. de Dios, C. Dania, M. Schläpfer, D. Basin, M. Clavel, and M. Egea. SSG: A model-based development environment for smart, security-aware GUIs. In *Proceedings of the 32nd ACM/IEEE International Conference on Software Engineering*, volume 2, pages 311–312, Cape Town-South Africa, 2010. ACM.

[19] B. Dutertre and L. Moura. Yices: An SMT solver. http://yices.csl.sri.com/, 2008.

[20] Eclipse Model to Model (M2M) Project. The operational QVT transformation engine. http://www.eclipse.org/modeling/m2m/, 2011.

[21] Eclipse Model to Text (M2T) Project. The Java emitter template (JET) framework for code generation. http://www.eclipse.org/modeling/m2t/, 2011.

[22] M. Egea, C. Dania, and M. Clavel. MySQL4OCL: A stored procedure-based MySQL code generator for OCL. *Electronic Communications of the EASST*, 36, 2010.

[23] E. Fernandez-Medina, J. Trujillo, and M. Piattini. Model driven multidimensional modeling of secure data warehouses. *European Journal of Information Systems*, pages 374–389, 2007.

[24] E. Fernández-Medina, J. Trujillo, R. Villarroel, and M. Piattini. Developing secure data warehouses with a UML extension. *Information Systems*, 32:826–856, September 2007.

[25] K. Fisler, S. Krishnamurthi, L. Meyerovich, and M. Tschantz. Verification and change-impact analysis of access-control policies. In *Proceedings of the 27th International Conference on Software Engineering (ICSE'05)*, pages 196–205. ACM, 2005.

[26] J. Fox and J. Jürjens. Introducing security aspects with model transformations. In *Proceedings of the 12th IEEE International Conference on the Engineering of Computer-Based Systems (ECBS'05)*, pages 543–549, Washington, DC, USA, 2005. IEEE Computer Society.

[27] C. Haley, J. Moffet, R. Laney, and B. Nuseibeh. A framework for security requirements engineering. In *Proceedings of the 2006 Software Engineering for Secure Systems Workshop (SESS'06)*, pages 35–42, New York, USA, 2006. ACM.

[28] R. Hubert. *Convergent Architecture: Building Model Driven J2EE Systems with UML*. John Wiley & Sons, 2001.

[29] J. Jürjens. UMLsec: Extending UML for secure systems development. In J. M. Jézéquel, H. Hussmann, and S. Cook, editors, *Proceedings of the 5th International Conference on the Unified Modeling Language (UML'02)*, volume 2460 of *LNCS*, pages 412–425. Springer-Verlag, 2002.

[30] G. Klein et al. sel4: formal verification of an OS kernel. In *Proceedings of the ACM SIGOPS 22nd symposium on Operating systems principles*, SOSP '09, pages 207–220, New York, NY, USA, 2009. ACM.

[31] T. Lodderstedt. *Model Driven Security, from UML Models to Access Control Architectures*. PhD thesis, Unversity of Freiburg, Germany, 2003.

[32] T. Lodderstedt, D. Basin, and J. Doser. SecureUML: A UML-based modeling language for model-driven security. In J.-M. Jézéquel, H. Hussmann, and S. Cook, editors, *Proceedings of the 5th international Conference on the Unified Modeling Language: Model Engineering, Concepts, and Tools (UML'02)*, volume 2460 of *LNCS*, pages 426–441. Springer-Verlag, 2002.

[33] F. Marschall and P. Braun. Model transformations for the MDA with BOTL. Technical report, University of Twente, 2003.

[34] F. Marschall and P. Braun. Bidirectional object oriented transformation language (BOTL). http://sourceforge.net/projects/botl/, 2005.

[35] Object Management Group. Model driven architecture guide v. 1.0.1. Technical report, OMG, 2003. OMG document available at http://www.omg.org/cgi-bin/doc?omg/03-06-01.

[36] Object Management Group. *Object Constraint Language specification Version 2.2*, February 2010. OMG document available at http://www.omg.org/spec/OCL/2.2.

[37] M. Schläpfer, M. Egea, D. Basin, and M. Clavel. Automatic generation of security-aware GUI models. In A. Bagnato, editor, *Proceegings of the 1st European Workshop on Security in Model Driven Arquitecture (SEC-MDA'09)*, pages 42–56, Enschede, the Netherlands, 2009. CTIT Workshop Proceedings WP09-06.

[38] K. Sohr, G. J. Ahn, M. Gogolla, and L. Migge. Specification and validation of authorisation constraints using UML and OCL. In S. di Vimercati, P. Syverson, and D. Gollmann, editors, *Proceedings of the 10th European Symposium on Research in Computer Security (ESORICS '05)*, volume 3679 of *LNCS*, pages 64–79. Springer-Verlag, 2005.

[39] K. Sohr, T. Mustafa, X. Bao, and G.-J. Ahn.

Enforcing role-based access control policies in web services with UML and OCL. In *Proceedings of the 24th Annual Computer Security Applications Conference (ACSAC'08)*, pages 257–266, Washington DC, USA, 2008. IEEE Computer Society.

[40] B. Vela, E. Fernandez-Medina, E. Marcos, and M. Piattini. Model driven development of secure XML databases. *ACM Sigmod Record*, 35(3):22–27, 2006.

[41] D. von Oheimb and V. Lotz. Formal security analysis with interacting state machines. In D. Gollmann, G. Karjoth, and M. Waidner, editors, *Proceedings of the 7th European Symposium on Research in Computer Security (ESORICS'02)*, volume 2502 of *Lecture Notes in Computer Science*, pages 212–228. Springer Berlin / Heidelberg, 2002.

[42] H. Wang, Y. Zhang, J. Cao, and J. Yang. Specifying role-based access constraints with object constraint language. In *Proceedings of the 6th Asia-Pacific Web Conference (APWeb '04)*, volume 3007 of *LNCS*, pages 687–696. Springer-Verlag, 2004.

[43] C. Wolter, M. Menzel, A. Schaad, P. Miseldine, and C. Meinel. Model-driven business process security requirement specification. *Journal of Systems Architecture*, 55(4):211–223, 2009.

[44] A. Yie, R. Casallas, D. Deridder, and R. V. D. Straeten. Multi-step concern refinement. In *Proceedings of the 2008 AOSD workshop on Early Aspects (EA-AOSD'08)*, pages 1–8, New York, NY, USA, 2008. ACM.

[45] N. Zhang, M. Ryan, and D. Guelev. Evaluating access control policies through model checking. *Information Security*, pages 446–460, 2005.

[46] N. Zhang, M. Ryan, and D. Guelev. Synthesising verified access control systems through model checking. *Journal of Computer Security*, 16(1):1–61, 2008.

APPENDIX

A. ANALYZING ACCESS CONTROL

As discussed in Section 3, analyzing the scenarios that are consistent with a given security-design model requires reasoning about what is entailed by the model's permissions and associated constraints, as well as any invariants of the underlying design model.

Our current approach to analyzing access-control scenarios is based on a mapping from OCL to first-order logic [14]. In a nutshell, this mapping is defined recursively over the structure of OCL expressions. Boolean expressions are translated to formulas, mirroring their logical structure; integer expressions are basically copied. Collections are translated to predicates, whose meaning is defined by auxiliary formulas generated by the mapping. Association-ends are translated to predicates, which are also defined by auxiliary formulas. Finally, attributes are translated to uninterpreted functions and classes are translated to predicates.

Based on this mapping, we can answer questions about the consistency of a scenario satisfying a given property, with respect to an access control policy model, using satisfiability modulo theories (SMT) solvers. For example, given the access control policy model of Figure 4, consider the property of someone being able to change his own salary. We use the SMT solver Yices [19] to analyze the consistency of scenarios satisfying this property with respect to this model.

First, using our mapping, we formalize in Yices the information contained in the (underlying) data model, i.e., the model shown in Figure 3.

```
(define Employee::(-> int bool))
(define supervisedBy::(-> int int bool))
(define supervises::(-> int int bool))

; type properties of supervisedBy and supervises
(assert (forall (x::int) (forall (y::int)
  (=> (supervisedBy x y) (Employee y)))))
(assert (forall (y::int) (forall (x::int)
  (=> (supervises y x) (Employee x)))))

; multiplicity of supervisedBy
(assert (forall (x::int) (forall (y::int)
  (=> (and (Employee x) (and (Employee y)
        (supervisedBy x y)))
    (forall (z::int)
      (=> (and (Employee z)
            (supervisedBy x z))
  (= y z)))))))

; relationship between supervisedBy and supervises
  (assert (forall (x::int) (forall (y::int)
(=> (supervisedBy x y) (supervises y x)))))
(assert (forall (x::int) (forall (y::int)
  (=> (supervises y x) (supervisedBy x y)))))

; invariant: nobody is his (or her) own supervisor:
(assert (forall (x::int)
    (=> (Employee x) (not (supervisedBy x x)))))
```

Second, we also use our mapping to formalize the OCL expression stating that someone satisfies the contraint for changing his own salary, namely:

```
Employee.allInstances()->exists(self, caller|
    self.supervisedBy->includes(caller)
    and self=caller)
```

The resulting assertion in Yices is the following:

```
(assert (exists (self::int) (exists (caller::int)
  (and (Employee self) (and (Employee caller)
  (and (supervisedBy self caller)
  (and (= self caller)
```

Finally, to check that the access control policy model prevents anyone from changing his own salary, we check if all of the above assertions are satisfiable. As expected, the answer automatically provided by Yices is unsat.

Deriving Role Engineering Artifacts from Business Processes and Scenario Models

Anne Baumgrass, Mark Strembeck
Institute of Information Systems, New Media Lab
Vienna University of Economics and Business
(WU Vienna), Austria
{firstname.lastname}@wu.ac.at

Stefanie Rinderle-Ma
Workflow Systems and Technology
Faculty of Computer Science
University of Vienna, Austria
stefanie.rinderle-ma@univie.ac.at

ABSTRACT

Scenario-driven role engineering is a systematic approach to engineer and maintain RBAC models. Such as every engineering process, this approach heavily depends on human factors and many of the corresponding engineering tasks must be conducted manually. However, based on the experiences we gained from our projects and case studies, we identified several tasks in role engineering that are monotonous, time-consuming, and can get tedious if conducted manually. These tasks include the derivation of candidate RBAC artifacts from business processes and scenario models. In this paper, we present an approach to automatically derive role engineering artifacts from process and scenario models. While our general approach is independent from a specific document format, we especially discuss the derivation of role engineering artifacts from UML activity models, UML interaction models, and BPMN collaboration models. In particular, we use the XMI (XML Metadata Interchange) representation of these models as a tool- and vendor-independent format to identify and automatically derive different role engineering artifacts.

Categories and Subject Descriptors

D.4.6 [**Operating Systems**]: Security and Protection—*Access Controls*; K.6.5 [**Management of Computing and Information Systems**]: Security and Protection

General Terms

Security

Keywords

Role Engineering, RBAC, UML, BPMN, XMI

1. INTRODUCTION

In recent years, role-based access control (RBAC) [8, 9, 22] – together with various extensions – has developed into a de facto standard for access control. In the context of RBAC, roles model

different job-positions and scopes of duty within a particular organization or within an information system. *Scenario-driven role engineering* is a systematic approach for defining customized RBAC models, including roles, role-hierarchies, permissions, and constraints [23, 24, 26]. Since its first publication in 2002 [18], we gained many experiences with scenario-driven role engineering and the approach has been adopted by a number of consulting firms and international projects (see, e.g., [5, 15]).

1.1 Scenario-driven Role Engineering

In scenario-driven role engineering, we use scenario and process models as a primary communication and engineering vehicle. We model usage scenarios of an information system and use the respective scenario and process models to derive permissions. In general, a scenario describes a possible or actual action and event sequence (see, e.g., [13]). Thus, to perform a certain scenario, a subject needs to be equipped with the exact number of permissions that are needed to complete each step of the respective scenario. After deriving the permissions, we therefore group the scenarios to form tasks and work profiles. These work profiles serve as preliminary roles and are an important step toward the definition of a customized RBAC model (for details see [18, 23, 24, 26]). Figure 1 shows the main relations between role engineering artifacts and corresponding RBAC model artifacts.

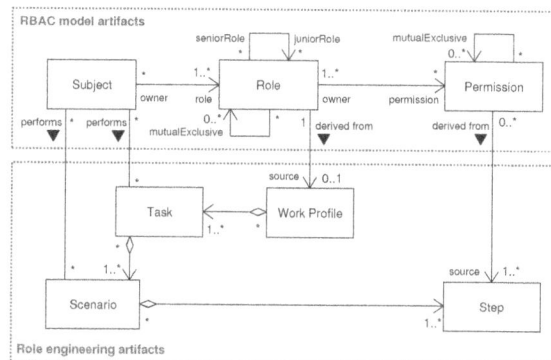

Figure 1: Role engineering and RBAC artifacts [24]

Such as every engineering process, the process of role engineering significantly depends on human factors. For this reason, many steps of the process cannot be automated (or at most partially). However, based on the experiences we gained from our role engineering projects and case studies (see Section 4), we identified several tasks in role engineering that are monotonous, time-consuming and can get tedious if conducted manually. These tasks include the derivation of candidate RBAC artifacts from scenario and process models. In this paper, we are especially concerned with the derivation of role engineering artifacts from UML activity, UML interaction, and BPMN collaboration models.

1.2 Approach Synopsis

In order to ease scenario-driven role engineering, we aim to automate the derivation of role engineering artifacts from different types of scenario and process descriptions. In general, scenario and process models can be defined in a wide variety of (modeling) languages, such as Unified Modeling Language (UML) activity and interaction models, event-driven process chains (EPCs), Business Process Model and Notation (BPMN) models, or via the Business Process Execution Language (BPEL). To automate the derivation of role engineering artifacts, we therefore chose an approach that is independent of the language which is used to define the scenarios and processes. In particular, we first assess the respective (modeling) language and specify a mapping between modeling language artifacts and role engineering artifacts. This mapping especially results in an integrated meta-model (see Figure 2). Based on this integrated meta-model we built a tailored analyzer component that extracts role engineering artifacts from corresponding scenario and process models.

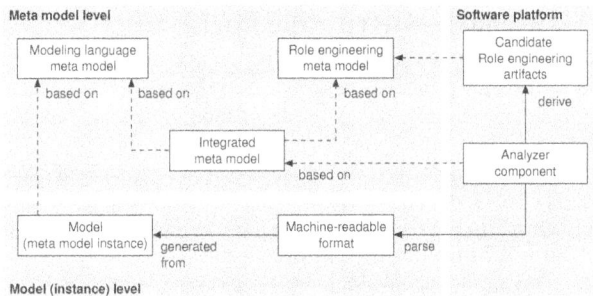

Figure 2: Generic approach for the automated derivation of role engineering artifacts from scenario and process models: conceptual overview

Thereby, our approach is independent of a certain modeling language or format. However, a detailed and dedicated investigation of different modeling languages is essential since modeling language meta models partly differ with respect to the representation of relevant artifacts (see Sections 2 and 3).

In this paper, we describe the derivation of role engineering artifacts from UML activity and interaction models as well as BPMN collaboration models. In particular, we use the XML Metadata Interchange (XMI) [20] representation of these models as a tool- and vendor-independent format to identify and derive different candidate role engineering artifacts.

The remainder of this paper is structured as follows. In Section 2, we give an overview of the different UML and BPMN models, and show how we use them for scenario and process modeling in the role engineering context. Subsequently, Section 3 presents our approach for the automated derivation of role engineering artifacts from the corresponding scenario and process models. Next, Section 4 discusses the practical relevance of our approach. Section 5 gives an overview of related work, and Section 6 concludes the paper.

2. USING UML AND BPMN FOR SCENARIO AND PROCESS MODELING

UML is a de facto standard for the definition of software-based systems. In scenario-driven role engineering, we use UML activity

and interaction models as standard means to visualize scenario and process models (see also [24]). Moreover, in recent years BPMN emerged as a new standard for the definition of process models that was quickly adopted in both research and industry.

2.1 UML Activity Models

Activity models specify processes and define the control and object flow between different actions. Figure 3 shows an excerpt of the UML2 meta-model that depicts selected elements of activity models (see [21]). In Section 3.1, we will use some of these activity elements to derive role engineering artifacts.

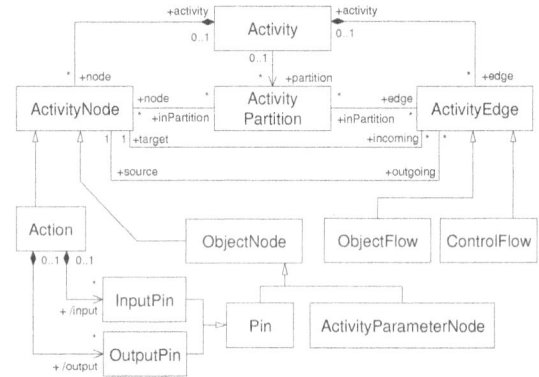

Figure 3: Selected elements of UML2 activity models

The left-hand side of Figure 4 shows the example of a simple credit application process modeled as UML activity diagram. An activity model may include (sub)partitions, and each partition may have a name. Partitions can be used to group actions that have common characteristics, for example the execution of all actions in a partition by the same actor. The example from Figure 4 includes three partitions using the so called swimlane notation (see [21]), the partitions are named "Credit Application Web-Frontend", "Bank Clerk A", and "Bank Clerk B".

Activity models have a token semantics, similar (but not equal) to petri nets. In general, two different types of tokens can travel in an activity model. Control tokens are passed along control flow edges and object tokens are passed along object flow edges (for details see [21]). To model object flows between actions, one uses corresponding object nodes. Pins are a specific type of object node and are visualized as small rectangles that are attached to action symbols. For example, in Figure 4 we have an object flow between the two actions "Negotiate contract" and "Approve contract". The object flow connects the two pins attached to the respective actions and accepts object tokens of type "Contract".

Each edge may be associated with a so called "guard" condition. The guard determines if a particular token is allowed to travel along the respective edge. A decision node is represented by a diamond-shaped symbol and has one incoming and multiple outgoing edges. A merge node is represented by a diamond-shaped symbol and has multiple incoming and one outgoing edge.

The right-hand side of Figure 4 shows an excerpt of the XMI representation of the activity model depicted on the left-hand side. The XML Metadata Interchange (XMI) specification (see [20]) defines an interchange and storage format and (among other things) allows for the transformation of graphical UML models to a generic (tool- and vendor-independent) model representation. Each element in an XMI document has an identifier defined through the `xmi:id` attribute. Via this identifier elements can reference other elements (see below). For demonstration purposes, Figure 4 highlights two

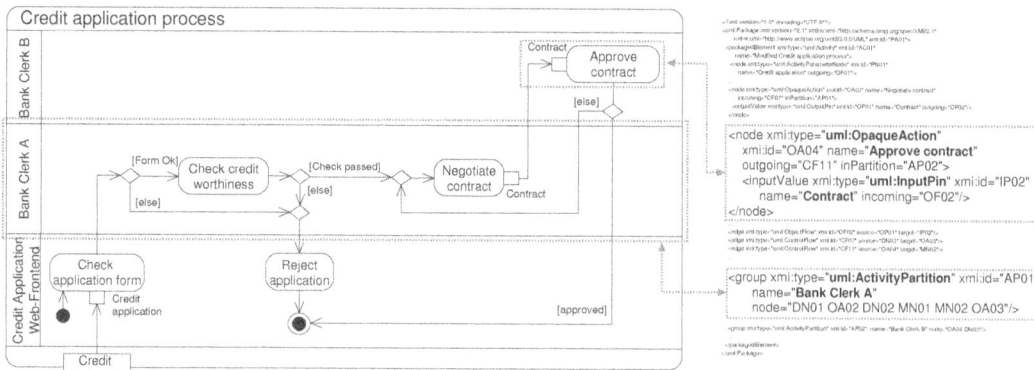

Figure 4: Example of an UML2 activity model and its XMI representation

areas of the activity model and the corresponding XMI representation, in particular:

- In the XMI representation, activity partitions are defined via a `group` element with the `xmi:type` attribute set to `uml:ActivityPartition`. Nodes/elements included in a partition are referenced via the `node` attribute. For example, in Figure 4 the partition with `name` "Bank Clerk A" includes the nodes DN01, OA02, DN02, MN01, MN02, and OA03[1].

- Actions are defined as `node` of the activity model and include an `xmi:type` attribute that specifies the corresponding action type. The action highlighted on the right-hand side of Figure 4 is of type `uml:OpaqueAction` and has the `name` "Approve contract". The `inPartition` attribute references the id of the activity partition that includes the respective action (see also Figure 3). In this example, the "Approve contract" action is included in partition AP02 (short for "Activity Partition 02") named "Bank Clerk B". Moreover, this action is connected to an InputPin that has the `name` "Contract".

- Input pins as well as output pins (see Figure 3) are defined as subelements of the action they are attached to. Input pins are included in an `inputValue` element and their `xmi:type` is set to `uml:InputPin` (see Figure 4). Likewise, output pins are `outputValue` elements of the type `uml:OutputPin`.

2.2 Refining/Concretizing Activity Models via Interaction Models

While activity models describe the control flows and object flows between different actions on a higher abstraction level, interaction models are used to define the interactions of different actors in detail. Figure 5 shows an excerpt of the UML2 meta-model that depicts selected elements of interaction models (see [21]). In Section 3.1, we will use some of these interaction elements to derive role engineering artifacts.

In particular, interaction models describe a sequence of messages that are send between different lifelines. Here, a lifeline represents an actor that is participating in a particular interaction. In general, an actor may be a human user or a technical (software-based) system. UML includes different (sub)types of interaction models (see [21]). In scenario-driven role engineering, we especially use UML sequence diagrams to model interactions and to specify the actions modeled in an activity model in detail (see also [24]). The right-hand side of Figure 6 shows an example of a sequence diagram

---
[1]DN = Decision Node, MN = Merge Node, OA = Opaque Action

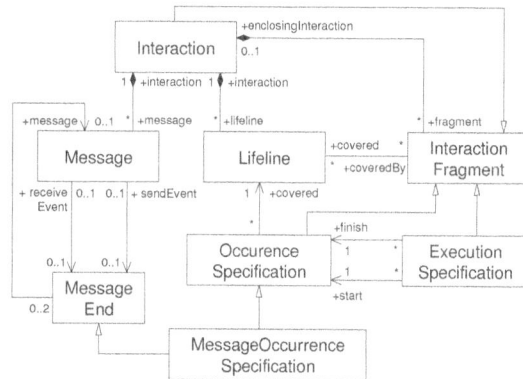

Figure 5: Selected elements of UML2 interaction models

which describes the "Check credit worthiness" action from Figure 4 in detail.

The Interaction from Figure 6 includes three lifelines, representing a "Bank Clerk", a (sub)system called "CustomerMgmt" and a (sub)system called "CustomerRating". Each message send between the lifelines defines a particular act of communication and is modeled via a directed edge pointing from the message sender's lifeline to the message receiver's lifeline. In UML, the start and end of the directed edges representing a message are called MessageEnds and define a so called MessageOccurrenceSpecification (see Figure 5), i.e. the occurrence of a respective send or a receive event on the corresponding lifeline. Asynchronous messages have an open arrow head, synchronous messages have a filled arrow head, and reply messages are drawn as a dashed line with an open arrow head (see Figure 6). Moreover, so called "execution specifications" specify the execution of a certain behavior or command within a lifeline (i.e. the execution of a behavior by the corresponding actor). ExecutionSpecifications are represented by thin rectangles on the lifeline, and may be nested/overlapping. Thus, execution specifications define when an actor (represented via a lifeline) is busy.

Moreover, interaction models may include CombinedFragments. A combined fragment models an interaction fragment which occurs in case a certain condition becomes true. In general, different types of CombinedFragments exist, e.g. to model alternative behaviors, optional behavior, loops, or breaking scenarios (for details see [21]). The example from Figure 6 includes a CombinedFragment modeling an optional behavior (indicated by the "opt" operator in the upper left corner of the fragment) that is executed if the "[decision is positive]" condition in the CombinedFragment evaluates to true.

13

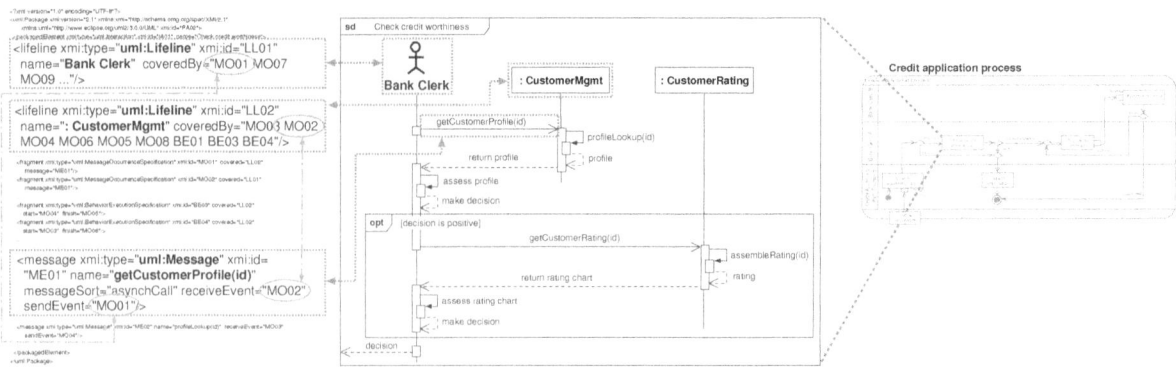

Figure 6: Example of an UML2 interaction model and its XMI representation

The left-hand side of Figure 6 shows an excerpt of the XMI representation of the interaction model depicted on the right-hand side. For demonstration purposes, Figure 6 highlights three areas of the interaction model and the corresponding XMI representation. In particular, the highlighted areas include the following elements:

- In the XMI representation, lifelines are defined via a `lifeline` element with the respective `xmi:type` attribute set to `uml:Lifeline`. Moreover, each lifeline includes a `coveredBy` attribute which contains id-references to the occurrence specifications of this particular lifeline. In the topmost highlighted area from Figure 6, the lifeline with `name` "Bank Clerk" is covered by a number of message occurrences ("MO01, MO07, MO09, ...")[2].

- A Message is defined via a `message` element with the corresponding `xmi:type` attribute set to `uml:Message`. Moreover, the `sendEvent` and `receiveEvent` attributes refer to the respective MessageOccurrenceSpecifications (see also Figure 5) that define the start and end points of a certain message. In the example from Figure 6, the message with `name` "getCustomerProfile(id)" connects the `sendEvent` "MO01" (which is covered by the lifeline "Bank Clerk") and the `receiveEvent` "MO02" (which is covered by the lifeline "CustomerMgmt").

2.3 BPMN Collaboration Models

BPMN2 provides three diagram types named Process, Collaboration, and Choreography respectively (for details see [19]). For our purposes, we especially focus on BPMN collaboration diagrams which model interactions between different entities (so called Participants).

Figure 7 shows an excerpt of the BPMN meta-model that depicts selected elements of BPMN collaboration models. In Section 3.2 we will use some of these elements to derive role engineering artifacts. Figure 8 shows an example of a descriptive BPMN model.

In a collaboration a participant is responsible for the execution of the process enclosed in a so called pool. In BPMN processes group the flow or sequence of different process steps. The steps within a process are categorized and organized via Lanes encapsulated by a LaneSet, whereas each lane can consist of sub-lanes to further partition the included process steps (for details see [19]). In version 2.0, BPMN introduces process modeling conformance classes to simplify the interchange between modelers and developers [19]. Below, we use the descriptive conformance class. The *Descriptive Conformance* class allows to establish a high-level understanding between modelers. The *Common Executable Conformance* class enables a detailed definition of the corresponding processes.

---

[2]MO = Message Occurrence

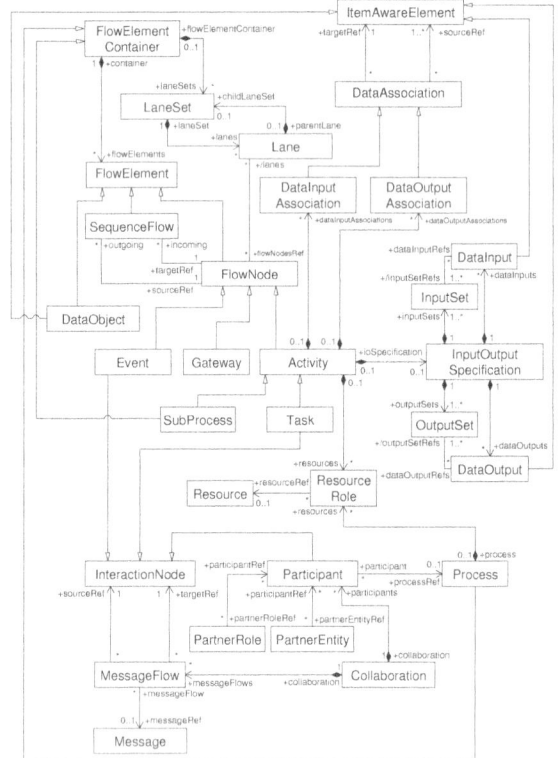

Figure 7: Selected elements of BPMN 2.0 collaboration models

Figure 8 shows our credit application example modeled via a BPMN model using the descriptive conformance class. It includes one Pool named "Bank Company" consisting of the three lanes named "Credit Application Web-Frontend", "Bank Clerk A", and "Bank Clerk B".

While BPMN tasks are atomic process steps, subprocesses can be broken down to a finer level of detail. In Figure 8, the process step "Check credit worthiness" represents a collapsed subprocess, while all other steps in this figure are tasks. The control flow in a process is defined via events and gateways. Gateways coordinate the direction and choices of the process flow, while events can directly affect this flow. Our example process shows five exclusive Gateways (diamonds), a Start Event (circle) to indicate where to begin the process and a End Event (circle with thick line) to indicate where the path of the process will end. So called Data Objects are used to store and convey items during process execution. Data Associations model how data is extracted from a data object into a

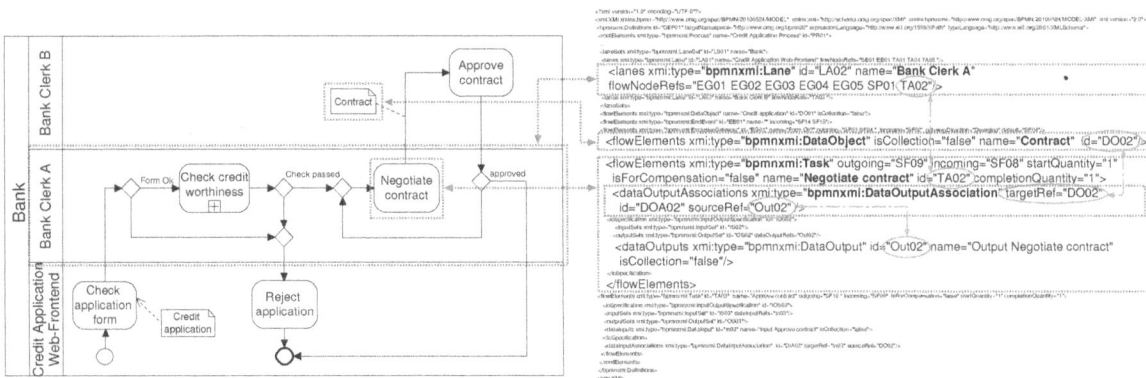

Figure 8: Example of a BPMN 2.0 collaboration model in descriptive conformance class and its XMI representation

task. In particular, this is done via the DataInput included in a task's InputSet. Similarly, a newly created data object is extracted from a task's DataOutput in the respective OutputSet (see also Figure 7). In our example the data object "Credit application" is connected to the task "Check application form" via a Data Input Association. A data object that is passed from one task to another can be attached directly to the sequence flow connecting these tasks. In Figure 8, this visualization option is shown for the data object "Contract".

The right-hand side of Figure 8 shows an excerpt of the XMI representation of the BPMN 2.0 collaboration model depicted on the left-hand side[3].

For demonstration purposes, Figure 8 highlights three areas of the BPMN model and the corresponding XMI representation. In particular, the highlighted areas include the following elements:

- Lanes partitioning the process are defined via `lanes` elements with the `xmi:type` attribute set to `bpmnxmi:Lane`. Each flow node that belongs to this lane is referenced by its id in the `flowNodeRefs` attribute. For example, the lane named "Bank Clerk A" includes the flow nodes EG01, EG02, EG03, EG04, EG05, SP01, TA02[4].

- Data Objects are defined as `flowElements` with the `xmi:type` attribute set to `bpmnxmi:DataObject`. Figure 8 shows the XMI representation of the data object "Contract".

- Elements describing the flow in a process are also defined as `flowElements`. These elements are flow nodes and sequence flows (see also Figure 7). Figure 8 shows the XMI representation of the "Negotiate contract" task as `flowElements` element of the type `bpmnxmi:Task`.

- Data associations between data objects and tasks are defined as subelement of a task. They are either defined as `dataOutputAssociations` or `dataInputAssociations`. Figure 8 shows that the "Contract" data object is related to "Negotiate contract" as output and to "Approve contract" as input. In Figure 8 the "Contract" data object is referenced via its id "DO02" (short for "Data Object 02") in the `dataOutputAssociations` element of the "Negotiate contract" task.

---

[3]The transformation to XMI from BPMN is conducted via a XSLT document that is provided as part of BPMN specification (see [19]).
[4]EG=Exclusive Gateway, SP=Sub-Process, TA=Task

3. DERIVING ROLE ENGINEERING ARTIFACTS FROM PROCESS AND SCENARIO MODELS

In this section, we show how we derive role engineering artifacts from the XML Metadata Interchange (XMI) [20] representation of UML activity, UML interaction, and BPMN collaboration models.

However, note that the role engineering artifacts derived from the XMI documents are only *candidate artifacts* and are subject to a subsequent selection and/or refinement performed by human role engineers. This means that after the role engineering artifacts are fed into the role engineering tool they can be renamed or deleted (see, e.g., [23]). For example, a certain candidate artifact can be deleted if two different artifacts refer to the same role engineering entity, as it may be the case with two candidate roles "Bank Clerk A" and "Bank Clerk B" which will most likely refer to a single role called "Bank Clerk".

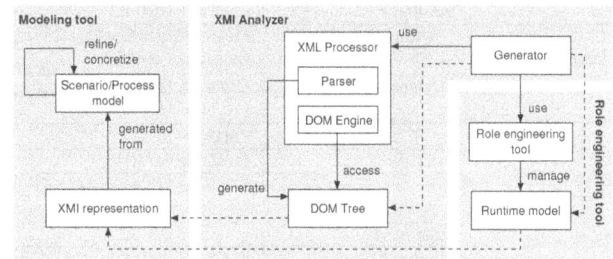

Figure 9: Deriving role engineering artifacts from scenario/process models: Structural overview

In particular, a special-purpose XMI Analyzer component transforms XMI model representations to candidate role engineering artifacts. Figure 9 depicts a structural overview of this XMI Analyzer while Figure 10 depicts the different steps of this transformation.

The XMI Analyzer uses a XML processor to parse the respective XML document and generate a corresponding DOM tree (see [2, 11, 12]). The DOM tree is an in-memory representation of the respective XML document and makes the corresponding document content accessible to software components. The Generator component then accesses the DOM tree to derive/extract role engineering artifacts and feeds them into a role engineering tool (such as the xoRET tool [23]). In turn, the role engineering tool produces a corresponding runtime model and provides an interface for human users (role engineers) to further manipulate/refine the respective role engineering artifacts and to build a tailored RBAC model (see also [23, 24]).

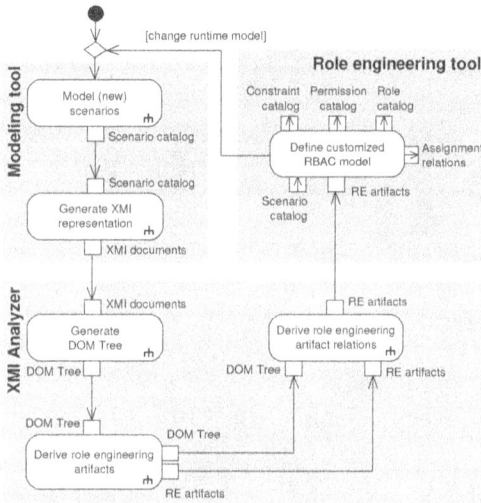

Figure 10: Deriving role engineering artifacts from scenario/process models: Task sequence

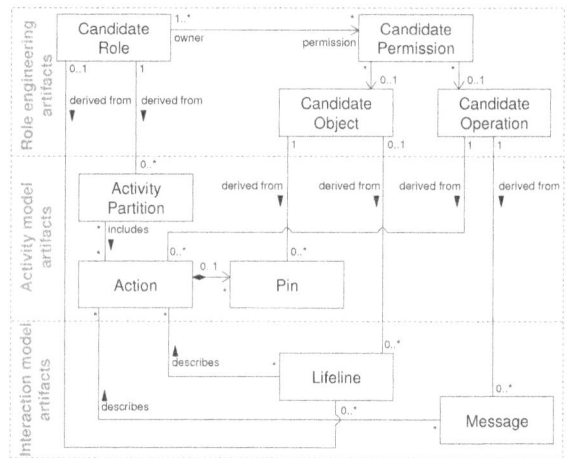

Figure 11: Derivation of role engineering artifacts from UML activity and interaction models: Integrated meta-model

Table 1 gives an overview what role engineering artifacts can be derived from the XMI representation of UML2 and BPMN 2.0 models. The details of this derivation are described in the following sections.

Table 1: Model elements to derive role engineering artifacts from UML2 and BPMN 2.0 models in XMI representation

	xmi:Type attribute	Role engineering artifacts
UML Activity Diagram	ActivityPartition	Candidate ROLE
	OpaqueAction	Candidate PERMISSION and Candidate OPERATION
	OutputPin	Candidate OBJECT
	InputPin	Candidate OBJECT
UML Interaction Diagram	Lifeline	Candidate ROLE or Candidate OBJECT
	Message	Candidate PERMISSION and Candidate OPERATION
BPMN Descriptive Collaboration Model	Lane	Candidate ROLE
	Participant	Candidate ROLE
	Task	Candidate PERMISSION and Candidate OPERATION
	DataObject	Candidate OBJECT
	Message	Candidate OBJECT
BPMN Common Executable Collaboration Model	Resource	Candidate ROLE
	PartnerEntity	Candidate ROLE
	PartnerRole	Candidate ROLE
	Task with implementation attribute	Candidate OBJECT

3.1 Deriving Role Engineering Artifacts from UML Models

Figure 11 shows the integrated meta-model for the derivation of role engineering artifacts from UML activity and interaction models. In particular, it indicates which UML model elements are used to derive corresponding role engineering artifacts: In a nutshell, we use ActivityPartitions and Lifelines to identify candidate roles, Pins and Lifelines to identify candidate objects, as well as Actions and Messages to identify candidate operations.

3.1.1 Derivation from Activity Models

Figure 12 shows an example of how we use the XMI representation of activity models to identify role engineering artifacts. In

particular, Figure 12 highlights an excerpt of Figure 4 and shows what role engineering artifacts can be derived from the corresponding XMI representation. In general, the following derivation rules are applied (see also Figures 2, 9, 10, and 11, as well as Table 1):

- We use `group` elements of the type `uml:ActivityPartition` to identify candidate roles. These candidate roles are then associated with the candidate permissions that are derived from actions included in the respective ActivityPartition. For example, the activity partition with name "Bank Clerk B" is used to derive a corresponding candidate role (see Figure 12).

- We use `node` elements of type `uml:OpaqueAction` to identify candidate operations. Moreover, the name of the respective action is also used to determine the name of the corresponding permission candidate. In Figure 12, we can thus use the `uml:OpaqueAction` with name "Approve contract" to derive the corresponding artifacts.

- We use `inputValue` elements with the `uml:InputPin` type and `outputValue` elements with the `uml:OutputPin` type to identify candidate objects. The candidate objects are then associated with the candidate operation that is identified from the corresponding action defined as `node` element of type `uml:OpaqueAction` (see also Figure 11). For instance, from Figure 12 we can derive the "Contract" candidate object for action "Approve contract" from the respective input pin.

In addition to the role engineering artifacts described above, we can also derive candidate *mutual exclusive constraints* (ME) from activity models. Mutual exclusive constraints enforce conflict of interest policies (see, e.g., [1, 3, 7, 25]). Conflict of interest arises as a result of the simultaneous assignment of two mutual exclusive tasks or roles to the same subject. In general, we use `group` elements of the type `uml:ActivityPartition` to identify candidate ME constraints. In particular, we assume that the actions included in different activity partitions must be executed by different actors. For instance, in the example from Figure 4 we can derive a candidate ME constraint on the actions "Negotiate contract" and "Approve contract". In the further course of the role engineering process, we would further refine this candidate ME constraint into a dynamic ME constraint on the corresponding permissions defined for the "Bank Clerk" role. This means, each user assigned to the

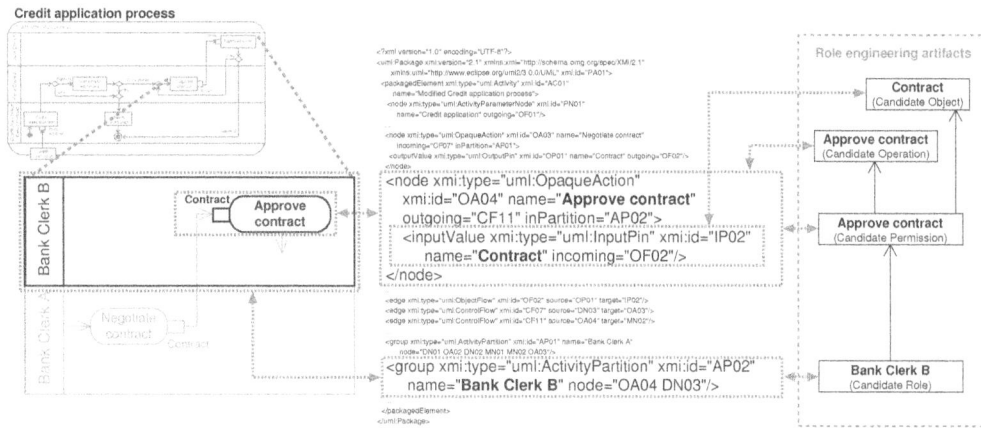

Figure 12: Example for the derivation of role engineering artifacts from activity models

"Bank Clerk" role owns both permissions and can, in principle, perform both tasks. However, due to the dynamic ME constraint on the respective permissions one always needs two different individuals acting in the "Bank Clerk" role to complete the credit application process (as it is reflected in the graphical model via two different swimlanes labeled "Bank Clerk A" and "Bank Clerk B").

3.1.2 Derivation from Interaction Models

Figure 13 shows an example how we use the XMI representation of interaction models to identify role engineering artifacts. In particular, Figure 13 highlights an excerpt of Figure 6 and shows what role engineering artifacts can be derived from the respective XMI representation. In general, the following derivation rules are applied (see also Figures 2, 9, 10, and 11, as well as Table 1):

- We use `message` elements to identify candidate operations and candidate permissions. Moreover, the `receiveEvent` and `sendEvent` attributes are used to determine the respective candidate object and the corresponding candidate role (see below).

- We use `lifeline` elements to identity candidate roles and candidate objects:

  - We derive a *candidate role* if one of the `sendEvents` covered by the respective lifeline is part of a `message` which is received by another lifeline. For instance, in Figure 13 the `sendEvent` of the `message` with name "getCustomerProfile(id)" is covered by the "Bank Clerk" lifeline, while the `receiveEvent` of this message is covered by the "CustomerMgmt" lifeline. Therefore, we derive a candidate role from the "Bank Clerk" lifeline.

  - We derive a *candidate object* if one of the `receiveEvents` covered by a lifeline is part of an `message` element which was sent by another lifeline. In the example from Figure 13, we therefore derive a candidate object from the "CustomerMgmt" lifeline, because it receives the "getCustomerProfile(id)" message from the "Bank Clerk" lifeline[5].

---

[5]Note that a candidate role as well as a candidate object may be derived from the very same lifeline in case the respective lifeline is both a sender and a receiver of `messages`. However, this is perfectly in sync with the typical object/component-based nature of today's software systems where different objects/components are connected and mutually invoke each others methods/procedures.

Because interaction models concretize and/or refine activity models, they are a valuable source to identify role engineering artifacts that cannot be derived from more abstract activity models.

3.2 Deriving Role Engineering Artifacts from BPMN Collaboration Models

Figure 14 shows the integrated meta-model for the derivation of role engineering artifacts from BPMN collaboration models. In particular, it indicates what BPMN model elements are used to derive corresponding role engineering artifacts: We use participants and lanes to identify candidate roles. Tasks are used to identify candidate operations, and Messages, Data Objects as well as the implementation of a task are used to identify candidate objects. All elements related to participants and lanes, such as resource, sublanes, PartnerRole and PartnerEntity are used to further refine candidate roles and to identify candidate role-hierarchies.

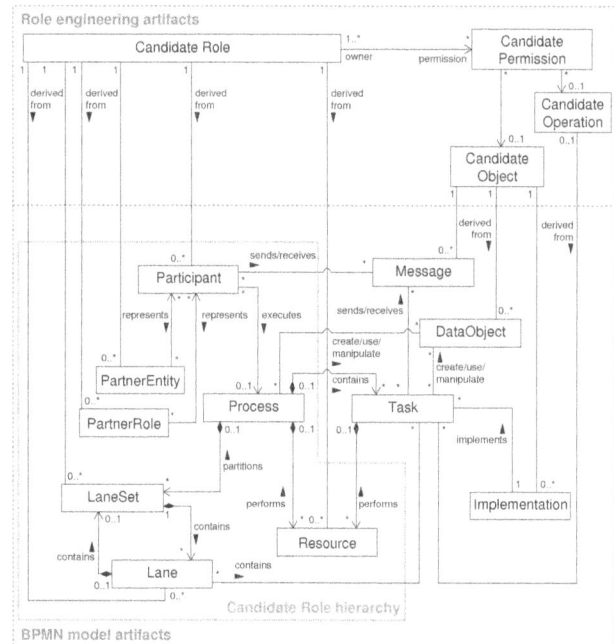

Figure 14: Derivation of role engineering artifacts from BPMN collaboration models: Integrated meta-model

Figure 13: Example for the derivation of role engineering artifacts from interaction models

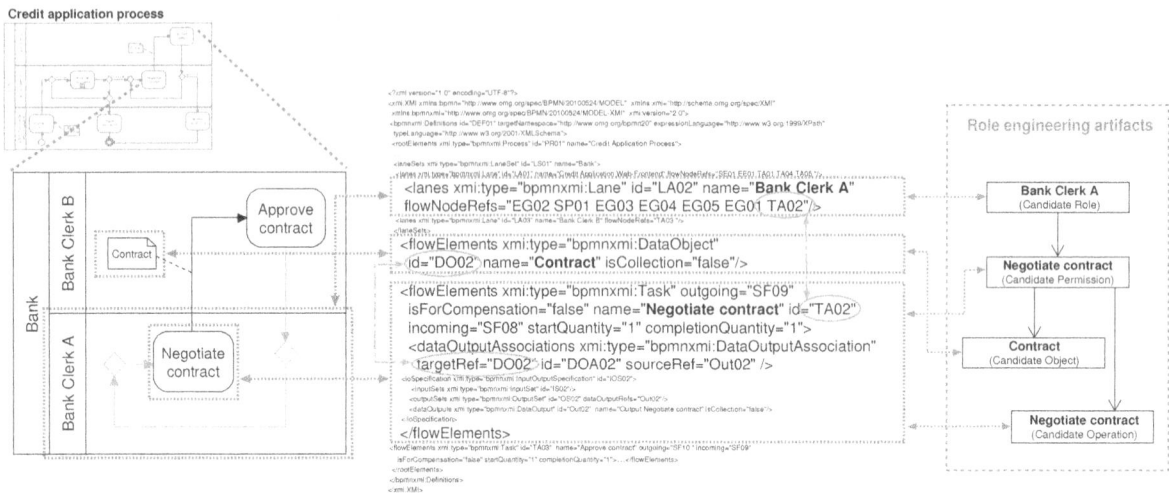

Figure 15: Example for the derivation of role engineering artifacts from collaboration models in descriptive conformance class

Figure 15 shows an example of how we identify role engineering artifacts from the XMI representation of BPMN collaboration models in the descriptive conformance class. In particular, Figure 15 highlights an excerpt of Figure 8 and shows what role engineering artifacts can be derived from the corresponding XMI representation. In general, the following derivation rules are applied (see also Figures 2, 9, 10, and 14, as well as Table 1):

- We use `lanes` elements to derive candidate roles. Tasks, including their input and output, are used to derive corresponding candidate permissions. For example, the "Bank Clerk A" lane shown in Figure 15 results in such a candidate role.

- We use `flowElements` of the type `bpmnxmi:Task` to derive candidate operations. Moreover, the name of the respective task element is also used to determine the name of the corresponding permission candidate. For example, in Figure 15 we see the "Negotiate contract" candidate permission and candidate operation.

- We use `flowElements` of the `bpmnxmi:DataObject` type to derive candidate objects. We use the data associations (either `bpmnxmi:DataOutputAssociation` or `bpmnxmi:DataInputAssociation`) of a data object to associate the candidate objects with the corresponding candidate permission. In the example, we can derive the candidate object "Contract" for the candidate permission "Negotiate contract" (see Figure 15).

Similar to UML activity models (see Section 3.1), we can also derive candidate mutual exclusion constraints (ME) from BPMN collaboration models. In BPMN models, we use the `lanes` element to identify candidate ME constraints. In particular, we assume that

the tasks included in different lanes have to be executed by different actors. In the example from Figure 8 we can derive such a candidate ME constraint for the "Negotiate contract" and "Approve contract" tasks.

In general, the derivation rules presented above are valid for BPMN collaboration models of all conformance classes. Moreover, models in the common executable conformance class are more detailed and can further concretize a BPMN collaboration model. Thereby, these more detailed models can be used to further refine the automated derivation of role engineering artifacts, similar to the refinement of activity models via interaction models discussed in Section 3.1. Due to the page restrictions, we had to cut the derivation rules and examples for BPMN models in the common executable conformance class from the paper. On our webpage, we provide an extended version of this paper where we re-inserted the text we had to cut from the paper.

4. PRACTICAL RELEVANCE AND DISCUSSION

Since its first publication in June 2002, numerous consulting firms and international projects have adopted the scenario-driven role-engineering process. The most visible of which is probably the Health Level 7 (HL7) role-engineering process defined by the US National Healthcare RBAC Task Force (see [5]). Among other things, the task force applied this process to produce HL7 RBAC healthcare scenarios and a HL7 RBAC healthcare permission catalog. In addition to such international projects, we are continuously conducting role engineering projects and gained many experiences in this area (see, e.g., [15, 18, 23, 24]). For example, in 2008 we conducted a role engineering project with the Austrian

Federal Ministry of Finance[6], in 2009 we conducted a corresponding case study with the German branch of ABB[7], in 2009/10 we were involved in a rights management project with Ernst & Young[8], and currently we are conducting a role engineering project with the Vienna City Municipality[9]. In each of these (as well as in other) projects we received requests for an extended automation support of different role engineering tasks. In particular, these requests revealed the demand for an automation support of the monotonous derivation of role engineering artifacts from scenario and process models.

The automatically derived candidate artifacts serve as input for the definition of a customized RBAC model for the respective organization or information system. However, note that the candidate artifacts are subject to a subsequent selection and refinement by human role engineers and domain experts. This is because an automated derivation is well-suited to derive a first version of the respective candidate artifacts, yet it cannot produce a set of tailored, integrated, and non-redundant role engineering artifacts. For example, the subsequent refinement aims to identify redundancies resulting from the automatic derivation such as the "Bank Clerk A" and "Bank Clerk B" candidate roles which will most likely be combined into a single "Bank Clerk" role (see Section 3). Nevertheless, although the candidate artifacts require a subsequent refinement, the automated derivation facilitates a monotonic and thus error-prone task, and thereby significantly eases the tasks of human role engineers.

5. RELATED WORK

Role mining is related to role engineering and aims to derive RBAC policy sets from permissions and role definitions that exist in the software systems of an organization. In [14], Kuhlmann et al. apply data mining techniques to detect patterns in a set of access rights. Subsequently, they use these patterns to derive candidate roles combined with business (organizational and functional) information. In [10], Frank et al. present an approach for hybrid role mining. In particular, they first review preexisting business information to determine their relevance for the role mining process. Afterwards, they include the preexisting business information, such as the organizational hierarchy or job descriptions, in the role creation step of role mining. Colantonio et al. [4], present a similar approach to use business information in a role mining approach. The approach is applied to identify the roles that are to be included in a candidate role set. Molloy et al. [17] applied role mining techniques to identify roles with semantic meaning. In case subject-to-permission relations are the only information available, they apply formal concept analysis to find roles. If certain user-attribute information is also available (e.g. job positions, departments, or job responsibilities) they propose to derive roles from such user-attribute expressions. Our approach is complementary to role mining approaches and can be used in combination with role mining.

Similar to our approach, Wolter et al. derive access control policies from BPMN 1.0 models in the domain of Web Services [27]. They provide authorization constraint artifacts as extension for the BPMN meta-model. These constraints can be assigned to groups, lanes, and respective activities to define separation of duty and binding of duty constraints. To automate the extraction of security policies from process models, they propose a mapping from selected meta-model entities of BPMN and XACML (eXtensible

Access Control Markup Language). XSLT is applied to automate the generation of enforceable XACML policies.

Fernandez and Hawkins [6] suggested an early approach to determine role rights from use cases. In particular, they propose to extend the textual description of use cases in order to define security requirements for use cases. Authorization rules are then derived from the specifications defined in the use case descriptions. In addition, they complement the use case descriptions with scenario diagrams to discover role rights. In [16], Mendling et al. introduced an approach to extract RBAC models from BPEL (Business Process Execution Language) processes. The approach integrates BPEL and RBAC on the meta-model level and describes how certain RBAC artifacts can be automatically derived from BPEL processes. Similar to the approach presented in this paper, the approach from [16] can be used to automate steps of the role engineering process.

Our work complements the contributions mentioned above by providing an approach for the automated derivation of role engineering artifacts from UML activity models, UML interaction models and BPMN collaboration models. In principle, it can be combined with each of the above mentioned approaches.

6. CONCLUSION

The scenario-driven role engineering process provides a systematic approach to engineer and maintain customized RBAC models. In recent years, we gained many experiences which resulted in an evolutionary enhanced role engineering process and a much better understanding of related activities and artifacts. In addition to our own projects and case studies, scenario-driven role engineering is used by several consulting firms and in international projects (see Section 4).

Such as every engineering process, the role engineering process depends significantly on human factors and cannot be completely automated. However, the automated derivation of role engineering artifacts from scenario and process models can significantly ease role engineering tasks. In particular, the automation of certain role engineering steps can help to facilitate monotonic and thereby error-prone tasks. In this paper, we presented an approach to derive role engineering artifacts from UML activity models, UML interaction models and BPMN collaboration models. However, our general approach for the derivation of role engineering artifacts is based on meta-model integration and is therefore independent of the UML, BPMN, or any other modeling language (see Section 1.2).

Human role engineers as well as domain experts from the respective organization can adapt and refine the derived candidate role engineering artifacts in order to specify a tailored RBAC model. Furthermore, to ease the work of role engineers and to reduce ambiguities in the derived role engineering artifacts, we recommend the following simple modeling guidelines for UML and BPMN: a) the name of an UML interaction model should be identical to the name of the action it refines; b) the names of subjects and objects should be consistent across the models (i.e. in UML the same subject or object is always referenced via the same identifier string or id, such as the "CustomerMgmt" sub-system or the "Bank Clerk" actor from our example) c) a clear understanding of lanes in a model should be defined, since BPMN leaves the meaning of lanes up to the modelers and d) the usage of PartnerRoles, PartnerEntities and Resources across all BPMN models for participants, lanes and tasks should be accurately defined.

In our future work, we will further investigate how we can derive different types of candidate constraints (such as context constraints, see [26]) from UML and BPMN models. In addition, we

---

[6]http://english.bmf.gv.at/

[7]http://www.abb.com/

[8]http://www.ey.com/

[9]http://www.wien.gv.at/ma14/

are currently investigating the options to combine the derivations from scenario and process models based on different languages to automatically propose a candidate RBAC model. Moreover, we plan to investigate further options to integrate role engineering and related role mining and process mining approaches.

7. REFERENCES

[1] G. J. Ahn and R. Sandhu. Role-Based Authorization Constraints Specification. *ACM Transactions on Information and System Security (TISSEC)*, 3(4), November 2000.

[2] V. Apparao, S. Byrne, M. Champion, and et. al. Document Object Model (DOM) Level 1 Specification. available at: http://www.w3.org/TR/1998/REC-DOM-Level-1-19981001/, October 1998. W3 Consortium Recommendation.

[3] D. Clark and D. Wilson. A Comparison of Commercial and Military Computer Security Policies. In *Proc. of the IEEE Symposium on Security and Privacy*, April 1987.

[4] A. Colantonio, R. Di Pietro, A. Ocello, and N. V. Verde. A Formal Framework to Elicit Roles with Business Meaning in RBAC Systems. In *Proc. of the 14th ACM Symposium on Access Control Models and Technologies (SACMAT)*, June 2009.

[5] E. Coyne and J. Davis. *Role Engineering for Enterprise Security Management*. Artech House, 2008.

[6] E. B. Fernandez and J. C. Hawkins. Determining Role Rights from Use Cases. In *Proc. of the 2nd ACM Workshop on Role-Based Access Control (RBAC)*, New York, NY, USA, 1997.

[7] D. Ferraiolo, J. Barkley, and D. Kuhn. A Role-Based Access Control Model and Reference Implementation within a Corporate Intranet. *ACM Transactions on Information and System Security (TISSEC)*, 2(1), February 1999.

[8] D. Ferraiolo and D. Kuhn. Role-Based Access Controls. In *Proc. of the 15th National Computer Security Conference (CSC)*, October 1992.

[9] D. Ferraiolo, D. Kuhn, and R. Chandramouli. *Role-Based Access Control, Second Edition*. Artech House, 2007.

[10] M. Frank, A. P. Streich, D. A. Basin, and J. M. Buhmann. A Probabilistic Approach to Hybrid Role Mining. In *Proc. of the 16th ACM Conference on Computer and Communications Security (CCS)*, 2009.

[11] A. L. Hors, P. L. Hegaret, L. Wood, and et. al. Document Object Model (DOM) Level 2 Core Specification. available at: http://www.w3.org/TR/2000/REC-DOM-Level-2-Core-20001113/, November 2000. W3 Consortium Recommendation.

[12] A. L. Hors, P. L. Hegaret, L. Wood, G. Nicol, J. Robie, M. Champion, and S. Byrne. Document Object Model (DOM) Level 3 Core Specification, Version 1.0. available at: http://www.w3.org/TR/DOM-Level-3-Core, April 2004. W3 Consortium Recommendation.

[13] M. Jarke, X. Bui, and J. Carroll. Scenario Management: An Interdisciplinary Approach. *Requirements Engineering Journal*, 3(3/4), 1998.

[14] M. Kuhlmann, D. Shohat, and G. Schimpf. Role Mining - Revealing Business Roles for Security Administration using Data Mining Technology. In *Proc. of the 7th ACM Symposium on Access Control Models and Technologies (SACMAT)*, New York, NY, USA, 2003.

[15] S. Kunz, S. Evdokimov, B. Fabian, B. Stieger, and M. Strembeck. Role-Based Access Control for Information Federations in the Industrial Service Sector. In *Proc. of the 18th European Conference on Information Systems (ECIS)*, June 2010.

[16] J. Mendling, M. Strembeck, G. Stermsek, and G. Neumann. An Approach to Extract RBAC Models from BPEL4WS Processes. In *Proc. of the 13th IEEE International Workshops on Enabling Technologies: Infrastructures for Collaborative Enterprises (WETICE)*, June 2004.

[17] I. Molloy, H. Chen, T. Li, Q. Wang, N. Li, E. Bertino, S. Calo, and J. Lobo. Mining roles with semantic meanings. In *Proc. of the 14th ACM Symposium on Access Control Models and Technologies (SACMAT)*, pages 21–30, New York, NY, USA, 2008. ACM.

[18] G. Neumann and M. Strembeck. A Scenario-driven Role Engineering Process for Functional RBAC Roles. In *Proc. of 7th ACM Symposium on Access Control Models and Technologies (SACMAT)*, June 2002.

[19] OMG. Business Process Modeling Notation (BPMN). available at: http://www.omg.org/spec/BPMN/2.0/Beta2/, May 2010. Version 2.0 - Beta 2, dtc/2010-06-04, The Object Management Group.

[20] MOF 2.0 / XMI Mapping Specification. available at: http://www.omg.org/technology/documents/formal/xmi.htm, December 2007. Version 2.1.1, formal/2007-12-01, The Object Management Group.

[21] OMG Unified Modeling Language (OMG UML): Superstructure. available at: http://www.omg.org/technology/documents/formal/uml.htm, February 2009. Version 2.2, formal/2009-02-02, The Object Management Group.

[22] R. Sandhu, E. Coyne, H. Feinstein, and C. Youman. Role-Based Access Control Models. *IEEE Computer*, 29(2), February 1996.

[23] M. Strembeck. A Role Engineering Tool for Role-Based Access Control. In *Proc. of the 3rd Symposium on Requirements Engineering for Information Security (SREIS)*, August 2005.

[24] M. Strembeck. Scenario-Driven Role Engineering. *IEEE Security & Privacy*, 8(1), January/February 2010.

[25] M. Strembeck and J. Mendling. Generic Algorithms for Consistency Checking of Mutual-Exclusion and Binding Constraints in a Business Process Context. In *Proc. of the 18th International Conference on Cooperative Information Systems (CoopIS), Lecture Notes in Computer Science (LNCS), Vol. 6426, Springer Verlag*, October 2010.

[26] M. Strembeck and G. Neumann. An Integrated Approach to Engineer and Enforce Context Constraints in RBAC Environments. *ACM Transactions on Information and System Security (TISSEC)*, 7(3), August 2004.

[27] C. Wolter, A. Schaad, and C. Meinel. Deriving xacml policies from business process models. In M. Weske, M. Hacid, and C. Godart, editors, *Web Information Systems Engineering, WISE 2007 Workshops*, volume 4832 of *Lecture Notes in Computer Science*, pages 142–153. Springer Berlin / Heidelberg, 2007.

An Integrated Approach for Identity and Access Management in a SOA Context

Waldemar Hummer[1], Patrick Gaubatz[2], Mark Strembeck[3], Uwe Zdun[2], and Schahram Dustdar[1]

[1]Distributed Systems Group
Information Systems Institute
Vienna University of Technology
{lastname}@infosys.tuwien.ac.at

[2]Software Architecture Group
Faculty of Computer Science
University of Vienna
{firstname.lastname}@univie.ac.at

[3]Information Systems Institute
Vienna University of
Economics and Business
mark.strembeck@wu.ac.at

ABSTRACT

In this paper, we present an approach for identity and access management (IAM) in the context of (cross-organizational) service-oriented architectures (SOA). In particular, we defined a domain-specific language (DSL) for role-based access control (RBAC) that allows for the definition of IAM policies for SOAs. For the application in a SOA context, our DSL environment automatically produces WS-BPEL (Business Process Execution Language for Web services) specifications from the RBAC models defined in our DSL. We use the WS-BPEL extension mechanism to annotate parts of the process definition with directives concerning the IAM policies. At deployment time, the WS-BPEL process is instrumented with special activities which are executed at runtime to ensure its compliance to the IAM policies. The algorithm that produces extended WS-BPEL specifications from DSL models is described in detail. Thereby, policies defined via our DSL are automatically mapped to the implementation level of a SOA-based business process. This way, the DSL decouples domain experts' concerns from the technical details of IAM policy specification and enforcement. Our approach thus enables (non-technical) domain experts, such as physicians or hospital clerks, to participate in defining and maintaining IAM policies in a SOA context. Based on a prototype implementation we also discuss several performance aspects of our approach.

Categories and Subject Descriptors

D.4.6 [**Operating Systems**]: Security and Protection—*Access Control*; C.2.4 [**Computer-Communication Networks**]: Distributed Systems—*Client/server, Distributed applications*; D.2.11 [**Software**]: Software Architectures—*Domain-specific architectures, Languages, Service-oriented architecture*

General Terms

Design, Languages, Management, Security

Keywords

Identity and Access Management, SAML, SOAP, WS-BPEL, WS-Security

1. INTRODUCTION

In recent years, Service-Oriented Architectures (SOA) [24] have emerged as a suitable means to develop loosely coupled distributed systems. Today, Web services are a commonly used technology that build the foundation of SOAs and both intra- and cross-organizational business processes. Electronic business collaborations require enforcement of high-level security constraints such as ensuring the identity and competencies of end users, restricted access to resources, or protection of private data. In our previous work, we identified the need for modeling support of identity and access control models from the experiences gained in the area of role engineering (see, e.g., [34–37]). However, to enforce the corresponding access control policies in a software system, the resulting models must also be mapped to the implementation level.

Different aspects of identity and access management (IAM) in distributed environments and SOAs have been studied previously. In fact, our work builds on a number of existing approaches and standards. An important point with regards to electronic business processes spanning multiple services and cross-organizational units is the concept of Single Sign-On (SSO, e.g., [17, 25]), which simplifies user authentication for the individual services by establishing trust relationships across security domains. SSO allows the business process to obtain a signed authentication token for a security domain d, which is also accepted by other security domains that trust domain d. The Security Assertion Markup Language (SAML) [20] provides a standard way of expressing signed assertions about the identity and attributes of a system participant. The Web Services Security (WS-Security) [21] SAML Token Profile defines how SAML assertions can be transported securely in Web service invocations, i.e., by including a security token element in the header of the SOAP (Simple Object Access Protocol) invocation message.

Cross-organizational IAM involves stakeholders with different background and expertise. The technical IAM model which expresses well-defined semantics and supports detailed security audits may be suited for software architects and developers, but for non-technical domain experts an abstracted view is desirable. In the context of model-driven development (MDD) [28,29,33], a systematic approach for DSL (*domain-specific language*) development has emerged in recent years (see, e.g., [15, 32, 38, 42]). A DSL is a tailor-made (computer) language for a specific problem domain. In general, DSLs provide relevant domain abstractions as first class language elements and can be designed and used on different abstraction layers, ranging from DSLs for technical tasks to DSLs for tasks on the business-level. Thus, DSLs can also be defined for non-technical stakeholders, such as business analysts or biologists, for example. In general, a DSL makes domain-knowledge explicit.

That is, the DSL is built so that domain experts can understand and modify DSL code to phrase domain-specific statements that are understood by an information system. To ensure compliance between models and software platforms, the models defined in a DSL are mapped to source code artifacts of the software platform via automated model-transformations (see, e.g., [14, 30, 41]).

This paper presents an approach to define and enforce IAM policies in cross-organizational SOA business processes. The approach is based on the Web Services Business Process Execution Language (WS-BPEL) [22], which has in the previous years emerged as the de-facto standard for defining Web service compositions and business processes. WS-BPEL is an XML-based special-purpose language whose features range from invocation of external Web services, message correlation and asynchronous invocations to control flow structures (e.g., loops, branches, parallel flows), XML data transformation and modification of SOAP message headers. Our implementation builds on well-established standards including SAML and WS-Security, and supports the concept of single-sign-on (SSO) to authorize and secure the individual steps in the business process. The use of a domain-specific language (DSL) for Role Based Access Control (RBAC) [4, 5, 27] allows us to abstract from technological details and to involve domain experts in the security modeling process. SOA experts and software developers utilize the identity and access models to define security constraints while designing electronic business processes in WS-BPEL. At deployment time, the WS-BPEL process is instrumented with special activities to ensure its compliance to the IAM policies at runtime.

The remainder of this paper is structured as follows. In Section 2, we introduce an illustrative scenario for IAM in a distributed SOA context. We then present in Section 3 our approach for integrated modeling and enforcement of identity and access control in SOA business processes, and discuss the mapping from the modeling to the implementation level. Details on the implementation are given in Section 4, and in Section 5 we evaluate different aspects of our solution. Section 6 contains a discussion of related work, and Section 7 concludes the paper with an outlook for future work.

2. SCENARIO: IAM IN A SOA BUSINESS PROCESS CONTEXT

We illustrate the concepts of this paper based on a motivating scenario taken from the e-health domain. Our example scenario models the workflow of an orthopedic hospital which treats fractures and other serious injuries. The hospital is supported by an IT infrastructure organized in a SOA, implemented using Web services. The SOA provides services for patient data, connects the departments of the hospital and facilitates the routine processes. The hospital exchanges data with other partner hospitals. As patient data constitute sensitive information, security must be ensured and a tailored domain-specific RBAC model needs to be enforced.

A core procedure in the hospital is the patient examination. The corresponding technical business process is depicted in Business Process Modeling Notation (BPMN) in Figure 1. We assume that the process is implemented using WS-BPEL and that each BPMN service task (depicted as gray rounded rectangles) denotes the invocation of a Web service. The arrows between the tasks indicate the control flow of the process. The BPMN groups in the figure are annotated with *Role* and *Context* labels, the purpose of which will be detailed later in this section. Note that all tasks are backed by Web services, however, part of the tasks are not purely technical but involve some sort of human labor or interaction. For instance, the activation of the task *Obtain X-Ray Image* triggers an invocation

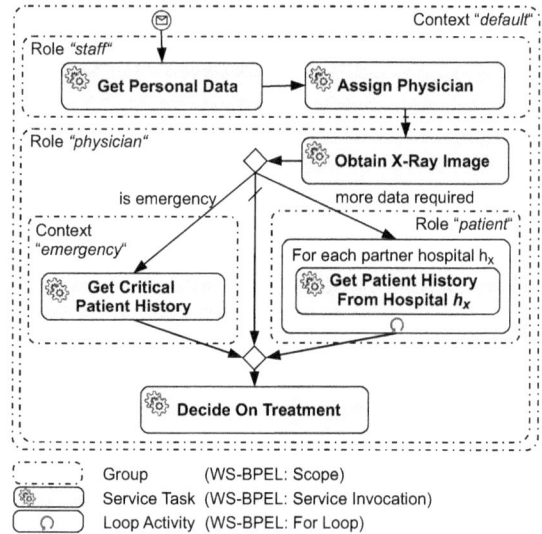

Figure 1: Hospital Patient Examination Scenario in BPMN

to the Web service http://h1.com/xray, but the task itself is performed by the hospital staff (and the patient).

The first step in the examination process is to retrieve the personal data of the patient. To demonstrate the cross-organizational character of this scenario, suppose that the patient has never been treated in our example hospital (H1) before, but has already received medical treatment in a partner hospital (H2). Consequently, H1 obtains the patient's personal data from H2 via a Web service residing under the URL http://h2.com/patients. Secondly, the patient is assigned to an available physician, which is performed using an examination service. These first two tasks need to be performed by a general staff member (role "staff"). In the process definition in Figure 1, this requirement is expressed as a BPMN *group* (rounded rectangle with dashed border) with a corresponding label. In the implementation of the process, this group is mapped to a BPEL *scope* with an extensibility attribute role. Similar to a scope in a regular programming language, a WS-BPEL scope embraces a set of instructions and defines boundaries for the lifetime of variables and event handlers defined in this scope. Analogously, the role attribute is valid within the boundaries of its owner scope.

After the patient has been assigned, the responsible physician requests an x-ray image using the Web service of the x-ray department (http://h1.com/xray). This activity runs under a new group (or scope), which requires the role "physician". The physician then analyzes the received x-ray image and decides whether additional data are required. For instance, the patient may have had a similar fraction or injury in the past, in which case special treatment is required. Hence, the business process requests historical data from partner hospitals, which also participate in the SOA. Due to privacy issues, the historical data are only disclosed to the patient herself, and the *Get Patient History* service task executes under the role "patient". Note that this role change and the identity management is enforced by the platform, which will be discussed in Section 3. Another situation that requires additional data is the case of an emergency. If the emergency demands for immediate surgery, it is important to determine historical data about any critical conditions or diseases that might interfere with the surgery. This critical information is stored in a secured repository which can be accessed via the Web service http://h1.com/emergency. Access to the critical historical data requires the context "emergency", which is also indicated via an enclosing scope in Figure 1. Finally, after acquiring the necessary data, the process switches back to the context "default" and the role "physician". The invocation of the operation `decideOnTreatment` constitutes the end of the examination and triggers the subsequent treatment activities.

The following list summarizes the stakeholders and their key requirements concerning the SOA-based IT system of the hospital.

- The IT system facilitates the hospital *staff* in their daily work and employs a clear role concept for separation of concerns.
- Besides receiving an efficient treatment, the main interest of the *patient* is that all personal data remain confidential and protected from abuse.
- The *security experts* of the hospital need not necessarily be technical experts and hence require an intuitive interface to model identities, roles and security restrictions in the system.
- The IT *architects and developers* who implement Web services and business processes desire an integrated solution, in which identity and access control can be easily plugged in based on the models defined by the hospital's management.

In the course of this paper, we focus on two aspects concerned with mapping security constraints from a higher-level model to the implementation level: 1) enabling domain experts to map the identity and access model from its abstract representation to a DSL, and mapping of DSL expressions to the implementation level, 2) enabling architects and developers to easily author SOA business processes in WS-BPEL which enforce the security constraints.

3. INTEGRATED APPROACH FOR IAM IN A SOA CONTEXT

This section presents our integrated approach for identity and access management and enforcement in a SOA context. The core assets in a SOA are the services, and the participants that perform operations on these services are either humans or other services. It has been shown that SOA models can be mapped to (extended) RBAC models (e.g., [1]). We build on these findings and provide a declarative DSL for RBAC, integrated with an end-to-end solution for simplified development of secured SOA business processes. The tight integration of the DSL allows to trace identity and access control specifications from the modeling level down to the implementation code, enabling the detailed audit of security compliance.

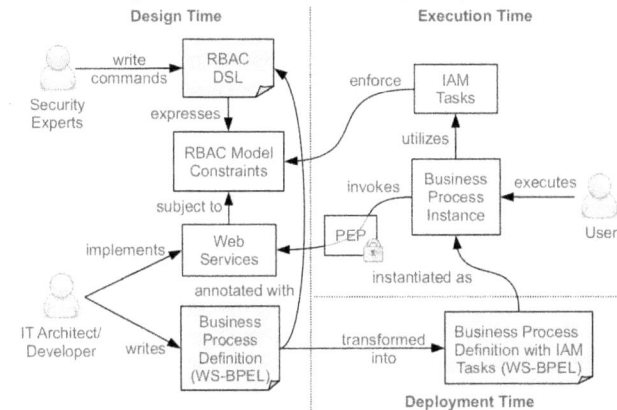

Figure 2: Approach Overview

Figure 2 depicts a high-level overview of our approach, including the involved stakeholders and system artifacts and the relationships between them. At design time, the security experts write RBAC DSL commands to define the RBAC model constraints. The IT spe-

cialists implement Web services and define WS-BPEL processes on top of the services. The WS-BPEL definition is annotated with elements from the RBAC DSL, in order to define which parts in the process require which access privileges. At deployment time, the WS-BPEL file is automatically enriched with IAM tasks that conform to the security annotations. The business process is instantiated and executed by human individuals (for example patients and staff members), and the IAM tasks have the process conform to the constraints defined in the RBAC model. A PEP component intercepts all service invocations and blocks unauthorized access.

In the following, we firstly discuss the core language model of the RBAC DSL and show its mapping to the textual representation and further down to the implementation level. Secondly, we present our approach for automatic enforcement of the access control constraints using the extensibility mechanism in WS-BPEL processes.

3.1 DSL-Based RBAC Modeling for SOA

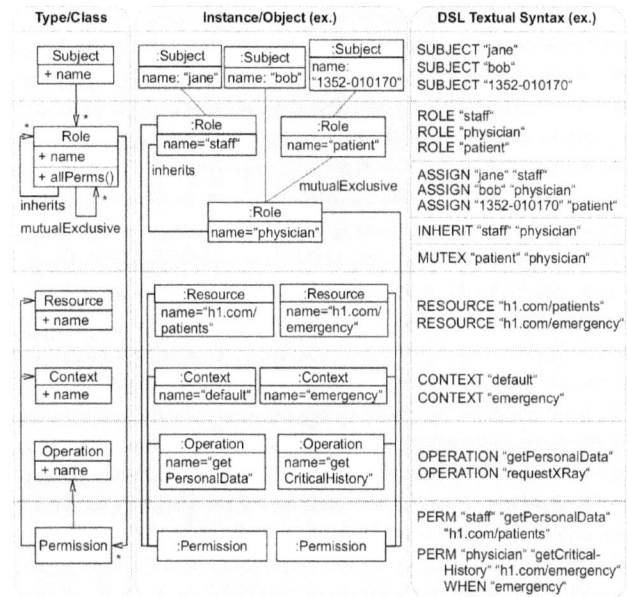

Figure 3: RBAC Model and DSL Language Elements

Figure 3 depicts an example that shows the different abstraction layers of our RBAC DSL. In particular it depicts a (simplified) class diagram of the DSL language elements, an excerpt of the object diagram for the hospital scenario from Figure 1, and a textual representation of the example specified with our RBAC DSL. `Subjects` are identified by a `name` attribute: hospital staff receive a unique name, and for the patients' name we use their social security number, which serves as a unique identifier. Subjects are associated with an arbitrary number of `Roles`, which are themselves associated with `Permissions` to execute certain `Operations`. Roles may inherit from other role instances (association `inherits`), and two roles can be defined as being mutually exclusive (association `mutualExclusive`). We use a context-specific extension of the traditional RBAC model, which has been proposed previously in a similar form (e.g., [6, 8, 26]). The `Context` element allows for a more fine-grained definition of permissions and maps directly to the context requirements in the scenario process definition (see Figure 1). In our approach, we directly associate Web service instances with `Resources`, service invocations with RBAC `Operations`, and `Contexts` with scopes in a Web services business process. A scope in WS-BPEL builds a group of related tasks and limits the lifetime and validity of its enclosed variables, partner links, correlation sets and event handlers. The RBAC permissions are expressed with regard to a certain context in which they are applicable. When a WS-BPEL scope is associated with a certain context (e.g., *emergency*), then all activities (i.e., operations) contained in that scope must execute under this context, and, consequently, the subject executing the process must be allowed to invoke the service operations under this context (see Section 3.2). For instance, when the physician named *bob* is about to retrieve the critical patient history in our scenario, then *bob* needs to have the role *physician*, which allows him to execute the Web service operation `getCriticalHistory` in the context *emergency* (see Figure 3). The *default* context always exists and is automatically assumed if no context is explicitly provided.

DSL Command	Effect (OCL)
SUBJECT "jane"	Subject.allInstances()->select(s | s.name='jane')->size() = 1
ASSIGN "jane" "staff"	Subject.allInstances()->select(s | s.name='jane').role->select(r | r.name='staff')->size() = 1
INHERIT "staff" "physician"	Role.allInstances()->select(r1 | r1.name='staff').allPerms()->forAll(p1 | Role.allInstances()->select(r2 | r2.name='physician').allPerms() ->exists(p2 | p1=p2))
MUTEX "patient" "physician"	Subject.allInstances()->forAll(s | not (s.role->exists(r | r.name='physician') and s.role->exists(r | r.name='patient')))

Table 1: Excerpt of RBAC DSL Semantics in OCL

An excerpt of the RBAC DSL constructs and their effect expressed as an OCL (Object Constraint Language) expression is printed in Table 1. The first exemplary command, SUBJECT "jane" has the effect that, upon execution, exactly one instance of the class *Subject* with name attribute *"jane"* exists. The effect of the second instruction is that the *Subject* named *jane* has an associated *Role* object with name *"staff"*. The INHERIT command takes two parameters, a junior-role and a senior-role name, and causes the senior-role to inherit all permissions of the junior-role. The operation *Role.allPerms()* returns all associated permissions of a Role instance and its ancestor roles. Finally, the statically mutual exclusive roles *"patient"* and *"physician"* are defined via the DSL command MUTEX, which specifies that no *Subject* instance must ever be assigned both of these roles simultaneously . We currently do not use the alternative form of dynamic mutually exclusive constraints which disallow combinations of certain roles to be activated by one user in the same session or process instantiation, but this is planned for future work. The four OCL constraints illustrate the mapping from the abstract RBAC domain model to the level of an intermediate language (DSL), which is easy to use and comprehend for domain experts, and abstracts from the underlying complexity. The remaining OCL constraints for our example have been left out for brevity.

3.1.1 Collaborative Identity and Access Modeling for Single-Sign On

The goal of the patient examination scenario is that hospitals are able to *collaboratively* model the identity and access control information. To avoid a single point of failure and because each hospital reserves the right to define their own (internal) access control policies, the RBAC information is not stored centrally, but each hospital maintains their own model. However, the ability to retrieve the model data from partner hospitals is vital in order to support SSO and cross-organizational access to resources. For instance, the loop in the business process in Figure 1 retrieves the patient

history from partner hospitals using a secured Web service operation `getPatientHistory`, which is provided by all hospitals. The idea is to store data in a decentralized manner, i.e., when a patient is registered or examined in hospital X, then X creates a patient record that is stored locally, but can be accessed by the partner hospitals. The invocation of the `getPatientHistory` operation is secured with a SAML header asserting the identity of the patient. Consider the patient is identified under a subject name "1352-010170" (cf. Figure 3). This requires that the RBAC models of the partner hospitals also contain a subject with this identifier, and that this subject is associated with the role "patient".

To achieve an integrated view on a distributed RBAC model, different strategies have been proposed. The special-purpose language PCL (Policy Combining Language) defined in [10] allows combining of access control policies expressed in XACML. In another work, integration of policies from different organizations is performed based on the similarity of XACML rules [12]. Since the RBAC DSL essentially provides a subset of the functionality of XACML, we are able to utilize these existing solutions for policy integration and collaborative modeling of access control constraints across the different hospitals in the scenario.

3.2 Security Enforcement in WS-BPEL Processes using Annotations

Section 3.1 discussed how the RBAC model is constructed by means of the RBAC DSL, and how the access constraints relate to services, operations, and scopes in SOA business processes. To enforce these constraints at runtime, the business process needs to follow a special procedure. For instance, invoking the `getPersonalData` operation of Hospital 1 requires the process to execute under the role "staff". That is, this service operation requires the presence of a corresponding SAML WS-Security token in the SOAP header of the request. The token contains a SAML assertion that confirms the identity of the subject executing the process operation, as well as the attribute claims for that subject. Integrity of this token and the contained attributes is ensured by applying an XML signature [40] using the X.509 certificate issued for Hospital 1. The attribute claims contain the information under which *role* ("staff") and in which *context* ("default") the subject executes the operation. To obtain the signed SAML assertion, the process needs to invoke the operation `requestSAMLAssertion` of the SAML Identity Provider (IdP) service of Hospital 1. The patient data service relies on the IdP to identify and authenticate the subject (process user), hence the user credentials (e.g. subject name and password) are required for invocation of `requestSAMLAssertion`.

Since one execution of the patient examination process involves different subjects (a staff member, a physician, a patient), the user credentials cannot be hard-coded into the process definition, but are requested from a separate, decoupled *Credentials Provider* (CrP) service. This service offers a `getUserAuthentication` operation, which provides the actual user credentials to be used for a specific process scope. Upon invocation, this operation will cause a username/password input prompt to be displayed to the staff member sitting at the reception desk. After the user has been authenticated, the user credentials can also be stored in a local session configuration file on the reception desk computer. To avoid plaintext passwords from being transmitted over the network, the returned user credentials are encrypted using WS-Security [21]. During execution, the *Credentials Provider* service is always invoked when the process enters a scope that requires a change of subject.

The detailed procedure is illustrated in Figure 4, which shows the sub-part of the hospital scenario process that executes under

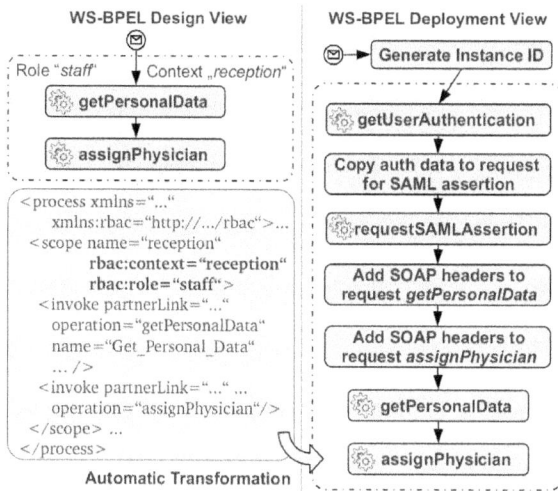

Figure 4: Transformation of WS-BPEL Process Definition

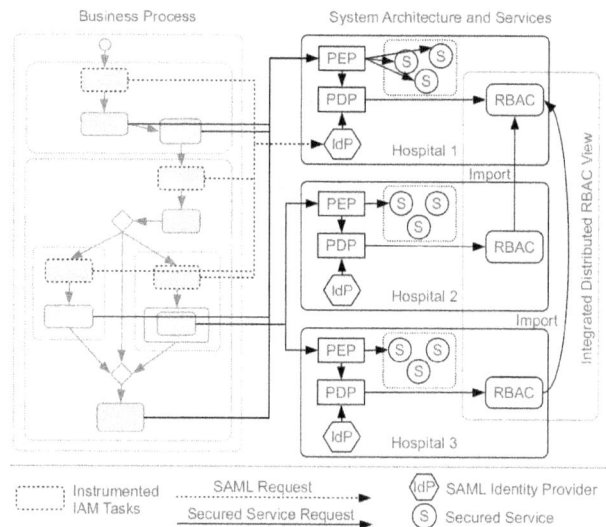

Figure 5: Example Process in System Architecture

the role "staff" and the context "reception". The left part of the figure shows the process definition at design time. Note the annotation attributes `rbac:context` and `rbac:role` which define the required context and role for the scope. At deployment time, the necessary additional process tasks are inserted into the WS-BPEL definition by means of an automatic transformation. At the start of the transformed process, an activity is inserted which generates a unique process instance identifier (ID). The instance ID is sent along as a SOAP header in all subsequent invocations of the WS-BPEL process. This ID helps the CrP service to correlate previous invocations of the process instance, and to keep track of the process state in order to provide the credentials from the correct subject. For instance, when the CrP's operation `getUserAuthentication` is first called with the generated ID, the user credentials are requested from the reception desk employee. The second invocation with the same instance ID will cause the CrP to request the user credentials from the assigned physician, and so on (cf. Figure 1). Note that the CrP service is application-specific and constitutes a tailor-made decoupled component that orchestrates the retrieval of user credentials of changing subjects. The injected process tasks that follow the CrP invocation retrieve the required SAML assertion from the IdP and copy a corresponding SAML header to all service requests of the scope. Details on the implementation of the automatic WS-BPEL transformation are provided in Section 4.

4. IMPLEMENTATION

In the following, we describe the prototype implementation of our approach for integrated SOA identity and access control. This section is divided into four parts: firstly, we outline the architecture of the system and the relationship between the individual services and components; secondly, the SAML-based SSO mechanism is described; the third part briefly discusses the implementation of the RBAC DSL; finally we present the algorithm for automatic transformation of WS-BPEL definitions containing security annotations.

4.1 System Architecture

Figure 5 sketches the high-level architecture and relationship between the example process and the system components. The patient examination example scenario is implemented using WS-

BPEL [22] and deployed in a Glassfish[1] server with WS-BPEL module. The example scenario involves three hospitals, which host the protected services for patient management and examination. All service invocations are routed through a Policy Enforcement Point (PEP), which acts as a central security gateway, intercepts every incoming service request and either allows or disallows its invocation. Using the Java API for XML Web services (JAX-WS), the PEP has been implemented as a SOAP message handler (interface `SOAPHandler`). This handler can be plugged into the Web service's runtime engine in a straightforward manner. Once activated, the interceptor is able to inspect and modify inbound and outbound SOAP messages as well as to abort the service invocation.

Each hospital runs an instance of the SAML IdP service, which is used to issue the SAML assertions that are required in the WS-BPEL process. The responsibilities of the IdP are twofold: firstly, it checks whether the subject (i.e., the user currently executing the process) has provided valid credentials; secondly, the IdP assures the identity of a subject and its associated attributes (roles, contexts) by issuing an SAML assertion which is used as a SOAP header in subsequent service invocations by this subject (i.e., the process scope for which it is valid).

The actual decision whether an invocation should be prevented or not is typically delegated to another entity, the Policy Decision Point (PDP). When deciding over the access to a service resource the PDP has to make sure that the subject attempting to access the resource has the permission to do so. In our concrete implementation, the PDP uses the RBAC repository to determine whether the requesting subject is permitted to access the target resource (service) under the specified context and role. Thereby, the PDP can rely on the SAML tokens in the SOAP header of the request messages, which assert the identity of the subject as well as the context and role it operates under. The policy information in the RBAC repository is based on the DSL commands authored by domain experts. Each repository defines both local rules and integrates rules from RBAC repositories of trusted partner hospitals (see, e.g., [10, 12]). The combined information of all RBAC repositories creates an integrated view on the distributed RBAC model.

The advantage of our approach is that changing security requirements in the course of the process execution are handled automati-

---

[1]https://glassfish.dev.java.net/

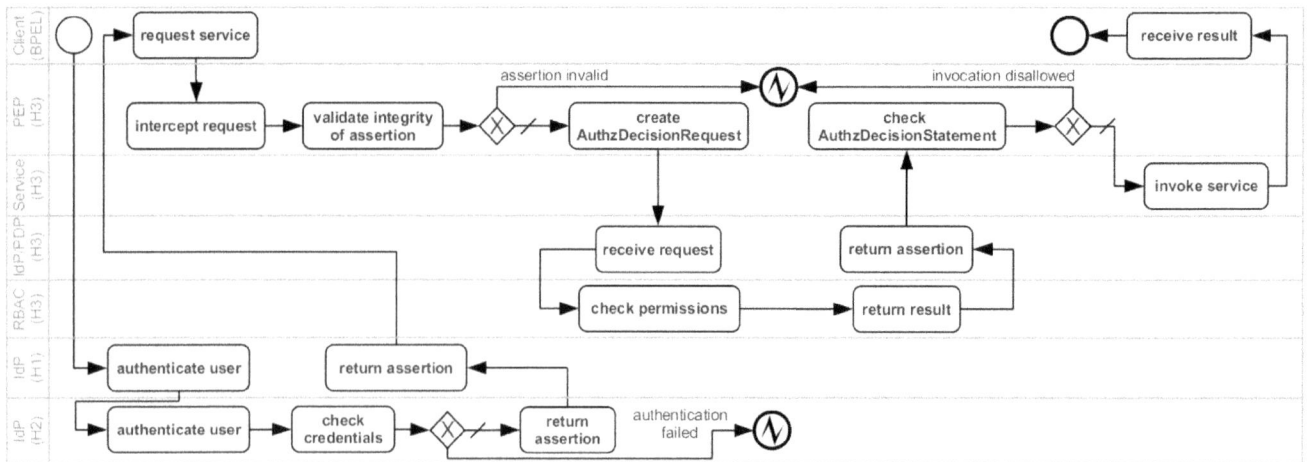

Figure 6: Identity and Access Control Enforcement Procedure

cally. Each time the process changes the scope and requires a new role or context, we utilize the *Instrumented IAM Tasks* which get injected into the WS-BPEL process automatically, as described in Section 3.2. The IAM tasks invoke the IdP and request a new security assertion token for the current subject, role, and context. The security token is then added to the header of all invocations in the same scope. This procedure is repeated for all sub-scopes which require a new role or context. More details concerning the automatic generation of the IAM tasks in WS-BPEL are given in Section 4.4.

4.2 SAML-based Single Sign-On

Figure 6 depicts an example of the Identity and Access Control enforcement procedure modeled via BPMN. To illustrate the SSO aspect of the scenario, we assume that a patient with subject name "1352-010170" (cf. Figure 3), who is registered in hospital 2 (H2), is examined in hospital 1 (H1) and requests its patient history from previous examinations in hospital 3 (H3). The procedure is initiated by the Web service client that demands the execution of a protected Web service. Note that we use the generic term *client*, whereas in our scenario this client is the WS-BPEL engine executing the patient examination process. Prior to issuing the actual service request, the client has to authenticate using the SAML IdP. The latter queries the user database (DB) to validate the credentials provided by the client. In our approach, the credentials (e.g., username-password combinations) are stored in a separate DB and are hence decoupled from the RBAC model. However, the username in the DB equals the subject name in the RBAC model. As the credentials of user "1352-010170" are not stored in the DB of H1, the IdP contacts the IdP of H2, which validates the credentials.

If the user credentials could not be validated, the process is terminated prematurely and a SOAP fault message is returned. In our example scenario, the business process receives the fault message and activates corresponding WS-BPEL fault handlers. Otherwise, if the credentials are valid, the IdP creates a signed assertion similar to the one shown in Listing 1 and passes it back to the client. From now on the business process attaches this assertion to every service request. The request to the protected service is then intercepted by the PEP of H3, which extracts the attached assertion, validates its integrity, and aborts the service invocation if the assertion is invalid (i.e., has been manipulated). Otherwise, it generates an Authorization Decision Request message which is passed to the PDP. The PDP then asks the RBAC repository if the client is allowed to access the requested service. The PDP's decision is expressed as an

Authorization Decision Statement. Wrapped into an assertion similar to the one shown in Listing 2, the statement is then passed back to the PEP. Based on the assertion's enclosed information the PEP then either effects the actual service invocation or returns a fault.

The example SAML assertion in Listing 1 illustrates the information that is encapsulated in the header token when the scenario process invokes the `getPatientHistory` operation of the patient Web service of H3. The assertion states that the subject named `1352-010170`, which has been successfully authenticated by the IdP of the hospital denoted by the `Issuer` element (H2), is allowed to use the context `default` and the role `patient`. Note that the subject can be a human being, but it may as well be a service itself that attempts to invoke another service as part of a service composition. The included XML signature element ensures the integrity of the assertion, i.e., that the assertion content indeed originates from the issuing IdP (H2) and has not been modified in any way. When the PEP of H3 intercepts the service invocation with the SAML SOAP header, its first task is to verify the integrity of the assertion. The signature verification requires the public key of the IdP that signed the assertion; this key is directly requested from the corresponding IdP (under `http://h2.com/IdP`) using SAML Metadata [19].

```
1    <Issuer>http://h2.com/IdP</Issuer>
2    <ds:Signature>...</ds:Signature>
3    <Subject><NameID>1352-010170</NameID></Subject>
4    <Conditions NotBefore="2010-12-17T09:48:36.171Z"
5                NotOnOrAfter="2010-12-17T10:00:36.171Z"/>
6    <AttributeStatement>
7      <Attribute Name="context">
8        <AttributeValue>default</AttributeValue>
9      </Attribute>
10     <Attribute Name="role">
11       <AttributeValue>patient</AttributeValue>
12     </Attribute>
13   </AttributeStatement>
14 </Assertion>
```

Listing 1: SAML Assertion Example (1)

After the PEP of H3 has verified the message integrity (and thereby authenticated the subject), it needs to determine whether the subject is authorized to access the requested service operation. This is achieved by the PDP service of H3 that allows the PEP to post an SAML Authorization Decision Query. The PDP answers this query by returning an assertion containing at least one SAML Authorization Decision Statement. Using these Decision Statements the PDP is able to express the RBAC service's authorization decision using "plain" SAML. Listing 2 shows an example SAML assertion which informs the PEP that our patient is allowed to invoke the action (operation) `getPersonalData` of the resource (Web service) `http://h1.com/patient`. The `Issuer` name of the PDP is the same as for the IdP (`http://h3.com/IdP`).

```
 1   <Assertion>
 2     <Issuer>http://h3.com/IdP</Issuer>
 3     <ds:Signature>...</ds:Signature>
 4     <Subject>
 5       <NameID>1352−010170</NameID>
 6     </Subject>
 7     <AuthzDecisionStatement Decision="Permit"
 8       Resource="http://h3.com/patient">
 9       <Action>getPersonalData</Action>
10     </AuthzDecisionStatement>
11   </Assertion>
```

Listing 2: SAML Assertion Example (2)

4.3 RBAC DSL Implementation

In Section 3.1 we have described the mapping of the RBAC model elements to the textual DSL representation. The mapping of the RBAC DSL commands to executable code on the implementation level is illustrated in Figure 7. We follow a *hybrid* approach to DSL development, which combines *preprocessing* with *embedding* [42]. Embedding means that the DSL platform makes use of an existing *host language* and uses the interpreter and development tools of that language. Preprocessing denotes the process of converting the DSL commands into the machine-readable syntax of the host language using (light-weight) transformations. We evaluated the performance and syntactical flexibility of different (scripting) languages and have chosen Ruby, a language frequently used for DSL development. Ruby provides an interpreter named *JRuby*[2], which is implemented in pure Java and can be integrated using the Java Bean Scripting Framework[3] (BSF).

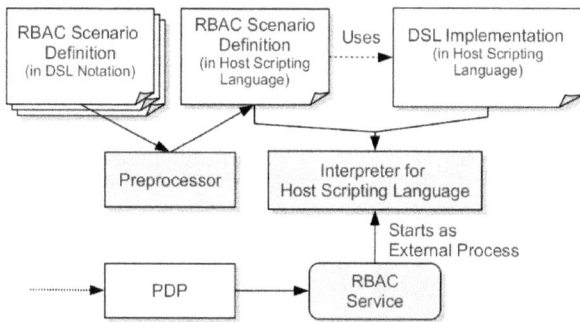

Figure 7: Execution of RBAC Requests

The Preprocessor component transforms the RBAC scenario definition from the DSL notation to the syntax of the host scripting language. An example of a light-weight transformation is to convert `ASSIGN "jane" "staff"` to `ASSIGN "jane","staff"` when using Ruby as the host scripting language. While the first command cannot be parsed by JRuby, the transformed command is well-formed for the interpreter, and is interpreted as a call to the function `ASSIGN` with the two string parameters, which looks up the `Subject` instance and assigns the given role. The remaining DSL constructs are interpreted analogously, and the implementation ensures that all constraints (e.g., mutually exclusive roles, see

[2] http://jruby.org/
[3] http://jakarta.apache.org/bsf/

Table 1) are fulfilled. The preprocessor also serves a second purpose, namely checking whether the DSL code conforms to the allowed syntax or uses any disallowed commands; since the textual DSL is the user interface to the security-critical RBAC model, it is important to identify potentially harmful commands. Another point to consider is that the host language potentially provides features that are undesired for use in the DSL context, such as input/output operations. Hence, the interpreter for the host scripting language executes in a separate Java process, for which we apply restrictive permissions in the Java security policy settings, such as file system access (`java.io.FilePermission`) or network access (`java.net.NetPermission`).

4.4 Automatic Transformation of WS-BPEL Process Definition

At deployment time of the business process, the WS-BPEL definition is automatically transformed to ensure correct execution of identity and access control at runtime. Note that the WS-BPEL process is responsible for the choreography of CrP service, SAML IdP, as well as the core business logic services for patient examination.

Figure 8 depicts the relationships between the five scopes (s_1, s_2, s_3, s_4, s_5) of the scenario process. A hierarchical relationship indicates that the child scope (arrow target) is contained in the parent scope (arrow source). Attributes that are not defined in a child scope are inherited from the parent scope. For instance, scope s_3 inherits the context from its parent s_1. The existence of a sequential relationship between two scopes s_x (arrow source) and s_y (arrow target) means that the control flow is passed from s_x to s_y. More specifically, the last task of scope s_x has a control flow link to the first task of s_y in the process definition. This is the case for the scopes s_2 and s_3, where task *Assign Physician* has a control flow link to *Obtain X-Ray Image* (cf. Figure 1). The scope relationships graph is the basis for determining at which points in the process definition the IAM tasks need to be injected.

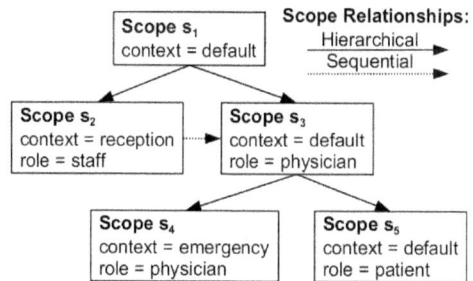

Figure 8: Scope Relationships in Scenario Process

The automatic WS-BPEL transformation is described in Algorithm 1. Variable names are printed in *italics*, and XML markup and XPath expressions are in `typewriter` font. The input is a WS-BPEL document *bpel* with security annotations. Firstly, four required documents need to be imported into the WS-BPEL process using `import` statements: the XML Schema Definitions (XSD) of SAML and WS-Security, and the WSDL (Web Service Description Language) files describing the CrP service and the IdP service.

Then the `partnerLink` declarations for these two services are added to *bpel*, and six `variable` declarations are created (input/output variables for operations `getUserAuthentication` and `requestSAMLAssertion`, a variable to store the assertion, and a variable for additional information such as the instance ID). Next, the algorithm loops over all `scope` elements s with a `role` or `context` attribute, and stores hierarchical and sequential relationships to the array variable *rel*. Although the implementa-

27

Algorithm 1 WS-BPEL Transformation Algorithm

1: **Input:** WS-BPEL document *bpel*
2: **Output:** transformed BPEL document
3: add `<import ../>` statements to *bpel*
4: add `<partnerLink ../>` definitions to *bpel*
5: add `<variable ../>` declarations to *bpel*
6: *rel* ← new array // use variable *rel* for scope relationships
7: **for all** *bpel*//`scope` as *s* **do**
8:    *rel*[*s*] ← ∅
9:    **if** *s*/@`role` or *s*/@`context` **then**
10:       *rel*[*s*] ← *rel*[*s*] ⋃ *s*/`ancestor::scope[1]`
11:       *rel*[*s*] ← *rel*[*s*] ⋃ *s*/`preceding-sibling::scope[1]`
12:    **end if**
13: **end for**
14: **for all** indexes *s* in *rel*, *r* in *rel*[*s*] **do**
15:    **if** scopes *r* and *s* have different security requirements **then**
16:       // add IAM tasks to *s*: `<invoke>` for IdP and CrP services, `<assign>` (SAML SOAP header) for each `<invoke>` in *s*
17:    **end if**
18: **end for**

tion also considers more complex cases, we assume that a sequential relationship exists if *s* has a preceding XML sibling element (i.e., an element on the same level as *s* in the element tree, sharing the parent element with *s*) named `scope`. The parent scope in a hierarchical relationship can be addressed using the XPath `ancestor::scope[1]`. After all scope relationships have been determined, we loop over all related scopes *r* and *s* (conforming to the notation in Figure 8, an arrow points from *r* to *s*) and check whether the security requirements are different (in terms of different security annotations). If so, the IAM tasks are injected to the beginning of scope *s*. The IAM tasks consist of two `invoke`s for the invocations to CrP and IdP, as well as several `assign` tasks which add the security SOAP headers to the requests of the remaining service invocations in scope *s*. Note that the first scope in the process always receives the IAM tasks, although it has neither a parent nor a preceding sibling element.

5. DISCUSSION AND EVALUATION

We evaluated various aspects of the presented solution, and the main evaluation results are discussed in the following. The key aspects are the runtime performance of identity and access control enforcement, and the discussed WS-BPEL transformation algorithm.

To evaluate the scalability of the approach we have defined, deployed, and executed ten test processes with the Glassfish WS-BPEL engine. The processes contain an increasing size (1,2,…,10) of scopes that are annotated with `rbac:role` and `rbac:context` attributes. Each scope contains one `<invoke>` task, which invokes one of the Web service operations of the hospital scenario. The average response time of each service is roughly 200 milliseconds. The processes have been deployed in Glassfish, once with enforced security (i.e., annotated with security attributes, automatically transformed at deployment time), and once in an unsecured version. The deployed processes were executed 10 times and we have calculated the average value to minimize the influence of external effects. Figure 9 illustrates different measurements of the process execution time in milliseconds for both the secured and the unsecured version. The secured version incurs a large overhead, which is hardly surprising considering the fact that for each business logic service the process needs to invoke

the CrP, IdP and RBAC services, and applies and checks the XML signatures. However, the measured results indicate that the current implementation leaves room for additional optimization.

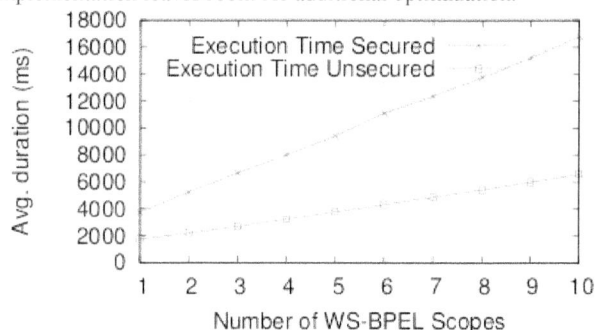

Figure 9: Process Execution Times – Secured vs Unsecured

In Section 4.1 we presented our concrete implementation of an SAML IdP and its duty to issue SAML Assertion tokens. These Assertion tokens are embedded in the header of every subsequent request to secured Web services. Each Assertion contains at least one Attribute Statement that includes the service's required role and context attribute. As the Assertion contains exactly one single context as well as one single role attribute, this means that the Assertion is only valid for one single subject, role, and context. Furthermore this also means, that whenever one of these three change, a new SAML Assertion has to be issued by the IdP. In terms of performance, this approach may not be the most effective, but it has the advantage, that it can be implemented using "plain" SAML. If performance is a critical issue, we propose the following solution: Instead of creating lots of specialized Assertions, the IdP should issue just one generic Assertion per subject. Contrary to the specialized Assertion, the generic one contains a list of all context and role attributes that the subject is allowed to use (instead of just one in each case). This means, that the generic Assertion can be re-used for multiple role/context changes in the WS-BPEL process. Consequently, the IdP's workload can be effectively reduced (provided that there is at least one role/context change present in the WS-BPEL process). The drawback of this solution is that a new custom SOAP header needs to be introduced, in which the client specifies which context and which role (chosen from the Assertion's list of allowed ones) it wants to use. Since the WS-BPEL engine acts as the client, it is the engine's duty to select and attach the correct header to every Web service request. Hence this functionality has to be embedded in the WS-BPEL process definition which, again, increases its size and complexity substantially.

Concerning the evaluation of the WS-BPEL transformation algorithm, we again consider the ten test processes described earlier in this Section. Figure 10 shows the number of WS-BPEL elements of the process definition before and after the automatic transformation. The results indicate that the size of the WS-BPEL definition rises sharply with increasing number of scopes. While our test process with a single scope contains 33/115 WS-BPEL elements before/after transformation, the process definition for 10 scopes grows to 60/484 WS-BPEL elements before/after transformation, respectively. These numbers are determined by counting all XML (sub-)elements in the WS-BPEL file using the XPath expression `count(//*)`. At the beginning of the transformation, 41 elements are added (`import`, `partnerLink` and `variable` declarations), and for each new scope 41 elements are added for the IAM task definitions (note that both values are 41 coincidentally). We observe that the ability to define security annotations in WS-BPEL greatly reduces the required effort at design time.

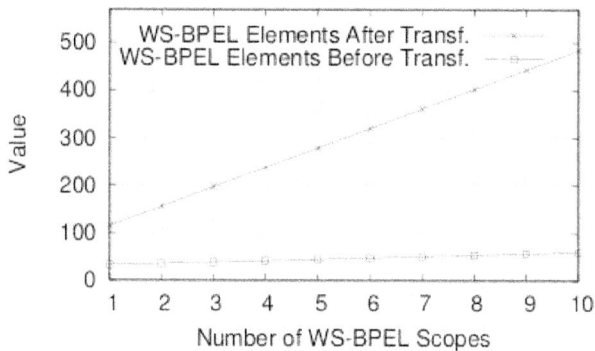

Figure 10: Process Size before and afer Transformation

The textual DSL is used as an interface to the policy rules stored in the RBAC repository. In case a UML binding is required, it is straightforward to integrate our DSL with domain-specific UML extensions for process-related RBAC models (see, e.g., [36]).

6. RELATED WORK

This section discusses related approaches in the area of model-driven IAM and their application to SOA.

Skoksrud et al. present Trust-Serv [31], a solution for model-driven trust negotiation in Web service environments. The platform supports modeling of trust negotiation policies as state machines, and the policy enforcement is transparent to the involved Web services. Different strategies for policy lifecycle management and migration are proposed. Our approach is less concerned with iterative creation of trust relationships, but builds on an IAM model and uses an integrated enforcement in Web service based business processes.

An integrated approach for Model Driven Security, that promotes the use of Model Driven Architectures in the context of access control, is presented by Basin et al. [2]. The foundation is a generic schema that allows creation of DSLs for modeling of access control requirements. The domain expert then defines models of security requirements using these languages. With the help of generators these models are then transformed to access control infrastructures.

The approach by Wolter et al. [39] is concerned with modeling and enforcing security goals in the context of SOA business processes. Similar to our approach, their work suggests that business process experts should collaboratively work on the security policies. A computational independent model (CIM) defines high-level goals, and the CIM gets mapped to a platform independent model (PIM) and further to a platform specific model (PSM). At the PIM level, XACML and *AXIS 2*[4] security configurations are generated. Whereas their approach is more generic and attempts to cover diverse security goals including integrity, availability and audit, we focus on IAM in WS-BPEL business processes.

Kulkarni et al. [9] describe an application of context-aware RBAC to pervasive computing systems. As the paper rightly states, model-level support for revocation of roles and permissions is required to deal with changing context information. Whereas their approach has a strong focus on dynamically changing context (e.g., conditions measured by sensors) and the associated permission (de-)activation, context in our case is a design-time attribute that is part of the RBAC model definitions.

A related access control framework for WS-BPEL is presented by Paci et al. in [23]. It introduces the *RBAC-WS-BPEL* model

---

[4]http://axis.apache.org/axis2/java/core/

and the authorization constraint language *BPCL*. Similar to our approach, the BPEL activities are associated with required permissions (in particular, we associate permissions for `invoke` activities that try to call certain service operations). However, one main difference is related to the boundaries of the validity of user permissions: RBAC-WS-BPEL considers pairs of adjacent activities (a_1 and a_2, where a_1 has a control flow link to a_2) and defines rules among them, including separation of duty (a_1 and a_2 must execute under different roles) and binding of duty (a_1 and a_2 require the same role or user); our approach, on the other hand, is to annotate scopes in BPEL processes, which allows to apply separation and binding of duties in a sequential, but also in a hierarchical manner.

A dynamic approach for enforcement of Web services Security is presented in [16] by Mourad et al. The novelty of the approach is mainly grounded by the use of Aspect-Oriented Programming (AOP) in this context, whereby security enforcement activities are specified as *aspects* that are dynamically weaved into the WS-BPEL process at certain *join points*. Essentially, our approach can also be regarded as a variant of AOP: the weaved aspects are the IAM tasks, and join points are defined by security annotations in the process. A major advantage of our approach is the built-in support for SSO and cross-organizational IAM. An interesting extension could be to decouple security annotations from the WS-BPEL definition and to dynamically adapt to changes at runtime.

Various other papers have been published that are related to our work or have influenced it, some of which are mentioned in the following. The platform-independent framework for Security Services named SECTISSIMO has been proposed by Memon at al. [13]. A multilayer mandatory access control (MAC) architecture tailored to Web applications is presented by Hicks et al. [7]. Lin et al. [11] propose policy decomposition to support collaborative access control definition. In [3] an approach to speeding up credential-based access control operations – in particular in the web context – is proposed by Carminati et al.

XACML [18] is an XML-based standard to describe RBAC policies in a flexible and extensible way. Our DSL could be classified as a high-level abstraction that implements a subset of XACML's feature set. Using a transformation of DSL code to XACML markup, it becomes possible to integrate our approach with the well-established XACML environment and tools for policy integration (e.g., [12]).

7. CONCLUSION

We presented an integrated approach for Identity and Access Management in a SOA context. The solution is centered around model-driven development of RBAC constraints, and runtime enforcement of these constraints in Web services based business processes. Our approach fosters cross-organizational authentication and authorization in service-based systems, and greatly simplifies development of SSO-enabled WS-BPEL processes. Although tailor-made SSO solutions (coded explicitly in the business process) may yield a performance gain over the generic approach, from a practical viewpoint our approach has the advantage of being highly reusable and simple to apply. As part of our ongoing work, we are developing alternative ways to define and assign RBAC permissions at runtime, also taking into account dynamic mutual exclusion. We further investigate the use of additional security annotations and an extended view of context information.

8. REFERENCES

[1] M. Alam, M. Hafner, and R. Breu. A constraint based role based access control in the SECTET a model-driven approach. In *Int. Conf. on Privacy, Security and Trust*, 2006.

[2] D. Basin, J. Doser, and T. Lodderstedt. Model driven security: From UML models to access control infrastructures. *ACM Transactions on Software Engineering Methodology*, 15:39–91, 2006.

[3] B. Carminati and E. Ferrari. AC-XML documents: improving the performance of a web access control module. In *10th ACM SACMAT*, pages 67–76, 2005.

[4] D. F. Ferraiolo and D. R. Kuhn. Role-Based Access Controls. In *15th National Computer Security Conference*, 1992.

[5] D. F. Ferraiolo, D. R. Kuhn, and R. Chandramouli. *Role-Based Access Control*. Artech House, second edition, 2007.

[6] O. Garcia-Morchon and K. Wehrle. Efficient and context-aware access control for pervasive medical sensor networks. In *IEEE Int. Conf. on Pervasive Computing and Communications Workshops*, pages 322 –327, April 2010.

[7] B. Hicks, S. Rueda, D. King, T. Moyer, J. Schiffman, Y. Sreenivasan, P. McDaniel, and T. Jaeger. An architecture for enforcing end-to-end access control over web applications. In *15th ACM SACMAT*, pages 163–172, 2010.

[8] V. Koufi, F. Malamateniou, and G. Vassilacopoulos. A Mediation Framework for the Implementation of Context-Aware Access Control in Pervasive Grid-Based Healthcare Systems. In *4th Int. Conf. on Advances in Grid and Pervasive Computing*, pages 281–292, 2009.

[9] D. Kulkarni and A. Tripathi. Context-aware role-based access control in pervasive computing systems. In *13th ACM SACMAT*, pages 113–122, 2008.

[10] N. Li, Q. Wang, W. Qardaji, E. Bertino, P. Rao, J. Lobo, and D. Lin. Access control policy combining: theory meets practice. In *14th ACM SACMAT*, pages 135–144, 2009.

[11] D. Lin, P. Rao, E. Bertino, N. Li, and J. Lobo. Policy decomposition for collaborative access control. In *13th ACM SACMAT*, pages 103–112, 2008.

[12] P. Mazzoleni, B. Crispo, S. Sivasubramanian, and E. Bertino. XACML Policy Integration Algorithms. *ACM Transactions on Information System Security*, 11:4:1–4:29, February 2008.

[13] M. Memon, M. Hafner, and R. Breu. SECTISSIMO: A Platform-independent Framework for Security Services. In *Modeling Security Workshop at MODELS '08*, 2008.

[14] T. Mens and P. V. Gorp. A Taxonomy of Model Transformation. *Electronic Notes in Theoretical Computer Science*, 152:125–142, 2006.

[15] M. Mernik, J. Heering, and A. Sloane. When and How to Develop Domain-Specific Languages. *ACM Computing Surveys*, 37(4):316–344, December 2005.

[16] A. Mourad, S. Ayoubi, H. Yahyaoui, and H. Otrok. New approach for the dynamic enforcement of Web services security. In *8th Int. Conf. on Privacy Security and Trust*, pages 189 –196, 2010.

[17] B. Neuman and T. Ts'o. Kerberos: an authentication service for computer networks. *Communications Magazine, IEEE*, 32(9):33–38, Sept. 1994.

[18] OASIS. eXtensible Access Control Markup Language. http://docs.oasis-open.org/xacml/2.0, 2005.

[19] OASIS. Metadata for the OASIS Security Assertion Markup Language (SAML). http://docs.oasis-open.org/security/saml/v2.0/saml-metadata-2.0-os.pdf, 2005.

[20] OASIS. Security Assertion Markup Language. http://docs.oasis-open.org/security/saml/v2.0/saml-core-2.0-os.pdf, March 2005.

[21] OASIS. Web Services Security: SOAP Message Security 1.1. http://docs.oasis-open.org/wss/v1.1/wss-v1.1-spec-os-SOAPMessageSecurity.pdf, 2006.

[22] OASIS. Web Services Business Process Execution Language. http://docs.oasis-open.org/wsbpel/2.0/OS, 2007.

[23] F. Paci, E. Bertino, and J. Crampton. An Access-Control Framework for WS-BPEL. *Int. J. f. Web Services Research*, 5(3):20–43, 2008.

[24] M. P. Papazoglou, P. Traverso, S. Dustdar, and F. Leymann. Service-Oriented Computing: State of the Art and Research Challenges. *Computer*, 40(11):38–45, 2007.

[25] A. Pashalidis and C. J. Mitchell. A taxonomy of single sign-on systems. In *8th Australasian Conference on Information Security and Privacy*, pages 249–264, 2003.

[26] W. rong Jih, S. you Cheng, J. Y. jen Hsu, and T. ming Tsai. Context-aware access control in pervasive healthcare. In *EEE Workshop: Mobility, Agents, and Mobile Services*, 2005.

[27] R. Sandhu, E. Coyne, H. Feinstein, and C. Youman. Role-based access control models. *Computer*, 29(2):38 –47, 1996.

[28] D. C. Schmidt. Model-Driven Engineering – Guest Editor's Introduction. *Computer*, 39(2), February 2006.

[29] B. Selic. The Pragmatics of Model-Driven Development. *IEEE Software*, 20(5), 2003.

[30] S. Sendall and W. Kozaczynski. Model Transformation: The Heart and Soul of Model-Driven Software Development. *IEEE Software*, 20(5), 2003.

[31] H. Skogsrud, B. Benatallah, and F. Casati. Model-Driven Trust Negotiation for Web Services. *IEEE Internet Computing*, 7:45–52, November 2003.

[32] D. Spinellis. Notable design patterns for domain-specific languages. *J. of Systems and Software*, 56(1):91–99, 2001.

[33] T. Stahl and M. Völter. *Model-Driven Software Development*. John Wiley & Sons, 2006.

[34] M. Strembeck. A Role Engineering Tool for Role-Based Access Control,. In *3rd Symposium on Requirements Engineering for Information Security*, 2005.

[35] M. Strembeck. Scenario-driven Role Engineering. *IEEE Security & Privacy*, 8(1), January/February 2010.

[36] M. Strembeck and J. Mendling. Modeling Process-related RBAC Models with Extended UML Activity Models. *Information and Software Technology*, 53(5), May 2011.

[37] M. Strembeck and G. Neumann. An Integrated Approach to Engineer and Enforce Context Constraints in RBAC Environments. *ACM Trans. on Inf. and System Security*, 7(3), 2004.

[38] M. Strembeck and U. Zdun. An Approach for the Systematic Development of Domain-Specific Languages. *Software: Practice and Experience (SP&E)*, 39(15), October 2009.

[39] C. Wolter, M. Menzel, A. Schaad, P. Miseldine, and C. Meinel. Model-driven business process security requirement specification. *J. Syst. Archit.*, 55:211–223, 2009.

[40] World Wide Web Consortium (W3C). XML Signature Syntax and Processing. http://www.w3.org/TR/xmldsig-core/, 2008.

[41] U. Zdun and M. Strembeck. Modeling Composition in Dynamic Programming Environments with Model Transformations. In *5th Int. Sym. on Software Composition*, 2006.

[42] U. Zdun and M. Strembeck. Reusable Architectural Decisions for DSL Design: Foundational Decisions in DSL Projects. In *14th European Conference on Pattern Languages of Programs (EuroPLoP)*, July 2009.

xDAuth: A Scalable and Lightweight Framework for Cross Domain Access Control and Delegation

Masoom Alam†, Xinwen Zhang‡, Kamran H Khan†, and Gohar Ali†
†Security Engineering Research Group IMSciences Pakistan
{masoom.alam,kamran,gohar}@imsciences.edu.pk
‡Huawei America Research Center, Santa Clara, CA, USA
xinwen.zhang@huawei.com

ABSTRACT

Cross domain resource sharing and collaborations have become pervasive in today's service oriented organizations. Existing approaches for the realization of cross domain access control are either focused on the model level only without concrete implementation mechanisms, or not general enough to provide a flexible framework for enterprise web applications. In this paper, we present *xDAuth*, a framework for the realization of cross domain access control and delegation with RESTful web service architecture. While focusing on real issues under the context of cross domain access scenarios such as no predefined trust relationship between a service provider domain and service requestor domain, xDAuth leverages existing web technologies to realize desired security requirements while supporting flexible and scalable security policies and privacy protection with low performance overhead. We have implemented xDAuth in a medical module in OpenERP, an open source ERP system. Our evaluation demonstrates that xDAuth is a feasible framework towards general cross domain access control for service oriented architectures.

Categories and Subject Descriptors

K.6.5 [**Management of Computing and Information Systems**]: Security and Protection

General Terms

Design, Security

Keywords

cross domain access control, permission delegation, authentication, authorization, RESTful, web services security

1. INTRODUCTION

The boom of online services has challenged traditional enterprises to open their legacy systems for cross domain access. Consequently, many business processes become more dependent on services provided by others out of their own domains. For example, in a hospital information domain, sharing of patient medical records among other healthcare and insurance service providers is required for many reasons. Similarly, it is a common practice for many organizations to consume services from financial institutions such as audit and financial statement analysis, by sharing their information in online service manner.

The transition in business processes introduce new security challenges. In particular, as autonomous and self-governing administration exists in individual domains, authentication and access control mechanisms need to consider access from external users in efficient and scalable way with least trust to external entities. In addition, delegation has been considered as a critical requirement in cross domain resource sharing and collaborations [18, 13, 29, 17, 23, 28]. Beyond administrative authorizations, a user can delegate partial or complete permissions to others from different domains in a discretionary manner, which can result undesired permission propagation and information leakage.

Cross domain access control and permission delegation have been widely studied in research literatures. Du and Joshi [14] have presented the solution to assign roles to users from different domains and consider issues with role hierarchies. In particular, they have discussed the possibility of exchange of role model among domains. Hasebe et al. [17] have introduced the notion of capability into the RBAC96 for achieving capability-based delegation (CRBAC) in cross domain scenarios. Atluri et al. [8] have presented delegation model and policies in workflow management system. There are also extensive research efforts in general delegation in single control domain context (cf. Section 7). However, these approaches focus on issues of access control and delegation model and policy specifications only. They do not propose concrete enforcement mechanisms, especially practical solutions in service oriented cross domain environment.

Many web-based open standard authentication and authorization protocols have been widely deployed by Internet services. OpenID [24] is a widely used protocol to delegate authentication functions to online identity providers (e.g., Google, Yahoo, MySpace). Single sign-on services such as Microsoft Live ID [6] and Google Accounts API [1] authenticate users for multiple web applications and services. OAuth [4] is a prominent open standard authentication and authorization protocol between web domains, which allows a user to share her private resources stored on one web site to another site without having to share her credentials, typically a username and password. These solutions, on the other side, focus more on open standard functions and APIs, while provide less support for fine-grained and domain-specific access control and delegation policies. Furthermore, these protocols usually focus on Internet-based services, and it is usually difficult to directly use them in legacy enterprise information systems, where each domain still has autonomous authority on authentications and authorizations.

In this paper, we present *xDAuth*, a general framework for the realization of cross domain access and delegation control. xDAuth leverages a trusted delegation service to serve as a decision making point for cross domain access requests. Each resource sharing (or service provider) domain can publish security policies to the delegation service via open RESTful [15] web service interfaces. Upon an access request [1], the service provider redirects the user client (e.g., a web browser) to the delegation service for authentication and authorization. Instead of authenticating the user itself, the delegation service further redirects the user to an authentication service, e.g., the one in her own domain. The delegation service then obtains the user's attributes upon successful authentication and makes decision if the access request should be allowed, and redirects the user client back to the service provider domain if so. In this way, xDAuth provides strong privacy protection: the delegation service does not learn the authentication credential of a cross domain user, and the service provider can define policies to hide the information of shared resources from the delegation service. In addition, the separation of policy decision point (the delegation service) and policy definition (the service provider) enables very flexible and scalable deployment of the framework. Very importantly, with the unique position of the delegation services for authorization, xDAuth can seamlessly support many access control and delegation constraints in cross domain environment, such as separation of duty (SoD) and the Chinese Wall policy.

There are several design and implementation challenges for xDAuth. First, as the delegation service is a central trust point, efficient decision making is mandatory. Secondly, when proxying the authorization for a service provider domain and the authentication of a service requestor domain, the delegation service should maintain seamless session management between the two redirections. Last but not least, xDAuth should have built-in revocation mechanism, not only for authorization policy revocation from a resource sharing domain, but also for revoking a user with already authorized permissions in an active session.

We have implemented xDAuth in a medical module of OpenERP, an open source ERP system. Our implementation supports a set of flexible access control and delegation policies for a medical information domain, to share medical records to other health care services. Built on top of maturing RESTful web service architecture and protocols, xDAuth provides friendly experience for web users. Our evaluation demonstrates that xDAuth is a feasible and lightweight framework for general cross domain access control and permission delegation in service oriented architectures.

Outline: The rest of the paper is organized as follows. Section 2 presents some motivating use cases towards a flexible but lightweight cross domain access control framework and summarizes our design principles. Section 3 gives an

---

[1] We consider cross domain access only in this paper.

overview of the xDAuth framework and Section 4 presents its design details. Implementation and evaluation of xDAuth in OpenERP are presented in Section 5, followed by discussions on variant extensions in Section 6. Finally, Section 7 presents related work in cross domain access control and delegation, and Section 8 concludes this paper.

2. MOTIVATING USE CASES AND SYSTEM DESIGN PRINCIPLES

We present two motivating use cases where cross domain access control and permission delegation are essential for their security problems. We then identify overall design requirements towards practical solutions.

2.1 Motivating Use Cases

Distributed health care information system In nationwide health information network (NHIN) architecture [22], multiple health care providers form a virtual coalition to share health care data and provide sophisticated and efficient online services. Traditionally, health care data of a hospital is provided to an authorized user (e.g., a physician) in the same domain, which is authenticated with a username and password. In a coalition, external physicians belonging to other hospitals may also need access the electronic health records (EHR) of a patient not registered at their hospitals. A trivial solution is to create a new account for every external physician and assign proper permissions. Obviously, this leads to a situation where the security administrator of the hospital domain has to handle many of external accounts in on-demand way. Alternatively, a primary doctor [17] or a patient [10] in the hospital can explicitly delegate corresponding permissions (access rights on the EHR) to an eternal physician. On one hand, it is risky to enable complete discretionary delegation between users in cross domain scenarios, as a typical user may not have the knowledge or awareness of sensitive permissions which can cause serious information leak or privacy compromising. On the other hand, complete security administrator controlled solution fails on authorization flexibility, e.g., when an external physician needs to access the EHR under emergency situation and while there is no pre-defined delegation policy for the physician by the security administrator.

Inter-organizational workflows Commercial organizations often take consultancy services from financial institutions, such as financial statement analysis and audit. Different employees from a financial institution need to inspect the information of a target domain. Therefore, explicit delegation relationship is usually needed to allow the access. The situation becomes complex when one user has access to multiple organizations financial data. Trivially, each user obtains multiple delegation credentials for accessing data of many client systems, which is obviously not scalable and cost effective on security administration, especially when the set of users to access variant target domains is not fixed. Furthermore, performing both authentication and authorization at the resource sharing domain make it difficult to enforce many dynamic security constraints such as the Chinese Wall policy. Existing approaches use cryptographic protocols for handling delegation. However, management of such mechanisms is a very tedious task such as permission revocation [11, 12]. An adaptable framework is needed where the user can be authenticated in her own domain, and then be authorized for accessing external services based on her authentication attributes.

2.2 System Design Principles

The above two use cases represent many cross domain situations where a general framework is desired for flexible, scalable, and lightweight access control and permission delegation. Among many requirements, we highlight several here which represent the salient features and objectives of our design.

Requirement#1: Flexible constraints and scalable security: The desired solution should support flexible security policies for cross domain environments, especially when an access request is from a user without authentication credential at the resource provider domain. In particularly, the framework should be extensible to support dynamic and scalable application specific constraints such as separation of duty and the Chinese Wall policy among multiple domains.

Requirement#2: Trade-off between scalability/efficiency and trust: As aforementioned, performing both authentication and authorization at resource provider domain introduces the scalability and flexibility issues. However, delegating authentication to external entities is not an option in our design as it significantly increases the trust base. Instead, the framework should leverage existing authentication mechanism of a resource requestor's home domain. On the other side, we can assume some trust for a resource provider domain to a centralized entity for authorization decision deriving purpose, while authorization policies are still defined by the security administrator or individual users in the resource sharing domain. This enhances the scalability of cross domain authorization as there is no need for a resource sharing domain to explicitly trust and link to the authentication mechanisms of all possible resource requestors' domains.

Requirements#3: Preserving privacy for access requestor and resources: An access requestor's credentials are used for authentication and result attributes are used for deriving authorization decisions. Ideally, a resource sharing domain does not need to know the requestor's authentication credentials and attributes in her home domain, except an identity. Furthermore, the authorization decision making entity should not know what real resources and permissions that a requestor is accessing.

3. OVERVIEW OF XDAUTH

In real world, enterprises often delegate the security verification of incoming people (to its premises) to companies which have specialized skill set in doing such job. Based on stated policies of an organization, these security companies verify various credentials of incoming people, before they are allowed to enter the premises of the organization. Limited time permits are often issued, thus, not every person needs a security clearance.

Our approach mimics these human verification systems. As Figure 1 shows, a *service provider* (SP, e.g., an enterprise web application) delegates authentication and authorization tasks for cross domain access to a service called *delegation service* (DS). Instead of performing authentication by itself, the DS further delegates the authentication task to the existing mechanism of the *service requestor* (SR) domain. Therefore, the DS acts as a mediator between the SP domain – the enterprise, and the SR domain – e.g., the user's

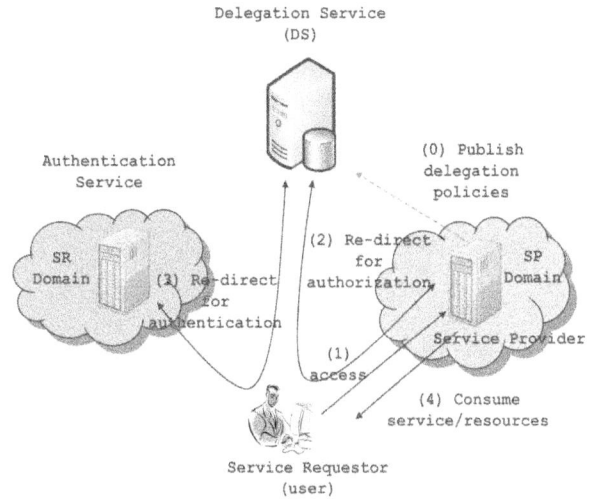

Figure 1: Overview of xDAuth.

home domain. In general, an SP domain can be an SR domain of another, and a single DS can work for multiple SP and SR domains.

xDAuth ensures the essential control of an SP domain with two facts: authorization decisions made by the DS are based on access control and delegation policies from the SP domain, and each authorization is based on authenticated information of the user from her home domain. More specifically, when the SP receives an access request from a user, the user's client (e.g., a browser) is redirected to the DS for authorization decision. After the user is redirected to the DS, a list of domains are presented. The SR selects her home domain (or any other domain that she can be authenticated) from the list and is redirected again to the authentication service interface of the SR domain for authentication. After successful authentication, the user is redirected back to the DS along with her identity and security attributes (e.g., roles and clearance). These attributes are then verified and evaluated by the DS against pre-defined policies by the SP domain. The DS then redirects the user back to the SP along with her identity, domain information, and authorization result, which takes corresponding actions based on the result.

Several benefits can be achieved with this *delegated* authentication and authorization mechanism in cross domain access scenarios. First, an SR domain is made aware of accessing a service by a user to another domain, which enables auditing seamlessly. Also, further security policies can be enforced in the SR domain, e.g., cross domain access to a particular SP is only allowed to certain users only. Therefore, the domain might refuse to authenticate a user after evaluating its own cross domain security policies. Secondly, an SR has no authentication credentials (e.g., username and password) on the DS except her home domain information (e.g., the URL of the authentication service). By handling two different sessions, rather than two different accounts, xDAuth increases the efficiency and flexibility of cross domain authorizations.

From privacy perspective, the stated paradigm has two advantages. Firstly, the privacy of the user is protected as there is no user credentials or attributes provided to the SP domain. All user attributes are verified at the DS end only and the DS does not have the user's authentication credentials. Secondly, the privacy of an SP is also protected as the DS has no knowledge of the resource (at the SP end) and permissions that the SR is asking. Easily, the security policies defined by SP domain can use pseudonyms of resources and permissions without revealing real internal information to the DS when publishing policies.

As a centralized service, the DS has the knowledge of concurrent cross domain accesses from an SR, therefore can enforce many flexible security constraints such as dynamic separation of duty. Optionally, the DS can maintain historic information of the access requests from variant SR domains, which enables it to enforce other general constraints such as the Chinese Wall policy. These constraints are specified by individual SP domains as part of cross domain security policies.

The role of the DS in xDAuth is very similar to the WRYF service in Shibboleth [21]. However, there is significant difference on the design of xDAuth from Shibboleth, which achieves different security objectives. Specifically, in Shibboleth, the WRYF service just maintains a list of home organization access points of users. When a user is redirected from an SP to the WRYF, the user selects her home organization and the WRYF redirects her to the access point. After that, the interactions are purely performed between the SP and SR – SR does authentication and SP does authorization. That is, the WRYF service is simply a redirection proxy and does not obtain authentication results of users and evaluate authorization decisions. In xDAuth, the DS performs authorization evaluation based on user authentication results. With the central position of the DS, many flexible security constraints crossing multiple domains can be enforced such as dynamic separation of duty and the Chinese Wall policy, which are not viable in Shibboleth. At the same time, xDAuth still maintains strong privacy protections to both SPs and individual users.

Threat and Trust Assumptions The main objective of xDAuth is to prevent unauthorized access to protected resources in an SP domain from external users. Therefore, any access request to an SP which is not authorized by the SP or DS is a potential threat.

By delegating the authorization decision to the DS, we assume that the SP trusts the DS to make right decisions based on pre-defined and published policies. This also implies that the SP trusts that DS keeps the integrity of the policies. However, we do not assume that each SP trusts all possible SR domains explicitly. That is, we do not require the web of trust between domains of SPs and SRs; instead, xDAuth leverages the DS as a proxy of trust. After an SR user is authenticated at her parent domain, and successfully authorized at the DS end, a transitive trust relationship is established between the SR and SP through the DS. With this, we eliminate the complexity of trust management between SP and SR domains. For example, an SP does not need to store credentials (e.g. , public key certificate) of each SR domain in order to verify the message authenticity and integrity, while the trust burden is handled by the DS in the middle.

We also trust the SP user's client agent such as web browser. We do not consider attacks on the cryptography used in protecting the integrity and authenticity of messages between SP, DS, and SR.

4. DESIGN OF XDAUTH

This section first gives the bootstrap of xDAuth including policy specification, domain registration, and policy publishing. We then illustrate the authorization and authentication protocols for cross domain access control, cross domain constraint enforcement, and revocation mechanisms.

4.1 xDAuth Policy

In xDAuth, a user from an SR domain is allowed to access resources in an SP domain, if allowed by cross access or delegated policies of the SP. Without loss of generality, we explain how *delegation policy* can be defined and enforced in this section, while cross domain access control policies can be easily supported with similar mechanisms. For cross domain delegation, a user or an administrator in the SP makes a delegation request to an internal authorization service. The delegation request is verified against a set of *delegation control policies* in the SP. Therefore, an xDAuth policy is generated by combining the information contained in the delegation request and that in the delegation control policies.

Formally, a delegation control policy is defined as a set of *rules*, each of which stating the *delegation_status* of individual permissions and constraints. In general, a permission p is defined as a pair (o, A), where o is an object (or resource) and A is a non-empty set of actions. Therefore, a permission essentially identifies possible access actions on an object within a particular domain. A constraint c defines conditions such as the life time of a delegated permission, the *delegatee*'s attributes such as roles or domain names. Therefore, a delegation control policy mandates an explicit approval of the delegation of a permission. The *delegation_status* is a boolean value specifying whether a permission is delegatable or not for a *delegator* (user or role) in the SP.

A delegation request is defined as a triple (s_i, p, s_j) where $s_i \in S$ is a subject playing the role of a delegator, p is a permission, and $s_j \in S$ is a subject playing the role of a delegatee. Each delegation request is evaluated against delegation control policies in the SP domain. If there is a delegation control policy that allows the request, it is approved by the internal authorization service of the SP, and a cross domain delegation policy is generated with the (s_j, p, c), where c is the constraint corresponding to the delegation control policy. Formally:

$xDAuthPolicyGen: (DR \otimes P) \rightarrow \{xDAuthP \mid Error\}$,

where $xDAuthPolicyGen$ is a mapping from a set of delegation requests DR and set of control policies P to a set of xDAuth policies $xDAuthP$ or an error. $\otimes$ operator matches a particular delegation request against the set of delegation control policies. We note that there can be multiple control policies that can satisfy one request, where multiple authorization polices can be generated.

As an example, consider a delegation request made by a doctor in an hospital for the blood tests of a patient. This requires access to the medical record of the patient. The following delegation query (DLQ) is being made:

$DLQ(Doc001, Lab001, readPatientRecord,$

$designation ='' pathologist'' \ and \ lifetime = 300mins)$,

where Doc001 requests the delegation of read permission on the patient record to another domain lab001 with the delegation constraint that designation of a user from lab001 should be pathologist. The delegation control policy in this case, verifies that whether a xDAuth policy exists that can satisfy the above delegation request. In case, an xDAuth policy exists, the above delegation request will not be approved.

4.2 Domain Registration

Consider an SP domain which provides services via http://sp.com, and the DS http://ds.com. In order to share resources, an administrator of the SP domain should first register on the DS via a web service interface http://ds.com/register. The registration requires information of the SP including service name, service access URL, and other metadata such as the services it offered (e.g. blog, finance solution, social networking, etc). Similar registration is required for an SR domain. In addition, a call back interface (e.g., http://sr.com/authenticate) is also provided by the sR domain to the DS, which is used by the DS for redirecting authentication requests.

As the results of an registration, the DS returns a domain key and secret pair. The domain key is a 30-byte public string that is unique to identify the domain, and the secret is a 10-byte shared secret between the DS and the domain. Table 1 lists necessary web interfaces for the DS and individual domains.

4.3 Publishing Policy

Each SP domain has an internal authorization service that approves delegation requests made from local users. When an administrator wants to delegate any permission of accessing resources to others in different domains, we assume the local authorization service provides necessary interfaces and tools to help the user make appropriate selections, such as corresponding objects and set of access actions which she wants to delegate, and applicable constraints such as valid time period. Upon this specification, the authorization service can approve the request based on pre-defined delegation control policies in the domain. In reality, the approval of a delegation request can be done automatically by system, or manually approved by administrators.

After a delegation request is approved, the authorization service creates a real cross domain delegation policy with the delegated permission information and constraints, and publishes it to the DS via a service interface https://ds.com/policy/publish. Each policy can be identified with an id by the authorization service such that it can be referred later, e.g., for update or revocation. For privacy purpose, the permission information in the delegation policy can be pseudonyms such that the real information of shared resources is hidden from the DS.

4.4 xDAuth Protocol

Consider a user from an SR domain wants to access a resource of a service provider in an SP domain by accessing http://sp.com. Figure 2 shows the work flow of xDAuth protocol to authorize this request. We assume that the user has not been granted for any access before this request at the SP. Therefore, she does not present any delegation permit with her access request. We also assume that the SP does know that the request is from external, e.g., via the client IP address of the HTTP request.

In order to authorize the request, the SP first generates a request token, and then redirects the user's browser to the DS for authentication and authorization. The HTTP redirection request includes the request token and permission

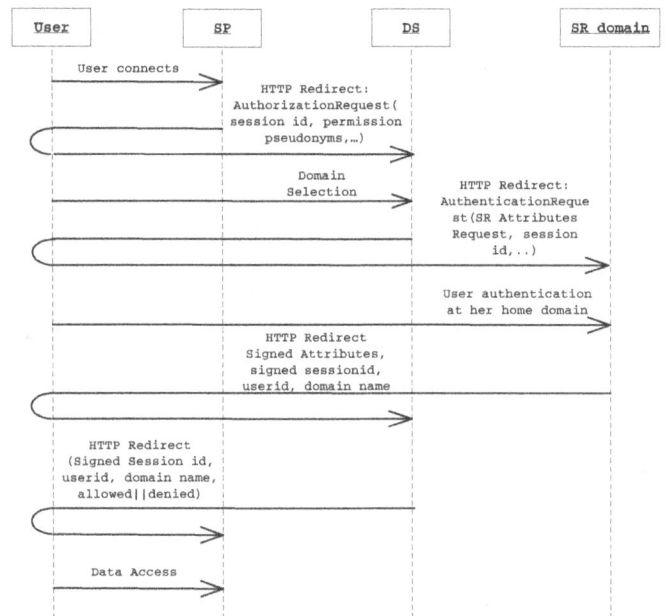

Figure 2: xDAuth protocol.

information required by the user's access, e.g., permission pseudonyms. A unique session id is also used in the HTTP request to prevent replay attacks.

After the user is redirected at the DS, she is asked to select her home domain from a list of registered SR domains. Upon the selection, the user is in turn redirected by the DS to the authentication service interface of SR with the domain name, which is provided to the DS during the SR domain registration process. This HTTP redirection includes the domain name and other information of the SP, as well as the session id. The user then authenticates herself, e.g., by login with username and password. Local security policies of the SR domain may be enforced within the authentication service, e.g., by checking if the user is allowed to access the SP's resources. We note that if the user is already authenticated in the SR domain, the authentication service can directly obtain the results, e.g., by reading the cookie at the user's browser. Overall, the authentication mechanism in the SR domain can be variant but provide single interface to the DS.

Upon successful authentication and authorization in the SR domain, the user is redirected back to the DS along with authentication results, such as roles, identities, or other attributes. The HTTP redirection is signed by the shared secret between the DS and SR, such that the DS can verify the integrity and authenticity of the authentication results. When the DS receives these, it first evaluates the user's access request based on the authentication results and pre-published delegation policies by the SP domain authorization service. Note that as the same session id is used when the user is redirected back from the SR, the DS can link the authentication results to the user who make the original access request to SP. The DS then redirects the user back to the SP, along with the authorization result (allowed or denied), the request token, the session id, and the necessary user identity information if the access is allowed (e.g., for logging and auditing purposes at the SP side).

Table 1: Web Service Interfaces of DS and Individual Domains

URL	Function Description
`http://ds.com/`	Main interface for authorization.
`http://ds.com/register`	Register individual domains, called by domain administrators.
`https://ds.com/policy`	Publish, update, and revoke cross domain access control policies, called by an SP domain authorization service.
`https://ds.com/update`	Update and revoke an authenticated user, called by an SR authentication service.
`https://sr.com/authenticate`	Authenticate a user in SR domain, called by DS.
`https://sp.com/revoke`	Revoke an authenticated user who has been allowed in a cross domain access session, called by DS.

Once receives and verifies the authenticity of the HTTP response, the SP generates an access token based on the request token, and allows the access of the user to required resources. The access token is used in all following transactions of the same session. Moreover, the access token along with different attributes is stored in the browser of the user as a delegation permit.

4.5 Cross Domain Constraint Enforcement

Enforcing cross domain security constraints is one of the major benefits of xDAuth. As the policy decision point (PDP) for cross domain access, the DS has the capability to enforce very flexible constraints. We use the Chinese Wall policy as an example to explain this capability. Consider a simple Chinese Wall policy which states that two SP domains are in conflict of interest such that resources in SP1 should not be accessed by a user who has an active session with SP2 at the same time. With the DS's record of active authorized sessions, it maintains two simple lists of SR domains that have active sessions in SP1 and SP2, respectively. When a new request from an SR domain for authorization of SP1, the DS simply checks if the same SR appears in the active list of SP2. If so then the request is denied due to the Chinese Wall policy. In order to support general Chinese wall policy which is a constraint for multiple sessions, the DS implements a function that records the history of accesses to conflicting domains. Moreover, in the current xDAuth, a single DS is used among a set of federated domains. We note that with Shibboleth and OAuth-like protocols, as there is no record of active sessions, cross domain constraints are difficult to enforce. Similarly, more general and fine-grained constraints such as dynamic separation of duty (DSoD) [27, 20] in user and role levels can be enforced with same mechanism.

4.6 Authorization Revocation

Revocations can happen in xDAuth in two levels: policy revocation, and access token revocation. The revocation of a delegation policy is relatively simple with the help of a dedicated web interface provided by the DS. This service URL is provided to each SP domain as the result of domain registration. When revoking a policy, the authorization service in an SP domain sends the domain name and policy id to the DS. After verifying the authenticity of the revocation request, i.e., with the signatured generated from the shared secret between the DS and SP, the DS removes the policy in its local database.

There can be several scenarios to revoke an active access token issued by the SP to a cross domain access session. First of all, if a user within the SP domain or the

SP service wants to revoke an active accessing session, it can directly revoke the access token issued for that session. Immediately, the user cannot access the resource. A more complex situation appears when any of the accessing user's attributes in her home domain is changed, e.g., a role is deactivated or even revoked by the SR domain. In this case, the SR authentication service needs to send the updated user information to the DS, via a dedicated web interfaces `http://ds.com/update`, given by the DS during registration phase. This HTTP request should include previous session id that is obtained from the DS for original authentication request, therefore the DS can re-evaluate the user's permission based on updated information. If the user's access should be revoked, the DS issues an revocation request to the SP via a web interface `http://sp.com/revoke`. The same session id is used so that the SP can make corresponding actions on the active session. The lifetime of the session id and access token are global system parameters, e.g., from a few minutes to hours.

5. IMPLEMENTATION & EVALUATION

In this section, we provide the implementation details of xDAuth framework along with a case study for a medical domain. The underlying information system playing the role of the SP is an open source enterprise resource planning (ERP) system called OpenERP [5]. We then evaluate the performance of xDAuth with our implementation and suggest performance improvement strategies.

5.1 xDAuth for Healthcare

Medical [2] is an open source module in OpenERP that provides a complete electronic medical record (EMR) system with patient information and other medical information. It also contains a hospital information system (HIS) integrated with other OpenERP modules like inventory and financial management.

As OpenERP does not support cross domain access, in current Medical module, each user must have an local account with username/password in order to access medical objects. Therefore, in the current settings, it is not possible for an external laboratory to connect to an OpenERP server and process the medical record of a patient. To enable cross domain access, we have developed a module called `xauth` in OpenERP. The module is derived from the OAuth Python library [4], which consists of a server module called `provider` and a client library `test.py` to provide xDAuth functionalities.

Our implementation consists of three servers: the SP domain running a Medical information system [2], the DS server running a Python web service, and the SR authen-

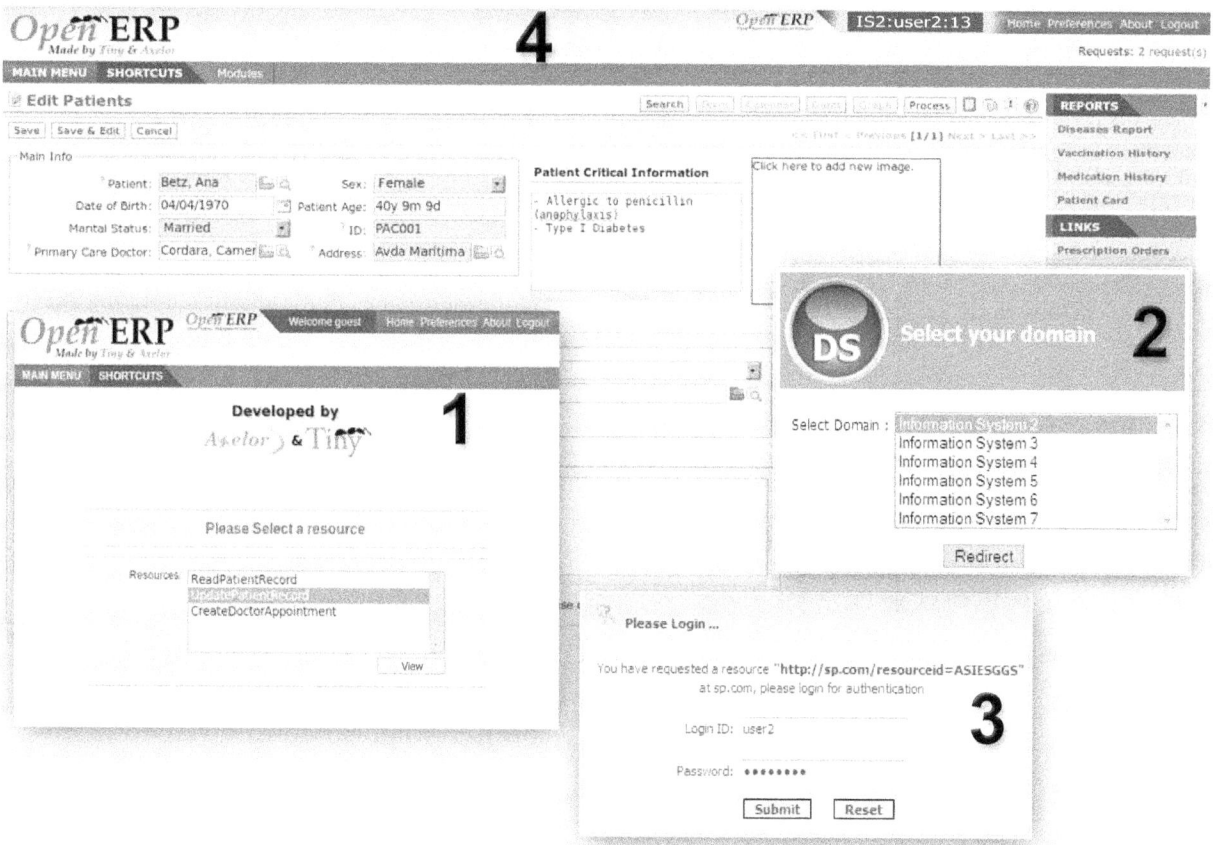

Figure 3: A snapshot of the xDAuth protocol: (1) view list of shared resources at the SP, (2) domain selection at the DS, (3), authentication at the SR home domain, and (4) resource access at the SP.

tication server running a PHP service which provides typical username/password login. The username/password database is extract from the Medical in SP domain to the SR authentication server. Figure 3 shows a snapshot of the xDAuth work flow for an external user to access Medical EMR of a patient. Once the user selects a particular resource and presses the view button in Medical main web page (cf. Fig 3 – Part 1), the client part of the `xauth` is called and redirects the user's browser to the DS service along with the unique link through which the necessary permission is identified at SP. It is important to note that the actual resource information such as `ReadPatientRecord` is not forwarded as part of the redirection for privacy, while only a pseudonym is used, which is the same name used when a delegation policy is created in the Medical domain for reading patient EMR. The user is prompted with a list of registered SR domains (cf. Fig 3 – Part 2). After the user selects her home domain, the browser is redirected to the SR authentication page (cf. Fig 3 – Part 3). After successful authentication, the user is redirected back to the DS, which evaluates the delegation policies defined by the Medical domain, and then redirected back to the original resource web page. If the access is allowed, the user can view the requested patient record (cf. Fig 3 – Part 4).

The reminder of this section gives more details of xDAuth policy in XACML and the implementation of `xauth` module and the DS service, followed by our performance evaluation.

5.2 xDAuth Policy in XACML

As a de-facto standard, XACML [3] is a natural choice for xDAuth policies specification. The reason is that the DS works like a central policy decision point for multiple service providers, therefore XACML can be used to express and evaluate policies from a variety of SPs using a single language.

In our implementation, the `<Subject>` element of an XACML policy identifies the domain of the delegatee subject. A more detailed information about a delegatee can also be included here such as roles or even identities. The `<Resource>` element refers to the resource URL in an SP domain, and the `<Rule>` element specifies the corresponding constraints which the DS must evaluate regarding a request. In our implementation we focus on enforcing cross domain constraints. Specifically, the XACML policy specifies simple mutual conflict of interests among individual SP domains, such that a user cannot have active sessions in both domains in a conflict pair concurrently. Another possible setting could be to include the SR's domain information within the `<Rule>` element of XACML. Therefore, policy encoding in the same way helps the DS in the organization of a set of xDAuth policies from various SPs.

5.3 `xauth` Module

The `xauth` module extends the `base` module in Open-ERP with an extra class called `res_delegation`. The `res_delegation` class is responsible for handling delegation requests from the local users and generating xDAuth policies. It further adds an extra attribute `external` in the `res_users` class by using the inheritance mechanism in OpenERP. This attribute is used to distinguish a local user from an external user. In addition to that, within the `res_delegation` class, a Python function is defined called `delegationRequestHandler`, which handles the incoming delegation requests from the local users and creates or update an existing xDAuth policy at the DS.

5.4 Implementation of DS

The DS is a standalone service which implements the server part of the `xauth` module. This library contains all the functions which an SP or SR can call. Besides, two other important functions are implemented. Firstly, as the DS proxies two HTTP redirections, we use the function `xauth_request_token`, the handler of the first redirection at the DS side, to initiate the second redirection with the SR authentication server by calling the `test.py` at the SR service side. Secondly, `xauth` integrates a Python XACML engine [7] to evaluate XACML delegation policies.

Delegation Decision Making As multiple delegation policies might exist that can be applied on a single user, it is the responsibility of the DS to efficiently evaluate an access request. Several strategies can be employed to efficiently evaluate a set of delegation policies applied to an SR user. In OAuth protocol, for each query from a web consumer to a backend service regarding user data (for example, user contact list), a separate function is defined at the backend service. These functions are responsible for providing data of a user to the consumer. We extend this mechanism to include a function that can also answer some logical queries such as whether an SR user's role is or senior to a particular role x (i.e., $role \geq x$) in the SR domain. For example, if the DS has a delegation policy with delegatee's domain is the SR, but with a condition that access is not allowed to an SR user with role lower than x. In this case, the DS can efficiently evaluate the authorization of an SR user without asking all the attributes from the SR domain. Similarly, multiple logical queries can be defined. Negative delegation policies can also be enabled for efficient evaluation, by first evaluating these policies.

Delegation Revocation As the SP trusts the DS on authorization and authentication, logically, it is the responsibility of the DS to intimate the SP regarding any change in the attributes of the user in SR domain during an active session. For this, whenever a change occurs about the user's attributes in her domain, the DS should be notified by the corresponding SR domain, so that this change can be propagated to the SP domain if a delegated permission should be revoked.

In order to handle revocation efficiently, the SR domain updates to the DS regarding those attributes only, for which the DS has asked during the authentication step of the xDAuth protocol. The DS then re-evaluates the delegation policies to decide if the active session should be revoked. For example, suppose the SR domain updates the DS regarding a local revocation of attribute x for the user. According to

a delegation policy which specifies a delegation constraint of $x \wedge y$, the delegation permission should be denied, and a revocation signal is sent to the SP's corresponding interface.

5.5 Performance Evaluation

In our testbed, the DS, SP, and SR run on individual Dell Optiplex desktops with Ubuntu 10.4, 2.8GZ Core2Quad, and 4 GB RAM, within 100MB LAN. The overhead of an xDAuth session includes the two HTTP redirections, and policy loading and evaluation times at the DS. Based on our 50 measurements, the average time for the first redirection from the Medical service to the DS takes about 800ms. The second redirection can occur in 560m or 3s, depending on the factor that whether the user is already authenticated in her home domain or not. We note that the times taken by redirections are almost constants in the xDAuth protocol, with slight variant according to network connection status. We do not count the time taken by a user to login her SR domain, which can vary according to different authentication mechanisms.

Table 2: Performance Evaluation of DS

No. of Policies	Load Time	Evaluation Time (w/o cache)	Evaluation Time(with cache)
10	5ms	48ms	38ms
100	15ms	64ms	46ms
1000	29ms	88ms	64ms

On the other hand, the time taken by the DS for xDAuth policy loading and evaluation is heavily dependent on the number of policies. We evaluate this performance overhead with 10, 100, and 1000 delegation policies, respectively. As Table 2 shows, The major overhead at the DS side is taken by policy evaluations. To improve the performance, we implement a cache mechanism in the XACML evaluation engine. As we can see in Table 2, with authorization decision cache support, the performance of the evaluation engine is improved 25% by average. For large number of policies from many different domains, another strategy can be employed to have policy index such that the policy loading time can be reduced by loading only policies for a particular SR domain.

6. DISCUSSION

In order to reduce the attack window, the permit token expiration time can be set to minimum. Therefore, in critical situations, a delegation permit can be made only good for a single session. This means that delegation permits have to be reissued each time the user logs into a cross domain service and have a very limited lifetime. However, delegation permits expiry time must be chosen adequately to balance usability so that users are not prompted for authentication too frequently.

According to our understanding, OpenERP defines permissions at the class level and not at the business object level. Once a user has been granted read/write permissions on a class, he/she can view all the object's data which are instances of this class. This limitation is inherent in our implementation. Therefore, multiple delegatees having permissions on the same object can view each other's data. Tracking the identity of a local user who has made a delegation can be a problem in cases where multiple users have delegated the same set of rights on the same objects. An SP creates a temporary identity of an SR by augmenting the domain information taken from the DS and identity of the local user who has enabled this delegation with each other.

In the cross domain access scenarios, one of the major concerns is the privacy protection of a user. An SP usually needs the identity of a user for tracking changes in its system. On the other side, disclosing the identify of a user to an SP might not be desirable due to several reasons. For example, financial monitoring departments often perform inspections of financial institutions. In this case, disclosing the identity of a particular inspector is prohibited, although inspections rights are delegated. This feature is can be easily supported by xDAuth by not forwarding the user identity from the DS to the SP, once the cross domain access is authorized.

Multi-step delegation has been discussed extensively in many delegation models [9, 29, 13]. In cross domain context, multi-step delegation has two alternatives: a user can delegate her authorized permission of an active session to a local user (i.e., in the same SR domain), or to another user in a different domain. xDAuth can be extended to support both cases. For the first one, the local authorization service in SR domain can approve the delegation request, and file the request to the DS, which can evaluate the permission based on delegation policies from the SP domain. Once allowed, the DS can send a request to a dedicated SP interface for this further delegation. The SP can revoke the original active access token and issue a new access token to the new delegatee. For the second case, the original delegatee can file a delegation request to her local authorization service (in SR domain), and if allowed, the authorization service can send a *re-delegation policy* to the DS. Users from the third SR domain can use the permission with the same xDAuth protocol. However, we argue that multi-step delegation in xDAuth in general is a complex process including more than two nested HTTP redirections. Certificate based delegation mechanisms [11, 12] may be integrated with xDAuth for practical multi-step delegations, which is the topic of our future research direction.

7. RELATED WORK

Delegation in Role-based and Workflow Management Systems Among those approaches, RBDM0 [9] was the first approach that aims at modeling user-to-user delegation in the RBAC model. RDM2000 [29] proposes hierarchical roles and multi step delegation. Delegation Logic (DL) [19] and PBDM [30] limits the delegation scope to individual permissions and roles. Crampton et al. [13] presented a formal model for administrative scope of delegations in the context of workflow systems. The main difference between these existing theoretical approaches and that we are concerned is the implementation issues with the enforcement of cross domain delegations using existing web standards.

Cross Domain Access Control and Delegation Crampton et al. [14] presents an approach where a restrictive role hierarchy mechanism is used for external users. Whenever an SR user requests a set of permissions, an authentication service verifies which role can satisfy the requested permissions and uses an assistant matrix to determine the minimum of roles that can satisfy the requested permissions. The authentication service in their architecture ensures that an external user cannot activate inherited permissions in the SP domain. Their architecture can be supported by xDAuth

using an authentication service at the SP side. CRBAC [17] provides the formal details of the integration of capability based access control in to RBAC96. The concept of capability is exclusively used to represent permissions that can be delegated in cross domain access scenarios in order to reduce administration cost. Therefore, any user having a special permission `create` can create a capability and assign it to an external user. xDAuth provides a classical mechanism for capability delegation described in CRBAC. In addition, an internal authorization service in SP governs the delegation of permissions to external domains. Shafiq et al. [26] proposed a framework for integrating access control policies of heterogeneous and autonomous domains to form global policy. This integration of access control policies might cause some conflict which are removed in a way that semantics of the global policy are preserved without changing the the autonomy of each individual domain. Our focus is this paper is on the enforcement of a delegation authority that can take decisions on the behalf of various domains. Community authorization service (CAS) is an authorization mechanism between virtual groups in Grid computing [23]. The main difference between xDAuth and CAS is that in CAS, a user first requests a capability from the CAS service before initializing the access at a resource provide side, while in xDAuth, we use web redirections to obtain more friendly user experience.

Web-based Authorization and Delegation OAuth is a de-fato protocol for authentication of web application regarding the data of individual users OAuth. Our inspiration for the OAuth protocol is due to token exchange mechanism for authentication. However in the original OAuth protocol, both authentication and authorization of users are performed at a backend server side, therefore it does not fit the design goal of xDAuth. Permitme [16] has introduced the concept of a delegation authority for providing delegation permits to mashup web applications, for accessing user data at back end services. Regarding the introduction of a delegation authority, Permitme is similar to our approach. However there are some fundamental differences as Permitme assumes that the delegation authority and backend services share information regarding user data. This means that whenever there is a change in the user data, the backend service has to intimate the delegation authority regarding the change. In xDAuth a user has no account on the delegation service, then authentication takes place in her home domain only. Shibboleth [21] is the closest technology to xDAuth. As we have discussed in Section 3, there is significant difference on the design of xDAuth from Shibboleth, especially on the role of the DS, which makes xDAuth ideal for cross domain constraint enforcement. DAuth [25] is an extension of OAuth to split an access token into multiple sub-tokens and assign them to different components of a distributed web consumer. Therefore DAuth can support very fine-grained permission control for accessing user data in service providers. However, like OAuth, DAuth does not support cross domain access and delegation as xDAuth does.

8. CONCLUSION

In this paper, we have presented a cross domain access control and permission delegation framework called xDAuth for service oriented organizations. xDAuth leverages a trusted delegation service to serve as a decision making point for cross domain access requests. Each resource sharing domain can publish security policies to the delegation service via open RESTful web service interfaces. Delegation in xDAuth occurs at two places: A local user or an administrator delegates rights on her owned resources to other domain users, provided that the delegation at this level is allowed by a delegation control policy of her domain. Secondly, each domain delegates the evaluation of cross domain authorization policies called xDAuth policies to a central policy decision point called delegation service. We implement xDAuth framework within a medical module in OpenERP, an open source ERP system. Currently, we are extending xDAuth framework for multi-step delegation and working on providing it as a open source module in the OpenERP project repository.

9. REFERENCES

[1] Authentication and authorization for google apis, http://code.google.com/apis/accounts/docs/AuthForWebApps.html.

[2] Medical–The Universal Hospital and Health Information System. medical.sourceforge.net/.

[3] OASIS, journal=OASIS: www.oasis-open.org/committees/xacml/repository/csxacml-specification-1.1.pdf, 2003.

[4] OAuth official web site. http://www.oauth.net/code.

[5] OpenERP systems. http://www.openerp.com/.

[6] Windows live id, https://accountservices.passport.net/ppnetworkhome.srf?lc=1033&mkt=EN-US.

[7] XACML 2.0 implementation in Python. http://pypi.python.org/pypi/ndg-xacml/0.4.0.

[8] V. Atluri and J. Warner. Supporting conditional delegation in secure workflow management systems. In *Proceedings of the tenth ACM symposium on Access control models and technologies*, 2005.

[9] E. Barka and R. Sandhu. A role-based delegation model and some extensions. In *Proceedings of National Information Systems Security Conference*, 2000.

[10] J. Benaloh, M. Chase, E. Horvitz, and K. Lauter. Patient controlled encryption: ensuring privacy of electronic medical records. In *Proceedings of the 2009 ACM workshop on Cloud computing security*, 2009.

[11] M. Blaze, J. Feigenbaum, and A. Keromytis. KeyNote: Trust management for public-key infrastructures. In *Security Protocols*, pages 625–625. Springer, 1999.

[12] D. Clarke, J.E. Elienb, C. Ellison, M. Fredette, A. Morcos, and R.L. Rivest. Certificate chain discovery in SPKI/SDSI. *Journal of Computer Security*, 9(4):285–322, 2001.

[13] J. Crampton and H. Khambhammettu. Delegation in role-based access control. *International Journal of Information Security*, 7(2):123–136, 2008.

[14] S. Du and J.B.D. Joshi. Supporting authorization query and inter-domain role mapping in presence of hybrid role hierarchy. In *Proceedings of the eleventh ACM symposium on Access control models and technologies*, 2006.

[15] R. T. Fielding and R. N. Taylor. Principled design of the modern web architecture. *ACM Transactions on Internet Technology*, (2), 2002.

[16] R. Hasan, M. Winslett, R. Conlan, B. Slesinsky, and N. Ramani. Please permit me: Stateless delegated

[17] K. Hasebe, M. Mabuchi, and A. Matsushita. Capability-based delegation model in RBAC. In *Proceeding of the 15th ACM symposium on Access control models and technologies*, 2010.

[18] J.B.D. Joshi and E. Bertino. Fine-grained role-based delegation in presence of the hybrid role hierarchy. In *Proceedings of the eleventh ACM symposium on Access control models and technologies*, 2006.

[19] N. Li, B.N. Grosof, and J. Feigenbaum. Delegation logic: A logic-based approach to distributed authorization. *ACM Transactions on Information and System Security (TISSEC)*, 6(1):128–171, 2003.

[20] N. Li, M.V. Tripunitara, and Z. Bizri. On mutually exclusive roles and separation-of-duty. *ACM Transactions on Information and System Security (TISSEC)*, 10(2), 2007.

[21] RL Morgan, S. Cantor, S. Carmody, W. Hoehn, and K. Klingenstein. Federated Security: The Shibboleth Approach. *Educause Quarterly*, 27(4):6, 2004.

[22] T.H. Payne, D.E. Detmer, J.C. Wyatt, and I.E. Buchan. National-scale clinical information exchange in the United Kingdom: lessons for the United States. *Journal of the American Medical Informatics Association*, 18(1):91, 2011.

[23] L. Pearlman, V. Welch, I. Foster, C. Kesselman, and S. Tuecke. A community authorization service for group collaboration. In *Policies for Distributed Systems and Networks, 2002. Proceedings. Third International Workshop on*, 2002.

[24] D. Recordon and D. Reed. OpenID 2.0: a platform for user-centric identity management. In *Proceedings of the second ACM workshop on Digital identity management*, 2006.

[25] J. Schiffman, X. Zhang, and S. Gibbs. DAuth: Fine-grained Authorization Delegation for Distributed Web Application Consumers. In *Proc. of IEEE Symposium on Policies for Distributed Systems and Networks*, 2010.

[26] B. Shafiq, J.B.D. Joshi, E. Bertino, and A. Ghafoor. Secure interoperation in a multidomain environment employing RBAC policies. *IEEE transactions on knowledge and data engineering*, pages 1557–1577, 2005.

[27] R.T. Simon and M.E. Zurko. Separation of duty in role-based environments. In *Proc. of Computer Security Foundations Workshop*, 2002.

[28] J. Wainer, A. Kumar, and P. Barthelmess. DW-RBAC: A formal security model of delegation and revocation in workflow systems. *Information Systems*, 32(3):365–384, 2007.

[29] L. Zhang, G.J. Ahn, and B.T. Chu. A rule-based framework for role-based delegation and revocation. *ACM Transactions on Information and System Security (TISSEC)*, 6(3):404–441, 2003.

[30] X. Zhang, S. Oh, and R. Sandhu. PBDM: a flexible delegation model in RBAC. In *Proceedings of the eighth ACM symposium on Access control models and technologies*, 2003.

Program Synthesis in Administration of Higher-Order Permissions

Glenn Bruns
Bell Labs, Alcatel-Lucent
grb@bell-labs.com

Michael Huth
Imperial College, London
M.Huth@imperial.ac.uk

Kumar Avijit
Carnegie Mellon University
kavijit@cs.cmu.edu

ABSTRACT

In "administrative" access control, policy controls permissions not just on application actions, but also on actions to modify permissions, on actions to modify permissions on *those* actions, and so on. One context of work in administrative policy is "administrative RBAC", in which policy controls the permissions of roles, the membership of roles, and other elements of RBAC access-control state.

Here we study and extend the UARBAC model for administrative RBAC from the perspective of usability and expressiveness. Using tools from logic and program verification, we formulate UARBAC logically and develop an algorithm that produces "administrative plans" that achieve specified permissions through permitted actions. This work is closely related to work on the safety problem in administrative access control, but aims to aid legitimate users in understanding how to reach a desired access-control state. We then show how this machinery can be used so that administrative actions at any desired depth, and so plans as well, can be uniformly simulated in the UARBAC model.

Categories and Subject Descriptors

D.4.6 Operating Systems [**Security and Protection**]: Access Control; D.3.1 Programming Languages [**Formal Definitions and Theory**]: Semantics

General Terms

Languages, Security, Theory

Keywords

Access-control policy languages, Role-based access control

1. INTRODUCTION

An access-control policy describes whether entities have permissions on actions in some application domain. An obvious question is: who has permission to change permissions? Without such "second-order" permissions, users could simply modify policy to obtain whatever permissions they desire. For example, suppose the dean of an academic department wants access to a potential student's application, but does not have permission. Without access control on the policy, the dean could simply modify permissions on the application, or could give herself the role of "member of the admissions committee", because users in this role have access to students' applications.

If second-order permissions are supported, then it makes sense to control them using third-order permissions, and so on. A policy that contains its own higher-order permissions is sometimes called an "administrative" access-control policy.

We briefly mention some desirable features of administrative access-control policy. First is *expressiveness*: it should be possible to express permissions of any order. For example, it should be possible to say that the dean of a department has the right to remove from a faculty member the right to give to a student permission to purchase a book using department funds. Second is *uniformity*: a single style of specifying permissions and a single method of enforcing them should be used. For example, in administrative RBAC, a single rule for defining permissions should be used at all levels of permissions. Third is *scope*: all aspects of policy should be controlled by policy. For example, permissions on modifying role membership, and the objects governed by policy, should be expressed in and controlled through policy. Last is the *use of logic*: access-control states and permissions should be defined logically to allow existing theory and tools to be leveraged in policy design and analysis.

Work on administrative RBAC seeks to use RBAC-style mechanisms to define higher-order permissions on RBAC policies. This work has focused on two main questions. First: how should RBAC be applied to RBAC? (See, e.g., [22, 8, 18, 15].) For example, should administrative roles be separate from ordinary roles? Second: how difficult is it to analyze administrative RBAC policies? (See, e.g., [11, 26, 16, 13, 28].) For example, is it decidable (and if so at what cost) to determine whether a user can legally modify the policy to reach a specified state?

The question of whether one can make such modifications to a policy is sometimes called the "safety problem" [11]. The idea is that one would like to know whether certain policy states, seen as undesirable, can be reached by an "attacker".

Here we examine administrative RBAC in the context of the UARBAC [15] formalism. The goal of UARBAC is to improve the uniformity of administrative RBAC. In this paper we attempt to build on UARBAC in several ways:

We describe UARBAC using logic, providing improved

uniformity across administrative and non-administrative actions in Section 2. We assess UARBAC from the point of view of the features we have listed above in Section 3. In Section 3, we then develop an algorithm to compute "administrative programs" for UARBAC that achieve specified permissions through permitted actions. And in Section 5, we show how permissions on administrative actions of a higher degree than supported in UARBAC can be simulated within UARBAC. We also discuss issues and perspectives for future work in Section 6. Our conclusions are in Section 7.

Our work on computing administrative programs is similar to work on the safety problem in administrative RBAC, but from a very different perspective. While the safety problem is concerned with preventing "attacks", we are concerned with helping legitimate users understand how they can achieve permissions through legal and expected administrative actions. For example, we would like a system to help the dean to learn that she can modify the policy state – in this case, membership of the admission committee – to access the application. In other words, our interest is not in reachability *per se*, but in the synthesis of plans that can help users achieve permissions they desire.

Related work

Much work on administrative RBAC inherits from the work on ARBAC97 [22]. Like most work on administrative RBAC, the aim in ARBAC97 is to administer RBAC with RBAC. However, the goal is not fully achieved, as a new class of administrative roles is introduced, and new relations for administrative permissions are defined. Furthermore, only two levels of administration are supported. ARBAC99 [23] and ARBAC02 [18] are refinements of ARBAC97 that attempt to allow for more expressive policy, but go no further than ARBAC97 in the aim of using RBAC to administer RBAC. Work on SARBAC [8] and A-ERBAC [12] are other variants, both using concepts of groups, or "scopes", to provide expressiveness beyond ARBAC97. A-ERBAC eliminates any technical distinction between normal and administrative roles. UARBAC [15] also contains no new class of role, and eliminates new relations for administrative permissions, instead using derived permissions for administrative actions. However, a new category of actions are introduced that are neither application-specific nor modify the access-control state. In the work on extended privilege inheritance in RBAC [9], administrative actions are defined simply as a broader class of actions under control of RBAC, and administrative privileges are inherited via roles just as in RBAC. None of these last-mentioned works support administrative policy analysis.

Trust management [6, 14], which focuses on delegation, is like administrative RBAC in that delegations are actions that have associated permissions, and that modify access-control state. In most trust-management frameworks, permissions on delegation are only loosely controlled through policy, but are controlled more through the "discretion" of delegators. From the point of view of our work, trust management is quite limited as a form of administrative access control. More precise controls could be put on delegation powers; for example in controlling who can delegate, who can grant delegation powers, etc.

There is much work on the analysis of the "safety problem" in access control. We shall not discuss the body of work concerning analysis of fixed (i.e., non-administrative)

policies. However, we note that the use of model checking in the analysis of access-control policies (e.g., [13]) is useful because there is a wide range of safety questions that can be asked of a policy.

Other work looks at the safety problem in administrative access control. In [11] a simple, generic model of administrative access control is defined, and the safety problem for this model is shown to be undecideable. In this model there is no bound on the size of the access-control state.

The relevance and correctness of the work in [11] is examined in [16, 17]. Most importantly, in [16] it is argued that the model of [11] is incomparable to Discretionary Access Control (DAC) models, and the decidability results of [11] are therefore not always applicable to DAC. A cubic-time algorithm is presented for deciding safety in the Graham-Denning DAC scheme.

In [10, 30] the authors present a logic-based formalism for administrative access control, a means of expressing goals, and an algorithm for checking the reachability of goals. Termination of the algorithm is guaranteed by finiteness of the access-control state.

In [28], algorithms and complexity results are provided for safety analysis in ARBAC97 policies. In [27], the authors defined a parameterized form of ARBAC, named PAR-BAC, and show the same kinds of results for policies of this model. The algorithms rely on the principle of *separate administration*, which partitions roles into administrative and non-administrative ones.

In [3, 4], authentication logics are developed in which permissions are derived from inference rules that separate updates of access-control states from constraints that decide the applicability of such rules. This separation is hoped to aid comprehension and maintainability of authorization policies. In [3], a proof system is the basis for a goal-oriented search algorithm that finds minimal sequences of transactions that lead to desired authorization state.

In [24], the authors study the analysis of policies written in ARBAC. They identify a connection between the analysis of access-control policies and planning as developed in artificial intelligence. They then exploit this connection to prove complexity results for the reachability problem in ARBAC. In particular, they show that plans for reaching specified target states in ARBAC may not have polynomial size.

The work in [31, 21] defines and studies a modeling language X-*Policy*, designed for applications within the space of collaborative web-based systems. Permissions focus on who can read or write what resources under which constraints. Model-checking techniques are being proposed for automated analysis of security properties.

2. OVERVIEW OF UARBAC

UARBAC is described in [15], referred to as "Li/Mao" henceforth. The key idea of UARBAC is that administration of RBAC can be done using RBAC itself: "permissions about users and roles are administered in the same way as permissions about other kinds of objects" [15]. This idea is clearly related to our requirement of using a single specification system and a single enforcement method.

Our technical presentation of UARBAC varies from [15], but retains the essential technical features. We assume the existence of a finite set C of class names, and a finite set Obj of objects. The set of class names includes the names role and user but may contain domain-specific names as well.

$$\alpha \ ::= \ \beta \ | \ \gamma$$
$$\beta \ ::= \ f(c) \ | \ f(x,c)$$
$$\gamma \ ::= \ op(\mathtt{PA},(\alpha,r)) \ | \ op(\mathtt{RH},(r_1,r_2)) \ |$$
$$op(\mathtt{OB},(c,x)) \ | \ op(\mathtt{UA},(u,r))$$

Figure 1: Abstract syntax of actions α. An action α can be a basic action β or an administrative action γ. Symbol f ranges over operator names, op ranges over administrative operators $\{add, remove\}$, x ranges over object names, c ranges over class names, u ranges over elements of $Dom(\mathtt{user})$, and r ranges over elements of $Dom(\mathtt{role})$.

For example, book might be a class name, and "Manager" (an object of class role), "Larry" (an object of class user), and "Firewalls" (an object of class book) might be objects.

We also assume a function $classOf : Obj \to C$ giving the class of each object. The function $Dom : C \to 2^{Obj}$ is derived from $classOf$ as follows

$$Dom(c) := \{x \in Obj \mid classOf(x) = c\}$$

When we refer to a *role*, we mean an object in $Dom(\mathtt{role})$, and similarly for *user*. Set $Dom(\mathtt{role})$ is assumed to contain the special administrative role name sso, which stands for "system security officer".

Li/Mao define a set of actions that can be requested. The abstract syntax of actions is defined in Figure 1. In the figure α is an action, γ is an administrative action, and β is a basic (i.e. non-administrative) action. The names in $\{\mathtt{OB}, \mathtt{UA}, \mathtt{PA}, \mathtt{RH}\}$ pertain to the functions and relations defined by an access-control state (see below). An operator name can be either an application-specific operation, such as read for a file read, or the name of one of UARBAC's built-in operations: admin, empower, grant, and create.

The syntax of Fig. 1 supports administration of actions of any "order". An example of an administrative action is add(PA, (buy(*book*), Engineer)). This action extends the role-permission relation PA so that action buy(*book*) is permitted for role Engineer.

Li/Mao support only administrative actions that do not contain administrative actions. For example, action

$$add(\mathtt{PA}, (buy(book), \mathsf{Engineer}))$$

is supported in Li/Mao, but the "second-order" administrative action

$$add(\mathtt{PA}, (add(\mathtt{PA}, (buy(book), \mathsf{Engineer})), \mathsf{Manager}))$$

is not. In other words, the syntax of actions supported by Li/Mao is like that of Fig. 1 except that clause $op(\mathtt{PA}, (\alpha, r))$ of γ is replaced by $op(\mathtt{PA}, (\beta, r))$. Below, we often write a to denote *atomic* administrative actions, which are those that do not contain administrative actions themselves.

An *access-control state* (or *AC state* for short) is a set of atoms, each of one of the following forms:

$$atom ::= OB(c,x) \ | \ UA(u,r) \ | \ PA(\beta,r) \ | \ RH(r_1,r_2)$$

where c ranges over class name, x over object names, u over users, r over roles, and β over non-administrative actions. We write s_{OB} for the set of OB atoms in s, and similarly for the other atoms.

```
OB(role, Director)    // other roles elided
OB(user, Larry)       // other users elided
OB(book, b)
RH(Director, Manager)
RH(Manager, Engineer)
UA(Larry, Director)
UA(Lisa, Manager)
UA(Greg, Engineer)
PA(admin(book),Manager)
PA(empower(role,Engineer), Manager)
PA(admin(role,Manager), Director)
```

Figure 2: An example of an AC State.

Intuitively, the elements of an AC state define some relations and functions. The OB atoms define the set $\{x \mid OB(c,x)\}$ of objects that "currently exist" for class c. The UA atoms define a user/role relation $\{(u,r) \mid UA(u,r) \in s\}$. The PA atoms define the set $\{\beta \mid PA(\beta, r)\}$ of basic actions permitted for role r. The RH atoms define a role hierarchy relation, which is required to be irreflexive and acyclic. We write $\mathcal{AC}$ for the set of all AC states and write $\mathcal{R}$ as a shorthand for $Dom(\mathtt{role})$.

Example. Figure 2 depicts a simple AC state. The first OB atoms indicate the existence of roles, users, and other objects. The RH atoms define that Directors lie above Managers, and Managers above Engineers in the role hierarchy. The UA atoms show that Larry is a Director, Lisa is a Manager, and Greg is an Engineer. Finally, the PA atoms give permissions on basic actions. For example, a Manager can administer book objects. **(End of Example.)**

We write $perm(\alpha, r)$ to indicate whether action α is permitted by a member of role r. For basic actions, it is derived as follows:

$$perm(f(c), r) \ := \ PA(f(c), r)$$
$$perm(f(c, o), r) \ := \ PA(f(c, o), r) \lor PA(f(c), r) \quad (1)$$

Figure 3 defines $perm$ for atomic administrative actions. The figure does not include conditions related to basic well-formedness of actions, such as that the role parameter of an action is a valid role.

Example. Returning to the example of Fig. 2, we consider some actions of users governed by the policy. First, suppose that Lisa wishes to give Engineers the permission to purchase books. To do so, Lisa would attempt to perform the administrative action

$$\mathsf{add}(\mathtt{PA}, (\mathsf{buy}(book), \mathsf{Engineer}))$$

By Figure 3, Lisa, as Manager, has permission to perform this operation, because

$$\mathtt{PA}(\mathsf{empower}(\mathtt{role}, \mathsf{Engineer}), \mathsf{Manager})$$
$$\mathtt{PA}(\mathsf{admin}(book), \mathsf{Manager})$$

both hold. As a result, the atom $\mathtt{PA}(\mathsf{buy}(book), \mathsf{Engineer})$ is added to the AC state. Now Greg has permission to buy book b, using basic action

$$\mathsf{buy}(book, b)$$

The AC state is unaffected by this action. Continuing with our example, suppose Larry is unhappy that Engineers now

a	$perm(a,r)$
$add(\texttt{OB},(c,o))$	$perm(\texttt{create}(c),r)$
$remove(\texttt{OB},(c,o))$	$perm(\texttt{admin}(c,o),r)$
$add(\texttt{UA},(u,r'))$	$perm(\texttt{grant}(\texttt{role},r'),r) \wedge perm(\texttt{empower}(user,u),r)$
$remove(\texttt{UA},(u,r'))$	$perm(\texttt{admin}(\texttt{role},r'),r) \vee perm(\texttt{admin}(user,u),r) \vee$
	$(perm(\texttt{grant}(\texttt{role},r'),r) \wedge perm(\texttt{empower}(user,u),r))$
$add(\texttt{RH},(r_1,r_2))$	$perm(\texttt{grant}(\texttt{role},r_1),r) \wedge perm(\texttt{empower}(\texttt{role},r_2),r)$
$remove(\texttt{RH},(r_1,r_2))$	$perm(\texttt{admin}(\texttt{role},r_1),r) \vee perm(\texttt{admin}(\texttt{role},r_2),r) \vee$
	$(perm(\texttt{grant}(\texttt{role},r_1),r) \wedge perm(\texttt{empower}(\texttt{role},r_2),r))$
$add(\texttt{PA},(f(c,o),r'))$	$perm(\texttt{admin}(c,o),r) \wedge perm(\texttt{empower}(\texttt{role},r'),r)$
$remove(\texttt{PA},(f(c,o),r'))$	$perm(\texttt{admin}(c,o),r) \vee perm(\texttt{admin}(\texttt{role},r'),r)$
$add(\texttt{PA},(f(c),r'))$	$r = \texttt{sso}$
$remove(\texttt{PA},(f(c),r'))$	$r = \texttt{sso} \vee perm(\texttt{admin}(\texttt{role},r'),r)$

Figure 3: Atomic administrative action a of UARBAC (left column) and condition $perm(a,r)$ (right column) specifying whether role r has permission to perform a in UARBAC. These conditions make use of permissions on *pseudo-actions* admin, create, empower, and grant.

have the right to buy books. Larry can perform the action

$$remove(PA,(admin(book),\textsf{Manager}))$$

that removes the power of Managers to administer books because, by Fig. 3, to do so it is enough that atom PA(empower (*role*, *Manager*), Director) belongs to the AC state. The effect of this action is to remove PA(admin(*book*), Manager) from the AC state. However, it does not remove the permission that Engineers have to buy books. It may seem that, as a member of a role above Manager, a Director should be able to remove administrative powers over books because Managers can do so. But UARBAC does not fix whether administrative actions are inherited according to the role hierarchy. (**End of Example.**)

Our formalization of UARBAC differs from the presentation in [15]. We use the single concept of action for both administrative and non-administrative operations; Li/Mao use the term "permission" for our basic action, and the term "administrative operation" for our atomic administrative action. We define access-control states simply as models of first-order logic, which is helpful in defining logics of permissions. In some cases we define the semantics of administrative actions differently than in [15]. For example, Li/Mao define the administrative operation createObject such that the user performing the operation gets administrative permissions on the object. For simplicity we did not model this aspect, but we could do so, and the change would not impact the methods developed later in this paper.

3. ASSESSING UARBAC

We now list some of the features and limitations of UARBAC (in the version of [15]) most relevant to our interest in administrative policy. First, in UARBAC there are only two levels of action: basic actions, and atomic administrative actions. As explained already, one cannot express nested administrative actions in UARBAC.

UARBAC has two types of basic actions: application-specific ones and the "pseudo-actions" create, admin, grant, and empower. These actions are curious because they are not application-specific; but they are not administrative either, as they do not modify the AC state. Indeed, they are not really actions (hence our use of "pseudo"), as they can neither be requested nor performed. Instead, they serve only to define permissions on administrative actions.

A closely-related point is that permissions in UARBAC cannot be set directly on administrative actions. Instead, permissions on administrative actions are derived in a fixed manner from permissions on pseudo-actions. It is helpful to think of pseudo-actions as a mechanism to define constraints between administrative permissions. For example, because of the way administrative permissions are derived from permissions on pseudo-actions, in UARBAC any role with permission to remove an object also has permission to give some other role permission on an action on that object. This is reflected in the second disjunct in (1). Also, permission conditions on actions built from operators f are uniform in, and independent from, the choice of f.

One of our desiderata for administrative policy is that a single method be used for determining permissions on administrative and non-administrative permissions. In Li/Mao it is stated that UARBAC allows RBAC mechanisms to administer RBAC. But this is true only in a limited way, since permissions on administrative actions and permissions on basic actions are not defined by a single rule, as one might expect in an RBAC framework.

Permissions on basic actions follow the usual RBAC approach: a role r has permission on an action β if (r',β) belongs to the current permission relation, where r' is r itself or a lesser role. But according to Li/Mao, there is no fixed notion of permissions on administrative actions. Also, since permissions cannot be set for administrative actions, the rule just described for basic actions cannot be applied.

Finally, Li/Mao do not describe how one might analyze UARBAC policies.

4. PLANS AS AUTHORIZED PROGRAMS

In administrative access control, a common scenario is that a user modifies the policy – according to permissions in the policy itself – to add or remove permissions of other users. However, a user can also attempt to modify the policy to increase her own or someone else's permissions. Thus, a user can ask: if I do not have a permission now, do I have permission on modification actions to the policy that will give me my desired permission? This problem is a variant of the widely-studied reachability problem in access control. Here we consider a version of the problem in the context of UARBAC. (Related work on the reachability problem in access control was discussed in Section 1.)

$$\phi \ ::= \ A(t) \ \mid \ t_1 = t_2 \ \mid \ \neg\phi \ \mid$$
$$\phi_1 \wedge \phi_2 \ \mid \ \phi_1 \vee \phi_2$$
$$t \ ::= \ x \ \mid \ f(t_1, \ldots, t_n) \ \mid \ (t_1, \ldots, t_n)$$

$$s \models A(t) \ := \ A(\llbracket t \rrbracket) \in s$$
$$s \models (t_1 = t_2) \ := \ \llbracket t_1 \rrbracket = \llbracket t_2 \rrbracket$$

Figure 4: At left is the abstract syntax of formulas ϕ and terms t, where x ranges over constant symbols, f ranges over function symbols, and A ranges over predicate symbols. The meaning of terms is just their syntax. At right is semantics of formulas; $s \models \phi$ means that access-control state s satisfies formula ϕ.

In the remainder of this section we present a logic of permissions, allowing one to express complex permissions in terms of basic permissions. Then we define a "program" as a sequence of atomic administrative actions, and show how to synthesize programs from the current access-control state and a logical formula expressing the desired permissions. If any such program exists, all of the steps of the program will be permitted, and the program will terminate with the desired permissions in place.

4.1 Logical Formulas

We define a simple quantifier-free and variable-free first-order logic on permissions. Informally, a formula in the logic is built up from atoms of form $A(t_1, \ldots, t_m)$ and $t_1 = t_2$ using propositional connectives. An atom $A(t_1, \ldots, t_m)$ holds of an AC state s simply if $A(t_1, \ldots, t_m)$ is in s. An atom $t_1 = t_2$ holds if t_1 and t_2 denote syntactically identical terms.

For simplicity we define the logic generically, and then instantiate for UARBAC. The vocabulary of the logic consists of a set of constant symbols, a set of function symbols, and a set of predicate symbols. The abstract syntax of terms and formulas of the logic is then defined in Fig. 4 (left). We also allow symbol `true` as a formula; it can be regarded as shorthand for $t = t$, where t is any term.

Formulas of the logic are interpreted relative to models that consist of a set of atoms of the form $A(t)$. We use a Herbrand-style semantics by letting the meaning $\llbracket t \rrbracket$ of terms t be just their syntax t:

$$\llbracket t \rrbracket := t$$

The semantics of formulas is defined in Fig. 4 (right). We write $s \models \phi$ if a model s satisfies a formula ϕ. We have omitted the clauses for the propositional connectives and truth constants, which are standard.

To instantiate this logic for UARBAC, we let the constant symbols be class names and object names, and let the predicate symbols be the elements of $\{OB, UA, PA, RH\}$. An access-control state then becomes a logical model.

An example formula of the logic is

$$\mathsf{UA}(Greg, \mathsf{Engineer}) \wedge \mathsf{PA}(\mathsf{buy}(book), \mathsf{Engineer})$$

which holds of an AC state if both

$$\mathsf{UA}(Greg, Engineer)$$
$$\mathsf{PA}(buy(book), Engineer)$$

exist in that state. Intuitively, Greg has permission to buy books, since user $Greg$ is an Engineer. Another example is

$$\mathsf{PA}(\mathsf{admin}(\mathsf{File}, f_1), \mathsf{Doctor}) \wedge \mathsf{PA}(\mathsf{empower}(\mathsf{Nurse}, \mathsf{Doctor}))$$

which, by Fig. 3, expresses that a doctor can modify the AC state so that a nurse can perform an action on file f_1. Note

$$\phi \ ::= \ \delta \ \mid \ \neg A(t) \ \mid \ \phi_1 \vee \phi_2 \ \mid \ \psi$$
$$\psi \ ::= \ \delta \ \mid \ \psi_1 \vee \psi_2 \ \mid \ \psi_1 \wedge \psi_2$$
$$\delta \ ::= \ A(t) \ \mid \ t_1 = t_2 \ \mid \ t_1 \neq t_2 \ \mid$$

Figure 5: Syntax of negation-flat formulas ϕ, where the syntax of terms is as in Fig. 4

$$p \ ::= \ () \ \mid \ \gamma \ \mid \ p_1; p_2$$

$$[()](s) \ := \ s$$
$$[add(A, t)](s) \ := \ s \cup \{A(t)\}$$
$$[remove(A, t)](s) \ := \ s \setminus \{A(t)\}$$
$$[p_1; p_2](s) \ := \ [p_2]([p_1](s))$$

Figure 6: Syntax of programs (top), where γ ranges over administrative actions. We write $\mathcal{P}$ for the set of all programs. Semantics of programs (bottom) as total function of type $\mathcal{P} \to (\mathcal{AC} \to \mathcal{AC})$, mapping programs to transformers of AC states (bottom).

that all conditions on the right of Fig. 3 are well-formed formulas of this logic.

A *positive* formula is one containing no negation symbols. A *negation-flat* formula is one in which negation does not appear within the scope of conjunction, as defined in Fig. 5.

4.2 Programs

A *program* is a sequence of atomic administrative actions. The syntax and semantics of programs is shown in Fig. 6. For the *add* and *remove* operators, each element A of the AC state is understood as a set; if A is a function or relation, we treat it as the graph of that function or relation. For example, $add(PA, (\alpha, r))$ interprets PA as a binary relation and means to add pair (α, r) to it.

A program is *positive* if it contains no *remove* actions. Positive programs preserve positive formulas.

PROPOSITION 1. *For all positive programs p, positive formulas ϕ, and AC states s: if $s \models \phi$ then $p(s) \models \phi$.*

We now define a permission condition on programs. The idea is that a program is permitted if its first action is, and if performing the action leads to an AC state where the second action is permitted, etc.

We formalize the notion of program permissions using function wp, defined in Fig. 7. Formula $wp(p, \phi)$ is the *nec-*

$$\begin{aligned}
wp((), \phi) &:= \phi \\
wp(add(A,t), A(t')) &:= A(t') \vee (t = t') \\
wp(add(A,t), A'(t')) &:= A'(t') \qquad (A \neq A') \\
wp(add(A,t), t_1 = t_2) &:= t_1 = t_2 \\
wp(add(A,t), \phi_1 \wedge \phi_2) &:= wp(add(A,t), \phi_1) \\
&\qquad \wedge\, wp(add(A,t), \phi_2) \\
wp(remove(A,t), A(t')) &:= A(t') \wedge (t \neq t') \\
wp(remove(A,t), A'(t')) &:= A'(t') \qquad (A \neq A') \\
wp(remove(A,t), t_1 = t_2) &:= t_1 = t_2 \\
wp(remove(A,t), \phi_1 \wedge \phi_2) &:= wp(remove(A,t), \phi_1) \\
&\qquad \wedge\, wp(remove(A,t), \phi_2) \\
wp(p_1; p_2, \phi) &:= wp(p_1, wp(p_2, \phi)) \\
wp(p, \neg\phi) &:= \neg wp(p, \phi)
\end{aligned}$$

$$\begin{aligned}
perm((), r) &:= \texttt{true} \\
perm(\gamma, r) &\qquad \text{Defined in Fig. 3} \\
perm(p_1; p_2, r) &:= perm(p_1, r) \wedge wp(p_1, perm(p_2, r))
\end{aligned}$$

Figure 7: Definition of functions $wp\colon \mathcal{P} \times \mathcal{L} \to \mathcal{L}$ **and** $perm\colon \mathcal{P} \times \mathcal{R} \to \mathcal{L}$.

essary and sufficient condition required of an AC state so that ϕ holds after program p executes from that state. For example, for

$$\begin{aligned}
\phi &:= \mathsf{PA}(\mathsf{buy}(b2, book),\ \mathsf{Engineer}) \\
p &:= add(\mathsf{PA}, (\mathsf{buy}(b1, book),\ \mathsf{Engineer}))
\end{aligned}$$

the condition $wp(p, \phi)$ needed to establish that ϕ holds after program p executes is

$$\mathsf{PA}(\mathsf{buy}(b2, book),\ \mathsf{Engineer})) \ \vee\ b1 = b2.$$

We now state the correctness of wp formally.

THEOREM 1. *Let s be an AC state, p be a program, and ϕ be a formula. Then $s \models wp(p, \phi)$ iff $p(s) \models \phi$.*

Using wp we can define $perm(p, r)$, which is the formula that holds of an AC state s if role r has permission to run program p. Function $perm$ is defined at the bottom of Fig. 7. The following is a sanity check on the definition of $perm$.

PROPOSITION 2. *Let p_1, p_2 be programs, r be a role, and s be an AC state. Then $s \models perm(p_1; p_2, r)$ iff both $s \models perm(p_1, r)$ and $p_1(s) \models perm(p_2, r)$.*

We define formula $\overline{wp}(p, r, \phi)$ to be

$$wp(p, \phi) \wedge perm(p, r).$$

Formula $\overline{wp}(p, r, \phi)$ holds at an AC state if role r has permission to run the program, and doing so leads to a state satisfying ϕ. We shall later use some simple properties of $\overline{wp}$, which we now list. For formulas ϕ_1 and ϕ_2, expression $\phi_1 \Rightarrow \phi_2$ holds if, for all AC states s, relation $s \models \phi_1$ implies $s \models \phi_2$. Also, $\phi_1 \Leftrightarrow \phi_2$ holds if $\phi_1 \Rightarrow \phi_2$ and $\phi_2 \Rightarrow \phi_1$ hold.

PROPOSITION 3. *Let p be a program, r be a role, and ϕ, ϕ_1, ϕ_2 be formulas. Then the following all hold:*

1. $\overline{wp}(p_1; p_2, r, \phi) \Leftrightarrow \overline{wp}(p_1, r, \overline{wp}(p_2, r, \phi))$

2. $\overline{wp}(p, r, \phi_1 \wedge \phi_2) \Leftrightarrow \overline{wp}(p, r, \phi_1) \wedge \overline{wp}(p, r, \phi_2)$

3. If $(\phi_1 \Rightarrow \phi_2)$ then $(\overline{wp}(p, \phi_1) \Rightarrow \overline{wp}(p, \phi_2))$

4. $\overline{wp}(add(A,t), r, A(t)) \Leftrightarrow perm(add(A,t), r)$

5. $\overline{wp}(remove(A,t), \neg A(t)) \Leftrightarrow perm(remove(A,t), r)$

4.3 Program Synthesis

The predicate $perm(\alpha, r)$ holds of an AC state if a user in role r has permission on action α. But in administrative access control, a user may wish to know not only if an action α can be performed – permission in the *strong* sense – but whether administrative actions could be performed that would change the AC state such that α could be performed. This is permission in the *weak* sense.

Fig. 8 defines function *progs*. The value $progs(s, r, \phi, \Phi)$ is a set of programs that r is permitted to run in s, and that all terminate in a state satisfying ϕ. Parameter Φ is used to ensure termination. The function can be understood as a backward-chaining planning algorithm, in which AC state s is the initial state, formula ϕ is the goal condition, and the possible actions are those listed in the left column of Fig. 3. Also, for any $P, Q \subseteq \mathcal{P}$ we write $P; Q$ for the subset $\{p; q \mid p \in P, q \in Q\}$ of $\mathcal{P}$ and write $P; q$ for $P; \{q\}$.

The algorithm works by considering and simplifying the structure of the goal condition ϕ. Suppose ϕ is a basic predicate of the form $A(t)$. Then the empty program () achieves the goal if ϕ is satisfied in initial state s; otherwise the goal can be achieved by action $add(A,t)$. If the latter, then the permission for action $add(A,t)$ is made the new goal. If ϕ is a formula of the form $\neg A(t)$, then the processing is similar, except $remove(A,t)$ is the action and the permission for $remove(A,t)$ is the new goal.

If the goal condition is a disjunction, then the problem is decomposed, with each disjunct becoming a goal, and similarly for conjunction. In the case of disjunction, a program for any disjunct is a program for the disjunction as a whole. For the case of conjunction, a program built sequentially from the programs for all conjuncts is a program for the conjunction as a whole. Intuitively, this treatment of conjunction works because the conjuncts must be positive, and therefore do not "interfere" with each other.

The next theorem establishes that the function *progs* terminates, is sound, and is complete, in the sense that a program will be produced, if one exists, that will achieve the desired condition.

THEOREM 2. *Let p be a program, r be a role, s be an AC state, ϕ be a negation-flat formula, and Φ be a set of formulas. Then:*

1. $progs(s, r, \phi, \Phi)$ *terminates.*

2. *If $p \in progs(s, r, \phi, \Phi)$ then $s \models \overline{wp}(p, r, \phi)$.*

3. *If $progs(s, r, \phi, \emptyset) = \emptyset$, then there is no program $p \in \mathcal{P}$ such that $s \models \overline{wp}(p, r, \phi)$.*

One may think of the computed set $progs(s, r, \phi, \emptyset)$ as a tree with internal nodes "$\cup$" and ";", and leaves "$\emptyset$" and "$\{()\}$". Also, only branch points for $\wedge$ and $\vee$ compute subtrees that are *both* non-trivial. The complexity of *progs* is

ϕ	$progs(s,r,\phi,\Phi)$	
$A(t)$	$\emptyset$	if $\phi \in \Phi$
	$\{()\}$	if $\phi \notin \Phi$ and $s \models \phi$
	$progs(s,r,perm(add(A,t),r),\Phi \cup \{\phi\}); add(A,t)$	otherwise
$\neg A(t)$	$\emptyset$	if $\phi \in \Phi$
	$\{()\}$	if $\phi \notin \Phi$ and $s \models \phi$
	$progs(s,r,perm(remove(A,t),r),\Phi \cup \{\phi\}); remove(A,t)$	otherwise
$t_1 = t_2$	$\{()\}$	if $s \models \phi$
	$\emptyset$	otherwise
$t_1 \neq t_2$	$\{()\}$	if $s \models \phi$
	$\emptyset$	otherwise
$\phi_1 \vee \phi_2$	$progs(s,r,\phi_1,\Phi) \cup progs(s,r,\phi_2,\Phi)$	
$\phi_1 \wedge \phi_2$	$progs(s,r,\phi_1,\Phi); progs(s,r,\phi_2,\Phi)$	

Figure 8: Definition of function $progs\colon \mathcal{AC} \times \mathcal{R} \times \mathcal{L} \times 2^{\mathcal{L}} \to 2^{\mathcal{P}}$. **Formula** ϕ **(left) ranges over elements on** $\mathcal{L}$ **in negation-flat form. The corresponding expression on the right defines** $progs(s,r,\phi,\Phi)$ **for** $\Phi \subseteq \mathcal{L}$.

therefore directly related to the width and depth of that tree. The depth is bounded by the well-founded ordering used in the termination analysis of this algorithm. The width is bounded by the number of nestings of disjunctions and conjunctions encountered in the computation.

The correctness of function *progs* depends on parameter ϕ being in negation-flat form. Alternatively, one could write a brute-force synthesis algorithm that would cope with any formula in our logic. Also, function *progs* could easily be modified to return only a single program to achieve the specified goal, rather than what could potentially be a large set.

In what follows we often write $progs(s,r,\phi)$ as shorthand for $progs(s,r,\phi,\emptyset)$. Also, we write *Act* and *BAct* for the sets of all α, respectively β, generated in Fig. 1.

COROLLARY 1. *Let s be in $\mathcal{AC}$, r in $\mathcal{R}$, and α in Act. Then for any p in $progs(s,r,perm(\alpha,r))$ we have that $s \models perm(p;\alpha,r)$.*

Thus a user who wants to reach a specified state of permissions can use function *progs* to find a program whose execution will reach that state.

Example. We now illustrate the use of *progs* using the example of Figure 2. In Section 2 we explained that director Larry might not want managers to have permission to give engineer's permission to buy books. Consider how function *progs* could be used by Larry to find a program to reach this goal. His goal is:

$$\neg perm(add(\mathsf{PA}, (buy(book), \mathsf{Engr})), \mathsf{Mgr})$$

which states that a manager does not have permission to give Engineers book-buying permission (we use abbreviated role names in this example to save space). By the definition of *perm* this is equivalently:

$$\neg(\mathsf{PA}(admin(book), \mathsf{Mgr}) \wedge \mathsf{PA}(empower(role, E), \mathsf{Mgr}))$$

which by DeMorgan's law is equivalently:

$$\neg\mathsf{PA}(admin(book), \mathsf{M}) \vee \neg\mathsf{PA}(empower(role, E), \mathsf{Mgr})$$

Let us refer to this formula as $\phi_1 \vee \phi_2$.

Next we try to find programs to reach this goal function *progs*: The function application $progs(s, \mathsf{Dir}, \phi_1 \vee \phi_2, \emptyset)$ expands to

$$progs(s, \mathsf{Dir}, \phi_1, \emptyset) \cup progs(s, \mathsf{Dir}, \phi_2, \emptyset)$$

Evaluating the first sub-expression yields:

$$progs(s, \mathsf{Dir}, perm(remove(\mathsf{PA}, (admin(book), \mathsf{Mgr})), \mathsf{Dir}), \phi_1);$$
$$remove(\mathsf{PA}, (admin(book), \mathsf{Mgr}))$$

Evaluating the *progs* call, we have:

$$progs(s, \mathsf{Dir},$$
$$perm(remove(\mathsf{PA}, (admin(book), \mathsf{Mgr})), \mathsf{Dir}), \phi_1)$$
$$= progs(s, \mathsf{Dir},$$
$$\mathsf{PA}(admin(book), \mathsf{Dir}) \vee \mathsf{PA}(admin(role, \mathsf{Mgr}), \mathsf{Dir}), \phi_1)$$
$$= progs(s, \mathsf{Dir}, \mathsf{PA}(admin(book), \mathsf{Dir}), \{\phi_1\}) \cup$$
$$progs(s, \mathsf{Dir}, \mathsf{PA}(admin(role, \mathsf{Mgr}), \mathsf{Dir}), \{\phi_1\})$$

Note that $\mathsf{PA}(admin(role, \mathsf{Mgr}), \mathsf{Dir})$ is an atom of the AC state. Therefore

$$progs(s, \mathsf{Dir}, \mathsf{PA}(admin(role, \mathsf{Mgr}), \mathsf{Dir}), \{\phi_1\}) = \{()\}$$

This means that no action is needed to reach goal

$$PA(admin(role, \mathsf{Mgr}), \mathsf{Dir})$$

Therefore the empty program () is also contained in

$$progs(s, \mathsf{Dir}, perm(remove(\mathsf{PA}, (admin(book), M)), \mathsf{Dir}), \{\phi_1\})$$

and therefore we have both set memberships

$$remove(\mathsf{PA}, (admin(book), \mathsf{Mgr})) \in progs(s, \mathsf{Dir}, \phi_1, \emptyset)$$
$$remove(\mathsf{PA}, (admin(book), \mathsf{Mgr})) \in progs(s, \mathsf{Dir}, \phi_1 \vee \phi_2, \emptyset)$$

In short, using *progs*, Larry has learned he has permission to perform program

$$remove(\mathsf{PA}, (admin(book), \mathsf{Mgr}))$$

and doing so will result in goal condition

$$\neg perm(add(\mathsf{PA}, (buy(book), E)), \mathsf{Mgr})$$

holding in the AC state. (**End of Example.**)

5. SIMULATING NON-ATOMIC ADMINISTRATION IN UARBAC

UARBAC, as defined by Li/Mao in [15], only supports *atomic* administrative actions. We now show that there is a way to check, within Li/Mao's UARBAC, permissions of non-atomic administrative actions. Furthermore, there is a way for users (when permitted) to operate on the AC state to achieve these permissions.

The idea we use is that a modified notion of permission will be used for non-atomic administrative actions. To see the idea, suppose that a director wishes to add permission for managers to remove permission for engineers to purchase books. This permission can't be expressed in Li/Mao's UARBAC. But director Larry can achieve the desired outcome if he can modify the AC state such that a manager can modify the AC state such that engineers *cannot* modify the control state to get permission to purchase books. We can express and check such "weak" permissions.

What property should we want weak permissions to possess? We can make an analogy to a property that holds of permissions on atomic administrative actions: if an operation to add (β, r) to PA is permitted, then applying the action leads to a state in which β is permitted for r. For example, if AC state s satisfies $\mathrm{PA}(add(\mathrm{PA}, (\alpha, r)), r')$ then modified state $add(\mathrm{PA}, (\alpha, r))$ satisfies $\mathrm{PA}(\alpha, r)$. A similar property holds of *remove* actions.

Weak permissions should possess a similar property: if an operation to add (α, r) to PA is weakly permitted, then there should exist a permitted program p that leads to a state in which α is weakly permitted for r. For example, if s satisfies $perm'(add(\mathrm{PA}, (\alpha, r)), r')$, then there exists a program p such that s satisfies $perm(p, r')$ and $p(s)$ satisfies $perm'(\alpha, r)$. Here $perm'$ is a weak permission predicate, and α can be an administrative action.

A difficulty with this property is that it uses the idea of existential quantification over *programs*. We would like to capture that property logically, and so need a way to express in logic that there exists a program with which a member of a role can reach an AC state satisfying some condition.

The following theorem states that function Ep, defined in Fig. 9, when given a role r and formula ϕ, returns formula $Ep(r, \phi)$ that holds at an AC state s if there exists a program p such that $s \models \overline{wp}(p, r, \phi)$.

THEOREM 3. *Let s be an AC state, r be a role, and ϕ be a formula. Then $s \models Ep(r, \phi)$ iff there exists a program p such that $s \models \overline{wp}(p, r, \phi)$.*

Using Ep we define function $perm'$ at the bottom of Fig. 9. Logical formula $perm'(\alpha, r)$ expresses weak permission for role r on action α. This notion of weak permission satisfies the property that we have said we expect of it.

PROPOSITION 4. *Let s be an AC state. Then:*

1. *For any α of form $add(\mathrm{PA}, (\alpha', r'))$ with $s \models perm'(\alpha, r)$ there exists a program p such that $s \models perm(p, r)$ and $p(s) \models perm'(\alpha', r')$.*

2. *For any α of form $remove(\mathrm{PA}, (\alpha', r'))$ such that $s \models perm'(a, r)$ there exists a program p such that $s \models perm(p, r)$ and $p(s) \not\models perm'(\alpha', r')$.*

It should be highlighted that $Ep(r, \phi)$ is a formula of our logic, and so we have captured the notion of reachability through a policy as a formula that can be checked of an AC state. Ep is closely tied to function $progs$: for all s r, and ϕ it is the case that $s \models Ep(r, \phi)$ iff there is some p in $progs(s, r, \phi)$. Similarly, $perm'(\alpha, r)$ is a formula of our

logic, and so a weak permission can be checked of an AC state.

To summarize, we have shown how permissions on non-atomic administrative actions, absent in Li/Mao's UARBAC, can be simulated in it. Next we define the effect of the application of a non-atomic administrative action in Li/Mao's UARBAC.

For an administrative action γ, we define in Fig. 10 the desired effect of γ as a postcondition $post(\gamma)$. The definition says that by performing a non-atomic *add* action one seeks to enable the given action, and by performing a non-atomic *remove* action one seeks to disable it.

Now, let γ be any administrative action. A user in role r can use any program in $progs(s, r, post(\gamma))$ to accomplish the desired effect of action γ.

COROLLARY 2. *Let s be an AC state, r and r' be roles, and a be an administrative action. Then:*

1. *For every p in $progs(s, r, post(add(r', a)))$ we have that $p(s) \models perm'(r', a)$.*

2. *For every p in $progs(s, r, post(remove(r', a)))$ we have $p(s) \not\models perm'(r', a)$.*

6. DISCUSSION

We now discuss some issues of our approach, and point out avenues for future work that these issues provide.

6.1 Plans for Roles Versus Plans for Users

Our technical development supports plans relative to roles. This answers questions such as "Can a Director perform administration so that Engineers can no longer buy books?"

It is obviously of interest to ask and answer similar questions at the level of users. For example, we may ask "Can Colin perform administration so that Engineers can no longer buy books?" and the variant "Can Colin perform administration so that Barbara can no longer buy books?"

Our technical development can be adjusted and extended in order to accommodate support for such user-centric plans. We hint at how this can be realized; a complete exposition is deferred to a full paper. The predicates $perm(\alpha, r)$, $\overline{wp}(p, r, \phi)$, and $progs(s, r, \phi, \Phi)$ change so that roles r are replaced with users u. For example, we would set

$$perm(p_1; p_2, u) := perm(p_1, u) \wedge wp(p_1, perm(p_2, u))$$

where it is crucial that programs p_1 and p_2 can be performed by the same user u but potentially in different roles.

Similarly, the definition of $perm(\alpha, u)$ reflects the RBAC model that permissions for users are mediated through permissions on their roles. Thus, we would set

$$perm(a, u) := \bigvee_{r \in \mathcal{R}} \mathrm{UA}(u, r) \wedge perm(a, r)$$

for atomic administrative actions a.

6.2 Atomicity of Plan Execution

An authorized synthesized program is only a solution to our planning problem if it can execute without interference. But the access-control architecture may be such that access requests that are not part of the plan are interleaved with the plan execution and potentially granted. This may in fact corrupt the aim of plan execution. There are at least two responses of interest to this concern.

$$
\begin{aligned}
Ep(r, t_1 = t_2) &:= t_1 = t_2 \\
Ep(r, A(t)) &:= A(t) \lor Ep(r, perm(add(A, t), r)) \\
Ep(r, \neg A(t)) &:= \neg A(t) \lor Ep(r, perm(remove(A, t), r)) \\
Ep(r, \phi_1 \land \phi_2) &:= Ep(r, \phi_1) \land Ep(r, \phi_2) \\
Ep(r, \phi_1 \lor \phi_2) &:= Ep(r, \phi_1) \lor Ep(r, \phi_2)
\end{aligned}
$$

$$
\begin{aligned}
perm'(\alpha, r) &:= Ep(r, perm(\alpha, r)) \quad (\alpha \text{ basic or atomic administrative}) \\
perm'(add(\mathtt{PA}, (\alpha, r')), r) &:= Ep(r, perm'(\alpha, r')) \\
perm'(remove(\mathtt{PA}, (\alpha, r')), r) &:= \neg Ep(r, perm'(\alpha, r'))
\end{aligned}
$$

Figure 9: Definition of functions Ep and $perm'$.

$$
\begin{aligned}
post(add(A, x)) &:= A(x) \quad &&\text{(atomic administrative case)} \\
post(remove(A, x)) &:= \neg A(x) \quad &&\text{(atomic administrative case)} \\
post(add(\mathtt{PA}, (\alpha, r))) &:= perm'(\alpha, r) \\
post(remove(\mathtt{PA}, (\alpha, r))) &:= \neg perm'(\alpha, r)
\end{aligned}
$$

Figure 10: Definition of function $post$. Formula $post(\gamma)$ gives the desired effect of administrative action γ.

One response would be to use techniques developed for run-time verification [2]. Whenever a plan wants to execute the next step and finds it unauthorized, one would re-synthesize a desired plan from the current AC state and (if such a plan exists) execute that new plan.

Another response would be to use techniques developed for design synthesis [19]. The idea is here to try to compute a plan that will lead to a desired goal state no matter what actions the environment may choose to do during plan execution. A plan would then not be a sequence of actions but a tree of such actions, technically, a winning strategy in an infinite 2-person game played between a system (the user who wants to get to a goal state) and an environment (all other or a set of "hostile" users).

6.3 Coalition Plans

Agent-based approaches to verification and validation, e.g. the temporal logic ATL [1], can compute reachability under the assumption that a designated coalition of agents collaborate in order to reach the target set of states.

In our context, agents are users. In a positive reading, coalitions would analyze whether they can collaborate in order to realize desired permissions to get necessary work done. In a negative reading, coalitions could do the same analysis to determine whether permissions could be realized with which insider attacks [20] could be launched. As most scientific methods, our approach is agnostic to these interpretations.

Adapting our approach to support coalitions is straightforward for plan synthesis. In the reachability problem we considered above, we would simply consider every action that is authorized and involves a role (or user) from the given coalition.

6.4 Use of Constraints

Constraints are often needed in the enforcement of access control. Seperation of duty, e.g., may require that two ac-

tions be performed by different users. RBAC models may support, for example, user/role constraints and role activation constraints. This raises the question of whether authorized plans can be synthesized that meet such constraints.

We think that this problem is related to that of computing authorized work-flow schemes [5]. Such schemas have tasks that need to be assigned to authorized users, where certain tasks must precede certain others and where constraints on user/task assignment have to be met. Computing solutions for such schemas is typically NP-complete or NP-hard [29].

We believe that, for an important class of constraints such as those in [7], the synthesis of authorized, constrained plans for higher-order permissions can be achieved by satisfiability checking of suitable fragments of linear-time propositional temporal logic, e.g. the NP-complete fragment of LTL [25].

Another question pertaining to constraints is whether our version of UARBAC can be extended so that permissions are enriched with pre-conditions over authorization state. The use of such constraints is also expected to be useful when trying to extend our work to the parameterized version of UARBAC in [15].

7. CONCLUSIONS

In this paper we studied the issue of whether and how standard tools from planning and program verification can provide needed support for users of access-control systems that are governed not just by basic permissions, but also by higher-order (so called "administrative") permissions.

The support we had in mind was to answer whether users can reach specific access-control goal states and, if so, how planning can synthesize administrative programs whose execution is authorized and will reach a desired goal state.

We focused our attention on the RBAC family of access-control models and identified the UARBAC model as a promising candidate for developing such user support. The principal technical contributions of this paper, therefore, were a logical reconstruction of UARBAC that not only allows for such support, but also provides a uniform enforcement rule, and the ability to simulate higher-order administrative actions within the original UARBAC model.

Acknowledgements

Glenn Bruns and Kumar Avijit were supported in part by US National Science Foundation grant 0244901. We thank the anonymous reviewers for their detailed and very thoughtful comments.

8. REFERENCES

[1] R. Alur, T. A. Henzinger, and O. Kupferman. Alternating-time temporal logic. In *Proc. of 38th Ann. Symp. on Found. of Computer Science*, 1997.

[2] A. Bauer, M. Leucker, and C. Schallhart. Runtime verification for LTL and TLTL. *ACM Transactions on Software Engineering and Methodology*, 2009. in press.

[3] M. Y. Becker and S. Nanz. A logic for state-modifying authorization policies. In *Proc. of ESORICS 2007*, pp. 203-218, LNCS 4734, Springer, 2007.

[4] M. Y. Becker. Specification and Analysis of Dynamic Authorisation Policies. In *Proc. of Comp. Security Found. Symp.*, pp. 203-217, IEEE, 2009.

[5] E. Bertino, E. Ferrari, and V. Atluri. The specification and enforcement of authorization constraints in workflow management systems. *ACM Trans. Inf. Syst. Secur.* 2:65–104, February 1999.

[6] M. Blaze, J. Feigenbaum, and J. Lacy. Decentralized trust management. In *Proc. of Symposium on Security and Privacy*, pp. 164–173. IEEE, 1996.

[7] J. Crampton. A reference monitor for workflow systems with constrained task execution. In *Proc. of SACMAT '05*, pp. 38–47. ACM, 2005.

[8] J. Crampton and G. Loizou. Administrative scope: A foundation for role-based administrative models. *ACM Trans. Inf. Syst. Secur.* 6:201–231, May 2003.

[9] M. A. C. Dekker, J. G. Cederquist, J. Crampton, and S. Etalle. Extended privilege inheritance in RBAC. In *Proc. of ASIACCS*, pp. 383–385. ACM, 2007.

[10] D. P. Guelev, M. Ryan, and P.-Y. Schobbens. Model-checking access control policies. In *Information Security*, LNCS 3225. Springer, 2004.

[11] M. A. Harrison, W. L. Ruzzo, and J. D. Ullman. Protection in operating systems. *Commun. ACM* 19:461–471, August 1976.

[12] A. Kern, A. Schaad, and J. Moffett. An administration concept for the enterprise role-based access control model. In *Proc. of SACMAT '03*, pp. 3–11. ACM, 2003.

[13] E. Kleiner and T. Newcomb. On the decidability of the safety problem for access control policies. *Electron. Notes Theor. Comput. Sci.* 185:107–120, 2007.

[14] N. Li, B. N. Grosof, and J. Feigenbaum. Delegation logic: A logic-based approach to distributed authorization. *ACM Trans. Inf. Syst. Secur.* 6:128–171, Feb. 2003.

[15] N. Li and Z. Mao. Administration in role-based access control. In *Proc. of ASIACCS*, pp. 127–138. ACM, 2007.

[16] N. Li and M. V. Tripunitara. On safety in

[17] N. Li and M. V. Tripunitara. The foundational work of Harrisson-Ruzzo-Ullman revisited. Technical Report CERIAS TR 2006-33, Purdue University, 2006.

[18] S. Oh, R. Sandhu, and X. Zhang. An effective role administration model using organization structure. *ACM Trans. Inf. Syst. Secur.* 9(2):113–137, 2006.

[19] A. Pnueli and R. Rosner. On the synthesis of a reactive module. In *Proc. of POPL '89*, pp. 179–190. ACM, 1989.

[20] C. W. Probst, J. Hunker, and M. Bishop, editors. *Insider Threats in Cyber Security*, volume 49 of *Advances in Information Security*. Springer, 2010.

[21] H. Qunoo and M. Ryan. Modelling Dynamic Access Control Policies for Web-Based Collaborative Systems. In *Proc. of Conf. on Data and Applications Security and Privacy*, LNCS 6166, pp. 295-302, Springer, 2010.

[22] R. Sandhu, V. Bhamidipati, and Q. Munawer. The ARBAC97 model for role-based administration of roles. *ACM Trans. Inf. Syst. Secur.* 2:105–135, Feb. 1999.

[23] R. Sandhu and Q. Munawer. The ARBAC99 model for administration of roles. In *Proc. of ACSAC'99*, pp. 229–238. IEEE, 2002.

[24] A. Sasturkar, P. Yang, S. D. Stoller, and C. R. Ramakrishnan. Policy Analysis for Administrative Role Based Access Control. In *Proc. of Computer Security Foundations Workshop*, pp. 124-138. IEEE, 2006.

[25] A. P. Sistla and E. M. Clarke. The complexity of propositional linear temporal logics. *J. ACM* 32:733–749, July 1985.

[26] J. A. Solworth and R. H. Sloan. A layered design of discretionary access controls with decidable safety properties. *IEEE Symposium on Security and Privacy*, pp. 56-67, 2004.

[27] S. D. Stoller, P. Yang, M. Gofman, and C. R. Ramakrishnan. Symbolic reachability analysis for parameterized administrative role based access control. In *Proc. of SACMAT '09*, pp. 165–174. ACM, 2009.

[28] S. D. Stoller, P. Yang, C. R. Ramakrishnan, and M. I. Gofman. Efficient policy analysis for administrative role based access control. In *Proc. of CCS '07*, pp. 445–455. ACM, 2007.

[29] Q. Wang and N. Li. Satisfiability and resiliency in workflow authorization systems. *ACM Trans. Inf. Syst. Secur.* 13:40:1–40:35, December 2010.

[30] N. Zhang, M. Ryan, and D. Guelev. Evaluating access control policies through model-checking. In *8th Information Security Conference*. Springer, 2005.

[31] N. Zhang, M. Ryan, and D. P. Guelev. Synthesizing verified access control systems through model checking. *J. of Computer Security* 16(1):1-61, 2008.

Relationship-Based Access Control Policies and Their Policy Languages

Philip W. L. Fong   Ida Siahaan
Department of Computer Science
University of Calgary
Calgary, Alberta, Canada
{ pwlfong, isrsiaha }@ucalgary.ca

ABSTRACT

The Relationship-Based Access Control (ReBAC) model was recently proposed as a general-purpose access control model. It supports the natural expression of parameterized roles, the composition of policies, and the delegation of trust. Fong proposed a policy language that is based on Modal Logic for expressing and composing ReBAC policies. A natural question is whether such a language is representationally complete, that is, whether the language is capable of expressing all ReBAC policies that one is interested in expressing.

In this work, we argue that the extensive use of what we call Relational Policies is what distinguishes ReBAC from traditional access control models. We show that Fong's policy language is representationally incomplete in that certain previously studied Relational Policies are not expressible in the language. We introduce two extensions to the policy language of Fong, and prove that the extended policy language is representationally complete with respect to a well-defined subclass of Relational Policies.

Categories and Subject Descriptors

D.4.6 [**Security and Protection**]: Access Controls

General Terms

Security, Language, Theory

Keywords

Access control policies, modal logic, policy languages, relationship-based access control, social networks

1. INTRODUCTION

The advent of social computing introduces the world to a new paradigm of access control, in which interpersonal relationships are explicitly tracked by the protection system for the purpose of authorization. Gates coined the term *Relationship-Based Access Control (ReBAC)* to refer

to this paradigm of access control [17]. In a typical ReBAC system, the protection state consists of a knowledge base of primitive relationships (e.g., friend) between individual users [8], and an access control policy (e.g., friend-of-friend) is expressed in terms of composite relationships induced by the primitive relationships (e.g., friend ∘ friend).

While previously proposed ReBAC systems are designed mostly for social computing applications [23, 9, 8, 34, 35, 16], a formal ReBAC model was proposed recently as a general-purpose access control model [15]. The model features poly-relational social networks with asymmetric relations, as well as a context-dependent authorization procedure that limits the scope of relationships to their applicable contexts. Fong articulates three benefits of the ReBAC paradigm in general, and of his ReBAC model in particular. First, formulating policies in terms of binary relationships between users supports the natural expression of authorization decisions that are based on the relative attributes of the accessor as perceived by the resource owner (e.g., trust, professional association, etc). Traditional access control systems base their authorization decisions on some unary predicates of the users (e.g., identities, roles, etc) that is defined by a central authority. The limitations of such an approach becomes evident as notions such as *parameterized roles* [29] (or *role templates* [19]) creep into RBAC systems: e.g., the parameterized role manager(john) signifies the role assumed by the manager of John. In many emerging application domains, such as social computing and Electronic Health Records Systems, in which the protection of user-contributed contents is prominent, accessibility depends not on the intrinsic attributes of the accessor, but on the relationship between the accessor and the owner (e.g., the professional relationship) [5, 30]. ReBAC provides natural support for such situations. Second, relationship-based access control policies support a richer form of policy composition. With policies that are based on unary predicates, the only interesting form of policy composition would be boolean combinations (i.e., ∧, ∨, ¬), which can be captured readily by, say, a role hierarchy. Binary relations, however, supports a much richer form of composition, including relational composition (friend∘friend) and transitive closure (friend$^+$). Third, a composite binary relation supports delegation of trust in a natural way: e.g., by adopting the policy friend-of-friend, I am delegating to my friends to decide who can access.

Fong also proposed a policy language for expressing ReBAC policies [15]. The language is based on a basic modal logic, and it has been shown to be capable of expressing complex, composite relationships between an owner and an accessor, such as those found in an Electronic Health Records (EHR) system [4]. One natural question to ask is whether the policy language of Fong is representationally complete, that is, whether it is capable of expressing all the ReBAC policies we would like to express. In this work, we give a negative answer to the question, we extend the policy language to cover its shortcomings, and we formally characterize the expressive power of the extended policy language. In this last respect, this research has close affinity to enforceability research, as exemplified in [33, 26, 13, 21, 36, 27, 28], which formally characterizes the structural relationships between naturally occurring policy families, and the family of policies enforceable by a given enforcement mechanism.

Our contributions are threefold:

1. A distinguished feature of ReBAC is its extensive use of what has come to be known as **relational policies** [1]. We demonstrate, in Section 2, that a number of relational policies previously studied in the context of Facebook-style Social Network Systems [16] cannot be expressed in the policy language of Fong.

2. We introduce, in Section 3, two new features into the ReBAC policy language, and demonstrate that the resulting language is capable of expressing the above-mentioned relational policies.

3. In Section 4, we formally characterize the expressiveness of the extended policy language by proving both an "upper bound" and a "lower bound" for the family of ReBAC policies expressible in the language. The upper-bound result shows that, every policy expressible in the extended policy language belongs to the family of owner-checkable policies. The lower-bound result identifies a natural subclass of relational policies, namely, finitary relational policies, that are provably expressible in the extended language: the extended language is representationally complete with respect to finitary relational policies.

2. INADEQUACY OF B

This section gives an overview of the background on which this work is based, and articulates the representational incompleteness of the basic policy language of Fong [15].

2.1 Notation

Given a binary relation $R \subseteq X \times Y$ and individuals $x \in X$ and $y \in Y$, we write $R(x, y)$ iff $(x, y) \in R$. We write 2^X for the powerset of X (i.e., the set of *all* subsets of X), $[X]^k$ for the set of all subsets of X that have a cardinality k, and $[X]^{<\omega}$ for the set of all *finite* subsets of X. We write $f : X \rightharpoonup Y$ whenever f is a function with a *subset* of X as its domain and Y as its co-domain. We write $\emptyset$ for a function with an empty domain. Consider a function $f : X \rightharpoonup Y$ and individuals $x_0 \in X$ and $y_0 \in Y$. We write $f[x_0 \mapsto y_0]$ to denote the function $f' : X \rightharpoonup Y$ defined as follows: $f'(x) = y_0$ if $x = x_0$, but $f'(x) = f(x)$ if $x \neq x_0$.

2.2 Social Networks and Relation Identifiers

We assume that an SNS defines a *finite* set $\mathcal{I}$ of **relation identifiers**. Each identifier denotes a type of relationships that is tracked by the system (e.g., parent-child, patient-physician, etc). A typical member of $\mathcal{I}$ is denoted by i.

A social network is essentially a directed graph with multiple kinds of edges. While individuals are represented by vertices, each kind of directed edges represents a distinct type of relationship between users. Formally, a **social network** G is a relational structure [6] of the form $\langle V, \{R_i\}_{i \in \mathcal{I}} \rangle$, where:

- V is a finite set of vertices, each representing an individual in the social network.

- $\{R_i\}_{i \in \mathcal{I}}$ is a family of binary relations. The binary relation $R_i \subseteq V \times V$ specifies the pairs of individuals participating in relationship type i.

We write $V(G)$ and $R_i(G)$ respectively for the V and R_i components of the social network G.

Standard graph-theoretic concepts apply to social networks in an expected manner. We outline a few to fix thoughts. We write $G \subseteq G'$ whenever $V(G) \subseteq V(G')$ and $R_i(G) \subseteq R_i(G')$ for every $i \in \mathcal{I}$. G is said to be a **subgraph** of G'. Suppose $U \subseteq V(G)$. We write $G[U]$ to denote the social network $\langle U, \{R'_i\}_{i \in \mathcal{I}} \rangle$, where $R'_i = R_i(G) \cap (U \times U)$. $G[U]$ is said to be the **subgraph of G induced by** U. Two social networks G, G' are **isomorphic** iff there is a bijective function $\pi : V(G) \to V(G')$ such that $(u, v) \in R_i(G)$ whenever $(\pi(u), \pi(v)) \in R_i(G')$. In this case, we write $G \cong G'$, and call π an **isomorphism** between G and G'.

Given a social network G, we define the **acquaintance graph** $\mathsf{acq}(G)$ to be the simple graph $\langle V(G), E \rangle$, where $E = \{\{u, v\} \in [V(G)]^2 \mid \exists i \in \mathcal{I} . (u, v) \in R_i(G)\}$. That is, an acquaintance graph shares the same vertex set as the social network, and there is an undirected edge between two *distinct* vertices in the acquaintance graph iff there is a typed, directed edge between the same pair of vertices in the social network. Note that, although loops may occur in the social network, the acquaintance graph is a simple graph, and thus it contains no loops. The purpose for defining the acquaintance graph is to reuse connectivity-related concepts from standard graph theory. Specifically, notions such as distance, connected-ness, and components can be applied to a social network. For example, two vertices in a social network G are said to be **connected** iff there is an undirected path[1] between them in $\mathsf{acq}(G)$; the **distance** between two connected vertices in G is the length of the shortest path between them in $\mathsf{acq}(G)$; an **(extended) neighbourhood** of a vertex u in G is the set $N^*_G(u)$ of vertices connected to u in $\mathsf{acq}(G)$; the **component** of G to which u belongs is the social network $C_G(u)$, which is defined to be $G[N^*_G(u)]$. Lastly, we write $C_G(u; v)$ to denote the social network $G[N^*_G(u) \cup \{v\}]$, which is called an **augmented component**. The idea is to form the component of G to which u belongs, but with the augmentation of vertex v. If u and v are connected, then $C_G(u) = C_G(u; v)$. Otherwise, $C_G(u; v)$ contains $C_G(u)$ plus an additional, isolated vertex v.

Suppose $\mathcal{U}$ is a countable set of user identifiers. We denote by $\mathcal{G}(\mathcal{U}, \mathcal{I})$ the set of all *finite* social networks defined for user set $\mathcal{U}$ and relation identifier set $\mathcal{I}$. That is, $\mathcal{G}(\mathcal{U}, \mathcal{I}) = \{\langle V, \{R_i\}_{i \in \mathcal{I}} \rangle \mid V \in [\mathcal{U}]^{<\omega}, R_i \subseteq V \times V\}$. $\mathcal{G}(\mathcal{U}, \mathcal{I})$ contains all the social networks with a vertex set that is a finite subset of $\mathcal{U}$. Since $\mathcal{I}$ is finite, such a social network has only finitely many edges. Note that, although every member of $\mathcal{G}(\mathcal{U}, \mathcal{I})$ is finite in size, the size of such a member is not bounded.

---

[1] We consider a vertex to be connected to itself by a length-zero path. Consequently, u is always a member of $N^*_G(u)$.

2.3 ReBAC Policies

In [15] a formal model of ReBAC is introduced. The state of a ReBAC system is a collection of social networks, as defined above. State transition involves the mutation of the social networks (e.g., addition and deletion of relationship edges). An access attempt involves an **accessor** requesting access to a **resource** owned by an **owner**[2]. When an access is attempted at a given state, the policy that controls the accessibility of the requested resource will be evaluated against a certain social network induced by the current state. The policy either allows or denies the request. In the following, we formally specify what a ReBAC policy is.

A ReBAC policy defines a desired binary relation between resource owners and resource accessors in the context of a given social network. Suppose we are given a fixed set $\mathcal{U}$ of users and a fixed set $\mathcal{I}$ of relation identifiers. A **ReBAC policy** is a family of binary relations over $\mathcal{U}$, indexed by social networks from $\mathcal{G}(\mathcal{U}, \mathcal{I})$. More specifically, a policy is a function $P : \mathcal{G}(\mathcal{U}, \mathcal{I}) \to 2^{\mathcal{U} \times \mathcal{U}}$, such that $P(G) \subseteq V(G) \times V(G)$ for every social network $G \in \mathcal{G}(\mathcal{U}, \mathcal{I})$. Intuitively, a policy P specifies, for each social network G, a binary relation $P(G)$ that relates each resource owner to those accessors that the policy grants access. That is, $(u, v) \in P(G)$ iff owner u grants access to accessor v in the context of social network G. Note that $P(G)$ contains only finitely many pairs because G has only finitely many vertices. Using the notation defined in Section 2.1, we write $P(G)(u, v)$ whenever $(u, v) \in P(G)$.

In a typical ReBAC system, only a certain vocabulary of ReBAC policies is supported. For example, in Facebook, the policy vocabulary includes ReBAC policies such as me, friend, friend-of-friend, everyone, etc. A resource owner will adopt a supported policy from the policy vocabulary to protect a resource. The following are examples of ReBAC policies. They were previously proposed in [16] in the study of Facebook-style Social Network Systems (FSNSs). They have been adapted here as examples of ReBAC policies.

EXAMPLE 1 (DISTANCE). *Suppose the set of relational identifiers is* $\mathcal{I} = \{\mathsf{friend}\}$. *Suppose further that the relation identified by* friend *is symmetric (but not necessarily irreflexive). We call such social networks* **pseudo-Facebook social networks** *(the* friend *relation of a genuine Facebook-style social network is irreflexive). Define the policy* dist_k *such that* $\mathsf{dist}_k(G)(u, v)$ *iff* u *and* v *is at a distance* k *or less from one another. This policy is a generalization of the friend-of-friend policy in Facebook. Specifically, the distance between two vertices is taken as a measure of the strength of trust between two individuals.*

EXAMPLE 2 (COMMON FRIENDS). *Consider again pseudo-Facebook social networks. Define the policy* cf_k *such that* $\mathsf{cf}_k(G)(u, v)$ *iff (a)* $u = v$, *or (b)* v *is a neighbour of* u, *or (c) there are* k *(or more) common neighbours between* u *and* v. *Intuitively, access is granted to a stranger if* k friends *of the owner witness to the trustworthiness of this stranger. This policy is another generalization of the friend-of-friend policy in Facebook. Specifically, the number of common neighbours is taken as a measure of the strength of trust between two strangers. Having the trust level exceeding the threshold* k *results in access granting.*

EXAMPLE 3 (CLIQUE). *Consider yet again pseudo-Facebook social networks. Define the policy* clique_k *such that* $\mathsf{clique}_k(G)(u, v)$ *iff (a)* $u = v$, *or (b)* u *and* v *belong to a* clique[3] *of size* k *(or more) in* $\mathsf{acq}(G)$. *Intuitively, access is granted if the accessor and the owner belong to a close-knit community of size* k *(or more). This policy is a generalization of the friend policy in Facebook. Specifically, the size of the largest common clique to which two neighbouring individuals belong is taken as a measure of the strength of trust between them. Having a trust level exceeding the threshold* k *results in access granting. Other notions of close-knit communities [10], such as clans, plexes and cores, can also be modelled in a similar way.*

2.4 Relational Policies

Anwar *et al.* identify a family of policies, called relational policies, the use of which distinguishes ReBAC from traditional access control paradigms [1]. Intuitively, a relational policy is special in two ways. First, a relational policy does not base authorization decisions on the identities of the owner or the accessor. Instead, only the topological structure the social network is analyzed for authorization. Second, a relational policy specifies how the owner and the accessor shall be related in the social network (e.g., the owner and the accessor are at a distance no more than k), rather than individual properties of the owner or the accessor (e.g., the accessor has a vertex degree no less than k). These two characteristics are captured in the following definitions, which we generalized from those in [1].

DEFINITION 4. *A policy P is* **topology-based** *iff, for every pair of isomorphic social networks* $G, G' \in \mathcal{G}(\mathcal{U}, \mathcal{I})$ *with isomorphism* $\pi : V(G) \to V(G')$, *we have* $(u, v) \in P(G)$ *whenever* $(\pi(u), \pi(v)) \in P(G')$.

In short, a topology-based policy depends only on the topological information of the social network, but not on the identities of the users.

The next definition characterizes policies that specify how the owner and the accessor are related to one another.

DEFINITION 5. *A policy P is* **local** *iff, given* $G \subseteq G'$ *and* $u, v \in V(G)$ *for which* $(u, v) \in P(G) \backslash P(G') \cup P(G') \backslash P(G)$, *there exists* $i \in \mathcal{I}$ *such that* $R_i(G') \backslash R_i(G)$ *contains a pair* (u', v') *for which each of* u' *and* v' *is connected to each of* u *and* v *in* G'.

The intuition of the definition is the following. Suppose P is a local policy. Suppose further that the authorization decision of P is altered for a pair of individuals (u, v) after one adds vertices and edges into the social network G to obtain social network G'. Then G' must have received a new edge (u', v') of some relationship type i, such that each of u', v' is connected to each of u, v. In short, adding vertices or edges outside of the shared component of the owner and the accessor never alters the authorization decision of a local policy. Put more succinctly, the ends of every edge that has an influence on authorization decisions must connect both the owner and the accessor. That is, such an edge must contribute to the "connectedness" between the owner and the accessor. In this way, we capture the intuitive requirement that the policy must specify how the owner and the accessor

---

[2]In [15], an access attempt also involves an access context. We ignore the latter as it is irrelevant to this work.

[3]A clique is a complete subgraph. Here we mean that u and v are part of a complete subgraph of the social network.

are related to one another, rather than specifying individual graph properties of the owner or the accessor.

DEFINITION 6. *A policy is **relational** iff it is both topology based and local.*

Note that the three example policies (i.e., distance, common friends and cliques) are all relational policies.

2.5 The ReBAC Policy Language B

Fong proposed a policy language for expressing ReBAC policies [15]. We call his language B to differentiate it from the extended language E to be presented in the sequel. The language B is a basic modal logic [6]. Each formula in B expresses a ReBAC policy: i.e., a desirable relationship between two individuals in a social network. The syntax of a B formula, which is based on a set $\mathcal{I}$ of relation identifiers, is given below[4]:

$$\phi, \psi ::= \top \mid a \mid \neg\phi \mid \phi \wedge \psi \mid \langle i \rangle \phi \mid \langle -i \rangle \phi$$

where $i \in \mathcal{I}$ is a relation identifier.

A policy (i.e., a formula) ϕ is interpreted in the context of a social network $G \in \mathcal{G}(V, \mathcal{I})$ and individuals $u, v \in V(G)$. Specifically, the semantics of B is given in a satisfiability relation $G, u, v \models_B \phi$, which asserts that, in social network G, owner u and accessor v possess the relationship prescribed by policy ϕ.

- $G, u, v \models_B \top$.

- $G, u, v \models_B a$ iff $u = v$.

- $G, u, v \models_B \neg\phi$ iff it is not the case that $G, u, v \models_B \phi$.

- $G, u, v \models_B \phi \wedge \psi$ iff both $G, u, v \models_B \phi$ and $G, u, v \models_B \psi$.

- $G, u, v \models_B \langle i \rangle \phi$ iff there exists $u' \in V(G)$ such that $(u, u') \in R_i(G)$ and $G, u', v \models_B \phi$.

- $G, u, v \models_B \langle -i \rangle \phi$ iff there exists $u' \in V(G)$ such that $(u', u) \in R_i(G)$ and $G, u', v \models_B \phi$.

Intuitively, $\top$ is a relationship satisfiable by any pair of individuals; a asserts that the accessor is the owner; $\langle i \rangle \phi$ asserts that the owner has an i-neighbour that is related to the accessor in the manner specified by ϕ; $\langle -i \rangle \phi$ asserts that the owner is the i-neighbour of some individual that is related to the accessor in the manner specified by ϕ. The difference between $\langle i \rangle$ and $\langle -i \rangle$ is that the former traverses *along* the direction of an edge, while the latter traverses *against* the direction of an edge. Standard derived forms are defined:

$$\bot = \neg\top \qquad\qquad [i]\phi = \neg\langle i \rangle \neg\phi$$
$$\phi \vee \psi = \neg(\neg\phi \wedge \neg\psi) \qquad [-i]\phi = \neg\langle -i \rangle \neg\phi$$

Intuitively, $[i]\phi$ asserts that every i-neighbour of the owner is related to the accessor in the manner specified by ϕ.

A ReBAC policy P is **definable in** B iff there is a B formula ϕ such that $P(G)(u, v)$ whenever $G, u, v \models_B \phi$. It has been demonstrated that many complex relational policies are definable in B. Specifically, Fong [15] was able to use B

---

[4]The modal operator $\langle -i \rangle$ is not found in [15]. Instead, it is assumed in [15] that social networks are "inverse-closed." The two achieve the same effect: the authorization procedure can freely traverse either along or against the direction of an edge.

to capture all the trust delegation policies identified in the Electronic Health Records case study developed by Becker and Sewell [4]. We illustrate the usage of B with a few examples. Consider social networks with relation identifiers $\mathcal{I} = \{\text{parent}, \text{child}, \text{spouse}, \text{sibling}\}$, which signify respectively the child-parent relation, its inverse, the symmetric spouse-spouse relation, and the reflexive symmetric sibling-sibling relation. The following policies are definable in B:

"Grant access to grand parents." The B formula that expresses this policy is "$\langle \text{parent} \rangle \langle \text{parent} \rangle$ a".

"Grant access to a sibling who is not married." The B formula that expresses this policy is:

$$\langle \text{sibling} \rangle (a \wedge [\text{spouse}] \bot)$$

"Grant access if accessor is the only child of the owner." A formula to express the policy is:

$$\langle \text{child} \rangle a \wedge [\text{child}] a$$

2.6 Limitations of B

B is not without limitations. It turns out that some relational policies are not definable in B.

EXAMPLE 7. *Assume the setting of Example 2. The policy cf_k, for every $k > 2$, is not definable in B. The reason is that the models for these policies are bisimilar to cf_1, and thus indistinguishable by a formula of B [6]. For instance, consider cf_2. A naive attempt to express cf_2 in B yields the following formula:*

$$a \vee \langle \text{friend} \rangle a \vee (\langle \text{friend} \rangle \langle \text{friend} \rangle a \wedge \langle \text{friend} \rangle \langle \text{friend} \rangle a)$$

The intention is that the disjuncts "a" and "$\langle \text{friend} \rangle$ a" respectively express requirements (a) and (b) in Example 2, while the third disjunct expresses requirement (c). Supposedly, each of the two conjuncts "$\langle \text{friend} \rangle \langle \text{friend} \rangle$ a" identifies a common friend of the owner and the accessor. Unfortunately, this formula does not express cf_2. Consider the scenario in which the owner and the accessor share exactly one common neighbour. Since conjunction is idempotent, the formula above is satisfied even though cf_2 should fail.

In the formula above, the original intention is that the two conjuncts specify two **disjoint sets of intermediaries** (i.e., two distinct common friends). Unfortunately, boolean conjunction fails to capture this requirement. This illustrates the need for an ReBAC policy language to provide a non-idempotent version of conjunction for specifying disjoint sets of intermediaries.

EXAMPLE 8. *The policy $clique_k$ is not definable in B, for every $k > 2$. For instance, consider $clique_3$. A naive attempt to express the policy is the following formula:*

$$a \vee (\neg a \wedge \langle \text{friend} \rangle a \wedge \langle \text{friend} \rangle (\neg a \wedge \langle \text{friend} \rangle a))$$

The intention is that the disjunct "a" expresses requirement (a) in Example 3, while the second disjunct expresses requirement (b). In the second disjunct, we assert that the owner is not the accessor ($\neg a$), the accessor is a friend of the owner ($\langle \text{friend} \rangle$ a), and the accessor is a friend of a friend of the owner ($\langle \text{friend} \rangle (\neg a \wedge \langle \text{friend} \rangle a)$). Yet, the following two social networks are not distinguishable by B formulas.

Specifically, the sub-formula "$\langle$friend$\rangle\,(\neg\mathsf{a} \wedge \langle$friend$\rangle\,\mathsf{a})$" fails to ensure that the owner (u) and the intermediary ($\bullet$) are two distinct vertices.

The above example illustrates an important shortcoming of the policy language B, namely, its lacking a **vertex identification** mechanism: i.e., the ability to name vertices and subsequently test if they are revisited.

As pointed out in [16], relational policies such as cf_k and clique_k are rich in social significance, and thus the lacking of disjoint intermediaries and vertex identification in B needs to be remedied.

3. THE REBAC POLICY LANGUAGE E

In the previous section, we identified two limitations of the policy language B, namely, disjoint intermediaries and vertex identification. We now look at how the two features can be incorporated into a ReBAC policy language. The result is an extended ReBAC policy language we call E.

Syntax.

As before, E is defined in the context of a countable set $\mathcal{U}$ of vertices and a countable set $\mathcal{I}$ of relation identifiers. We assume that there is a countably infinite set $\mathcal{P}$ of propositional symbols. We write p and q for typical members of $\mathcal{P}$. We also assume that $\mathcal{P}$ contains a distinguished member a.

The syntax of E is given below:

$$\phi, \psi ::= \top \mid p \mid \neg\phi \mid \phi \wedge \psi \mid \langle i \rangle\,\phi \mid \langle -i \rangle\,\phi \mid @p.\phi \mid \phi \otimes \psi$$

where $p \in \mathcal{P}$ is a propositional symbol, and $i \in \mathcal{I}$ is a relation identifier. Intuitively, $@p.\phi$ introduces a propositional symbol for identifying the owner. Specifically, the proposition symbol p can be used inside ϕ to test if a vertex is the owner. The formula $\phi \otimes \psi$ holds whenever the relationships prescribed by ϕ and ψ both hold between the accessor and the owner, but the set of intermediary vertices used for establishing these two relationships are disjoint. A more precise definition of the semantics of these new constructs is given below.

The notion of **free** and **bound** occurrences of propositional symbols can be defined in a standard way. For example, in the formula $(p \wedge @q.\langle i \rangle\,q)$, the propositional symbol p occurs free but q occurs bound. A formula is **a-closed** if no propositional symbol other than a occurs free in the formula. Otherwise the formula is **a-open**.

Semantics.

Given a social network G, a function $\Sigma : \mathcal{P} \rightharpoonup V(G)$ is called a **binding environment**[5]. A binding environment interprets a propositional symbol as a vertex.

The semantics of E is defined via the satisfaction relation $G, u, v \models_\mathsf{E} \phi$, which is specified in terms of an auxiliary relation $G, \Sigma, u \Vdash \phi$, where Σ is a binding environment.

- $G, \Sigma, u \Vdash \top$.

---

[5] Note that our binding environment plays the role of a valuation or labelling function in the standard literature of modal logic [6], in which a valuation is a function with signature $\mathcal{P} \to 2^{V(G)}$, and a labelling function is a function with signature $V(G) \to 2^{\mathcal{P}}$. In our logic, a propositional symbol is interpreted as a single vertex. We therefore adapt the definition to ease presentation.

- $G, \Sigma, u \Vdash p$ iff $\Sigma(p) = u$.

- $G, \Sigma, u \Vdash \neg\phi$ iff it is not the case that $G, \Sigma, u \Vdash \phi$.

- $G, \Sigma, u \Vdash \phi \wedge \psi$ iff both $G, \Sigma, u \Vdash \phi$ and $G, \Sigma, u \Vdash \psi$.

- $G, \Sigma, u \Vdash \langle i \rangle\,\phi$ iff there exists $u' \in V$ such that $(u, u') \in R_i$ and $G, \Sigma, u' \Vdash \phi$.

- $G, \Sigma, u \Vdash \langle i \rangle\,\phi$ iff there exists $u' \in V$ such that $(u', u) \in R_i$ and $G, \Sigma, u' \Vdash \phi$.

- $G, \Sigma, u \Vdash @p.\phi$ iff $p \neq \mathsf{a}$ and $G, \Sigma[p \mapsto u], u \Vdash \phi$.

- $G, \Sigma, u \Vdash \phi \otimes \psi$ iff the following holds:

  Let v be $\Sigma(\mathsf{a})$. There exists two subsets V_1 and V_2 of $V(G)$, such that $V(G) = V_1 \cup V_2$, $V_1 \cap V_2 = \{u, v\}$, and both $G[V_1], \Sigma, u \Vdash \phi$ and $G[V_2], \Sigma, u \Vdash \phi$ hold.

Lastly, $G, u, v \models_\mathsf{E} \phi$ iff $G, \emptyset[\mathsf{a} \mapsto v], u \Vdash \phi$.

Derived Forms.

We define the derived forms $\bot$, $\phi \vee \psi$, $[i]\,\phi$ and $[-i]\,\phi$ as before. In addition, we introduce the following derived form:

$$\phi \oplus \psi = \neg(\neg\phi \otimes \neg\psi)$$

The connective $\oplus$ is the dual of $\otimes$. Specifically, $G, \Sigma, u \Vdash \phi \oplus \psi$ iff the following holds:

  Let v be $\Sigma(\mathsf{a})$. For every two subsets V_1 and V_2 of $V(G)$ such that $V(G) = V_1 \cup V_2$, $V_1 \cap V_2 = \{u, v\}$, either $G[V_1], \Sigma, u \Vdash \phi$ or $G[V_2], \Sigma, u \Vdash \phi$ holds.

In other words, $G, \Sigma, u \Vdash \phi \oplus \psi$ whenever, for every subset V of $V(G)$ such that $\{u, \Sigma(\mathsf{a})\} \subseteq V$, either $G[V], \Sigma, u \Vdash \phi$ or $G[V], \Sigma, u \Vdash \phi$ holds.

Definability.

A policy P is **definable in** E iff there is an a-closed formula ϕ in E such that $P(G)(u, v)$ whenever $G, u, v \models_\mathsf{E} \phi$.

Examples.

The following examples illustrate how the new features of E address the needs for disjoint intermediaries and vertex identification.

EXAMPLE 9. *The policy cf_2 is definable in E, via the following formula:*

$\mathsf{a} \vee \langle$friend$\rangle\,\mathsf{a} \vee ((\langle$friend$\rangle\,\langle$friend$\rangle\,\mathsf{a}) \otimes (\langle$friend$\rangle\,\langle$friend$\rangle\,\mathsf{a}))$

EXAMPLE 10. *The policy clique_3 is definable in E, via the following formula:*

$\mathsf{a} \vee (\neg\mathsf{a} \wedge \langle$friend$\rangle\,\mathsf{a} \wedge @p.\langle$friend$\rangle\,(\neg p \wedge \neg\mathsf{a} \wedge \langle$friend$\rangle\,\mathsf{a}))$

4. EXPRESSIVENESS OF E

It has been pointed out in Section 2.4 that ReBAC is distinguished by its extensive use of access control policies are *relational*: i.e., authorization decisions consume only topological information of the social network (topology-based), and express how the owner and the accessor are related in the social network (local). In this section, we will examine the expressiveness of E by identifying what family of relational policies are definable in E. We will first establish, in

Section 4.1, an "upper bound" of the policies definable in E: i.e., identifying a natural family of ReBAC policies to which every E-definable policy belongs. We will then establish, in Section 4.2, a "lower bound" of the expressiveness of E. That is, we will identify a natural subclass of relational policies that are definable in E. In other words, we establish the representational completeness of E with respect to that subclass of relational policies. We conclude the section with a structural analysis of the hierarchy of policy families identified along the way (Section 4.3).

4.1 Owner-checkable policies

We begin our discussion with the family of topology-based policies that can be enforced by an agent that traverses a neighbourhood of the owner.

DEFINITION 11. *A topology-based policy P is **owner-checkable (OC)** iff $P(G)(u,v) \Leftrightarrow P(C_G(u;v))(u,v)$. A topology-based policy P is **accessor-checkable (AC)** iff $P(G)(u,v) \Leftrightarrow P(C_G(v;u))(u,v)$.*

Intuitively, the authorization decision of an OC policy can be determined by examining *only* the component of social network in which the owner is located, plus the additional knowledge of whether the accessor is in that component ($C_G(u;v)$). That is, even if there may be vertices and edges outside of the owner's component, they never influence the authorization decision. The intuition of an AC policy is analogous.

An OC policy is special in two ways. Firstly, an OC policy presents a tractability advantage. In particular, an OC policy can be evaluated by a "crawler" that traverses only the owner's component (i.e., neighbourhood), starting at the owner vertex. Venturing outside of the owner's component is never necessary. An AC policy shares the same tractability advantage if the traversal begins at the accessor's vertex. Secondly, an OC policy provides a security advantage. Although an AC policy provides the same tractability advantage as an OC policy, only an OC policy provides this form of security advantage. The checking of an AC policy can be conducted by a "crawler" that traverses the accessor's component, starting at the accessor. Yet, an AC policy may lead to a denial-of-service attack by the accessor. Specifically, the accessor may carefully craft its neighbourhood in such a way that would lead the "crawler" (i.e., the authorization procedure) to explore a graph neighbourhood that is expensive to traverse (with respect to the policy in question). Even if access is not granted, an accessor may repeatedly request access, leading the authorization procedure to waste precious computational resources. An OC policy prevents this form of manipulation, in the sense that the accessor cannot dictate the computational cost of authorization.

Relational policies are related to OC and AC policies.

PROPOSITION 12. *A relational policy is both OC and AC.*

(A proof of this proposition can be found in Appendix A.)

The following theorem represents an "upper bound" to the expressiveness of E.

THEOREM 13. *A policy definable in E is OC.*

(A proof of this theorem can be found in Appendix A.)

A corollary of Theorem 13 is that, if a policy can be expressed as an E formula, then there is no need for an additional syntactic analysis to ensure that the policy is OC.

This contrasts with the use of alternative policy languages (e.g., Datalog), whereby an additional analysis is needed to ensure the policy is indeed OC.

4.2 Finitary Relational Policies

We now turn to the "lower bound" of E's expressiveness. The authorization decisions of a ReBAC policy can be determined in two ways. One is to grant access when certain relationships are present in the social network, the other is to grant access when certain relationships are absent. The evaluation of a policy of the second kind requires complete knowledge of the entire social network, while the evaluation of a policy of the first kind requires only a fragment of the social network to provide an existential proof of compliance. The following definition formalizes the idea.

DEFINITION 14. *A policy P is **monotonic** iff $G \subseteq G'$ implies $P(G) \subseteq P(G')$.*

That is, adding relationships into a social network never reduces accessibility, and removing relationships never expands accessibility. Such a policy makes authorization decisions by verifying the presence of relationships rather than the absence of relationships. The notion of monotonicity was originally proposed in [16] for Facebook-style Social Network Systems. Here we generalize the notion for ReBAC policies.

Adopting policies that are exclusively monotonic enables a decentralized implementation of ReBAC in the style of trust management systems [7, 37, 25, 24]. Specifically, an accessor who seeks authorization may present to the reference monitor a fragment of the social network (e.g., a collection of certificates of relationships) as a proof of compliance. We are therefore interested in policies that are both monotonic and topology based.

DEFINITION 15. *A policy P is **positive** iff it is both topology based and monotonic.*

We review here a characterization of positive policies. Our characterization is phrased in terms of birooted graphs.

DEFINITION 16. *A **birooted graph** $G_{(u,v)}$ is a triple $\langle G, u, v \rangle$ such that G is a social network and $u, v \in V(G)$. The vertices u and v are the **roots** of $G_{(u,v)}$, and they need not be distinct. Specifically u is the **owner root**, and v is the **accessor root**. We write $\mathcal{B}(S, \mathcal{I}) = \{G_{(u,v)} \mid G \in \mathcal{G}(S, \mathcal{I}), u, v \in V(G)\}$ to denote the set of all birooted graphs based on vertex set S. $G'_{(u,v)}$ is a **(birooted) subgraph** of $G_{(u,v)}$, written as $G'_{(u,v)} \subseteq G_{(u,v)}$, iff $G' \subseteq G$. (Note the matching roots.) We say that $G_{(u,v)}$ and $G'_{(u',v')}$ are **isomorphic** iff there exists an isomorphism $\pi : V(G) \to V(G')$ between social networks G and G', such that $\pi(u) = u'$ and $\pi(v) = v'$. In this case we write $G_{(u,v)} \cong G'_{(u',v')}$. We also write $G'_{(u',v')} \lesssim G_{(u,v)}$ whenever there is a birooted graph $G''_{(u,v)}$ such that $G'_{(u',v')} \cong G''_{(u,v)}$ and $G''_{(u,v)} \subseteq G_{(u,v)}$.*

We are now ready to state the characterization theorem for positive policies.

DEFINITION 17. *The policy **positively induced** by a set $\mathcal{B}$ of birooted graphs is the policy $P_{\mathcal{B}}^+$ for which*

$$P_{\mathcal{B}}^+(G)(u,v) \text{ iff } \exists G'_{(u',v')} \in \mathcal{B} . G'_{(u',v')} \lesssim G_{(u,v)}$$

Intuitively, the birooted graph set $\mathcal{B}$ specifies topological "patterns" that must exist between an owner and an accessor in the social network in order for access to be granted by the policy. It was proven in [1] that every positive policy can be characterized by a set of birooted graph patterns. The result was originally established for Facebook-style Social Network Systems. Here, we adapt the result to the more general context of ReBAC.

THEOREM 18. *Every positive policy is positively induced by a set of birooted graphs. The minimal set of birooted graphs to positively induce a given policy P is defined to be the set $\mathcal{B}$ for which there exists no proper subset of $\mathcal{B}$ that also positively induces P. This minimal set does not contain a pair of distinct birooted graphs $G_{(u,v)}$ and $G'_{(u',v')}$ such that $G_{(u,v)} \lesssim G'_{(u',v')}$. Such a minimal set always exists, and is unique up to birooted graph isomorphism.*

Intuitively, every positive policy can be uniquely characterized by a smallest set of birooted graph patterns.

We are particularly interested in a special kind of positive policies.

DEFINITION 19. *A positive policy P is **finitary** iff the minimal set of birooted graphs to positively induce P is a finite set.*

Finitary policies can be characterized by a finite number of birooted graphs. While positive policies can be evaluated by checking for the presence of relationships, the finitary requirement ensures that only a bounded number of such relationships need to be enumerated. This requirement is computationally significant in two ways. Firstly, this translates to a bound in the search effort for a centralized implementation of the authorization procedure, for the search tree now has bounded depth. Secondly, in a distributed implementation of ReBAC, this constraint implies that a proof of compliance consists of a bounded number of certificates.

We are now ready to state the main theorem of this work.

THEOREM 20. *Every finitary OC policy is definable in* E.

The theorem provides a "lower bound" of what can be expressed in E. The proof of this theorem can be found in Appendix A.

Recall that our core interest is in expressing relational policies, rather than OC policies. The following corollary, which follows directly from proposition 12, identifies a subclass of relational policies definable in E.

COROLLARY 21. *Every finitary relational policy is definable in* E.

Note that all the three example policies (i.e., distance, common friends, and clique) are finitary relational policies.

We can further strengthen the above result. Suppose P_1 and P_2 are definable in E via the formulas ϕ_1 and ϕ_2. Consider the policy P defined such that $P(G) = P_1(G) \cap P_2(G)$. That is, P grants access whenever both P_1 and P_2 grant access. It is easy to see that P is also definable in E, via the formula $\phi_1 \wedge \phi_2$. The same can be said about other boolean combinations (disjunction and negation).

COROLLARY 22. *The family of policies definable in* E *is closed under boolean combinations. Consequently, boolean combinations of finitary relational policies are definable in* E*. Note that such boolean combinations of finitary relational policies are still relational policies, although they are not necessarily finitary.*

This corollary gives us an easy extension of the definability result in Corollary 21.

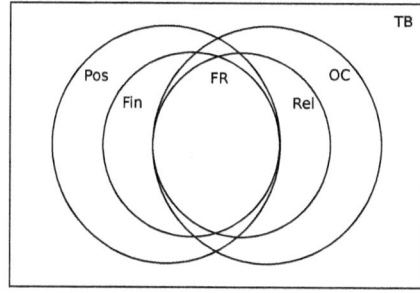

Figure 1: **The hierarchy of policy families identified in this work: TB:** topology-based policies; **OC:** owner-checkable policies; **Rel:** relational policies; **Pos:** positive policies; **Fin:** finitary policies; **FR:** finitary relational policies.

4.3 Discussion

Figure 1 depicts the hierarchy of policy families identified in this section. Note that *every inclusion in Figure 1 is proper*. To demonstrate this, the following list states a member policy for each set difference.

TB\(Pos ∪ OC): The social network contains no more than k vertices (including the owner and the accessor).

Pos\Fin: The owner and the accessor are connected.

Fin\FR: The accessor has at least k neighbours.

OC\Rel: The owner has no more than k neighbours.

Rel\FR: The owner and the accessor are not connected.

5. RELATED WORK

The term Relationship-Based Access Control (ReBAC) was first coined by Gates [17] when she articulated the need for an access control paradigm that is based on interpersonal relationships. A number of ReBAC models and/or systems have been proposed for social computing applications [23, 9, 8, 34, 35, 16]. The targets of study include the distributed evaluation of trust [9], the employment of semantic web technology to encode social networks and ReBAC policies [8], the automatic generation of ReBAC policies [34], multiple ownership of resources [35], the generalization of Facebook-style Social Network Systems [16], and the characterization of relational policies [1]. Fong advocates the employment of ReBAC in application domains outside of social computing [15], and demonstrates the utility and feasibility of doing so by the specification of a general-purpose ReBAC model and a ReBAC policy language. He points out that the various constructs in his ReBAC model arise naturally out of the generalization of foundational concepts such as roles, role hierarchy, sessions and constraints in Role-Based Access Control (RBAC) [31, 12]. His work also raises the question of representational completeness, which is the focus of this work. The core contribution of this work is (a) demonstrating that Fong's policy language fails to encode a number of relational policies previously studied in [16], (b) incorporating the support of disjoint intermediaries and vertex identification into a ReBAC policy language that is based on modal logic, and (c) providing both an upper bound and a lower bound to the family of policies expressible in the extended policy language.

The question of representational completeness is related to enforceability research [33, 26, 13, 21, 36, 27, 28]. The goal of enforceability research is to establish the structural relationships between naturally occurring policy families (e.g., safety policies), and the family of policies enforceable by a specific kind of enforcement mechanisms (e.g., program monitors that have access only to the execution history). Rather than relating policy families to *enforcement mechanisms*, this work establishes upper bound and lower bound for the family of policies definable in a *policy language*.

Policies such as cf_k (for $k > 2$) are not definable in B. The reason is that the models for these policies are bisimilar to cf_1, and thus indistinguishable by a formula of B [6]. Therefore, in E a new connective $\otimes$ is introduced to require disjoint partitioning of the social network during a satisfiability check (except for the accessor and the owner). This approach is similar to *manifold roles* by Li *et al.* in RT^T [25]. The credential using $\otimes$ in RT^T is a union of the sets where the intersection of such sets is empty. The concept of *threshold structure* by Li *et al.* in Delegation logic [24] is also similar to $\otimes$. In a threshold structure, k out of N principals are required, where each of the k is unique.

6. FUTURE WORK

Some extensions to the ReBAC model have been suggested in [15]. We discuss in the following future directions that are specific to ReBAC policy languages.

A natural future work is to improve the precision of the characterization of policies definable in E. Specifically, there is a "gap" between the "upper bound" and "lower bound" presented in Section 4. As demonstrated in Section 4.3, the inclusion of FR in OC is proper. It is desirable if one can close the gap, and provide a precise identification of the family of policies definable in E.

One of the motivations for designing a policy language for ReBAC policies is to facilitate policy analysis. It has been shown [14] that proper static analysis can be applied to the configuration of Facebook-style Social Network Systems to ensure the absence of Sybil attacks. It is interesting to explore if this or other policy analyses can be translated into an equivalent syntactic analysis for policies written in a ReBAC policy language.

Both this work and [15] assume the ReBAC system tracks relationships explicitly, and the relations are in turn identified by a fixed vocabulary of relation identifiers. This assumption has made the design of rich policy languages possible. In some applications, however, the presence of a relationship is induced by complex external factors. For example, consider a network consisting of users and devices such as mobile phones, in which the presence of a relationship is the result of the states of the mobile phones (e.g., battery level) and their relative proximity. Rational modelling of such external dependence would allow us to reuse ReBAC and our policy languages even in these application domains.

Another future direction is to combine the strengths of both RBAC and ReBAC, thereby allowing the access control system to reason about both the relationships between individuals, and the hierarchical organization of user roles. One possibility is to employ Description Logic (DL) technology [2] as the basis of both the policy language and the authorization engine. Highly related to modal logics [32], DL is a mature technology, with language families of various levels of tractability, and the support of efficient reasoners (e.g., RACER [20] and FaCT [22]). A previous work on applying DL to access control is that of RelBAC [18, 38], in which DL is employed to construct an access control model akin to Domain-Type Enforcement (DTE) [3]. Further work is needed to integrate ReBAC and RBAC in one model.

7. CONCLUSION

This work examined the relative expressiveness of two ReBAC policy languages. We began by demonstrating that there are known relational policies, such as cf_k and $clique_k$, that cannot be expressed in the ReBAC policy language B. We pointed out that the limitations were due to the lack of support for disjoint intermediaries and vertex identification. The two features were then incorporated into B, resulting in an extended policy language E. We showed that ReBAC policies definable in E are owner-checkable policies, a superset of relational policies. We also showed that every finitary relational policy is definable in E, meaning that E is representationally complete with respect to that policy family. We have therefore identified a policy language that is representationally adequate for expressing useful ReBAC policies.

Acknowledgements

This work is supported in part by an NSERC Discovery Accelerator Supplements.

8. REFERENCES

[1] M. Anwar, Z. Zhao, and P. W. L. Fong. An access control model for Facebook-style social network systems. Tech. Rep. 2010-959-08, Dept. of Computer Science, University of Calgary, AB, Canada, July 2010.

[2] F. Baader, D. Calvanese, D. L. McGuinness, D. Nardi, and P. F. Patel-Schneider, editors. *The Description Logic Handbook*. Cambridge, 2007.

[3] L. Badger, D. F. Sterne, D. L. Sherman, K. M. Walker, and S. A Haghighat. Practical domain and type enforcement for UNIX. In *Proceedings of the 1995 IEEE Symposium on Security and Privacy (S&P'95)*, pages 66–77, Oakland, CA, USA, May 1995.

[4] M. Y. Becker and P. Sewell. Cassandra: Flexible trust management, applied to electronic health records. In *Proceedings of the 17th IEEE Computer Security Foundations Workshop (CSFW'04)*, Pacific Grove, CA, USA, June 2004.

[5] K. Beznosov. Requirements for access control: US healthcare domain. In *Proceedings of the 3rd ACM Workshop on Role-Based Access Control (RBAC'98)*, page 43, Fairfax, VA, USA, October 1998.

[6] P. Blackburn, M. de Rijke, and Y. Venema. *Modal Logic*. Cambridge, 2001.

[7] M. Blaze, J. Feigenbaum, and J. Lacy. Decentralized trust management. In *Proceedings of the 1996 IEEE Symposium on Security and Privacy (S&P'96)*, pages 164–173, Oakland, CA, USA, May 1996.

[8] B. Carminati, E. Ferrari, R. Heatherly, M. Kantarcioglu, and B. Thurainsingham. A semantic web based framework for social network access control. In *Proceedings of the 14th ACM Symposium on Access Control Models and Technologies (SACMAT'09)*, pages 177–186, Stresa, Italy, June 2009.

[9] B. Carminati, E. Ferrari, and A. Perego. Enforcing access control in Web-based social networks. *ACM Transactions on Information and System Security*, 13(1):1–38, October 2009.

[10] D. Chakrabarti and C. Faloutsos. Graph mining: Laws, generators, and algorithms. *ACM Computing Surveys*, 38, March 2006.

[11] T. H. Cormen, C. E. Leiserson, R. L. Rivest, and C. Stein. *Introduction to Algorithms*. MIT Press, 3rd edition, 2009.

[12] D. F. Ferraiolo, R. Sandhu, S. Gavrila, D. R. Kuhn, and R. Chandramouli. Proposed NIST standard for role-based access control. *ACM Transactions on Information and System Security*, 4(3):224–274, 2001.

[13] P. W. L. Fong. Access control by tracking shallow execution history. In *Proceedings of the 2004 IEEE Symposium on Security and Privacy (S&P'04)*, pages 43–55, Oakland, CA, USA, May 2004.

[14] P. W. L. Fong. Preventing Sybil attacks by privilege attenuation: A design principle for social network systems. In *Proceedings of the 2011 IEEE Symposium on Security and Privacy (S&P'11)*, Oakland, CA, USA, May 2011.

[15] P. W. L. Fong. Relationship-based access control: Protection model and policy language. In *Proceedings of the First ACM Conference on Data and Application Security and Privacy (CODASPY'11)*, pages 191–202, San Antonio, Taxas, USA, February 2011.

[16] P. W. L. Fong, M. Anwar, and Z. Zhao. A privacy preservation model for Facebook-style social network systems. In *Proceedings of the 14th European Symposium on Research In Computer Security (ESORICS'09)*, volume 5789 of *LNCS*, pages 303–320, Saint Malo, France, September 2009. Springer.

[17] Carrie E. Gates. Access Control Requirements for Web 2.0 Security and Privacy. In *IEEE Web 2.0 Privacy and Security Workship (W2SP'07)*, Oakland, CA, USA, 2007.

[18] F. Giunchiglia, R. Zhang, and B. Crispo. RelBAC: Relation based access control. In *Proceedings of the Fourth International Conference on Semantics, Knowledge and Grid (SKG'08)*, pages 3–11, Beijing, China, December 2008.

[19] L. Giuri and P. Iglio. Role templates for content-based access control. In *Proceedings of the 2nd ACM Workshop on Role-Based Access Control (RBAC'97)*, pages 153–159, Fairfax, VA, USA, November 1997.

[20] V. Haarslev and R. Möller. RACER system description. In *Proceedings of the 1st International Joint Conference on Automated Reasoning (IJCAR'01)*, pages 701–705, Siena, Italy, 2001.

[21] K. W. Hamlen, G. Morrisett, and F. B. Schneider. Computability classes for enforcement mechanisms. *ACM Transactions on Programming Langanguages And Systems*, 28(1):175–205, January 2006.

[22] I. R. Horrocks. Using an expressive description logic: FaCT or fiction? In *Proceedings of the 6th International Conference on Principles of Knowledge Representation and Reasoning (KR'98)*, pages 636–649, Trento, Italy, 1998.

[23] S. R. Kruk, S. Grzonkowski, A. Gzella, T. Woroniecki, and H.-C. Choi. D-FOAF: Distributed identity management with access rights delegation. In *Proceedings of the 1st Asian Semantic Web Conference (ASWC'06)*, volume 4185 of *LNCS*, pages 140–154, Beijing, China, September 2006. Springer.

[24] N. Li, B. N. Grosof, and J. Feigenbaum. Delegation logic: A logic-based approach to distributed authorization. *ACM Transactions on Information and System Security*, 6(1):128–171, February 2003.

[25] N. Li, J. C. Mitchell, and W. H. Winsborough. Design of a role-based trust-management framework. In *Proceedings of the 2002 IEEE Symposium on Security and Privacy (S&P'02)*, pages 114–130, Berkeley, California, USA, May 2002.

[26] J. Ligatti, L. Bauer, and D. Walker. Edit automata: Enforcement mechanisms for run-time security policies. *International Journal of Information Security*, 4(1–2):2–16, February 2005.

[27] J. Ligatti, L. Bauer, and D. Walker. Run-time enforcement of nonsafety policies. *ACM Transactions on Information and Systems Security*, 12(3), 2009.

[28] J. Ligatti and S. Reddy. A theory of runtime enforcement, with results. In *Proceedings of the 15th European Symposium on Research in Computer Security (ESORICS'10)*, volume 6345 of *LNCS*, Athens, Greece, September 2010. Springer.

[29] E. Lupu and M. Sloman. Reconciling role based management and role based access control. In *Proceedings of the 2nd ACM Workshop on Role-Based Access Control (RBAC'97)*, pages 135–141, Fairfax, VA, USA, November 1997.

[30] L. Rostad and O. Edsberg. A study of access control requirements for healthcare systems based on audit trails from access logs. In *Proceedings of the 22nd Annual Computer Security Applications Conference (ACSAC'06)*, Miami Beach, FL, USA, December 2006.

[31] R. S. Sandhu, E. J. Coyne, H. L. Feinstein, and C. E. Youman. Role-based access control models. *IEEE Computer*, 19(2):38–47, February 1996.

[32] K. Schild. A correspondence theory for terminological logics: preliminary report. In *Proceedings of the 12th International Joint Conference on Artificial intelligence (IJCAI'91)*, pages 466–471, 1991.

[33] F. B. Schneider. Enforceable security policies. *ACM Transactions on Information and System Security*, 3(1):30–50, 2000.

[34] A. Squicciarini, F. Paci, and S. Sundareswaran. PriMa: An effective privacy protection mechanism for social networks. In *Proceedings of the 5th ACM Symposium on Information, Computer and Communications Security (ASIACCS'10)*, pages 320–323, Beijing, China, April 2010.

[35] A. C. Squicciarini, M. Shehab, and J. Wede. Privacy policies for shared content in social network sites. *The VLDB Journal*, 2010. To appear.

[36] C. Talhi, N. Tawbi, and M. Debbabi. Execution monitoring enforcement under memory-limitation constraints. *Information and Computation*, 206:158–184, 2008.

[37] S. Weeks. Understanding trust management systems. In *Proceedings of the 2001 IEEE Symposium on Security and Privacy (S&P'01)*, pages 94–105, Oakland, California, USA, May 2001.

[38] R. Zhang, F. Giunchiglia, B. Crispo, and L. Song. Relation-based access control: An access control model for context-aware computing environment. *Wireless Personal Communications*, 55(1):5–17, September 2010.

APPENDIX

A. PROOF

PROPOSITION 12. *A relational policy is both OC and AC.*

PROOF. Suppose P is a relational policy. We show that P is OC. (The proof of the assertion that P is also AC is symmetrical.) Consider the social network G and vertices $u, v \in V(G)$. It is obvious that $C_G(u; v) \subseteq G$. There is no $i \in \mathcal{I}$ such that $R_i(G) \backslash R_i(C_G(u; v))$ contains a pair (u', v') for which each of u' and v' is connected to u in G. Consequently, by Definition 5, $P(C_G(u; v)) \backslash P(G) \cup P(G) \backslash P(C_G(u; v))$ is an empty set, and thus $P(G)(u, v) \Leftrightarrow P(C_G(u; v))(u, v)$. $\square$

THEOREM 13. *A policy definable in* E *is OC.*

PROOF. Had it not been for the construct @$p.\phi$, this theorem could have been proven in a straightforward manner via structural induction on the abstract syntax tree of a formula. The subtlety arises from the fact that ϕ may contain free occurrences of variables.

To address the presence of free variables, we prove a claim regarding a pair (Σ, ϕ), where Σ is an environment, and ϕ is a formula. A formula ϕ is said to be Σ-***closed*** iff every free variable of ϕ belongs to the domain of Σ. A pair (Σ, ϕ) is a ***closure*** iff ϕ is Σ-closed. We also write $\pi(\Sigma)$ to denote the environment Σ' defined over the same domain as Σ, such that $\Sigma'(p) = \pi(\Sigma(p))$.

Claim: Given a closure (Σ, ϕ) such that $\Sigma(\mathsf{a})$ is defined, the following conditions hold:

1. Let π be an isomorphism between social networks G and G'. Then $G, \Sigma, u \Vdash \phi$ iff $G', \pi(\Sigma), \pi(u) \Vdash \phi$.
2. $G, \Sigma, u \Vdash \phi$ iff $C_G(u; \Sigma(\mathsf{a})), \Sigma, u \Vdash \phi$.

The theorem follows directly from the above claim. The proof of the claim is a straightforward structural induction on the abstract syntax tree of the formula in the closure. $\square$

The proof of Theorem 20 relies on the following lemma.

LEMMA 23. *Suppose P is both positive and OC. Let $\mathcal{B}$ be the minimal set of birooted graphs to positively induce P. For all $G_{(u,v)} \in \mathcal{B}$, every $v' \in V(G) \backslash \{v\}$ is connected to u.*

The proof of the lemma is elementary.

THEOREM 20. *Every finitary OC policy is definable in* E.

PROOF. We describe a sketch of the proof. Suppose P is a finitary OC policy. As P is positive, let $\mathcal{B}$ be the minimal set of birooted graphs to positively induce P. Since P is finitary, $\mathcal{B}$ is finite. We outline in the following the construction of an E formula ϕ for each birooted graph $G_{(u,v)} \in \mathcal{B}$ such that, for every $G'_{(u',v')} \in \mathcal{B}(U, \mathcal{I})$, $G_{(u,v)} \lesssim G'_{(u',v')}$ implies $G', u', v' \models_{\mathsf{E}} \phi$. The formula required by the theorem is the disjunction of the constructed formulas (recall that there are only finitely many of such formulas as $\mathcal{B}$ is finite).

Given birooted graph $G_{(u,v)} \in \mathcal{B}$, we construct a corresponding formula $\phi(u)$ as follows:

Step 1: We label each vertex by a distinct propositional symbol. (Since we have countably infinitely many propositional symbols, we always have enough symbols to work with.) In the following, we write p_x for the propositional symbol associated with a vertex x.

Step 2: Since P is both positive and OC, Lemma 23 implies that the vertices in G (perhaps with the exception of v) are connected to u. With u as the root, one can therefore build a depth-first search tree T. We assume that the search algorithm may traverse either along or against the direction of an edge. That is, a tree edge linking a parent vertex and a child vertex may go in either direction. Following standard terminology, we call the non-tree edges in G ***back edges***. A back edge always link a descendent vertex with an ancestor vertex. (Again, a back edge may either point from a descendent vertex to an ancestor vertex, or point the other direction.) For more details regarding DFS trees, consult a standard text such as [11]. Note that v may or may not be part of T, but all other vertices are in T. Also, every edge in G is either a tree edge or a back edge.

Step 3: For each vertex x in search tree T, construct a formula $\phi(x) = \psi_1 \wedge \psi_2 \wedge @p_x.(\psi_3 \wedge \psi_4)$, where:

- If x is not the root of T (i.e., $x \neq u$), then $\psi_1 = \neg p_{x_1} \wedge \neg p_{x_2} \wedge \ldots \wedge p_{x_k}$, where $x_1, x_2, \ldots, x_k$ are the proper ancestors of x (i.e., excluding x itself). In case $x = u$, then $\psi_1 = \top$.
- If $x = v$, then $\psi_2 = \mathsf{a}$. Otherwise, $\psi_2 = \neg \mathsf{a}$.
- If x is a leaf of T, then $\psi_3 = \top$. Otherwise, a subformula is constructed for each child of x in T. Suppose $(x, y) \in R_i(G)$ is a tree edge linking x with its child y in T. The subformula corresponding to y is $\langle i \rangle \phi(y)$. If the tree edge points in the other direction (i.e., $(y, x) \in R_i(G)$), then we use $\langle -i \rangle$ instead. Let $\psi_3^1, \psi_3^2, \ldots, \psi_3^m$ be the subformulas constructed in this way. We construct $\psi_3 = \psi_3^1 \otimes \psi_3^2 \otimes \ldots \otimes \psi_3^m$.
- If x is not incident on a back edge in G, then $\psi_4 = \top$. Otherwise, ψ_4 is a conjunction of formulas, one for each back edge linking x with one of its ancestors. Suppose $(x, y) \in R_i(G)$ is one such back edge. The conjunct corresponding to this back edge is $\langle i \rangle p_y$. If the back edge points in the other direction (i.e., $(y, x) \in R_i(G)$), then we use $\langle -i \rangle$ instead.

The construction proceeds recursively, with $\phi(y)$ constructed prior to $\phi(x)$ whenever y is a child of x. The recursion terminates properly because T is a tree of finite size. The intuition behind the construction is that $\phi(u)$ is an encoding of G, including both the subgraph T and all the back edges. More precisely, $\phi(u)$ encodes a DFS that an authorization procedure can deploy to confirm that a birooted graph contains a subgraph isomorphic to the "pattern" $G_{(u,v)}$. The detailed proof of this last claim is mechanical. $\square$

xfACL: An Extensible Functional Language for Access Control

Qun Ni
Purdue University
Department of Computer Science
W. Lafayette, IN 47906, USA
ni@cs.purdue.edu

Elisa Bertino
Purdue University
Department of Computer Science
W. Lafayette, IN 47906, USA
bertino@cs.purdue.edu

ABSTRACT

The main goal of modern access control policy languages is to offer high-level languages, by using which security officers and application developers can express a large variety of access restrictions and isolate the security logic from the application logic. However, the current state-of-the-art language, XACML, suffers from some design flaws and lacks important features, such as those that characterize the RBAC model. Therefore, we propose an access control language that combines the benefits of both XACML and RBAC while avoiding their drawbacks.

Categories and Subject Descriptors

C.2.0 [**Computer Communication Networks**]: General—*security and protection*; D.4.6 [**Operating Systems**]: Security and Protection—*Access Controls*; K.6.5 [**Management of Computing and Information Systems**]: Security and Protection

General Terms

Management, Security, Standardization

Keywords

Access Control, Policy, Language

1. INTRODUCTION

Current access control policy languages and architectures make it possible to isolate the security logic from the application logic. Access control policy languages thus enable developers to move hard-coded security check points out of applications. Such a separation makes it easier to update and revise the security logic without the need to modify the code, which is usually either very expensive or highly impractical. Therefore it is unsurprising to see that several access control policy languages/models have been recently proposed, e.g. XACML, RBAC, EPAL, TRBAC, and P-RBAC [8, 1, 4, 13, 12, 9].

Among these proposals, XACML [1] and RBAC, both of which have been standardized [15, 4], are perhaps the most widely adopted. RBAC typically helps security officers in reducing the number of access control policies and enforcing some well established security principles, e.g. the least privilege principle. Also it is conceptually simple and supports a specification of access control policies which is close to the organization of enterprises. RBAC has, thus, been adopted in several leading identity management solutions, and commercial operating systems and database management systems. Another important standard access control language is XACML, an XML encoded and attribute-based policy language, which supports a flexible specification of access control policies through the use of permit and deny rules within the same access control policy, and the combination of (possibly different) decisions from different rules by policy combining algorithms. Therefore, XACML has also been selected by several ongoing industrial and academic projects, e.g. the HL7 healthcare application infrastructure.

A main drawback of RBAC is that it is just a conceptual model, and unlike XACML does not have a standardized policy language. As such, its implementations in different products are very different [16, 5]. Therefore whenever one has to deal with heterogeneous domains, which today are quite common, policy administration could become very complicated. One possible solution to this problem would be to use the RBAC profile of XACML. Unfortunately, XACML only provides limited support for RBAC, e.g. no sessions (least privilege). Moreover, the design of XACML suffers from some non-trivial drawbacks, e.g. inconsistent policy combination [10] and erroneous policy evaluation truth tables [10]. Therefore, we believe that there is a strong need for an access control language that combines the benefits of XACML and RBAC without their drawbacks. The goal of this paper is to provide the foundations for such a new access control language by proposing an eXtensible Functional Language for Access Control (xfACL). The language has the following distinct features.

- *It is attribute-based.* Access control decisions are made based on the attributes of the involved entities, e.g. subjects, operations, objects, recipient subjects, and environments. An attribute-based approach ensures that the language is able to directly support the specification of high-level policies.

- *It is context-centric.* The collection of attributes involved in an access request constitutes the *context* of the access request. The context is dynamic in that its contents may change during the evaluation of the access request. As the context contents are crucial in evaluating access decisions, dynamic context changes need to be controlled by some

---

[1] In this paper, XACML means XACML 1.0, 2.0, and 3.0 (draft).

special policies, referred to as *auxiliary policies*. As a result xfACL has two types of access control policies: (a) authorization policies, specifying permissions on protected objects; (b) auxiliary policies, specifying updates to access request contexts, that greatly improve its expressiveness.

- *It supports sophisticated error handling and returns informative decisions.* Other access control languages only support rather limited access decisions. For example XACML supports Permit, Deny, Not Applicable, and Indeterminate. However, even with these four possible decisions, critical information in access decisions may be lost because Indeterminate represents too many different access control decisions [10]. Such information loss may result in a wrong final access decision [10]. xfACL supports more informative decisions (discussed in Section 5.4) and provides a mechanism to record the reason resulting in abnormal decisions.

- *It is extensible in certain language constructs.* xfACL allows policy authors to specify their own specific attribute categories and whatever types of attributes they need. xfACL also ensures that policy authors are able to define their own implementation dependent error messages.

- *Its syntax is based on a functional language.* We use the OCaml language [6], a functional programming language, to specify xfACL syntax. The use of OCaml has several advantages. First, the type definition of types can be easily translated into BNF and encoded by XML Schemas if required. However, because of the variant type supported by OCaml, we obtain a terser language specification than that we would have obtained by using BNF, especially for complicated expressions. Policies specified by xfACL become terser as well. Second, the xfACL language specification can be directly used in the implementation of an xfACL interpreter and xfACL PDPs based on the F Sharp Language. F Sharp is the first commercial implementation of functional languages and is integrated with MS Visual Studio 2010 and .NET version 4 (Windows) and Mono project (Linux). Therefore, security sensitive applications developed in .NET can be easily integrated with the implementation of xfACL. However, note that even though we use OCaml to specify the xfACL language, xfACL could be implemented using other common programming languages, such as C and Java.

The most novel contributions of our model are the notion of dynamic contexts, the notion of auxiliary policies for managing such contexts, and solutions to problems resulting from the use of auxiliary policies. An example of dynamic context change occurs in RBAC when, because of session policies that restrict the privileges applicable to an access request, some roles of a subject may be deactivated. The deactivation may further require to deactivate the junior roles of these roles. All these changes arise before the access decision is made, but existing access control languages, e.g. XACML, are not able to support the specification of policies to control context changes. xfACL through the notion of auxiliary policies makes it possible to exactly specify the changes that can occur in the context of an access request.

Even though auxiliary policies can be applied in many different ways, the best example of their applicability is in the support of RBAC functionalities. Through the support of auxiliary policies, xfACL is the first fine-grained access control policy language fully supporting all the functionalities required by the RBAC standard. For instance, role hierarchies, user assignments, and ses-

sion policies can be directly specified by auxiliary policies (detailed in Section 6.3).

The rest of the paper is organized as follows. Next section outlines the main requirements that have driven the design of xfACL. Sections 3 outlines xfACL, whereas Sections 4 and 5 provide a detailed description of the main elements of the language, such as attributes, contexts, and policies, and of key concepts, such as authorization decisions and their aggregation, and the ternary logic. Section 6 focuses on auxiliary policies and addresses some problems resulting from the introduction of auxiliary policies. Section 7 discusses related work, and finally Section 8 outlines some conclusions.

2. DESIGN OBJECTIVES OF XFACL

The design of xfACL is driven by the following requirements, some of which have also driven the design of XACML [8]:

- xfACL should be a general purpose policy language for access control. The language should not be designed based on a specific application, e.g. healthcare. To address this requirement, the language should provide a method for making authorization decisions based on values of object attributes and subject attributes and on the contents of the information retrieved, e.g. query results. Attributes should be allowed to have multiple values, e.g. roles. Both positive policies and negative policies should be supported. A standard interface between access requests and access control policies should also be provided. Such an interface isolates the policy author from the details of the application development environment.

- The evaluation of xfACL should be deterministic. Operations that can be expressed in the language must be defined clearly, including logical operations on values of subject and object attributes, and aggregations of different decisions. More importantly, abnormal situations must be taken into account when evaluating xfACL policies.

- xfACL should be a language that can be easily integrated with well-known development environments. Integration with such environments is crucial in order to deploy the language in real application domains.

3. OUTLINE OF XFACL

To clarify the high level design of xfACL, it is important to show how, given a request context, the xfACL policies are evaluated to a final access decision. As shown in Fig. 1, the evaluation consists of three steps:

1. Context Modification. A request context is sent to an auxiliary PDP first. The auxiliary PDP evaluates auxiliary policies one by one. Once the PDP determines that an auxiliary policy is applicable to the request, it generates a new request context. This new request context is used as input for the evaluation of the next applicable auxiliary policy whose evaluation in turn will generate a new request context. Such process continues until all applicable auxiliary policies have been evaluated.

2. Authorization Evaluation. The final request context generated by the previous step is then sent to an authorization PDP. The PDP then evaluates authorization policies one by one. Different applicable authorization policies may evaluate to possibly different responses, including access decisions and status, accordingly. For instance, policy 1 might evaluate to permit while policy 2 might evaluate to deny.

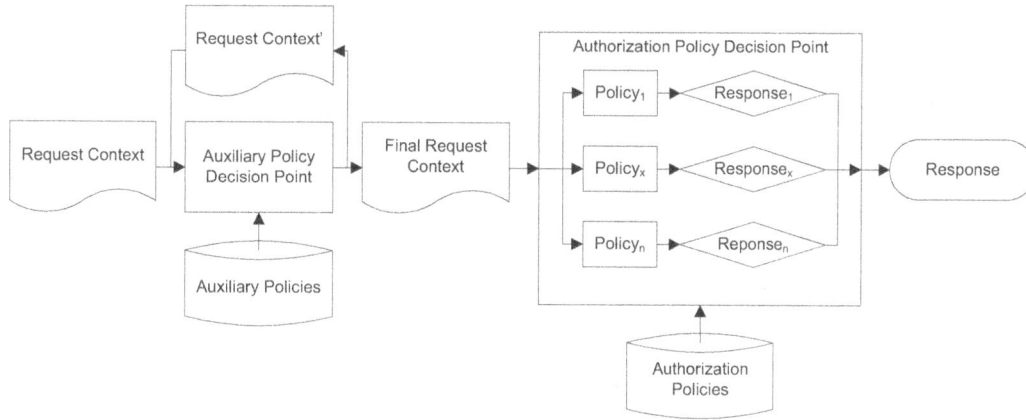

Figure 1: xfACL policy evaluation flow

3. Decision Aggregation. All responses generated by the applicable policies are aggregated by the authorization PDP based on some predefined method to generate the final response.

The high level design of the xfACL is roughly mapped onto the aforementioned policy evaluation flow. The core construct of xfACL is the expression, as the majority of concepts defined in xfACL correspond to different expressions, described in what follows.

- Normal expressions. They represent the values of primary types appearing in various applications, e.g. integer, real, date, time and string, variables of these types, and the application of common numeric functions or string functions to these values and variables. Normal expressions are the connection between xfACL PDPs and the external applications. In other words, normal expressions are used to describe and retrieve the required attribute values from applications that are further applied in the context modification and the authorization evaluation.

- Context expressions. They represent a request context, an auxiliary policy, and an auxiliary policy set. A simplest request context is a group of (attribute, value) pairs that represent the attribute values of a given request. The request context is the standard interface between applications and xfACL policies and describes the required attribute values. The evaluation result of an auxiliary policy or an auxiliary policy set is a request context, thus, they are also context expressions.

- Ternary expressions. They represent the truth values of ternary logic, i.e. True, False, and Unknown, logical operations on these values, and the application of comparison functions to two normal expressions. Ternary expression are used to specify predicates on attributes of subjects and objects. An access decision in an authorization policy is made based on the value of a ternary expression. Likewise, an attribute value in an auxiliary policy is updated based on the value of a ternary expression.

- Decision expressions. They represent the response from an authorization policy, the application of decision aggregation functions to responses, an authorization policy, and an authorization policy set. The evaluation result of an authorization policy or a policy set is a decision expression. Therefore, an authorization policy or a policy set are decision expressions as well.

4. ATTRIBUTES, REQUEST CONTEXTS, AND RESPONSES

In this section, we define attributes, request contexts, and responses that are used to specify the interface between policies and security applications.

4.1 Attributes and Values

Attributes are one of the basic concepts of xfACL and thus we define their structures first. Without loss of generality, we use a tuple constructor from OCaml to define the structure of attributes. We define an attribute as a tuple with the following elements: an attribute id, an issuer id (optional), an issuing time instant (optional), and finally an attribute value. The following OCaml type definition formally specifies our attribute notion:

```
type attributeT = attributeIdT * issuerIdT option
                  * datetimeT option * valueT
```

To simplify, we define the attribute id, and the issuer id as primitive string types. Such a design choice ensures that policy authors can define whatever they want to be the attribute id. An attribute id must be at least unique in its attribute category detailed in next section. Some typical examples of attribute id are URN ids, GUID ids, or PK-based ids.

The issuer id and the issuing time instant (`datetimeT`) are optional. Some internal applications might not need the attribute issuer information but others, e.g. customer applications in a financial institution, might require an issuer id authenticated by well-know organizations, such as VeriSign. The attribute value (`valueT`) contains the primary data type specification of xfACL.

```
type dateT = Date of int * int * int
type timeT = Time of int * int * int
type datetimeT = dateT * timeT
type valueT = (* XML Schema primitive type values *)
        DecimalV of int (* an interger *)
      | BooleanV of bool (* a boolean *)
      | FloatV of float32 (* a float *)
      | DoubleV of float (* a double *)
      | StringV of string (* a string *)
      | DateTimeV of datetimeT (* a datetime *)
      | TimeV of timeT (* a time *)
      | DateV of dateT (* a date *)
      | HexBinaryV of string (* a hex binary *)
      | Base64BinaryV of string (* a base64 binary *)
      | AnyUriV of string (* a AnyURI *)
      | YearMonthDurationV of int * int
      | MonthDayDurationV of int * int
      | CollectionV of valueT list
```

In the xfACL specification, we intentionally choose the XML Schema primitive data types as its primitive types. Such a design choice has two benefits. First, the XML Schema primitive data types are sufficient for an access control language. Second, there is a straightforward mapping between the functional language-based specification and its XML encoded specification. The only exception is represented by the collection type which will be discussed in Section 6.

Example. The following attribute describes a "name" attribute, issued by "VeriSign" at 20:6:15 on March 26, 2010, with its value string type "Alice".

```
("name", Some "VeriSign", Some (Date (2010,3,26),
  Time (20,6,15)), StringV "Alice")
```

Please note that both "VeriSign" and "(Date (2010,3,26), Time (20,6,15))" are option types, so "Some" is used to indicate that they are optional values.

4.2 Request Contexts

Many different entities are relevant to access control decisions. Without loss of generality, these entities may be categorized as follows:

- access subject: the subject who initiates the access, e.g. user Alice;
- recipient subject: the subject who receives the object, e.g. user Bob;
- intermediary subject, the subject who is involved in the access, e.g. user Charles;
- machine subject: the computer system from where the access request is issued, e.g. machine Obelix;
- process subject: the process that issues the access request, e.g., process custo.exe;
- session subject: the session during which the access request is issued, e.g., session Data Analysis;
- object: the entity which is accessed, e.g. table Customer;
- operation, the entity through which the access is performed, e.g. command Select;
- environment: the entity which represents external factors, e.g. location, date, or time.
- other: xfACL allows policy authors to define their specific attribute category to extend the language. These customized categories can be applied in policies just as other predefined categories.

Each entity may have its own attributes. Therefore, we define the collection of relevant attributes for a specific entity as an *attribute group*. Such a design is motivated by the typical organization of a real identification cards, e.g. the driver license, which usually groups important attributes of a specific individual. Each group only contains attributes within a specific attribute category. Moreover, users may define their own custom attribute category types by using the "Other" constructor if necessary. Finally, a *request context* is a collection of relevant attribute groups. This simple yet flexible design makes it possible for policy authors to specify various kinds of request contexts. For instance, an access request containing two recipients can be described by two recipient subject attribute groups. Other context expressions are discussed in Section 6.

```
type attrCategoryT =
  | AccessSubject | RecipientSubject
  | IntermediarySubjet | ProcessSubject | SessionSubject
  | MachineSubject | Object | Operation | Environment
  | Other of string
type attrGroupT = attrCategoryT * attributeT list
type contextExprT = | Request of attrGroupT list | ...
```

Example. The access request "Bart Simpson, with e-mail 'bs@simpsons.com', wants to read his medical record maintained at Medi Corp." may be specified as the following request context:

```
Request [ (AccessSubject, [("id", Some "VeriSign", None,
  StringV "bs@simpsons.com")]);
  (Object, [("id", None, None,
  AnyUriV "file://med/record/patient/BartSimpson")]);
  (Operation, [("id", None, None, StringV "read")]) ]
```

In the above example, "None" is a special value indicating that no value is available for an optional attribute.

4.3 Responses

A response is the output of an authorization PDP (a function) given a request context and a set of authorization policies. The first component of a response is of course the access decision. In some situations, e.g. some attribute value is not available, we may have to include a second component, status, to clearly indicate what went wrong during the evaluation of this access request. Some authorization policies may also include obligations as part of a response. Therefore, we define the response, the first decision expression, in xfACL as follows.

```
type decisionT = | Null | Permit | Deny | NA | PNA
                           | DNA | PD | PDNA
type obligationT = string
type statusT =
  | Normal
  | NotAvailable of attrCategoryT * attributeIdT
  | Null of attrCategoryT * attributeIdT
  | Error of int * string
  | Other of string
type decisionExprT =
  | Response of decisionT
      * (policyIdT * statusT) list
      * obligationT list option
  | ...
```

xfACL supports both positive, i.e. Permit, and negative, i.e. Deny, authorization policies. Negative policies are typically used to specify some exceptions in a group of positive policies, and thus may help reduce the number of required policies. Moreover, negative policies are also useful to preclude undesired resource accesses or information disclosures due to wrongly specified positive authorization policies, if the Deny takes precedence over Permit approach is used to solve conflicts among authorization policies. Therefore, the decision type of xfACL, decisionT, includes both Deny and Permit. Other values in the decision components will be discussed later. The obligation type in the current xfACL specification is just a place holder and will be implemented in a future version of xfACL. An authorization policy may specify several obligations, thus a response contains an optional collection of obligations.

One distinct feature of xfACL is the introduction of a detailed log mechanism for the evaluation result of each potentially applicable policy in the language itself instead of its implementation. By doing so, xfACL provides a standard way to record policy evaluation logs for auditing purposes or policy analysis purposes while avoiding interoperability issues in log analysis resulting from different xfACL PDP implementations. The evaluation logs are based on statusT type that consists of five different status values.

- Normal: there is no error during the evaluation of a policy.
- NotAvailable of attrCategoryT * attributeIdT: the specific attribute (attrCategoryT * attributeIdT) required by a policy evaluation is not available in the request context.

- Null of attrCategoryT * attributeIdT: the specific attribute value required by a policy evaluation is NULL.
- Error of int * string: there is some run-time error with an error ID and its description. Some common errors include "insufficient memory" and "buffer overflow".
- Other of string: xfACL allows policy authors to write their own abnormal messages that can be referenced in their policies.

A status value is combined with its policy id as one component in the response. During the decision aggregation, the decision of a policy may be overridden but the status of the policy evaluation will not be overridden. By contrast, the status value will be inserted in the status list and finally be transferred back to the Authorization PDP. Depending on the configuration, the status information may be periodically logged into external storage for later usages, e.g. for auditing purposes or error analysis purposes.

Example. A response "Deny" is obtained. In the evaluated policies, the attribute "ActivatedRole" of "AccessSubject" in policy "P001" is not available in the request context. Such response is expressed as follows.

```
Response (Deny, [("P001", NotAvailable (AccessSubject,
    "ActivatedRole"))], None)
```

5. AUTHORIZATION POLICIES

In this section, we elaborate on the specification of authorization policies.

5.1 Attribute Queries, Content Queries, and Normal Expressions

Intuitively, an authorization policy specifies predicates against the following values:

- attribute values in a request context, and/or
- content values in some protected objects, and/or
- some predefined values.

Based on the values of these predicates, the policy specifies different access decisions. Therefore, the first question is how we obtain the required attribute values in the request context. We, thus, define a variant type AttrQuery to retrieve a desired attribute value from the current request context.

```
type expressionT =
  | ValueE of valueT
  | VarE of string
  | ApplyE of functionIdT * expressionT option
  | AttrQuery of attrCategoryT * attributeIdT
      * issuerIdT option * datetimeT option
  | ContentQuery of contentIdT * attributeIdT
      * ternaryExprT
```

AttrQuery is one of four variant types of normal expressions, expressionT, in xfACL. Its execution semantics is to return the value of the required attribute specified by an attribute category, an attribute id, an attribute issuer id (optional), and an issuing time instant (optional). Because the current request context is known to a PDP when interpreting AttrQuery, the context is not included in the AttrQuery construction tuple. AttrQuery must be implemented in a PDP of xfACL.

Example. An attribute query for the value of the identifier of "AccessSubject", issued by "VeriSign", in the request is expressed as follows [2]:

```
AttrQuery (AccessSubject, "id", Some "VeriSign", None)
```

---

[2] For simplicity, we use string "id" as the identifier here.

If the attribute query is executed on the request context example in Section 4.2, the evaluation value is

```
ValueE (StringV "bs@simpsons.com").
```

In some cases, we may want to use some values of the protected object, e.g. the Gender field in a record of the Customer table, in some access predicates. We thus define a ContextQuery as well. A ContextQuery retrieves the desired values from the protected object content. Note that, unlike an AttrQuery which is implemented by an authorization PDP, a ContentQuery must be implemented by the application because it is application dependent. In a typical C implementation of xfACL a ContentQuery can be implemented as a function pointer that will be called back by an authorization PDP during policy evaluation. Support for ContentQuery is optional in xfACL.

Content attributes are different from object attributes. For instance, assuming that the object to be accessed is some portion of the Customer table, then the object attribute values might be the table's properties, e.g. the table creation time or the table owner, while the content attributes usually refer to the table content, e.g. customer.salary.

Example. A ContentQuery to retrieve the salary of Zoe with name "zoe@gmail.com" from the Customer table is expressed as follows:

```
ContentQuery ("customer", "customer.salary",
    ApplyT ("match",VarE "customer.name",
    ValueE (StringV "zoe@gmail.com")))
```

"ApplyT" represents an application of the ternary logic function "match" and returns True, False, or Unknown based on whether its arguments are the same or not. This topic is further discussed in the next section.

The ValueE expression represents the value of an expression and is of course based on valueT type. The VarE expression represents a variable that is usually used in content queries for referring to some interesting attribute. We may also apply some numeric or string functions to existing expressions to generate a new expression, discussed in Appendix A.

5.2 Ternary Logic and Ternary Expressions

We usually expect that the evaluation of predicates on attributes always results in either True or False. However, real cases are more complicated. When processing an AttrQuery or a ContentQuery, abnormal situations can happen. For instance, the AccessSubject attributes are not available in the request context, a critical attribute in the ContentQuery has a Null value, or there are some run-time errors during the processing of the ContentQuery.

Several access control systems do not take into account the possibility of such abnormal situations. Other systems adopt a simple solution, that is, stopping the evaluation of the policy and returning an error message (usually a Deny is finally returned to the access requester). However, such a simple solution is not always the best. In the case of a disjunction of a predicate on the result of an abnormal ContentQuery and another predicate evaluating to True, perhaps we should return True because the predicate result based on the abnormal ContentQuery (either True or False) will not affect the final evaluation. Therefore, the access decision relevant to the predicate result (True) should be returned.

The classical Boolean logic adopted in traditional programming languages and access control languages is unable to deal with this situation. Therefore we introduce an old ternary logic [3]

---

[3] As reviewers of this paper mentioned, the ternary logic, i.e. Lukasiewicz logic, was well studied a long time ago. We use the

Table 1: Ternary Truth Value

A	B	A OR B	A AND B	Not A
True	True	True	True	False
True	Unknown	True	Unknown	False
True	False	True	False	False
Unknown	True	True	Unknown	Unknown
Unknown	Unknown	Unknown	Unknown	Unknown
Unknown	False	Unknown	False	Unknown
False	True	True	False	True
False	Unknown	Unknown	False	True
False	False	False	False	True

in xfACL to precisely evaluate predicates on attribute values in access control policies. Formally, the xfACL Ternary Expressions are defined as follows.

```
type ternaryValueT = True | False | Unknown
type ternaryExprT =
    | ValueT of ternaryValueT
    | Not of ternaryExprT
    | And of ternaryExprT * ternaryExprT
    | Or of ternaryExprT * ternaryExprT
    | ApplyT of functionIdT * expressionT
                * expressionT
```

As it can be seen from the above syntax fragment, a third logic value, called *Unknown*, is introduced in addition to True and False. The semantics of Unknown is either True or False but we are not sure. The semantics of the ternary logic is shown in Table 1. Ternary expressions in xfACL can be built using the conjunction, disjunction, and negation logic connectives as usual.

The comparison between different attribute values, defined as normal expressions in xfACL, is supported by means of ternary logic functions discussed in Appendix A. One example is the "match" function applied in the previous example. These comparison functions will generate a ternary logic value based on different cases. Specifically, these comparison functions generate an Unknown value in the following cases:

- An error happens during the evaluation of predicates.
- The required attribute is not available in the request context.
- The retrieved attribute value is Null and the value is not compared to a Null value.

In order to distinguish these different Unknown results, relevant information, that is, the reason of the Unknown result, is inserted in the status list component of the final decision.

Example. To determine whether the access subject's name is "bs@simpsons.com" in the request context the following function is used:

```
ApplyT ("match",
    AttrQuery (AccessSubject, "Id",
        Some "VeriSign", None),
    ValueE (StringV "bs@simpsons.com"))
```

This ternary expression applies a "match" function to the access subject id and to the string value "bs@simpsons.com". The execution semantics of the "match" function is an equality test (defined in Appendix A).

5.3 Authorization Policies and Decision Expressions

As mentioned earlier, we define an authorization policy (Auth-Policy) as a variant type of the decision expression in xfACL. The intuition behind this design is that the evaluation result of an authorization policy is a decision expression.

term "ternary" here purely for an easier explanation of its values and semantics.

```
type decisionT =
    | Null | Permit | Deny | NA | PNA | DNA| PD | PDNA
type decisionExprT =
    | Response of decisionT * (policyIdT * statusT) list
        * obligationT list option
    | ApplyD of functionIdT * decisionExprT
        * decisionExprT
    | AuthPolicy of policyIdT * ternaryExprT
        * decisionT * obligationT list option
        * decisionT * obligationT list option
        * decisionT * obligationT list option
    | AuthPolicySet of policySetIdT
        * functionIdT * decisionExprT list
```

The decision type "decisionT" is explained in next section. There are four kinds of decision expressions. The response has already been discussed in Section 4.3. A function application to two decision expressions returns a decision expression, referred to as a decision function, which represents the application of various different decision aggregation methods suggested in our previous work [10] and is discussed in next section and Appendix A.1. Other two expressions, AuthPolicy and AuthPolicySet, are more complicated and explained below.

In xfACL, an authorization policy (AuthPolicy) contains the following components:

- a policy id (policyIdT) which uniquely identifies a policy and is also used to indicate in the response which policy is the source of the abnormal evaluation;
- a ternary expression (ternaryExprT) which is used to determine which decision should be made based on its logical value;
- the first decisionT which represents the decision to take if the ternary expression evaluates to True;
- the second decisionT which represents the decision to take if the ternary expression evaluates to False;
- the third decisionT which represents the decision to take if the ternary expression evaluates to Unknown;
- each decision may be followed by an optional collection of obligations.

Example. An authorization policy "Any user with an e-mail address in the 'med.example.com' namespace is allowed to perform any action on any resource." is expressed in xfACL as follows:

```
AuthPolicy ( "P002", ApplyT ( "Contain",
    AttrQuery (AccessSubject, "Email", None, None),
    ValueE (StringV "@med.example.com") ),
    Permit, None, NA, None, PNA, None )
```

The policy ID is "P002". We apply a "Contain" function to determine whether the "Email" attribute of the access subject in the request context contains string value "@med.example.com". If the function evaluates to True, the policy decision is Permit without obligation. If the function evaluates to False, the decision is NA (Not Applicable). If the function evaluates to Unknown, the decision is PNA that is either Permit (True) or Not Applicable (False) but we do not know.

If we set the first decision expression to Permit, the second decision expression to Deny, and the third decision to PD (either Permit or Deny) in an authorization policy, the authorization policy becomes a policy that is always applicable to any access request, returning either Permit, Deny, or PD, even when some evaluation error happens.

Like XACML, xfACL supports organizing policies into policy sets for better policy administration. As we can see from the specification, a policy set AuthPolicySet contains the following components:

66

- a policy set id (policyIdT) which is used for administration purposes;
- a function id (functionIdT) which represents a decision aggregation function; the function is used to aggregate possibly different decisions from different applicable policies; these functions are discussed in the next section;
- a collection of policies or policy sets (decisionExprT); a policy set can contain either policies or other policy sets which are of course decision expressions.

The final decision of a policy set is the execution of the decision aggregation function (discussed in Appendix A.1) pair-wisely on decisions resulting from the evaluation of the containing policies and policies sets.

5.4 Decision Aggregation

Except for Permit and Deny, the semantics of other six decisions is as follows.

- Null: No decision. If we have an empty policy set, the decision of the policy set is Null (no decision) given any access requests.
- NA: Not Applicable. The policy is not specified for the specific situation.
- PNA: Either Permit or Not Applicable.
- DNA: Either Deny or Not Applicable.
- PD: Either Permit or Deny.
- PDNA: Either Permit, Deny, or Not Applicable.

Suppose that, given a request context, three authorization policies evaluate to Permit, Deny, and NA, respectively. If we do not have preference, e.g. Deny takes precedence, with respect to these decisions, the final decision should be either Permit, Deny, or NA but we are not sure, which in xfACL is represented by PDNA.

Obviously, a final PDNA decision does not make any sense because we know that the final decision should be PDNA even if we do not have any access control policies. To generate a meaningful final decision, some aggregation methods are therefore required, e.g., deny overrides (DO) or permit overrides (PO). If we adopt the DO method, the final decision should be Deny in the case mentioned in the beginning of this section.

However, because we support the evaluation of policies in abnormal situations, decisions like PNA, DNA, PD, and PDNA still may appear during policy evaluation and/or decision aggregation even if we adopt some aggregation methods. Therefore, the decision aggregation is more complicated than it looks like. For instance, the decision aggregation of Permit and DNA is Permit if the PO method is adopted, and it is PD if the DO method is adopted. In our previous work [10], we have proposed a formal algebra for aggregating these different decisions. The truth table for the PO method is shown in Table 2. The decision functions in xfACL implement these aggregation methods [10].

6. AUXILIARY POLICIES AND CONTEXT EXPRESSIONS

In xfACL, request contexts are defined as context expressions. Given a request context, an auxiliary PDP, based on the applicable auxiliary policies, may add, update, or remove some attributes and/or their values. The evaluation result of an auxiliary policy is an updated request context. Therefore, context expressions in xfACL are defined by request contexts and auxiliary policies. Formally, context expressions are defined as follows.

```
type contextExprT =
  | Request of attrGroupT list
```

```
  | AuxPolicy of policyIdT * ternaryExprT
    * attrGroupT list
    * attrGroupT list
    * policyIdT list option
  | AuxPolicySet of policySetIdT
    * contextExprT list
```

The Request variant type is used to describe a request context and represents the value of a context expression. The AuxPolicy contains five components:

- an auxiliary policy id (policyIdT) which is used to indicate the source when evaluation errors happen;
- a ternary expression which is used to determine whether an auxiliary policy is applicable to a given request context;
- the first attribute group collection which represents attributes that will probably be added or updated in the original request context;
- the second attribute group collection which represents attributes that will probably be removed from the original request context;
- the optional collection of policy ids (policyIdT list) which indicates a collection of auxiliary policies that are possibly affected by the auxiliary policy.

If the ternary expression of an auxiliary policy evaluates to True, the policy is applicable to the given request context. Both attribute group collections in the policy will affect the request context only if the policy is applicable to the request context. If the ternary expression evaluates to False, the policy is not applicable and will not affect the request context.

6.1 Abnormal Situations and Worst Case Preservation Method

In the evaluation of authorization policies, some abnormal situations in policy evaluation may not affect the final access decision. However, abnormal situations in the evaluation of auxiliary policies result in more complicated situations. It is not completely impossible to predicate whether the abnormal situation will affect the final decision, but it is very hard to do so. Abnormal situations in the auxiliary policy evaluation means that different combination of attribute values in a request context are possible, which in turn may result in different auxiliary policies to be applicable and finally authorization policies may evaluate to different decisions. Unlike the case of authorization decisions in which we have a rather limited set of possible decisions to aggregate, in the case of an abnormal evaluation of auxiliary policies, we have a very large state space, resulting from the huge number of different combinations from context attribute values, to analyze. It is inefficient to analyze them during the policy evaluation stage.

A naive solution may simply disallow abnormal situations from happening during the evaluation of auxiliary policies. If such an abnormal situation arises, the policy evaluation will be terminated immediately and an error message returned. However, we notice that once an attribute may take different values due to an abnormal situation in the evaluation of an auxiliary policy, its effect on policy evaluation, including both the evaluation of authorization policies and that of auxiliary policies, is no worse than the case in which the attribute value is NULL or the attribute is not available [4]. Based on this observation, we propose the following worst case preservation method to continue processing the access request as much as possible.

---

[4] In the current version of xfACL, the semantics of a NULL attribute value and that of a not-available attribute are different, but their effect on policy evaluation is the same. In the future version of our language, we may process them differently.

Table 2: Permit-Overrides Truth Table

	Null	Permit	Deny	NA	PD	PNA	DNA	PDNA
Null	Null	Permit	Deny	NA	PD	PNA	DNA	PDNA
Permit	Permit	Permit	Permit	Permit	Permit	Permit	Permit	Permit
Deny	Deny	Permit	Deny	Deny	PD	PD	Deny	PD
NA	NA	Permit	Deny	NA	PD	PNA	DNA	PDNA
PD	PD	Permit	PD	PD	PD	PD	PD	PD
PNA	PNA	Permit	PD	PNA	PD	PNA	PDNA	PDNA
DNA	DNA	Permit	Deny	DNA	PD	PDNA	DNA	PDNA
PDNA	PDNA	Permit	PD	PDNA	PD	PDNA	PDNA	PDNA

- If the ternary expression can evaluate to a deterministic value, i.e. either True or False, in an abnormal situation, the policy is processed as usual.

- If the ternary expression cannot evaluate to a deterministic value, then the applicability of the policy is not deterministic either. In this case, since the values of the affected attributes become non-deterministic, the values of the attributes in the first attribute group and the second attribute group are reset to the NULL value. After that, the auxiliary policy is processed as usual.

The method may not be the best, but it ensures that we still may obtain a deterministic access decision if the affected attributes are not critical or can be safely replaced with other attributes in policies *without additional computational overhead*.

6.2 Cascading Effect

Since the intention of auxiliary policies is to update the attribute values, it is not surprising to see that some previous, i.e. evaluated, non-applicable auxiliary policies become *applicable*, referred to as cascading effects of auxiliary policies.

The cascading effect can be illustrated by means of role assignment policies in role hierarchies. Suppose that a senior role A consists of two junior roles B and C; we thus have the following three auxiliary policies:

...
P007: assign role B to role A
P008: assign role C to role A
P009: assign role A to user X
...

If user X submits an access request, when evaluating policy P007 and P008, the user cannot be assigned to roles B and C because the user has not yet been assigned to role A.

As mentioned earlier, the outcome of some auxiliary policies may affect the applicability of other auxiliary policies. Those affected auxiliary policies, even if they have already been evaluated, may need to be evaluated again given the updated request context. Consider again the previous example, once policy P009 has been evaluated, policies P007 and P008 should be evaluated again.

Obviously, reevaluating all evaluated policies is not a good idea. We also notice that the number of affected policies is usually pretty small in practice. Such an observation motivates the optional collection component, i.e. the collection of affected policy ids. The execution semantics of the collection in an auxiliary policy is that if the policy is applicable to an access request, all policies in the collection that have already been evaluated should be evaluated again.

Policy authors may manually specify affected policy ids. However, for large organizations with complicated policies, an automatic tool may be required in order to automatically determine the ids of the affected policies. A tool based on the concept of a fixed-point construction is under development and will be discussed in future work.

6.3 Auxiliary PDP Function

In this section, we present the algorithm (see Algorithm 1) in pseudo code to show how an auxiliary PDP evaluates a request context given a list of auxiliary policies. Each auxiliary policy will be evaluated one by one against the request context to determine its applicability.

When an auxiliary policy is applicable to a given request context, i.e., its ternary expression evaluates to True, the returning request context is updated by the first attribute group collection (collection A) based on the following rules, as shown in Line 8-14.

- If an attribute in collection A is not available in the request context, the attribute and its value, and relevant attribute group, if necessary, will be added into the resulting request context.

- If the attribute in collection A is in the request context and is not a collection type (List), the attribute value in the resulting request context is updated with the new value.

- If the attribute in collection A is in the request context and is a collection type (List), the attribute value in the resulting request context is the concatenation of these two lists.

Similarly, when an auxiliary policy is applicable to a given request context, the returning request context is updated by the second attribute group collection (collection B) based on the following rules, as shown in Line 15-22.

- If an attribute in collection B is in the request context and the attribute is not a collection type (List), and its value is the same value as that in the request context, the attribute and its value are removed from the resulting request context.

- If an attribute in collection B is in the request context and the attribute is not a collection type (List), and its value is different from that in the request context, the attribute and its value do not change in the resulting request context.

- If an attribute in collection B is in the request context and the attribute is a collection type (List), the attribute values in the resulting request context are the list of values that are generated by the following steps:

  1. If a value of the attribute is contained in both the request context and collection B, the value is removed from both the request context and collection B.

  2. Otherwise, the value is removed from collection B.

  3. Repeat step 1 and 2 until the attribute in collection B becomes empty. Return the request context as the resulting request context.

The following example illustrates the last rule.

Example. Consider the role hierarchy in Fig. 2. Suppose that the role attribute value in a request context is [R1, R2, R3, R4, R4] and that the role attribute value in an applicable auxiliary policy (collection B) is [R3, R4, R5]; then the role value in the resulting request context is [R1, R2, R4].

Input: APS → RQ → RQ'
Data: APS: the auxiliary policy set
Data: RQ: the request context
Data: RQ': the updated request context

```
1  set termination guard g to be 1000 times of the cardinality of
   APS and the number of evaluated policy i to be 0;
2  foreach ContextExpr ce ∈ APS do
3  │  insert policy id in ce to an evaluated policy list pl;
4  │  tv ← evaluate the ternary expression in ce;
5  │  copy RQ to RQ';
6  │  switch tv do
7  │  │  case "True"
8  │  │  │  foreach AttrGroup ag1 ∈ ce.AttrGroupOne do
9  │  │  │  │  foreach Attribute at1 ∈ ag1 do
10 │  │  │  │  │  if at1 ∉ RQ' then insert RQ' with at1;
11 │  │  │  │  │  if at1 ∈ RQ' && typeof(at1)! = List then
12 │  │  │  │  │  │  update value of the at1 in RQ' with new
   │  │  │  │  │  │  value of at1 from ag1;
13 │  │  │  │  │  else
14 │  │  │  │  │  │  concatenate values of the at1 in RQ'
   │  │  │  │  │  │  with new values of at1 from ag1;
15 │  │  │  foreach AttrGroup ag2 ∈ ce.AttrGroupTwo do
16 │  │  │  │  foreach Attribute at2 ∈ ag2 do
17 │  │  │  │  │  if at2 ∉ RQ' then No Operation;
18 │  │  │  │  │  if at2 ∈ RQ' && typeof(at1)! = List then
19 │  │  │  │  │  │  remove at2 and its value from RQ';
20 │  │  │  │  │  else
21 │  │  │  │  │  │  remove one copy of values of the at2
   │  │  │  │  │  │  from ag2 from the values of at2 from
   │  │  │  │  │  │  RQ';
22 │  │  │  │  │  │  if the some value of the at2 from ag2
   │  │  │  │  │  │  does not exist in the values of at2 from
   │  │  │  │  │  │  RQ' then the value has no effect;
23 │  │  │  foreach PolicyId id ∈ ce.PolicyIDList && id ∉ pl do
24 │  │  │  │  obtain the context expression p of auxiliary
   │  │  │  │  policy id;
25 │  │  │  │  insert p into the end of APS;
26 │  │  │  break;
27 │  │  case "Unknown"
28 │  │  │  foreach AttrGroup ag1 ∈ ce.AttrGroupOne do
29 │  │  │  │  foreach Attribute at1 ∈ ag1 do
30 │  │  │  │  │  if at1 ∈ RQ' then  reset the value of at1 from
   │  │  │  │  │  RQ' to be NULL;
31 │  │  │  foreach AttrGroup ag2 ∈ ce.AttrGroupTwo do
32 │  │  │  │  foreach Attribute at2 ∈ ag2 do
33 │  │  │  │  │  if at2 ∈ RQ' then  reset the value of at2 from
   │  │  │  │  │  RQ' to be NULL;
34 │  │  │  foreach PolicyId id ∈ ce.PolicyIDList && id ∉ pl do
35 │  │  │  │  obtain the context expression p of auxiliary
   │  │  │  │  policy id;
36 │  │  │  │  insert p into the end of APS;
37 │  │  │  break;
38 │  │  case "False"
39 │  │  │  continue;
40 │  if ++i == g then exit;
41 return RQ'
```

Algorithm 1: Auxiliary PDP Function

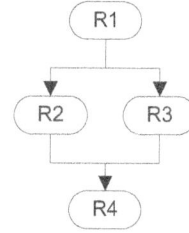

Figure 2: Role-Role assignments

The previous example also explains why we model collections using a list type which supports redundant values in the collections. Assume that we implemented the role attribute as a set and suppose that the role attribute value in a request context is [R1, R2, R3, R4]. If role R2 is deactivated by a session policy, R4 should be deactivated as well because R4 is a junior role assigned to R2. However, since R3 is still in the request context, R4 should be kept as well. We can clearly see that we must record additional information, e.g. paths to R4, to determine whether we should keep R4 after deactivating R2 in this set-based implementation. However, in our list-based implementation, we do not have this issue and we can simply deactivate R4 because there is exactly a copy of R4 in the collection resulting from R2. We still have another copy of R4 resulting from R3. It is obvious that the list-based implementation is more efficient.

Example. Role-role assignment, R4 to R2 in Fig. 2.

```
AuxPolicy ("P003",
  ApplyT ("contain",
    AttrQuery (AccessSubject, "ActivatedRole",
      None, None),
    ValueE (CollectionV [StringV "R2"])),
  [(AccessSubject,
    [("ActivatedRole", None, None, StringV "R4")])],
  [(AccessSubject,
    [("DeactivatedRole", None, None, StringV "R4")])],
  [...])
AuxPolicy ("P004",
  ApplyT ("contain",
    AttrQuery (AccessSubject, "DeactivatedRole",
      None, None),
    ValueE (CollectionV [StringV "R2"])),
  [(AccessSubject,
    [("DeactivatedRole", None, None, StringV "R4")])],
  [(AccessSubject,
    [("ActivatedRole", None, None, StringV "R4")])],
  [...])
```

The reader may wonder why we use two auxiliary policies to specify one role-to-role assignment. Indeed, the role-to-role assignment has two meanings: if R2 is activated, R4 should be activated (moving from the set of deactivated roles to the set of activated roles); if R2 is deactivated, R4 should be deactivated as well. Therefore, we need two policies for these two cases. It is worth noting that in this example we do not distinguish between assigned roles and activated roles because they are the same for the purpose of making access control decisions. If necessary, we can write auxiliary policies to make them different.

Example. Consider a session policy requiring that Role R2 only be deactivated in session "DataAnalysis". This policy is specified in xfACL as follows:

```
AuxPolicy ("P005",
  ApplyT ("match",
    AttrQuery (SessionSubject, "id", None, None),
    ValueE (StringV "DataAnalysis")),
  [(AccessSubject,
    [("DeactivatedRole", None, None, StringV "R2")])],
  [(AccessSubject,
```

69

```
[("ActivatedRole", None, None, StringV "R2")])],
["P004"])
```

The policy also indicates that it may affect another policy, that is, "P004".

When an abnormal situation arises, i.e. the ternary expression evaluates to Unknown, as mentioned in Section 6.1, the worst case preservation method is applied. The values of all affected attributes are reset to NULL, as shown in Line 28-33.

In both cases, i.e. "True" and "Unknown", of the value of the ternary expression, affected policy ids are provided to deal with cascading effects. These policies, retrieved based on their ids, are added to the end of the auxiliary policy list that is being evaluated if these policies have already been evaluated, as shown in Line 23-25 and Line 34-36. Thus, affected policies will be evaluated again. However, an important and negative effect resulting from cascading effects is that carelessly developed auxiliary policies may result in non-terminating evaluations. To mitigate this problem, we provide a simple solution in this paper based on an observation that there is an upper bound on the number of policies affected by each applicable policies in practice. The solution is based on a guard that is 1000 times larger than the number of auxiliary policies (Line 1) which, we believe, is large enough for most applications. In a different deployment, such a number may change if necessary. We record a counter for processed auxiliary policies. If the counter is larger than the guard, the processing of auxiliary policies is terminated, as shown in Line 40. Static policy analysis techniques may also be applied to address this problem which will be discussed future work. Since in practice we may safely assume that

- the upper bound on the number of attributes in any given request context is a constant, and
- the upper bound on the number of affected attributes in any auxiliary policies is a constant,

the complexity of Algorithm 1 is $O(n)$ assuming n to be the number of auxiliary policies.

7. RELATED WORK

Perhaps the closest work to xfACL is XACML. One major drawback in XACML 2.0, as indicated in our previous work [10], is the lack of informative access decisions. Some decision, such as Indeterministic, represents too many decisions including PD, PNA, DNA, and PDNA. Therefore, the decision aggregation in XACML in some cases may result in an information loss [10]. Such information loss in turn results in a wrong final decision. xfACL addresses this problem by directly supporting informative decisions and decision aggregation truth tables suggested by Ni et al. [10] in its authorization policies.

Another drawback in XACML is that it is difficult or impossible to specify RBAC specific policies. For instance, the XACML RBAC profile does not support session policies which can be described naturally by the auxiliary policies introduced by xfACL. The notion of context handler of XACML is mainly designed to assist PDP to retrieve necessary attribute values from PIP and resources. The corresponding components of xfACL are the processes running attribute query functions and content query functions. By contrast, xfACL deliberately extends the notion of request contexts, and is able to dynamically modify a request context based on auxiliary policies, and thus is able to meet needs well beyond standard RBAC specific policies. A good example is that xfACL is able to specify policies that can be expressed by some RBAC extensions. Temporal RBAC [1] and its generalized version GTRBAC [7] were proposed to deal with dynamic role activation/deactivation with temporal constraints. Such temporal constraints can be specified by xfACL auxiliary policies. The privacy-aware RBAC family of models [13, 12, 9] addresses the gap between privacy regulations and current RBAC models. Purposes, conditions, and obligations are introduced to specify fine-grained policies based on privacy regulations. Purposes can be specified as an operation attribute and conditions can be translated into ternary expressions in xfACL. Obligations will be supported in the future version of xfACL. Compared to xfACL, these proposals lack the advanced features of xfACL, e.g., flexible combination and error handling.

Flexible and error-tolerating access decision aggregation has been investigated by some recent work [2, 18, 10, 3]. Specifically, the authorization policy and policy decision aggregation functions are the direct application of results from [10]. A similar approach is also adopted in [3]. These proposals provide a solid foundation for xfACL taking the advantages of XACML decision aggregation methods while avoiding their drawbacks.

Risk-based access control is crucial when dealing with ad-hoc access requests in emergencies. A fuzzy inference-based approach was introduced by Ni et al. [11]. With the implementation of specific fuzzy inference functions in xfACL, e.g. membership function, and defuzzification functions, the language can be used to specify fuzzy inference rules and the authorization PDP can be used to generate the final fuzzy decisions.

The UCON models [17] focus on the continuous enforcement of usage policies on specific applications or products, e.g. playing copyright protected music files. Th obligation enforcement models suggested by UCON and P-RBAC [9] will complement the future version of xfACL with obligation support.

8. CONCLUSION

In this paper, we have proposed a novel access control language that combines the benefits of XACML and RBAC. The paper has discussed the language specification, its design objectives, and strategies.

We have implemented the standard functions, the authorization PDP function, and the auxiliary PDP function using Microsoft F Sharp 2010 and .NET 4 platform. The implemented PDP prototypes take request contexts and policies specified in xfACL specification and generate access control decisions.

As future work we plan to extend xfACL in the following directions: supporting obligations as function declarations; defining the semantics of obligation orchestrating functions and enforcing functions; developing static and dynamic policy analysis techniques; supporting user preferences and sticky policies [14]; supporting a script language to further extend xfACL functionality; providing a mechanism to limit (possibly dangerous) side effects in the policy evaluation; and supporting crypto-based access control policies.

9. ACKNOWLEDGMENTS

The work reported in this paper has been partially supported by the MURI award FA9550-08-1-0265 from the Air Force Office of Scientific Research.

10. REFERENCES

[1] E. Bertino, P. A. Bonatti, and E. Ferrari. Trbac: A temporal role-based access control model. *ACM Trans. Inf. Syst. Secur.*, 4(3):191–233, 2001.

[2] G. Bruns and M. Huth. Access-control policies via belnap logic: Effective and efficient composition and analysis. In *CSF*, pages 163–176. IEEE Computer Society, 2008.

[3] J. Crampton and M. Huth. An authorization framework resilient to policy evaluation failures. In D. Gritzalis, B. Preneel, and M. Theoharidou, editors, *ESORICS*, volume 6345 of *Lecture Notes in Computer Science*, pages 472–487. Springer, 2010.

[4] D. F. Ferraiolo, R. Sandhu, S. Gavrila, D. R. Kuhn, and R. Chandramouli. Proposed nist standard for role-based access control. *ACM Trans. Inf. Syst. Secur.*, 4(3):224–274, 2001.

[5] IBM. Tivoli Identity Manager. Available at http://www-01.ibm.com/software/tivoli/products/identity-mgr/.

[6] INRIA. The OCaml Language. Available at http://caml.inria.fr/.

[7] J. B. D. Joshi, E. Bertino, and A. Ghafoor. Temporal hierarchies and inheritance semantics for gtrbac. In *SACMAT '02: Proceedings of the seventh ACM symposium on Access control models and technologies*, pages 74–83, New York, NY, USA, 2002. ACM.

[8] T. Moses, editor. *eXtensible Access Control Markup Language (XACML) Version 2.0*. OASIS Open, Feb 2005.

[9] Q. Ni, E. Bertino, and J. Lobo. An obligation model bridging access control policies and privacy policies. In *SACMAT '08: Proceedings of the 13th ACM symposium on Access control models and technologies*, New York, NY, USA, 2008. ACM Press.

[10] Q. Ni, E. Bertino, and J. Lobo. D-algebra for composing access control policy decisions. In *ASIACCS '09: Proceedings of the 4th International Symposium on Information, Computer, and Communications Security*, pages 298–309, New York, NY, USA, 2009. ACM.

[11] Q. Ni, E. Bertino, and J. Lobo. Risk-based access control systems built on fuzzy inferences. In *ASIACCS '10: Proceedings of the 4th International Symposium on Information, Computer, and Communications Security*, pages 298–309, New York, NY, USA, 2010. ACM.

[12] Q. Ni, D. Lin, E. Bertino, and J. Lobo. Conditional privacy-aware role based access control. In *ESORICS '07: Proceedings of the 12th European Symposium On Research In Computer Security*, pages 72–89. Springer, 2007.

[13] Q. Ni, A. Trombetta, E. Bertino, and J. Lobo. Privcy aware role based access control. In *SACMAT '07: Proceedings of the 12th ACM symposium on Access control models and technologies*, New York, NY, USA, 2007. ACM Press.

[14] Q. Ni, S. Xu, E. Bertino, R. Sandhu, and W. Han. An access control language for a general provenance model. In *SDM '09: Proceedings of the 6th VLDB Workshop on Secure Data Management*, pages 68–88, Berlin, Heidelberg, 2009. Springer-Verlag.

[15] OASIS. eXtensible Access Control Markup Language (XACML) 2.0. Available at http://www.oasis-open.org/.

[16] Oracle. Identity Management. Available at http://www.oracle.com/us/products/middleware/identity-management/index.html.

[17] J. Park and R. S. Sandhu. The ucon$_{abc}$ usage control model. *ACM Trans. Inf. Syst. Secur.*, 7(1):128–174, 2004.

[18] P. Rao, D. Lin, E. Bertino, N. Li, and J. Lobo. An algebra for fine-grained integration of xacml policies. In B. Carminati and J. Joshi, editors, *SACMAT*, pages 63–72. ACM, 2009.

APPENDIX

A. STANDARD XFACL FUNCTIONS AND PDPS

As we can see from the design of xfACL, the expressiveness of xfACL depends on the functions supported by xfACL. We define a set of standard functions in xfACL and all implementations of xfACL should support these functions.

A.1 Standard Functions

xfACL supports four kinds of functions, as shown in the following.

- Attribute query functions: they take as input a request context and a desired attribute id as input and generate a normal expression.

- Normal functions: they take as input an expression list and generate a new expression. Typical examples are math functions and string functions.

- Ternary functions: they take as input two normal expressions and generate a ternary expression. Typical examples are the comparison functions of two attribute values.

- Decision functions: they take as input two decision expressions and generate a new decision expression.

There is only one standard attribute query function in the current version of xfACL: `attrQueryF`, which is defined and implemented as follows. The `attrQueryF` function recursively retrieves the values of a given attribute. Once a result is found, the result is added to the resulting collection. When all attributes are examined, the resulting expression is returned. xfACL supports several ternary functions for different types of values, e.g. numbers, strings, date and time, and collections.

- `matchF`: an equality test applied to all value types in xfACL, including lists.

- `containF`: a containment test applied to strings and lists.

- `lessthanF`: a relation test applied to numerical values.

xfACL also support several decision functions, as shown in the following.

- `permitOverridesF`: it returns a deny only if there is no permit decision. The function uses a decision truth table (e.g. Table 2) to generate the aggregated decision.

- `denyOverridesF`: it returns a permit only if there is no deny decision.

- `simpleVotingF`: it counts the number of permits and denies and returns the decision with the highest count number.

- `firstApplicableF`: it returns the first permit or deny decision given an authorization policy set.

- `onlyOneApplicableF`: it returns a decision only if there is only one applicable authorization policy.

A.2 Policy Decision Points

In the current version of xfACL, we support two kinds of decision points: authorization PDPs and auxiliary PDPs. An authorization PDP is implemented as a curry function AuthPdpF in xfACL. The function is defined as follows.

```
type AuthPdpF = decisionExprT -> contextExprT
    -> decisionExprT
```

Basically, a AuthPdpF takes an authorization policy set and a request context as input and generates an access decision. There are two major steps in the implementation of an authorization PDP function:

1. translation: it replaces the function identifiers in authorization policies with the corresponding xfACL functions, and translates these policy expressions into a new policy function;

2. execution: the policy function is executed on the request context and generates an access decision.

An auxiliary PDP is implemented as a curry function AuxPdpF in xfACL, and is defined as follows.

```
type AuxPdpF = contextExprT -> contextExprT
    -> contextExprT
```

Similarly, an AuxPdpF takes an auxiliary policy set and a request context as input and generates a new request context.

Rumpole: A Flexible Break-glass Access Control Model

Srdjan Marinovic
Department of Computing
Imperial College London, UK
srdjan@imperial.ac.uk

Robert Craven
Department of Computing
Imperial College London, UK
r.craven@imperial.ac.uk

Jiefei Ma
Department of Computing
Imperial College London, UK
j.ma@imperial.ac.uk

Naranker Dulay
Department of Computing
Imperial College London, UK
n.dulay@imperial.ac.uk

ABSTRACT

Access control operates under the assumption that it is possible to correctly encode and predict all subjects' needs and rights. However, in human-centric pervasive domains, such as health care, it is hard if not impossible to encode all emergencies and exceptions, but also to imagine *a priori* all the permissible requests. Break-glass is an approach that embodies the idea that under certain conditions it is possible for a subject to *break-the-glass* and explicitly override the denied request. Current break-glass models make this decision without considering and investigating what the reasons for issuing the denial are, and they have a fixed decision procedure to determine whether the override is permitted. Furthermore, they do not explicitly represent and reason over conflicting and missing information about subjects and the context; which in human-centric pervasive domains is a norm rather than an anomaly. This paper presents a novel break-glass model, Rumpole, that structures a break-glass policy by establishing why the access was denied. It uses Belnap's four-valued logic to represent conflicting and missing (unknown) information, allowing the policy to make a more informed decision when faced with missing or inconsistent knowledge. The model also provides a declarative query language that is used to specify an explicit break-glass decision procedure, rather than having an implicitly hard-coded one. This allows a policy writer to further condition and restrict when and how break-glass access is permitted.

Categories and Subject Descriptors

D.4.6 [**Operating Systems**]: Security and Protection

General Terms

Security, Languages, Theory

Keywords: access control, break-glass, emergency management, policy

1. INTRODUCTION

Computer systems often employ a security policy that governs which subjects, under which conditions, are permitted to use resources. The policy is often enforced through the access control model that uses a preventive protection strategy. A crucial assumption underlying the access control system is that the encoded security policy is complete and can anticipate and precisely formulate which subjects ought to be permitted to access a resource.

However, in domains where it is not possible to completely encode or anticipate who should be granted access under which conditions, this assumption can result in obstructing people in their tasks, thus creating more risk than it tried to prevent. Risannen et al. [20] refer to these situations as "not machine encodable". For example, precise encoding of an emergency may never be complete, yet it is necessary to allow some access in precisely those situations. Conversely, it may be well understood what an emergency is but not who ought to be permitted. The common access control approach to these situations is not to grant the access, thus preserving the confidentially and integrity of resources, but at the cost of restricting availability. Even adopting an *open* access control policy, where a subject is permitted unless explicitly denied, does not alleviate the problem. For example, a subject could be denied because there is no emergency (but this is incompletely encoded), or simply because it was not anticipated that the subject needs the access.

Break-glass access control has recently been proposed [19, 2] as a way to supplement traditional access control models in order to deal with these situations. The core idea of the approach is to allow the subject to override the access control decision, whilst imposing *obligatory* actions on the subject or the system itself. The main difference between standalone and break-glass policies is that the former encode the conditions for permitting access, while the latter encode the conditions under which overrides are permitted. The benefits of allowing overriding are established in pervasive computing domains such as emergency management [2] and health-care [11]—but even more traditional domains such as business applications are adopting break-glass concepts such as the Virsa Firefighter for SAP software [1].

An essential aspect of override permissions is comprehending why the denial was first issued. Clearly there is a difference between subjects' being explicitly *denied* and not being explicitly *permitted*. Equally, a subject may be typically permitted (e.g. has the right role or credentials) but a particular access will violate integrity constraints such as separation-of-duty. Current break-glass models do not attempt to represent precisely why the request was denied. This leaves the break-glass policy to be defined only in terms of contextual conditions without being able to constrain the break-glass overrides based on knowledge of the denial's causes.

Modality conflicts (where a subject is permitted and denied at the same time) commonly occur when making an access control decision and the access control model must employ a conflict-resolution strategy. But a *conflict* value can be useful to communicate to the break-glass policy, as it clearly shows that there is evidence to support both a permission and a denial. In a distributed system there could be many access decision points and their decisions could disagree (without any of them having internal conflict). However, when combining these decisions it is clear that the *conflict* value is needed to accurately determine the overall decision. There are also situations where the access control simply has too little information and it is unknown whether the subject is permitted or denied. In these situations some form of Closed World Assumption (CWA) is adopted, where the unknown value is assumed to be false, but *unknown* would be more useful. The need to evaluate a decision as *unknown* appears quite naturally in distributed scenarios where decision points can be unreachable. In pervasive systems these problems are even more acute as the decisions are based on sensor data (to establish the context) which can be conflicting or missing. Current break-glass approaches do not offer a framework to represent these different truth and knowledge levels and no way to define how such values are to be combined in order to reach a decision.

It is of vital importance to be able to constrain the overrides by imposing non-contextual conditions such as limit of overrides per subject or target, how much incomplete knowledge is allowed, the least number of available access decision points, etc. These fine-grained integrity constraints are not currently considered by break-glass models. Furthermore, current models have an implicit decision procedures which dictates how the break-glass decision is reached. A fixed decision procedure tells the PDP which break-glass policies, in which order, they are to be considered, thus the policy writer is forced to construct the break-glass policy according to this fixed decision procedure.

This paper presents a novel break-glass model, Rumpole, to be used as an extension of access control models. Rumpole's contributions are three. (1) It introduces notions of subjects' *competences* and *empowerments* to gain more insight into the causes for the access denial, (2) It uses Belnap's four-valued logic [6] to represent conflicting and incomplete information, and this logic underlies the semantics of rules used to encode how these facts are combined to evaluate how much is known about the subject and whether he may override. (3) The model has a declarative query language to specify a break-glass decision procedure, this allows a policy writer to condition and constrain the break-glass access permissions in a fine-grained manner by embedding integrity constraints into the decision procedure.

2. OVERVIEW OF RUMPOLE MODEL

This section provides an informal account of Rumpole model where a high-level break-glass policy is encoded using the following concepts:

- *Competences* – Encode whether a subject has necessary abilities to access the resource without causing harm to the resource or the system.

- *Empowerments* – Encode whether the necessary contextual conditions are met so that the access will not cause harm to the resource or the system.

- *Break-glass Rules* – Encode whether a subject is permitted or denied to override an access control denial based on what is known about his competences, empowerments and obligations that he has accepted or violated.

- *Resolution Query* – Encodes how the rules, and under what conditions, are consulted in order to reach an override decision.

2.1 Integration with Access Control Points

As indicated in the Introduction, Rumpole is not an extension of a particular access control model, such as presented in [12] for RBAC. This creates a clear separation of concerns between the two models and more importantly it allows the break-glass decision point to be able to consult different, and possibly distributed, access control knowledge bases. Figure 1 captures how this separation between the access control decision points (ACPs) and the break-glass decision point is organised. *PDP* represents a security policy decision point

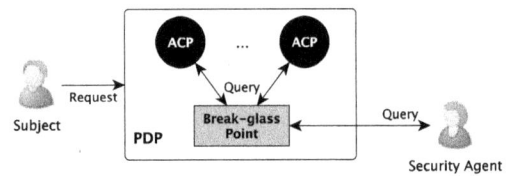

Figure 1: Integration of the break-glass decision point within a PDP

which consists of two types of decision points: access control points and a break-glass point. When the subject requests a particular access, the PDP will consult its access control point(s) to determine whether the access can be given. How their decisions are combined to reach a decision is independent of the break-glass policy. If the request is denied, the PDP will forward the request to the break-glass point to see if this decision can be overridden by the break-glass policy encoded through Rumpole. If the override can be given, the subject will be notified about the possible obligations that he will have to fulfil and asked to confirm that he accepts them. This *confirmation* interaction is not part of the model and is left to be enforced by the PDP implementation.

The *Query* abstraction represents the interaction between the break-glass point and an individual ACP, when a break-glass point attempts to determine why the denial was issued (we assume that the access control point can answer queries about the state of its knowledge base). Naturally, the question arises of what the query should contain, or how the denial should be represented. In this paper we propose that the denial is depicted by the concepts of competences and empowerments.

However, the break-glass point need not be reliant only on a set of access control points. We use the term *Security Agent* to refer to either human or computational agents who can testify for or against subjects' attributes. The reason why we explicitly separate an ACP and a security agent is that not all security agents are qualified to make an access control decision. This is especially prevalent in pervasive systems such as health care, where nurses can often supply security relevant information on the subjects or even make certain local security decisions.

2.2 Competence and Empowerment

Fundamentally, an access control model attempts to determine whether the subject requesting the access is permitted, given the context of the request. As put forward in Barker [4], all subjects are organised into categories (which could be roles, domains and so forth), and permissions hold between a subject's category and a requested action on a resource. Determining the *who* part of the permission means determining if the subject's category is sufficient for allowing the access, and the category inclusion can be contextually constrained.

On the other hand, the *contextual* conditions describe integrity constraints which are not part of the conditions that determine which category the subject falls into or which permissions a category has. Typical examples of these conditions represent separation-of-duty constraints, where a subject can *typically* access a resource but owing to his current open sessions or previous accesses cannot be permitted. Similarly, a particular access may not be allowed after working hours. Even though this condition could be encoded through the definition of a subject's categories, it is more naturally expressed as an integrity constraint.

It follows that the fundamental understanding of why the denial was issued lies in determining whether a subject's category (if it was assigned to any) has the necessary permissions and also whether such permissions broke any of the contextual constraints. We characterise these two aspects as: *(1) competence* and *(2) empowerment*.

The notion of competence subsumes the notion of *belonging to a permitted category* and attempts to capture whether the subject possesses abilities necessary for accessing the resource in a way that would not cause any undesired harm. For example, belonging to a *nurse* category implicitly carries the notion that the subject has the skills to perform certain nursing tasks on patients and should be given access to appropriate patient data. Competence could also be established by a set of certificates and credentials. However, the notion of competence does not have to be exclusively linked to a particular role, domain or credentials. Those attributes are used as *evidence* for a subject's competence. This can augmented by additional evidence that is not directly linked to a particular access control model. So, for example, a break-glass policy might say that after a certain number of reviewed and approved overrides a subject can be considered as competent.

The notion of *empowerment* subsumes these of resource-specific and contextually-specific integrity constraints, and captures whether the access should take place without considering whether some particular subject is competent to make it. For example, a subject, in a typical separation-of-duty constraint, may not be permitted to execute two workflow conflicting tasks, and this information could be used as evidence to support or diminish his empowerment. But much as is the case with competence, empowerment does not have to depend exclusively on integrity constraints.

From the given discussions, it follows that a minimal understanding of why a denial was issued can be obtained by using the access control knowledge base to provide evidence to support or disprove subjects' competences and empowerments. Thus having the necessary credentials can be used as positive evidence towards establishing competence, but breaking the integrity constraints is negative evidence for an empowerment. This kind of intimate understanding of the access control decision gives us a fine-grained way to structure break-glass policies.

Notice that apart from being *true* and *false*, both competences and empowerments can also be *unknown*. In other words, if the subject does not posses the necessary credentials it may be more appropriate to say that it is unknown whether it is competent rather than adopting the Closed World Assumption (CWA) and automatically assuming that it is not. On the other hand, not belonging to a particular category may be deemed as sufficient to establish that the subject is not competent. Clearly we need the additional *unknown* value to specify how the access control knowledge base is to be interpreted and used. Furthermore, if a particular distributed access control point, or a security agent, cannot be reached, then their knowledge should be evidently characterised as *unknown*.

Similarly, a subject may be deemed competent by one access control point and not competent by another. The appropriate value for the competence is therefore *conflict*. However, even locally some evidence may support a subject's competence (such as having the credentials) but other evidence such as broken obligations may go against it, resulting in the *conflict* value. A better understanding of whether a subject is competent and empowered can be achieved by expanding the truth-value space, rather than attempting to represent these attributes using the classical truth values of "true" and "false". Since there is a clear distinction between the four truth values of "true", "false", "conflict" and "unknown", they can be used to specify a more precise break-glass policy.

2.3 Break-glass Rules

Given what and how much is known about a subject's competences and empowerments, we need to specify how their truth values are to be combined in order to establish whether an override is permitted or not. The override decision can be further conditioned by the obligations that a subject has to agree upon or conditioned by contextual situations surrounding the request. These break-glass rules are split into two types: (1) permit rules and (2) deny rules.

Permit rules specify how much is known about whether an override is permitted. The meaning of the *true* value is that it is known that the subject is permitted. The *false* value indicates that it is known that the subject is not permitted. The *unknown* value tells the PDP that it cannot be established whether the override is permitted. Finally the *conflict* value indicates that there is evidence to support both cases. Hence, expanding the truth-value space is not only beneficial for reasoning about subjects' competences and empowerments but also for allowing a clear statement of what and how much is known about their override permissions as well.

Often it is needed to state more explicitly that a subject is denied an override, much like the integrity constraints are used in access control policies. We refer to these rules as deny rules. Strictly speaking it is not necessary to have deny rules: one may attempt to embed these constraints into permit rules and make sure that they are evaluated as false. This will, however, create complex rules that are hard to specify and manage. Not only can deny rules be used to create a less complex policy, they can also be used to give different semantic weight to denial constraints when considering them in conjunction with the permit rules. For example, in certain cases the *deny* may take precedence over the *permit* decision and similarly not permitted may be taken as stronger than not denied. This is addressed in more detail in Section 7.

2.4 Break-glass Resolution Query

A break-glass resolution query specifies how the break-glass decision point infers a binary override decision which either permits an override or not.

The resolution query specifies how to combine knowledge about whether the subject is permitted or denied. But it also allows us to define how much weight is given to each decision and how much knowledge is deemed sufficient in order to make a conclusive decision. For example, for some resources only full knowledge that the request is not explicitly denied may be required, but for more sensitive resources the request would have to be permitted as well. The resolution query thus gives a fine-grained way to specify whether to override access control based on understanding how much is known, how much is unknown, or in conflict.

Informally: the break-glass rules establish how much is known about whether the request is permitted or denied, and the resolution query then specifies how such information is used to instruct the PDP what to do.

3. BELNAP'S $\mathcal{FOUR}$ LOGIC

In [6] Belnap introduced a logic based on four different truth values: the *classical* values t (true) and f (false), and two additional ones, $\bot$, intuitively denoting lack of information (no knowledge), and $\top$, denoting inconsistency or conflict of information (*over*-knowledge). It is commonly referred to as the logic $\mathcal{FOUR}$. The main notion behind

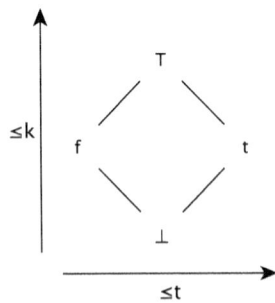

Figure 2: The Logic $\mathcal{FOUR}$ [6]

these truth values is to convey how much is known regarding the truth of a sentence, when the evidence is gathered from possibly multiple sources.

The truth values have two natural orderings (Figure 2). The first is the standard logical partial order $\leq_t$, which reflects differences in the *measure of truth* that every value represents. f is the least element, t is the greatest one, while $\top$ and $\bot$ are the intermediate values that are incomparable w.r.t. $\leq_t$. As Figure 2 indicates, these four values form a lattice with respect to the $\leq_t$ ordering. The finite meet and

join of this lattice, $\wedge$ and $\vee$ respectively, correspond to the classical truth operators. Negation is represented through an order reversing involution unary operator $\neg$, for which $\top = \neg\top$, $\bot = \neg\bot$. For the values t and f, the truth operators $\wedge$ and $\vee$ behave as in classical logic.

The second order, $\leq_k$, reflects the differences in the amount of knowledge or information that each truth value exhibits. Again the four values form a lattice such that $\top$ is the maximal element, $\bot$ is the minimal, and t and f are incomparable w.r.t. $\leq_k$. Fitting [13, 14] introduced symbols $\otimes$ and $\oplus$ to denote respectively the finite meet and join operations. The $\otimes$ can be seen as giving the most amount of information that the truth values can agree on, while the $\otimes$ can be seen as giving the most amount of information that can be derived. So for example $f \oplus t \equiv \top$, which fits into our intuitive notion that having supporting evidence for both the truth and falsity will give rise to a conflict. Similarly $\top \oplus A \equiv \top$ for all A, essentially says that once a conflict is established for a certain value adding any more information cannot change this. On the other hand $f \otimes t \equiv \bot$, which says that there is no information that is agreed upon. All binary operators are monotonic w.r.t both orderings (if $x_1 \leq_* y_1$ and $x_2 \leq_* y2$ then $x_1 \ op \ x_2 \leq_* y_1 \ op \ y_2$) but the negation operator is only monotonic w.r.t $\leq_k$ ordering.

The previously introduced idea that the break-glass policy (encoded in Rumpole) needs to differentiate whether a certain subject's property or a system state is known to be true or false, or unknown, or conflicting can be mapped to the Belnap truth values. So these truth values cover the sought-after truth space, while the Belnap operators provide the necessary connectives to describe how to combine various pieces of evidence.

4. LANGUAGE $\mathcal{L}_E$

The language $\mathcal{L}_E$ is used by Rumpole to encode rules that define how competences, empowerments and override permissions are determined. Every rule can be seen as a piece of evidence contributing towards this evaluation. The language $\mathcal{L}_E$ is a multi-sorted function-free language used for specifying correlations between Belnap predicates. It is defined over the $\mathcal{FOUR}$ truth values and we assume the usual logic programming notions of a term, literal, and a predicate. An atomic formula, or simply an atom, is an expression $p(t_1, ..., t_n)$ where p is a predicate of arity n and t_i is a term.

An interpretation I of a set of rules P is a function that to every ground atom from the Herbrand base of P assigns a Belnap truth value. Formulae of $\mathcal{L}_E$ are expressions build up from atoms using the introduced Belnap operators: $\neg$, $\wedge$, $\vee$, $\oplus$, $\otimes$, and constants $\{\top_\mathbf{4}, \bot_\mathbf{4}, t_\mathbf{4}, f_\mathbf{4}\}$.

DEFINITION 1. *The interpretation I is extended pointwise to Belnap formulae in the following manner:*

- $I(\top_4) = \top$ *and similarly for other constants as well.*

- $I(\neg\psi) = \neg I(\psi)$ *where ψ is an $\mathcal{L}_E$ formula.*

- $I(\psi \wedge \psi') = I(\psi) \wedge I(\psi')$ *where ψ and ψ' are $\mathcal{L}_E$ formulae, and similarly for operators: $\vee$, $\otimes$, and $\oplus$.*

$\mathcal{L}_E$ rules are split into two types, the unconditional and the conditional ones. In order to make the presentation of the semantics clearer, we shall first consider the unconditional rules and the semantics of the specification that only contains these rules; after that we shall expand the semantics to include the second type of rules as well.

DEFINITION 2. *An unconditional rule is an expression $A \Leftarrow \psi$, where A is an atom and ψ is a formula.*

An unconditional rule with a grounded atom as its head and a constant as its body is referred to as a fact.

The unconditional rule should intuitively be thought of as a rule of testimony that says that there is evidence for the atom A to have at minimum the truth value of ψ: in other words $I(A) \geq_k I(\psi)$ for every rule. Just as in the case for choosing an interpretation for the semantics of the normal logic programs, where the interpretation may be required to be minimal w.r.t. the number of true atoms, we would also like the interpretation I to be minimal in the amount of knowledge that it assigns. But it should also be supported in the sense that it assigns only as much knowledge as needed to satisfy all the rules. In order to construct this minimal and supported interpretation I, we will use a fixpoint operator T_P which maps an interpretation I onto interpretation I' in such a way that it applies the evidence rules over I to derive values for I'. We keep applying this operator in order to reach a fixpoint interpretation which we will show to be the minimal and supported interpretation that we are looking for.

The set of unconditional rules is first *grounded* and then with this grounded set of rules P a fixpoint operator T_P is associated, defined as:

$$T_P(I)(A) = \begin{cases} I(\psi_1 \oplus ... \oplus \psi_n) & \forall A \text{ where } A \Leftarrow \psi_i \in P \\ \bot & \neg \exists A \text{ where } A \Leftarrow \psi_i \in P \end{cases}$$

T_P maps an interpretation I onto interpretation I', such that for all A it holds that $I'(A) = T_P(I)(A)$. This defined operator is a modification of the operator that Fitting introduced in [13] where the ground atom A could appear in the head of exactly one ground rule. As these rules are used to formulate pieces of evidence for a particular attribute or property, they should be combined using $\oplus$ operator. The reason for this is that the intuitive meaning of the knowledge base's interpretation is that which assigns the least amount of knowledge such that all the rules are taken into account.

This way of combining the rules is in contrast to normal logic programs where the operator $\vee$ is used, and to further illustrate why we have chosen $\oplus$ instead of $\vee$ let us consider the set of rules P, $\{a \Leftarrow \top_4, a \Leftarrow \bot_4\}$. If the $\vee$ operator is used, $I_P(a) = t$, where the $\oplus$ will result in $I_P(a) = \top$. It seems counterintuitive that if we have evidence for a to suggest that it is both in conflict and unknown then the interpretation should convey that a is true.

Since all the Belnap operators are monotonic with respect to $\leq_k$ (and by structural induction all formulae ψ made out of these operators), it follows that the T_P is a *monotonic* operator, thus for any two interpretations it holds that:

$$I_1 \leq_k I_2 \Rightarrow T_P(I_1) \leq_k T_P(I_2)$$

Clearly this monotonicity does not extend the truth-ordering $\leq_t$ as negation is a non-monotonic operator with respect to truth-ordering. Furthermore Fitting has also established that the operator T_P is *(chain) continuous*, and for any chain of interpretations $I_1 \leq_k I_2 \leq ...$ it holds that:

$$T_P\left(\bigoplus_i I_i\right) = \bigoplus_i T_P(I_i)$$

By the Knaster-Tarski theorem the monotonic and continuous operator T_P [13, 14] has the least fixpoint $T_P{\uparrow}^\omega$ which can be constructed through:

$$I_P^0 \stackrel{def}{=} I_\bot$$
$$I_P^{n+1} \stackrel{def}{=} T_P(I_P^n)$$
$$...$$
$$T_P{\uparrow}^\omega \stackrel{def}{=} \bigoplus_{\alpha < \omega} I_P^\alpha$$

where $I_\bot$ represents an interpretation which assigns $\bot$ to every atom from P's Herbrand base. We follow Fitting and take this least fixpoint, $T_P{\uparrow}^\omega$ as a canonical interpretation for P's declarative semantics.

Given T_P's definition and its properties, T_P can be seen as accumulating knowledge by progressively using the given rules as evidence to establish the least amount of knowledge such that the head of every rule has as little knowledge as possible and still be $\geq_k$ than its $I(\psi)$. And the least fixpoint is *minimal* and *supported* as it requires no more information in order for its rules' heads to be $\geq_k$ than their bodies. Thus if the value of any A is lowered in the least fixpoint, some rule will have $A \not\geq_k I(\psi)$, meaning that this piece of evidence has effectively not been taken into account. If a set of $\mathcal{L}_E$ rules are taken as evidential rules for encoding competences, empowerments and break-glass rules, then the least fixpoint combines all the evidence for a particular attribute in such a way to maximise, as much as it has to, the amount of knowledge that can be established about these attributes.

Notice that the fixpoint is non-monotonic with respect to the truth ordering: adding more facts or rules to P may turn the truth value of some of its atoms from t to f or vice-versa.

As mentioned at the beginning of this subsection the T_P operator can be used over the set P of unconditional rules, and the reason why we refer to these rules as *unconditional* is that the T_P operator considers them unconditionally as pieces of evidence, since in every iteration every rule is used. But this presupposes that each piece of evidence should be used to establish the Belnap value of a rule's head. At first this may seem right, after all this is exactly how the normal logic program's clauses are used. But let us consider the following example: *A nurse is competent to do any action on any target at any time.* The policy writer may write the following rule:

$$competent(Sub, Act, Tar, T) \Leftarrow role(Sub, nurse)$$

This rule is deceptively simple and it can give rise to some potentially unwanted consequences. For example when f is assigned to $role(Sub, nurse)$, the Sub will be considered as not competent and similarly when $I(role(Sub, nurse)) = \top$, the fixpoint will tell us that the Sub has both evidence for and against her competence. Clearly this encoding is wrong since the intuitive notion of the example is to say that if the Sub is nurse, it is competent but it does not address what to conclude when the Sub is not a nurse.

The solution to this is to use the *role* condition as the rule's *applicability* condition; if it is true then other conditions are evaluated, otherwise the rule is skipped. In normal logic programs when clauses are used as low-level policies, there is no need to separate the conditions as they are conjoined with the $\wedge$ operator and they can entail the *true* value only when all conditions are *true*. This is no longer the case with the rules in Belnap logic: more values can be entailed and it must be clearly stated when these values should be entailed. To express these conditions we propose the following *applicability* operator:

$$I(\psi \ \textbf{if} \ \phi) = \begin{cases} I(\psi) & \text{if } I(\phi) = t, \\ \bot & \text{otherwise} \end{cases}$$

using which a condition rule is defined as:

DEFINITION 3. *A conditional rule of $\mathcal{L}_E$ is an expression of the form $A \Leftarrow \psi \ \textbf{if} \ \phi$.*

The intuition behind a conditional rule is that its formula ψ contributes to the value of the atom A if and only if $I(\phi) = t$, when this is the case we refer to the rule as being applicable. Unfortunately the applicability operator is non-monotonic with respect to $\leq_k$. This has two immediate consequences: (1) it cannot be expressed with the available operators (thus it cannot be expressed in Fitting's language [13]), and (2) it is no longer possible to guarantee that the least fixpoint $T_P\uparrow^\omega$ can be constructed. Clearly not having the *applicability* operator can limit the extent to which the policy language can be used; it is likely to be essential for expressing certain policies.

DEFINITION 4. *A set of conditional $\mathcal{L}_E$ rules P is hierarchically stratified in n strata as $P_1 \cup ... \cup P_n = P$, when the predicates in rules' heads in one stratum do not appear as heads in other strata, the predicates in ψ contain only those from the same stratum or a lower one, and the predicates in ϕ contain only predicates from the lower strata.*

Unconditional rules can always be treated as conditional rules by having t_4 as ϕ.

DEFINITION 5. *For a stratified set of $\mathcal{L}_E$ rules an iterated fixpoint interpretation I_P is defined as I_n:*

$$I_1 = T_{P_1}\uparrow^\omega$$
$$I_2 = T_{P_2 \cup I_1}\uparrow^\omega$$
$$...$$
$$I_n = T_{P_n \cup I_{n-1}}\uparrow^\omega$$

An interpretation I can be represented by a set of facts, where for every I's atom there is a conditional rule that has that atom as a head and the body has only a Belnap constant that corresponds to atom's value (given by I). The expression $P_{i+i} \cup I_i$ merges P_{i+1}'s rules with I_i's facts to create a knowledge base over which T_P is applied. We have to do this since T_P is not a progressive operator, and hence it cannot be guaranteed that for any starting interpretation I there exists the least fixpoint $T_P\uparrow^\omega(I)$.

PROPOSITION 1. *An iterated stratified interpretation I_P of a set of hierarchically stratified rules P is minimal (with respect to $\leq_k$ ordering) and supported.*

PROOF. The stratum P_1 contains only unconditional rules and thus I_1 is supported and a minimal interpretation. Adding I_1's facts to P_2 will essentially disable some conditional rules whose RHS of the applicability operator is not equal to t and this cannot change during the fixpoint construction. The immediate effect of this is that all the remaining rules can be treated as unconditional rules and T_{P_i} is thus monotonic and continuous. Hence I_2 is also supported and a minimal interpretation since the value of atoms in I_2 will not be changed by any higher strata. Therefore by induction the last interpretation I_n will also be supported and minimal. $\square$

In summary $\mathcal{L}_E$ represents a novel extension of the bi-lattice logic programming language introduced in [13] by adding a k-nonmonotonic operator **if** and defining a new stratified semantics for the fixpoint operator.

5. ENCODING A BREAK-GLASS POLICY

Rumpole encodes a break-glass policy in two parts:

(1) *Evidential rules* – These are encoded as $\mathcal{L}_E$ rules and are used to define how various pieces of information, that either attest or disprove subjects' and contextual attributes and conditions, are combined to establish how much is known about competences and empowerments. The $\mathcal{L}_E$ rules are also used to encode the break-glass rules that establish how much is known about whether the override is permitted or denied. The semantics of these rules is given by constructing the minimal interpretation for the rule set, as described in the previous section.

(2) *Resolution query* – The evidential rules construct an *evidence* base (defined by the constructed interpretation) that tells the PDP how much truth and knowledge has been established by them. Now, the PDP needs to be instructed what to do based on this evidential information. A resolution query is used for this purpose as it encodes how to combine the *permit* and *deny* information (and potentially other contextual information) in order to allow or deny the override. In order to be able to encode a fine-grained resolution query, we need to be able to constrain how much knowledge is needed for a particular predicate and which predicates are to be given more weight. This kind of expressivity is not directly encodable through the $\mathcal{L}_E$ rules. Accordingly we have designed a query language designed for constructing fine-grained queries over a Belnap interpretation.

This strategy of separating the knowledge base from the actual decision is inspired by the similar approach used in SecPAL [5].

5.1 Pre-defined Sorts and Predicate Sets

Evidential rules of any high-level break-glass policy have to use at least the following sorts. (1) A finite sort of subjects *Subject*; the variable *Sub* will be used (possibly with superscripts and subscripts) to represent members of this sort. (2) A finite sort of actions *Action*; the variable *Act* will be used (possibly with superscripts and subscripts) to represent members of this sort. (3) A finite sort of targets *Target*; the variable *Tar* will be used (possibly with superscripts and subscripts) to represent members from this sort.

The predicates used in the evidential policies are split into three disjoint sets $\mathcal{L}_E^{Core}$, $\mathcal{L}_E^{Obl}$, and $\mathcal{L}_E^{aux}$. The set $\mathcal{L}_E^{Core}$ contains the predicates *permit* (args *Subject* $\times$ *Target* $\times$ *Action*), *deny* (args *Subject* $\times$ *Target* $\times$ *Action*), *competent* (args *Subject* $\times$ *Target* $\times$ *Action*), and *empowered* (args *Subject* $\times$ *Target* $\times$ *Action*). These are used to represent competences and empowerments as well as the break-glass rules. The set $\mathcal{L}_E^{Obl}$ contains the following predicates:

1. *agreedObl* (args *Subject* $\times$ *Target* $\times$ *Action*) – used to denote whether the subject has agreed to perform the requested obligatory action on the designated target.

2. *violatedObl* (args *Subject* $\times$ *Target* $\times$ *Action*) – used to indicate that the specified obligation has been violated by the subject.

3. *fulfilledObl* (args *Subject* $\times$ *Target* $\times$ *Action*) – used to

indicate that the specified obligation has been fulfilled by the subject.

4. *activeObl* (args $Subject \times Target \times Action$) – used to denote that the given obligation is still active.

The set $\mathcal{L}_E^{aux}$ holds additional *auxiliary* predicates used for representing domain and access control policy specific properties.

6. EVIDENTIAL RULES

6.1 Competences and Empowerments

Rules defining competences and empowerments are used as pieces of evidence to contribute towards establishing subjects' competence or empowerment.

DEFINITION 6. *A competence/empowerment rule is a conditional rule that has a competent or empowered atom as its head and body atoms from* $\mathcal{L}_E^{Core} \cup \mathcal{L}_E^{Obl} \cup \mathcal{L}_E^{aux}$

The interpretation of Belnap truth values for these predicates is as follows:

- $[competent/empowered](Sub, Tar, Act) = t$ – It is known that Sub is competent/empowered to perform Act on Tar.

- $[competent/empowered](Sub, Tar, Act) = f$ – It is known that Sub is not competent/empowered to perform Act on Tar.

- $[competent/empowered](Sub, Tar, Act) = \bot$ – It is not known whether Sub is competent/empowered or not to perform Act on Tar.

- $[competent/empowered](Sub, Tar, Act) = \top$ – There is conflict between whether the Sub can be considered as competent/empowered to perform Act on Tar.

To illustrate how competence may be specified let us consider the following example: *A student is competent to assist a patient when the student's supervising nurse assigned that student to the patient.* One simple attempt could be:

$$competent(Sub, Patient, assist) \Leftarrow$$
$$assigned(nurse, Sub, Patient) \wedge student(Sub)$$

However, this states that the Sub is known not to be competent, i.e. $I(competent(Sub, Patient, assist) = f$, whenever the Sub does not hold the *student* role, i.e. $I(student(Sub)) = f$. This can result in a quite different decision over the override request from the intended, since the role atom contributes directly with its truth value towards establishing the competence's truth value. But formulating the rule as:

$$competent(Sub, Patient, assist) \Leftarrow$$
$$assigned(nurse, Sub, Patient) \textbf{ if } student(Sub)$$

is more appropriate as it is used only when the Sub holds the *student* role and otherwise the rule is not used.

Apart from specifying explicit competences and empowerment, these rules should be used to extract fine-grained reasons why the denial was issued in the first place. To illustrate this further we shall use the influential FAF access control model by Jajodia et al. [16]. The FAF model allows both positive and negative authorisations (*dercando* predicate) to be specified as well as integrity constraints (*error*

predicate). As mentioned, the notion of competence relates to authorisation based on the subject's inclusion in a particular role, or his place in a more general hierarchical domain. On the other hand, empowerments try to capture, not whether the subject has the necessary role, but whether such access can take place given the context. We can capture this analysis with the following rules:

$$competent(Sub, Tar, Act) \Leftarrow$$
$$dercando(Sub, Tar, +Act) \oplus \neg dercando(Sub, Tar, -Act)$$
$$empowered(Sub, Tar, Act) \Leftarrow \neg error(Sub, Tar, Act)$$

where $dercando(Sub, Tar, +Act)$ is a positive authorisation and $dercando(Sub, Tar, -Act)$ is a negative authorisation. Thus, the competence is gauged by combining the information about whether a positive and/or a negative authorisations were derivable. This leaves the *empowered* predicate to be used as a query about whether the integrity (i.e. contextual) constraints have been broken, in other words the *when* component of the access control decision. Thus these constraints can be used to tell the PDP whether restrictions, such as *separation-of-duty*, were broken. Other access control models such as GTRBAC [17] can be queried in the similar fashion. Depending on the complexity of an access control model additional $\mathcal{L}_E^{aux}$ predicates may be required to correctly capture competences and empowerments.

6.2 Break-glass Rules

Break-glass rules are represented as evidential rules defining how much is known about whether a subject is permitted or denied to override an access control denial.

DEFINITION 7. *A break-glass rule is a conditional rule that has permit or deny atom as its head and body atoms from the set* $\mathcal{L}_E^{Core} \cup \mathcal{L}_E^{aux} \cup \mathcal{L}_E^{Obl}$.

Intuitively the *permit* predicate is used to provide evidence to support the override whereas the *deny* policy represents the evidence to support the denial of the override. Their meaning is as follows:

- $[permit/deny](Sub, Tar, Act) = t$ – It is known that Sub is permitted/denied to override the access denial for Act on Tar.

- $[permit/deny](Sub, Tar, Act) = f$ – It is known that Sub is not permitted/denied to override the access denial for Act on Tar.

- $[permit/deny](Sub, Tar, Act) = \bot$ – It is not known whether Sub is permitted/denied to override the access denial for Act on Tar.

- $[permit/deny](Sub, Tar, Act) = \top$ – There is conflict of evidence between whether the Sub is permitted/denied the override.

For example: *a subject is permitted to override and append to a file only when it is competent to read it and has agreed to provide the reason for this.* This example can be captured in the following way:

$$permit(Sub, file, append) \Leftarrow competent(Sub, file, read)$$
$$\textbf{if } agreedObl(Sub, log, giveReason)$$

Notice that when the Sub is not competent this rule will result in the interpretation saying that Sub is not permitted which corresponds to the *only* condition in the wording of the policy. A slightly different example may say that an override is permitted for any access if the subject is known to be competent or if there is conflicting information about his competence, and he has not broken any obligations:

$$permit(Sub, Tar, Act) \Leftarrow competent(Sub, Tar, Act) \otimes t_4$$
$$\textbf{if } \neg violatedObl(Sub, Tar_2, Act_2)$$

The difference between this example and the previous one is that this example does not use competence as a way to dispute the override permission.

However, as has been discussed, we may need to provide some safeguards to constrain overrides and not expose resources to higher risks. The following examples capture some of these concerns: *A subject is not allowed to override when he exceeds the override limit*, and *during night shifts no overriding can take place if the subject is not empowered*:

$$deny(Sub, Tar, Act) \Leftarrow t_4$$
$$\textbf{if } overrideCount(Sub, N) \wedge exceededLimit(Sub, N)$$
$$deny(Sub, Tar, Act) \Leftarrow \neg empowered(Sub, Tar, Act)$$
$$\textbf{if } currentTime(T) \wedge nightShift(T)$$

These constraints are used to prevent potential abuse and also to limit overrides when needed. For example, during night shifts, there are fewer doctors present and thus potential emergencies caused by inappropriate overrides need to be kept to a minimum. These policies are used to encode evidence about a particular override request, and they are not supposed to be used as instructions for the PDP. Thus simply having encoded the break-glass policy is not enough to let the PDP make the decision over a certain request.

6.3 Evidence base

Previous subsections have shown how $\mathcal{L}_E$'s rules are used to encode evidence to represent a subject's attributes and to encode how much is known about whether a request is permitted or denied.

DEFINITION 8. *An evidence base EB of a high-level break-glass policy is a set of locally stratified (see Def. 4) $\mathcal{L}_E$ rules, where all rules that have permit, deny, competent, empowered are as in Definitions 6 and 7.*

PROPOSITION 2. *An evidence base has a minimal (with respect to $\leq_k$ ordering) supported interpretation.*

PROOF. Follows directly from Proposition 1. □

We take the iterated stratified fixpoint of the evidence base, I_{EB}, as its intended semantic interpretation.

7. BREAK-GLASS RESOLUTION QUERY

Given a break-glass policy and its interpretation I_{EB}, Rumpole needs to enforce an override decision for a request (s, t, a) where $s \in Subject$, $t \in Target$, and $a \in Action$. Before we define how the decision is reached, we first define an access control query over the I_{EB} of an encoded break-glass policy.

DEFINITION 9. *A break-glass resolution query Ω is defined as:*

$$\Omega ::= \phi \mid \Omega \wedge \Omega \mid \Omega \vee \Omega \mid \Omega \sqsupset_t \Omega \mid \Omega \sqsupset_f \Omega$$
$$\phi ::= b \mid p(x_1, ..., x_n) \mid \neg \phi \mid \phi \; op \; \phi$$

where $p(x_1, ... x_n)$ is a ground atom, $b \in \{t, f, \top, \bot\}$, and $op \in \{\wedge, \vee, \oplus, \otimes, \textbf{\textit{if}}\}$.

DEFINITION 10. *A break-glass resolution query Ω is satisfied by an I_{EB} for a request (s, t, a), written as $I_{EB} \models \Omega$, as specified by the structural induction (where $* \in \{t, k\}$ and $** \in \{t, f\}$):*

- $I_{EB} \models \phi_1 \; op \; \phi_2$ iff $I_{EB}(\phi_1) \; op \; I_{EB}(\phi_2)$, where $op \in \{=, \neq, \leq_*, \nleq_*\}$.

- $I_{EB} \models \Omega_1 \wedge \Omega_2$ iff $I_{EB} \models \Omega_1$ and $I_{EB} \models \Omega_2$

- $I_{EB} \models \Omega_1 \vee \Omega_2$ iff $I_{EB} \models \Omega_1$ or $I_{EB} \models \Omega_2$

- $I_{EB} \models \Omega_1 \sqsupset_{**} \Omega_2$ iff $I_{EB} \models \Omega_1 \sqsupset_{**} I_{EB} \models \Omega_2$

We have introduced the $\sqsupset_{[t/f]}$ operator as part of the query. This operator will be used to hierarchically structure subqueries within the resolution query. Its semantic evaluation over the I_{EB} is defined as:

$$I_{EB} \models \Omega_1 \; \sqsupset_t \; I_{EB} \models \Omega_2 \stackrel{def}{=} \begin{cases} true & \text{if } I_{EB} \models \Omega_1 \\ I_{EB} \models \Omega_2 & \text{otherwise} \end{cases}$$

$$I_{EB} \models \Omega_1 \; \sqsupset_f \; I_{EB} \models \Omega_2 \stackrel{def}{=} \begin{cases} false & \text{if } I_{EB} \models \Omega_1 \\ I_{EB} \models \Omega_2 & \text{otherwise} \end{cases}$$

Informally, the operator $\sqsupset_t$ says if the LHS formula is *true* then the whole expression is *true*, otherwise the truth value is determined by the RHS formula. The operator $\sqsupset_f$ says if the LHS is *true* then the whole expression is *false*, otherwise the truth value is determined by the RHS formula.

A PDP can only make a decision on whether to allow an override if it has a query to evaluate on a knowledge base. Therefore we define an encoded break-glass policy as:

DEFINITION 11. *An encoded break-glass policy is a tuple $\langle I_{EB}, \Omega \rangle$, where I_{EB} is the evidence base of the break-glass policy and Ω is the break-glass resolution query.*

DEFINITION 12. *A PDP will allow an override for the request (s, t, a) according to the encoded break-glass policy $\langle I_{EB}, \Omega \rangle$, iff $I_{EB} \models \Omega$ for the given s, t and a.*

The query can return only the two classical truth values *true* and *false*, and as the query is a propositional sentence it is decidable. To illustrate how a simple query can be constructed consider the following example:

$$\Omega_{conservative} \stackrel{def}{=} (permit(s, t, a) = t \wedge deny(s, t, a) = f)$$

where s, t and a are placeholders for the corresponding values grounded by the request. This can be considered as a conservative query as it allows an override only when it is known that the override is permitted and when it is known that it is not denied. We refer to it as a conservative query because it requires the knowledge to be fully established as known in both cases. Thus if a permission atom is unknown or in conflict the override will be denied.

A more tolerant query may allow an override as long as there is some evidence to support the override and no evidence to imply the denial in the following fashion:

$$\Omega_{tolerant} \stackrel{def}{=} (permit(s, t, a) \geq_t \top) \wedge (deny(s, t, a) \leq_t \bot)$$

The last example underlines that an essential part of a resolution query is stating how to treat conflicting and unknown

	permit	deny
Strong resolution conflict	t	t
Weak resolution conflict	$\top, \bot$	t
	t	$\top, \bot$
Strong resolution gap	f	f
Weak resolution gap	f	$\top, \bot$
	$\top, \bot$	f
Strong resolution incompleteness	$\bot$	$\bot$
Weak resolution incompleteness	$\top$	$\bot$
	$\bot$	$\top$

Table 1: Conflicts, Gaps and Incompletenesses

information in order to make an override decision. Clearly modality conflicts can occur when it is known that the request is both permitted and denied. However the expanded truth-space introduces additional situations which can occur when evaluating break-glass rules which are summarised in Table 1. The resolution gap represents a situation where it is known (fully or partially) that the request is neither permitted or denied. Resolution incompleteness occurs when it is not possible to reach a clear understanding of whether the request is permitted or denied. Thus, a resolution query can distinguish between these situations and potentially make a more cautious decision based on available or unavailable knowledge. For example in case of conflicting or unknown evaluations, the policy may decide to trust the subject and allow the request if the subject agrees to leave a fingerprint:

$$\Omega_{lax} \overset{def}{=} (permit(s,t,a) \geq_t \top) \wedge (deny(s,t,a) \leq_t \bot) \sqsupset_t$$
$$(deny(s,t,a) <_t t) \wedge agreedObl(s, fingerPrint, take)$$

Intuitively, the Ω_{lax} query allows an override if there is some evidence that it is permitted and it is known that it is not denied. If the first sub-query does not allow it, then the user can leave a fingerprint and still be allowed to override provided that at least it is known he is not denied.

However, the Ω_{lax} query may be seen as too risky when the override involves sensitive resources. The query can easily be restricted to address this issue in the following manner:

$$\Omega_{restricted\text{-}lax} \overset{def}{=}$$
$$(permit(s,t,a) \geq_t \top) \wedge (deny(s,t,a) \leq_t \bot) \sqsupset_t$$
$$(sensitive(t) \geq_t \top) \sqsupset_f$$
$$(deny(s,t,a) \leq_t t) \wedge agreedObl(s, fingerPrint, give)$$

Here the query evaluation is stopped if the target is a sensitive resource and the user has not been allowed an override before reaching this point. This results in the query only using the risky override for non-sensitive resources.

8. RELATED WORK

One of the earliest arguments for a break-glass concept was formulated by Povey [19], where it was argued that there will always be an expressiveness gap between what can be encoded and what the needs of an organisation are. The author introduced partially-formed transactions, whose effects can be *rolled-back*, and the core idea was to allow users to perform these transactions even if they do not have the permission but are willing to acknowledge that they are aware of this fact. Risannen et al. [20] have similarly argued that all requests cannot be anticipated and that many conditions are not completely encodable. Their model provides

the predicate *can* which permits the requestor to override a denied decision, but this has to be authorised and the model determines who this should be. Rumpole does not address this issue. The Break-glass concept has been introduced into the Role-based Access Control (RBAC) model within a medical information system [12, 11] where a user is permitted to override any access as long as he acknowledges the override. Brucker et al. [8] presented a generic break-glass model where subjects are permitted to override specific access control permissions. The access control policy consists of a partially ordered set of permissions; to each permission, override permissions are attached. These are enabled by activating pre-defined emergency levels. Ardagna et al. [3] present a break-glass model where the policies are separated into different categories starting with the access control policies, emergency policies and a break-glass policy. Unless the access is explicitly denied, it can be obtained by either finding an applicable emergency policy with obligations or, if that is not successful, the override is granted if the system is in some emergency state and the supervisor can be notified about the override.

These break-glass models hard-code the break-glass resolution procedure into the model itself rather than, as with Rumpole, expressing it as a declarative rule over the causes for the denied access, which can be varied from policy to policy. Thus a policy writer has to frame a break-policy according to a particular model's break-glass procedure which in turn can limit the expressivity of the intended break-glass policy. For example in Risannen et al.'s work, the policy cannot explicitly define override constraints, while Brucker et al.'s work relies on a predefined set of break-glass policies and emergencies and unless the emergency is activated, no override is permitted. In Ardagna et al.'s work explicit access control denials can never be overridden, and the override depends on correctly encoding and identifying emergency situations. In contrast our work attempts to structure the break-glass policy based on understanding which access control conditions were broken, thus avoiding explicit idea of an "emergency" state; furthermore Rumpole takes advantage of reasoning over unknown and contradictory knowledge to permit an override even if it is unknown or contradictory that there is an emergency. Similarly, in situations where if it is known that the subject does not have an override permission, one can still be given if the subject has not broken any prior obligations and if the override will not break any integrity constraints. This declarative way of expressing a break-glass policy empowers the policy writer to represent a more expressive break-glass policy that is not tied into any particular break-glass procedure. Rumpole can also encode the implicit break-glass resolution procedures present in all surveyed break-glass models.

Obligations in access control have an established presence [18, 7, 15]. These models augment an access control policy with obligations and are thus aimed at formulating extended access control policies rather than break-glass policies. The obligation models in these languages are more expressive than the obligations in this paper and we plan to explore how the break-glass obligations can be made more expressive by using these proposed solutions.

Bruns and Huth presented a policy language PBel [21, 9] which is also based on Belnap logic. PBel has a number of operators that are used to construct a policy as a composition of sub-policies. PBel's operators are syntactic constructs over Belnap operators and an additional operator $a \supset b$. This additional operator can be encoded as: $(b \text{ if } a \otimes t_4) \oplus (t_4 \text{ if } \neg(a \oplus f_4))$. Hence $\mathcal{L}_E$ could express PBel's operators if multiple **if** operators were used within a rule, which would not alter the presented stratified semantics in any way. PBel does not support policy variables, and it cannot express recursive policy definitions.

9. CONCLUSION AND FUTURE WORK

This paper presents a novel break-glass model, Rumpole, that takes a different approach to structuring a break-glass policy which is based on identifying causes for the denial, rather than on a set of emergencies or explicit override permissions. Rumpole uses a logic programming language defined over Belnap logic to explicitly reason about unknown and conflicting information. This reasoning over different amounts of knowledge, coupled with explicit override constraints, provides a flexible and generic break-glass model.

Our *proof-of-concept* implementation implements the T_P operator over grounded rules. Although the construction of the evidence base is polynomial with respect to the size of the rule base, this is not scalable as the grounding process can generate an exponential number of grounded instances. Also the *bottom-up* construction creates the whole evidence base whenever a new fact is inserted. To overcome these issues, we have a procedure which translates $\mathcal{L}_e$'s rules into a stratified Datalog program [10]. Proofs of soundness and completeness are forthcoming. The Datalog encoding can then take advantage of top-down polynomial resolution procedures to infer atoms' truth values. As mentioned in the paper, the current query resolution does not support variables in the query which is something that we are currently expanding the query semantics with. The queries will be then translated into a Datalog fragment as well.

Having multiple **if** operators in an $\mathcal{L}_E$ rule allows it to have any PBel [9] policy-composition expression as its body. Similarly we are looking into translating certain fragments of D-Algebra (specifically its P-Interpretation) [22] into a set of $\mathcal{L}_E$ rules. Thus we attempt to investigate to what extent $\mathcal{L}_E$ can be used as a general access control policy language.

10. ACKNOWLEDGMENTS

We thank the reviewers for their comments and suggestions. Marinovic and Dulay's research was supported by EU FP7 research grant 213339 (ALLOW). Craven and Ma's research was supported by the International Technology Alliance, sponsored by the U.S. Army Research Laboratory and the U.K. Ministry of Defence.

11. REFERENCES

[1] Virsa firefighter for sap, http://www.sap.com/uk/solutions/solutionextensions/virsa/index.epx.

[2] Break-glass: An approach to granting emergency access to healthcare systems. *White Paper, Joint NEMA/COCIR/JIRA Security and Privacy Committee (SPC)*, 2004.

[3] C. A. Ardagna, S. D. C. di Vimercati, S. Foresti, T. W. Grandison, S. Jajodia, and P. Samarati. Access control for smarter healthcare using policy spaces. *Computers & Security*, 29(8):848 – 858, 2010.

[4] S. Barker. The next 700 access control models or a unifying meta-model? In *SACMAT '09*, pages 187–196, 2009.

[5] M. Y. Becker, C. Fournet, and A. D. Gordon. Secpal: Design and semantics of a decentralized authorization language. *J. Comput. Secur.*, 18:619–665, 2010.

[6] N. D. Belnap. A useful four-valued logic. *Modern Uses of Multiple-Valued Logics*, pages 8–37, 1977.

[7] C. Bettini, S. Jajodia, X. S. Wang, and D. Wijesekera. Provisions and obligations in policy management and security applications. In *VLDB '02*, pages 502–513, 2002.

[8] A. D. Brucker and H. Petritsch. Extending access control models with break-glass. In *SACMAT '09*, pages 197–206, 2009.

[9] G. Bruns and M. Huth. Access-control policies via belnap logic: Effective and efficient composition and analysis. In *CSF '08*, pages 163–176, June 2008.

[10] S. Ceri, G. Gottlob, and L. Tanca. What you always wanted to know about datalog (and never dared to ask). *Knowledge and Data Engineering, IEEE Transactions on*, 1(1):146–166, Mar 1989.

[11] A. Ferreira, D. Chadwick, P. Farinha, R. Correia, G. Zao, R. Chilro, and L. Antunes. How to securely break into rbac: The btg-rbac model. In *ACSAC '09. Annual*, pages 23 –31, 2009.

[12] A. Ferreira, R. Cruz-Correia, L. Antunes, P. Farinha, E. Oliveira-Palhares, D. W. Chadwick, and A. Costa-Pereira. How to break access control in a controlled manner. In *CBMS '06*, pages 847–854, 2006.

[13] M. Fitting. Bilattices and the semantics of logic programming. *J. Log. Program.*, 11(2):91–116, 1991.

[14] M. Fitting. Fixpoint semantics for logic programming a survey. *Theoretical Computer Science*, 278(1-2):25 – 51, 2002.

[15] K. Irwin, T. Yu, and W. H. Winsborough. On the modeling and analysis of obligations. In *CCS '06*, pages 134–143, 2006.

[16] S. Jajodia, P. Samarati, M. L. Sapino, and V. S. Subrahmanian. Flexible support for multiple access control policies. *ACM Trans. Database Syst.*, 26(2):214–260, 2001.

[17] J. B. D. Joshi, E. Bertino, U. Latif, and A. Ghafoor. A generalized temporal role-based access control model. *IEEE Trans. on Knowl. and Data Eng.*, 17:4–23, January 2005.

[18] Q. Ni, E. Bertino, and J. Lobo. An obligation model bridging access control policies and privacy policies. In *SACMAT '08*, pages 133–142, 2008.

[19] D. Povey. Optimistic security: a new access control paradigm. In *NSPW '99*, pages 40–45, 2000.

[20] E. Rissanen, B. S. Firozabadi, and M. J. Sergot. Discretionary overriding of access control in the privilege calculus. In *Formal Aspects in Security and Trust*, pages 219–232, 2004.

[21] G. Bruns, D. S. Dantas, and M. Huth. A simple and expressive semantic framework for policy composition in access control. In *FMSE '07*, pages 12–21, 2007.

[22] Q. Ni, E. Bertino, and J. Lobo. D-algebra for composing access control policy decisions. In *ASIACCS '09*, pages 298–309, 2009.

SEAL: A Logic Programming Framework for Specifying and Verifying Access Control Models

Prasad Naldurg
Microsoft Research India
Bangalore, India
prasadn@microsoft.com

Raghavendra K. R.
Indian Institute of Science
Bangalore, India
raghavendra.kaundinya@gmail.com

ABSTRACT

We present SEAL, a language for specification and analysis of safety properties for label-based access control systems. A SEAL program represents a possibly infinite-state non-deterministic transition system describing the dynamic behavior of entities and their relevant access control operations. The features of our language are derived directly from the need to model new access control features arising from state-of-the art models in Windows 7, Asbestos, HiStar and others. We show that the reachability problem for this class of models is undecidable even for simple SEAL programs, but a bounded model-checking algorithm is able to validate interesting properties and discover relevant attacks.

Categories and Subject Descriptors

D.4.6 [**Operating Systems**]: Security and Protection—*access controls, verification*

General Terms

Security, Verification

Keywords

access control, label-based access, Windows 7, attacks, bounded model checking, logic programs

1. INTRODUCTION

The question of safety in access control was first studied in the 70s in the context of the HRU and Graham-Denning [13, 11] models, based on the access-control matrix abstraction due to Lampson [16]. The general safety question in this context, which formalizes the notion of authorized access was shown to be undecidable.

In practice however, there are restricted models for which safety is decidable [15, 5], and it can be shown that correct enforcement of authorized access requests preserves safety, using a reference monitor (RM) which mediates all accesses.

In most commercial and open-source operating systems, such as Windows 7 and different flavors of Linux, a modified discretionary access-control (DAC) model is implemented using this idea. The concept of ownership is used to define authorized access, which determines the ability to change permissions to resources. RMs mediate all requests from processes to resources and control access based on the instantaneous values in a virtual access matrix that captures the ownership relation. This automatically enforces safety, even though general safety properties require history for correctness. Since ownership implies authorization in these models, this notion is frequently exploited by attackers (e.g., using buffer overflow attacks to get "root-user" access), thereby making safety guarantees provided by enforcement using RMs meaningless.

In a bid to work around this weakness, in recent years, there is a growing interest in applying what we call label-based access control (LBAC) models to provide stronger confidentiality and integrity guarantees. Windows Vista and Windows 7 are the first commercial operating systems that use integrity labels to minimize the damage that can be caused by a compromised process running on behalf of an authenticated user. Windows' LBAC is called UAC (User Account Control). In UAC, applications can run only with low integrity levels by default, and cannot access trusted resources which are tagged with higher-integrity labels when compromised. Other examples of LBAC include SELinux[14] and IFEDAC[18], as well as Asbestos and Hi-Star [21, 22]. In all these models, customizable confidentiality or integrity labels are used to taint processes and resources that access sensitive data, thereby preventing them from being accessed or modified by processes with lower labels. Ownership-based discretionary access control is also allowed in these models.

LBAC models are inspired by the pioneering works on Multi-level Security (MLS) systems, exemplified by the Bell-LaPadula [3] and Biba [4] models, but differ from them in one crucial aspect. In traditional MLS models, labels assigned to processes and resources are immutable (fixed), and strong safety properties can be enforced by RMs that only need to compare the labels of processes and resources on access. A security lattice [12] of labels is defined, which imposes a partial-order on how information is allowed to flow between processes and resources, e.g., by disallowing write-ups in the lattice for integrity protection and preventing read-ups for confidentiality. However, immutable labels are not very useful in commercial operating systems [17]. Controlled and selective downgrading or upgrading of labels is required, to satisfy everyday information flow requirements, such as installing web applications. The safety question in this context is whether a high process can access a low resource (confidentiality violation), or whether a low process can write to a high resource (integrity violation). Once the labels are allowed to change, safety cannot be enforced by instantaneous lookup using an RM, without maintaining auxiliary information about the value of the label. History, e.g., as taint information, needs to be stored along with a process or resource's current label.

We present SEAL, a language for modeling and analyzing safety properties in LBAC systems. Using SEAL we can model the system state as the set of relevant access control relations. Transitions are events that change labels and create new associations or entries in these relations. A SEAL program induces a possibly infinite state non-deterministic transition system over these sets of relations. The safety problem (or really its negation) can be viewed as a reachability property in this system. We show that analyzing this property is undecidable even in a very restricted fragment of SEAL. This is in contrast to other models of access control, where even though the general case turns out to undecidable, we admit decidable fragments that are expressive enough for practical systems.

The syntax of SEAL resembles Datalog [6] or logic programming closely. In terms of semantics however, typical Datalog programs are interpreted over a given (closed) set of relations. SEAL programs, on the other hand, can be thought of as specifying dynamic state-transition systems on sets of relations.

Access control problems have been specified using logic programs in the past [1, 2, 19]. In these works, the mechanism of access control is expressed using an appropriate language, i.e., constraint logic programming (CLP) or safe stratified Datalog respectively. Given an access request, and a database instance, logic specialization is used to answer the query correctly and efficiently. The declarative aspect of these programs also adds flexibility in terms of allowing one to change access control mechanisms with little overhead. Given the state of the system and an access query, one can use these frameworks to tell whether the access is authorized or not.

In contrast, we examine the problem of verifying if a dynamic access control model admits unsafe behavior. More precisely, a SEAL LBAC specification is declared secure when no unauthorized accesses are possible, assuming that the system starts from a valid state and evolves adhering to the behavior given in the specification. The difference between the two approaches can be expressed as examining the satisfiability aspect of safety in abstract models, in contrast to verifying the validity of queries in a model instance.

SEAL is related to EON [8], a language for expressing dynamic access control systems where the *base relations* of an EON program are unary. This restriction is not natural in generalized LBAC systems, since it does not capture concepts such as binding resources to their named entities (e.g., link files), or in expressing the exact semantics of label associations. We show that extending EON with even one binary predicate makes the query reachability question undecidable.

For verification in SEAL, we propose an algorithm that systematically explores all possible states in the model, for a given depth, as in bounded model checking [10, 9], and validates if the property can be proved in the expansion. If

a counter-example is found, a finite state representation of this attack is automatically generated, and a corresponding RM can be built to track the history of states and transitions to enforce the property. The monitor will track changes to the state of the system and warn users before an unsafe state is imminent. If the property cannot be disproved in the bounded model, no safety guarantees can be asserted in general. However, bounded depth guarantees from the model can still carry over in natural use-cases in implementations appropriately.

We show how SEAL can be used to model state-of-the-art LBAC systems and models, including Windows 7, HiStar, and Asbestos. We present examples of vulnerabilities, including the UAC prompt elevation in the start menu, as well as the silent elevation-list vulnerability that were discovered by our bounded state-space exploration. These examples cannot be modeled by EON. For Asbestos, we show the absence of secrecy violations in bounded contexts for general safety properties. Finally we also discuss some limitations of SEAL, especially in the context of IFEDAC [18].

The rest of the paper is organized as follows: In Section 2 we introduce SEAL and present its syntax and operational semantics formally, and explain it informally with a relevant example. Section 3 explores the Windows 7 LBAC model and motivates the features of SEAL. Section 4 examines the query reachability problem in SEAL, and includes a brief description of our bounded state-space exploration algorithm. This is followed by our case studies in Section 5, where we highlight vulnerabilities found in Windows 7 as well as discuss its applicability to Asbestos and IFEDAC. Finally, we summarize our work in Section 6 and conclude with some pointers to future work.

2. SEAL LANGUAGE

In this section, we present the formal syntax and semantics of our logic programming language SEAL. SEAL uses a relational model to formulate the access control problem, i.e., every state of the modeled access control system is viewed as a set of relevant relations that are used to define the mechanism of access. To illustrate, the state $\{Process(a), File(b), Own(b, a)\}$, represents a model with one process a, and one file b whose owner is a. Note that at any instance (or snapshot), the relations have only a finite number of tuples.

2.1 SEAL Syntax

A SEAL program consists of three sections: a static part, a dynamic part and queries. The static part of a SEAL program encodes how the access relations can be constructed (or derived) from the base relations, capturing dependencies among the base relations appropriately. The dynamic part is the heart of SEAL and consists of a list of customized rules that specify how the base relations can be updated, under what conditions (if any).

The static part of a SEAL program P is identical in syntax to Datalog and denoted by $\widehat{P}$. We first give a brief description of the syntax of Datalog. For a full description of Datalog refer to [6]. A Datalog rule is of the form: $L_0 :- L_1, L_2, \ldots, L_n$, where L_i is a predicate with parameters. The parameters can either be constants (strings) or variables. L_0 is called the head of the rule. The head of the rule should not have constants as parameters. Datalog does not allow complex terms (such as functors) as arguments to these predicates, and imposes certain stratification restrictions on the use of negation and recursion i.e., the variable appearing in the negated predicate should also appear in some positive predicate in the body of the same rule. Further each variable in the head of a rule must also appear in some positive clause in the body of the rule. There are two types of predicates: base and derived. Base predicates occur only in the body of the rules, and derived predicates occur in at least one rule as head.

The syntax of the dynamic rules in SEAL is as follows:

$$\text{anext } \mathcal{B}(x_1, \ldots, x_m), \mathcal{B}'(y_1, \ldots, y_n) \ :\!\!- \\ \mathcal{R}(u_1, \ldots, u_k), \mathcal{R}'(v_1, \ldots, v_l).$$
$$\text{enext } \mathcal{B}(x_1, \ldots, x_m), \mathcal{B}'(y_1, \ldots, y_n) \ :\!\!- \\ \mathcal{R}(u_1, \ldots, u_k), \mathcal{R}'(v_1, \ldots, v_l).$$

In this rule, $\mathcal{R}(u_1, \ldots, u_k)$ denotes the conjunction of positive predicates with parameters from the variables $u_1, \ldots, u_k$, such that every $u_i, 1 \leq i \leq k$ occurs in some predicate. $\mathcal{R}'(v_1, \ldots, v_l)$ denotes the conjunction of negative predicates with parameters from the variables $v_1, \ldots, v_l$, and every $v_i, 1 \leq i \leq l$ also occurs in some positive predicate. Similarly, $\mathcal{B}(x_1, \ldots, x_m)$ denotes the conjunction of positive base predicates and $\mathcal{B}'(y_1, \ldots, y_n)$ denotes the conjunction of negative base predicates. All the variables of $\mathcal{R}'$ and $\mathcal{B}'$ occur in $\mathcal{R}$. Though the syntax of enext and anext are similar, the semantics is a little different. We explain this in detail in Section 2.2.

The dynamic rules can be normalized by restricting each rule to have only one positive guard (right-hand side) predicate, as it is equivalent to the above form. If the guard is not a single positive predicate, it has to be a conjunction of positive and negative predicates. This can be replaced with a single fresh predicate (containing all the variables appearing in the earlier guard predicates), without loss of generality. The original rule can now be replaced with a Datalog rule with the fresh predicate as the head and the earlier guard predicates as the body. Thus, a simplified (but equivalent) dynamic rule would look like:

$$\text{anext } \quad \mathcal{B}(x_1, \ldots, x_m), \mathcal{B}'(y_1, \ldots, y_n) \ :\!\!-R(u_1, \ldots, u_k)$$
$$\text{enext } \quad \mathcal{B}(x_1, \ldots, x_m), \mathcal{B}'(y_1, \ldots, y_n) \ :\!\!-R(u_1, \ldots, u_k)$$

In these rules, all the variables of $\mathcal{B}'$ occur in R.

We allow two kinds of queries: simple and temporal. A simple query is written as $Q(x_1, \ldots, x_n)?$ and a temporal query as $Q_1(x_1, \ldots, x_m); Q_2(y_1, \ldots, y_n)?$. We disallow duplication of variables in queries in a given SEAL program. Note that if duplication of variables is needed, one can introduce a new Datalog rule with a fresh query predicate. Hence it is enough to consider just the name of the query predicate (along with its arity) and not the argument variables. In the rest of the paper, we assume that the all the dynamic rules have a single positive predicate as the guard without duplication of variables.

2.2 SEAL Semantics

Given an initial set of base predicates I, a SEAL program P induces a transition system $M_P = (Q, \Sigma, \longrightarrow, s_0)$ where Q is a (possibly infinite) set of states, Σ is a set of dynamic rules in the program, the transition relation is given by $\longrightarrow \subseteq Q \times \Sigma \times Q$, and $s_0 \in Q$ is the starting state constructed from I. A state is a set (or database) of relations. Note that this transition system may be non-deterministic.

As mentioned earlier, we use $\widehat{P}(I)$ to denote the standard Datalog semantics for the Datalog portion of the SEAL program P against a given set of base predicates I. In other words, the Datalog rules of P are applied iteratively (and cumulatively) on the predicates of I and derived predicates are populated until they reach a fix-point. The conditions on the Datalog rules ensure the existence of a least fix-point [6]. We use s and t to denote such saturated sets of predicates. These saturated sets form the basic states in the induced state-transition system. The starting state $s_0 = \widehat{P}(I)$. We use $bp(s)$ and $bp(t)$ to denote only the set of base predicates in states s and t.

We now describe the semantics of the dynamic rules. Let $\alpha = \text{anext } \mathcal{B}(x_1, \ldots, x_m), \mathcal{B}'(y_1, \ldots, y_n) \ :\!\!-R(u_1, \ldots, u_k)$ in a SEAL program P, where all the variables of $\mathcal{B}'$ occur in R. Then we have a transition $s \xrightarrow{\alpha} s'$ where $s' = \widehat{P}(bp(s) \cup genan(\alpha, s) \setminus killan(\alpha, s))$ if the predicate R (with arity k) is non-empty in s, otherwise the a-transition is not enabled at s. The sets $genan$ and $killan$ are defined as:

$$
\begin{array}{|l|}
\hline
genan(\alpha, s) = \{B(a_1, \ldots, a_r) \mid \\
B \in \mathcal{B} \land R(c_1, \ldots, c_k) \in s\} \\
\text{where, for every } 1 \leq i \leq r, \\
a_i = \begin{cases} c_j & \text{if } x_i = u_j 1 \leq j \leq k \\ \text{a fresh constant} & \text{otherwise} \end{cases} \\
\hline
killan(\alpha, s) = \{B'(b_1, \ldots, b_t) \mid \\
B' \in \mathcal{B}' \land R(c_1, \ldots, c_k) \in s\} \\
\text{where, for every } 1 \leq i \leq t, \ b_i = c_j \\
\text{such that } y_i = u_j \text{ for some } 1 \leq j \leq k. \\
\hline
\end{array}
$$

Similarly, when $\alpha = \text{enext } \mathcal{B}(x_1, \ldots, x_m), \mathcal{B}'(y_1, \ldots, y_n) \ :\!\!-R(u_1, \ldots, u_k)$ where all the variables of $\mathcal{B}'$ occur in R, we have a transition $s \xrightarrow{\alpha} s'$ where $s' = \widehat{P}(bp(s) \cup genen(\alpha, s) \setminus killen(\alpha, s))$ if the predicate R with arity k is non-empty in s, otherwise the α-transition is not enabled at s. When the α-transition is enabled at s, pick one tuple $R(c_1, \ldots, c_k)$ from s and update the state as defined by $genen$ and $killen$ as follows:

$$
\begin{array}{|l|}
\hline
genen(\alpha, s) = \{B(a_1, \ldots, a_r) \mid B \in \mathcal{B}\} \\
\text{where, for every } 1 \leq i \leq r, \\
a_i = \begin{cases} c_j & \text{if } x_i = u_j 1 \leq j \leq k \\ \text{a fresh constant} & \text{otherwise} \end{cases} \\
\hline
killen(\alpha, s) = \{B'(b_1, \ldots, b_t) \mid B' \in \mathcal{B}'\} \\
\text{where, for every } 1 \leq i \leq t, \ b_i = c_j, \\
\text{such that } y_i = u_j \text{ for some } 1 \leq j \leq k. \\
\hline
\end{array}
$$

Note that in case of anext we consider all the tuples in R from s and in enext we non-deterministically pick one tuple of R in s. The semantics of enext is the source of non-determinism in the induced automaton. If there are multiple elements satisfying the guard of an enext rule e at a state s, the induced transition system has many transitions on s with the same label e accounting for every selection of the satisfying guard predicate in s. A dynamic rule without a guard is equivalent to having a zero-arity (constant) guard predicate true.

We now describe the semantics of SEAL query evaluation. A simple query $Q(x_1, \ldots, x_n)?$ holds from a set of a basic predicates I w.r.t. a SEAL program P if there exists a state s' and a sequence of dynamic rules $w = \alpha_1 \alpha_2 \ldots \alpha_m$ of P such that $\widehat{P}(I) \xrightarrow{\alpha_1} s_1 \xrightarrow{\alpha_2} \cdots \xrightarrow{\alpha_m} s'$ and the predicate Q (with arity n) is non-empty in s'. A temporal query of the form $Q_1(x_1, \ldots, x_m); Q_2(y_1, \ldots, y_n)$? holds from a state s w.r.t. a SEAL program P if there exist states s', s'' and two sequences of dynamic rules $u = \alpha_1\alpha_2\ldots\alpha_k, v = \beta_1\beta_2\ldots\beta_l$ of P such that $\widehat{P}(I) \xrightarrow{\alpha_1} s_1 \xrightarrow{\alpha_2} \cdots \xrightarrow{\alpha_k} s' \xrightarrow{\beta_1} t_1 \xrightarrow{\beta_2} \cdots \xrightarrow{\beta_l} s''$, the predicate Q_1 (with arity m) is non-empty in s' and Q_2 (with arity n) is non-empty in s''.

Temporal queries can equivalently be written as simple queries. Let $Q_1(x_1, \ldots, x_m); Q_2(y_1, \ldots, y_n)$ be a temporal query. This query may be replaced with a new simple query $Q(x_1, \ldots, x_m, y_1 \ldots, y_n)$, a dynamic rule

$$\text{enext } Done(x_1, \ldots, x_m) :- Q_1(x_1, \ldots, x_m)$$

where $Done$ is a fresh predicate, and a Datalog rule

$$Q(x_1, \ldots, x_m, y_1, \ldots, y_n) :- Q_2(y_1, \ldots, y_n), Done(x_1, \ldots, x_m)$$

We now state the problem of query-reachability formally. Given a snapshot of the system as a set of base relations I, a simple query predicate Q and a SEAL program P, does Q hold from $\widehat{P}(I)$ w.r.t. P. We also want to compute all such paths.

2.3 Example

We present a simple program written in SEAL, and explain our syntax and semantics informally with this example. Consider the following program that models the behavior of a user presented with a UAC prompt associated with a label change in Windows 7:

```
1. enext LowFile(x).
2. anext LinksTo(x,y):- LowFile(y), StdHighName(x).
3. AlwaysConsent(x) :- StdHighName(x).
4. StdHighName("regedit").
5. LinksTo(x,y),LowFile(y); AlwaysConsent(x)?
```

The first statement in our SEAL program is an enext rule, which specifies that a new low file (file with integrity label low) can be created by the user, or by a program running as low on behalf of the user at any point. Note that anext would not have made any difference here. The second statement is a guarded anext statement which specifies that we can create a link with a standard high name (say regedit, the registry editor) to a low file (a virus) and put it on the desktop. The third line is a regular Datalog rule that states that anything with standard high name always causes the user to accept prompt. The fourth statement is a database entry (or a database "fact"). The last statement is a query that says if we have a link to a low file on the desktop, can the user be fooled into giving consent?

This program induces a infinite state-transition system as shown in the Figure 1. We start with the initial state (say state 1) where regedit is the only entry in the StdHighName and AlwaysConsent relations, consistent with standard Datalog semantics. The first enext rule will cause the database to transition to a state where a new constant is added to the Low relation (state 2). Once this is added, no other Datalog rule can fire and this is the updated state. Now, the guard to the second anext rule is satisfied and a transition to a new state can occur, where the LinksTo relation can be updated appropriately. Note that the first enext rule is also enabled in state 2, and this transition creates another constant in the Low relation, and so on. Since there is only one constant in

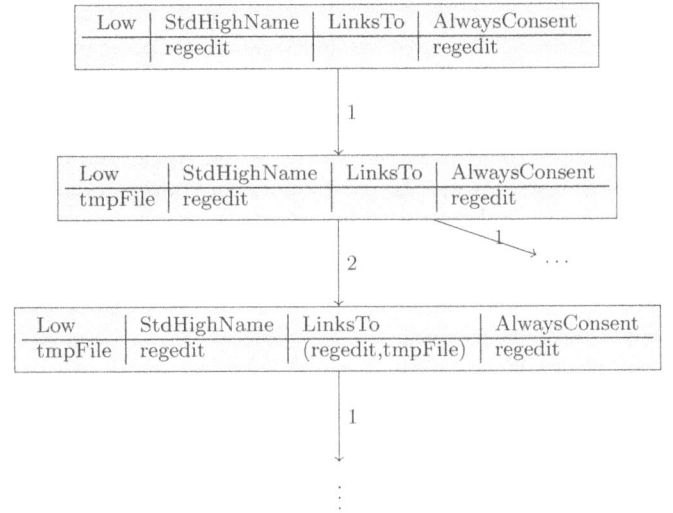

Figure 1: Induced transition system for the example

the StdHighName relation, we will end up eventually describing a world where there are many low links on the desktop to the high resource. It is easy to see that the query, about whether it is possible for a link to a low file (say a virus) to fool the user into accepting a UAC prompt(AlwaysConsent), is true in this model. We have intentionally kept this example simple, and hence a little contrived, attributing to user behavior semantics that is outside the scope of the specification given in the example.

3. MODELING IN SEAL

In this section, we call out specific requirements in state-of-the art access control systems that motivate our choice of features for SEAL. In particular, we focus on the LBAC component of Windows 7, which is called User Account Control (UAC). With the help of examples we show how existing formalisms (specifically EON) cannot capture the required semantics adequately.

The intuition behind UAC is to enable authorized users (typically PC owners) to log in as standard users and perform common tasks that do not require administrative privileges. The idea is when a user process is compromised (say by a buffer-overflow attack) and control hijacked, the attacker will have no more privileges than the default (low) privileges associated with standard user accounts. Therefore, when UAC is enabled, even a local administrator will run as a standard user account with reduced privileges. This is the case until (s)he attempts to run an application or task that has an administrative token (i.e., requires special privileges). When such a member of the local administrators group attempts to start a privileged application or task, they are prompted to consent to running the application as elevated.

UAC is implemented using a lattice of integrity labels. The integrity labels for each process (or thread) and resource on the Windows 7 installation are stored in its security descriptor. Windows 7 has four integrity labels (a total order): System, High, Medium and Low. By default, processes (and threads) on behalf of standard user accounts run as Medium and all resources created by these accounts can only be Medium or lower. Some applications however, such as Internet Explorer (IE), run with default low rights. Any resource downloaded from the Internet (say) is automatically assigned a Low label, and (explicit) consent from the user (who is Medium), is required by clicking on the UAC prompt in case of elevation. By default, for integrity protection, restrictions are placed on explicit information flows from lower levels to higher levels in the usual way. Write-up by a lower process to a higher resource is not allowed, and a read-down from a higher process to a lower user is not allowed, unless explicitly authorized by the user in response to a UAC prompt. Explicit authorization is allowed in UAC for functionality reasons. If a user is reasonably certain e.g., that they trust the source of the plugin (by checking the cryptographic hash of the binary with a trusted provider), the labels need to be upgraded naturally. Within IE it is possible to download and install plugins that need higher privileges. A separate process or thread is run on behalf of an existing process that requests additional privileges, and explicit user consent is required to make these label changes.

The formal model of UAC was presented by Chaudhuri et al in EON [7]. We present this model in SEAL, restricting our relations to unary base predicates to mimic the syntax of EON. This also sets the context to explain our extensions to this model in the next subsection.

The unary base relations used in the model example have the following informal meanings: P is a relation representing processes; Obj represents objects (including processes); and Low, Med, High, *etc.* represent processes and objects with those integrity labels (ILs).

```
enext Obj(x),Low(x).
enext Obj(x),Med(x).
enext Obj(x),High(x).

enext P(x) :- Obj(x).
...
```

Guarded enext rules specify how ILs of processes and objects can be changed. For instance, a Medium process can raise the IL of an object from Low to Medium if that object is not a process; it can also lower the IL of an object from Medium to Low. A High process can lower its own IL to Medium (*e.g.*, to execute a Medium object), consistent with the safe upgrading and downgrading in the context of integrity properties.

```
enext Med(y),!Low(y) :- Low(y),!P(y),Med(x),P(x).
enext Low(y),!Med(y) :- Med(y),Med(x),P(x).

enext Med(x),!High(x) :- High(x),P(x).
...
```

Datalog rules specify how processes can Read, Write, and Execute objects. A process x can Read an object y without any constraints. In contrast, x can Write y only if the IL of x is Geq (greater than or equal to) the IL of y. Conversely, x can Execute y only if the IL of y is Geq the IL of x.

```
Read(x,y) :- P(x),Obj(y).
Write(x,y) :- P(x),Geq(x,y).
Execute(x,y) :- P(x),Geq(y,x).

Geq(x,y) :- Med(x),Med(y).
Geq(x,y) :- Med(x),Low(y).
Geq(x,y) :- Low(x),Low(y).
...
```

Several interesting safety queries can be studied in this model. For instance, can a Medium object be read by a Medium process after it is written by a Low process? Can an object that is written by a Low process be eventually executed by a High process by downgrading to Medium?

```
Med(y); Low(x),Write(x,y); Med(z),Read(z,y)?
Low(x),Write(x,y); High(z); Med(z),Execute(z,y)?
```

When these queries were executed in EON, which has a sound and complete decision procedure, in addition to the obvious vulnerabilities that are introduced by explicit user consent, vulnerabilities were discovered that highlight the need to maintain the history of label-state of a process or a resource as the system evolves over time. This information is not explicitly available to the standard user when a UAC prompt is issued, and the attacks such as the one shown in our running-example can exist, due to additional native resource-access semantics that are not accounted for in the model.

In the next sub-section, we show how the EON language used to model UAC is not sufficient to analyze scenarios when UAC actions are composed with Windows native access semantics. While the results of modeling UAC with EON are useful, they do not specify interactions with components outside the direct scope of the access relations (such as file naming semantics etc.)

3.1 Windows 7 Folder Access

We motivate the need for a richer specification language, SEAL, by illustrating a behavior that captures the interaction between the UAC model and native Windows 7 folder-access semantics.

As mentioned earlier, Windows 7 attaches integrity labels: Low, Medium, High and System, to all resources and processes (threads) in an installation. While the UAC defines rules for safe upgrading and downgrading of integrity levels, we show with an example that the peculiar and no doubt useful semantics of the start Menu folder admits a behavior that cannot be modeled in EON.

In Windows, a user's start menu is populated with soft links (shortcuts to actual resources) from two separate folder locations. One is the user's local start menu folder and the other is a global folder, typically populated in enterprise networks with remotely sourced applications. These two locations are merged to create the start menu that the user sees. If the same shortcut exists in both the user's local folder and the global folder, upon access, the shortcut in the user's folder is given preference, and the application associated with the link is executed.

To model this behavior, we use the following base predicates to represent entities in our model:

P(x)	x is a process
Low(x)	x has a 'low' IL
High(x)	x has a 'high' IL
Adm(x)	x is an admin
File(x)	x is a file
Link(x)	x is a link
Folder(x)	x is a folder
FreshName(x)	x is a fresh name
LinksTo(x,y)	link name x points to resource y
Name(x,y)	Name of x appears as y
InLocalFolder(x)	x is in local start menu folder
InGlobalFolder(x)	x is in global folder

The modeling assumes that there are only two integrity levels: low and high (for simplicity), and that there is a high administrator process already running in the system.

The dynamic rules are from 1 to 7. The rules 1 and 2 model creation of a new low and a high process respectively.

```
1. enext P(y), Low(y) :- Adm(x).
2. enext P(y), High(y) :- Adm(x).
```

Rule 3 creates fresh names, which are used in naming the link files.

```
3. enext FreshName(x).
```

Rules 4 and 5 model the creation of a new low and high file respectively, where y is a fresh constant.

```
4. enext File(y), Low(y) :- P(x).
5. enext File(y), High(y):- P(x), High(x).
```

The rules 6 and 7 model the start menu semantics. Rule 6 creates a link in the global folder to a genuine executable which requires elevation. Rule 7 creates a link in the local folder to another executable with the same name as the link in the global folder, pointing to a low file.

```
6. enext LinksTo(y,z), High(y), Name(y, u),
   UsedName(u), !FreshName(u),
   InGlobalFolder(y) :- P(x), High(x),
   File(z), High(z), FreshName(u).

7. enext LinksTo(y,z), Low(y), Name(y, u),
   InLocalFolder(y) :- P(x), File(z),
   UsedName(u).
```

The rest of the rules are pure Datalog rules, with easy-to-read meanings.

```
SameName(x,y) :- Name(x,z), Name(y,z).

StartMenu(x) :- SameName(x,y),
  InLocalFolder(x), InGlobalFolder(y).

StartMenu(x) :- InLocalFolder(x),
               !InGlobalFolder(x).
StartMenu(x) :- InGlobalFolder(x),
               !SameName(x,y).
AddPrivilege(x) :- StartMenu(x).
```

Below is the query modeling a safety property. The state satisfying this query represents the vulnerable state of the system.

```
Low(x); AddPrivilege(x)?
```

Note that both LinksTo and SameName are binary predicates and cannot be represented as multiple unary predicates in EON, as they both range over infinite domains. In Section 5, we explain how we can analyze this specification and examine if it admits unsafe states.

4. QUERY REACHABILITY IN SEAL

While the specification shown in Section 3.1 captures the semantics of native Windows 7 file access, we show that the existence of even one binary predicate in a SEAL program makes the query reachability problem undecidable. We show this with a reduction from Hilbert's tenth problem. This result adds further restrictions to the proof presented by Chaudhuri et al. [8] where they showed undecidability using two binary predicates.

THEOREM 1. *The query reachability problem for SEAL with one binary base predicate is undecidable.*

PROOF. We prove that the simple query reachability problem for SEAL with just one binary base predicate is undecidable by reducing Hilbert's tenth problem.

Hilbert's Tenth Problem. Given a diophantine equation (n degree polynomial with m unknowns: $x_1 \ldots x_m$ and integer coefficients: $p_{11} \ldots p_{mn}, p$) of the form

$$
\begin{aligned}
&p_{11}x_1^1 + p_{12}x_1^2 + \cdots + p_{1n}x_1^n + \\
&p_{21}x_2^1 + p_{22}x_2^2 + \cdots + p_{2n}x_2^n + \\
&\vdots \\
&p_{m1}x_m^1 + p_{m2}x_m^2 + \cdots + p_{mn}x_m^n + p = 0
\end{aligned}
$$

does there exist natural number solution (zero included) for the unknowns? This problem is known to be undecidable. Hilbert initially defined the problem for an integer solution. However, the problem is equivalent for a natural number (zero included) solution. This follows from the fact that every natural number can be expressed as a sum of 4 squares, as proved by Lagrange.

We encode natural numbers using a single binary predicate and extend it to model Hilbert's Tenth problem (HTP). Given an instance of HTP: $p_{11} \ldots p_{mn}$, p, we construct a SEAL program with isZero and Succ as base predicates, with their natural meanings (Succ(x,x') represents x being the successor of x'). The predicate Succ is the only binary base predicate in the program. From this, we can generate all natural numbers. We use the standard ordered pair notation for representing integers: (a, b) for the integer $a - b$. We give the sketch of the program here:

```
enext isZero(x).
anext Succ(x,x') :- NaturalNum(x').

NaturalNum(x) :- isZero(x).
NaturalNum(x) :- Succ(x,y), NaturalNum(y).

Integer(x,y) :- NaturalNum(x), NaturalNum(y).

Plus(x,y,x) :- isZero(y).
Plus(x,y,z) :- Succ(y,y'), Plus(x,y',z'),
               Succ(z,z').

NMul(x,y,y) :- isZero(y).
NMul(x,y,z) :- Succ(y,y'), NMul(x,y',z'),
               Plus(x,z',z).
Mul(a,b,x,c,d) :- NMul(a,x,c), NMul(b,x,d).

NExp(x,y,z) :- isZero(y), isZero(z'),
               Succ(z,z').
NExp(x,y,z) :- Succ(y,y'), NExp(x,y',z'),
               NMul(x,z',z).

One(x) :- Succ(x,x'), isZero(x').
Two(x) :- Succ(x,x'), One(x').
  .
  .
  .
N(x) :- ...

P11(x,y) :- ...
  .
```

```
          .
          .
PMN(x,y) :- ...
P(x,y) :- ...

Equal(x,y) :- isZero(x), isZero(y).
Equal(x,y) :- Succ(x,x'), Succ(y,y'),
                   Equal(x',y').

Query(x1...xm) :-
 One(1), Two(2), ... , N(n),  P(pa,pb),
 NExp(x1,1,x11'), P11(p11a,p11b),
  Mul(p11a,p11b,x11',x11a,x11b),
 NExp(x1,2,x12'), P12(p12a,p12b),
  Mul(p12a,p12b,x12',x12a,x11b),
          .
          .
          .
 NExp(x1,n,x1n'), P1N(p1na,p1nb),
  Mul(p1na,p1nb,x1n',x1na,x1nb),
          .
          .
          .
 NExp(xm,1,xm1'), PM1(pm1a,pm1b),
  Mul(pm1a,pm1b,xm1',xm1a,xm1b),
          .
          .
          .
 NExp(xm,n,xmn'), PMN(pmna,pmnb),
  Mul(pmna,pmnb,xmn,xmna,xmnb),
 Plus(pa,x11a, y11a), Plus(y11a,x12a, y12a), ... ,
 Plus(.,xmna, ymna),
 Plus(pb,x11b, y11b), Plus(y11b,x12b, y12b), ... ,
 Plus(.,xmnb, ymnb), Equal(ymna,ymnb).

Query(x1...xm) ?
```

We give a brief explanation of the above program. The first dynamic rule creates an element representing zero. The second rule with the help of Datalog rules for `NaturalNum` create natural numbers. Note that the type of the dynamic rule would not make any difference for this program. As mentioned earlier an integer is represented using an ordered pair of natural numbers. The predicate `Plus`, `NMul` and `NExp` describe addition, multiplication and exponentiation of natural numbers respectively. The predicate `Mul` denotes the multiplication of an integer with a natural number. The predicates `One` till `N` are used to describe exponentiation constants of the equation. A positive integer coefficient q is represented as $(q, 0)$ and a negative coefficient $-q$ as $(0, q)$. The predicates `P11` till `PMN` and `P` represent the coefficients. The predicate `Equal` is true when both the arguments (natural numbers) are same. The query predicate `Q` describes the given equation and checks if the result is zero.

Now, if the query reachability problem is decidable then we will have an algorithm to solve HTP. Hence proved. □

The undecidability result implies that it is not possible to find an algorithm (or a decision procedure) to compute reachability for a general SEAL program. We have looked at various abstractions and over-approximations and a general algorithm to guarantee soundness, by defining an appropriate equivalence relation or appropriate finite abstractions is still open.

Instead, we implement a bounded model-checking algorithm, which is complete for a given depth-bound. The procedure is to start with an initial state and explore all possible (non deterministic) transitions from each reachable state iteratively, until the bound is reached. If a counterexample or an unsafe state is found in the bounded model, then it is a true error. In practice, as we show in our Case Studies, a depth of 8 to 10 uncovers many vulnerabilities, previously known or otherwise. While we cannot assert that a model that does not admit an attack (or unsafe state) within this bound is safe, it may be unlikely that an attacker would use methods that involve many more state change operations.

In the next section, we present three case studies, where we model and analyze different aspects of safety in Windows 7, Asbestos, and IFEDAC.

5. CASE STUDIES

In this section, we present results from our modeling of three different access control systems, Windows 7, Asbestos (and HiStar), and IFEDAC. In each of the studies we explain our findings, in terms of true vulnerabilities discovered/not discovered for different depths. The SEAL tool to implement the bounded state-space exploration was written in F# and is available for download.

5.1 Windows 7 vulnerabilities

The first case study is the specification of the behavior of dynamically created links in the start menu folder. Through our analysis we discover that the specification admits a vulnerability at exploration depth 8.

To explain this vulnerability [20], we present an attack scenario as follows: A malicious user can write a proxy infection tool, which can be downloaded as a Trojan (as low), when the user clicks on an interesting third-party application. When this tool is run by the user, it can write to the user's start menu folder and read the contents of the global start menu folder without requesting elevated permissions. This malicious program searches the global start menu folder for all applications that require elevation, and creates duplicate links to malicious virus code (still labeled low) in the user's local folder, with the same name as the trusted program in the global folder.

When the user attempts to run a program that has been duplicated, they see a UAC prompt. Because the program already requires elevated permission, the user would not be alarmed, and would give consent. The malicious program, with elevated privileges, executes the intended program, fooling the user into thinking everything is normal. Meanwhile, the malicious program can clean up any traces, and install itself somewhere with permanently-elevated privileges.

The steps required to mount this attack, in the context of the SEAL program presented in Section 3.1, are shown in Figure 2. The model has to explore the states to depth level of 7 before the attack is discovered. We implemented a reduced version of the specification which had about 100000 states.

The next behavior we model is something called the silent elevation list. The silent elevation list is an option to allow the operating system developer to define a list of applications that can always bypass the UAC prompt, without user consent. The intent is to populate this list with only trusted applications, and improve the user experience.

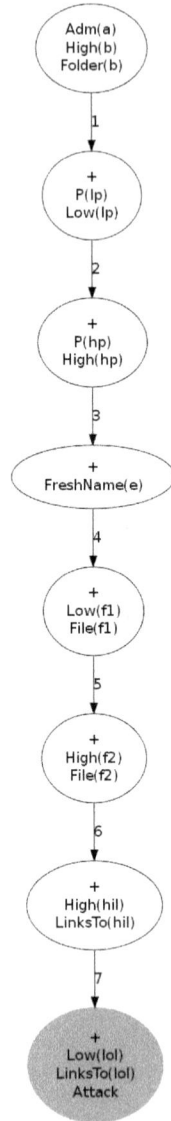

Figure 2: Start Menu Vulnerability

Popular third-party applications such as Adobe Reader and Flash Player occur in this list. These third-party applications are themselves untrusted and require explicit consent by the user to install as a plugin in the browser after they are downloaded. Once they are installed, they are automatically added to the silent elevation list. A SEAL program modeling this behavior is presented next:

```
1. enext Downloads(x,y), Low(y), App(y)
   :- Low(x), P(x).
2. High(y) :- Install(y), Low(y)
3. App(y), High(y) :- SEList(u), SameName(y,u).

4. Low(x); High(x)?
```

It is clear that a malicious plugin with the same name as a trusted binary on the Silent Elevation list can obtain administrative privileges, violating the safety requirement. A low process can download a low application, as specified in Step 1 and this can be installed as a plugin, assuming the source was trusted in Step 2. Now if this has the same name as an application in the Silent Elevation list, we have essentially bypassed the integrity guarantee as a High user can read a high application (this is not modeled in the example). This vulnerability was found in 5 steps in our tool. For the bounding depth of 5, our tool discovered over 6000 states.

Note that Windows 7 has an in-built tamper detection warning that automatically changes the color of the UAC prompt when an untrusted application is loaded. A trusted application whose integrity can be verified is presented with UAC window with a green border, and an untrusted application has a yellow border. This warning may prevent a vigilant user from falling victim to a start menu attack, but does not help much in the Silent Elevation attack, unless the browser validates the signature of the downloaded plugin outside the scope of the UAC prompt.

The vulnerabilities described were found by examining different components in the Windows 7 codebase that use UAC, and studying their behavior in the context of integrity guarantees (safety). In the future, we plan to examine all such interactions to systematically discover similar vulnerabilities (if any).

5.2 Asbestos

Asbestos is a Unix-based operating system developed by researchers that provides in-built support for creating confidentiality labels. The goal is to provide safety by implementing LBAC, by dynamically isolating trusted processes from untrusted ones using automatic tainting and taint propagation. Asbestos processes have both send and receive labels, corresponding to their clearance level and their taint level. Labels can also be set-valued, as in MLS compartments. The specification of Asbestos' LBAC provides a large number of choices. In EON, the authors have shown that it is possible to configure Asbestos labels in a manner that can cause unsafe behavior. However, safe defaults are suggested for send and receive labels. Even though these labels are set-valued, restricting the specifications to default values allows us to express it in EON and SEAL. For the example scenarios and configurations presented in the Asbestos work, EON was able to validate the safety properties effectively.

In terms of improving on EON, SEAL allows the use of multiary relations, reducing the size of the specifications, and potentially the complexity of verification for bounded models. For example, in EON, in order to create a user process and its associated port, with specific values for send and receive labels in the webserver example, we need the following relations:

```
enext Process(x), PortUW(x),
    LabelSendUcStar(x), LabelSendUtThree(x),
    LabelSendVcOne(x), LabelSendVtOne(x),
    LabelSendUwStar(x), LabelSendVwOne(x),
--
    LabelRecvUcStar(x), LabelRecvUtThree(x),
    LabelRecvVcTwo(x), LabelRecvVtTwo(x),
    LabelRecvUwStar(x), LabelRecvVwTwo(x),
--
    LabelPortUWUcTwo(x), LabelPortUWUtThree(x),
    LabelPortUWVcTwo(x), LabelPortUWVtTwo(x),
    LabelPortUWUwZero(x), LabelPortUWVwTwo(x) :- U.
```

In SEAL this can be specified using far fewer relations. In fact, this enext rule can be specified using only one relation, but we present an equivalent rule which uses four relations for readability:

```
enext Process(x, port),
ProcessSendLabels(x,s1, .. ,s6),
ProcessRecvLabels(x,r1, .. ,r6),
ProcessPortLabels(port,x,p1, .. ,p6).
```

Further, as in the case of Windows 7, exposing additional semantics to the access models may help in discovering new vulnerabilities. HiStar is an extension to Asbestos, and similar properties can be validated here.

5.3 IFEDAC

Information Flow enhanced DAC (IFEDAC [18]) is a proposed extension to the traditional DAC models that is specifically targeted at preventing Trojans. One of the problems with a DAC system is that a resource is associated with only one owner, whereas in real systems, the provenance of the resources, in terms of their past owners and their integrity plays an important part in arbitrating trust issues. To capture provenance, IFEDAC specifications extends the concept of ownership to include all principals that ever created or owned the file. This set of principals is used as a label to mark clearance or integrity level of a resource / process. These labels naturally form a lattice with set inclusion as the order. These labels may change as the system evolves (in accordance with the given IFEDAC specification).

The framework modeling the behaviors of IFEDAC specifications should account for these dynamic sets (labels). Let X and Y denote integrity label of a process p and *read protection class (rpc)* of an object o respectively. For the purpose of this illustration, it is enough to treat *rpc* of an object to be same as its integrity label. Let $\text{dom}(X,Y)$ denote X dominates Y, i.e., $X \supseteq Y$. A straight-forward translation of IFEDAC rule for a process p to read object o would read as follows.

```
reads(p,o) :- int(X,p), rpc(Y,o), dom(X,Y).
```

Note that here we are using an implicit quantification on set variables X and Y. SEAL does not allow quantification over set variables, and the IFEDAC model cannot be expressed in our framework. However, as in the case of Asbestos presented previously, it is possible to encode a particular instance of an IFEDAC system where these sets are fixed, and SEAL can be used in a limited way to verify safety when other relations can change dynamically. Verification with quantification over set-valued variables is outside the scope of SEAL.

6. CONCLUSIONS

We present SEAL, a language for specifying and analyzing dynamic LBAC systems using logic programs. SEAL improves on existing modeling languages such as EON by allowing for richer specifications, modeling behaviors that were not previously articulated. The safety problem in LBAC systems is reduced to query reachability in SEAL, and is shown to be undecidable even for a conservative program instance with one binary base predicate. This restriction poses an interesting open question about the existence of abstractions or over-approximations that can guarantee soundness in these models automatically.

Because of this restriction, we implement a bounded state-space exploration tool that is useful in analyzing the behavior of Windows 7, which is arguably the most widely used commercial LBAC system. While we cannot guarantee safety, any violation found by our tool is a true error. The vulnerabilities discovered by SEAL, including the Start Menu problem and the Silent Elevation list, highlight the need to define the interface between the access control model and modules that implement or require label-changes using UAC, more rigorously. We also study how SEAL can be used for modeling other LBAC systems, including Asbestos and IFEDAC. We recognize SEAL's limitations to handle IFEDAC models.

One natural direction to explore is to construct approximations. Ideally we would like to construct a finite state transition system containing all the behaviors (runs) of the induced possibly infinite state transtion system of a SEAL program. In this way, we can give guarantees on when a specification doesn't have a vulnerability.

Acknowledgements

The authors would like to thank their shepherd Steve Barker for his support, and thank the anonymous reviewers for their useful comments and suggestions that have improved the quality of this presentation greatly. We would also like to acknowledge the contributions of G. Ramalingam, Sriram Rajamani, and A. Baskar during our discussions about this work. Much of this work was done when the second author was an intern at Microsoft Research India.

7. REFERENCES

[1] S. Barker, M. Leuschel, and M. Varea. Efficient and flexible access control via jones-optimal logic program specialisation. *Higher Order Symbol. Comput.*, 21:5–35, June 2008.

[2] S. Barker and P. J. Stuckey. Flexible access control policy specification with constraint logic programming. *ACM Trans. Inf. Syst. Secur.*, 6:501–546, November 2003.

[3] D. E. Bell and L. J. LaPadula. Secure computer systems: Mathematical foundations and model. Technical Report M74-244, MITRE Corp., 1975.

[4] K. J. Biba. Integrity considerations for secure computer systems. Technical Report TR-3153, MITRE Corp., 1977.

[5] M. Bishop. Theft of information in the take-grant protection model. In *CSFW*, pages 194–218, 1988.

[6] S. Ceri, G. Gottlob, and L. Tanca. What you always wanted to know about datalog (and never dared to ask). *IEEE Transactions on Knowledge and Data Engineering*, 1(1):146–166, 1989.

[7] A. Chaudhuri, P. Naldurg, S. Rajamani, G. Ramalingam, , and L. Velaga. Eon: Modeling and analyzing dynamic access control systems with logic programs. Technical report, MSR-TR-2008-21, Microsoft Research, 2008.

[8] A. Chaudhuri, P. Naldurg, S. Rajamani, G. Ramalingam, and L. Velaga. Eon: Modeling and analyzing dynamic access control systems. In *Proceedings of the 15th ACM Conference on Computer and Communications Security (CCS'08)*, pages 381–390. ACM, 2008.

[9] E. Clarke, A. Biere, R. Raimi, and Y. Zhu. Bounded model checking using satisfiability solving. In *Formal Methods in System Design*, page 2001. Kluwer Academic Publishers, 2001.

[10] E. M. Clarke, O. Grumberg, and D. A. Peled. *Model Checking*. MIT Press, 2000.

[11] D. Denning. *Cryptography and Data Security*. Addison Wesley, 1982.

[12] D. E. Denning. A lattice model of secure information flow. *Commun. ACM*, 19(5):236–243, 1976.

[13] M. A. Harrison, W. L. Ruzzo, and J. D. Ullman. On protection in operating systems. In *SOSP '75: Proceedings of the fifth ACM symposium on Operating systems principles*, pages 14–24, 1975.

[14] B. Hicks, S. Rueda, L. St.Clair, T. Jaeger, and P. McDaniel. A logical specification and analysis for selinux mls policy. *ACM Trans. Inf. Syst. Secur.*, 13:26:1–26:31, July 2010.

[15] A. K. Jones, R. J. Lipton, and L. Snyder. A linear time algorithm for deciding security. *Symposium on Foundations of Computer Science*, 0:33–41, 1976.

[16] B. W. Lampson. Protection. *Proc. Fifth Princeton Symposium on Information Sciences and Systems*, 1971.

[17] P. Loscocco, S. Smalley, P. Muckelbauer, R. Taylor, J. Turner, and J. Farrell. The inevitability of failure: The flawed assumption of security in modern computing environments. Technical report, United Stated National Security Agency (NSA), 1995.

[18] Z. Mao, N. Li, H. Chen, and X. Jiang. Trojan horse resistant discretionary access control. In *SACMAT*, pages 237–246, 2009.

[19] P. Naldurg, S. Schwoon, S. Rajamani, and J. Lambert. Netra: seeing through access control. In *FMSE '06: Proceedings of the fourth ACM workshop on Formal methods in security*, pages 55–66, 2006.

[20] R. Paveza. User-prompted elevation of unintended code in windows vista. World Wide Web electronic publication, 2009.

[21] S. Vandebogart, P. Efstathopoulos, E. Kohler, M. Krohn, C. Frey, D. Ziegler, F. Kaashoek, R. Morris, and D. Mazières. Labels and event processes in the asbestos operating system. *ACM Trans. Comput. Syst.*, 25(4):11, 2007.

[22] N. Zeldovich, S. Boyd-Wickizer, E. Kohler, and D. Mazières. Making information flow explicit in histar. In *OSDI '06: Proceedings of the 7th USENIX Symposium on Operating Systems Design and Implementation*, pages 19–19, Berkeley, CA, USA, 2006. USENIX Association.

Transforming Provenance using Redaction

Tyrone Cadenhead, Vaibhav Khadilkar, Murat Kantarcioglu and
Bhavani Thuraisingham
The University of Texas at Dallas
800 W. Campbell Road, Richardson, TX 75080
{thc071000, vvk072000, muratk, bxt043000}@utdallas.edu

ABSTRACT

Ongoing mutual relationships among entities rely on sharing quality information while preventing release of sensitive content. Provenance records the history of a document for ensuring both, the quality and trustworthiness; while redaction identifies and removes sensitive information from a document. Traditional redaction techniques do not extend to the directed graph representation of provenance. In this paper, we propose a graph grammar approach for rewriting redaction policies over provenance. Our rewriting procedure converts a high level specification of a redaction policy into a graph grammar rule that transforms a provenance graph into a redacted provenance graph. Our prototype shows that this approach can be effectively implemented using Semantic Web technologies.

Categories and Subject Descriptors

F.4.2 [**Mathematical Logic and Formal Languages**]: Grammars and Other Rewriting Systems; D.4.6 [**Operating Systems**]: Security and Protection—*Access Control*

General Terms

Security

Keywords

Redaction, Provenance, RDF, Graph Grammar

1. INTRODUCTION

Provenance is the lineage, pedigree and filiation of a resource (or data item) and is essential for various domains including healthcare, intelligence, legal and industry. The utility of the information shared in these domains relies on (i) quality of the information and (ii) mechanisms that verify the correctness of the data and thereby determine the trustworthiness of the shared information. These domains rely on information sharing as a way of conducting their day-to-day

activities; but with this ease of information sharing comes a risk of information misuse. An electronic patient record (EPR) is a log of all activities including, patient visits to a hospital, diagnoses and treatments for diseases, and processes performed by healthcare professionals on a patient. This EPR is often shared among several stakeholders (for example researchers, insurance and pharmaceutical companies). Before this information can be made available to these third parties the sensitive information in an EPR must be circumvented from the released information. This can be addressed by applying redaction policies that completely or partially remove sensitive attributes of the information being shared. Such policies have been traditionally applied to text, pdfs and images using tools such as Redact-It[1]. Redaction is often required by regulations which are mandated by a company or by laws such as HIPAA. The risks of unintentional disclosure of sensitive contents of an EPR document can be severe and costly [15]. Such risks may include litigation proceedings related to non-compliance of HIPAA regulations [15].

Traditionally, we protect documents using access control policies. However, these policies do not operate over provenance which takes the form of a directed graph [4]. Our idea of executing an access control policy over a provenance graph is to identify those resources of the graph that a user is permitted/denied to view. The policy is used to determine whether a user is allowed access to a subset (a single node, a path or a sub-graph) of the provenance graph. Such a subset is found by queries that operate over graph patterns. A generalized XML-based access control language for protecting provenance was proposed in [21]. This language was further extended to show how to effectively apply access control over provenance graphs by extending SPARQL queries with regular expressions [6]. The work in [6], however, did not address graph operations suitable for executing redaction policies over a provenance graph. Commercially available redaction tools have been so far applied over single resources but not to provenance graphs. Therefore, we now explore new mechanisms for supporting redaction policies over a provenance graph.

The current commercially available redaction tools block out (or delete) the sensitive parts of documents which are available as text and images. These tools are not applicable to provenance since provenance is a directed acyclic graph (DAG) that contains information in the form of nodes and relationships between nodes. Therefore, new approaches are needed for redacting provenance graphs. In this paper, we

---

[1]http://www.redact-it.com/

apply a graph transformation technique (generally called graph grammar [24]) which is flexible enough to perform fine-grained redaction over data items and their associated provenance graphs. A graph is best described in a graphical data model, such as RDF [16], which is equipped with features for handling both, representation and storage of data items, and provenance. Our approach utilizes this graph data model for applying a set of redaction policies, which involves a series of graph transformation steps until all the policies are applied. At each step, a policy specifies how to replace a sensitive subset of the graph (such as a data item or a relationship between data items such as edge, path or subgraph) with another graph in order to redact the sensitive content. The final graph is then shared among the various stakeholders.

We implement a prototype that performs redaction over the information resources in a graph. This prototype uses an interface which mediates between our graph transformation rules and a high-level user policy specification language. This interface allows us to separate the business rules (or ways of doing business) from a specific software implementation, thus promoting easier maintenance and reusability. Further, we keep the policy specification closer to the domain rather than the software implementation, therefore allowing the business rules to be defined by domain experts.

Our main contribution in this paper is the application of a graph grammar technique to perform redaction over provenance. In addition, we provide an architectural design that allows a high level specification of policies, thus separating the business layer from a specific software implementation. We also implement a prototype of the architecture based on open source Semantic Web technologies.

Section 2 presents the graph grammar used to express redaction policies. Section 3 presents our architecture. Section 4 reviews previous work on securing information using graph transformation approaches. In closing, in Section 5 we provide our conclusions and future work.

2. GRAPH GRAMMAR

There are two steps to apply redaction policies over general directed labeled graphs: (i) Identify a resource in the graph that we want to protect. This can be done with a graph query (i.e. a query equipped with regular expressions). (ii) Apply a redaction policy to this identified resource in the form of a graph transformation rule. For the rest of this section, we will focus on a graph grammar (or a graph rewriting system) which transforms an original graph to one that meets the requirements of a set of redaction policies. We first describe two graph data models that are used to store provenance. Next, we present the graph rewriting procedure, which is at the heart of transforming a graph, by describing the underlying graph operations. We motivate the general descriptions of our graph rewriting system with use cases taken from a medical domain.

2.1 Graph Data Models

Graphs are a very natural representation of data in many application domains, for example, precedence networks, path hierarchy, family tree and concept hierarchy. In particular, we emphasize on applying graph theory to redaction by using two existing data models, namely a RDF data model [16] and the OPM provenance model [20]. In addition directed graphs are a natural representation of provenance [4, 6, 20,

27]. We begin by giving a general definition of a labeled graph suitable for any graph grammar system, and then we introduce a specific labeled graph representation for our prototype. This specific representation is referred to as RDF, which we will use to support the redaction procedure over a provenance graph.

DEFINITION 1. *(Labeled Graph) A labeled graph is a 5-tuple, $G_\ell = (V, E, \mu, \nu, \ell)$ where, V is a set of nodes, $E = V \times V$ is a set of edges, $\ell = \langle \ell_V, \ell_E \rangle$ is a set of labels, $\mu : V \to \ell_V$ is a function assigning labels to nodes, and $\nu : E \to \ell_E$ is a function assigning labels to edges. In addition, the sets ℓ_V and ℓ_E are disjoint.*

2.1.1 Resource Description Framework (RDF)

RDF is a W3C Recommendation for representing data on the web [16]. This data model has been successfully applied for provenance capture and representation [28, 11, 6]. The RDF data model is composed of three disjoint sets: a set $\mathcal{U}$ of URI references, a set $\mathcal{L}$ of literals (partitioned into two sets, the set $\mathcal{L}_p$ of plain literals and the set $\mathcal{L}_t$ of typed literals), and a set $\mathcal{B}$ of blank nodes. The set $\mathcal{U} \cup \mathcal{L}$ of names is called the vocabulary.

DEFINITION 2. *(RDF Triple) A RDF triple is defined as (s, p, o) where $s \in (\mathcal{U} \cup \mathcal{B})$, $p \in \mathcal{U}$, and $o \in (\mathcal{U} \cup \mathcal{B} \cup \mathcal{L})$.*

DEFINITION 3. *(RDF Graph) A RDF graph is a finite collection of RDF triples. A RDF graph used in this paper restricts Definition 1 as follows:*

1. *$\ell_V \subset (\mathcal{U} \cup \mathcal{B} \cup \mathcal{L})$*

2. *$\ell_E \subset \mathcal{U}$*

3. *A RDF triple (s, p, o) is a directed labeled edge p in G_ℓ with endpoints s and o.*

2.1.2 Open Provenance Model (OPM)

The open provenance model (OPM) [20] describes provenance as a directed acyclic graph that captures causal relationships between entities. This graph can be further enriched with annotations about time, location and other relevant contextual information. The OPM model identifies three categories of entities, which are artifacts, processes and agents. A restricted vocabulary is also used to label the relationships between these entities. In RDF representation, the vocabulary is used to label predicates as follows,

```
<opm:Process> <opm:WasControlledBy> <opm:Agent>
<opm:Process> <opm:Used> <opm:Artifact>
<opm:Artifact> <opm:WasDerivedFrom> <opm:Artifact>
<opm:Artifact> <opm:WasGeneratedBy> <opm:Process>
<opm:Process> <opm:WasTriggeredBy> <opm:Process>
```

Our provenance graph is a restricted RDF graph with the following properties:

1. Causality. For any RDF triple (s, p, o) (represented graphically as $s \xrightarrow{p} o$), s is causally dependent on o. We refer to s as the effect and o as the cause of s.

2. Acyclic. For any cause o and effect s there exists no path from o to s.

DEFINITION 4. *(Provenance Graph) Let $H = (V, E)$ be a RDF graph where V is a set of nodes with $|V| = n$, and $E \subseteq (V \times V)$ is a set of ordered pairs called edges. A provenance graph $G = (V_G, E_G)$ with n entities is defined as $G \subseteq H$, $V_G = V$ and $E_G \subseteq E$ such that G is a directed graph with no directed cycles.*

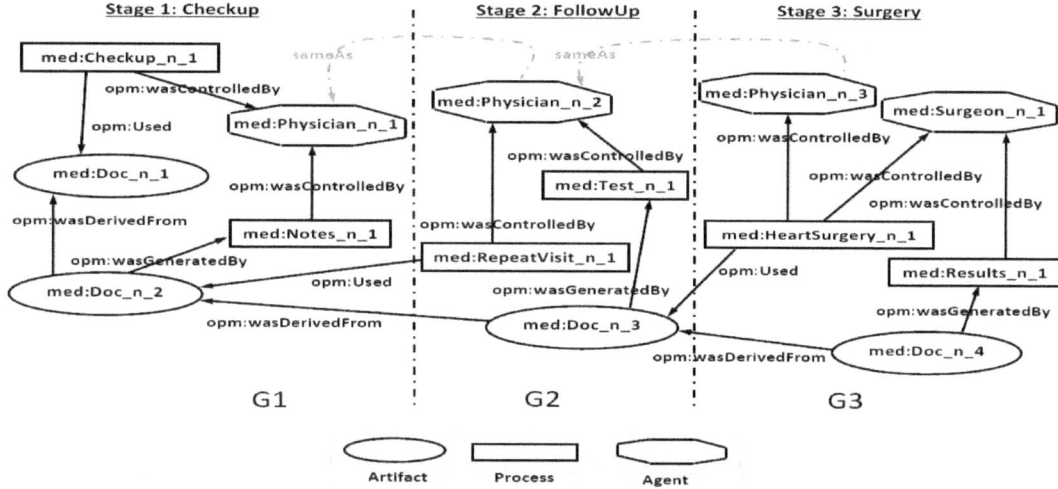

Figure 1: Provenance Graph

2.1.3 Use Case: Medical Example

Figure 1 shows a medical example as a provenance graph using a RDF representation that outlines a patient's visit to a hospital. This provenance graph is divided into three stages, namely a checkup procedure, a follow up visit and a heart surgery procedure. Note that at the point of undergoing the heart surgery procedure, the surgeon has access to the entire history of the patient's record. We assume that a hospital has a standard set of procedures that govern every healthcare service that the hospital provides. Therefore, each patient that needs to use a healthcare service will need to go through this set of procedures. We use a fixed set of notations in Figure 1 to represent an entity in the provenance graph, for example

```
<med:Checkup_n_1> .
```

The "n" denotes a particular patient who is undergoing a procedure at the hospital. Therefore, n = 1 identifies a patient with id = 1, n = 2 identifies a patient with id = 2, and so on. A larger number in the suffix of each process, agent and artifact signifies that the particular provenance entity is used at a later stage in a medical procedure. In practice, "n" would be instantiated with an actual patient id; this leads to the following set of RDF triples for a patient with id = 1 at stage 1,

```
<med:Checkup_1_1> <opm:WasControlledBy> <med:Physician_1_1>
<med:Checkup_1_1> <opm:Used> <med:Doc_1_1>
<med:Doc_1_2> <opm:WasDerivedFrom> <med:Doc_1_1>
<med:Doc_1_2> <opm:WasGeneratedBy> <med:Notes_1_1>
<med:Notes_1_1> <opm:WasControlledBy> <med:Physician_1_1>
```

This is not a complete picture of the provenance graph, it would be further annotated with RDF triples to indicate for example, location, time and other contextual information. Each entity in the graph would have a unique set of RDF annotations based on its type. Table 1 shows a set of compatible annotations for each type of provenance entity. A usage of these annotations in RDF representation for a physician associated with a patient with id = 1 would be,

Table 1: RDF Annotations

Entity	RDF Annotation
Process	PerformedOn
Agent	Name, Sex, Age and Zip Code
Artifact	UpdatedOn

```
<med:Physician_1_1> <med:Name> "John Smith"
<med:Physician_1_1> <med:Sex> "M"
<med:Physician_1_1> <med:Age> "35"
<med:Physician_1_1> <med:Zip> "76543"
```

2.2 Graph Rewriting

A graph rewriting system is well suited for performing transformations over a graph. Further, provenance is well represented in a graphical format. Thus, a graph rewriting system is well suited for specifying policy transformations over provenance. Graph rewriting is a transformation technique that takes as input an original graph and replaces a part of that graph with another graph. This technique, also called graph transformation, creates a new graph from the original graph by using a set of production rules. Popular graph rewriting approaches include the single-pushout approach and the double-pushout approach [24, 9]. For the purpose of this paper we define graph rewriting as follows,

DEFINITION 5. (Graph Rewriting System) A graph rewriting system is a three tuple, (G_ℓ, q, P) where,

G_ℓ is a labeled directed graph as given by Definition 1;

q is a request on G_ℓ that returns a subgraph G_q;

P is a policy set. For every policy $p = (r, e)$ in P, $r =$

(se, re) is a production rule, where se is a starting entity and re is a regular expression string; and e is an embedding instruction;

- *Production Rule, r: A production rule, $r : L \longrightarrow R$ where L is a subgraph of G_q and R is a graph. We also refer to L as the left hand side (LHS) of the rule and R as the right hand side (RHS) of the rule. During a rule manipulation, L is replaced by R and we embed R into $G_q - L$.*

- *Embedding Information, e: This specifies how to connect R to $G_q - L$ and also gives special post-processing instructions for graph nodes and edges on the RHS of a graph production rule. This embedding information can be textual or graphical.*

This general graph rewriting system can be used to perform redaction over a directed labeled graph, in particular a provenance graph. A graph query is used to determine the resources in the provenance graph that are to be shared with other parties. These resources take the form of a single node, a relationship between two nodes or a sequence of nodes along a path in the provenance graph. A set of redaction policies is used to protect any sensitive information that is contained within these resources. Such policies are a formal specification of the information that must not be shared. We formulate these policies in our graph grammar system as production rules in order to identify and remove any sensitive (e.g. proprietary, legal, competitive) content in these resources. These production rules are applied on the provenance graph as one of the following graph operations: a vertex contraction, or an edge contraction, or a path contraction or a node relabeling operation.

In order for our graph rewriting system to manipulate the provenance graph, we use a graph manipulation language over RDF called SPARQL [23]. In addition, we use one of the features in the latest extension of SPARQL [14], namely regular expressions, to identify paths of arbitrary length in a provenance graph. We give a brief overview of SPARQL followed by details of the various graph operations.

2.2.1 SPARQL

SPARQL is a query language for RDF that uses graph pattern matching to match a subgraph of a RDF graph [23].

DEFINITION 6. *(Graph pattern) A SPARQL graph pattern expression is defined recursively as follows:*

1. *A triple pattern is a graph pattern.*

2. *If P1 and P2 are graph patterns, then expressions (P1 AND P2), (P1 OPT P2), and (P1 UNION P2) are graph patterns.*

3. *If P is a graph pattern and R is a built-in SPARQL condition, then the expression (P FILTER R) is a graph pattern.*

4. *If P is a graph pattern, V is a set of variables and $X \in \mathcal{U} \cup V$ then (X GRAPH P) is a graph pattern.*

The current W3C recommendation for SPARQL lacks necessary constructs for supporting paths of arbitrary length [10]. Recent work has focused on extending the SPARQL language with support for paths of arbitrary length as given

in [10, 1, 19]. In addition, a W3C working draft for incorporating this feature into SPARQL can be found in [14].

We formulate our SPARQL queries around regular expression patterns in order to identify both, the resources being shared, and the LHS and RHS of the production rules of a policy set. The regular expressions are used to qualify the edges of a triple pattern so that a triple pattern is matched as an edge or a path in the provenance graph.

DEFINITION 7. *(Regular Expressions) Let Σ be an alphabet. The set $RE(\Sigma)$ of regular expressions is inductively defined by:*

- $\forall x \in \Sigma, x \in RE(\Sigma);$

- $\Sigma \in RE(\Sigma);$

- $\epsilon \in RE(\Sigma);$

- *If $A \in RE(\Sigma)$ and $B \in RE(\Sigma)$ then: $A|B, A/B, A^*, A^+, A? \in RE(\Sigma).$*

The symbols | and / are interpreted as logical OR and composition respectively.

2.2.2 Graph Operations

We now define the graph operations that manipulate a provenance graph in order to effectively apply a set of redaction policies. These graph operations remove or circumvent parts of the graph identified by a query. In addition, a graph rewriting system can be constructed so that the rules and embedding instructions ensure that specific relationships are preserved [3]. Therefore, we specify embedding information which will ensure that our graph rewriting system returns a modified but valid provenance graph. These graph operations are implemented as an edge contraction or a vertex contraction or a path contraction or a node relabeling.

Edge Contraction. Let $G = (V, E)$ be a directed graph containing an edge $e = (u, v)$ with $v \neq u$. Let f be a function which maps every vertex in $V \setminus \{u, v\}$ to itself, and otherwise maps it to a new vertex w. The contraction of e results in a new graph $G' = (V', E')$, where $V' = (V \setminus \{u, v\}) \cup \{w\}$, $E' = (E \setminus \{e\})$, and for every $x \in V$, $x' = f(x) \in V$ is incident to an edge $e' \in E'$ if and only if the corresponding edge, $e \in E$ is incident to x in G. Edge contraction may be performed on a set of edges in any order. Contractions may result in a graph with loops or multiple edges. In order to maintain the definition of a provenance graph given in Definition 4 we delete these edges. Figure 2 is an example of an edge contraction for our use case (see Figure 1). In this example, our objective is to prevent a third party from determining a specific procedure (i.e., a heart surgery) as well as the agent who performed that procedure (i.e., a surgeon). The triangle refers to a merge of the heart surgery process and the surgeon who performed the said process. The cloud represents predecessors, which could be the remaining provenance graph or a redacted graph.

We would like to make clear that an edge contraction will serve as the basis for defining both vertex contraction and path contraction: A vertex contraction can be implemented as an edge contraction by replacing two arbitrary vertices u, v and an edge drawn between them with a new vertex w. Similarly, a path contraction can be implemented as a series of edge contractions, where each edge is processed in turn

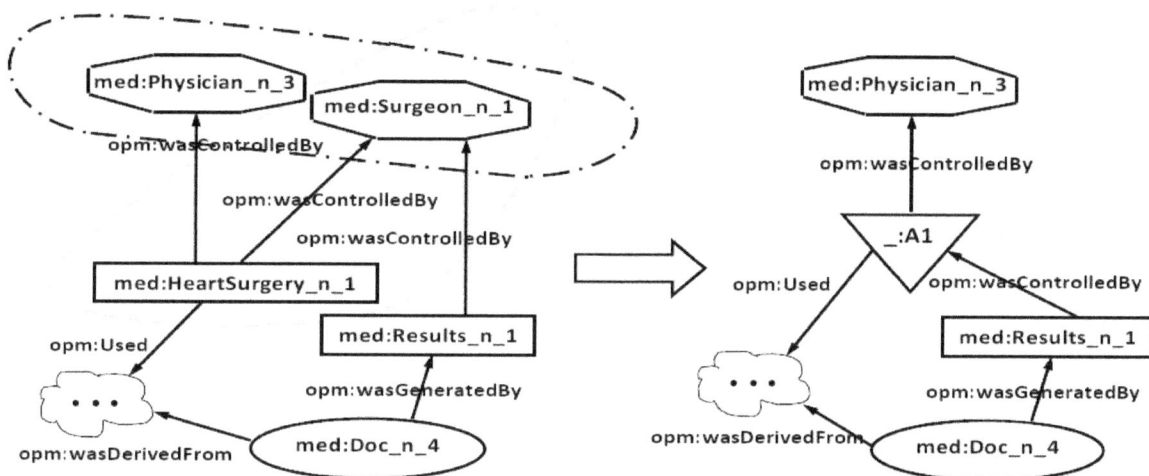

Figure 2: Edge Contraction

until we reach the last edge on the path. We will therefore exploit these two implementation details to make clear that both our vertex and path contractions are in fact edge contractions; therefore, they are both consistent with our graph rewriting system.

Vertex Contraction. This removes the restriction that contraction must occur over vertices sharing an incident edge. This operation may occur on any pair (or subset) of vertices in a graph. Edges between two contracting vertices are sometimes removed, in order to maintain the definition of a provenance graph given in Definition 4. A vertex contraction of the left hand side of Figure 2 would therefore replace Physician1_1 and Surgeon1_1 with a triangle that denotes a merge of these two nodes. This vertex contraction could show for example how a third party is prevented from knowing the identities of agents (i.e., both, a patient primary physician and surgeon) who controlled the processes (i.e., a heart surgery and a logging of results of a surgery into a patient's record).

Path Contraction. This occurs upon a set of edges in a path that contract to form a single edge between the endpoints of the path. Edges incident to vertices along the path are either eliminated, or arbitrarily connected to one of the endpoints. A path contraction over the provenance graph given in Figure 1 for a patient with id = 1 would involve circumventing the entire ancestry chain of Doc_1_4 as well as the entities affected by Doc_1_4. A path contraction is necessary when we want to prevent the release of the history of patient 1 prior to surgery as well as the details of the surgery procedure. We show the resulting triples after conducting path contraction on Figure 1.

```
<med:Doc_1_4> <opm:WasDerivedFrom> <_:A1>
<med:Doc_1_4> <opm:WasGeneratedBy> <_:A2>
```

Node Relabeling. A node relabeling operation replaces a label in a node with another label. This is generally a production rule whose LHS is a node in G_q and whose RHS is also a node normally with a new label. The entities shown in Figure 1 have generic labels but in practice each entity would be annotated with contextual information. This information serves as identifiers for the respective entity. Before

sharing information about these entities it is imperative that we remove sensitive identifiers from them. For example, a physician's cell phone number and social security number are considered unique identifiers and these should be redacted whenever this physician's identity is sensitive. Other attributes such as date of birth, sex and zip code, when taken together, may also uniquely identify a physician (see further details in work by Sweeney [25]). We motivate this idea of node relabeling with the following RDF triples taken from our use case.

```
<med:Physician_1_1> <med:Sex> "M"
<med:Physician_1_1> <med:Age> "35"
<med:Physician_1_1> <med:Zip> "76543"
```

After performing a node relabeling on the above set of RDF triples we would then share the following triples.

```
<med:Physician_1_1> <med:Sex> "X"
<med:Physician_1_1> <med:Age> "30-40"
<med:Physician_1_1> <med:Zip> "765XX"
```

2.3 An Example Graph Transformation Step

We show the general steps of the medical procedure only for one patient in Figure 1 for clarity. However, in reality Figure 1 would be a subgraph of a much larger graph that describes provenance for n patients. We now motivate the transformation step over Figure 1 with an example.

EXAMPLE 1. *After Bob underwent a heart surgery operation, the hospital must submit a claim to Bob's insurance company. In order to completely process the claim, the insurance company requests more information about the heart surgery procedure.*

In this example, the entity representing patient 1 in the provenance graph would be annotated with an attribute *name* and a value *Bob*. The hospital may wish to share this information in order to receive payment from *Bob*'s insurance company. However, based on guidelines related to this sharing of medical records with third parties, the hospital may not wish to share *Bob*'s entire medical history, as doing so could adversely affect *Bob*'s continued coverage from his insurance company. So in this case, the hospital shares the relevant information related to the surgery operation but not *Bob*'s entire medical history.

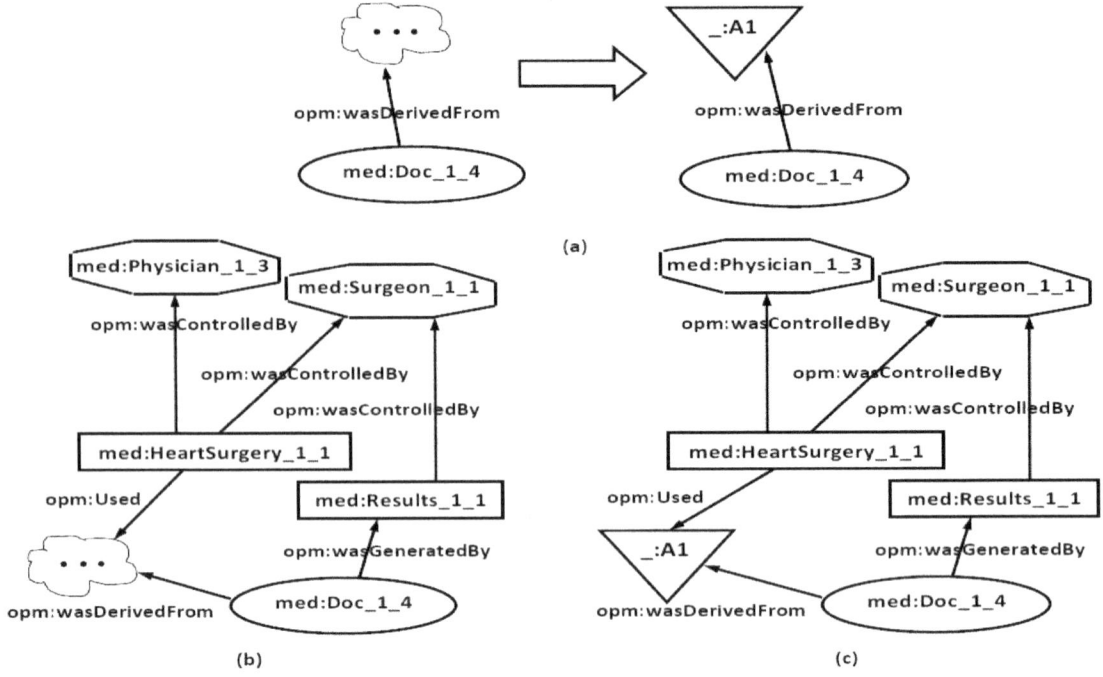

Figure 3: Graph Transformation Step

From Figure 1, the provenance of Doc1_4 involves all the entities which can be reached from Doc1_4 by following the paths which start at Doc1_4. The hospital's first step is to identify the resources in the provenance graph related to patient 1. For this we would evaluate a regular expression SPARQL query over the provenance graph G, by using the following graph patterns with Doc1_4 as the starting entity for the first graph pattern and HeartSurgery1_1 as the starting entity of the second graph pattern.

```
{ { med:Doc1_4 gleen:OnPath("([opm:WasDerivedFrom]+/
    ([opm:WasGeneratedBy]/[opm:WasControlledBy]))") }
    UNION { med:HeartSurgery1_1 gleen:OnPath("([opm:Used]|
    [opm:WasControlledBy])*") } }
```

This would return G_q as the following RDF triples:

```
<med:Doc_1_4> <opm:WasDerivedFrom> <med:Doc_1_3>
<med:Doc_1_3> <opm:WasDerivedFrom> <med:Doc_1_2>
<med:Doc_1_2> <opm:WasDerivedFrom> <med:Doc_1_1>
<med:Doc_1_3> <opm:WasGeneratedBy> <med:Test_1_1>
<med:Test_1_1> <opm:WasControlledBy> <med:Physician_1_2>
<med:Doc_1_2> <opm:WasGeneratedBy> <med:Notes_1_1>
<med:Notes_1_1> <opm:WasControlledBy> <med:Physician_1_1>
<med:Doc_1_4> <opm:WasGeneratedBy> <med:Results_1_1>
<med:Results_1_1> <opm:WasControlledBy> <med:Surgeon_1_1>
<med:HeartSurgery1_1> <opm:WasControlledBy> <med:Physician_1_3>
<med:HeartSurgery1_1> <opm:WasControlledBy> <med:Surgeon_1_1>
<med:HeartSurgery1_1> <opm:Used> <med:Doc_1_3>
```

We would then evaluate a set of production rules against these RDF triples, where each production rule has a starting entity in G_q. This set of rules governs the particulars relating to how information is shared based on the hospital procedures (or an even bigger set of regulatory guidelines eg., HIPAA). Figure 3(a) is the first production rule applied to G_q and Figure 3(b) and Figure 3(c) respectively show the transformation before and after applying the rule. This rule reveals some information about the heart surgery procedure which was done for patient 1, but not the entire history of the record, which may contain sensitive information. The graph

pattern for the regular expression SPARQL query used to generate the LHS of the rule in Figure 3(a) is:

```
{ { med:Doc1_4 gleen:OnPath("([opm:WasDerivedFrom]+/
    ([opm:WasGeneratedBy]/[opm:WasControlledBy])")
    UNION { med:RepeatVisit1_1 gleen:OnPath("([opm:Used]|
    [opm:WasControlledBy])") }
    UNION { med:Checkup1_1 gleen:OnPath("([opm:Used]|
    [opm:WasControlledBy])") } }
```

The graph representing the RHS would be given by _:A1 and the embedding instruction for gluing the RHS to $G_q - LHS$ is given by,

```
<med:HeartSurgery_1_1> <opm:Used> <:_A1>.
```

The transformed G_q would now be:

```
<med:Doc_1_4> <opm:WasDerivedFrom> <_:A1>
<med:Doc_1_4> <opm:WasGeneratedBy> <med:Results_1_1>
<med:Results_1_1> <opm:WasControlledBy> <med:Surgeon_1_1> .
<med:HeartSurgery1_1> <opm:WasControlledBy> <med:Physician_1_3>
<med:HeartSurgery1_1> <opm:WasControlledBy> <med:Surgeon_1_1>
<med:HeartSurgery1_1> <opm:Used> <_:A1>
```

2.4 Discussion

We acknowledge the impact of an adversarial model when doing an analysis of our approach. Asking who is the adversary violating privacy safeguards, in what ways they would do it, and what their capabilities are, is an art in itself and may not be something a community is capable of doing correctly. Also, with so many regulations restricting an institution's sharing ability and with a high demand for quality and trustworthy information, there is a need for very flexible redaction policies. However, redaction policies alone may not anticipate various potential threats which may occur after the information is released from our prototype system.

We identify a unit of provenance that is to be protected as a resource. We could describe this resource as a concept, where modifying the resource produces a description of a possibly new concept that may no longer be sensitive. This modification could be performed by an operation, such as deletion, insertion or relabeling. We could also describe a resource as a unit of proof; this means that the evidence for the starting entity (or some entity) exists in the rest of the resource. Tampering with this evidence would then reduce the utility of the resource. We attempt to strike the right balance between these two descriptions.

We note that for the standard procedures in our use case, a set of similar procedures give provenance graphs with similar topologies. This allows us to define the resources in the provenance graph by regular expressions, which match a specific pattern. These patterns are our concepts. An advantage of regular expressions in queries is that we do not need the contents of the provenance graph to determine the resource we are protecting, we only need the structure of the graph since all graphs generated in accordance with the same procedure have similar topologies.

One drawback with our prototype is that if we change (or sanitize) only the content of a single resource node before releasing it to a third party, other identifying characteristics still remain in the released resource. For example, if we hide the physician in stage 2 of Figure 1, the contextual information associated with that physician (such as age, zip code and sex) could reidentify the physician. Another drawback in releasing information is that the querying user, in the real world, usually has knowledge of the application domain. Let us assume a resource having the following regular expression pattern: opm:WasGeneratedBy/opm:WasControlledBy was released. Then, a user could infer the sequence of entities along the path identified by this regular expression pattern. In addition, if we apply this regular expression pattern to stage 2 of Figure 1, we could determine that only a physician could have performed/ordered the particular test.

In order to minimize the above drawbacks, we apply our graph grammar approach, which transforms a provenance graph to a new graph and at each stage of the transformation determines if a policy is violated before performing further transformations. When this transformation process is completed, we hope to successfully redact the piece of provenance information we share as well as maximize its utility.

3. ARCHITECTURE

Our system architecture is composed of three tiers, the interface layer, the graph transformation layer and the data storage layer. This design allows a user to seamlessly interact with the data storage layer through our graph rewriting system. We first describe the layers in our architecture followed by a prototype that implements the architecture using Semantic Web technologies.

3.1 Modules in our Architecture

The **User Interface Layer** hides the actual internal representation of a query and a redaction policy from a user. This allows a user to submit a high-level specification of a policy without any knowledge of grammar rules and SPARQL regular expression queries. This layer also allows a user to retrieve any information irrespective of the underlying data representation. The **High Level Specification Language Layer** allows the user to write the redaction policies in a language suitable for their application needs. This layer is not tied to any particular policy specification language. Any high level policy language can be used to write the redac-

tion policies as long as there is a compatible parser that translates these policies to the graph grammar specification.

We provide a simple default policy language for writing redaction policies. The syntax uses XML [5], which is an open and extensible language, and is both customizable and readily supports integration of other domain descriptions. The following is a high level specification of the rule in Figure 3(a) using our default policy language for patient 1.

```
<policy ID="1" >
   <lhs>
        start=Doc1_4
        chain=[WasDerivedFrom]+ artifact AND
        artifact [WasGeneratedBy] process AND
        process [WasControlledBy] physician|surgeon.
        start=RepeatVisit1_1
        chain=[Used][WasControlledBy].
        start=Checkup1_1
        chain=[Used][WasControlledBy].
   </lhs>
   <rhs>_:A1</rhs>
   <condition>
    <application>null</application>
    <attribute>null</attribute>
   </condition>
   <embedding>
    <pre>null</pre>
    <post>(HeartSurgery_1_1,Used, _:A1)</post>
   </embedding>
</policy>
```

The description of each element is as follows: The **lhs** element describes the left hand side of a rule. The **rhs** element describes the right hand side of a rule. Each path in the **lhs** and **rhs** begins at a starting entity. The **condition** element has two optional sub elements, the **application** defines the conditions that must hold for rule application to proceed, and the **attribute** element describes the annotations in LHS. Similarly, the **embedding** element has two optional sub elements, **pre** describes how LHS is connected to the provenance graph and the **post** describes how RHS is connected to the provenance graph.

The **Policy Parser Layer** is a program that takes as input a high-level policy set and parses each policy into the appropriate graph grammar production rule. In the case of our default policy, the parser would verify that the structure of the policy conforms to a predefined XML schema. The **Redaction Policy Layer** enforces the redaction policies against the information retrieved to make sure that no sensitive or proprietary information is released for unauthorized uses. This layer also resolves any conflicts that resulted from executing the policies over the data stores. The **Regular Expression-Query Translator** takes a valid regular expression string and builds a corresponding graph pattern from these strings. The **Data Controller** stores and manages access to data, which could be stored in any format such as in a relational database, in XML files or in a RDF store. The **Provenance Controller** is used to store and manage provenance information that is associated with data items that are present in the data controller. The provenance controller stores information in the form of logical graph structures in any appropriate data representation format. This controller also records the on-going activities associated with the data items stored in the data controller. This controller takes as input a regular expression query and evaluates it over the provenance information. This query evaluation returns a subgraph back to the redaction policy layer where it is re-examined using the redaction policies.

To implement the layers in our architecture we use various open-source tools. We implement the High Level Specification Language Layer using our default XML-based pol-

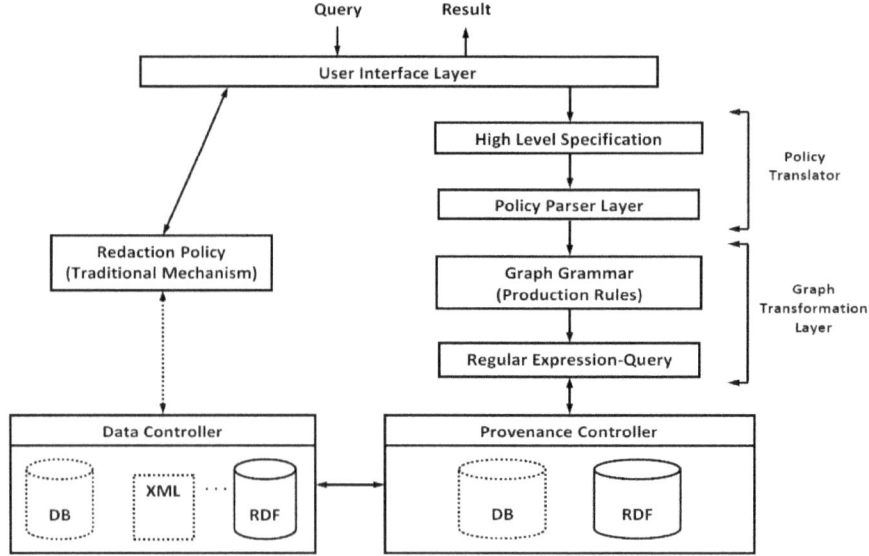

Figure 4: Architecture

icy language. To implement the Policy Parser Layer, we use Java 1.6 and the XML schema specification. The XML schema allows us to verify the structure of our policy file. This layer is also programmed to produce the production rules. We implement the Regular Expression-Query Translator layer using the Gleen[2] regular expression library, that extends SPARQL to support property path queries over a RDF graph [10]. We create our provenance graph using the OPM toolbox[3] instead of other available tools such as Taverna [22] which is not as easy to use as the OPM toolbox. Our experiments are conducted over in-memory models created using the Jena API[4][7].

3.2 Experiments

Our experiments were conducted on an IBM workstation with 8 X 2.5GHz processors and 32GB RAM. Our prototype is efficient for both, finding the shared resource over an original provenance graph and evaluating the production rules over the shared resource. We choose three conventions for pre-ordering the production rules: (1) the original ordering ($\mathcal{OO}$); (2) lowest to highest utility ($\mathcal{LHO}$); and (3) highest to lowest utility ($\mathcal{HLO}$). We believe that provenance is more useful when it is least altered. Therefore, we define utility as $(1 - \frac{\text{altered triples}}{\text{original triples in } G_q}) \times 100$ which captures this notion. For implementing the second and third conventions we use a sorting mechanism based on our definition of utility. This sorting mechanism is used in Algorithm 1 which is an overview of the redaction procedure discussed in Section 2.2.

Table 2 shows a comparison of the average redaction time for two graphs given to Algorithm 1 with the same rule patterns. Both graphs are constructed from the original provenance graph such that each of them start at the beginning of the longest path in the provenance graph. Further, the first

---

[2]Available at http://sig.biostr.washington.edu/projects/ontviews/gleen/index.html
[3]Available at http://openprovenance.org/
[4]http://jena.sourceforge.net/

Algorithm 1 REDACT(G_q, RS)

1: LI ← SORT(G_q, RS); {Initial sort of Rule Set (RS)}
2: **while** diff > 0 **do**
3:     $G'_q = G_q$
4:     p = LI.top
5:     $G_q ← p.e(p.r(G'_q))$ {$T_{Redact} += T_{Rule} + T_{Emb}$}
6:     LI = SORT($G_q, RS - p$) {$T_{Redact} += T_{Sort}$}
7:     diff = difference(G_q, G'_q) {$T_{Redact} += T_{Diff}$}
8: **end while**
9: **return** G'_q

Algorithm 2 SORT(G_q, RS)

1: SL = new List()
2: **for all** $r \in RS$ **do**
3:     **if** $r.se \in G_q$ **then**
4:         **if** $G_q \models r$ **then**
5:             SL.add(r)
6:         **end if**
7:     **end if**
8: **end for**
9: **return** SL

Table 2: Query Comparison in milliseconds

G_q	Order	T_{Redact}	T_{Rule}	T_{Emb}	T_{Sort}	T_{Diff}
1	$\mathcal{HLO}$	17304	19	3	17241	41
	$\mathcal{LHO}$	41012	1853	7	39137	15
2	$\mathcal{HLO}$	35270	28	2	35187	53
	$\mathcal{LHO}$	9044	2904	7	6106	27

graph retrieves all the ancestry chains for that starting entity while the second graph determines the agents that are two hops away from every artifact at least one hop away from the said starting entity. Algorithm 1 updates the redaction time at each graph transformation step. Our first observa-

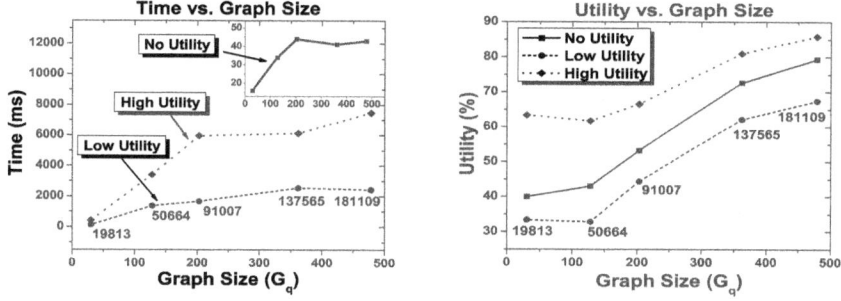

Figure 5: Comparison of Redaction Time and Utility vs. Graph Size

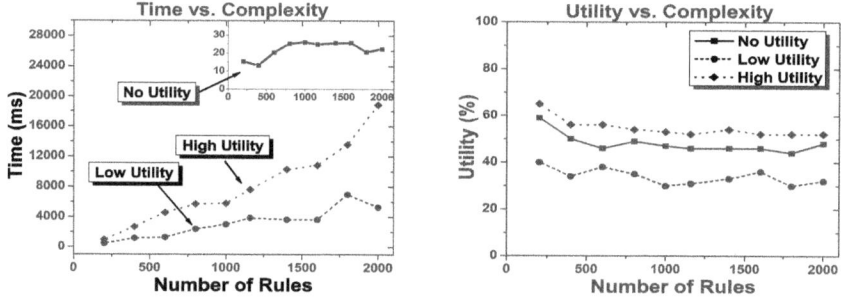

Figure 6: Experimental Comparison of Complexity

tion from Table 2 is that the major component of the redaction time is the time spent in sorting the rule set when using our notion of utility. We further explore the performance of Algorithm 1 using different graph sizes and rule patterns.

Figure 5 shows a comparison of the redaction time and utility vs. graph size while keeping the rule set size constant ($RS = 200$ rules). The labels on every point in Figure 5 show the actual provenance graph size. Figure 5(a) compares the redaction time for our three utility conventions as the input graph to Algorithm 1 increases in size. The inset to Figure 5(a) shows that $\mathcal{OO}$ takes the least redaction time because this strategy does not execute lines 1, 4 and 6 of Algorithm 1 for each rule in the rule set. The difference in times between the different strategies is compensated by the higher utility gained from applying the $\mathcal{HLO}$ as shown in Figure 5(b).

Figure 6 shows a comparison of the redaction time and utility as the size of the rule set increases while keeping the size of G_q constant ($G_q = 87$ triples). At each transformation step, Algorithm 1 picks a rule that alters the least triples in G_q for $\mathcal{HLO}$ while it picks a rule that alters the most triples in G_q for $\mathcal{LHO}$. Algorithm 1 picks any rule for $\mathcal{OO}$.

At each transformation step, Algorithm 1 transforms G_q by using rule p at line 5. Rule p is determined by applying either $\mathcal{LHO}$ or $\mathcal{HLO}$ to a sorted rule set returned by Algorithm 2. Line 4 of Algorithm 2 performs graph matching to determine if $G_q \models p.r$. This operation tests if $G_q \models s \xrightarrow{\rho} o$ where $\rho \in RE(\Sigma)$. This further evaluates whether $G_q \models t$ for each triple t along $s \xrightarrow{\rho} o$. In conclusion, the time and utility of the entire redaction process is dependent on (1)

the current G_q; (2) the current rule set, RS; (3) a given rule $r \in RS$ which transforms G_q; and (4) the given RHS of r and the embedding instruction, $p.e$.

4. RELATED WORK

Previous work on using graph transformation approaches to model security aspects of a system include references [17, 18]. In [8], an extension of the double pushout(DPO) rewriting, called Sesqui-pushout (S_qPO) was used to represent the subjects and objects in an access control system as nodes and the rights of a subject on an object as edges. In [17], the authors used the formal properties of graph transformation to detect and resolve inconsistencies within the specification of access control policies. References [4, 26, 21] focus on the unique features of provenance with respect to the security of provenance itself. While [21] prescribes a generalized access control model, the flow of information between various sources and the causal relationships among entities are not immediately obvious in this work. Our work is also motivated by [4, 6, 20, 27] where the focus is on representing provenance as a directed graph structure. We also found previous work related to the efficiency of a graph rewriting system in [12, 13, 2]. In the general case, graph pattern matching, which finds a homomorphic (or isomorphic) image of a given graph in another graph is a NP-complete problem. However, various factors make it tractable in a graph rewriting system [2]. In summary and to the best of our knowledge, our work, therefore, extends these previous approaches so that graph transformation, security and provenance can be combined to address redaction of provenance information before sharing it.

5. CONCLUSIONS

In this paper we propose a graph rewriting approach for redacting a provenance graph. We use a simple utility-based strategy to preserve as much of the provenance information as possible. This ensures a high quality in the information shared. We also implement a prototype based on our architecture and on Semantic Web technologies (RDF, SPARQL) in order to evaluate the effectiveness of our graph rewriting system. We plan to explore the following directions in the future: (i) This work focuses on using in-memory models to store provenance graphs. We propose to test our prototype with disk-based storage mechanisms. (ii) The order in which we apply rules is based on our definition of utility. We plan to investigate other techniques for ordering the policies such as policy subsumption based on least and most restrictiveness, as well as using the priority of policies, which also resolves the problem of conflicting policies.

6. REFERENCES

[1] F. Alkhateeb, J. Baget, and J. Euzenat. Extending SPARQL with regular expression patterns (for querying RDF). *Web Semantics: Science, Services and Agents on the World Wide Web*, 7(2):57–73, 2009.

[2] D. Blostein, H. Fahmy, and A. Grbavec. Issues in the practical use of graph rewriting. In *Graph Grammars and Their Application to Computer Science*, pages 38–55. Springer, 1996.

[3] D. Blostein and A. Schürr. Computing with graphs and graph rewriting. In *FACHGRUPPE INFORMATIK, RWTH*. Citeseer, 1997.

[4] U. Braun, A. Shinnar, and M. Seltzer. Securing provenance. In *Proceedings of the 3rd conference on Hot topics in security*, pages 1–5. USENIX Association, 2008.

[5] T. Bray, J. Paoli, C. Sperberg-McQueen, E. Maler, and F. Yergeau. Extensible markup language (XML) 1.0. *W3C recommendation*, 6, 2000.

[6] T. Cadenhead, V. Khadilkar, M. Kantarcioglu, and B. Thuraisingham. A Language for Provenance Access Control, 2011.

[7] J. J. Carroll, I. Dickinson, C. Dollin, D. Reynolds, A. Seaborne, and K. Wilkinson. Jena: implementing the semantic web recommendations. In S. I. Feldman, M. Uretsky, M. Najork, and C. E. Wills, editors, *WWW (Alternate Track Papers & Posters)*, pages 74–83. ACM, 2004.

[8] A. Corradini, T. Heindel, F. Hermann, and B. König. Sesqui-pushout rewriting. *Graph Transformations*, pages 30–45, 2006.

[9] A. Corradini, U. Montanari, F. Rossi, H. Ehrig, R. Heckel, and M. Löwe. Algebraic approaches to graph transformation. Part I: Basic concepts and double pushout approach. In *Handbook of graph grammars and computing by graph transformation*.

[10] L. Detwiler, D. Suciu, and J. Brinkley. Regular paths in SparQL: querying the NCI thesaurus. In *AMIA Annual Symposium Proceedings*, volume 2008, page 161. American Medical Informatics Association, 2008.

[11] L. Ding, T. Finin, Y. Peng, P. Da Silva, and D. McGuinness. Tracking RDF graph provenance using RDF molecules. In *Proc. of the 4th International Semantic Web Conference (Poster)*, 2005.

[12] M. Dodds and D. Plump. Graph transformation in constant time. *Graph Transformations*, pages 367–382, 2006.

[13] H. Dörr. *Efficient graph rewriting and its implementation*. Springer, 1995.

[14] S. Harris and A. Seaborne. SPARQL 1.1 Query Language. *W3C Working Draft*, 2010.

[15] G. Heath. Redaction Defined: Meeting Information Disclosure Requests with Secure Content Delivery. 1997.

[16] G. Klyne, J. Carroll, and B. McBride. Resource description framework (RDF): Concepts and abstract syntax. *W3C recommendation*. *http://www.w3.org/TR/rdf-concepts/*, 2004.

[17] M. Koch, L. Mancini, and F. Parisi-Presicce. Graph-based specification of access control policies. *Journal of Computer and System Sciences*, 71(1):1–33, 2005.

[18] M. Koch and F. Parisi-Presicce. UML specification of access control policies and their formal verification. *Software and Systems Modeling*, 5(4):429–447, 2006.

[19] K. Kochut and M. Janik. SPARQLeR: Extended SPARQL for semantic association discovery. *The Semantic Web: Research and Applications*, pages 145–159, 2007.

[20] L. Moreau, B. Clifford, J. Freire, Y. Gil, P. Groth, J. Futrelle, N. Kwasnikowska, S. Miles, P. Missier, J. Myers, et al. The Open Provenance Model—Core Specification (v1. 1). *Future Generation Computer Systems*, 2009.

[21] Q. Ni, S. Xu, E. Bertino, R. Sandhu, and W. Han. An Access Control Language for a General Provenance Model. *Secure Data Management*, pages 68–88, 2009.

[22] T. Oinn, M. Addis, J. Ferris, D. Marvin, M. Greenwood, T. Carver, M. Pocock, A. Wipat, and P. Li. Taverna: A Tool for the Composition and Enactment of Bioinformatics Workflows. *Bioinformatics*, 2004.

[23] E. Prud'hommeaux and A. Seaborne. SPARQL query language for RDF. *W3C Recommendation*, 2008.

[24] G. Rozenberg and H. Ehrig. *Handbook of graph grammars and computing by graph transformation*, volume 1. World Scientific, 1997.

[25] L. Sweeney. K-anonymity: A model for protecting privacy. *International Journal on Uncertainty, Fuzziness, and Knowledge-based Systems*, 10(5):557–570, 2002.

[26] V. Tan, P. Groth, S. Miles, S. Jiang, S. Munroe, S. Tsasakou, and L. Moreau. Security issues in a SOA-based provenance system. *Provenance and Annotation of Data*, pages 203–211, 2006.

[27] J. Zhao. Open Provenance Model Vocabulary Specification. *Latest version: http://purl.org/net/opmv/ns-20100827*, 2010.

[28] J. Zhao, C. Goble, R. Stevens, and D. Turi. Mining Taverna's semantic web of provenance. *Concurrency and Computation: Practice and Experience*, 20(5):463–472, 2008.

Data Leakage Mitigation for Discretionary Access Control in Collaboration Clouds

Qihua Wang
IBM Almaden Research Center
San Jose, California, USA
qwang@us.ibm.com

Hongxia Jin
IBM Almaden Research Center
San Jose, California, USA
jin@us.ibm.com

ABSTRACT

With the growing popularity of cloud computing, more and more enterprises are migrating their collaboration platforms from in-enterprise systems to Software as a Service (SaaS) applications. While SaaS collaboration has numerous advantages, it also raises new security challenges. In particular, since SaaS collaboration is increasingly used across enterprise boundaries, organizations are concerned that sensitive information may be leaked to outsiders due to their employees' inadvertent mistakes on information sharing. In this article, we propose to mitigate the data leakage problem in SaaS collaboration systems by reducing human errors. Built on top of the discretionary access control model in existing collaboration systems, we have designed a series of mechanisms to provide defense in depth against information leakage. First, we allow enterprises to encode their organizational security rules as mandatory access control policies, so as to impose coarse-grained restrictions on their employees' discretionary sharing decisions. Second, we design an attribute-based recommender that suggests and prioritizes potential recipients for users' files, reducing errors in the choices of recipients. Third, our system actively examines abnormal recipients entered by a file owner, providing the last line of defense before a file is shared. We have implemented a prototype of our solution and performed experiments on data collected from real-world collaboration systems.

Categories and Subject Descriptors

D.4.6 [**Operating Systems**]: Security and Protection—*Access controls*; K.6.5 [**Management of Computing and Information Systems**]: Security and Protection

General Terms

Algorithms, Security

1. INTRODUCTION

Enterprises increasingly subscribe to Software as a Service (SaaS) applications for collaboration, migrating from in-enterprise systems to collaboration clouds. Popular SaaS collaboration systems include IBM's LotusLive [6], Cisco's WebEx [4], Box.net [1],

and so on. A key motivating use case for SaaS collaboration is when work needs to occur across enterprise boundaries [3]. Unlike in-enterprise solutions, which are accessible only to the intranet users of an organization, a SaaS collaboration system is offered by a cloud provider and may serve clients from different organizations. After registering a company domain on the SaaS collaboration system, an organization may create affiliated accounts for its employees, who can then communicate and share files with other system users, including those outside of their organization.

The growing popularity of SaaS collaboration raises new security challenges. A key security concern with the migration from in-enterprise solutions to collaboration clouds is the data leakage problem, especially the leakage due to insiders' inadvertent mistakes on information sharing. For example, multiple instances on corporate data leakage have been reported where people inappropriately shared their calendar events on the cloud-based Google Calendar [7]. In the past when collaboration systems were kept within an organization's intranet, enterprise organizational boundaries have been key to the controls on sharing, providing both a social and technical barrier that can slow or stop potentially inappropriate sharing [3]. However, because SaaS collaboration is often used across enterprise boundaries, we can no longer rely on organizational boundaries for data leakage mitigation.

Information sharing is one of the most popular activities in collaboration systems. For example, a user may upload a file and grant access to her collaborators. A practical access control approach for collaborative information sharing should satisfy a number of properties. (1) *Fine-grained*: users oftentimes want to share only with specific collaborators rather than a large group. (2) *Flexible*: as a user's collaboration needs change over time, similar files may be granted to different people and similar people may be authorized to different files. (3) *User friendly*: the authorization scheme must be easy to use by business users who do not have much information security background. Due to such and other requirements, most existing collaboration systems employ the user-to-user (U2U) discretionary access control (DAC) mechanism, where a file owner discretionarily determines which individual users are authorized to access her files. However, this mechanism raises the risk of data leakage:

- Users are fully responsible to comply with organizations' security policies in their discretionary sharing decisions. In practice, an organization may have many such policies, including business conduct rules, non-disclosure agreements (NDA) with other parties, and so on. Even though most users will not intentionally violate organizational policies, information leakage is still possible when someone is unaware of a security restriction or is not careful.

- Choosing the right recipients for a file is not always an easy task. To decide on file recipients, a business user oftentimes needs to answer questions such as who need this file, will I gain benefits by sharing with these people, is there security risk if I share this file with them, and so on. Users do not always have clear answers to these questions, while real-world business conduct requires them to make sharing decisions rapidly. When a user does not have sufficient time for thorough consideration, she may make some default choices (such as making a resource accessible to everyone in an organization), which leads to poor security [17].

- Even when a user has a list of appropriate file recipients in mind, she might still make mistakes entering them into the system, either due to typos or incorrect auto-completion. The current SaaS collaboration systems are unable to tell whether what a user enters is what she really wants; they will simply take whatever input given by the user. Confidential information may thus slip through one's fingers.

In this paper, we propose to mitigate the data leakage problem in collaboration clouds by reducing human errors in file sharing. Our solution still employs U2U DAC as the core authorization mechanism, while introducing a series of protection mechanisms. First, our solution supports mandatory access control (MAC) policies specified by organizations. By encoding organizational security rules, such MAC policies impose coarse-grained restrictions on users' discretionary decisions. Furthermore, we design an attribute-based recipient recommender to help users make data sharing decisions better and faster, reducing inappropriate choices. Our recommender determines user attributes based on their past collaboration activities, and predicts likely recipients for a given file based on such attributes. To further reduce mistakes, the recommender actively examines user input and issues warnings should abnormal recipients be detected.

Our solution has a number of advantages with respect to security and usability.

- **Defense in depth:** The series of protections in our solution provide multiple layers of defense against those human errors that may result in data leakage.

- **Similarity:** Business users are already familiar with the existing data sharing mechanism in collaboration systems. If a solution changes the sharing process significantly, there will be a learning curve, making users reluctant to adopt the new approach. Our solution requires little change on the existing user-to-user discretionary data sharing process from the users' perspective. The MAC policies are specified by companies and are automatically enforced by the system; such policies are transparent to users except when violations occur. Recipient recommendation and abnormality warning may be seamlessly integrated into the existing recipient selection process as auxiliary features.

- **Simplicity:** Our solution demands low user effort. The input it takes from the user is simple and intuitive. It even takes advantages of existing mechanisms such as file tagging to acquire needed information, which further reduces the amount of additional input required.

- **Adaptivity:** Our solution is adaptive. It keeps learning from users' on-going collaboration activities and updates its knowledge base. It may also receive feedback from users and take their preferences into account in future services. On a finer scale, our interactive recommendation mechanism adaptively adjusts its suggestion based on what the users already entered, which further increases usability and accuracy.

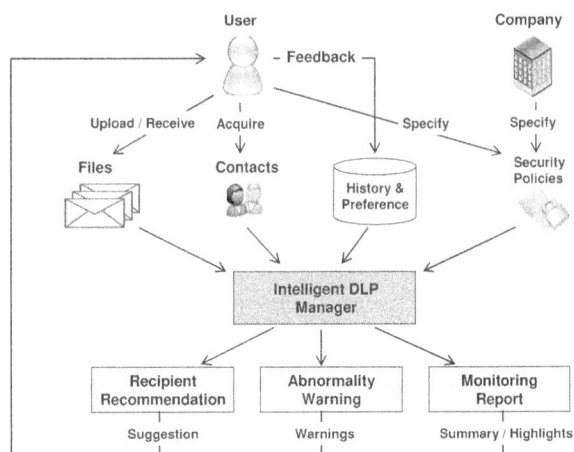

Figure 1: System architecture of our solution

Finally, the techniques in our solution may be applied to secure user information sharing in other systems, such as social networks. Our solution may also be extended to support Attribute-Based Access Control (ABAC) in collaborative working environments. We will discuss these topics in Section 7.

The rest of this paper is organized as follows. We will provide an overview of our solution in Section 2. We will study MAC policies, user modeling, and the recommender in Sections 3, 4, and 5, respectively. After that, we will describe evaluation methods and present experimental results in Section 6. The security and expansion of our approach will be discussed in Section 7. Finally, we will study related work in Section 8 and conclude in Section 9.

2. OVERVIEW

2.1 Preliminaries

We formally define the concepts appearing in this paper.

DEFINITION 1 (COLLABORATION SYSTEM). A *collaboration system* is represented as $\langle O, U, S \rangle$, where O is the set of all registered organizations, U is the set of all registered users, and $S = \{s_1, \ldots, s_m\}$ is the set of subsystems.

Most existing collaboration systems use a person's registered email address as his/her identity. Each subsystem in a collaboration system offers a certain type of collaboration service. Example services include file sharing, online meetings, and collaborative workflows (where users may contribute to a collaborative task that is divided into multiple steps).

DEFINITION 2 (COLLABORATION ACTIVITY). Given a collaboration system $\langle O, U, S \rangle$, a *collaboration activity* in the system is represented as $\langle U_i, s_j, W, t \rangle$, where $U_i \subseteq U$ is the set of users involved in the activity, $s_j \in S$ is the subsystem in which the activity is performed, W is the textual content of the activity, and t is time of the activity.

For example, assume that Alice shared a file related to "database security" with Bob and Carl on 01/31/10. This may be represented as $\langle \{Alice, Bob, Carl\}, s_{file}, \{database, security, \ldots\}, 01/31/10 \rangle$. Intuitively, the textual content of an activity describes what the activity is about.

DEFINITION 3 (USER AND CONTACT). Given a collaboration system $\langle O, U, S \rangle$, a *user* is represented as $\langle u, org, C \rangle$, where $u \in U$ is the user's identity, $org \in O$ is the user's affiliated organization, and $C \subseteq U$ is the user's *contacts* in the system.

There are a number of common ways for a user to acquire contacts in existing collaboration systems. First, the user may manually add contacts to her address book. Second, contacts may be automatically added to a user's address book through collaboration activities. If a user u participates an activity with another user, the latter will be automatically added to u's address book by the system. Third, contacts may be preloaded from organizational directories when applicable.

DEFINITION 4 (FILE). Given a collaboration system $\langle O, U, S \rangle$, a *file* is represented as $\langle f, L, W_k \rangle$, where f is the file's identity, L is its *security labels*, and W_k is a set of keywords.

For convenience, we refer to the user who uploads a file to the collaboration system as the *owner* of the file. The file owner is responsible for specifying the security labels and keywords upon uploading the file. If a file contains confidential information on an organization o_i, its owner should add o_i as a security label to L. A file may have more than one security label. If the file does not contain confidential information about any organization, L is empty. Applying security labels to files is a required or recommended practice in many business organizations. Note that a file f containing confidential information about the organizations in L does not indicate that f can only be shared with users from an organization in L. In practice, another organization may have intellectual property agreements with those in L, making it qualified to access f.

As to keyword specification, our current prototype employs the method of file tagging. Tagging, as a popular Web 2.0 offering, has been widely used by people to organize and retrieve web resources. Many SaaS collaboration systems, such as LotusLive, allow users to apply tags to files. By using a file's tags as keywords, our solution takes advantage of users' effort on file organization to serve a security task.

DEFINITION 5 (SHARING INSTANCE). Given a collaboration system $\langle O, U, S \rangle$, a *file sharing instance* is represented as $\langle u, U_a, f, t \rangle$, where $u \in U$ is the user who initiates the sharing, $U_a \subseteq U$ is the set of recipients selected by u, f is the identity of the target file, and t is the time when the instance is initiated.

A sharing instance may either represent a past sharing activity or a proposed one to be processed by the collaboration system.

2.2 System Architecture

The system architecture of our solution is given in Figure 1. The central component of our solution is a DLP manager that provides defense in depth against information leakage through file sharing. First, the DLP manager supports mandatory access control (MAC) policies specified by organizations. The MAC policies allow organizations to control the maximum sharing scopes of certain types of files. Such MAC policies essentially place coarse-grained security boundaries around the discretionary sharing decisions made by users, so as to stop certain undesirable information flows while keeping the flexibility of U2U DAC.

Second, the DLP manager creates attribute profiles for each user's contacts by mining their past collaboration activities. With the created contact profiles, it is able to recommend likely recipients for target files and examine user input for abnormalities. The goal of such recipient recommendation and abnormality examination is to reduce user errors in both the decision making and the input phases, preventing data leakage due to mistakes.

Third, the DLP manager periodically updates a user's contact profiles using his/her new collaboration information. This allows the DLP manager to adapt to users' changing collaboration needs. It also accepts feedback from users and adjusts its recommendation and examination strategies accordingly.

3. MANDATORY POLICIES

In this section, we define the mandatory access control (MAC) policies supported by our DLP manager.

DEFINITION 6 (MAC POLICY). Given a collaboration system $\langle O, U, S \rangle$, a *mandatory access control policy* is represented as $\langle \delta, O_q \rangle$, where δ is the *application scope function* that takes a sharing instance as input and returns a boolean value, and $O_q \subseteq O$ is the *qualification scope* of the policy.

Given a sharing instance $\tau = \langle u, U_a, f, t \rangle$ and a policy $p = \langle \delta, O_q \rangle$, we say that τ *violates* p if and only if both of these conditions hold: (1) $\delta(\tau)$ is true; (2) $\exists_{u' \in U_a} org(u') \notin O_q$, where $org(u')$ is the affiliated organization of u'.

We say that τ *satisfies* p, if τ does not violate p. Also, we say that the users in U_a are *qualified* for f with regards to p, if τ satisfies p.

The application scope function determines to which sharing instances a MAC policy is applicable. The concrete form of the function may vary from organization to organization, depending on the security rules that need to be encoded. In reality, an organization's MAC policies may only be applicable to the sharing instances initiated by its affiliated users. Other factors considered by the application scope function may include the security labels of the target file, the organizations of the recipients, and the time of the instance.

The qualification scope defines a security boundary at the organization level: to be qualified to receive the target file, a user must be affiliated with an organization in the qualification scope. The qualification scope aims to prevent applicable data from flowing out of the boundaries of certain organizations. We would like to emphasize that not all the users in a "qualified organization" are authorized for the target file. Authorization is performed discretionarily by the user who initiates the sharing; a MAC policy only provides an upperbound on his/her discretionary selections.

Theoretically, we could define finer-grained qualification scopes in MAC policies, e.g. at the granularity of roles. However, in reality, the MAC policy makers in an organization may not know the administrational structure of another organization, making it infeasible to define fine-grained scopes regarding the latter. Furthermore, based on our experiences, most practical Non-Disclosure Agreements (NDA) are at organization level. We will refine the qualification scopes in MAC policies should there be practical needs in the future.

EXAMPLE 1. Company X is a software provider on web security tools. Company Y is X's customer. In a recent agreement, Y opts-in to provide its web access logs to X and its research partners to support the research of new products. In exchange, Y will receive discounts on existing services. In the agreement, X is not responsible for sharing research findings with Y. Company Z is a research partner of X's. Z has signed an agreement with X, which allows it to access X's data and research results.

The companies X, Y and Z subscribe to a SaaS collaboration. X would like to control the information flows related to its research project on new products. In response to this, the security administrators of X specify a MAC policy p to encode the agreements with Y and Z: $p = \langle \delta_1, \{X, Z\} \rangle$, where δ_1 is an application scope function such that: $\delta_1(\langle u, U_a, f, t \rangle)$ is true if and only if u is affiliated with X and f is related to a new product.

Alice, who is a member of the research team in X, has prepared a quarterly report f_r, which she would like to share with her collaborators. After uploading f_r to the SaaS collaboration system, Alice applies security labels and keywords to f_r to specify that f_r is about a new product from X. First, Alice chooses to share the file with Bob, who is a developer in Z. The sharing is permitted since it does not violate the MAC policy p. Next, Alice thinks that

Carl, who is a manager in Y, may also be interested in f_r, since the report contains research results from Y's data. Alice is not aware that X considers the new product as a business secret and does not want to share related information to anyone other than its research partners. With the discretionary access control mechanism in existing SaaS collaboration systems, Alice would have mistakenly leaked sensitive information to Y through the sharing of f_r. In contrast, with the enforcement of organizational MAC policies, Alice's request to share f_r with Carl is denied as it violates the applicable policy p. As we can see, the support of MAC policies releases users from taking full responsibility of remembering and complying with every applicable organizational security rule.

4. USER MODELING

File sharing on collaboration systems is driven by real-world collaboration practices. A user's *collaboration patterns* include who she works with, on what topics, and when (i.e. who, what, and when). Collaboration patterns enable the system to determine the likely recipients for files on certain topics, which is important in both recipient recommendation and abnormality examination, which will be discussed in Section 5. For example, if Alice chooses to share a file on "web security" with someone who has never worked with her on the topic, such a decision might be due to a mistake and should be brought to Alice's attention.

In this section, we describe how to derive a user's collaboration patterns from her past collaboration activities on the SaaS collaboration system. Contact profiles are created to store a user's collaboration patterns and feedback. For convenience, we assume that the name of our target user is Alice.

4.1 Information Retrieval

As a first step in mining Alice's collaboration patterns, we retrieve her collaboration information from the SaaS collaboration system. Recall that the collaboration system may contain multiple subsystems. We process such subsystems one by one. For each subsystem, we crawl the past and ongoing collaboration activities of Alice's, and then represent each activity in the form given in Definition 2. Note that the textual content of an activity is subsystem-dependant. Certain activities, such as online meetings and collaboration workflows, contain textual description. Certain activities, such as a shared file or bookmark, are associated with user-applied tags, which may also be used as textual content. If an activity does not have any available text, we may leave its textual content blank.

4.2 Profile Creation

We create a profile for each of Alice's contacts. A contact profile contains *personal information*, a *preference tag*, and a *collaboration vector*. First, a contact's personal information includes the contact's name, email, and affiliation. Such information may be retrieved from Alice's address book. Second, the preference tag is set by Alice's past feedback on the corresponding contact. A preference tag may take one of these values: "white", "black", "green", and "red". A "white" tag means neutral or no feedback; "black" indicates that the contact has been placed into the blacklist by Alice; "green" means that the contact is one of Alice's preferred collaborators; a "red" tag sets an alarm on the contact. Third, the collaboration vector stores a list of tuples, each of which consists of a keyword and a real-number weight. Intuitively, a keyword represents a collaboration topic between Alice and the contact; the higher the weight of a keyword, the more important the contact currently is with regards to the topic for Alice.

Next, we discuss the creation of a collaboration vector in a contact profile. Given a contact u_i, let $A(u_i)$ be the set of Alice's collaboration activities in which u_i is involved. For every $a_j \in A(u_i)$,

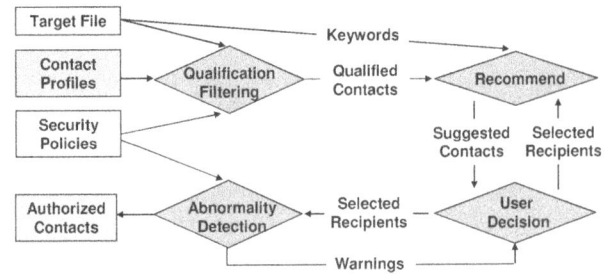

Figure 2: Data flows in file sharing

we extract the top y keywords (say $y = 10$) from its textual content. We may use existing keyword extraction algorithms such as the TF-IDF approach [10]. We then create the collaboration vector using the extracted keywords.

The next step is to determine the weight of each keyword in the collaboration vector. Let $A(u_i, t_l) \subseteq A(u_i)$ be the set of activities that contain t_l as keyword. The weight $g(t_l)$ of the keyword t_l in the collaboration vector for u_i is computed as

$$g(t_l) = \Sigma_{a_j \in A(u_i, t_l)} h(a_j)$$

where $h(a_j)$ is the importance value of activity a_j. The value of $h(a_j)$ is determined by the time of a_j, as practical collaboration relation is time-sensitive. For instance, two parties may put an end to their collaboration relation after a project or contract is finished. Hence, a recent activity should carry larger weight than an old one. Assume that a_j was performed k periods away from the current time. We have $h(a_j) = \alpha^k$, where $\alpha \in (0, 1]$ is a decay factor. The length of the time period may be manually specified or determined by the frequency of sharing activities performed by a user, while the value of α may be determined by training. Intuitively, if Alice and u_i have many recent collaboration activities on the topic t_l, the weight of t_l in u_i's collaboration vector is large. On the contrary, if Alice rarely works with u_i on the topic t_l or their related collaboration activities are old, u_i's weight on t_l is small.

4.3 Incremental Maintenance

Alice will continue using the collaboration system after the profiles of her contacts are created. She will participate in new collaboration activities and acquire new contacts. To stay updated with Alice's latest collaboration information, we update Alice's contact profiles periodically. We crawl the set A_1 of Alice's new collaboration activities since the last update from the collaboration system. We then integrate such new information into Alice's existing contact profiles. More specifically, we create profiles for new contacts and modify the collaboration vectors of existing ones. For each existing contact u_i, the weight of the keyword t_l in its collaboration vector is updated as:

$$g_1(t_l) = g_0(t_l) \times \alpha + |A_1(u_i, t_l)|$$

where $g_0(t_l)$ is the old weight, $g_1(t_l)$ is the new weight, $\alpha \in [0, 1]$ is a decay factor, and $|A_1(u_i, t_l)|$ is the number of activities in A_1 that involve u_i and contain t_l as a keyword. By applying the decay factor α, we attach more importance to recent collaboration activities than old ones.

5. RECOMMENDER

In this section, we study how to use the contact profiles created in the previous section to reduce the probability of data leakage in the file sharing process. Figure 2 presents the dataflow of the sharing process in our solution. For simplicity, assume that the target user's name is Alice. The process consists of the following steps:

1. **File uploading:** Alice uploads the target file and specifies its security labels and keywords.

2. **Policy retrieval:** The DLP manager retrieves the MAC policies that are applicable to the current sharing instance.

3. **Qualification filtering:** The DLP manager evaluates each of Alice's contacts against all the applicable MAC policies. A contact is qualified to be a candidate recipient if and only if it does not violate any MAC policy and the preference tag in its profile is not "black" (i.e. Alice has not placed the contact in the blacklist).

4. **Recipient recommendation:** The DLP manager computes a matching score between each candidate recipient and the file. It then sorts the list of candidates based on their matching scores and returns the top ones as recommended recipients. The recommendation process is interactive in the sense that whenever Alice selects or enters a recipient, the DLP manager will recompute the list of recommended recipients by taking Alice's input into account.

5. **User decision:** Alice selects recipients from the recommendation list and/or types in recipients manually. The input from Alice will be provided as feedback to the recommender.

6. **Abnormality detection:** When Alice finishes entering the list of recipients, the DLP manager examines the list. It removes recipients (which are manually entered by Alice) that violate any applicable MAC policy. It also issues warnings on unlikely recipients with regards to the target file, if any. Alice may choose to ignore the warnings or address them by modifying the list of recipients.

7. **Authorization:** The recipients on the final list are authorized access to the target file.

5.1 Attribute-Based Recommendation

Assume that we have created contact profiles for Alice to store her collaboration patterns. Given a file f to be shared by Alice, let C_q be the set of remaining contacts after qualification filtering. The DLP manager computes a list of suggested recipients for f through the following steps:

1. *Assessment*: For each contact $c_i \in C_q$, we compute a *likelihood score* between c_i and f. The higher the score, the more likely that Alice may share f with c_i.

2. *Prioritization*: We sort the contacts in descending order of their likelihood scores and return the top x ones (say, $x = 10$) as suggested recipients.

Step 2 is straightforward. We will study the computation of the likelihood scores in Step 1.

Our likelihood score computation is inspired by the TF-IDF approach, which is widely used in text mining. Recall that each file in the SaaS collaboration system is associated with a list of keywords specified by its owner. Let W_f be the list of keywords associated with the file f. The likelihood score $d(c_i, f)$ between f and the contact c_i is computed as:

$$d(c_i, f) = \Sigma_{t_j \in W_f} g(c_i, t_j) \times \log \frac{|C|}{|C_{t_j}|} \times b(pt_i) \quad (1)$$

where $g(c_i, t_j)$ is the weight of the keyword t_j in the contact c_i's collaboration vector ($g(c_i, t_j) = 0$ if t_j does not appear in c_i's collaboration vector), $|C|$ is the total number of Alice's contacts, $|C_{t_j}|$ is the number of Alice's contacts whose collaboration vector contains the keyword t_j, and $b(pt_i)$ is the adjustment value based on the preference tag pt_i in c_i's profile.

Intuitively, the more important c_i is with regards to the keywords in W_f, the larger $d(c_i, f)$ is. The degree of importance between c_i and a keyword $t_j \in W_f$ is measured by $g(c_i, t_j)$. Furthermore, not all keywords in W_f are equally effective in identifying which contacts should be recommended for f. More specifically, those keywords that are common among Alice's contacts are less effective than the rare ones. For example, assume that Alice is a security expert who is collaborating with Bob on "database security, with Carl on "OS security", and with Dave on "web security". In this case, the keyword "security" is not very effective in identifying likely recipients, because it does not distinguish a contact from the other two. In contrast, the keyword "database" immediately distinguishes Bob from Carl and Dave. Hence, we may want to assign more weight to the identifiable word "database" than to the common word "security". In the computation of $d(c_i, f)$, the degree of commonality of the keyword t_j is measured by $|C|/|C_{t_j}|$: the more contacts having t_j as a keyword, the smaller the value of $|C|/|C_{t_j}|$. We compute the logarithm of $|C|/|C_{t_j}|$ to prevent the value from becoming too dominant for those very rare words.

Finally, we take Alice's opinions on her contacts into account by adjusting the value of the likelihood score based on the preference tag pt_i in c_i's profile. More specifically, when pt_i is "green", we may apply a bonus β (say $\beta = 0.5$) to $d(c_i, f)$. In other words, we have $b(pt_i) = 1 + \beta$. Such a bonus will help promote Alice's preferred contacts in the recommendation list. There is no adjustment, when pt_i is "white" or "red". If desired, additional preference tags and adjustment values may be introduced.

5.2 Interactive Recommendation

We have presented a recipient recommendation approach that makes use of Alice's contact profiles. Next, we describe an interactive recommendation approach that aims to further improve the usability and accuracy of our recommender. Our interactive recommender takes into consideration which recipients have already been chosen by Alice and adjusts the remaining recommendation accordingly.

An observation is that certain contacts often appear together in a user's collaboration activities. Such co-occurrence information allows us to derive groups among the contacts. Should Alice selects a contact c_i as a recipient, other contacts belonging to the same groups as c_i become more likely to be chosen. This is similar to the grouping of one's friends in social networks, except that the groups in collaboration systems are more dynamic: collaboration groups may evolve quickly over time along with the changes of collaborative projects and the various roles each collaborator plays. Therefore, rather than deriving static groups from one's contacts, as existing work does in social networks [5], we design a time-sensitive probabilistic approach to model the dynamic grouping of contacts in collaboration systems.

Let $A(i)$ be the set of Alice's collaboration activities that include contact c_i. Also, let $A(i, j)$ be the set of Alice's collaboration activities that include both contacts c_i and c_j. The probability $p(c_j|c_i)$ that c_j currently belongs to the same collaboration group as c_i, or their *connection strength*, is computed as:

$$p(c_j|c_i) = \Sigma_{a_k \in A(i,j)} h(a_k) / \Sigma_{a'_k \in A(i)} h(a'_k)$$

where $h(a_k)$ is the time-sensitive weight of the activity a_k (introduced in Section 4.2). Recall that recent activities have larger weights than old ones.

Let $R = \{c_1, \ldots, c_m\}$ be a set of contacts. For each $c_j \notin R$, we compute the connection strength between c_j and R as:

$$p(c_j|R) = \Pi_{c_i \in R} p(c_j|c_i)$$

Note that the above formula computes the joint probability by treating the contacts in R as independent. Even though such independence assumption may not hold, it does greatly reduce the complexity of computation. We leave a more accurate but yet efficient estimation of the joint probability as interesting future work.

Furthermore, if c_i and c_j have never participated in the same collaboration activity, we will have $p(c_j|c_i) = 0$. When $p(c_j|c_i) = 0$ and $c_i \in R$, we always have $p(c_j|R) = 0$, regardless of the other contacts in R. This is undesirable as c_j may have strong connections with other contacts in R except for c_i. To address such an issue, we adopt a smoothing method by using $p(c_j)$ to estimate $p(c_j|c_i)$, when the latter is zero. We have

$$p(c_j) = \Sigma_{a_k \in A(j)} h(a_k) / \Sigma_{a'_k \in A} h(a'_k)$$

where A is the set of Alice's collaboration activities and $A(j) \subseteq A$ is the set of activities that involve c_j. Essentially, $p(c_j)$ is the time-sensitive probability of c_j among all of Alice's activities.

Next, we describe how to use the connection strength among contacts to perform interactive recommendation. Let R_f be the current set of recipients selected by Alice for file f. R_f is empty at the very beginning. The interactive recommendation consists of the following steps:

1. Alice selects a recipient c_i, which is then added to R_f.

2. For each remaining contact c_j that is not in R_f, we compute the connection strength $p(c_j|R)$ between c_j and R.

3. Let $d(c_j, f)$ be the likelihood score between c_j and f, which is computed using Formula 1 in Section 5.1. We compute a priority score $s(c_j, f)$ by combining $p(c_j|R)$ and $d(c_j, f)$.

4. We sort the remaining contacts based on their priority scores and return the top ones as recommended recipients.

5. Exit, if Alice has finished selecting all recipients for f; otherwise, goto Step 1.

By combining the likelihood score and the connection strength in the above Step 3, we essentially match the contact c_j with both the target file f and the recipients that have already been selected by Alice. The priority score of c_j keeps changing as Alice inputs more recipients. Intuitively, if Alice selects a recipient that is closely connected with c_j, c_j's relative priority score will increase, which may make it rank higher in the updated recommendation list; otherwise, if Alice selects someone irrelevant to c_j, c_j may have lower priority in the new recommendation list.

There are at least two possible ways to combine $p(c_j|R)$ and $d(c_j, f)$ into a the priority score $s(c_j, f)$. The first one is to compute $s(c_j, f)$ as the geometric mean of $p(c_j|R)$ and $d(c_j, f)$, that is, $s(c_j, f) = \sqrt{p(c_j|R) \times d(c_j, f)}$. The second way is to linearly combine $p(c_j|R)$ and $d(c_j, f)$, that is, $s(c_j, f) = \sigma p(c_j|R) + (1 - \sigma)d(c_j, f)$, where $\sigma \in [0, 1]$ determines the combination weights of the two factors. In our current implementation, we adopt the first method. As to the second method, determining an appropriate value of σ may not be easy. But using a parameter (i.e. σ) in the linear combination may enable the system to adapt to users' preferences by adjusting the value of σ for each user to achieve better personalized performance. Designing an adaptive linear combination approach is interesting future work.

5.3 Abnormality Detection

In reality, even the best recommender solution may fail to suggest all the file recipients Alice wants. Alice would have to manually type in those recipients that are missing in the recommendation list; errors may occur during such an input process. Unlike existing SaaS collaboration systems, our DLP manager does not accept user input passively. As the last line of defense, the DLP manager examines the recipients entered by Alice when she clicks the "share" button, with the goal to detect potential errors.

Let R_f be the set of recipients entered by Alice. The examination consists of the following three steps:

1. Let P be the set of applicable MAC policies. For every $c_i \in R_f$, if c_i violates one or more policies in P, c_i is removed from C_r. (Note that Alice might have manually typed in someone who violates an applicable MAC policy; such violators must be removed from the recipient list.)

2. For every $c_i \in R_f$, if the preference tag in c_i's profile is "red", a warning message is issued. The "red" preference tag indicates that Alice has expressed the desire to be alarmed when sharing a file with c_i. For example, Alice may not personally consider Bob to be trustworthy. In this case, she may set an alarm on Bob so that she does not accidentally share something sensitive to Bob, even if Bob is qualified to receive such files by organizational MAC policies.

3. Let C be the set of Alice's contacts. For every $c_i \in R_f$, if the likelihood score of c_i is in the bottom x percent (say, $x = 50\%$) among the scores of contacts in C, c_i is marked as an abnormal recipient and a warning message is issued. Intuitively, if a recipient has never or very rarely worked with Alice on the topics related to the target file, Alice might have entered such a recipient by mistake. Such abnormal choices should be brought to Alice's attention.

Upon warnings, Alice is given an opportunity to modify the recipients to address the warnings (note that each added/modified recipient will be evaluated against MAC policies). She may also choose to ignore some or all of the warning messages. The file will not be shared until all the warnings are addressed or ignored.

To help Alice address a warning, the DLP manager will try to propose a correction for each abnormal recipient. The DLP manager assumes that there might be typos in the recipient's identity and will look for a more likely candidate that is syntactically similar to the abnormal one. Assume that c_i is marked as abnormal. Also, let C_h be the list of contacts whose likelihood scores are in the top y percent (say, $y = 50\%$) among all the contacts of Alice's. For every $c_j \in C_h$, we compute the edit distance between c_i and c_j. If the edit distance between c_i and c_j is smaller than a threshold (say, 3), the DLP manager will propose c_j as a correction of c_i. The rationale behind such a proposal is that, c_j is a more likely recipient than c_i according to their likelihood scores with regards to the target file; due to their syntactical similarity, Alice might mean c_j but a few typos change the input to c_i.

6. EVALUATION

We have implemented a prototype of our solution. We would like to answer the following questions in our evaluation.

- How does our solution compare with other approaches?

- How does our solution perform on users with different amounts of collaboration information?

- How do different component methods, such as the interactive recommendation and abnormality detection, contribute to the overall effectiveness of our solution?

In our experiments, we focus on evaluating the analytical component, that is, the recommender, in our solution. We collect real-world collaboration information to create user models and then simulate users' information-sharing processes. Comparing to user study, simulation has a number of advantages. Most importantly, simulation allows us to analyze the effectiveness of various solutions in different settings with limited user effort. In the future, we plan to complement our findings from simulation with extensive user study. More specifically, we plan to (1) evaluate the usability and usefulness of MAC policies in real-world collaboration systems; (2) measure the effectiveness of our recommender on human-error reduction in practice.

6.1 Evaluation Methods

Data There are 25 Lotus Connections users who contributed their real-world collaboration information to our study. The data we collected includes activities from different collaboration sub-systems, such as file sharing, project wikis, work communities, and so on. On average, each user has 53 collaboration activities and 75 collaborators. The maximum numbers of activities and collaborators of a user are 116 and 1307, respectively, while the minimum numbers are 13 and 39, respectively. For each user, we use 50% of her collaboration activities as training cases and the other 50% as test cases. There is no overlap between the two sets of activities. The activities in the training set are used to create contact profiles at the very beginning of our experiments.

Baseline approaches We compare our solution with the following baseline approaches.

- The trivial approach None always returns an empty list of recipients. It models the current situation in existing collaboration systems, where there is no recipient recommender.

- The approach Greedy recommends recipients using the greedy strategy. Let A_u be the set of collaboration activities we have seen for the user u. For each of u's contacts, Greedy counts the number of activities in A_u that involve the contact. Given a file sharing instance of u's, Greedy recommends those contacts with the highest counts.

- The approach K.Neighbor is proposed in [3] as a recommender for discretionary access control. K.Neighbor employs the k-Nearest Neighbor strategy to suggest file recipients. Let F_u be the set of files that u has shared with others. Given a new file f, K.Neighbor retrieves the set F_k of the k files in F_u that are most similar to f (we use cosine similarity between the files' TF-IDF keyword vectors as similarity measure). K.Neighbor then suggests contacts based on how many files in F_k they have received from u.

Furthermore, in order to evaluate the effectiveness of different component methods in our solution, we create special versions of our recommender by disabling one or more component methods. For convenience, we denote the complete version of our solution as P.Complete. We disable both the interactive recommendation and the abnormality examination functionalities to create a plain profile-based recommender called Profile. In other words, Profile recommends recipients only once per file sharing instance and does not examine user input for abnormality. The approach P.Interactive (short for Profile plus interactive recommendation) is our solution with abnormality examination disabled. Similarly, the approach P.Abnormal (short for Profile plus abnormality examination) is our solution with interactive recommendation disabled.

Test method We evaluate the recommenders based on the amount of information that is leaked due to user mistakes. Given a file sharing instance $\langle u, U_a, f, t \rangle$ in the test cases, we simulate the process of u choosing recipients for f. The set U_a is considered to be the "correct answer" in the simulation and it is not visible to the recommenders. First, we ask the recommender to suggest up

---

Input: user u, file f, set of target recipients U_a, and an integer x
Output: data leakage rate d of the sharing instance

1. $U_r \leftarrow \emptyset$ and $U'_a \leftarrow U_a$
2. Ask the recommender to suggest a list L_s of up to x contacts based on u, f and U_r;
   $U_r \leftarrow U_r \cup (L_s \cap U'_a)$ and $U'_a \leftarrow U'_a - L_s$
3. If $U'_a = \emptyset$, go to Step 5;
   Otherwise, select $c_i \in U'_a$, $U'_a \leftarrow U'_a - \{c_i\}$, and
   - with probability ϵ_1, randomly select a contact c_j from u's address book and add c_j to U_r;
   - with probability ϵ_2, convert c_i to c'_i by changing up to 3 characters in c_i and add c'_i to U_r;
   - with probability $(1 - \epsilon_1 - \epsilon_2)$, add c_i to U_r
4. If $U'_a = \emptyset$, go to Step 5;
   Otherwise, if the recommender is interactive, go to Step 2;
   Otherwise, go to Step 3
5. If abnormality detection is not supported, go to Step 6;
   Otherwise, ask the recommender to examine U_r and return a list L_b of abnormal recipients and a list L'_b of suggested corrections;
   $U_r \leftarrow (U_r - L_b) \cap L'_b$
6. Return $d = |U_r - U_a|/|U_a|$

Figure 3: Simulating the process of sharing a file

Table 1: Performance of various approaches over different numbers of recommended recipients

Rec. Num.	None	Greedy	K.Neighbor	Profile	P.Complete
2	0.142	0.064	0.062	0.057	0.045
4	0.142	0.060	0.056	0.053	0.044
6	0.142	0.056	0.052	0.049	0.042
8	0.142	0.053	0.048	0.047	0.041
10	0.142	0.050	0.045	0.045	0.039

to x recipients for f, where x is a test parameter. Those suggested contacts that are in U_a will then be selected by u. Note that the value of x must be small (say, no larger than 10), as it is not practical to ask users to select from a long list of suggested recipients. Requiring x to be small also precludes the trivial approach that always recommends a user's entire list of contacts. For every contact $c_i \in U_a$ that has not been selected, u will try to enter it manually. Errors may occur during such manual process. More specifically, there is a probability ϵ_1 that u will enter another recipient rather than c_i, which models an inappropriate decision on who to share with; there is a chance ϵ_2 that u will make typos when entering c_i; with probability $(1 - \epsilon_1 - \epsilon_2)$, u will enter c_i correctly. In our simulation, we assumed that the probability that a user makes an error is small; we had $\epsilon_1 = \epsilon_2 = 0.01$. After entering a recipient, either correctly or incorrectly, an interactive recommender may adjust its recommendation list based on the new recipient. Also, after u finishes entering all recipients for f, the recommender may perform abnormality detection and suggest correction. Finally, the resulting list U_r of recipients from the simulation process is compared with U_a. The *data leakage rate* of the instance is computed as $|U_r - U_a|/|U_a|$, which is the percentage of final recipients that are not in U_a. Note that we always has $|U_r| = |U_a|$ at the end of a simulation instance. In particular, if a recommender does not return any suggestion, the user will have to manually enter $|U_a|$ recipients for f. The simulation algorithm is given in Figure 3.

6.2 Experimental Results

We have performed three sets of experiments to answer the three questions listed at the beginning of this section. Our experiments were performed on a workstation with a 3.2GHz Intel CPU and 3GB main memory.

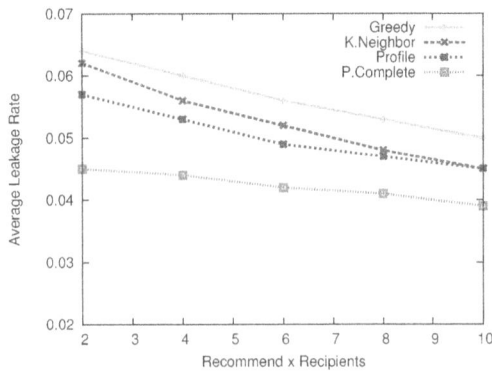

Figure 4: Performance of various approaches over different numbers of recommended recipients

Comparing recommenders The first set of experiments are designed to compare our solution with other baseline approaches. To get a comprehensive picture of the performance of each approach, we have evaluated the solutions over different numbers of recommended recipients. Intuitively, allowing a recommender to return more recipients each time will reduce the average data leakage, because a user is more likely to find the desired recipients in the recommendation list. However, in reality, a longer recommendation list will take the user more time to examine, which reduces efficiency. The average data leakage rates of the tests are given in Table 1 and visualized in Figure 4.

As we can see from Table 1, all the non-trivial recommenders (those other than None) were able to reduce the average data leakage rate by more than 50% when compared to None. The complete version of our solution (i.e. P.Complete) had the lowest average leakage rates, no matter how many recipients the recommenders were allowed to return per suggestion. In particular, from Figure 4, the smaller the number of recommended recipients, the larger the advantage of P.Complete over the other solutions. This indicates that P.Complete is effective in ranking the desired recipients high in the recommendation lists.

To remove the advantage that P.Complete employs interactive recommendation and abnormal examination while the baseline approaches do not, we have also compared Profile with the baseline. From Table 1, Profile always had lower average leakage rates than Greedy. Profile also had lower leakage rates than K.Neighbor when the number of recommendation was smaller than 8 (the difference is statistically significant at level 0.01); when the number of recommendation was 8 or larger, the performance of Profile and K.Neighbor was similar. Overall, Profile outperformed the two baseline approaches in this set of experiments with regards to average data leakage rate.

As to running time, the average time spent on 1000 test instances was 719 milliseconds for Greedy, 3953 milliseconds for Profile, and 7891 milliseconds for K.Neighbor. Greedy was the fastest, since it employs a very simple strategy; Profile was faster than our implementation of K.Neighbor (not including the time to build contact profiles, which is done off-line), because computing the similarities between keyword vectors in K.Neighbor is relatively expensive.

Active users v.s. less active users In reality, some users are more active than others in collaboration systems. The goal of the second set of experiments is to evaluate the performance of different solutions over users with different amounts of collaboration data. We divided the 25 users into three groups. The High group contains 8 users, each of who has at least 80 collaboration activities; the Medium group contains 7 users, each of who has 40 to 79 collabo-

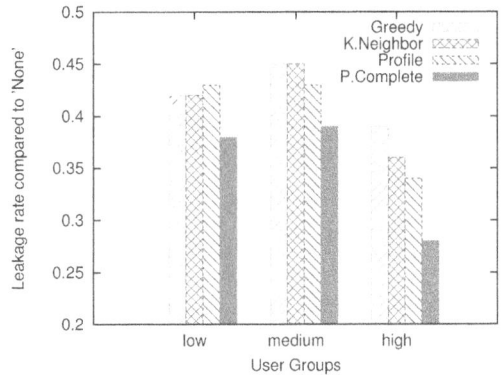

Figure 5: Performance over users with different amounts of available collaboration information

Table 3: Performance of different component methods

Rec. Num.	Profile	P.Interact	P.Abnormal	P.Complete
5	0.051	0.045	0.049	0.042
10	0.044	0.041	0.042	0.039

ration activities; the Low group contains 10 users, each of who has less than 40 collaboration activities. We performed experiments on each of the three groups. In the experiments, we found that the trivial method None had different average leakage rates in the three groups. In order to reduce the data bias among different groups, for each test method, we computed the percentage of its average leakage rate against that of None in the same group. For example, when recommending 5 recipients, the average leakage rate of Greedy in group Low is 0.058, while the rate of None in Low is 0.138. In this case, the percentage of Greedy over None in Low is $0.058/0.138 = 0.42$. Comparing such percentages of a method over different groups allow us to understand how the method improves over None in different groups. Our experimental results are listed in Table 2 and visualized in Figure 5.

From Figure 5, all the tested methods had the best performance in the group High. This may not be surprising as more information provides a better knowledge base for the recommenders. In particular, P.Complete and Profile scaled very well over the amount of available data as they had the largest improvement rates in High over Medium and Low. P.Complete had similar performance in Medium and Low, so did Profile. P.Complete outperformed the baseline approaches in all the three groups.

An interesting finding is that the average leakage rate of Greedy was no larger than those of K.Neighbor and Profile in the group Low. In reality, we might consider applying Greedy to new users to take advantage of its simplicity; after we gather more information for those users, we may then change to another strategy, as Greedy does not seem to improve as well as more sophisticated methods such as Profile and P.Complete over the amount of available data.

Effectiveness of different component methods The objective of the third set of experiments is to study whether each of the component methods in our solution is effective in mitigating data leakage. The component methods we consider are interactive recommendation and abnormality examination. If a component method does not have positive impact on the overall performance, it may be better to remove it from our solution for the sake of efficiency. In our experiments, we compared the performance of the four versions of our solution; they are Profile, P.Interactive, P.Abnormal, and P.Complete. The experimental results are given in Table 3 and visualized in Figure 6.

Table 2: Performance over users with different amounts of available collaboration information

Rec.Num.	Groups	None	Greedy		K.Neighbor		Profile		P.Complete	
			rate	percent	rate	percent	rate	percent	rate	percent
5	Low	0.138	0.058	0.42	0.058	0.42	0.060	0.43	0.052	0.38
	Medium	0.122	0.055	0.45	0.055	0.45	0.052	0.43	0.048	0.39
	High	0.148	0.058	0.39	0.053	0.36	0.050	0.34	0.041	0.28
10	Low	0.138	0.050	0.36	0.051	0.37	0.055	0.40	0.050	0.36
	Medium	0.122	0.051	0.42	0.052	0.43	0.049	0.40	0.046	0.38
	High	0.148	0.049	0.33	0.044	0.30	0.041	0.28	0.037	0.25

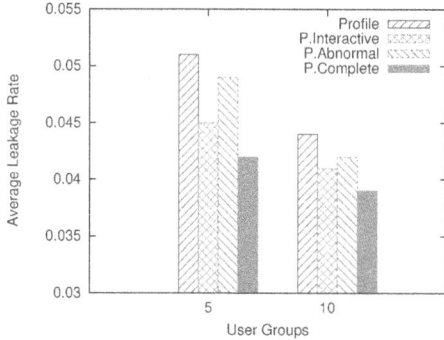

Figure 6: Performance of different component methods

`P.Interactive` and `P.Abnormal` had lower average data leakage rates than `Profile` (the differences are statistically significant at level 0.05). This indicates that both interactive recommendation and abnormality examination are effective when used alone. Also, `P.Complete` outperformed `P.Interactive` and `P.Abnormal`, meaning that the contribution of either component method is not subsumed by the other when the two are combined.

Finally, the average false positive rate of our abnormality examination approach was 18%. That is, approximately one out of five warnings was a false positive (i.e. the user indeed wanted to share with the recipient that is considered abnormal). Even though the current rate is acceptable, in the future, we plan to improve our abnormality examination solution to reduce the false positive rate.

7. DISCUSSION

Security Our solution is designed to alleviate the data leakage problem in existing collaboration systems under normal use, where users may make mistakes but will not intentionally leak sensitive information to others. If a user is malicious, he can bypass the MAC policies by not labeling his files correctly and then share the files with whoever he wants by ignoring the recommendation and abnormality warnings. However, we expect that malicious information leaking activities will go through channels other than enterprise collaboration systems. In reality, there are many information channels that are much less traceable than collaboration systems. For example, a malicious user may simply send a sensitive file using personal email or via personal instant messenger, which are almost impossible to track. There exist laws and business conduct rules that aim to prevent malicious data leakage in the physical world. Our goal here is to protect honest users from leaking information by mistake, which is a realistic security concern business organizations have on existing collaboration systems.

Social Networks The data leakage problem in collaboration systems share similarity with the privacy preservation problem in social networks. Both collaboration systems and social networks mainly employ user-to-user discretionary access control. In social networking sites such as Facebook, users decide who may have access to what information in their profiles so as to protect their privacy. We may apply the techniques in our solution to assist so-cial network users in making such information sharing decisions. First, we may apply the approach in Section 4 to create profiles for a user's friends using the social activities that are visible to the user. There are various types of activities on social activities that may be used, such as wall postings, calendar events, photo tagging, and so on. Second, we may use the recommender in Section 5 to suggest which friends should be granted access to a certain piece of profile information. The abnormality examination approach may also be handy in catching inappropriate decisions or errors.

On the contrary, existing privacy solutions may not be easily applied to collaboration systems for data leakage prevention due to a number of reasons. First, the users in collaboration systems are affiliated with organizations and are thus subject to organizational policies. In contrast, social network users have fully control on the information in their profiles and are not normally restricted by the security rules from others. Hence, existing privacy solutions for social networking sites do not support higher-level mandatory policies, which are desired in collaboration systems. Second, the collaboration relation is much more dynamic than friendship in social networks. Business users change their collaborators or collaboration topics more frequently than social network users change their friends. Many existing privacy solutions in social networks do not attach importance to the time factor when extracting features of one's friends. However, time plays a critical role in user modeling for collaboration systems. Our solution takes recency of events into account when creating/maintaining contact profiles and determining the connection strength among collaborators.

Attribute-Based Access Control Attribute-Based Access Control (ABAC) is a very useful mechanism for information distribution in enterprise environments [14]. For example, a user may grant the privilege to access her database proposal to all colleagues who have the attribute "database" so as to seek constructive feedback. By using ABAC, the user is able to reach a wide range of audience, while complying the security principle of need-to-know (compared to broadcasting the proposal to everyone in his organization). A major challenge in supporting ABAC in practice is how to determine users' attributes. Having dedicated personnel to manually specify the attributes of every user in the system is expensive and time-consuming, especially if broad attributes such as one's expertise are desired.

The recipient recommender in our solution is essentially attribute-based. It determines user attributes based on their past activities. Rather than returning a list of suggested users, the recommender may serve as an ABAC engine by authorizing the corresponding resource to the users on top of the recommendation list. Depending on the target adversary models, additional security features may be needed when we build an ABAC engine based on the recipient recommender in this paper. We leave this as interesting future work.

8. RELATED WORK

People increasingly share data on the web. The problem of preventing data leakage through information sharing has attracted significant interest in the research community. Today, social networking sites are one of the most popular places where people post and share their information. Many solutions have been proposed for privacy preservation on social networks [5, 12, 16]. We have discussed the differences between existing privacy solutions and our solution as well as why the former may not be applied to enterprise collaboration systems in Section 7.

Enterprise collaboration systems is another popular place on the web where sensitive information may be shared by users. With the migration from in-enterprise to cloud, collaboration systems are switching from a relatively closed platform to an open one. Data leakage prevention (DLP) is becoming more and more important in such systems. However, compared to the amount of research on social networks, much less attention has been paid to DLP in collaboration systems, especially in collaboration clouds. In [3], Chari et al. pointed out that assisting business users' discretionary access control decisions is crucial in reducing information leakage in SaaS collaboration systems. They proposed a recipient recommender based on file similarity, which has been described in Section 6.1. However, they did not evaluate their recommender in [3]. Unlike our solution, their recommender is not based on time-sensitive user models that are created from past collaboration activities from multiple collaboration sub-systems. Furthermore, their recommender does not perform interactive recommendation according to the connection strength among users, nor does it examine user input for abnormality detection.

As discussed in Section 7, our solution utilizes user attributes to perform authorization recommendation and may be extended to support Attribute-Based Access Control (ABAC) in enterprise. In [14], Wang and Jin proposed to enforce ABAC in collaborative working environments by deriving user attributes from people-tagging. The solution in this paper extends [14] by building user models from various collaboration activities rather than from people-tagging only. Furthermore, our solution supports organizational mandatory policies, interactive recommendation, and abnormality examination, none of which was discussed in [14].

This paper is also related to existing work on user modeling using data from social and collaboration systems. In [15], Wang et al. proposed to derive users' work patterns by semantically enriching and clustering collaboration activities. Their focus was user modeling and they did not provide a concrete way to use the derived work patterns. Wang et al. [13] also studied mining user preferences from public social and collaborative data to perform adaptive search personalization. Similarly, Carmel et al. [2] proposed to derive users' social relation from multiple social systems to personalize search results. Data protection features such as MAC policies and abnormality detection are not discussed in the above work. Even though none of the above work studied the data leakage problem, the recommender in our solution may be able to benefit from their user modeling techniques.

Finally, researchers [9, 8, 11] have studied information leakage from cloud environments in contexts other than data sharing in collaboration systems. These contexts include data indexing [11], virtual machine allocation [9], and so on. Due to space limitation, we are unable to discuss these works in detail.

9. CONCLUSION

We have proposed a framework to alleviate the data leakage problem in collaboration clouds. Our solution aims to reduce data leakage due to inappropriate discretionary sharing decisions and mistakes. It employs a defense-in-depth strategy by providing multiple layers of protection, including organization-level mandatory access control policies, attribute-based recipient recommender, and abnormality detection. We have implemented a prototype of our so-

lution. Evaluation has been performed by comparing our solutions with existing approaches using real-world data. Our experimental results demonstrated the effectiveness of our approach.

10. REFERENCES

[1] Box.net. http://www.box.net/.
[2] D. Carmel, N. Zwerdling, I. Guy, S. Ofek-Koifman, N. Har'el, I. Ronen, E. Uziel, S. Yogev, and S. Chernov. Personalized social search based on the user's social network. In *CIKM '09: Proceeding of the ACM conference on Information and knowledge management*, 2009.
[3] S. Chari, L. Koved, and M. E. Zurko. Using recommenders for discretionary access control. In *Proceedings of the Web 2.0 Security and Privacy (W2SP)*, 2010.
[4] Cisco WebEx. http://www.webex.com/.
[5] L. Fang and K. LeFevre. Privacy wizards for social networking sites. In *WWW '10: Proceedings of the international conference on World Wide Web*, 2010.
[6] IBM LotusLive. https://www.lotuslive.com/en/.
[7] Cybernetnews. http://cybernetnews.com/using-google-calendar-to-scoop-up-private-corporate-data/.
[8] D. Lin and A. Squicciarini. Data protection models for service provisioning in the cloud. In *SACMAT '10: Proceeding of the ACM symposium on Access control models and technologies*, 2010.
[9] T. Ristenpart, E. Tromer, H. Shacham, and S. Savage. Hey, you, get off of my cloud: exploring information leakage in third-party compute clouds. In *CCS '09: Proceedings of the ACM conference on Computer and communications security*.
[10] G. Salton, and C. Buckley. Term-weighting approaches in automatic text retrieval. In *Information Processing and Management*, 1988.
[11] A. Squicciarini, S. Sundareswaran, and D. Lin. Preventing information leakage from indexing in the cloud. *IEEE International Conference on Cloud Computing*, 2010.
[12] A. C. Squicciarini, M. Shehab, and F. Paci. Collective privacy management in social networks. In *WWW '09: the International Conference on World Wide Web*, 2009.
[13] Q. Wang and H. Jin. Exploring online social activities for adaptive search personalization. In *CIKM '10: Proceeding of the ACM conference on Information and knowledge management*, 2010.
[14] Q. Wang, H. Jin, and N. Li. Usable access control in collaborative environments: authorization based on people-tagging. In *ESORICS'09: Proceedings of the European conference on Research in computer security*.
[15] Q. Wang, H. Jin, and Y. Liu. Collaboration analytics: Mining work patterns from collaboration activities. In *CIKM '10: Proceeding of the ACM conference on Information and knowledge management*, 2010.
[16] E. Zheleva and L. Getoor. To join or not to join: the illusion of privacy in social networks with mixed public and private user profiles. In *WWW '09: Proceedings of the international conference on World wide web*, 2009.
[17] M. E. Zurko, C. Kaufman, K. Spanbauer, and C. Bassett. Did you ever have to make up your mind? what notes users do when faced with a security decision. In *ACSAC '02: Proceedings of the Annual Computer Security Applications Conference*, 2002.

Modeling Data Flow in Socio-Information Networks: A Risk Estimation Approach

Ting Wang†   Mudhakar Srivatsa‡   Dakshi Agrawal‡   Ling Liu†

†College of Computing, Georgia Institute of Technology, Atlanta, GA
‡IBM T.J. Watson Research Center, Hawthorne, NY
†{twang, lingliu}@cc.gatech.edu   ‡{msrivats, agrawal}@us.ibm.com

ABSTRACT

Information leakage via the networks formed by subjects (e.g., Facebook, Twitter) and objects (e.g., blogosphere) – some of whom may be controlled by malicious insiders – often leads to unpredicted access control risks. While it may be impossible to precisely quantify information flows between two entities (e.g., two friends in a social network), this paper presents a first attempt towards leveraging recent advances in modeling socio-information networks to develop a statistical risk estimation paradigm for quantifying such insider threats. In the context of socio-information networks, our models estimate the following likelihoods: *prior flow* – has a subject s acquired covert access to object o via the networks? *posterior flow* – if s is granted access to o, what is its impact on information flows between subject s' and object o'? *network evolution* – how will a newly created social relationship between s and s' influence current risk estimates? Our goal is not to prescribe a one-size-fits-all solution; instead we develop a set of composable network-centric risk estimation operators, with implementations configurable to concrete socio-information networks. The efficacy of our solutions is empirically evaluated using real-life datasets collected from the IBM SmallBlue project and Twitter.

Categories and Subject Descriptors

K.6.5 [**Computing Milieux**]: Management of Computing and Information Systems—*Security and Protection*

General Terms

Security, Management

Keywords

Risk estimation, social network, access control

1. INTRODUCTION

The ever-increasing complexity and dynamics of information sharing infrastructures have presented grand challenges for today's access control mechanisms. One key issue is the

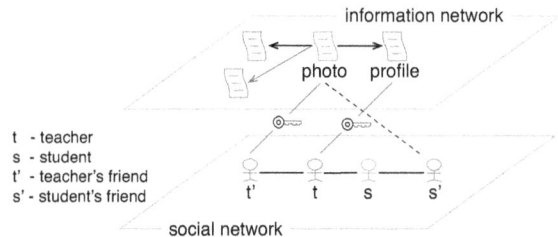

Figure 1: Networks of subjects and objects.

information leakage via the complex and dynamic networks formed by subjects and objects (e.g., social network and blogosphere): subject s who has access to object o may (un)intentionally leak it to a socially linked subject s', or object o' derived from o may reveal information about o.

Example 1. In [2], a high school teacher had to resign since she was tagged in a friend's photo with her holding a wine glass, which was then visible via her FACEBOOK profile to her students. As illustrated in Figure 1, this incident is essentially caused by an access channel in the socio-information network: "student → teacher → teacher's profile → photo".

Indeed information leakage via such socio-information networks often leads to unpredicted access control risks – more so in the presence of malicious insiders within such networks. While it may be impossible to precisely quantify information flows between two entities (e.g., two friends in a social network), this paper leverages statistical models of information flows in such networks (such as those proposed in [4, 16, 25, 8]) to develop a risk estimation paradigm for quantifying such insider threats. In the context of socio-information networks, our models estimate the following likelihoods:

- *prior flow* estimation: how likely is it for s to have acquired covert access to o (or a *fraction* of o) via the channels formed by relevant subjects N_s and objects N_o?
- *posterior flow* estimation: how would granting s access to o (denoted by $s \to o$) potentially affect the information flows with respect to N_s and N_o?

Loosely speaking, the risk of granting access ($s \to o$) is high if it would significantly increase (= *posterior flow – prior flow*) the information flow between certain subject $s' \in N_s$ and object $o' \in N_o$. Our goal is to develop risk estimation operators that capture such *network effects*, namely, that one access granting decision ($s \to o$) has on several other related subjects and objects ($s' \to o'$) in a socio-information network. To our best knowledge this work also represents the first attempt to study the impact of network effects (in socio-information networks) in Risk-based Access Control, an emerging security paradigm [10, 20].

The key contributions of our paper are as follows. First, we develop a set of composable network-centric risk estimation operators, with implementations configurable to concrete socio-information networks. To make the estimation practical, we further refine our estimates by taking account of factors including the evolution of networks and the incompleteness or uncertainty in network information. Second, we show that a range of state-of-the-art access control models can be enhanced by our risk estimation paradigm, typically by encoding the policy-enforced information flows as weighted links in the socio-information network. We note that our approach does not replace classical access control models; instead it addresses an orthogonal problem and augments classical access control models with risk assessments in the context of socio-information networks. Third, we develop a suite of scalable algorithms for implementing the operators on large networks.

The efficacy of our solution is empirically evaluated using real socio-informatics network datasets of varied network scale, collected from Twitter[1] (200K subjects) and the IBM SmallBlue project [18] (40K subjects). Specifically, on Twitter an user s_i that *follows* another user s_j may *re-tweet* (re-post) the messages sent by s_j to its (s_i's) followers, which can be considered as one type of leakage (though not necessarily unwanted information flow). We show that our model is able to effectively capture such leakage behavior. Further, using the multiple snapshots (separated by six month time interval) of socio-information network in the Smallblue dataset, we show how our solution is able to incorporate the inherent dynamic aspects of social-information network, such as evolution, granted/revoked accesses, etc.

The remainder of this paper is organized as follows. Section 2 formalizes the mathematical model of our risk estimation paradigm; the library of composable risk estimation operators is introduced in Section 3; Section 4 details scalable implementation of these operators followed by experimental evaluation in Section 5; Section 6 concludes the paper.

2. NETWORK-CENTRIC RISK LOGIC

2.1 Basic Model

In network-centric risk estimation, a multi-layer network model is used to capture subject-subject, object-object, and subject-object relationships, wherein relationships are encoded as intra-network or inter-network links (see Figure 1). Specifically, the interconnected objects form an *object network* (or information network), $G_O = (O, L_O)$, with nodes O and links L_O representing the set of objects and their relationships. Analogously, a *subject network* (or social network), $G_S = (S, L_S)$, captures the relationships between subjects, where S and L_S denote the set of subjects and their connections. Further, a collection of inter-network links L_I between the subject and object networks encode their interactions (e.g., access and leakage history).

We apply a generic information flow model to quantify the qualification of a subject to access an object, wherein information is viewed as fluid that flows along links in socio-information networks. The dynamics of fluid flow may be different (e.g., gossips in subject-subject links, database triggers in object-object links, access history in subject-object links, etc.). The weight on a (directed) network link is in-

[1]http://www.twitter.com

dicative of the propensity of information flow along the link. Our goal is to regulate the flow of information between subjects and objects by controlling subject-object links, namely, subject-object links (L_I) created as a consequence of granting access requests. More specifically, in our information flow model, each intra-network or inter-network link is associated with two attributes:

- *Enforced flow capacity*, $\text{enf}(\cdot)$, that specifies flows permitted by an underlying access control model. It is typically encoded as either "1" or "0", with "1" indicating that information is free to flow (e.g., from low security to high security, or from high integrity to low integrity), and "0" indicating that no information flow is permitted. For instance, two subjects s and s' have $\text{enf}(\overline{ss'}) = 1$ if the role of s' dominates s (e.g., *employee* < *manager*); two objects o and o' have $\text{enf}(\overline{oo'}) = \text{enf}(\overline{o'o}) = 1$ if they are not "mutually exclusive" in Chinese-wall policy. In Appendix A we show that a wide range of conventional access control models may be emulated by our model by suitable parameterization (e.g., setting link weights).

- *Leakage flow capacity*, $\text{leak}(\cdot)$, that specifies flows introduced by potential information leakage via networked subjects and objects. It is typically a real number within the interval $[0, 1]$. For object network, $\text{leak}(\overline{oo'})$ may specify the fraction of information object o that is inferable from o' (called *residual information*), which can usually be measured using information-theoretic metrics, e.g., Kullback-Leibler divergence; while for subject network, $\text{leak}(\overline{ss'})$ may be interpreted as the likelihood that s leaks (intentionally or unawarely) information to s'. In general, such leakage likelihood may be discriminative with respect to specific objects and subjects under consideration, i.e., a function of object metadata [23] and the corresponding social relationship.

Given access request $(s \rightarrow o)$, our network-centric risk estimation gauges the overall enforced flow $f_e(o \rightarrow s)$ (details in Appendix A) and leakage flow $f_c(o \rightarrow s)$ (details in Section 4) from object o to subject s. More specifically, $f_e(o \rightarrow s) = 1$ if the flow from o to s is allowed by the access control model, and 0 otherwise; while $f_c(o \rightarrow s)$ comprises two estimates: f_c^{frac}, the fraction of information of o leaked to s, and f_c^{like}, the likelihood of such leakage.

2.2 Access Request Evaluation

In our risk estimation paradigm, the risk of an access request is no longer solely based on the requesting subject and the concerned object; rather, within the context of socio-information network, it depends on (i) relevant subjects and objects, and (ii) their profound network influence before (and after) approving this access. Towards this end, we propose two fundamental operations, *prior*-flow and *posterior*-flow estimation, as the foundation of access risk evaluation.

Prior-Flow Estimation

Given a new request $(s \rightarrow o)$, we first evaluate the existing enforced and leakage flows $f_e(o \rightarrow s)$ and $f_c(o \rightarrow s)$. Conceivably, if $f_e(o \rightarrow s) = 1$, i.e., the flow is allowed by the access control policies, this access should be granted. Meanwhile, when the flow is disabled by the policies (i.e., $f_e(o \rightarrow s) = 0$), but the leakage flow is significant, i.e., $f_c^{frac}(o \rightarrow s) \geq \epsilon$ and $f_c^{like}(o \rightarrow s) \geq \delta$ (ϵ and δ are threshold parameters)[2], it may make limited sense to impose strict control over s to access o. Intuitively, in addition to evaluating the qualification of s with respect to o, prior-flow estimation provides an important risk-based exception handling mechanism. Formally, request $(s \rightarrow o)$ is granted only if the following condition is met (necessary condition):

$$(i)\, f_e(o \rightarrow s) = 1 \vee f_c(o \rightarrow s) \geq \epsilon$$

Example 2. In Figure 1, on evaluating request (student $\rightarrow$ photo), one may notice that teacher has possession of profile (as indicated by the inter-network link profile – teacher), which semantically refers to photo (as indicated by the reference relationship photo – profile). The leakage flow photo $\rightarrow$ profile $\rightarrow$ teacher $\rightarrow$ student may carry sufficient information for student to completely infer photo, which makes simple comparison of classification level class(photo) and clearance level clear(student) non-informative.

Posterior-Flow Estimation

While prior-flow captures existing information flows before an access $(s \rightarrow o)$ is granted, posterior-flow estimation evaluates how the access once granted would impact the information flows for relevant subjects and objects. Essentially, posterior-flow estimation measures the potential risk of approving an access request. Let $f_e'(\cdot)$ and $f_c'(\cdot)$ be the enforced and leakage flows[3], after an inter-network link $\overline{so}$ is created. If the posterior enforced flow invalidates a previously approved access, or the posterior leakage flow enables a previously disabled access, a violation is raised. Formally,

$$(ii)\, \nexists\, o' \in O, s' \in S, \text{ s.t. } f_e(o' \rightarrow s') = 1 \wedge f_e'(o' \rightarrow s') = 0$$

$$(iii)\, \nexists\, o' \in O, s' \in S, \text{ s.t. } \begin{cases} f_e(o' \rightarrow s') = 0 \\ f_c(o' \rightarrow s') < \epsilon \\ f_c'(o' \rightarrow s') \geq \epsilon \end{cases}$$

Here condition (ii) dictates that the requested access should not invalidate any previously (potentially) approved access $(s' \rightarrow o')$; while condition (iii) states that it should not increase leakage flow capacity beyond the threshold ϵ.

Example 3. Recall the example in Figure 1. The approval of access (student's friend $\rightarrow$ photo) may significantly change the leakage flow $f_c'(\text{photo} \rightarrow \text{student})$, given the close relationship student – student's friend. If $f_e(\text{photo} \rightarrow \text{student}) = 0$ and $f_c(\text{photo} \rightarrow \text{student}) < \epsilon$, this increased leakage may result in a violation of existing access control policy.

To summarize, conditions (i), (ii), and (iii) together form the sufficient condition for granting an access request: if significant prior leakage flow exists, request $(s \rightarrow o)$ may be granted even if the security level of s is inadequate to access o; meanwhile, if access $(s \rightarrow o)$ incurs the risk of information leakage that violates access control policies, $(s \rightarrow o)$ may not be approved even if the security level of s is sufficient to access o. It is worth noting that as more accesses are granted, the average leakage flow (i.e., risk) in the networks tends to increase; after the overall risk reaches certain "frozen point", no more accesses would be granted. Fortunately, the value of tactical information typically decays over

---

[2] In following, we assume that the leakage likelihood threshold δ is fixed, and use $f_c(\cdot)$ to denote $f_c^{frac}(\cdot)$ if $f_c^{like}(\cdot) \geq \delta$, and 0 otherwise.

[3] For dynamic models (e.g., Chinese-wall, History-based Access Control models (HBAC)), granted accesses may change enforced flows.

op.	input	output
D	object o	objects depending on o
U	object o	objects depended by o
J	object o, objects N_o	overall information of o at N_o
S	subject s, threshold δ	subjects with leakage to s of likelihood above δ
T	subject s, threshold δ	subjects with leakage from s of likelihood above δ
A	subjects s	subjects connected with s
X	subjects N_s	objects N_o accessed by N_s

Table 1: List of atom operators.

operation	algebra
estimate prior flow	$J(o, \text{X} \cdot \text{S}(s, \kappa))$
estimate posterior flow	$\triangleright s' \in \text{T}(s, \kappa), \triangleright o' \in \text{U}(o) : J(o', \text{X} \cdot \text{S}(s', \kappa))$
add new object	$\triangleright o' \in \text{U}(o) : J(o', \{o\})$
update existing object	$\triangleright o' \in \text{U}(o), \triangleright o'' \in \text{D}(o) : J(o', \{o''\})$
add new subject link	$\triangleright s' \in \text{A}(s), \triangleright o \in \text{X} \cdot \text{A}(s) : J(o, \text{X} \cdot \text{S}(s', \kappa))$

Table 2: Risk estimation algebra.

time [22]; it is thus possible to incorporate such time sensitivity to maintain the system operability, which we consider as one ongoing research direction.

3. RISK ESTIMATION ALGEBRA

In this section we describe the realization of our risk estimation paradigm. Conceptually, we construct an expressive algebra framework (e.g., estimating leakage flow, updating existing network, and predicting network evolution) by composing a library of fundamental *atom operators*. Following we briefly introduce the set of atom operators. The summaries of atom operators and risk estimation algebra are listed in Table 1 and 2.

- *Downstream* - D. It returns the set of objects that refer to (or are derived from) a source object o (directly or indirectly), i.e., they contain the information of o.

- *Upstream* - U. It is the reverse operator of D. It returns a set of objects referred by a target object o.

- *Join* - J. It measures the overall fraction of information of a source object o in a set of target objects N_o.

The next two operators are designed for subject network.

- *Source* - S. It takes as input a subject s and returns the set of subjects that have high leakage likelihood (above threshold δ) to s.

- *Target* - T. It is the reverse operator of S. For a given subject s, it finds the set of subjects that feature high leakage likelihood from s.

- *All* - A. This operator identifies all subjects N_s connected (transitively) to a given subject s.

The final operator extracts subject–object relationships.

- *Cross* - X. For a given set of subjects N_s, it identifies the set of objects N_o that have been accessed by N_s.

Further, we use $\cdot$ to denote the composition of two operators, and $\triangleright$ to denote an iterator which iterates over the set of elements (for each). Next we describe how these atom operators may be combined to estimate prior and posterior leakage flow capacities between subjects and objects.

Operation 1: Prior Leakage Flow Estimation

$$\text{J}(o, \text{X} \cdot \text{S}(s, \delta))$$

For given access request $(s \rightarrow o)$, the operation of *prior-flow* estimation determines the leakage flow $f_c(o \rightarrow s)$ from object o to subject s in the current network before the request is granted. It may be implemented by composing J-,

X- and S-operator: (i) We first use S to determine the set of source subjects N_s featuring high leakage likelihood (above δ) from s. (ii) We then apply X over N_s to find the set of objects N_o accessible to N_s. (iii) Taking N_o and o as input, we use J-operator to estimate the residual information of o at N_o. If the residual information is above certain threshold ϵ, the leakage flow is considered as informative enough for s to learn o via the socio-information networks.

Operation 2: Posterior Leakage Flow Estimation

$$\triangleright s' \in \mathtt{T}(s,\delta), \triangleright o' \in \mathtt{U}(o) : \mathtt{J}(o', \mathtt{X} \cdot \mathtt{S}(s',\delta))$$

For given request $(s \to o)$, the operation of *posterior-flow* estimation identifies subject-object pairs whose flows change significantly because of granting $(s \to o)$. It may be implemented in the following steps. (i) We first apply T-operator on s to identify the set of subjects N_s featuring high leakage likelihood from s. (ii) We then identify the set of objects N_o referred by o. (iii) For each subject s' of N_s, and object o' of N_o, we follow the procedure of prior-flow estimation (with and without link $\overline{so}$) to measure the flows from o' to s'. (iv) A pair (s', o') is identified if its flow changes significantly (i.e., $f_c(o' \to s') < \epsilon \wedge f'_c(o' \to s) \geq \epsilon$) due to $(s \to o)$.

Further, since we intend to evaluate if granting an access may result in violations to access control policies, the search space can be reduced by focusing on subject-object pairs (s', o') that carries zero enforced flow, i.e., $f_e(o' \to s') = 0$.

The next set of operations are designed to support changes to security policy and personnel, i.e., administrative model. A bulk of work is available on administrating enforced flow (conventional access control models) (e.g., [11]). We therefore focus on the leakage flow part; particularly, we are interested in *incremental* update, e.g., new subjects or objects are added, new links are created, etc., and similar discussion applies to *decremental* update.

Operation 3: Adding A New Object

$$\triangleright o' \in \mathtt{U}(o) : \mathtt{J}(o', \{o\})$$

It is noted that each object may depend on (refer to) multiple other objects, e.g., one blog refers to multiple blogs; hence, on inserting a new object, we need to consider all these referring objects. We assume that the objects are inserted according to their orders of dependency (or creation time); that is, an object can be inserted only after all its dependent objects have been inserted.

Let o be the object to insert. (i) We first apply U-operator over o to identify all objects K_o directly or indirectly depended by o (closure). (ii) For each object $o' \in K_o$, we apply J-operator to estimate the residual information of o' at o. Note that this operation affects the existing information flow between objects and subjects only through new access of o, which is implemented mainly by Operation 2.

Operation 4: Updating An Existing Object

$$\triangleright o' \in \mathtt{U}(o), \triangleright o'' \in \mathtt{D}(o) : \mathtt{J}(o', \{o''\})$$

This operation updates the content of an existing object o. We assume that the acyclic directed structure of the object network is preserved after the update. Clearly, the update will affect the residual information of objects referred by o. Following the dependency relationships, we incrementally apply J-operator to update the estimation of residual information at affected objects. Note that the update influences

leakage information flow only after new accesses have been executed upon o. We place a "red" flag on o to indicate that existing access privileges on o need to be re-evaluated.

Operation 5: Adding A Link in Subject Network

$$\triangleright s' \in \mathtt{A}(s), \triangleright o \in \mathtt{X} \cdot \mathtt{A}(s) : \mathtt{J}(o, \mathtt{X} \cdot \mathtt{S}(s',\kappa))$$

This operation evaluates the risk of adding a new link (let s be either one of the involved subject) to the existing subject network. Essentially, it could influence all the covert information flows for all subjects K_s relevant to s.

The implementation is as follows. (i) We first find the set of subjects K_s relevant to s using A-operator. (ii) We further apply X-operator to collect all objects K_o accessed by K_s. (iii) For each pair (s', o) ($s' \in K_s$, $o \in K_o$), if it carries zero enforced flow, i.e., $f_e(o \to s') = 0$, we evaluate the leakage flow $f_e(o \to s')$. The asymptotic complexity of this operation is $O(|K_s| \times |K_o|)$; while in our scenarios, we focus on the subject-object pairs with zero enforced flow, which significantly reduces the search space. Further, scalable evaluation methods exist for a range of leakage measures [21].

If the inserted link results in any violation of access control policies, further actions may be taken, e.g., revoking existing access privileges.

Operation 6: Adding A New Subject

This operation inserts a new subject into the network. For a new subject whose leakage behavior is not clear (with unknown leakage flows), one may simply apply the enforced flow estimation only. As new observations are collected, one can creates its links with relevant subjects, following the procedure of Operation 5. Details are omitted here.

4. ATOM OPERATORS

We have thus far described an expressive algebra for supporting network-centric risk estimation. In this section we present one possible implementation of the atom operators. We note that while this algebra is general-purpose (applicable across a wide range of information and social networks), the concrete realizations of these operators (and their space-time complexity) are inherently tied to the complexity of information flow models in these networks. In this section we first highlight the complexity of information flow models by comparing it against the classical network flow problem [13] and then delve into concrete realizations of risk operators under specific assumptions on information flow models in the networks.

In contrast to a classical network flow problem, studying information flow in social and information networks features unique challenges. (i) Information flows violate *flow conservation*: outbound flow may exceed inbound flow at a network node (e.g., when one creates an identical (or partial) copy of an object). (ii) Information flows are *non-additive*: a set of information flows may merge into a new flow; however, this merge may be non-additive (e.g., merge of flows f_1 and f_2 results in f_1 if f_2 is derived from f_1, even though the residual information in f_2 is non-zero). (iii) Information flows in social networks are *stochastic*; it may be possible to derive statistical properties of such flows (e.g., using contact time distribution between subjects – email frequency). (iv) Network evolution must be taken account in order to refine information flow estimation over a period of time. (v) The solution should be able to support large-scale networks (up to hundreds of thousands of nodes), and handle stream-manner updates. To the best of our knowledge, our work presents a first of a kind solution to address this information flow problem.

4.1 Operators for Information Network

We assume a class of information networks wherein information flows are restricted to a directed acyclic graph (DAG) [9], i.e., links in the network capture directed dependency among objects. Such dependency prevails in real life, in the form of *reference*, *derivation*, and *inheritance* (e.g., links between blogs, tweets, etc.). Assuming that the information network is a DAG, the implementations of *upstream* (U) and *downstream* (D) operators are fairly straightforward. Our following discussion focuses on *join* (J) operator.

For given source o_i, J-operator estimates the (fractional) *residual information* of o_i existing in a set of (target) objects $\{o_j\}$. We start with the case of a single target object o_j.

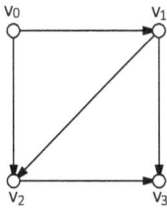

Figure 2: Diffusion and fusion in network.

If o_i and o_j are adjacent, e.g., o_j directly refers to (or inherits) certain parts of o_i, it is typically feasible to quantify the residual information r_{ij}, using information theoretic metrics [4, 19]. We thus specify the leakage flow capacity w_{ij} of direct link $\overline{o_i o_j}$ as $w_{ij} = r_{ij}$. The difficulty lies in estimating the residual information r_j[4] where o_i and o_j are not neighbors, particularly, when there exist multiple directed paths from o_i to o_j.

Example 4. Figure 2 illustrates this scenario: the information of v_0 flows through several overlapping paths to v_3. Before discussing in detail our method, we first introduce a set of fundamental concepts.

For given object o_i, the *flow* of a directed link $\overline{o_k o_j}$, f_{kj}, is the residual information of o_i passed through it. It is estimated by $f_{kj} = r_k \cdot w_{kj}$. Another key concept is the *union* of residual information (regarding o_i) over a set of flows $F = \{f_{k_1 j_1}, \ldots, f_{k_n j_n}\}$, denoted by $\oplus F = f_{k_1 j_1} \oplus \ldots \oplus f_{k_n j_n}$.

The problem of estimating the residual information r_j can then be formulated in an iterative manner:

$$\begin{cases} r_j = \oplus_{o_k \in P_j} f_{kj} \\ f_{kj} = r_k \cdot w_{kj} \end{cases} \quad (1)$$

where P_j represents the set of parents (direct ancestors) of o_j in the network.

Clearly, the union operation $\oplus$ is the key to estimating r_j. Following, we detail its implementation. Consider a set of flows F. We can establish the following bounds.

$$\max_F f \le \oplus F \le \min\{\sum_F f, 1\} \quad (2)$$

We focus on establishing a tighter upper bound, based on the following observation. It is observed that for two flows f_{kj_1} and f_{kj_2} going out of o_k, the residual information of their union cannot exceed that of o_k, i.e., $f_{kj_1} \oplus f_{kj_2} \le \min\{r_k, f_{kj_1} + f_{kj_2}\}$. Next we first introduce the concept of *cut*. Let all the flows of F (no inheritance relationship) inject into a virtual sink o_{sink}. A set of links are called a cut of F if they separate o_i and o_{sink}. Intuitively, all the flows of F must go through every cut of F.

For given flow f, we attempt to bound its effective part responsible for generating F (called *effective flow*, denoted

---

[4] Following, without ambiguity, we omit the referred source object o_i in the notations.

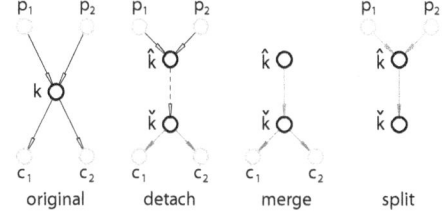

Figure 3: Primitives of constructing effective-flow graph. The effective flows in blue are materialized, and those in red are being updated.

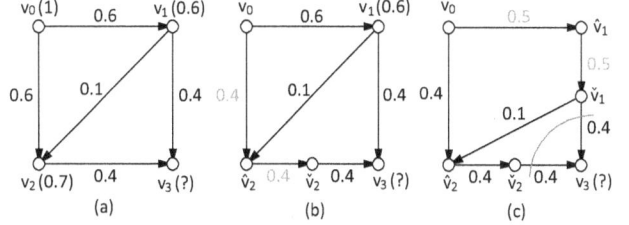

Figure 4: Construction of effective-flow graph.

by $\underline{f}$) using the observation above. Estimating the upper bound of $\oplus F$ is equivalent to finding a cut that carries the minimum (upperbound) effective flow with respect to F. We now show how to estimate the upper bound of effective flow for involved links.

We achieve this in a bottom-up manner: starting from F, following the reverse topological order, we trace back to the root o_i. At each step, we apply the following three primitives, as illustrated in Figure 3:

- *detach.* For each object o_k encountered in the process, we detach o_k into two nodes $o_{\hat{k}}$ and $o_{\check{k}}$, and connect them with a link $\overline{o_{\hat{k}} o_{\check{k}}}$; $o_{\hat{k}}$ is connected to the parent flows of o_k, while $o_{\check{k}}$ is connected to the child flows of o_k. The flow on $\overline{o_{\hat{k}} o_{\check{k}}}$, $f_{\hat{k}\check{k}}$, is set as r_k.

- *merge.* For the set of outbound flows of o_k (now $o_{\check{k}}$), $\{f_{\check{k}c_1}, \ldots, f_{\check{k}c_n}\}$, whose effective parts have been estimated, we update the effective flow of $\overline{o_{\hat{k}} o_{\check{k}}}$ as follows (i.e., the effective flow on $\overline{o_{\hat{k}} o_{\check{k}}}$ cannot exceed the sum of the effective parts in all its child flows):

$$\underline{f}_{\hat{k}\check{k}} = \min\{f_{\hat{k}\check{k}}, \sum_{l=1}^n \underline{f}_{\check{k}c_l}\}$$

- *split.* Given the set of inbound flows of o_k (now $o_{\hat{k}}$), $\{f_{p_1 k}, \ldots, f_{p_m k}\}$, we update the estimation regarding their maximum effective flows using the rule:

$$\underline{f}_{p_l k} = \min\{f_{p_l k}, \underline{f}_{\hat{k}\check{k}}\} \quad (1 \le l \le m)$$

Intuitively, the effective flow on each incoming link can not exceed that of $\overline{o_{\hat{k}} o_{\check{k}}}$.

If the effective flows on all the links have been estimated, finding the upper bound of $\oplus F$ is equivalent to finding a minimum cut of this *effective-flow* graph, where the capacity of each link is defined as its effective flow. Now, J-operator can be implemented as follows. For each target object o_j, we create a link $\overline{o_j o_{sink}}$ to a virtual sink o_{sink} with $w_{j,sink} = 1$, $F = \{f_{j,sink}\}$, then construct the effective-flow graph using the three primitives above, and find the minimum cut of the graph, with detailed algorithm in Algorithm 1.

Example 5. This operation over the network in Figure 3 is illustrated in Figure 4. In (a) the maximum residual information of objects v_1 and v_2 (regarding v_0) has been esti-

117

```
Input: object network $G_O = (O, L_O)$, a set of flows $F$
Output: upper bound of $\oplus F$
create a virtual object $o_j$ in $G_O$ collecting all flows in $F$;
$S \leftarrow$ sources of $F$;
// topological sorting
sort $S$ in decreasing order;
while  $S \neq \varnothing$ do
    $o_k \leftarrow$ pop the head of $S$;
    // detach + merge + split operation
    detach $o_k$;
    $O \leftarrow O \setminus \{o_k\} \cup \{o_{\hat{k}}, o_{\check{k}}\}$;
    // $CF_k$:  child flows of $o_k$
    merge $CF_k \cap F$;
    // $PF_k$:  parent flows of $o_k$
    split $PF_k$;
    // update $S$ and $F$
    $F \leftarrow F \setminus CF_k \cup PF_k$;
    $S \leftarrow S \cup$ sources of $PF_k$;
end
// remove irrelevant objects
remove from $G_O$ all unvisited objects;
// min-cut process
find the minimum $o_i - o_j$ cut $w$;
output $w$ as the upper bound of $\oplus F$;
```

Algorithm 1: Sketch of J-operator.

mated (shown in parenthesis); in (b) and (c), we apply the primitives over objects v_2 and v_1, respectively. The maximum residual information of v_3 is estimated using the cut of the effective-flow graph in (c).

In addition to the upper and lower bounds of the union of a flow set F, we show that computing the expected value, $\mathbb{E}(\oplus F)$ is equivalent to a maximization problem over a graph (which is NP-hard) and present a Monte Carlo sampling approach to estimate $\mathbb{E}(\oplus F)$ (details can be found in [1]).

4.2 Operators for Social Network

In contrast with object network, subject network demonstrates dynamic aspects: the leakage behavior of each subject may only stochastically follow certain pre-defined formation. Hence, we are particularly interested in estimating the likelihood that one subject leaks (or shares) its information to another subject in the network (leakage likelihood).

We assume complete information regarding the social network. Later we will lift this assumption and take account of possible information incompleteness/uncertainty. We assume that each link $\overline{s_i s_j}$ (from subject s_i to s_j) in the social network is associated with a leakage flow capacity (or *leakage likelihood*) w_{ij}, indicating the likelihood that s_i leaks (shares) received information to s_j. This quantity has a variety of instantiations in realistic networks [12]. For instance, in online social networks, it can be estimated as the amount of information in the blogs re-posted by s_i, relative to the total information of the blogs viewed by s_i; in enterprise social networks, it can be estimated as the quantity of information in outbound emails from s_i to s_j relative to the overall information in s_i's incoming emails.

We capture the behavior of network-wise information leaking using *random walk with restart* (RWR) model [3, 24]: the leaked information is modeled as a random particle that originates at the source subject s_i. It iteratively transmits to a neighboring subject with probability proportional to the corresponding leakage flow capacity. Further, at each step, it has certain probability of stopping propagation (i.e., it is kept confidential). The likelihood that s_i leaks information to s_j, denoted by r_{ij}, can be measured by the steady-state probability that the particle is observed at s_j. This model features several desirable properties for our purpose: (i) it

embeds all the likelihoods of leaking information or keeping confidentiality; (ii) it considers the multi-facet relationships between two subjects; (iii) it captures the global structure of the subject network. Next, we formalize this model, and construct Source (S) and Target (T) operators based on it.

Consider a subject s_i as the source subject. Let N_i denote the set of outgoing neighbors of s_i. For each subject $s_j \in N_i$, we specify the probability that the information (particle) transmits through $\overline{o_i o_j}$ as: $p_{ij} = w_{ij} / \sum_{j' \in N_i} w_{ij'}$. At each step, the probability c_i that the information stops propagation is specified as: $c_i = w_{ii} / (w_{ii} + \sum_{j \in N_i} w_{ij})$. If we stack the steady-state probability that the information (particle) is observed at each subject of the network into a column vector r_i, the definition of RWR gives us:

$$r_i = (1 - c_i) \cdot A \cdot r_i + c_i \cdot e_i \qquad (3)$$

where A is the column normalized adjacent matrix of the subject network, such that $A_{ji} = p_{ij}$ if $o_j \in N_i$ and 0 otherwise, and e_i is the starting vector for s_i with the i-th entry set as 1 and 0 otherwise. Furthermore, we have the following matrix formation: $R = A \cdot R \cdot (I - C) + C$. Here R denotes the stack of the leakage probabilities with respect to all subjects, $R = [r_1, r_2, \ldots]$, I is an identity matrix, and C represents the diagonal matrix with the i-th diagonal element as c_i. Scalable algorithms are available to compute R (e.g., [15]).

Based on this formulation, the implementations of S and T operators are as follows. For given target s_j, S operator identifies the set of subjects that feature high leakage likelihood (above a threshold δ_i) to s_j, which correspond to the elements s_i in the j-th row of R with $R_{ji} \geq \delta_i$[5], denoted by $S(s_j) = \{s_i | R_{ij} \geq \kappa_i\}$. Meanwhile, for given source subject s_i, T operator returns the set of subjects that feature high leakage likelihood from s_i, i.e., $T(s_i) = \{s_j | R_{ji} \geq \delta_i\}$.

5. EMPIRICAL EVALUATION

This section presents an empirical study of our network-centric access control paradigm. The experiments are specifically designed to center around the following metrics: (i) its validity in terms of capturing leakage flow, (ii) its efficacy in quantifying unpredicted risk incurred by ignoring the network effects among subjects and objects, (iii) its effectiveness in incorporating the impact of network evolution over risk estimation, and (iv) its execution efficiency. We start with describing the setup of the experiments.

5.1 Experimental Setting

Our experiments used three datasets collected from real-life social and information networks (attributes of interest to us are listed in Table 3).

The Twitter dataset contains 18,617,827 tweet messages, involving 203,222 users, over three weeks of 2009. The social network is constructed according to the following/followed relationships among users: one user s_i follows another user s_j if s_i wishes to receives tweets from s_j; also, s_i can *re-tweet* (re-post) the viewed tweets to its followers.

The SmallBlue dataset describes the social network of IBM employees who participated in the SmallBlue project. It consists of two snapshots of as of January 2009 and July 2009, involving 41,702 and 43,041 individuals, respectively,

---

[5]The parameter δ for each subject needs to be normalized to accommodate the difference of subjects' influence in the network. In implementation, we set $\delta_i = \delta / (\sum_{j \neq i} \mathbf{1}_{R_{ji} > 0})$.

Attribute	Description
	Twitter dataset
createdat	timestamp of message post
tweetid	unique message id
text	plain message content
userid	id of the message author
rtstatus	re-tweeted message id (by this one)
rtuser	id of the re-tweeted message author
	Smallblue dataset
location	working location
position	managerial position
division	working department
tie strength	volume of exchanged emails
	Dogear dataset
email	email address of user s (identifier of subject)
url	url o bookmarked by s (identifier of object)
tags	bookmark tags made by s regarding o
time	time-stamp that s accesses o

Table 3: Attributes of datasets.

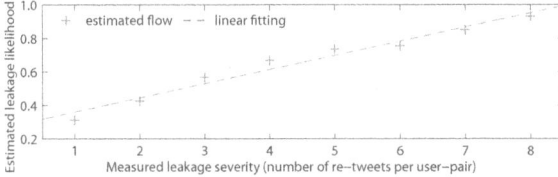

Figure 5: Estimated leakage likelihood with respect to actually observed leakage severity (number of re-tweets per user-pair).

We construct the social network according to the social connections among individuals.

The Dogear dataset consists of 20,870 bookmark records, relevant to 7,819 urls. The *email* and *url* attributes uniquely identify a user (subject) and a webpage (object), respectively, and *tags* encodes the semantics of the object. We construct the object network as follows. Let t_i be the collection of tags suggested by users regarding object o_i. We consider both potential temporal and semantic dependency among objects. For object o_j, we assume that it is directly dependent on the minimum set of (temporally) most recent objects O_j with the union of tags maximally possibly covering t_j, i.e., $\max \cup_{o_i \in O_j} t_i \quad t_j$. The weight of link $\overline{o_i o_j}$ is defined as $w_{ij} = |t_i \cap t_j|/|t_i|$.

All the core algorithms (the library of operators) are implemented in Java. The experiments are conducted on a workstation with 3.20GHz Intel Celeron CPU and 2GB RAM, running Windows XP.

5.2 Experimental Results

In the first set of experiments, we use the Twitter dataset and Enron archive to validate the leakage flow model on real social and information network platform.

Validity of Leakage Model

We set up the experiments as follows. On Twitter, the social network is constructed according to the following/followed relationships: one user (subject) s_j opts to follow another user s_i if s_j wishes to receive messages (*tweets*) from s_i; also, s_j can "leak" (*re-tweet*) the tweets from s_i, which may be further leaked by followers of s_j. Clearly, such leakage can happen between two remotely connected users due to the network effects.

We intend to apply the leakage flow model to quantify the likelihood that the information (tweets) possessed by one subject leaks to another subject in the network, and compare the estimated leakage flow with actually measured leakage (number of re-tweets). We use the data corresponding to

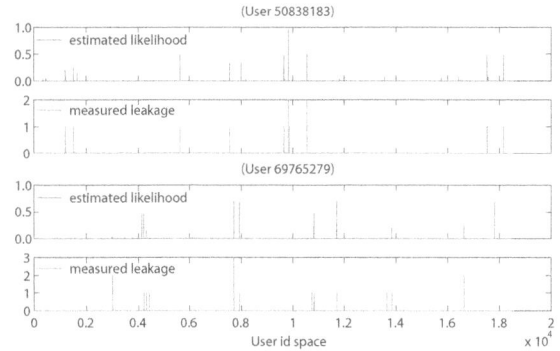

Figure 6: Individual level comparison of estimated leakage likelihood and observed leakage severity.

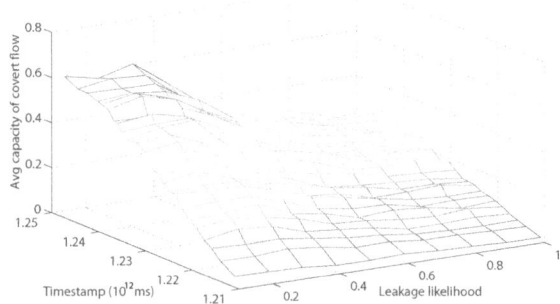

Figure 7: Average covert information flow measured at different time-stamps.

October 2009 to collect the overall statistics regarding each user, particularly the number of received tweets and among them the number of re-tweets, which we use to set up the parameters $\{w\}$ and $\{c\}$ as in Appendix 4.2. We apply the model to predict the leakage likelihood for the period of November 2009.

For a specific pair of users s_i and s_j, we consider the severity of leakage as the number of re-tweets s_j posts with original tweets from s_i during the considered time period. For each specific level of observed leakage severity, Figure 5 shows the corresponding estimated leakage flow (leakage likelihood) averaged over pairs of users demonstrating such severity. One can notice the high correlation between the estimated flow and the actual leakage severity, indicating that the leakage flow model captures the essence of leakage patterns. We further perform individual level comparison of estimated leakage flow and observed leakage severity. We randomly pick two (sources) users, measure their leakage severity to the rest users, and compare the results with the estimated likelihood by our model. As shown in Figure 6, it is noticed that the predicted "peaks" match well with the actually measured results.

Impact of Leakage Flow

Next we intend to evaluate the impact of leakage flow existing in the social and information networks over the risks associated with access control decisions, specifically, the risk of information leakage that would be under-estimated if ignoring the network effects among subjects and objects.

We use the SmallBlue and Dogear datasets to construct the socio-information network. We consider an bookmarking action as an access; hence, each access request q is associated with a time-stamp t_q. At each specific time-stamp t^*, we assume that the set of requests before t^*, $\{q|t_q \leq t^*\}$, have

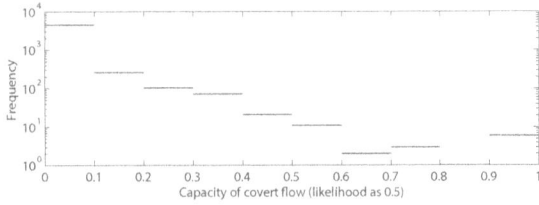

Figure 8: Distribution of leakage flows of 5K randomly generated requests (likelihood fixed as 0.5).

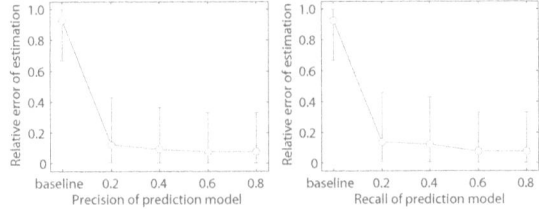

Figure 9: Estimation error with respect to the accuracy of 2-hop link prediction model, where no prediction is employed in the baseline approach.

been granted; we then randomly generate a set of access requests, and evaluate their corresponding leakage flows.

More concretely, we consider the history from 12/01/2005 to 07/20/2009, 20,870 access requests in total. At a step of 1,000 requests, we evaluate the leakage flows for 5K randomly generated requests. The average leakage flow with respect to time-stamp and leakage likelihood is plotted in Figure 7. It is noticed that as more requests are granted, the average flux increases significantly. This is explained by that the newly-created inter-network links between social and information networks generally increase the leakage flow capacity between the two networks, which also implies the non-negligible impact of the network effects among subjects and objects over access control risks.

We further look into the distribution of leakage flows of subject-object pairs. For the time-stamp of 07/20/2009, we measure the leakage flows for 5K randomly generated requests. Figure 8 shows the result. The distribution demonstrates a long tail, which is mainly attributed to the heterogeneity of social and information networks; that is, there exist "hot" spots in both networks, which feature large leakage flows; the existence of "hot" spots necessitates careful risk estimation before making access control decisions.

Incorporation of Network Evolution

One critical feature that makes our paradigm useful is its capability of incorporating predicted network evolution in current risk estimation procedure. In our experiments, we focus on on the impact of social network evolution. We consider the two snapshots of the social network, and focus on the set of individuals appearing in both snapshots, which contains 32,028 users. From January to July 2009, 81,592 new relationships were created among these subjects. We assume the prediction model [17] that predicts new links that spans two hops.

We intend to study the robustness of our estimation model against the prediction error incurred by the prediction model. For 0.5K randomly generated access requests, we measure the leakage flow over the network snapshot as of July 2009 (measured flow), and compare the result with that estimated based on the snapshot as of January 2009, in conjunction of the prediction model (estimated flow). We evaluate the rela-

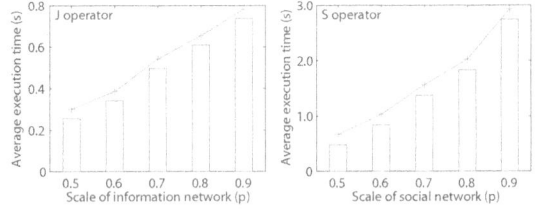

Figure 10: Average execution time of J-operator and S-operator as a function of network scale.

tive estimation error as a function of the accuracy of prediction model, with default recall and precision set as 0.5. The result is shown in Figure 9. In both cases, the estimation made by the baseline approach (without prediction) considerably deviates from the actually measured result, with relative error around 0.9. Employing the prediction model significantly improves the estimation accuracy; even with recall fixed as 0.2, the average error is reduced around 0.2. However, as the precision (or recall) increase, the further accuracy improvement is flat; this is explained by that the model only considers 2-hop links, while other types of links account for 49% of new relationships.

Scalability of Risk Estimation

In this set of experiments, we investigate the overhead of risk estimation over the access control infrastructure. Each risk estimation operation (Section 3) is constructed by composing a set of atom operators, whose complex interactions make it fairly difficult to directly characterize their impact over the scalability of risk estimation. We therefore focus our discussion at the level of atom operators. Due to the space limitation, we particularly study J-operator and S-operator, given their high frequency of usage.

We evaluate their execution time with respect to the scale of social and information networks. To do so, we create a set of network copies of different scales by randomly removing certain number of nodes (and their associated links) from the original network; a p-scale network indicates that $100 * (1-p)\%$ nodes are removed. Figure 10 shows the result. It is clear that both operators scale approximately linearly with the size of the networks, which empirically substantiates the analysis in Section 4.

6. DISCUSSION AND CONCLUSION

This work advances the state-of-the-art in risk-based access control by presenting a novel network-centric access control paradigm that explicitly accounts for the network effects in information flows. We show that a broad range of traditional node-centric models can be enhanced in terms of risk estimation using this general framework. While our framework is rich and flexible, several key challenges need to be addressed before it can be readily adopted. First, our approach relies on measures of information flow in socio-information networks. We believe that recent advances in network science research make it feasible (in part) to estimate such information flows. Second, we believe that applications in the future will be risk-based, i.e., they will exploit risk estimates to guide their decision-making (e.g., using budget based policies or exception handling mechanisms). Third, we believe that incorporating the time dimension (e.g., due to network evolution or due to decay in sensitivity of information) into risk estimation is essential to make sound decisions; while our approach handles network evolution, it does not explicitly address information items whose sensitivity decays over time. Despite these limitations, we believe that our proposed approach offers a new approach to modeling data flows in socio-information networks.

7. REFERENCES

[1] *Network-centric access control: models and techniques.* Georgia Tech Technical Report, GIT-CERCS-10-08, http://www.cercs.gatech.edu/tech-reports/.

[2] Teacher fired over Facebook sues district: http://www.cbsatlanta.com/news/21573759/detail.html.

[3] D. Aldous and J. A. Fill. Reversible markov chains, 1994.

[4] M. Backes, B. Kopf, and A. Rybalchenko. Automatic discovery and quantification of information leaks. In *SP*, 2009.

[5] D. E. Bell and L. J. LaPadula. Secure computer system: unified exposition and multics interpretation. In *MITRE Corporation*, 1976.

[6] E. Bertino, P. A. Bonatti, and E. Ferrari. Trbac: A temporal role-based access control model. *ACM Trans. Inf. Syst. Secur.*, 4(3):191–233, 2001.

[7] D. D. F. Brewer and D. M. J. Nash. The chinese wall security policy. *SP*, 1989.

[8] B. Carminati, E. Ferrari, S. Morasca, and D. Taibi. A probability-based approach to modeling the risk of unauthorized propagation of information in on-line social networks. In *CODASPY*, 2011.

[9] J. R. Challenger, P. Dantzig, A. Iyengar, M. S. Squillante, and L. Zhang. Efficiently serving dynamic data at highly accessed web sites. *IEEE/ACM Trans. Netw.*, 12(2):233–246, 2004.

[10] P.-C. Cheng, P. Rohatgi, C. Keser, P. A. Karger, G. M. Wagner, and A. S. Reninger. Fuzzy multi-level security: An experiment on quantified risk-adaptive access control. In *IEEE Security and Privacy Symposium*, 2007.

[11] J. Crampton. Understanding and developing role-based administrative models. In *CCS*, 2005.

[12] D. Easley and J. Kleinberg. *Networks, Crowds, and Markets: Reasoning About a Highly Connected World.* Cambridge University Press, 2010.

[13] J. Edmonds and R. M. Karp. Theoretical improvements in algorithmic efficiency for network flow problems. *J. ACM*, 19(2):248–264, 1972.

[14] D. Ferraiolo and R. Kuhn. Role-based access control. In *15th NIST-NCSC National Computer Security Conference*, 1992.

[15] D. Fogaras, B. Rácz, K. Csalogány, and T. Sarlós. Towards scaling fully personalized pagerank: Algorithms, lower bounds, and experiments. *Internet Mathematics*, 2(3), 2005.

[16] Y. Kanzaki, H. Igaki, M. Nakamura, A. Monden, and K.-i. Matsumoto. Characterizing dynamics of information leakage in security-sensitive software process. In *ACSW Frontiers*, 2005.

[17] J. Leskovec, L. Backstrom, R. Kumar, and A. Tomkins. Microscopic evolution of social networks. In *KDD*, 2008.

[18] C.-Y. Lin, N. Cao, S. X. Liu, S. Papadimitriou, J. Sun, and X. Yan. Smallblue: Social network analysis for expertise search and collective intelligence. In *ICDE*, 2009.

[19] S. McCamant and M. D. Ernst. Quantitative information flow as network flow capacity. In *PLDI*, 2008.

[20] I. Molloy, P.-C. Cheng, and P. Rohatgi. Trading in risk: using markets to improve access control. In *NSPW*, 2008.

[21] H. H. Song, T. W. Cho, V. Dave, Y. Zhang, and L. Qiu. Scalable proximity estimation and link prediction in online social networks. In *IMC*, 2009.

[22] M. Srivatsa, D. Agrawal, and S. Reidt. A metadata calculus for secure information sharing. In *CCS*, 2009.

[23] M. Srivatsa, P. Rohatgi, S. Balfe, and S. Reidt. Securing information flows: A metadata framework. In *QoISN*, 2008.

[24] H. Tong, C. Faloutsos, and J.-Y. Pan. Fast random walk with restart and its applications. In *ICDM*, 2006.

[25] N. Zeldovich, S. Boyd-Wickizer, and D. Mazières. Securing distributed systems with information flow control. In *NSDI*, 2008.

Acknowledgements

The research of this work was sponsored by the U.S. Army Research Laboratory and the U.K. Ministry of Defence and was accomplished under Agreement Number W911NF-06-3-0001. The views and conclusions contained in this document are those of the author(s) and should not be interpreted as representing the official policies, either expressed or implied, of the U.S. Army Research Laboratory, the U.S. Government, the U.K. Ministry of Defence or the U.K. Government. The U.S. and U.K. Governments are authorised to reproduce and distribute reprints for Government purposes notwithstanding any copyright notation hereon. The first and last authors are also sponsored by grants under NSF NetSE and NSF Cybertrust program, an IBM SUR grant and a grant from Intel Research Council.

APPENDIX

A. RECASTING CLASSICAL MODELS

Access control policies encode the rules used to regulate the qualification of $s \in S$ to access $o \in O$. In composing such policies, traditional models typically adopt a *node-centric* paradigm; they either treat each subject and object in isolation, or only partially account for the relationships between subjects, between objects and between subjects and objects.

Next we use three representative access control models as concrete examples to show the compatibility of our network-centric paradigm; how to extend to more complicated models (e.g., FuzzyMLS [10]) is also discussed; further we address how the dynamic aspects of access control models including administrative update of security setting and exception handling (e.g., the upgrade/downgrade of subjects' security levels in MLS model, the periodic role enabling and disabling in temporal RBAC model [6]) are implemented.

A.1 Multi-Level Security (MLS) Model

We use Bell-LaPadula (BLP) model, a classic MLS access control model, as the first concrete example. In its simplest form, the policies in BLP are described by two terms, the *security attributes* of the objects/subjects concerned and the rules for access. BLP attaches security labels to both objects (classification levels) and subjects (clearance levels) (more precisely, the combination of classification/clearance and a set of compartments); the classification/clearance scheme is described in terms of a lattice. Further, BLP has a *simple-security* and a *-property* rule, which can be characterized as "no read up, no write down":

- Simple security. Read access is allowed only if the subject's clearance is above the object's classification.
- *-property. Write access is granted only if the subject's clearance is below the object's classification.

Under the network-centric framework, the implementation of BLP is fairly straightforward:

- The subject and object networks consist of the set of subjects S and objects O.
- The inter-network links encode the clearance/classification comparison of subjects and objects. Specifically, for subject s and object o, $\mathtt{enf}(\overline{os}) = 1$ if $\mathtt{clear}(s) > \mathtt{class}(o)$, $\mathtt{enf}(\overline{so}) = 1$ if $\mathtt{class}(o) > \mathtt{clear}(s)$, and 0 otherwise.
- An access request $(s \to o)$ is granted only when the enforced flow $f_e(s \to o) = 1$ for a read access, or $f_e(o \to s) = 1$ for a write access.

Variations in MLS can be accommodated by modifying this basic construction in different ways.

A.2 Fuzzy MLS

Unlike the simple dichotomic comparison of the classification $\mathtt{class}(o)$ of object o and clearance $\mathtt{clear}(s)$ of subject s

in conventional MLS [5], Fuzzy MLS computes a quantified *risk* for an access request $(s \rightarrow o)$ based on the gap between $\texttt{clear}(s)$ and $\texttt{class}(o)$, and specifies a region on the risk scale (which can be further divided into bands). It allows access with risk below the lower-bound of the region (soft boundary), denies access with risk above the upper-bound of the region (hard boundary), and charges access with risk laying between soft and hard boundaries by its difference to the soft boundary against subject's risk credit. Each subject is periodically (say, monthly) allotted a risk budget.

We can implement Fuzzy MLS using the network-centric paradigm as follows. Let $\texttt{risk}(s, o)$ represent the risk associated with the access $(s \rightarrow o)$, L and U denote the soft and hard boundaries, and $\texttt{budget}(s)$ be the budget allotted to s initially (all in the unit of risk credit). For given subject s, we create a link $\overline{os}$ if $\texttt{risk}(s, o) < \texttt{U}$, and specify its enforced flow capacity initially as $\texttt{enf}(\overline{os}) = \infty$ if $\texttt{risk}(s, o) \leq \texttt{L}$, or $\texttt{enf}(\overline{os}) = \texttt{budget}(s)$ if $\texttt{risk}(s, o) > \texttt{L}$. An access $(s \rightarrow o)$ is granted only if $\texttt{enf}(\overline{os}) > 0$. After the access, all links of s update their enforced flow capacities by decreasing $(\texttt{risk}(s, o) - \texttt{L})$. After the periodic allocation of risk budget, the flow capacities of links $\overline{os}$ with $\texttt{L} < \texttt{risk}(s, o) < \texttt{U}$ are restored to $\texttt{budget}(s)$.

A.3 Role-based Access Control (RBAC) Model

RBAC models explicitly capture the relationships among subjects by organizing them according to their functional roles. A typical RBAC [14] model uses the following conventional notations: S, the set of subjects, R, the set of *roles*, which describe authorization levels, and P, the set of permissions, which represent the approval of access to concerned objects. Access control policy can be described by the following three mappings:

- Subject assignment, $SA \subseteq S \times R$, which is a many to many subject to role assignment relation;
- Permission assignment, $PA \subseteq P \times R$, which is a many to many permission to role assignment relation;
- Role hierarchy, $RH \subseteq R \times R$, which is a partially ordered role hierarchy. Two roles $r \geq r'$ means r inherits the permissions of r'.

Under the network-centric paradigm, we intend to encode these three mappings via the subject and object networks and the inter-network relationships. One possible implementation could be as follows:

- In the subject network G_S, in addition to the set of subjects S, for each role $r \in R$, we create a corresponding node r. For each $s \in S$, a link $\overline{rs}$ ($\texttt{enf}(\overline{rs}) = 1$) is created to indicate that s is assigned role r, i.e., SA mapping. The sub-network G_R over the set $\{r \in R\}$ encodes the role hierarchy RH: two nodes r and r' are adjacent over the link $\overline{rr'}$ ($\texttt{enf}(\overline{rr'}) = 1$) if they are adjacent in RH and $r \geq r'$.
- Due to role inheritance, if subject s is associated with any two roles r and r' with $r \geq r'$, only the link $\overline{rs}$ is necessary, which implies the link $\overline{r's}$.
- The object network G_O is a set of nodes, each corresponding to one object $o \in O$.
- The inter-network relationships between G_O and the sub-network G_R encode the permission assignment PA. Each link $\overline{or}$ between object o and role r indicates that r has access to o, and the access mode is contained in the type information of $\overline{or}$.
- An access request is granted only if the enforced flow $f_e(o \rightarrow s) = 1$ (the type of inter-network link must be equivalent to the requested access mode) in this network.

The basic model can be further enriched to support features such as session-based role activation, constraints on subjects/objects/roles, and multiple security domains.

A.4 Chinese-wall Model

Beyond other conventional access control models, Chinese-wall model [7] and its variations further take into consideration the conflict of interest in objects. It also has a dynamic aspect that accounts for the the access history of subjects regarding the objects concerned. In a simplified Chinese-wall model, each object o is associated with two label x_o indicating the commercial database holding o, and y_o indicating its *conflict of interest class*. The basic Chinese-wall policy can be described as:

- Simple security. An access $(s \rightarrow o)$ is granted only if o has the same label x_o as an object o' already accessed by s, i.e., within the wall, or has an entirely different label y_o to all the objects already accessed by s.
- *-property. Write access is granted only if the simple security rule is honored, and no accessible object o' contains unsanitized information and has a different label $x_{o'}$ to the requested one o.

Under the network-centric framework, one implementation of Chinese-wall model could be as follows:
- The subject network is a set of nodes, each corresponding to a subject $s \in S$.
- In the object network, a pair of objects o and o' are bi-directionally adjacent if (i) $x_o = x_{o'}$ or (ii) $y_o \neq y_{o'}$ (both $\texttt{enf}(\overline{oo'}) = 1$ and $\texttt{enf}(\overline{o'o}) = 1$). Further, each object is labeled by either *sanitized* or *unsanitized*.
- Once subject s has accessed object o, an inter-network link $\overline{os}$ ($\texttt{enf}(\overline{os}) = 1$) is added to the network.
- If subject s has not yet accessed any object, i.e., no inter-network link exists for s, an access request $(s \rightarrow o)$ is granted by default. Otherwise, the request is granted only if the enforced flow estimation $f_e(o \rightarrow s) = 1$ for a read access; and (i) $f_e(o \rightarrow s) = 1$, (ii) $\nexists o', f_e(o' \rightarrow s) = 1, x_o \neq x_{o'}'$, o' is unsanitized for a write access.

A.5 Dynamic Aspects

To accommodate changing application environments, many access control models introduce dynamic aspects: e.g., down-grade/upgrade of subjects' sensitivity labels in MLS [5], dynamic role dependencies in temporal RBAC [6]. Here, we use the periodic role enabling/disabling in TRBAC as an example to show how to implement such dynamic aspects in network-centric paradigm.

We still follow the generic information flow model introduced in Section 2. In addition to labeling network links, we also assigns labels to network nodes. Now, nodes act like *switches*, which can block or unblock enforced flows. Particularly, in periodic role enabling/disabling, each role is associated with a *periodic expression* that indicates the activation period of the role, e.g., $all \cdot Year + \{1, 4\} \cdot Months \triangleright 2$ represents the set of intervals starting at the first and fourth month of every year, and having a duration of two months [6]. We can attach such expression to the corresponding role node (see Appendix A.3), and activate the node only when the expression is true. This way, all permissions associated with a disabled role are detached from the subjects associated with the role (zero enforced flows).

An Authorization Scheme for Version Control Systems

Sitaram Chamarty
Tata Consultancy Services
Hyderabad, India
sitaram@atc.tcs.com

Hiren D. Patel
ECE Department
Univ. of Waterloo, Canada
hdpatel@uwaterloo.ca

Mahesh V. Tripunitara
ECE Department
Univ. of Waterloo, Canada
tripunit@uwaterloo.ca

ABSTRACT

We present gitolite, an authorization scheme for Version Control Systems (VCSes). We have implemented it for the Git VCS. A VCS enables versioning, distributed collaboration and several other features, and is an important context for authorization and access control. Our main consideration behind the design of gitolite is the balance between expressive power, correctness and usability in realistic settings. We discuss our design of gitolite, and in particular the four user-classes in its delegation model, and the administrative actions a user at each class performs. We discuss also our ongoing work on expressing gitolite precisely in first-order logic, to thereby give it a precise semantics and establish correctness properties. gitolite has been adopted in open-source software development, university and industry settings. We discuss our experience with these deployments, and present some performance results related to access enforcement from a real deployment.

Categories and Subject Descriptors

D.4.6 [**Operating Systems**]: Security and Protection—*Access Controls*; D.2.7 [**Software Engineering**]: Distribution, Maintenance, and Enhancement—*Version control*

General Terms

Security, Design

Keywords

Authorization, Version Control Systems, Git

1. INTRODUCTION

We present gitolite [3], a new authorization scheme for Version Control Systems (VCSes). Authorization deals with the specification and management of the rights users have to resources. (The terms "authorization" and "access control" mean the same in this paper.) It is an important aspect of the security of a system. A VCS is used when resources (e.g., software programs) are in flux, and the history of changes need versioning. Typically, a VCS needs to allow multiple users to access, modify and update the resources.

gitolite has been implemented for the Git VCS [2] and is sufficiently general to be applicable to other VCSes such as SVN [1].

Our particular focus in this paper is our design of controlled delegation that is part of the scheme. Traditional authorization schemes for VCSes have a single administrator for an instance of a VCS that specifies authorization rules for accessors. Our scheme is more flexible and scalable as it has a finer-grained delegation model. We have validated the scheme with real-world deployments in large-scale open-source software development projects, universities and industry (see Section 5).

In the context of designing an authorization scheme for VCSes, we have set a broader goal for ourselves: to design a scheme that simultaneously addresses expressive power, usability and correctness. The scope of this paper is more modest that our overall goal — we seek to introduce gitolite, convey its salient features, and argue that it is indeed different in its expressive power from prior schemes. In this context, our intent is only for our scheme to be applicable to VCSes; it is not designed to be as expressive as more general schemes from the research literature. A natural question then is whether schemes that have been proposed previously, such as those for Discretionary Access Control (DAC) [12], Role-Based Access Control (RBAC) [9, 25] and Trust Management [7, 18], are expressive enough to subsume our scheme. We discuss this issue in more detail in Section 6. Our observation is that other schemes do not capture gitolite in a manner that is useful for real-world deployments. This should not be surprising: it has been observed before that even from a more rigorous standpoint, given two authorization schemes, neither may be as expressive as the other [31]. Furthermore, the application-domain has a significant influence on the design of an authorization scheme and its expressive power. Therefore, it is likely that schemes from different application-domains are incomparable with one another.

Novelty A number of authorization schemes have been proposed in the research literature. Also, there are several schemes that are deployed in various application domains such as file and database systems. The elements of our scheme are not new. However, the manner in which we put the elements together into a composite scheme is novel. For example, delegation is a well-studied notion in authorization. However, in the context of a new scheme such as ours, one still needs to make a number of choices regarding, for example, the depth of delegation that is allowed, and the sorts of power an individual at a particular depth has.

There are two mindsets that we see in past work on authorization schemes. One is work that is agnostic to the application domain. A lot of past work on RBAC, for example, appears to be based on this mindset. The other mindset is that the application domain influences the authorization scheme significantly. Our design is based on this latter mindset, and our design is validated by our experience from several deployments, as we discuss in Section 5.

Layout The remainder of this paper is organized as follows. In the next section, we introduce VCSes. In Section 2 we discuss how we perform access enforcement. In Section 3, we discuss our authorization scheme. In Section 4, we discuss our ongoing work on giving our scheme a precise encoding in first-order logic. In Section 5, we discuss our experience from deployments. We discuss related work in Section 6, and conclude in Section 7.

1.1 Version Control Systems

A VCS provides the ability to version resources such as data files. (We use the phrase "a VCS" to mean "an instance of a VCS.") Considerable functionality is associated with modern VCSes; some examples are distributed development, non-linear development and the maintenance of history (versions) [1, 2]. A VCS comprises objects such as repositories and branches that help realize such functionality. An authorization scheme for a VCS specifies how these objects are protected, while respecting the semantics of the relationships between the objects.

Version Control System ::= {Repo}

Repo ::= Branch {Branch}

Branch ::= {Folder} {File} {Tag}

Folder ::= {Folder} {File}

Figure 1: A Version Control System in BNF. The notation ::= stands for "comprises," and {·} means 0 or more occurrences.

In Figure 1, we show the components of a VCS from the standpoint of authorization in Backus-Naur Form (BNF) [16], and give an example below. A VCS is a collection of repositories. A repository can be seen as a collection of data for a single project. A repository comprises branches. A branch is a thread of work on the data in a repository. A repository has at least one branch – its main branch. After a user edits some of the data in a branch, she may merge her changes with another branch.

A branch comprises folders, files and tags. Files contain data, and folders contain files and other folders; they are similar to folders and files in conventional file systems. A tag represents a "commit point" in a branch. Thus, a branch can be seen as comprising tags. From the standpoint of our authorization scheme, there is a function from the set of branches to the set of repositories, the set of tags to the set of branches, and the set of files and folders to the set of branches.

2. AUTHENTICATION AND ACCESS ENFORCEMENT

Before we discuss our authorization scheme, we describe authentication and access enforcement with `gitolite`. Our approach is quite general; however, there are some implementation aspects that are specific to Git. Our main point with this section is to discuss how we have been able to realize `gitolite` as middleware, and largely agnostic to changes to Git. `gitolite` works with version 1.6.2 and later versions of Git "out of the box." Furthermore, given our implementation as middleware, we expect `gitolite` to be compatible with future versions of Git.

In Figure 2, we show the relevant entities and the process. Git relies on SSH for access by a client, and authentication. As we

show in the figure, four entities are relevant in the context of authentication and access enforcement. One is the VCS client, which issues access requests to objects maintained by the VCS server. The communication is mediated by the SSH server, and access requests are mediated by the `gitolite` Reference Monitor. A VCS client communicates a command that is intended for `gitolite` and Git, which is opaque to the SSH server. The SSH server authenticates the client based on its public key (pubKey in Figure 2). The SSH server is configured to map the client's pubKey to its `gitolite` username. (Every Git client has to have a username to be authorized by `gitolite`– see Section 3.)

A command from a VCS client comprises two components: the name of a repository (repoName), and what we call a VCS object (vcsObject). The vcsObject is opaque to the SSH server and the `gitolite` Reference Monitor, and must be "unwrapped" by the VCS server. From the standpoint of access enforcement, the vcsObject contains a branchName, the data within the branchName to which the access request pertains, and the manner in which the client wishes to access the data.

The modes of access are classified into two: read and write. There is only one kind of read access; there are several kinds of write access (see Section 3.3). As Figure 2 indicates, access enforcement is split into two stages based on whether the request pertains to a read or write access. We label these (1) and (2) in the figure.

As we discuss in Section 3.3, any write right to a branch of a repository implies read access to the repository. Consequently, in stage (1) of access enforcement, the `gitolite` Reference Monitor first checks whether userName is authorized to read some branch of repoName. If the check succeeds, the access check labelled (1) passes. As we explicate in Section 3.4, a client needs to have read access to only any branch in the repository to have read access to the entire repository. Consequently, there is no need for the `gitolite` reference monitor to access any part of vcsObject to make an access decision related to read.

The access check labelled (2) is triggered by the VCS server, if necessary. It is not necessary if the client wishes read access only. The manner in which this is implemented in `gitolite` is by what is called a "hook" in Git. A hook allows one to associate a call-back function with Git. In our case, the hook is used for access enforcement. The VCS server is able to interpret the contents of vcsObject. It invokes the call-back function within `gitolite` with the name of the branch (branchName) and the particular write operation (writeOp) to which the request pertains. The `gitolite` reference monitor consults its policy and issues a binary decision on the access request.

As we discuss in Section 3, the access policy comprises rules which are compiled into an Access Control List (ACL). In Section 5.4, we present performance results with our approach to access enforcement that we discuss above. Our results indicate that our approach is pragmatic. This has also been validated by our experience with deployments (see Section 5).

3. AUTHORIZATION SCHEME

Our authorization scheme is discretionary [12]. We discuss in Section 3.2 how users specify rules. These rules are compiled into an ACL that is used for access enforcement; we discuss this in Section 3.4. An ACL, in our context, is a set of triples, each of the form ⟨Resource, Right, User⟩. It indicates that User possesses the Right to the Resource. There are two kinds of negative (deny) rights; we discuss these in Section 3.3.

The authorization rules include administrative actions such as delegations. We being, in the following section, with a discussion

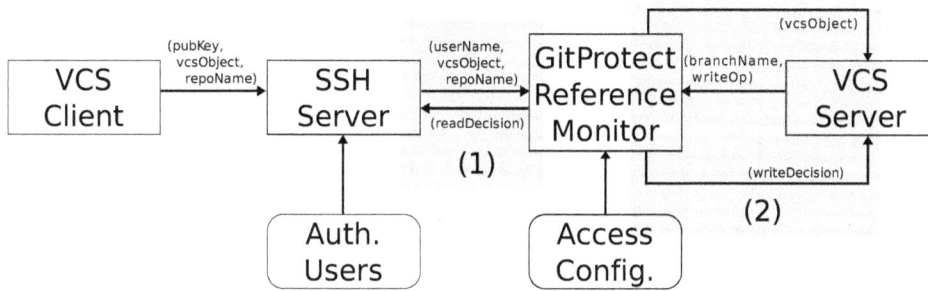

Figure 2: Access enforcement to VCS objects using the `gitolite` reference monitor.

of our classification of users into four user-classes, three of which comprise users that are allowed to specify authorization rules that pertain to administration.

3.1 Classes of Users

Traditional VCSes have only two classes of users: an administrator, and an accessor. As we discuss in Section 6, this is often the case in other application domains such as file systems as well. An administrator configures authorization rules, and an accessor is allowed access based on those rules. In `gitolite`, we have four classes of users, as we show in Figure 3. These classes and their relationships are fixed. Consequently, the depth of delegation is at most four. This design choice of a fixed delegation depth is similar to some schemes from prior work such as ARBAC97 [24] which has a delegation depth of two, and dissimilar to schemes such as RT [18] which allow delegation of arbitrary depth.

As we express in the figure, our four classes of users are: VCS Admin, Repo Admin, Repo Owner and Accessor. A solid arrow represents "may delegate to." We point out that the transitive closure of that relation is appropriate in our context. For example, we indicate in Figure 3 that a VCS Admin may delegate to a Repo Admin. However, he may delegate also to Repo Owner and Accessor.

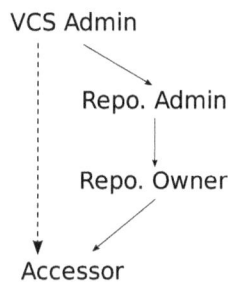

Figure 3: We have four classes of users. The dotted arrow shows what is in traditional VCSes -- only two classes of users, VCS Admin and Accessor. We, in addition to those, have Repo Admin and Repo Owner. The transitive closure of the arrows represents "may delegate to."

We give a broad characterization of each user-class here, and make it more precise in the following sections. A VCS Admin administers an entire installation of a VCS. In a typical enterprise, we anticipate that this is a classical systems administrator. We anticipate that a VCS Admin is not involved in projects that are represented by repositories.

A Repo Admin administers a set of repositories. The set typically represents a large project within which may exist smaller projects. The term "within" has no meaning in the context of repositories

in a VCS such as Git; there is no such thing as a "sub-repository." Consequently, each smaller project is associated with a repository, but the authorization scheme must somehow capture the intuition that a set of repositories are administered together. This is why we have designed our scheme to have the notion of a Repo Admin.

A Repo Owner administers a repository. In `gitolite`, we have the notion of the creator of a repository as well. We assume in this paper that the Repo Owner is the creator of the repository. A Repo Admin determines who may create (and hence, own) repositories, and delimits the identities of those repositories. Only one user may be the Repo Owner of a repository. An Accessor accesses VCS objects such as repositories and branches.

A typical chronological flow of actions is as follows. A VCS is installed by the VCS Admin. Initially, and over time the VCS Admin adds users that may access parts of the VCS. The VCS Admin also broadly divides the VCS into sets of repositories for administration by Repo Admins. These repositories may not exist yet; the specification is done using regular expressions. A Repo Admin is involved in projects in an intimate way. He designates Repo Owners for sub-projects that have some limited discretion in handing our access rights to other users. We discuss more concrete uses of `gitolite` in Section 5.

3.2 Administrative and Authorization Specifications

In this section, we discuss the specifications that a user in each class that we present in the previous section may make. Our user-classes are organized in a hierarchy (see Figure 3). Anything a user at a particular class can do may also be done by a user at a higher class for that instance of the hierarchy. That is, a user at a higher class of the hierarchy may delegate some power directly to a user at a class lower than the one immediately below his.

We call each specification of authorization for an entire VCS a *configuration*, and an element of a configuration a *rule*. For example, the VCS Admin may designate *Alice* to be a valid user. He does so using a rule in the configuration for that VCS.

VCS Admin The following are rules that only a VCS Admin may specify.

- The set of valid usernames for the VCS. This set is the domain to which the SSH Server maps public keys at the time of access (see Section 2).

- A set of mnemonics. Examples of such mnemonics are READERS and WRITERS. The intent is for these to be used by a Repo Owner to specify who may read and write objects. A mnemonic may be seen as a group or role. However, there are some differences between what we call a mnemonic, and groups and roles. We discuss these differences in Section 6.

Indeed, `gitolite` has a separate notion of a group that may be specified in place of a user in an ACL entry.

- Who may act as a Repo Admin. The VCS Admin is able to delimit the set of repositories over which a Repo Admin has purview. He does this by specifying regular expressions for the names of the repositories. (Repositories within a VCS are identified uniquely by name.) More than one Repo Admin may be associated with a set of repositories. This may happen, for example, if two regular expressions match the same string. The VCS Admin assigns a strict priority to a Repo Admin's authorization rules.

From the standpoint of authorization, we need certain conditions to hold with regards to delegations and definitions that the VCS Admin has made. We capture these in the effective rights that users have, which we discuss in Section 3.4.

Repo Admin The following are rules that only a Repo Admin or VCS Admin may specify.

- Associate a right with a mnemonic. For example, a Repo Admin may associate the right "read" with the mnemonic READERS, and "read" and "write" with WRITERS.

- Who may act as a Repo Owner, and of which repositories a user may be the Repo Owner. A Repo Admin may also delimit a Repo Owner's ability to give out rights. One manner in which he does this is by designating a repository to be "private." We discuss this below. Another manner is that he can deny a particular user some rights, which a Repo Owner cannot override.

Repo Owner The following are rules and actions that only a Repo Owner or Repo Admin of a repository, or the VCS Admin may specify and perform.

- Create a repository. A repository may be created only if one with the same (fully-resolved) name does not exist, and a corresponding Repo Admin has authorized it.

- Assign users to mnemonics. As we mention above in our discussions on Repo Admins, we constrain a Repo Owner in that he is unable to directly assign rights to users. All he is allowed to do is assign a user to a mnemonic, via which the user may acquire rights. This is a design choice that balances flexibility (expressive power) and security.

3.3 Objects and Rights

In this section, we specify the access rights that accessors may have to VCS objects. The different kinds of VCS objects and the relationship between them from the standpoint of authorization are shown in Figure 1. The objects are: repositories, branches, tags, folders and files. Rights are classified into read and write. There is only one read right. We designate `read` as the right that gives read rights to a repository. The kinds of write rights are the following.

- `write` – this is the right to write or commit an object. This right may be specified for any VCS object.

- `rewindBranch` – this is the right to be able to revert a branch to an original version. It may be specified for a repository or branch only. If it is specified for a repository, then it applies for every branch in the repository.

- `createBranch` – this is the right to be able to create a branch within a repository. It may be specified for a repository only.

- `deleteBranch` – this is the right to be able to delete a branch within a repository. It may be specified for a repository only.

- `createRepo` – this is the right to be able to create a repository.

- `deleteRepo` – this is the right to be able to delete a repository.

There are also two "negative" rights that explicitly deny the corresponding right to an accessor. These may be used, for example, by a Repo Admin to disallow a Repo Owner from giving the right to an accessor. In Section 3.4, we discuss how these negative rights are reconciled with their "positive" counterparts.

- `denyWrite` – this is the "negative" of `write`.

- `denyRewindBranch` – the "negative" of `rewindBranch`.

3.4 Compilation

As we mention in Section 3.2, in our system, rules are specified in a configuration. There is one configuration per VCS; the configuration is split across one or more files. The VCS Admin has a particular configuration file in which he specifies his rules, such as the legitimate usernames (the concrete values that correspond to the predicate definesUser) and the definitions of mnemonics (definesMnemonic). Similarly, each Repo Admin has his own configuration file.

In this section, we discuss how the configurations that are specified as we discuss in Sections 3.2 and 3.3 are compiled into an ACL. Compilation, therefore, translates a configuration into a list of effective rights that each user has to resources, encoded as an ACL. Compilation takes as input a specification of the authorization scheme as we discuss in the previous two sections, and outputs an ACL, which comprises ⟨Resource, Right, User⟩ triples. The reason for this intermediate step of compilation, rather than directly checking a request against the configuration rules is efficiency at the time of access enforcement. We relate our discussions in this section to our discussion on access enforcement in Section 2. Also, in Section 5.4, we present data on the performance of access enforcement from a real deployment.

We use Git to administer Git. That is, our configuration files are maintained as part of the Git repository which is the VCS instance. As we mention in Section 3.2, an aspect of our scheme is our prioritization of Repo Admins and rules within a Repo Admin's specification. Our prioritization is implemented by sequencing the configuration files in a particular order during compilation. This is simple, but effective in achieving what we need, which is imposing a strict priority on Repo Admins and rules respectively. All a VCS Admin does, for instance, is specify in what order the `gitolite` compiler should process the configuration files, and this expresses his prioritization.

For User to have Right over Resource, the following two conditions are necessary.

1. The User must be valid, as specified by VCS Admin, and,
2. The user must either (a) directly be assigned Right (by Repo Admin), or, (b) there must exist a valid mnemonic (as specified by the VCS Admin) to which User is assigned (by the Repo Owner), and that mnemonic must have in its effective set of rights, Right.

Consequently, the first set of processes that the compiler runs comprises assembling the following from the configuration rules.

3. The set of valid users.

4. The set of valid mnemonics.

5. The set of authorizations of rights directly assigned to users, and the corresponding priority.

6. The set of authorizations of rights assigned to mnemonics and the corresponding priority.

7. The set of user to mnemonic assignments per resource.

The pieces of information (3)–(7) are read by the compiler directly from the configuration rules. The compiler must then process the above information and make inferences regarding the effective rights per user to resources. This comprises the following steps.

8. Infer the rights a user may have to resources via mnemonics. This involves putting the information from Steps (6) and (7) together. The compiler also records the priority with which each such assignment is associated.

9. For each right to which a user is authorized, either directly or indirectly via a mnemonic, infer other rights. We discuss below how this inference is done. An example of such an inference is that any (positive) right to a resource implies read access to the repository that corresponds to the resource.

10. Decide whether the user indeed has a right to a resource by considering the highest priority rule that grants him the right. If there is a "deny" counterpart of this right in a rule of higher priority, then the user does not have the right.

After Steps (8)–(10) are completed, the compiler is able to output ACL entries of the form ⟨Resource, Right, User⟩ for each Right and Resource to which the User is authorized. The final ACL comprises only those positive rights that a user possesses. Consequently, checking whether a user has a right or not against the ACL is efficient – see Section 5.4 for some data related to the performance of access enforcement.

In Step (9), we refer to inferring that a user has a right to a resource if he has another right to a resource. Following is our specification.

a. If a user has any positive right to a resource, then he has read to the repository associated with that resource.

b. Every right other than read is of type write. If a user has any right of type write to a resource, then he has write to that resource.

c. If a user has createBranch to a branch, then he has rewindBranch to that branch.

d. If a user has deleteBranch to a branch, then he has createBranch to that branch.

The reason that underlies the above inferences regarding rights is that it does not make sense to possess a right and not another in the specific cases that we address with the inferences. For example, it does not make sense for a user to have any right of type write to a resource unless he is able to read that resource. Also, in practice, there is no need for the read right to be at a finer granularity than to an entire repository.

4. TOWARDS A PRECISE ENCODING

It is our goal to establish a precise semantics and correctness properties for our scheme. A comprehensive description of those aspects is beyond the scope of this paper. Indeed, these aspects are ongoing work. In this section, we provide some discussion of how we go about achieving this goal.

We conjecture that our scheme can be expressed precisely in first-order logic [14]. To express a configuration, we specify predicates and functions. We then specify the manner in which we compute the effective rights (see Section 3.4) as inference rules in first-order logic. In the following section, we discuss the predicates and functions that we adopt to express a configuration. We discuss also an subset of the inference rules that we adopt to infer effective rights. We introduce "intermediate" predicates for ease of exposition.

What we seek is to define predicates that map directly to elements in a configuration. Then, we are able to make such a predicate concrete in a model [14] by populating it with values directly from the configuration. In Section 4.2 we discuss how we intend to specify a precise semantics along these lines.

4.1 Authorizations

In this section, we discuss the predicates and functions that we adopt to express a configuration. We discuss also a subset of the inference rules that are used to infer the effective rights. We follow the same flow as in Section 3.2.

VCS Admin We associate the following predicates with actions that a VCS Admin performs.

- definesUser(u, v) indicates that u is defined to be a valid user by the user v.

- definesMnemonic(m, u) indicates that m is a mnemonic that has been defined by user u.

- definesRepoAdmin(u, R, v) indicates that u is designated a Repo Admin to the repository R by the user v.

As we mention in Section 3.2, more than one Repo Admin may be associated with a set of repositories. A VCS Admin associates a priority with each Repo Admin for the authorization rules. We specify the following functions.

- $vcsAdmin$ – this is the constant function that identifies the VCS Admin.

- The function $adminPrio(u, r, v)$ is the strict priority that the user u has to administer the repository r according to v.

Repo Admin We associate the following predicates with the actions that pertain to a Repo Admin.

- mnemonicHasRight(m, ρ, o, u) indicates that the mnemonic m is assigned the right ρ to the VCS object o by the user u.

- userHasRight(u, ρ, o, v) indicates that the user u is assigned the right ρ to o by the user v. Only a Repo Admin or VCS Admin may directly assign rights to users. We discuss the manner in which a Repo Owner assigns rights in our discussions on Repo Owner below.

- isRepoOwner(u, R, v) indicates that the user u is specified to be a potential Repo Owner of all the repositories in the set R by the user v. We say "potential," as more than one user may be designed to be a Repo Owner, and the user that creates the repository with a particular name ends up being its only owner.

We define also the following functions.

- $priv(r)$ – a Repo Admin may designate a repository to be private. What this means is that the Repo Owner is disallowed from giving out any rights to that repository (even though he may create it). This somewhat coarse-grained restriction is useful in practice. The repository r is private if and only if $priv(r) = $ true.

$$\text{auth}(u, \texttt{read}, o) \longleftarrow \exists \rho \in \text{RIGHTS}^+ \ \text{auth}(u, \rho, o) \tag{1}$$

$$\text{auth}(u, \texttt{write}, o) \longleftarrow \exists \left(\rho \in \text{RIGHTS}^+ - \{\texttt{read}\} \right) \text{auth}(u, \rho, o) \tag{2}$$

$$
\begin{aligned}
\text{auth}(u, \rho, o) \longleftarrow \ & (\text{authByOwner}(u, \rho, o) \wedge \neg\text{deniedByRepoAdmin}(u, \rho, o) \wedge \\
& \neg\text{deniedByVCSAdmin}(u, \rho, o)) \vee \\
& (\text{authByRepoAdmin}(u, \rho, o) \wedge \neg\text{deniedByVCSAdmin}(u, \rho, o)) \vee \\
& \text{authByVCSAdmin}(u, \rho, o)
\end{aligned}
\tag{3}
$$

$$
\begin{aligned}
\text{authByOwner}(u, \rho, o) \longleftarrow \ & \neg priv\,(repo(o)) \wedge \\
& \exists m\,(\text{validMnemonic}(m) \wedge \text{isMember}\,(u, m, o, creator(repo(o))) \wedge \\
& \text{authMByRepoAdmin}(u, m, \rho, o))
\end{aligned}
\tag{4}
$$

$$\text{validMnemonic}(m) \longleftarrow \text{definesMnemonic}(m, vcsAdmin) \tag{5}$$

$$\text{isMember}(u, m, o, v) \longleftarrow \text{isMember}(u, m, repo(o), v) \vee (br(o) \neq \epsilon \wedge \text{isMember}(u, m, br(o), v)) \tag{6}$$

$$
\begin{aligned}
\text{authMByRepoAdmin}(u, m, \rho, o) \longleftarrow \ & \exists v\,(\text{validRepoAdmin}(v, repo(o)) \wedge \text{highestRightPrio}(u, m, \rho, o, v) \wedge \\
& (\forall w \ \text{validRepoAdmin}(w, repo(p)) \wedge \text{mnemonicHasRight}(m, \rho, o, w) \wedge \\
& (adminPrio(v, r, vcsAdmin) > adminPrio(w, r, vcsAdmin))))
\end{aligned}
\tag{7}
$$

$$
\begin{aligned}
\text{validRepoAdmin}(u, r) \longleftarrow \ & (vcsAdmin = u) \ \vee \\
& \text{definesRepoAdmin}(u, r, vcsAdmin)
\end{aligned}
\tag{8}
$$

$$
\begin{aligned}
\text{highestRightPrio}(u, m, \texttt{createBranch}, o, v) \longleftarrow \ & \text{mnemonicHasRight}(m, \texttt{createBranch}, o, v) \wedge \\
& (\forall n \ \text{isMember}(u, n, o, creator(repo(o))) \wedge \\
& (rightPrio(m, \texttt{createBranch}, o, v) > rightPrio(n, \texttt{createBranch}, o, v)))
\end{aligned}
\tag{9}
$$

$$
\begin{aligned}
\text{highestRightPrio}(u, m, \texttt{write}, o, v) \longleftarrow \ & \text{mnemonicHasRight}(m, \texttt{write}, o, v) \wedge \\
& (\forall n \ \text{isMember}(u, n, o, creator(repo(o))) \wedge \\
& (rightPrio(m, \texttt{write}, o, v) > rightPrio(n, \texttt{write}, o, v))) \wedge \\
& (\forall n \ \text{isMember}(u, n, o, creator(repo(o))) \wedge \\
& (rightPrio(m, \texttt{write}, o, v) > rightPrio(n, \texttt{denyWrite}, o, v)))
\end{aligned}
\tag{10}
$$

Figure 4: A portion of our inference rules for our authorization scheme. RIGHTS$^+$ = {read, write, rewindBranch, createBranch, deleteBranch}.

- $rightPrio(mORu, \rho, o, v)$ is a function that specifies the strict priority that the rule that assigns the right ρ has been assigned by the user v over object o to the mnemonic or user $mORu$. Rights can conflict with one another. Within a particular user's grants, this is disambiguated by this priority. Rights can also conflict across granters. This is resolved via the inference rules.

Repo Owner As with the other user-classes, we associate the following predicate with actions relevant to a Repo Owner.

- isMember(u, m, o, v) indicates that user u is assigned to be a member of the mnemonic m for object o by a user v.

We define also the following function.

- $creator(r)$ – the Repo Owner of r. If the repository r does not exist, then $creator(r) = \epsilon$, where ϵ is a special symbol in the range of $creator$. A repository that exists has exactly one creator.

Inferences We show an example of inferring authorized access to an object in Figure 4. The predicate auth(u, ρ, o) is used to indicate whether the user u has the right ρ to the object o. Figure 4 has a partial list of inference rules that are relevant for $\rho = $ createBranch, and $\rho = $ write. We point out that the former does not have a corresponding negative right, while the latter does.

In Figure 4, Inference (1) asserts that possession of any positive right to o implies possession of read to o. Inference (2) asserts that possession of any positive right other than read to o implies possession of write to o. The rights read and write are the only ones for which such implication holds. The reason is that this is the most sensible design. For example, it does not make sense of a user to have the createBranch right to a repository unless he is able to read and write the repository.

Inference (3) presents the cases for user u to have right ρ to object o. The right ρ may be positive or negative. The three disjuncted clauses express the three possibilities. They are as follows.

- User u has ρ to o if he is granted it by the Repo Owner, and not denied it by either a Repo Admin or the VCS Admin. "Denied" in this context is somewhat non-straightforward to determine as we have priorities associated both with Repo Admins (as assigned by the VCS Admin), and to rules within a Repo Admin's ruleset.

- The second case is that u is authorized to ρ over o by the Repo Admin and not denied it by the VCS Admin. In this case, any rules of the Repo Owner are superceded by the rules of the Repo Admin.

- The third case is that u is authorized to ρ over o by the VCS Admin, which supercedes any denials by a Repo Admin.

Inference (4) clarifies when authByOwner is true. The only way for a Repo Owner to grant a right is by assigning a user to a mnemonic (see Section 3.2). For this, the repository in which o is cannot be private. Also, the right is assigned to the mnemonic by a Repo Admin; this is the reason we introduce the predicate authMByRepoAdmin.

Inference (5) clarifies that a valid mnemonic is one that is defined by the VCS Admin. Inference (6) asserts that if user v specifies that u is assigned to mnemonic m for an object (repository or branch) that contains o, then this implies that v assigns u to m for o.

Inference (7) specifies what we mean by a right being authorized to a mnemonic m by a Repo Admin. The Repo Admin must be valid, as specified by the VCS Admin. Also, within his set of rules for the object o, the assignment of ρ to the mnemonic m must supercede (by priority) any other assignments for o that pertain to ρ. We use the example of $\rho = \mathtt{createBranch}$, which is somewhat simpler than, for example, write, as the latter has a corresponding negative right, denyWrite. Consequently, for write, we need to check also whether the Repo Admin has denyWrite of higher priority that any rules that grants write to the user via the mnemonic.

Inference (8) expresses what we mean by a "valid" Repo Admin. It must be someone to whom the vcsAdmin has delegated power. Finally, Inference (9) expresses how we use priorities within the authorization rules of a Repo Admin for the case that $\rho = \mathtt{createBranch}$. Inference (10) expresses how the right write is assigned to a user by the Repo Owner. The highest priority Repo Admin must not have a higher priority rule that assigns the user the denyWrite right.

4.2 Semantics

For a semantics, we specify a model, $\mathcal{M}$, in which we instantiate sets of tuples for each predicate [14]. We consider only those environments in which variables are mapped meaningfully to concrete values that are meaningful. For example, the set of concrete values, A that we associate with $\mathcal{M}$ includes A_u, the set of users of the system, and A_r, the set of all rights that we specify in Section 3.3. We associate the variable u in Inference (1) of Figure 4, for example, only with elements from A_u, and not A_r. Similarly, we assign ρ only elements from A_r.

Our scheme has a well-founded semantics. We use negation in the inference rules. Examples are in Inference (4) in Figure 4 and in inference rules that involve the negative rights. However, the negation is stratified [11]. $\mathcal{M}$ is the least fix point from applying the inference rules to the model $\mathcal{M}_0$ with which we start. In $\mathcal{M}_0$, we populate the relations that make our predicates concrete with values directly from the authorization configuration files. For example, for every user u that the VCS Admin defines, we include the tuple $\langle u, vcsAdmin \rangle$ in definesUser$^{\mathcal{M}_0}$. Similarly, for every user v that associates a mnemonic m with a right ρ for object o, we include the tuple $\langle m, \rho, o, u \rangle$ in mnemonicHasRight$^{\mathcal{M}_0}$.

We are able to assert also that our algorithm to compute $\mathcal{M}$ (and $\mathcal{M}$ itself) is sound and complete. Soundness comprises two subproperties. One is that if there exists an environment in which auth$^{\mathcal{M}} \ni \langle u, \rho, o \rangle$ is entailed by $\mathcal{M}$, then this can be only because u is indeed authorized to ρ on o by one of the conditions we discuss in the previous section. The second soundness subproperty is that we do not infer any contradictions with respect to negative rights. That is, we never infer that a user is authorized to both write and denyWrite, or rewindBranch and denyRewindBranch to the same object. Completeness is the property that for any instance of our scheme, our algorithm to compute $\mathcal{M}$ terminates.

5. EXPERIENCE FROM DEPLOYMENTS

In this section, we discuss our experience from deploying our authorization scheme. As we mention in Section 1, our scheme has been validated in two settings: university and open-source software development.

5.1 University

We have deployed gitolite within a university research team for managing access to repositories that contain versioning content for code, projects, papers, proposals, courses, and private repositories for users. At present, our deployment is one year old, and it has approximately fifty repositories and thirty users. Our users include professors, graduate students, undergraduate students, and collaborators. Amongst these users, we have one VCS Admin, one Repo Admin, and the rest of the users are either Repo Owners and/or Accessors. The VCS Admin is a professor, the Repo Admin is a graduate student, all collaborators are Accessors, and the remaining users are either Repo Owners and/or Accessors. The VCS Admin delegates the responsibility of managing access to the the projects, papers and code repositories to the Repo Admin. Only the VCS Admin administers control to proposals, courses and private repositories.

We describe a typical scenario where a student writes a paper for a conference. This involves a user creating a repository, and then delegating access to other users if there are co-authors. Note that every user possesses the ability to create repositories except for collaborators. This is because we characterize collaborators as external to the university, and we require that they are given access to the repository explicitly either by the Repo Owner or one of the administrators. A student who is the first author creates a repository for the paper. This makes the student a Repo Owner of that repository. At this point, only the Repo Owner can read and write to this repository. If there are Accessors that are co-authors of this paper, then Repo Owner must explicitly add them to the READERS or WRITERS mnemonic for that repository. Notice that even after the co-authors have access to the repository, they are only Accessors; only one user can be a Repo Owner.

We provide every professor and student with a set of repositories that are private, and only accessible to them. These repositories are used for version controlling confidential documents such as recommendations and financial summaries. While a professor or student can create a repository, they are not allowed to delegate access to other users. This means users can create repositories and thereby becoming Repo Owner but they cannot further delegate. Recall from Figure 3 that a Repo Owner may delegate to Accessors. For private repositories, we do not allow Repo Owners to do this.

We also give every professor and student a *scratch* space of repositories. These repositories are used for both personal and collaborative efforts on class projects, technical reports, and independent programming projects. In our entire deployment, we use the default set of mnemonics: WRITERS, READERS and CREATORS. Users associated with the WRITERS mnemonic have read and write permissions, READERS have only read permissions, and CREATORS have read, write and rewind permissions. This means that only the creator can issue commands that delete segments of the branches.

We heavily use the ability to let users create repositories and then delegate access to other users in our deployment. Students have the ability to create paper and project repositories, and professors can create proposal and course repositories. Once a student or a professor becomes an Repo Owner, he/she can determine which other users to allow access. None of our repositories are created by the VCS Admin or the Repo Admin. As a result, a minimal amount of involvement from either administrators to manage the repositories once the initial deployment was successful.

5.2 Open-source Software Development

We describe the deployment experience of KDE as an open-source software project. Currently, KDE's deployment has approximately 1,730 users and 130 repositories as shown in Table 1. Approximately 60 of these repositories are created by either a VCS Admin or Repo Admin. These repositories are the projects that already exist in KDE's deployment of SVN, and they are directly transitioned and setup by the administrators. The remaining repositories are created by Repo Owners. These are mainly used for the beginnings of new projects, project notes, and configuration files. KDE's policy gives read and write permissions to repositories to developers, and read access to all accessors. There are some repositories that are private that have specific access control rules. Examples of private repositories are those that are exclusively used by the system administrators and board of directors.

KDE makes extensive use of the ability to allow users to create repositories, and delegate permissions using mnemonics. Their deployment uses four mnemonics: WRITERS, MANAGERS, DANGERS, and CREATORS. WRITERS associates users with the permissions to read, write and create branches, MANAGERS with read, write, create and delete branches, DANGERS with read, write, create, delete and rewind branches, and CREATORS with all the permissions of DANGERS including the ability to create repositories. This deployment ensures that CREATORS and DANGERS have full control over the repository with the exception that only CREATORS can delegate. A Repo Owner associating a user with DANGERS effectively allows the user to have the same permissions as the owner (aside from delegation). This mnemonic allows creators of the repository to provide equal permissions to the owner of the repository to other users. MANAGERS, on the other hand, are not allowed to rewind or force push onto the branches. Such repositories are commonly used for starting up new projects that are typically features of existing projects.

The current deployment heavily employs the mnemonics, creation and Repo Owner delegation. While only a small subset of KDE's software collection is currently managed using gitolite, the number of users and repositories will increase significantly once the transition to Git is complete. System administrators responsible for this transition and deployment mention that after the initial deployment, the administration using gitolite requires minimal effort. Their overall experience in using gitolite is positive.

5.3 Some Organizations that use gitolite

In Table 1, we list some of the organizations that use gitolite, and who were willing to share their deployment information to the public domain. The number of repositories and users in Table 1 are approximated and were taken at the time of collecting the survey data from the system administrators. We qualitatively describe the usability of gitolite in the last column. A good rating means that the administrators spent approximately twenty minutes a day

to administer gitolite. Of this, they mentioned that most of it was spent in adding users and not any significant alterations to the access rules.

5.4 Performance of Access Enforcement

Figures 5a and 5b present the time for access checks when using gitolite. We use Fedora Linux's configuration, which contains approximately 11,600 repositories with 1,000 users as shown in Table 1. Our experiments are run on an Intel dual-core Corei7 1.2Ghz with 8GB of DRAM. We measure the elapsed time on the server hosting Git, and gitolite. Therefore, we do not incorporate the network latency that often dominates.

We describe the performance of gitolite under two scenarios. The first scenario in Figure 5a shows the read, write and combined access check times when using gitolite. We vary the number of repositories from 100 to 11,600 repositories. The graph separates the access check time for readDecision and writeDecision as described in Figure 2, and it shows a line that combines the two labelled combined. The access time for readDecision is less than that of writeDecision.

We expect this result because the permission checks for readDecision are simple. However, the checks for writeDecision are more complex, which requires checks for a variety of permissions such as branches, files, and folders. Figure 5a shows that it takes approximately 0.16 seconds to perform a combined read and write access when a VCS has 11,600 repositories. 11,600 repositories is a large number of repositories, and yet the access check times are less than half a second. We recognize that measurements under a second may contain jitter such as operating-system context switches, but it allows us to claim that the access check times in gitolite are negligible for large numbers of repositories.

In the second scenario shown in Figure 5b, we evaluate the effect of increasing the number of access rules per repository on the access check times. We only perform this on one repository because an access is only done for a single repository. Our experiment varies the number of rules for the repository from 100 to 2,000 rules, and the combined access check time for 2,000 rules is less than 0.20 seconds. Note that the typical number of rules per repository in our experience is around 10 rules. This means that the typical access check time is also negligible.

6. RELATED WORK

A number of authorization schemes have been proposed in the research literature, and a comprehensive discussion is beyond the scope of this paper. Our scheme pulls together several aspects that have been proposed before, such as the use of ACLs, delegation and resolving conflicts between rules using some sort of prioritization. In the context of VCSes, we are unaware of work on authorization that has been published in a research venue. The book by Pilato, Collins-Sussman and Fitzpatrick [22] on SVN includes a discussion on SVN's authorization scheme. It is a good example of traditional authorization schemes as used in VCSes in the past. In our work, we also use logic for modeling our scheme. The use of logic has a long history in access control, including the work of Abadi et al. [4], and more recent work [6, 10, 18, 26]. Our interest is not in developing a new logic for authorization, but rather in using first-order logic for precision, and for correctness properties.

We are primarily interested in the expressive power of our scheme relative to schemes that have been proposed in the past. Our objective in designing the scheme was to have a scheme that is sufficiently flexible (expressive) so administrators can configure it as they need to in practice, yet not make it so complex as for it to be unusable. Our deployment experiences (see Section 5) suggest

Setting	Name	# Repo.	# Users	Usability
University	MIT	20	40	Good
	University of Waterloo	50	30	Good
Open-source	KDE Project	130	1730	Good
	Fedora Project	11600	1000	Good
	Gentoo Linux	200	1000	(unknown)
	Racket	100	34	Good
Industry	Reaktor	100	40	Good

Table 1: Organizations that use `gitolite`.

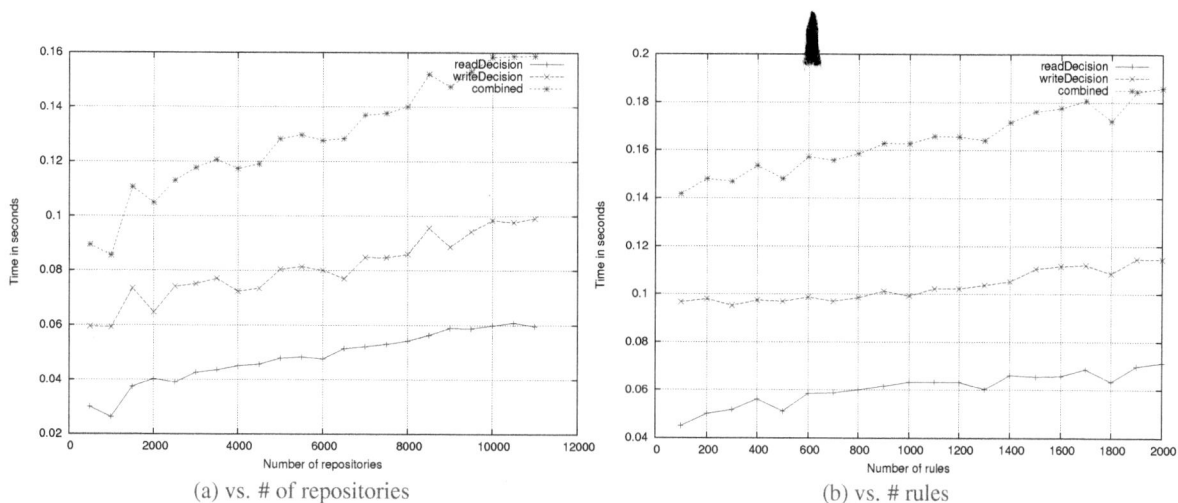

(a) vs. # of repositories

(b) vs. # rules

Figure 5: Performance of `gitolite`— access check times.

that we have hit the right balance. Consequently, the question as to whether our scheme is more expressive that another scheme is not of interest in the context of this paper.

One may pose the question in the other direction: whether there exist schemes from the literature that can capture our scheme. To our knowledge, the answer to this question is no. At the minimum, we assert that there does not seem to be a natural encoding of our scheme in other schemes. For some example schemes from the literature, we discuss the basis for our above assertion.

Consider, for example, DAC schemes that are used to protect filesystems. There are two differences between such schemes and ours. One is that resources that are protected in filesystems are different, and have different relationships with one another than in VCSes. The second is that typically, such schemes, such as the ones in POSIX-compliant systems [27] and Windows ACLs [29, 30], have only two levels of administrators: a superuser ("root") and the owner of a file or directory. The owner has full discretion in handing out rights to resources that he owns. One may argue that the notion of a mnemonic in our scheme is the same as the notion of a group in such systems. However, there are some important differences. One is that in existing filesystems, the superuser not only defines a group (the mnemonic), but also assigns users to the group. We have adopted the approach wherein the VCS Admin only defines the mnemonic, but the assignment of users is discretionary to the Repo Owner. This has significant consequences to the administrative ease of the system.

There have also been administrative schemes for RBAC such as ARBAC97 [24], SARBAC [8] and UARBAC [17]. It may be argued that a mnemonic in our scheme is exactly a role as perceived in such schemes. However, there are some important differences

between such schemes and our scheme. One is that we have three levels of administrators where these schemes have two only. It is unclear that our mid-level administrators (Repo Admin and Repo Owner) can be captured using the constructs provided within such schemes. Also, the rules by which a user (a Repo Owner) assigns users to mnemonics is discretionary, whereas in such schemes it is guarded by preconditions on users' memberships to other roles.

There are also schemes that are presented as logics, but may be perceived as authorization schemes in their own right; an example is DynPal [6]. It is quite possible that DynPal can capture our scheme. However, an issue with such a scheme is that it is too expressive. For example, we observe that DynPal permits delegations of unbounded depth. Furthermore, policy verification (safety analysis) is undecidable in general in DynPal. We do not delve into policy verification in the context of `gitolite` in this paper; however, we conjecture that it is decidable, and even tractable, even though our domain is infinite.

7. CONCLUSIONS AND FUTURE WORK

We have presented aspects of our design and implementation of `gitolite`, an authorization scheme for Version Control Systems (VCSes). Access enforcement relies on Access Control Lists (ACLs), and there is a new syntax that we have developed for specifying authorization rules that are compiled into an ACL. In ongoing work, we are using first-order logic to express our scheme precisely, and also give it a precise semantics, and to assert soundness and completeness properties. Our scheme has several deployments, and we have discussed our experiences from such deployments. We have also discussed how access enforcement works, and its performance relative to the number of repositories and ACL entries.

There is considerable scope for future work. One is to conduct a comprehensive usability test of our deployments to find out whether `gitolite` is indeed as usable as it can be. An aspect for us to assess in this context is whether we can fine-tune the balance between flexibility and usability. Another topic for future work regards an expression of our scheme precisely. It may be possible to use some automated proof technique and maintain the formal specification of our scheme in such a syntax even as it evolves. We plan also to explore the issue of policy verification in the context of our scheme.

8. REFERENCES

[1] Apache subversion. http://subversion.apache.org/ (Accessed Dec. 2010).

[2] Git – the fast version control system. http://git-scm.com/ (Accessed Dec. 2010).

[3] S. Chamarty. Gitolite. https://github.com/sitaramc/gitolite/ (Accessed Mar. 2011).

[4] M. Abadi, M. Burrows, B. Lampson, and G. Plotkin. A calculus for access control in distributed systems. *ACM Transactions on Programming Languages and Systems*, 15(4):706–734, Oct. 1993.

[5] P. Ammann and R. S. Sandhu. Safety analysis for the extended schematic protection model. In *Proceedings of the 1991 IEEE Symposium on Security and Privacy*, pages 87–97, May 1991.

[6] Moritz Y. Becker. Specification and analysis of dynamic authorisation policies. In *Proceedings of the 22nd IEEE Computer Security Foundations Symposium*, July 2009.

[7] M. Blaze, J. Feigenbaum, and J. Lacy. Decentralized trust management. In *Proceedings of the 1996 IEEE Symposium on Security and Privacy*, pages 164–173. IEEE Computer Society Press, May 1996.

[8] Jason Crampton and George Loizou. SARBAC: A new model for role-based administration. Technical Report BBKCS-02-09, Birbeck College, University of London, UK, March 2002.

[9] D. F. Ferraiolo, D. R. Kuhn, and R. Chandramouli. *Role-Based Access Control*. Artech House, Apr. 2003.

[10] D. Garg, L. Bauer, K. D. Bowers, F. Pfenning, and M. K. Reiter. A linear logic of authorization and knowledge. In *ESORICS*, pages 297–312, 2006.

[11] A. V. Gelder, K. A. Ross, and J. S. Schlipf. The well-founded semantics for logic programming. *Journal of the ACM*, 38(3):620–650, 1991.

[12] G. S. Graham and P. J. Denning. Protection — principles and practice. In *Proceedings of the AFIPS Spring Joint Computer Conference*, volume 40, pages 417–429. May 16–18 1972.

[13] M. A. Harrison, W. L. Ruzzo, and J. D. Ullman. Protection in operating systems. *Communications of the ACM*, 19(8):461–471, Aug. 1976.

[14] M. Huth and M. Ryan. *Logic in Computer Science*. Cambridge University Press, UK, 2nd edition, 2004.

[15] S. Jha, N. Li, M. Tripunitara, Q. Wang, and W. Winsborough. Towards formal verification of Role-Based Access Control policies. *IEEE Transactions on Dependable and Secure Computing(TDSC)*, 5(4):242–255, Oct. 2008.

[16] D. E. Knuth. Backus Normal Form vs. Backus Naur Form. *Communications of the ACM*, 7(12):735–736, 1964.

[17] Ninghui Li and Ziqing Mao. Administration in Role-Based Access Control. In *Proceedings of the 2nd ACM Symposium on Information, Computer and Communications Security*, ASIACCS '07, pages 127–138, New York, NY, USA, 2007.

[18] N. Li, J. C. Mitchell, and W. H. Winsborough. Design of a role-based trust management framework. In *Proceedings of the 2002 IEEE Symposium on Security and Privacy*, pages 114–130. IEEE Computer Society Press, May 2002.

[19] N. Li, J. C. Mitchell, and W. H. Winsborough. Beyond proof-of-compliance: Security analysis in trust management. *Journal of the ACM*, 52(3):474–514, May 2005. Preliminary version appeared in *Proceedings of 2003 IEEE Symposium on Security and Privacy*.

[20] N. Li and M. V. Tripunitara. On Safety in Discretionary Access Control. In *Proceedings of the 2005 IEEE Symposium on Security and Privacy*, May 2005.

[21] N. Li and M. V. Tripunitara. Security analysis in role-based access control. *ACM Transactions on Information and Systems Security (TISSEC)*, 9(4):391–420, Nov. 2006.

[22] M. Pilato, B. Collins-Sussman, and B. W. Fitzpatrick. *Version Control with Subversion*. O'Reilly, Sept. 2008.

[23] R. S. Sandhu. Undecidability of the safety problem for the schematic protection model with cyclic creates. *Journal of Computer and System Sciences*, 44(1):141–159, Feb. 1992.

[24] R. S. Sandhu, V. Bhamidipati, and Q. Munawer. The ARBAC97 model for role-based aministration of roles. *ACM Transactions on Information and Systems Security*, 2(1):105–135, Feb. 1999.

[25] R. S. Sandhu, E. J. Coyne, H. L. Feinstein, and C. E. Youman. Role-based access control models. *IEEE Computer*, 29(2):38–47, February 1996.

[26] F. B. Schneider, K. Walsh, and E. G. Sirer. Nexus authorization logic (nal): Design rationale and applications. Cornell Computing and Information Science Technical Report, Sept. 2009. Available from http://www.cs.cornell.edu/People/egs/papers/nal.pdf.

[27] Security Working Group, IEEE Computer Society. IEEE 1003.1e and 1003.2c: Draft Standard for Information Technology–Portable Operating System Interface (POSIX)–Part 1: System Application Program Interface (API) and Part 2: Shell and Utilities, draft 17. Available from http://ece.uwaterloo.ca/~tripunit/Posix1003.1e990310.pdf, October 1997.

[28] M. Soshi. Safety analysis of the dynamic-typed access matrix model. In *Proceedings of the Sixth European Symposium on Research in Computer Security (ESORICS 2000)*, pages 106–121. Springer, Oct. 2000.

[29] Michael M. Swift, Peter Brundrett, Cliff Van Dyke, Praerit Garg, Anne Hopkins, Shannon Chan, Mario Goertzel, and Gregory Jensenworth. Improving the granularity of access control in windows nt. In *Proceedings of the sixth ACM symposium on Access control models and technologies*, SACMAT '01, pages 87–96, New York, NY, USA, 2001.

[30] Michael M. Swift, Anne Hopkins, Peter Brundrett, Cliff Van Dyke, Praerit Garg, Shannon Chan, Mario Goertzel, and Gregory Jensenworth. Improving the granularity of access control for windows 2000. *ACM Trans. Inf. Syst. Secur.*, 5:398–437, November 2002.

[31] M. Tripunitara and N. Li. A theory for comparing the expressive power of access control models. *Journal of Computer Security*, 15:231–272, 2007.

An Approach to Modular and Testable Security Models of Real-world Health-care Applications

Achim D. Brucker
SAP Research
Vincenz-Priessnitz-Str. 1
76131 Karlsruhe, Germany
achim.brucker@sap.com

Lukas Brügger*
Information Security
ETH Zurich
8092 Zurich, Switzerland
lukas.bruegger@inf.ethz.ch

Paul Kearney
Security Futures Practice
BT Innovate & Design
Adastral Park, Ipswich, UK
paul.3.kearney@bt.com

Burkhart Wolff†
Université Paris-Sud
Parc Club Orsay Université
91893 Orsay Cedex, France
wolff@lri.fr

ABSTRACT

We present a generic modular policy modelling framework and instantiate it with a substantial case study for model-based testing of some key security mechanisms of applications and services of the NPfIT. NPfIT, the National Programme for IT, is a very large-scale development project aiming to modernise the IT infrastructure of the National Health Service (NHS) in England. Consisting of heterogeneous and distributed applications, it is an ideal target for model-based testing techniques of a large system exhibiting critical security features.

We model the four *information governance principles*, comprising a role-based access control model, as well as policy rules governing the concepts of patient consent, sealed envelopes and legitimate relationships. The model is given in Higher-order Logic (HOL) and processed together with suitable test specifications in the HOL-TESTGEN system, that generates test sequences according to them. Particular emphasis is put on the modular description of security policies and their generic combination and its consequences for model-based testing.

Categories and Subject Descriptors

D.4.6 [**Software**]: Operating Systems—*Security and Protection*

General Terms

Security, Languages

---

*This work was partly supported by BT Group plc.
†This work was partly supported by the Digiteo Foundation.

Keywords

Security testing, model-based testing, electronic health-care record, NPfIT

1. INTRODUCTION

The National Health Service (NHS) in England's National Programme for Information Technology (NPfIT) is one of the most ambitious and challenging ongoing IT projects worldwide [9].[1] At the heart of the project lies the development of a nationwide on-line service, also known as the *Spine*, enabling health professionals and patients to access electronic health records. Many lessons can be learnt from studying the security mechanisms of a real-world system—perhaps most notably, that the traditional borderline between *security* and *safety*, (where security is understood as "protecting the confidentiality, integrity and availability of information systems" and safety is viewed as "protection of health and life of humans"), becomes pretty artificial, since erroneous or missing health-care records can lead to serious harm to patients [2, 10]. In contrast to such "compartmentalised thinking," the analysis of real-world scenarios needs a more interdisciplinary approach combining formal methods, formal testing, computer security, and software engineering.

The security requirements—called Information Governance (IG) in the NPfIT terminology—are informally specified in many official documents (e. g. [17, 18]). Ensuring that all of the applications and services of the NPfIT individually and collectively comply with these policies, is a very difficult task. An approach based on verification is impossible to be successful in such a complex scenario with a heterogeneous and distributed code-base. Model-based Testing (MBT) is an ideal approach to address these problems and can help to increase confidence in the security mechanisms of the NPfIT. We advocate a technique to create a model of the relevant requirements, automatically generate test sequences from the model and run them against the real system to both validate our formalisation as well as finding bugs in the various implementations. The challenges of *modelling* these Information Governance principles are manifold:

---

[1]Possible future and recently announced changes in name and scope of the programme by the government are not considered in this paper.

- The access control rules for patient-identifiable information are complex and reflect the trade-off between patient confidentiality, usability, functional, and legislative constraints. Traditional discretionary and mandatory access control models as well as standard Role-based Access Control (RBAC) [1] are insufficiently expressive to capture complex policies such as *Legitimate Relationships* (LR), *Sealed Envelopes* (SE), or *Patient Consent* (PC) management. Therefore, both a framework for their *uniform* modelling as well as their combination is needed.
- The access rules of such a large system comprise not only elementary rules of data-access, but also access to security policies themselves enabling *policy management*. The latter is, for example, modelled in administrative RBAC [1, 30] models.
- The requirements are mandated by laws, official guidelines and ethical positions (e. g. [16, 32]) that are prone to change. Such changes have to be enforced throughout a distributed and heterogeneous system, i. e. the Spine and the applications that access it from various sites. Moreover, the accessing applications also have to conform to local policies.

This world of informal, high-level information governance descriptions is in contrast to the formalised world of policies in *Higher-order Logic* (HOL). We have developed a somewhat non-standard view on the fundamental concept of *policies*. This view has arisen from prior experience in the modelling of network (firewall) policies [13]. Instead of regarding policies as relations on resources, sets of permissions, etc., we emphasise the view that a policy is a *policy decision function* that grants or denies access to resources, permissions, etc. In other words, we model the concrete function that implements the policy decision point in a system. An advantage of this view is that it is compatible with many different policy models. Furthermore, this function is typically a large cascade of nested conditionals, using conditions referring to an internal state and to security contexts of the system or a user. This cascade of conditionals can easily be decomposed into a set of test cases similar to transformations used for Binary Decision Diagrams (BDDs). From the modelling perspective, our system uses HOL as its input language, offering all the expressive power of a functional programming language, including the possibility to define higher-order combinators. In more detail, we model policies as partial functions (written as $\_ \rightharpoonup \_$) based on input data of type α (e. g., arguments, system state, security context) to output data of type β:

types $\alpha \mapsto \beta = \alpha \rightharpoonup \beta$ decision ,

where the enumeration type β decision just consists of the two variants allow β and deny β. *Partial* functions are used since we describe elementary policies by partial system behaviour, which are glued together by operators such as function override and functional composition.

A particular instance of this generic concept of policy is the *transition policy*. Transition policies have the form:

$$\alpha \times \sigma \mapsto \beta \times \sigma$$

where σ refers to some system state. Transition policies are, as we will see later, isomorphic to state-exception monads and therefore amenable to the approach of HOL-TESTGEN [14] to sequence testing (based on models in HOL). Since policies in our sense—e. g. a decision function or decision table for an

RBAC model—are possible elements of a system state σ, we can have policies that transform policies in our framework:

$$(\alpha \times (\gamma \mapsto \delta)) \mapsto (\beta \times (\gamma \mapsto \delta))$$

Since these constructs in HOL have a type of order two, we call this form of transition policies *second order policies*.

Our contributions are three-fold:
1) we present a modular modelling framework for security policies,
2) we instantiate our modelling framework with a large, real-world case study in the health-care domain,
3) we show how to generate test sequences for this case study using HOL-TESTGEN [11, 12]. The generated test sequences can be used for testing, e. g. Web Service-based, applications that access the Spine.

The organisation of the paper is as follows: in Section 2 we explain our background, i. e. the NPfIT and HOL-TESTGEN, in Section 3 we present briefly our framework for modelling security polices and in Section 4 its instantiation with the NPfIT concepts. In Section 5 we discuss the generation of test data on the basis of *test specifications*, i. e. concrete properties of the system.

2. BACKGROUND

2.1 Overall System Architecture of the NPfIT

At the core of the National Programme for Information Technology (NPfIT) is the *Spine*, a collection of services provided centrally and used by applications installed locally in hospitals, doctors practises, etc. The most important of these services is the *Care Records Service* (CRS), providing authorised health care staff (here called *users*) access to an electronic health record (called *Summary Care Record* (SCR)) for every *patient* in England.

The rights of the information subject to privacy, and the need to provide an efficient and effective service to the customer (who is often also the information subject) pose conflicting information access requirements, and defining policies that balance the two is a challenge. This holds in particular for applications in the health care domain in which very sensitive data is handled, but withholding that data may endanger the patient's health. For example, an emergency paramedic could harm an accident victim by administering emergency treatment without knowing about allergies and other medication being used.

The Information Governance (IG) principles are expressed in terms of four main concepts: Role-based Access Control (RBAC), Legitimate Relationships (LR), Sealed Envelopes (SE) and Patient Consent (PC) Management.

2.1.1 Role-Based Access Control (RBAC)

NPfIT uses a variant of administrative RBAC [30] to control who can access what system functionality.[2] Each user is assigned one or more *User Role Profile* (URP). Each URP permits the user to perform several *activities*. Activities are generic descriptions of business functionality grouped in a hierarchy. Each application that is part of the NPfIT, must define its set of application functions which have to be controlled by RBAC. Each of these functions is mapped to one or more activities. Thus, each permitted activity gives a user

---

[2]In this paper, we follow the naming convention of the NPfIT documents which, in some cases, deviates from widely-used RBAC definitions such as [1, 30].

134

access to a set of application functions. A URP contains the following main elements:

Job Role: a generic description of the job of a user, e.g. General Practitioner (GP).

Areas of Work: e.g. mental health. Partly, in combination with a specific role, confer additional access rights.

Additional Activities: used to grant additional permissions to an individual user. This adds flexibility and minimises the number of roles required. They grant a user permissions which he otherwise would not have.

Thus, there are three reasons to grant a user rights to perform an activity: a) It is a generic requirement of a Job Role b) It is a requirement of members of a Job Role working in a specialised discipline c) It is an explicit requirement of the individuals job. The mappings for the first two points are common throughout the NPfIT and stored in a national database on the Spine, containing the set of activities granted for each role and role-area of work combination.

2.1.2 Legitimate Relationships (LR)

Whereas RBAC expresses the need to use application functions, Legitimate Relationships (LR) express the need to view or change records of particular patients. A user is only allowed to access the data of patients in whose care he is actually involved. Users are assigned to hierarchically ordered *workgroups* that reflect the organisational structure of a workplace.

There are ten different types of LRs. Eight of them are between a patient and a workgroup, two between a patient and a single user. LRs can either be active or frozen. Loosely speaking an active LR denotes a current relationship, whereas a frozen LR indicates a previous relationship. A frozen LR only allows access to data created before a specific time in the past. All LRs carry an expiry date. There is a complex set of rules governing the dynamic behaviour of these LRs. Sometimes, users can also self-claim an LR (e.g. in case of an emergency), but this always triggers a message to the responsible privacy officer (the Caldicott Guardian).

While the circumstances under which LRs can be created are clearly defined, this is done by each application itself, usually transparently to a user as part of the workflow within an application. For example, when a General Practitioner (GP) refers a patient to a hospital clinic, the recipient application will automatically create an LR for the workgroup associated with the clinical team. The applications report the changes of the LRs to the Spine, which stores all the current LRs together with the workgroup memberships and their hierarchy. Applications can query the Spine to find out if a user has an LR with a patient. The Spine itself does not enforce correct treatment of the LRs by the applications.

2.1.3 Patient Consent (PC)

Patients can opt out of having a Summary Care Record (SCR) at all, in which case no health care details will be uploaded to the Spine; a blank SCR will be created. If an SCR is created, the patient may choose to be asked every time a user attempts to add or read data and can refuse this. Alternatively, a patient can grant this right once and for all. If a patient with an SCR decides to opt out later, his care record will be suppressed. A complete deletion of a record is only possible in special cases.

Some of the data will always be shared, even if users dissent, e.g. demographic data and information about a patient's GP.

2.1.4 Sealed Envelopes (SE)

The sealing concept is used to hide parts of a health care record from users. There are three different kinds of seals:

Seal: Sealed information is hidden except from users in the same workgroup as the creator of the seal. Other users can detect sealed parts and unlock a seal in specific cases.

Seal and lock: Like *seal*, but without the possibility of detection of sealed parts.

Clinician seal: Used to hide data from a patient. Users are able to detect sealed parts and to unlock them, but are supposed to keep them confidential from the patient. A patient cannot detect parts sealed in this way when accessing his record directly.

Patients cannot create seals themselves; only users can do this on their behalf. Some data is sealed automatically, e.g. test results, while other data can never be sealed.

Not all of the concepts mentioned have been implemented yet, some are not yet completely specified and are subject to change. In particular, the concept of Sealed Envelopes has recently been dropped from the NPfIT. In our model, we therefore sometimes had to use simplified approximations in the spirit of the policies. In rare cases where we could not get access to the latest policy documents, we made our own assumptions or used earlier specifications. While we tried to stay as close as possible to the "real" policy, our model cannot be viewed as a true description of what is in place now or will be there in a final system implementation.

2.1.5 Example

As an example, consider a situation in which Alice is both a *clinical practitioner* and a *clerical*, Bob and John are *nurses*. Bob may add or remove people to or from workgroups. Alice, in her role as clinical practitioner, and John belong to the workgroup *surgery*. Alice, in her role as clerical, and Bob belong to the workgroup *orthopedics*. Now assume two patients Paula and Pablo whose patient records should be (partially) available to Alice, Bob, and John. Modelling such a scenario in traditional security models such as ANSI conform RBAC [1] or Bell-LaPadula [8] is at least difficult, if not impossible. In the NPfIT framework we can model dynamic relationships between patients and their medical practitioners. For example, we can model that Paula has a *legitimate relationship* with the working group *surgery*, Alice is his general practitioner. Her record has three entries. The first one is sealed (open) for *surgery*, the second one is sealed (open) for *orthopedics*, the third one is open. Pablo has a legitimate relationship with *orthopedics*, and no entries in his patient record.

2.2 A Note on HOL-TestGen

HOL-TESTGEN is an interactive, i.e. semi-automated, test tool for specification-based tests built upon Isabelle/HOL. Isabelle [26] is an interactive modelling and theorem proving environment; among other logics, Isabelle supports Higher-order Logic (HOL) [15]. HOL is a classical logic with equality, enriched by total higher-order functions; thus, it offers the usual logical connectives $\neg A$, $A \land B$, $A \to B$, $A = B$ and $\forall x.\ P(x)$, etc. HOL is a language typed with Hindley/Milner polymorphism; type variables are denoted by α, β, γ, etc. Function types are written by $\alpha \Rightarrow \alpha'$, functions by λ-notation. Support for datatype definitions like:

datatype α option = Some α| None

introducing the option type as an enumeration with the alternatives Some x and None, and the usual pattern matching notation give Isabelle/HOL a similar flavour like functional programming languages like F# or Haskell, except that the combined language comprises logical quantifiers and logical, extensional equality. Thus, it often allows a very natural way of specification. Isabelle/HOL provides also a large collection of theories like pairs, sets, lists, multisets, maps, orderings, and various arithmetic theories. Of particular importance for the models described here is the type of *partial functions* $\alpha \rightharpoonup \beta$, modelled as synonym to functions $\alpha \Rightarrow \beta$ option, which also provides the usual concept of domain dom$f$ and range ran$f$ on them.

HOL-TESTGEN is an extension to Isabelle/HOL designed to support model-based testing. It offers support for the typical phases of a model-based testing process: 1) writing the *test theory*, i.e. a collection of basic types and auxiliary functions formalising the problem domain, 2) writing the *test specification*, TS, specifying the concrete property to be tested, 3) the *test case generation* phase, i.e. an automated conversion of TS into a sequence of *test cases*, TC, (or: partitions) representing classes of possible input, 4) the *test data generation* phase, during which concrete members are constructed for the TC, and 5) the *test execution* phase when HOL-TESTGEN generates a *test script* driving the actual testing. Once a test theory is completed, documents can be generated that represent a formal test plan, including test theory, test specifications, configurations of the test data and test script generation commands.

The core of the test case generation procedure lies in case splittings up to a certain depth for each free or universally quantified (input) variable in the test specification; depth and form of the case split depend on the type of the variable. The resulting test cases, TC$_i$, have the form $C_1\ x \wedge \cdots \wedge C_n\ x \rightarrow P(\mathsf{PUT}\ x)$, where PUT is a place-holder for the program under test, x is the input vector and P is the oracle or postcondition telling that the output of PUT complies with the test specification. Test data generation from test cases boils down to a constraint resolution process finding an x satisfying the constraints C_i. The reader interested in more details is referred to [11, 12].

2.3 Monads for Sequence Testing

Modelling and reasoning over computations requires mechanisms to deal with states and state transitions within the logic. HOL, however, as a purely functional specification formalism has no such built-in concepts. Using *monads*—a concept made popular for purely functional programming languages by Peyton Jones and Wadler [28]—is one way to overcome this apparent limitation. Abstractly, a monad is a type constructor with a unit and a bind operator, enjoying unit and associativity properties. Due to well-known limitations of the Hindley-Milner type system, it is not possible to represent monads *as such* in HOL, only concrete instances. We define such an instance for our purpose, the state-exception monad, which models precisely partial state transition functions of type

types (o, σ) MON$_{SE}$ = $\sigma \rightharpoonup$(o $\times \sigma$)

Using monads, we can view our programs under test, PUT, as *i/o stepping functions* of type $\iota \Rightarrow$ (o,σ)MON$_{SE}$, where each stepping function may either fail for a given state σ and input ι, or produce an output o and a successor state.

The usual concepts of *bind* (representing sequential composition with value passing) and *unit* (representing the embedding of a value into a computation) are defined for the case of the state-exception monad as follows:

definition bind$_{SE}$ :: (o,σ)MON$_{SE}$ $\Rightarrow$(o $\Rightarrow$(o',σ)MON$_{SE}$) $\Rightarrow$ (o', σ)MON$_{SE}$

where bind$_{SE}$ f g $\equiv \lambda \sigma$. case f σ **of** None $\Rightarrow$None | Some(out, σ') $\Rightarrow$ g out σ'

definition unit$_{SE}$ :: o $\Rightarrow$(o, σ)MON$_{SE}$
where unit$_{SE}$ e $\equiv \lambda \sigma$. Some(e,σ)

We write x$\leftarrow$f; g for bind$_{SE}$ f(λ x. g) and return for unit$_{SE}$. On this basis, the concept of a *valid test sequence* can be specified:

$$\sigma \models o_1 \leftarrow \mathsf{PUT}\ i_1;\ ...;\ o_n \leftarrow \mathsf{PUT}\ i_n;\ \mathsf{return}\ (P\ o_1\ ...\ o_n)$$

where $\sigma \models$m is defined as (m $\sigma \neq$ None $\wedge$ fst (the (m σ))) and where the (Some x) = x. For iterations of i/o stepping functions, we also use an mbind operator, which takes a list of inputs ιs = $[i_1,...,i_n]$, feeds it subsequently into PUT and stops when an error occurs. Using mbind, valid test sequences can be reformulated by:

$$\sigma \models os \leftarrow \mathsf{mbind}\ \mathsf{PUT}\ \iota s;\ \mathsf{return}\,(P\ os)$$

which is the standard way to represent sequence test specifications in HOL-TESTGEN.

3. MODELLING POLICIES IN HOL: UPF

In this section, we present the Unified Policy Framework (UPF), a generic framework for the modular modelling of testable security policies.

3.1 Foundation: Policies as Functions

We model the concept of a policy by partial policy decision functions. *Partial* functions are used since we describe elementary policies by partial system behaviour, which are glued together by operators such as function override and functional composition. In more detail, the partial policy decision functions are based on input data α (e.g., arguments, system state, security context) to output data β:

types $\alpha \mapsto \beta = \alpha \rightharpoonup \beta$ decision

where the enumeration type decision is defined as:

datatype α decision = allow α | deny α

This definition gives rise to a clear separation of the set of decisions into the allowance-set or A $\equiv\{$x | $\exists$ y. x = allow y$\}$ and the analogously defined deny-set D.

We introduce a number of common operations over policies p: these include *update*

p(x$\mapsto$t) $\equiv \lambda$ y. if y = x then Some t else p y

and its variants

p(x+$\mapsto$t) $\equiv$p(x$\mapsto$allow t) and p(x−$\mapsto$t) $\equiv$p(x$\mapsto$deny t)

Elementary policies are

$\emptyset$ $\equiv \lambda$ x. None
$\forall A_f$ $\equiv \lambda$ x. Some (allow f x)   (*AllowAll*)
$\forall D_f$ $\equiv \lambda$ x. Some (deny f x)   (*DenyAll*)

The operation *override* $\_\bigoplus\_ :: [\alpha \rightharpoonup \beta, \alpha \rightharpoonup \beta] \Rightarrow \alpha \rightharpoonup \beta$ allows elementary policies (*rules*) to be combined to more complex ones in a first-fit manner, e. g.:

$$p_1 \bigoplus \cdots \bigoplus p_n \bigoplus \forall D_f$$

where the last rule serves as "catch-all" (for a given function f producing the default return value, if any).

There are the notions of a *domain* dom p :: $[\alpha \rightharpoonup \beta] \Rightarrow \alpha$ set and a *range* ran p :: $[\alpha \rightharpoonup \beta] \Rightarrow \beta$ set. Inspired by the Z notation [31], we introduce the concept of *domain restriction* $S \lhd p \equiv \lambda x.$ if $x \in S$ then p x else None and *range restriction* $p \rhd S$, defined analogously.

As an example, consider the Permission Assignment (PA) of Core RBAC [1]:

types $PA_{CoreRBAC}$ = (ROLES $\times$ PRMS) $\mapsto$ unit,

where the type unit (not to be confused with the unit operator for monads) consists of only one element written (). It is used for policies having no output.

As another example, consider firewall policies as introduced in [13]:

types FP = packet $\mapsto$ packet,

which also covers network address translations, i.e. the policy may allow a certain packet only after modification of its source or destination address.

3.2 Combining Policies

In the "policy-as-function"-view, policies are easy to combine using (higher-order) combinators. A number of generic combinators is provided in the UPF for common situations. There is a wide range of different semantic flavours that can be used in combination (similar to the policy combining algorithms of the eXtensible Access Control Markup Language (XACML) [27]). Consider the following semantics for combining two policies. Each of these can be desirable in different applications:

- First defined rule applies (this corresponds to the override $\_\bigoplus\_$ discussed previously)
- If allowed by any policy, return allow (called $\_\bigotimes_{\vee A}\_$)
- If denied by any policy, the decision is deny (called $\_\bigotimes_{\vee D}\_$)
- Only allow if allowed by both policies (called $\_\bigotimes_{\wedge A}\_$)
- Only deny if denied by both policies (called $\_\bigotimes_{\wedge D}\_$)

The latter four policies are inspired by parallel composition of automata: each policy makes an (independent) step, and the result is a step relation on the Cartesian product of states. As an example, consider *parallel-or-deny*:

definition $\_\bigotimes_{\vee D}\_ :: (\alpha \mapsto \beta) \Rightarrow (\gamma \mapsto \delta) \Rightarrow (\alpha \times \gamma \mapsto \beta \times \delta)$
where   p1 $\bigotimes_{\vee D}$ p2 = ($\lambda(x,y)$. (case p1 x of
        Some (allow d1) $\Rightarrow$ (case p2 y of
            Some (allow d2) $\Rightarrow$ Some (allow (d1,d2))
            | Some (deny d2) $\Rightarrow$ Some (deny (d1, d2))
            | None $\Rightarrow$ None)
        | Some (deny d1) $\Rightarrow$ (case p2 y of
            Some (allow d2) $\Rightarrow$ Some (deny (d1, d2))
            | Some (deny d2) $\Rightarrow$ Some (deny (d1, d2))
            | None $\Rightarrow$ None)
        | None $\Rightarrow$ None))

The other cases proceed analogously. Since policies may have output in general, another fundamental combination concept is sequential composition. Similar to the parallel composition, four essential cases are to be distinguished and lead to the composition operators $\_\circ_{\vee D}\_$, $\_\circ_{\vee A}\_$, $\_\circ_{\wedge D}\_$, and $\_\circ_{\wedge A}\_$, which all have the type: $(\beta \mapsto \gamma) \Rightarrow (\alpha \mapsto \beta) \Rightarrow (\alpha \mapsto \gamma)$.

It may be necessary to adapt the input type or output type of a policy to a more refined context. This boils down to variants of functional composition for functions that do not have the format of a policy. With the standard function composition $\_\circ\_$ it is possible to change the input domain

of a policy $p :: (\beta \mapsto \gamma)$ to $p \circ f :: (\alpha \mapsto \gamma)$, provided that f is a coercion function of type $\alpha \Rightarrow \beta$. The same effect can be achieved for the range with the ∇-operator defined by:

(f,g) ∇ p $\equiv \lambda x.$ case p x of
        Some(allow x) $\Rightarrow$ Some(allow (f x))
        | Some(deny x) $\Rightarrow$ Some(deny (g x))
        | None $\Rightarrow$ None

It turns out that the two families of product and sequence operators are essentially enough to define a core language, which enjoys a number of properties, which we proved formally in Isabelle: For all sum, product, and sequential operators $\emptyset$ is neutral (i.e. p $\bigotimes_{\vee D} \emptyset = \emptyset \bigotimes_{\vee D}$ p $= \emptyset$), all these operators are associative, enjoy some form of commutativity or pseudo-commutativity (i.e. p $\bigoplus$ q = q $\bigoplus$ p if dom p and dom q are disjoint, or p $\bigotimes_{\vee D}$ q = $(((\lambda(x,y). (y,x)) \circ_f (q \bigotimes_{\vee D}$ p$))) \circ (\lambda(a,b).(b,a))$ where g $\circ_f$ p is an abbreviation for (g,g) ∇ p), and various forms of distributivity. All these algebraic laws established as derived rules give rise to a tool to normalise policies in order to simplify the task of an automated equivalence proof or test-case generation. For the special case of firewall policies, this technique has been successfully applied in [13] and has led to a breakthrough in the efficiency of the overall procedure.

3.3 Linking Transition Policies to Execution Sequences

A particular instance of the policy concept is the second-order *transition policy* of the form:

$\iota \times \sigma \mapsto o \times \sigma$

where σ refers to some system state. Such transition policies are isomorphic to $\iota \Rightarrow$ (o decision ,σ) MON$_{SE}$; thus, *i/o stepping functions* and *transition policies* are closely linked concepts and there are two conversion functions linking these two. Here, we will only present:

definition policy2MON :: $(\iota \times \sigma) \mapsto (o \times \sigma) \Rightarrow \iota \Rightarrow$ (o decision,σ)MON$_{SE}$
where policy2MON p = ($\lambda \iota \sigma$. case p (ι, σ) of
        Some (allow (o, σ')) $\Rightarrow$ (Some (allow o, σ'))
        | Some (deny (o, σ')) $\Rightarrow$ (Some (deny o, σ'))
        | None $\Rightarrow$ None)

It is easy to check that policy2MON is a bijection to state exception monads of the form: (o decision ,σ)MON$_{SE}$. As mentioned earlier, this link is import for the sequence testing approach of HOL-TESTGEN (see Section 5).

4. MODELLING NPFIT POLICIES

In this section, we show the instantiation of the UPF with a model of the Information Governance principles of the NPfIT. These principles are a typical example of a complex and realistic access-controlled system consisting of a range of different policy concepts. Thus, the instantiation allows us to present a typical usage of the UPF and proves its applicability in real-world scenarios.

While the individual policy parts will be quite different in other systems, the employed modelling strategy is typical and shows how the UPF can often be used. Abstractly speaking, the strategy is the following:

- Model the generic concepts of the scenario, here health records, the desired system operations, etc.
- Model the different policy parts in small units, here typically using a policy type of the form ($\iota \times \sigma \mapsto$ unit), with different kinds of states σ.

- Model the system behaviour, again in a modular way, leading to two automaton: one for the normal behaviour, one for the exceptional behaviour.
- Use the combinators of the UPF to combine these parts (according to the desired test scenario, different combinations might be desired).
- Transform the combined policy into a state-exception monad to enable use of HOL-TESTGEN's sequence testing framework.

In the following, we only briefly outline how the individual parts of the systems can be modelled, and focus on their combination.

4.1 NPfIT Concepts and Operations

First, we describe how we model those main concepts of the NPfIT system which are relevant for the policy. The most important part is the set of Summary Care Records (SCRs), as the IG principles mainly govern access to them. An SCR is modelled containing some basic information including various status flags, plus references to demographic information (held by the Personal Demographics Service (PDS)), and to the proper care record content. Only last of these is governed by the concepts of LR, PC, and can be sealed. PC information is held in the main SCR, while seals are part of the content entries.

```
record entry  =  entry_id          ::  entry_id
                 entry_type        ::  entry_type
                 seal              ::  seal
                 provider          ::  user
                 entry_content     ::  content
record SCR  =  patient_id  ::  patient
               flag        ::  consent_flag
               GP          ::  user
                            :
                            :
               PDS         ::  entry_id  ⇀  PDS_entry
               content     ::  entry_id  ⇀  entry
```

We view the *Spine* as a partial function from patients to SCRs. We do not use it in the same meaning as in the NPfIT terminology.

types Spine = patient ⇀ SCR

Whenever a user wants to access a system function, he needs to present a User Role Profile (URP). While a user may have several URPs, only one at a time is active during an application session. URPs are defined by a record:

```
record urp  =  nhs_id      ::  user
               org         ::  org_id
               role        ::  Role
               aows        ::  AoW set
               activities  ::  Activity set
```

The *user context* v stores all attributed URPs. This is needed as a user may only access the system with a URP that belongs to him:

types v = user ⇀ (urp set)

Next, we model 29 operations, which are generic abstractions of functional behaviours governed by the IG principles that may be implemented in applications. All of them are about creating, editing, reading, and deleting an SCR or parts of it, including consent information and seals, or changing or querying the user or security context (see 4.4). Note that these operations are not equal to the activities mentioned earlier. They are part of the model only and restricted to policy-related parts of the system. When per-

forming the tests, these operations need to be mapped to concrete functions. Here we only show a selection of them:

```
datatype Operation = createSCR urp patient name address
                                dob consent_flag user
                   | extendSCR urp patient entry
                   | readSCR urp patient
                   | deleteSCR urp patient
                   | removeEntry urp patient  entry_id
                   | editEntry urp  patient  entry_id entry
                   | readEntry urp  patient  entry_id
```

In some cases we might be interested in the output of an operation. We model the possible outputs as enumeration, including one element with an arbitrary string and the possibility to concatenate several outputs.

```
datatype Output = OutEntry entry | OutSCR SCR | ...
               | OutMsg string | Conc Output Output (infixl $ 80)
```

As an example (see Section 2.1.5), the following sequence of operations describes a system execution where first user Bob presenting one of his URPs adds a URP of user John to a specific workgroup, and then John wants to read the SCR of patient Pablo.

[(addToWG urp_bob 1 {urp_john}), (readSCR urp_john pablo)]

4.2 NPfIT RBAC

In this section, we formalise the RBAC part of the NPfIT policy. As described in 2.1.1, the main ingredients of RBAC are User Role Profiles (URPs), roles, Areas of Work (AoW), activities, and functions.

The policy consists of several mappings: a) A mapping between roles and activities b) The hierarchy on the activities c) A mapping between roles and Areas of Work and activities d) A mapping between an application's functions and activities. The first three mappings are relatively static and the same for every application, while the last one is application-dependent. All of them are modelled as simple relations.

Depending on the test scenario, we need to come up with different kinds of RBAC policies:

- Function $\times$ user $\times$ urp $\times$ v $\mapsto$ unit when we want to test the correctness of the RBAC implementation of a specific application.
- Operation $\times$ v $\mapsto$ unit where the operations are mapped to an application's functions, if this policy is combined with other concepts to test the correct Information Governance (IG) implementation of a specific application.
- Operation $\times$ v $\mapsto$ unit where the operations are mapped to activities, if this policy is combined with other concepts to test the IG principles independently from a concrete application.

All of them are built up by using the provided relations, a mapping for the operations, and a decision function that implements the RBAC behaviour (e.g. a function is granted to a user if he presents a valid URP that allows him to perform an activity that is mapped to the desired function).

4.3 Patient Consent (PC)

The concept of Patient Consent (PC) governs whether a care record can be created and data be uploaded to it. To enforce this, every SCR contains a flag which can take on five different values:

```
datatype consent_flag = opt_out | ask | dontask | suppressed
                      | unknown
```

They have the following meaning: opt_out: The patient has explicitly chosen not to have a care record. It is not possible to upload medical data, however there is still a record containing demographic information. ask: The patient wants to have a care record, however users must ask him every time they want to upload any new data. dontask: The patient wants to have a care record, however he does not want to be asked again before uploading. suppressed: The patient had an SCR but has chosen to have it deleted. Some information will however be retained and made available for reading for some time for administrative and legal reasons. unknown: If the wish of the patient is unknown. Currently, this is interpreted as ask.

The rules about patient consent have the following type:

types PCPolicy = (Operation ×Spine) ↦ unit

As only a limited number of operations is governed by these rules, we specify the set PC_Relevant_Ops.

Next, we define the individual rules modelling the desired semantics of the consent flag. As an example the following one allows all operations if the flag is set to dontask:

```
definition dontaskPolicy :: PCPolicy where
  dontaskPolicy = (λ(op,sp). ( if op ∈ PC_Relevant_Ops
    then (case SCROp (op,sp) of
        Some s ⇒ (case flag s of dontask ⇒ Some (allow ())
                               |  _ ⇒ None)
      | _ ⇒ None)
    else None))
```

Here, SCROp (op,sp) returns Some SCR as specified by the input of the operation op and the Spine sp or None if it does not exist. The other rules are similar and the full PC policy is the override (⊕) of all these rules, with the default AllowAll rule for the non-matching inputs.

4.4 Legitimate Relationship (LR)

There are ten different types of Legitimate Relationships (LR), which need to be distinguished:

datatype LR_Type = PatientReferral | SelfClaimed (...)

The LRs also have a status, which can take any of the following values:

datatype LR_Status = active | inactive | frozen | expired

The workgroups are sets of User Role Profiles (URPs) and have a unique identifier. While eight of the LRs are between a patient and a workgroup, two of them are between a patient and a single user. This is modelled as follows:

datatype lr_to = WG wg_id | User urp

An LR is a record containing the following elements:

```
record LR = lr_id  ::  lr_id
            lr_patient  ::  patient
            lr_to  ::  lr_to
            lr_type  ::  LR_Type
            lr_status  ::  LR_Status
```

The policy about Legitimate Relationships (LR) needs as context information all the existing LRs and the workgroup memberships. These are stored in a security context Σ:

types Σ = (patient ⇀ LR set) × (wg_id ⇀ workgroup)

An LR policy is of the following type:

types LRPolicy = (Operation ×Σ) ↦ unit

The function hasLR returns True if the given user has an active LR of any type with a specific patient in given security context. A typical rule about the concept of LRs then looks as follows:

LRPolicy1 ((editEntry u p e_i e), Σ) = (if hasLR u p Σ
            then Some (allow ()) else Some (deny ()))

Other rules (mainly those about how LRs can be transferred) additionally need to take the concrete type and status of an LR into account. Again, all the LR rules can be combined straightforwardly.

As an example, user John in the example mentioned earlier will only be able to read Pablo's SCR, if he is in a workgroup which has an active LR to Pablo. Here, this is achieved by Bob adding him to workgroup 1 just before.

4.5 Sealed Envelopes (SE)

Each content entry of an SCR has a flag showing the sealing status of that entry. The flag can take on any of five values:

seal_open wg: The entry is sealed with an open seal, only users in the workgroup with id wg can read this entry, but others may know that the entry exists, and override the seal when this is justified.

seal_lock wg: The entry is sealed with a locked seal, only users in the workgroup with id wg can read this entry or know that the entry exists.

seal_patient: The entry is hidden from the patient.

not_sealed: The entry is not sealed.

not_sealable: The entry must never be sealed.

The rules about Sealed Envelopes (SE) use information from the care records and the workgroup memberships. Thus, their type is:

types SEPolicy = (Operation ×Spine × Σ) ↦ unit

A user is allowed to read an entry directly (i. e. without breaking a seal), if the entry is either not sealed or, else, he is a member of the respective workgroup. Such a rule can be modelled as follows, where userHasAccess checks membership in an allowed workgroup if required:

```
definition readEntry :: SEPolicy
where readEntry x = (case x of
 (readEntry u p e_id ,S,( lrs ,wgs)) ⇒
        (case get_entry S p e_id of
            None  ⇒ None
          | Some e ⇒ ( if (userHasAccess u wgs e)
                         then Some (allow ())
                         else Some (deny ()))))
| x ⇒ None)
```

The other rules are similar. We must, however, not forget rules specifying that only a seal_open seal can be broken and that a not_sealable seal must never be sealed.

4.6 State Transitions

As we want to test a system that changes over time, we need to model state transitions. The relevant state in this case consists of three individual parts: the Spine, the security context, and the user context. The state transitions are triggered by an operation and there are usually two cases: a transition if the operation is allowed by the policy, and a transition if the operation is denied by the policy. We model each of these state transitions individually, thus leading to six different transitions. The output is modelled similarly. In the following, we show an excerpt of the state transition for an allowed operation on the Spine.

```
fun ST_A_Spine :: (Operation × Spine) ⇀ Spine
where ST_A_Spine ((extendSCR u p e), S) =
    (case S p of None ⇒ Some S
          | Some x ⇒ Some (S(p↦x(|content := (content x)
            ((SOME y. y ∉(dom (content x)))↦e)|))))
```

The individual state transitions can be combined to a single big one using the UPF operators. The following, e.g., is a model of the system behaviour if there were no policy:

definition ST_Allow ::
Operation $\times$ Spine $\times \Sigma \times v \rightharpoonup$ Output $\times$ Spine $\times \Sigma \times v$
where
ST_Allow = ((OUTPUT_A p_m (ST_A_Spine o_st ST_A_Σ
                                                    o_st ST_A_v))
           o (λ (a,b,c,d). ((a,b),(a,b,c,d)))))

where o_st and p_m are operators from the UPF for parallel combinations of state transitions or partial functions respectively. ST_Deny is defined similarly.

4.7 Combination

So far, we have modelled only small individual parts of the system and its policy. In the end, all of them have to be combined to a transition policy to model to desired real behaviour. Despite the individual parts being rather distinct from each other, their combination is quite easy using the operators of the UPF. First, all the policy parts can be combined:

definition appPolicy :: (Operation $\times$ Spine $\times \Sigma \times v) \mapsto$ unit
where   appPolicy = C_1 o$_f$ ((C_1 o$_f$ ((C_1 o$_f$
                     (PCPolicy
                     $\otimes_{\vee D}$ SEPolicy) o C_2)
                     $\otimes_{\vee D}$ LRPolicy) o C_3)
                     $\otimes_{\vee D}$ AppRBACPolicy) o C_4

where AppRBACPolicy is the RBAC policy of some application being part of the NPfIT. The coercion functions C_1 = λ(a,b). a, C_2 = λ(a,b,c). ((a,b),(a,b,c)), C_3 = λ(a,b,c). ((a,b,c),a,c) and C_4 = λ(a,b,c,d). ((a,b,c),(a,d)) serve to a mere technical *repackaging* of the underlying state and input formats involved in the composition. This policy can then be combined with the previously combined two state transitions as follows, where C_5 = λa. (a,a):

definition app_ST_Policy ::   (Operation $\times$ Spine $\times \Sigma \times v$)
                          $\mapsto$ (Output $\times$ Spine $\times \Sigma \times v$)
where
app_ST_Policy = C_1 o$_f$ (((appPolicy $\rhd$A)
                                              $\otimes_{\vee A}$ ($\forall Ax$. ST_Allow x)) o C_5)
             $\oplus$ (((appPolicy $\rhd$ D)
                                              $\otimes_{\vee A}$ ($\forall Dx$. ST_Deny x))) o C_5)

And, finally, transformed into a state transition monad:

definition appMon
where   appMon = policy2MON app_ST_Policy

Possible usages of such a monad are described in the next section.

5. SECURITY TESTING OF THE NPFIT

In this section, we discuss several test purposes and test scenarios resulting in different test specifications and briefly describe how the generated test cases can be used for testing Web Service-based applications.

5.1 Test Specifications and Test Data

From an application perspective, we can distinguish two types of test specifications, i.e. properties that the system under test should fulfil: first, test specifications that ensure certain "quality criteria" of the modelled policy (e.g. is the policy always defined) and, second, test specifications that ensure that the applications conform to the policy and are compliant to legal regulations such as the Caldicott Report [32], or the NHS Confidentiality Code of Practice [16].

We start by generating test cases showing that our policy meets some *basic quality criteria*. For example, for every potential **access** X, the evaluation of the policy should give a well-defined result, i.e. allow or deny:

$\neg$(PUT X = None)

Applying HOL-TESTGEN to this test specification results, among others, in the following test data representing arbitrary attempts to access the system:

PUT((readEntry urp1_alice patient1 2),σ0) = Some(deny())

As an example for a scenario testing a critical situation, we might want to validate that the personal GP of a patient is always allowed to read his SCR.

$\llbracket$UC u = Some urps_u; urp_u $\in$ urps_u; Sp patient = scr;
  gp scr = u$\rrbracket \Longrightarrow$
Policy ((readSCR urp_u patient), Sp, SC, UC) = Some(allow())

A similar scenario, but this time exploring not only a single state transition but a sequence thereof, is that the consent status of a patient who is at one point declared as deceased should never be allowed to change, unless the patient is undeceased (i.e. his death status was an error) by an earlier operation.

A policy specified in a wide range of formal and informal documents, guidelines, etc. is prone to be underspecified or to contain ambiguities. In the case of the NPfIT this has already been observed before [6]. In such known cases, where a policy specification can be interpreted in several ways, we can create tests to check to which interpretation a specific application conforms.

For example an early ambiguity detected by Becker [6] is whether users are able to seal data they are not allowed to read. We can test this property as follows:

$\llbracket$Policy ((readEntry u p e), spine, sc, uc) = Some (deny ())$\rrbracket$
$\Longrightarrow$ PUT (createSeal u p e s, spine, sc, uc)= Some (deny ())

Generating test cases that *ensure the compliance to standards and regulations* like the principles from the Caldicott Report [32] or stipulations such as a requirement that test results can only be accessed after breaking a seal usually require test specifications for sequence tests. The general format of such sequence tests is:

σ0 $\models$os $\leftarrow$mbind is PolicyMonad; return (os=X) $\Longrightarrow$
σ0 $\models$os $\leftarrow$mbind is PUT; return (os = X)

meaning that if the formalised policy returns X beginning in some state σ0, so should the program under test.

Often, such tests are too general and we need to limit the possible inputs; e.g. consider the following test specification

$\llbracket$users is $\subseteq \{$ urp1_alice , urp2_alice , urp_john, urp_bob$\}$;
σ0 $\models$os $\leftarrow$mbind is appMon; return (os = X)$\rrbracket \Longrightarrow$
σ0 $\models$os $\leftarrow$mbind is PUT; return (os = X)

which can be used to generate test data for the small example introduced in Section 2.1.5. Here, only Alice, Bob and John are allowed to perform an operation. This test specification produces test data like the following:

σ0 $\models$os $\leftarrow$mbind [(readSCR urp_john pablo),
                   (addToWG urp_bob 1 {urp_john}),
                   (readSCR urp_john pablo)] PUT;
    return (os = [(deny OutNo),(allow OutSuccess),
               (allow (OutSCR SCR_pablo))])

specifying the output that the PUT must produce when receiving the three operations in sequence (here, John is first denied access to Pablo's SCR, but is later allowed after Bob has added him to the workgroup *surgery*).

Limiting the possible inputs allows for limiting the adversary to special kinds of operations. As an example, we might make the assumption that an attacker can only access the system using a valid URP, reflecting measurements in place which are not part of our models (e. g. access only possible using smart cards).

5.2 Testing Web Services

HOL-TESTGEN supports the generation of test-scripts (written in SML) that allow for the automated testing of real implementations (see [14]) for details). In its current form, HOL-TESTGEN only supports the automated testing of local implementations, i. e. distributed services-based systems are not supported. As modern distributed applications support, in large parts, WSDL compliant Web Service interfaces, we extended the test-script generation of HOL-TESTGEN to support the testing of WSDL-compliant Web services using the .net platform. In more detail, we

- ported the framework that executes the test-scrips to F#, a member of the ML family that is supported by the .net plattform.
- using the WSDL support of the .net plattform, we generated client libraries that allow to access the Web services under test using F#.
- we ported the test-scripts generated by HOL-TESTGEN to F#. While this was done manually in our current prototype, we see no difficulties in developing a test-script generator that directly generates F#.

A simplified excerpt of the test-script testing a Web-service in our small example (cf Section 2.1.5) looks as follows:

```
let _ = System.Console.Write("Test Case 38:")
let pre_38  = []
let post_38 = valid
  ((fun a -> a = [deny OutNo
        allow OutSuccess
        allow (OutSCR SCR pablo])), Unity)
  (fun a -> mbind sendToWS
      [readSCR urp john pablo
        addToWG urp bob 1 {urp john}
        readSCR urp john pablo])
let res_38  = HolTestGen.TestHarness.check
                    retlet pre_38 post_38
```

This setup paves the way for automated unit and sequence tests of WSDL-compliant Web services with HOL-TESTGEN.

6. CONCLUSION AND RELATED WORK

6.1 Related Work

With Barker [4], our Unified Policy Framework (UPF) shares the observation that a broad range of access control models can be reduced to a surprisingly small number of primitives together with a set of combinators or relations to build more complex policies. We also share the vision that the semantics of access control models should be formally defined. In contrast to [4], UPF uses higher-order constructs and, more importantly, is geared towards machine support for (formally) transforming policies and supporting model-based test case generation approaches.

While there is a large body of literature adapting access control models to the specific needs of health care systems in general, e. g. [3, 5, 6, 19, 24], only a few (i. e. [5, 6, 19]) discuss the particular needs of the NHS in England.

On the modelling part, the closest related work is that of Becker [5, 6], presenting a formal model of the Information Governance (IG) policy using the authorisation policy language Cassandra [7]. While his model does cover some more details such as the management of credentials, it lacks, compared with our model, a modular organisation. Moreover, the focus of this work is on the (efficient) enforcement of policies and not on the generation of test cases for validating compliance of an implementation. Overall, we agree with Becker that the requirements of NHS cannot be modelled directly in traditional access control frameworks such as RBAC [30] or Bell-LaPadula [8]. This is an instance of a more general lesson; that real-world applications tend to be loosely inspired by abstract frameworks rather than to implement them faithfully. Finally, Eyers et al. [19] implemented a NHS care record service that supports the runtime enforcement of the RBAC-based sub-policies.

As regards testing, the closest related works are those of Hu et al. [21], Martin and Xie [25] presenting a test case generation approach (based on change-impact analysis, respectively, mutation testing) for a subset of XACML [27] and that of Hu and Ahn [20] presenting a conformance testing approach for RBAC models using SAT solving techniques. Traon et al. [33] present a conformance testing approach that generates test cases for checking that an OrBAC [23] policy (an extension of RBAC also modelling the organisational contexts) complies with high-level compliance goals. Finally, there are several approaches, e. g. [22, 29], applying combinatorial testing to RBAC models. All approaches have in common that they consider only RBAC models or simple extensions thereof. In contrast, we used a uniform framework for security policies that is expressive enough to model sophisticated real-world policies such as the ones of NPfIT.

6.2 Model-based Testing In The Real World

The work presented in this paper has reinforced our conviction that MBT tools have the potential to satisfy a genuine practical need, in combination with complementary techniques such as penetration testing. Compliance of healthcare applications with the NPfIT IG policy is a good example of where model-based testing could usefully augment the IT governance toolset:

- non-compliance has serious implications in terms of patient privacy and potentially safety, and may leave the service and software providers exposed to prosecution and litigation;
- the policy is complex, structured and subject to ongoing change;
- it applies to a range of application types from multiple providers.

Combined, these properties mean that the sizable investment of time and money in building the model could plausibly be justified in terms of mitigated risk, less problematic introduction of the software into service, and improved user experience.

However, building the model still requires specialised expertise, which remains a factor holding back the practical application of MBT. To improve this situation, more research in high-level graphical or textual languages and the use of reusable patterns and templates for the UPF is required. Integration of MBT tools into mainstream software development environments and testing suites would be a further way forward to enable their commercial use.

6.3 Conclusion and Future Work

We have presented a uniform framework for modelling security policies. This might be regarded as merely an interesting academic exercise in the art of abstraction, especially given the fact that underlying core concepts are logically equivalent, but presented remarkably different from—apparently simple—security textbook formalisations. However, we have successfully used the framework to model fully the large and complex information governance policy of a national health-care record system as described in the official documents (e.g. [17, 18]). Thus, we have shown the framework being able to accommodate relatively conventional RBAC mechanisms alongside less common ones such as Legitimate Relationships. These security concepts are modelled separately and combined into one global access control mechanism. Moreover, we have shown the practical relevance of our model by using it in our test generation system HOL-TestGen, translating informal security requirements into formal test specifications to be processed to test sequences for a distributed system consisting of applications accessing a central record storage system.

Besides applying our framework to other access control models, we plan to develop specific test case generation algorithms. Such domain-specific algorithms allow, by exploiting knowledge about the structure of access control models, respectively the UPF, for a deeper exploration of the test space. Finally, this results in an improved test coverage.

References

[1] *American National Standard for Information Technology – Role Based Access Control.* INCITS 359-2004.

[2] R. Anderson. *Database State.* Joseph Rowntree Reform Trust Ltd, 2009. ISBN 9780954890247 (pbk.).

[3] C. A. Ardagna, S. D. C. di Vimercati, S. Foresti, T. W. Grandison, S. Jajodia, and P. Samarati. Access control for smarter healthcare using policy spaces. *Computers & Security*, 2010.

[4] S. Barker. The next 700 access control models or a unifying meta-model? In *SACMAT*, pages 187–196. ACM Press, 2009.

[5] M. Y. Becker. A formal security policy for an NHS electronic health record service. Technical Report UCAM-CL-TR-628, University of Cambridge, 2005.

[6] M. Y. Becker. Information governance in NHS's NPfIT: A case for policy specification. *International Journal of Medical Informatics*, 2007.

[7] M. Y. Becker. and P. Sewell. Cassandra: flexible trust management, applied to electronic health records. In *CSF*, pages 139–154. IEEE Computer Society, 2004.

[8] D. E. Bell and L. J. LaPadula. Secure computer systems: A mathematical model, volume II. In *Journal of Computer Security 4*, pages 229–263, 1996.

[9] S. Brennan. *The NHS IT project: the biggest computer programme in the world - ever!* Radcliffe Publishing, 2005.

[10] A. Browne. Lives ruined as NHS leaks patients' notes. The Observer, June 25th, 2000.

[11] A. D. Brucker and B. Wolff. Symbolic test case generation for primitive recursive functions. In J. Grabowski and B. Nielsen, editors, *FATES*, number 3395 in LNCS, pages 16–32. Springer, 2004.

[12] A. D. Brucker and B. Wolff. Test-sequence generation with HOL-TestGen – with an application to firewall testing. In B. Meyer and Y. Gurevich, editors, *TAP*, number 4454 in LNCS, pages 149–168. Springer, 2007.

[13] A. D. Brucker, L. Brügger, P. Kearney, and B. Wolff. Verified firewall policy transformations for test-case generation. In *ICST*, pages 345–354. IEEE Computer Society, 2010.

[14] A. D. Brucker, L. Brügger, M. P. Krieger, and B. Wolff. HOL-TestGen 1.5.0 user guide. Technical Report 670, ETH Zurich, 2010.

[15] A. Church. A formulation of the simple theory of types. *Journal of Symbolic Logic*, 5(2):56–68, 1940.

[16] Department of Health. Confidentiality. Code of Practice, 2003.

[17] Department of Health. The Care Record Guarantee. Our Guarantee for NHS Care Records in England, 2009.

[18] Department of Health. Information Governance (IG) Concepts, 2010. http://www.connectingforhealth. nhs.uk/systemsandservices/infogov.

[19] D. Eyers, J. Bacon, and K. Moody. OASIS role-based access control for electronic health records. In *IEE Software*, volume 153, pages 16–23. IEE, 2006.

[20] H. Hu and G.-J. Ahn. Enabling verification and conformance testing for access control model. In *SACMAT*, pages 195–204. ACM Press, 2008.

[21] V. Hu, E. Martin, J. Hwang, and T. Xie. Conformance checking of access control policies specified in XACML. In *COMPSAC*, volume 2, pages 275–280, 2007.

[22] V. Hu, D. Kuhn, and T. Xie. Property verification for generic access control models. In *EUC*, volume 2, pages 243–250, 2008.

[23] A. A. E. Kalam, S. Benferhat, A. Miège, R. E. Baida, F. Cuppens, C. Saurel, P. Balbiani, Y. Deswarte, and G. Trouessin. Organization based access control. In *POLICY*, pages 120–131. IEEE Computer Society, 2003.

[24] J. Longstaff, M. Lockyer, and M. Thick. A model of accountability, confidentiality and override for healthcare and other applications. In *Role-based access control*, pages 71–76. ACM Press, 2000.

[25] E. Martin and T. Xie. Automated test generation for access control policies via change-impact analysis. In *SESS*, pages 5–5, 2007.

[26] T. Nipkow, L. C. Paulson, and M. Wenzel. *Isabelle/HOL—A Proof Assistant for Higher-Order Logic*, volume 2283 of *LNCS*. Springer, 2002.

[27] OASIS. extensible access control markup language (XACML), version 2.0, 2005.

[28] S. L. Peyton Jones and P. Wadler. Imperative functional programming. In *POPL*, pages 71–84. ACM Press, 1993.

[29] A. Pretschner, T. Mouelhi, and Y. Le Traon. Model-based tests for access control policies. In *ICST*, pages 338–347. IEEE Computer Society, 2008.

[30] R. Sandhu, V. Bhamidipati, and Q. Munawer. The ARBAC97 model for role-based administration of roles. *ACM TISSEC*, 2(1):105–135, 1999.

[31] J. M. Spivey. *The Z Notation: A Reference Manual.* Prentice Hall, Inc., 2nd edition, 1992.

[32] The Caldicott Committee. Report on the Review of Patient-Identifiable Information, 1997.

[33] Y. L. Traon, T. Mouelhi, and B. Baudry. Testing security policies: Going beyond functional testing. In *ISSRE*, pages 93–102, 2007.

Security Validation Tool for Business Processes*

Wihem Arsac
SAP Research,
Sophia-Antipolis, France
wihem.arsac@sap.com

Luca Compagna
SAP Research,
Sophia-Antipolis, France
luca.compagna@sap.com

Samuel Paul Kaluvuri
SAP Research,
Sophia-Antipolis, France
samuel.kaluvuri@sap.com

Serena Elisa Ponta
SAP Research,
Sophia-Antipolis, France
serena.ponta@sap.com

ABSTRACT

To evaluate whether a business process (BP) under-design enjoys certain security desiderata is hardly manageable by business analysts without a proper tool support, as the BP runtime environment is highly dynamic, e.g., delegation. We describe a novel security validation tool for BPs that employs model checking for evaluating security-relevant aspects of BPs in dynamic environments and offers accessible user interfaces and apprehensive feedback for business analysts. As proof-of-concept we integrate our tool within SAP NetWeaver Business Process Management.

Categories and Subject Descriptors

D.2.4 [**Software Engineering**]: Software/Program Verification—*Formal methods, Model checking, Validation*; K.4.1 [**Computers and Society**]: Public Policy Issues—*Privacy, Regulation, Use/abuse of power*; K.4.4 [**Computers and Society**]: Electronic Commerce—*Security*

General Terms

Security, Verification

1. INTRODUCTION

Compliance with regulations and directives as well as fraud prevention require BPs to be carefully designed and executed so to guarantee critical security desiderata. Industrial BPM systems aim to enforce security, but are of little help in guaranteeing that the BP fulfills the security desiderata. This, combined with the high dynamicity of the environments in which BPs are run (e.g., delegation), makes these security desiderata evaluation a very hard task for business analysts. Model checking can provide a high level of assurance by validating all the execution paths of the BP under-design against the expected security desiderata but require a strong logical and mathematical background.

In this paper, we describe a security validation tool for evaluating security-relevant aspects of BPs that implements

*This work was partially supported by the FP7-ICT Projects AVANTSSAR (no. 216471, www.avantssar.eu) and SPaCIoS (no. 257876, www.spacios.eu)

the approach we detailed in [1]. It employs model checking and makes it accessible for business analysts who are neither a model checking practitioners nor a security experts by automatically *(i)* generating the formal model on which to run the analysis as well as *(ii)* translating the model checking results in a graphical notation. This tool has been integrated within the SAP NetWeaver BPM system (NW BPM).

2. MOTIVATING EXAMPLE

Let us consider a scenario where a BP analyst designs a Loan Origination Business Process (LOBP). The process is characterized by a flow of human tasks that have sets of data, that have to be performed by users according to an RBAC access control model extended with delegation (more detail in [1]). Regulations (e.g., Basel II, EU directives) and risks for frauds demand the bank to set strict policies and to ensure challenging security principles and desiderata.

(S1) **Need-to-know:** Users should access only those sensitive data strictly necessary to accomplish their tasks.

(S2) **Separation of duty (SoD):** The execution of critical tasks should involve multiple users in order to mitigate the risk of frauds.

(S3) **Binding of Duty:** Certain tasks should be performed by a single user so as to ensure the integrity of the data.

(S4) **Data confidentiality:** The access to sensitive data should be restricted to certain users.

It is indeed difficult for the business analyst to be sure that security desiderata are fulfilled by the BP under-design given the high dynamicity of the environment.

3. ARCHITECTURE

The *Security Validator for Business Processes*, outlined in Fig. 1, integrates a validation procedure within standard BP modeling environments enabling the validation of security desiderata. First, the business analyst uses the modeling environment to define the *BP model* intended here as the workflow, the data objects as input and output to tasks, and task assignments to principals. The `Security Desiderata Specification` module offers the business analyst with accessible user interfaces an easy way to specify *Security Desiderata*. In particular the system we developed supports the specification of general security desiderata for (S1)-(S4). The security validation procedure automatically checks whether the BP model enjoys these desiderata. In

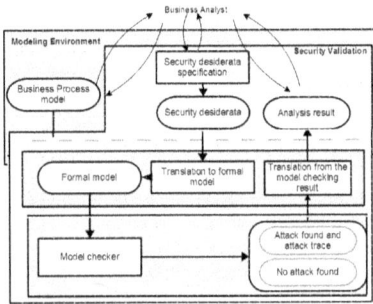

Figure 1: Our Security Validator within a BPM modeling environment

particular, a *Formal Model* capturing both the BP model and the security desiderata is generated and then analyzed via a `Model Checker` that explores all the potential execution paths of the BP model. Notice that system-dependent features, e.g. specific delegation rules, are also automatically retrieved and captured in the formal model. The results of the analysis are retrofitted to the business analyst upon a translation of the raw model checking output to an easy-to-understand, graphical *Analysis Result*. This transformation, carried out by the `Translation from the Model Checking result` module, allows the business analyst to quickly understand the attack reported (if any) and to take proper counter-measures to fix it.

4. IMPLEMENTATION

We have implemented our approach within NW BPM by augmenting the Process Composer, that enables business analysts to design and deploy BPs, with a plug-in that implements our Security Validation and that business analysts can run to validate security desiderata. The plug-in, entirely developed in Java, implements the modules presented in Section 3. The `Security Desiderata Specification` module provides *wizards*, through which the business analyst can easily provide the key information for the security desiderata to be validated. The `Translation to Formal Model` retrieves the *BP Model* and the security desiderata and generates the corresponding formal model in the ASLan language (www.avantssar.eu/pdf/deliverables/avantssar-d2-1.pdf). The `Model Checker` module invokes the SATMC model checker as a service (http://satmc.ai.dist.unige.it/avantssar/) and retrieves the result of the formal validation. The `Translation from model checking result` module inspects the response. If no attack is found, the module reports it through a dialog box. If the model checker returns an attack trace (Fig. 5, top), this is graphically translated and reported with all the details as well as with controls to replay the attack step-by-step (Fig. 5, bottom).

5. ASSESSMENT

Let us consider a business analyst left with the problem of evaluating if the LOBP fulfills instances of the security desiderata (S1-S4). In order to specify the security desiderata, the business analyst can access wizards to provide the key information, e.g. the set of critical tasks subject to SoD. Once the security desiderata are specified, the business analyst presses a button and the validation starts. Following the approach described in Section 3, the formal model is generated. If there exists an execution path that violates

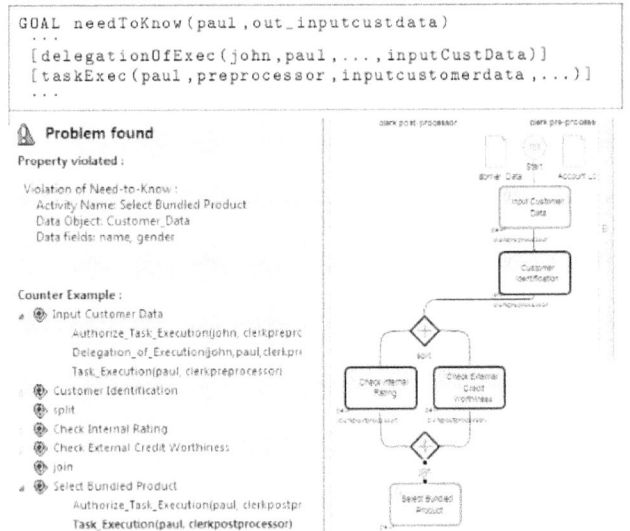

Figure 2: Need-to-know property counter-example

one of the security desiderata, such a violation is discovered by SATMC, returned to our plug-in, and automatically presented via the `Analysis result` GUI of Fig. 5 (bottom). The business analyst can thus see which desiderata has been violated—in this case (S1)—and play the attack trace step-by-step. This graphical representation is critical to allow the business analyst to understand the root cause of the violation (if any) and to take proper counter-measures to fix the issue in the model. We have evaluated the performance of the plug-in by considering processes with increasing complexity. In addition to the LOBP in Section 2 and detailed in [1], we have considered an aviation maintenance case study featuring 6 roles, 64 activities, and multiple loops and gateways. The experiments performed shows that, as model checking suffers of the state explosion problem, the time required for the analysis considerably increases with the complexity of the BP or the depth of the attack trace, i.e., the number of steps to reach the attack state. In order to improve the scalability of the approach, we have devised optimizations in the formal model by considering only the parts of the BP which are relevant for the security desiderata under analysis in line with standard slicing. As expected, the preliminary results shows that violations are found in few seconds as long as the desiderata involve a small number of activities, independently of the complexity of the BP.

6. CONCLUSION

In this paper we have detailed a novel security validation approach for BPs that employs model checking for evaluating security-relevant aspects of BPs in dynamic environments, and still features accessible user interfaces and apprehensive feedback for business analysts. As proof of concept we have implemented our approach as an Eclipse plug-in within SAP NW BPM and assessed it against real BPs from the banking area or aviation domain. Our approach increases the quality, robustness and reliability of BP under design, mitigating the risk of deploying non-compliant BPs.

7. REFERENCES

[1] Arsac, W., Compagna, L., Pellegrino, G., Ponta, S.E.: Security validation of business processes via model-checking. In: Proc. of ESSoS (2011) 29–42

System for Automatic Estimation of Data Sensitivity with Applications to Access Control and Other Applications

Youngja Park, Stephen C. Gates, Wilfried Teiken, Suresh N. Chari
IBM T. J. Watson Research Center
P.O. Box 704
Yorktown Heights, NY 10598, USA
{young_park, scgates, wteiken, schari}@us.ibm.com

ABSTRACT

The Enterprise Information Security Management (EISM) system aims to semi-automatically estimate the sensitivity of enterprise data through advanced content analysis and business process mining. We demonstrate a proof-of-concept of EISM that crawls all the files in a personal computer and estimates the sensitivity of individual files and the overall sensitivity level of the computer. The system can identify 11 different personally identifiable information (PII) types and 11 sensitive data categories, and estimate data sensitivity based on the identified sensitive information in the data. Furthermore, the tool produces the evidences of the discovered sensitive information including the surrounding context in the document to help users understand what kinds of sensitive information are stored in their computer. The evidences allow users can easily redact the sensitive information or move it to a more secure location. Thus, this system can be used as a privacy enhancing tool as well as a security tool.

Categories and Subject Descriptors

H.4 [**Knowledge Management**]: Information Security

General Terms

Algorithms, Measurement, Security

Keywords

Data Sensitivity, Data-centric Security, Data Leakage Protection

1. INTRODUCTION

Identity theft and large-scale data leakage incidents are rapidly growing in recent years [1]. Due to recent large-scale data breaches, companies have realized that protection of their high-value data is critical, but they do not have a systematic way to identify where their sensitive data resides. Recently, many data loss protection (DLP) solutions have been proposed to prevent sensitive information from being leaked externally [3, 4, 5]. The state-of-the-art technologies for DLP aim to discover sensitive information in data (e.g., for regulatory compliances such as HIPAA and PCI-DSS,

but do not have any automated mechanisms to measure the value or sensitivity of individual data items.

We propose a new systematic end-to-end system, called Enterprise Information Security Management (EISM), for automatically measuring the sensitivity of data. The system envisions to provide fine-grained security on high-value enterprise data and help large enterprises manage the security risks associated with their data. For instance, the fine grained classification and the resulting estimation of sensitivity values can be used in many access control applications. First, the sensitivity estimation of the document along multiple dimensions can be used to define dynamic version of the category classifications in traditional access control models such as Bell-Lapadula [6]. More directly, one could define simple access control policies based on granting access to content with sensitivity levels up to a defined threshold. Another application of the dynamic computation of sensitivity values is in risk based methods to access controls [7]. These methods typically rely on bounding the worst case damage due to incorrect access control decisions. The ability to dynamically estimate the sensitivity values would make risk based methods effective and applicable in practice where it is difficult to have static labels of sensitivity values.

In this demo, we demonstrate the data sensitivity measurement process for a set of sensitive data categories including PII, PHI, PCI-DSS and intellectual property data. The demo system will analyze a set of documents in various file formats, and produces a sensitivity score for each file, and the total sensitivity score for the document set. Furthermore, the system will produce the evidences of the discovered sensitive information including the surrounding context in the document to help users understand what kinds of sensitive information are stored in their computer.

2. DATA SENSITIVITY ESTIMATION PROCESS

Figure 1 depicts the data sensitivity measurement process comprising of file scanning, file content extraction, data classification, sensitivity mapping and evidence generation steps.

File Scanning: The component scans the hard disk of a computer and selects files for analysis. The system currently supports Windows, Linux and Mac OS X platforms and various file formats including plain text files, html files, pdf files, Microsoft Office documents (i.e., doc, ppt and xls) and zip files. We allow the users easily customize the file retrieval process. Users can limit the scanning to a certain

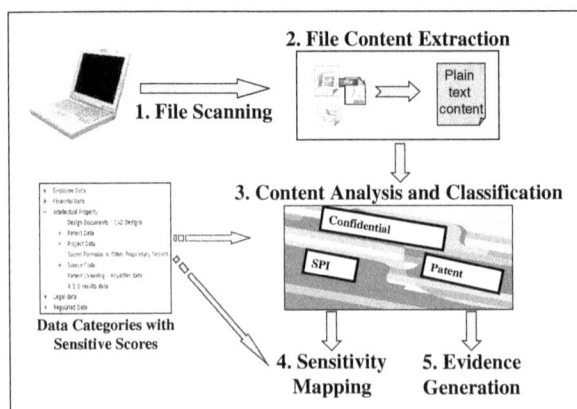

Figure 1: Process for measuring data sensitivity

Figure 1 shows the system's GUI visualizing the progress of the scanning. The leftmost panel displays the elapsed time, the number of files scanned, number of files containing sensitive information, and the statistics of each sensitive type. The pie charts on the right hand display the statistics in a more visual form.

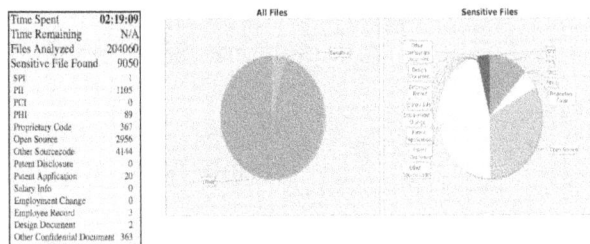

Figure 2: EISM System Run

directories or certain type of files, or can exclude certain directories or files from the scanning.

File Content Extraction: Upon retrieval of a file, it converts a non-textual file (e.g., MS PowerPoint files and Adobe PDF files) into plain text for content inspection. This process extracts only text from the original file, and looses graphical information and other formatting information.

Content Analysis and Classification: This component comprises a suite of text analytics and classification engines that categorize unstructured text into a set of sensitive data types. Currently, the system can identify 11 sensitive data categories, which are mostly concerning regulatory compliance and intellectual property. The categories include *Sensitive Personal Information (SPI), Personal Health Information (PHI), Payment Card Industry Information (PCI), Document with PII, Design Documents, Patent Disclosure, Patent Application, Employee Record, Salary Information, Proprietary Source Code,* and *Confidential Documents.*

Note that we need to recognize personal information to identify the SPI, PHI, PCI and PII categories. Currently, the system can identify the following personal information types: *Social Security Number, Passport Number, Lotus Notes Email Address, Internet Email Address, Employee Name, Non-employee Person Name, Address, Phone Number, Date of Birth, Credit Card Number,* and *Disease and Treatment Names.*

Sensitivity Mapping: When the classification process is completed, the component then maps the classification results into their sensitivity scores. Note that the sensitivity scores are based on the value of a single data (e.g., one credit card number) or a single document (e.g., one source code file), so we count the number of occurrences of each type of sensitive information to estimate the overall sensitivity of a document and a laptop.

Evidence Generation: In addition to producing the sensitivity scores, the demo system also generates the context and the location in the document, where the identified sensitive information is found. The evidences help the users to validate and to take an appropriate action to protect the sensitive information. When the system is used in a real environment, the evidence generation component can easily be disabled.

3. CONCLUSIONS

In this paper, we demonstrate a semi-automated method for estimating sensitivities of enterprise data. To the best of our knowledge, this is the first systematic attempt for estimating data sensitivity quantitatively. This system can automatically discover sensitive data types and estimate the sensitivities of employees' laptops and can bring a significant value to both companies and end users.

4. REFERENCES

[1] Open Security Foundation: OSF datalloss db. (*http://datalossdb.org/*)

[2] Ponemon Institute LLC: Five countries: Cost of data breach. http://www.ponemon.org/local/upload/fckjail/generalcontent/18/file/2010GlobalCODB.pdf (2010)

[3] Mogull, R.: Dlp content discovery: Best practices for stored data discovery and protection. http://www.emea.symantec.com/discover/downloads/DLP-Content-Discovery-Best-Practices.pdf (2008)

[4] Liu, S., Kuhn, R.: Data loss prevention. In: IT Professional. Number 2 (2010) 10–13

[5] Parno, B., McCune, J.M., Wendlandt, D., Andersen, D.G., Perrig, A.: Clamp: Practical prevention of large-scale data leaks. IEEE Symposium on Security and Privacy (2009) 154–169

[6] Bell, D.E., Padula, L.J.L.: Secure computer systems: Mathematical foundations. MTRŰ2547, The MITRE Corporation **1** (1973)

[7] Molloy, I., Dickens, L., Morisset, C., Cheng, P.C., Lobo, J., Russo, A.: Risk-based access control decisions under uncertainty. In: IBM Research Technical Report, RC25121. (2011)

[8] Sokolova, M., El Emam, K., Rose, S., Chowdhury, S., Neri, E., Jonker, E., Peyton, L.: Personal health information leak prevention in heterogeneous texts. In: Proceedings of the Workshop on Adaptation of Language Resources and Technology to New Domains. AdaptLRTtoND '09, Association for Computational Linguistics (2009) 58–69

[9] Park, Y.: A text mining approach to confidential document detection for data loss prevention. In: IBM Research Technical Report RC25055. (2010)

Visualizing Security in Business Processes

Ganna Monakova
SAP Research
Vincenz-Priessnitz-Str. 1

76131 Karlsruhe, Germany
ganna.monakova@sap.com

Andreas Schaad
SAP Research
Vincenz-Priessnitz-Str. 1

76131 Karlsruhe, Germany
andreas.schaad@sap.com

ABSTRACT

Defining constraints at the business process level is an often demanded feature. Our approach guides a business user in the analysis of threats to resources used in a business process, and provides the means to specify appropriate controls on the identified threats. These controls are of a highly visual nature and address both – safety as well as security concerns.

Categories and Subject Descriptors

D.2.2 Design Tools and Techniques.

General Terms

Design, Security

Keywords

Business Process Security

1. INTRODUCTION

As business processes become more complex, analysis of the resources involved in the process and security issues associated with these resources becomes significantly harder. While the business expert concentrates on the specification of the business aspects of a process, other aspects, such as security, remain mostly neglected (if at all understood). The reasons for this are lack of the security knowledge on the business side as well as unwillingness to "pollute" the business process with additional information perceived as non-business related. Security, and in a wider sense, compliance, of a business process, however, are critical to any organization, as for example an unauthorized modification of a variable (which could represent a node in a purchase order) can have major implications on the process outcome. Therefore, there is a clear necessity for a business level security specification mechanism. We present an approach that allows a business user to easily identify and specify resource controls on the business process level.

2. CONCEPTUAL MODEL

Figure 1 gives an overview over the main concepts used in our approach. An asset can be either a data object or a physical resource used by a process activity during its execution. Threats related to an asset are based on certain asset characteristics. We provide the end user with a possibility of specifying asset characteristics using *tags*. Different tags or tag sets imply different threats.

For example, a resource tagged with *food* has a threat of *contamination* and a resource tagged as *private data* has a threat of *information disclosure*. Threats can be refined or broken down into sub-threats by adding more characteristics (tags) to the asset. For example, adding a *deep frozen* tag to the *food* tag will identify a sub-threat of *contamination* as *storage temperature is too high*.

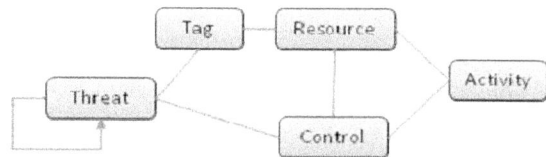

Figure 1: Concepts Overview

After the threats have been identified, the user can apply controls that would countermeasure these threats. For example, the threat of a resource temperature being too high can be countermeasured by observing the temperature of the environment the resource is exposed to. Applicable countermeasures or controls can be applied. Our approach allows specification of controls at three stages of a business process activity execution: on activity start, during the activity execution and on activity completion.

Controls defined at start time of an activity control the incoming states of resources, for example an activity might want to ensure that a received *order request document* is signed before the activity starts its execution. Similar, controls at activity completion time check the outgoing state of the resources. Controls defined on the activity execution, or internal controls, monitor resource state during the activity execution, which is useful for the monitoring of physical resource states, such as temperature or location. Internal controls are especially useful in case of the asset being a physical resource, where the continuous monitoring through the activity execution can be realized using different sensors to observe the state of different resource properties.

3. PROTOTYPE

Our prototype[1] is based on Windows Workflow Foundation 4.0. We extended the existing modeling environment with the visual representation of the variables used in the business process. A variable represents either a physical resource, in which case it contains a resource identification (or resource reference), or a data object, in which case it contains the actual data used by the business process. Figure 2 shows an example pizza transportation process.

---

[1] Work sponsored as part of joint BMBF / ANR Project RescueIT (13N10963)

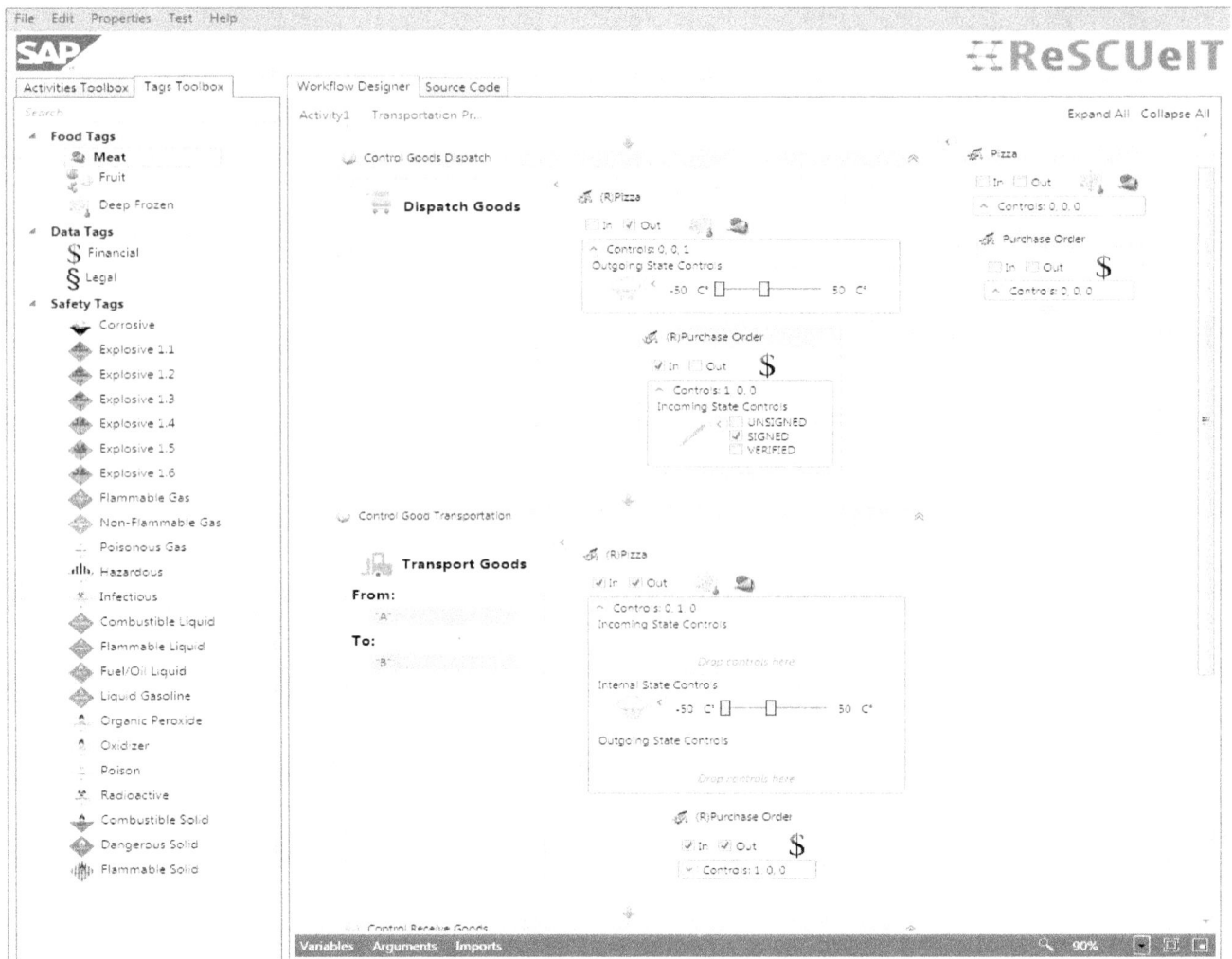

Figure 2: Security & Safety Constraint Modeling and Example Transportation Process

The process contains two variables - *Pizza* and *Purchase Order*, which are visible in the right lane. *Pizza* variable represents a physical resource and is annotated with the *deep frozen* and *contains meat* tags. *Purchase Order* is a data variable and is annotated with the *financial* tag.

The tags are displayed at the top of the variable object, the user can add new tags to a variable by drag & drop a new tag from the tag pane, visible on the left. When a new tag is added to a variable, a query is sent to a database containing knowledge about possible threats applicable to the current set of tags.

The query returns a set of controls needed to countermeasure the threats. The returned controls are compared with the existing controls and the user is notified if a control is missing.

Each variable container contains a placeholder for the three types of controls – incoming state controls, internal state controls and outgoing state controls.

We implemented a set of control scopes, that contain a variable pane that visualizes variables used in the scope. Variables defined on the parent scope are visible in all children activities. Different children activities might need to specify different controls on the same variables. To enable this, all parent activity variables are propagated to all children activities. In the given example, variables are defined in the scope of Transportation Process and propagated to the children control scopes: Control Good Dispatch; Control Good Transportation; and Control Good Receive. This allows children control scopes to define their own controls on these variables, while correlation between the variables is preserved through the parent scope.

Activity *Dispatch Good* is contained inside a control scope that defines an input state control on the *Purchase Order*, specifying that it must be signed when received by this activity, as well as a control on its output state, specifying that it must be encrypted by the time it leaves this scope. *Pizza* resource also contains an outgoing state control, specifying that its temperature must be below 12°C. The scope containing Transport Goods defines an internal control on the pizza temperature.

Access Control for a Federated Police Information System

Matthew Hudnall
Center for Advanced Public Safety
The University of Alabama
Tuscaloosa, AL 35487-0290
(001) 205-348-0856
mhudnall@cs.ua.edu

Maury Mitchell
Alabama Criminal Justice Info. Center
201 South Union Street, Suite 300
Montgomery, AL 36130
(001) 334-517-2400
maury.mitchell@alacop.gov

Allen Parrish
Center for Advanced Public Safety
The University of Alabama
Tuscaloosa, AL 35487-0290
(001) 205-348-3749
parrish@cs.ua.edu

ABSTRACT
In this paper, we present the elements of a system for demonstration that supports a federated infrastructure for a collection of police agencies.

Categories and Subject Descriptors
D.4.6 [**Operating Systems**]: Security and Protection – *Access controls, authentication.*

General Terms
Security

Keywords
Role-based authentication, federated systems.

1. INTRODUCTION
This proposal is for a demonstration of an access control system called *ADAPT* (Active Directory Authentication Processing Tool). ADAPT is used to control access to a group of applications that are part of the *AlaCOP* portal, which is a statewide police portal used within the State of Alabama. The AlaCOP portal is an umbrella for a number of police applications that are used on a statewide basis within Alabama. ADAPT provides single sign-on access to these applications to any registered police officer within Alabama; there are currently approximately 15,000 registered ADAPT users.

ADAPT is a privilege-based system where privileges are assigned to officers based on roles. Privileges are customized for each application, and their degree of restrictiveness is determined by the application. ADAPT was developed in 2003 and has been the production system for access control for state-managed police applications within Alabama since that time. There are over 20 separate applications controlled by ADAPT.

2. SYSTEM ARCHITECTURE
There are three major components to the overall ADAPT system architecture:

- Users
- Privileges
- Applications

As noted in the introduction, there are approximately 15,000 users in the ADAPT system. These users are generally police officers in one of Alabama's nearly 400 police agencies. Each agency manages its own users through an *agency information security officer (AISO)*. The agency's AISO is responsible for adding new officers and deleting officers who have left the agency.

The AISO also is responsible for administering privileges for each of the agency's users. Privileges are controlled by a hierarchy starting with the state's central criminal justice technology agency – the Alabama Criminal Justice Information Center (ACJIC). ACJIC grants the appropriate privileges to each of 8 region administrators; such privileges are granted at a level that permits further propagation. Each region administrator then propagates appropriate privileges across the region to each agency's AISO. The AISO also receives propagate permission, and is permitted to grant each privilege received (as appropriate) to each of his/her agency's users. Figure 1 shows how privileges are propagated across this hierarchy.

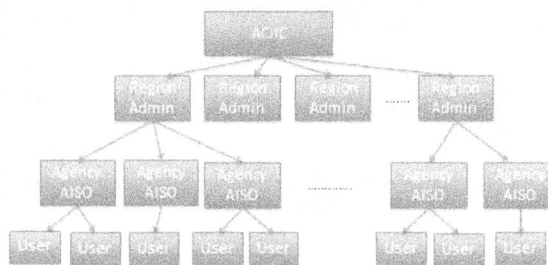

Figure 1 – Privilege Propagation

To support this propagation, a given privilege may be granted at several different levels:

- Allow
- Full management/allow
- Limited assignment/allow
- Deny

If a privilege is granted at the "allow" level, then the assignee simply inherits the privilege with no further propagation rights. "Full management/allow" gives the assignee the right to inherit the privilege, as well as the right to propagate all rights (including further propagation rights) to the privilege to assignees. "Limited assignment/allow" gives the assignee the right to inherit the privilege, as well as the right to assign the privilege to others; however, the right to propagate the privilege to assignees for (potentially) further propagation is withheld. "Deny" explicitly denies a privilege for an assignee, and can be used to revoke privileges. Figure 2 shows the ADAPT screen for adding and removing user privileges.

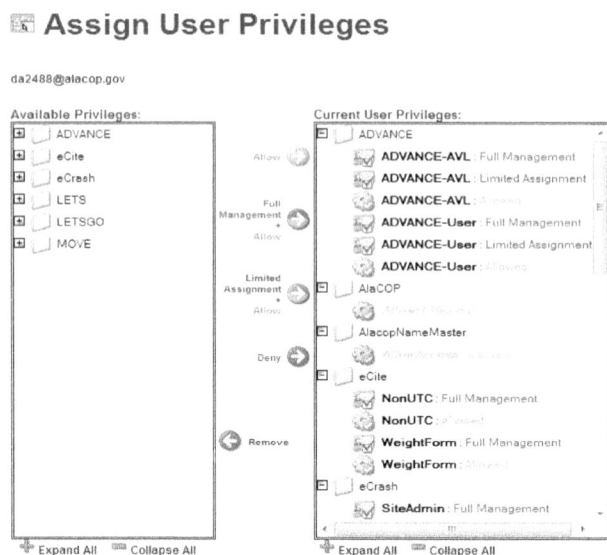

Figure 2 – User Privilege Assignment

There are a number of different applications that are accessible through the portal. These applications each have controlling privileges that determine the level of access available to particular users. The semantics of a privilege are application-dependent; applications are implemented so that possession of a privilege controls the type of access to the application. For example, the privilege "AllowHSAccess" permits access to homeland security information within the AlaCOP application. The AlaCOP application is then coded in such a way that AlaCOP users without this privilege have access to the application, but without the homeland security information. Figure 3 depicts the overall relationship between users, privileges and applications.

ADAPT is built using Microsoft Active Directory to manage user accounts. Privileges are stored in a SQL Server database that is external to the underlying Active Directory system. The system is constructed using a service-oriented architecture, which allows both Windows and Web-based applications to be controlled by this approach. This service-oriented architecture also allows the system to be adapted to standards such as GFIPM and other federated security standards as needed.

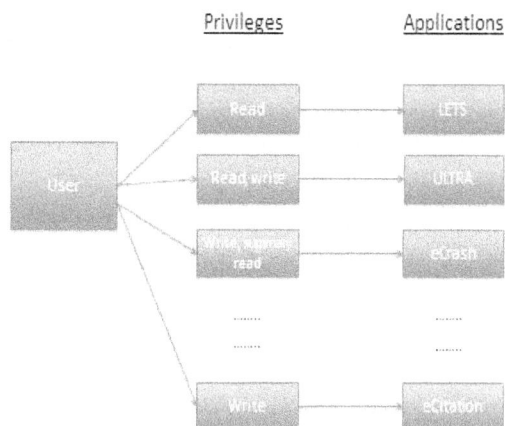

Figure 3– Users, Privileges and Applications

3. DEMONSTRATION SCENARIOS

This application will be demonstrated using three basic scenarios:

1. Adding a new user
2. Assigning user privileges
3. Demonstration of an application for which privileges have been assigned.

These three scenarios will demonstrate the full range of services provided by ADAPT. In particular, adding a user will show the full range of data maintained on a particular user. Assigning that user privileges will provide a sense of the types of privileges that are available for the various applications, and then demonstrating an application will show how the privileges are utilized by the various applications.

4. SUMMARY

Demonstration of the ADAPT system will provide attendees with exposure to a real-world access control system that is widely used (with over 15,000 users) in a large-scale, geographically distributed environment. Police agencies using ADAPT are scattered over the entire State of Alabama. Applications controlled by ADAPT consist of both Windows and Web applications, and also include mobile applications that are designed to be used in a network disconnected setting (in cases where field cellular data service is weak or spotty). Managing access in such a variety of settings over a broad area to a large number of users presents unique challenges that will be discussed in the course of this presentation.

Data-centric Multi-layer Usage Control Enforcement: A Social Network Example

Enrico Lovat
Karlsruhe Institute of Technology
Karlsruhe, Germany
enrico.lovat@kit.edu

Alexander Pretschner
Karlsruhe Institute of Technology
Karlsruhe, Germany
alexander.pretschner@kit.edu

ABSTRACT

Usage control is concerned with how data is used after access to it has been granted. Data may exist in multiple representations which potentially reside at different layers of abstraction, including operating system, window manager, application level, DBMS, etc. Consequently, enforcement mechanisms need to be implemented at different layers, in order to monitor and control data at and across all of them.

We present an architecture for usage control enforcement mechanisms that cater to the data dimension, grasping the distinction between data (e.g a picture or a song) and its representations within the system (e.g a file, a window, a network packet, etc.). We then show three exemplary instantiations at the level of operating system, application, and windowing system. Our mechanisms enforce data-related policies simultaneously at the respective levels, offering a concrete multi-layer enforcement and laying the grounds for a combined inter-layer usage control enforcement.

In this demo, we consider a use case from a social network scenario. A user can, on the grounds of assigned trust values, protect his data from being misused after having been downloaded by other users. In particular, our mechanisms prevent sensitive data in the browser window from being printed, saved or copied to the system clipboard, avoid direct access to the cached copy of the file and forbid taking a screenshot of the window where data is shown.

Categories and Subject Descriptors: D.2.11 [Software Architectures]: Data abstraction

General Terms: Security

Keywords: Policy enforcement, Usage control

1. INTRODUCTION

Usage control is an extension of access control concerning actions that can and have to be performed over data after access has been granted. Usage control requirements, such as "delete after 30 days" or "notify owner upon access", are expressed in so-called policies. These policies can and should be enforced [4] at different levels of abstraction (LoA) in the system. Among others, this has been done at the levels of operating system [1], X11 [3], Java, enterprise service bus, social network [2] or in the context of DRM.

The reason for this variety of enforcement mechanisms is that the data that has to be protected comes in different rep-

resentations: as network packets, as attributes in an object, as window content, etc. In principle, all of them eventually boil down to some representation in memory, but it turns out to be more convenient to protect them at higher LoA. For instance, taking screenshots is easily inhibited at the X11 level; disabling the print command is easily done at the browser level; prohibiting dissemination via a network requires little effort at the operating system level; etc.

In this work we discuss a generic architecture for usage control mechanisms that can be instantiated to arbitrary LoA. We present three exemplary instantiations at the level of operating system, browser application and windowing system and describe a use case in a social network scenario.

2. ARCHITECTURE

Our architecture is built on top of three main blocks: a *Policy Enforcement Point* (PEP), which observes and possibly modifies events in the system; a *Policy Decision Point* (PDP), where usage control decision are finally taken; and a *Policy Information Point* (PIP), which provides additional information to the PDP.

The role of the PEP is to intercept desired and actual events, forward them to the PDP and, according to the response, allow, inhibit or modify them. On the grounds of such events, the PDP evaluates the policies using standard runtime verification techniques. The PDP component represents the usage control logic of the architecture and due to its generic behavior, its implementation can be the same for several LoA (provided that the semantic binding (events in the system - events in the policies) is given).

PDP decisions sometimes may require additional information about distribution of data among different representations. For this reason the PDP queries the PIP. The PIP is a data-flow tracking system, that simply groups all the representations of the same data. Every time an event happens, the PIP updates its mapping according to a predefined semantic. For instance, if event "copy file1 to file2" is detected, then the PIP records the information that file2 is another representation of the same data stored in file1.

The three components are designed to communicate using a network protocol, so they can be deployed in a distributed way. However, due to their level-dependent nature, PEPs are bound to specific LoA. The inclusion of other components, e.g. for policy management, is work in progress. In particular, so far we can only have independent instantiations of our architecture at different LoA. A future work will be a PIP that "vertically" connects representations of the same data at different LoA (i.e. a synergy of PIPs at different levels). For the purpose of this demo, these aspects have been hard-coded (see Section 4).

3. IMPLEMENTATION

We instantiate our generic architecture at three different LoA: operating system, application level and windowing system. Note that identical implementations of PDP and PIP, due to their layer-independent nature, have been used in all the examples and are not presented here for space reasons.

At the application level, we implemented a usage control mechanism for the Firefox web browser [2]. In this context, events are user commands, like "save the page", "copy & paste", "print", etc., and data is represented by the content of the web page. We implemented a Firefox extension that replaces the original mapping between user interface and core functionalities with a javascript instantiation of our PEP. Each user command is hence intercepted and, according to the PDP response, allowed, modified or inhibited (and eventually additional actions executed).

At the operating system level, relevant events are system calls, performed over data representations such as files, network packets, memory regions, etc. Hence, we implemented our second PEP leveraging *Systrace*, a tool for system call interposition in Unix-like operating systems [1].

A third instance of our architecture was deployed for the X Window System (X11, [3]), a distributed system and a protocol for GUI environments on Unix-like systems. In X11, events are network packets that contain requests, replies, events and errors, and are invoked on specific X11 resources (potentially carriers of sensitive information), like windows, pixmaps (memory areas for drawing functions), attributes and properties (variables attached to windows), etc. For this implementation, we developed a wrapper for the X server based on *Xmon*, an interactive X protocol monitoring tool.

4. USE CASE

We consider a use case from a social network scenario where the usage of profile data is restricted according to the relationship between the requester and the owner. If a user logs in and visits another user's page, the server delivers the profile data together with a policy defined on the grounds of their relationship ("best friend" vs "friend" vs "acquaintance", etc.). Such a policy is received and enforced by the visitor's system. Integrity measurements and guarantees that mechanisms are in place and have not been tampered cannot be discussed here because of space restrictions.

In our use case, described in Figure 1, Bob, being Alice's best friend, can see her profile page, print it, save it and, in general, do everything he wants with it (case 1). After a dispute, Alice declassifies Bob from her "best friend" to just an "acquaintance" (case 2(a)). Now Bob still sees Alice's profile page, but he cannot print, save, or copy and paste from it anymore. Moreover he can't take a screenshot of the browser window (case 2(b)) nor directly access a browser cache file (case 2(c)) if these contain (part of) the page.

The policy we enforce is *"Any part of this page cannot be printed nor copied to the clipboard (not even in form of a screenshot) nor saved to disk and its cached version can be used only by Firefox."*. The implementation-level policies in XML are not provided here for space reasons.

If Bob requests Alice's profile page, Firefox downloads it together with the aforementioned policy. Upon reception by the web browser, the web page's content takes new represen-

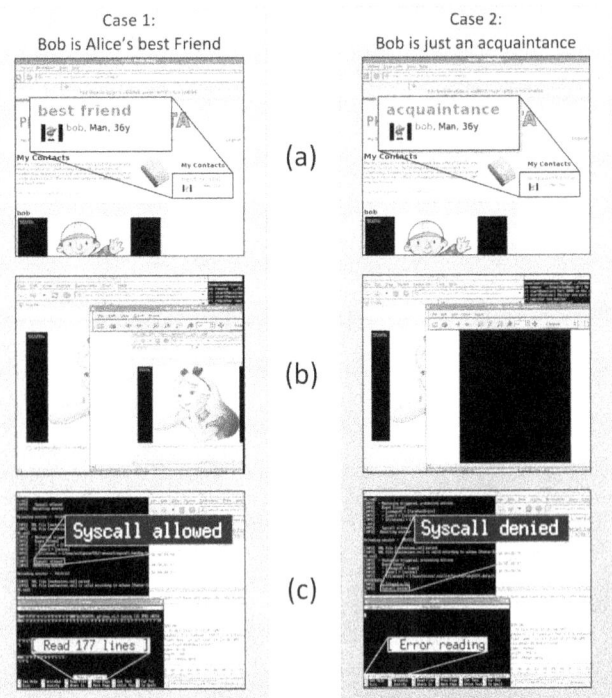

Figure 1: Cross-layer policy enforcement. Row (a) is a view from Alice's account. Rows (b) and (c) are from Bob's perspective, trying to take a screenshot of the page (b) or open a cache file directly (c).

tations at different LoA: it is rendered as a set of pixels in the browser window, it is cached as a file, and it is internally represented by the browser as a node in the DOM tree. To protect all these representations, the Firefox monitor adds some runtime information (like the name of the cache file and the id of the window), deploys tailored policies to the operating system and X11 layers. This is the hard-coded part mentioned above. Afterwards, the Firefox monitor allows rendering the page and creating the cache file.

From now on, several instantiations of the policy are enforced at different LoA, as shown in the following usage attempts. First, Bob tries to print the page; the attempt is intercepted, evaluated against the policy and forbidden. In the second example, taking a screenshot of the browser window is intercepted by the X11 monitor; according to the policy, the request is modified to returning a black rectangle. The last example shows how opening the cache file of a page element (e.g., a profile picture), is prohibited because the the system call is denied unless the caller process is Firefox.

5. REFERENCES

[1] M. Harvan and A. Pretschner. State-based Usage Control Enforcement with Data Flow Tracking using System Call Interposition. In *Proc. 3rd Intl. Conf. on Network and System Security*, pages 373–380, 2009.

[2] P. Kumari, A. Pretschner, J. Peschla, and J.-M. Kuhn. Distributed data usage control for web applications: a social network implementation. In *Proc. 1st ACM Conf. on Data and application security and privacy*, pages 85–96, 2011.

[3] A. Pretschner, M. Buechler, M. Harvan, C. Schaefer, and T. Walter. Usage control enforcement with data flow tracking for x11. In *Proc. 5th Intl. Workshop on Security and Trust Management*, pages 124–137, 2009.

[4] A. Pretschner, M. Hilty, D. Basin, C. Schaefer, and T. Walter. Mechanisms for Usage Control. In *Proc. ACM Symposium on Information, Computer & Communication Security*, pages 240–245, 2008.

Panel

Usable Access Control for All

Organizer:
Robert W. Reeder
Microsoft
Redmond, WA 98052
roreeder@microsoft.com

PANEL SUMMARY

Managing access-control policies has traditionally been the domain of information security experts or system administrators, but is increasingly performed by individual consumers who may have no technical expertise. A variety of new applications create the need for consumers to use access control, including online social networks, online healthcare records databases, location-based mobile applications, mobile application stores, and cloud-based file shares. With these applications, data that is both personal and highly sensitive is being moved online, where it can be conveniently accessed by others. There are great benefits to be gained by making this sensitive data available to some---for example, by making an individual's medical history available to healthcare providers---and great risks to making the data available to others---for example, making location data available to stalkers. Access-control technologies thus become the gateway to enabling applications to provide value through sharing data while keeping that data safe from those who should not be allowed to have it.

Making access control usable by everyday users introduces a variety of new challenges. Requiring users to have a conceptual access control framework in their heads, e.g., an understanding of the Biba or Bell-LaPadula models, is unrealistic. Instead, access control models must strike a careful balance between flexibility and simplicity and user interfaces for managing them must expose management options while being intuitive enough that no training or advanced knowledge is required.

For models, an important question is what level of granularity to provide to users. On the one hand, coarse grained models that allow for turning access on or off to all principals may be essential for simple management or for handling emergencies. For example, a user concerned about sharing their location may want a control that simply, easily, and verifiably turns off al access to their location. As

another example, a patient in an emergent medical situation would likely want doctors to have immediate, full access to all health records. On the other side of the granularity debate, fine-grained models are needed to accommodate the many nuances of online data-sharing. The user of an online-social network may be happy to share personal news with all of their friends, except for a few who are professional contacts. The user of a health records database may want to share their entire health record with a personal trainer, except for one lab test for a sensitive disease.

For user interfaces, an important consideration is when to prompt users to manage access-control. One approach is to allow proactive management, in which the user initiates access-control management by opening a user interface to set access-control policy. Another approach is reactive management, in which a platform (e.g., an online social network or the operating system on which mobile applications run) prompts the user to make access-control decisions at critical times---e.g., when access requests are received. Both approaches have benefits and drawbacks, and the best approach for a given domain may be a hybrid of the two. User interfaces also introduce important challenges like how to visually represent access-control policies, how to draw users' attention to access-control issues, and how to explain the semantics of a given access-control policy setting.

It is also important to realize that models and user interfaces for access control affect each other. Models can affect the usability of user interfaces, and user interfaces can modulate the complexity of models.

In addition to these new technical challenges for access-control models and user interfaces, consumer-oriented applications raise a few interesting ethical questions for access-control platforms. For example: Should an access-control platform in some cases provide false data on behalf of a user? Who should be in control of a patient's health-record privacy settings when the patient is medically incapacitated? Should parents have access to their teenager's social-networking account?

This panel will discuss the rise of applications requiring consumer management of access control and the corresponding challenges for development of access control models and user interfaces. Each panelist will address three topics:

1. Describe an end-user access control application domain, such as online social networks, online healthcare records databases, location-based mobile applications, mobile application stores, or cloud-based file shares.

2. Introduce one key challenge to developing usable access-control systems for that domain.

3. Identify the top research questions they'd like to have answered to improve access control for end users in that domain.

Panelists will be asked to stimulate a broad discussion of application domains requiring usable consumer-oriented access control, with two primary goals: (1) to inspire new ideas and directions for access-control research; and (2) to help bring out common themes and problems across the various domains, so that researchers and practitioners in different domains can seek common solutions.

Categories & Subject Descriptors: H.1.2 User/Machine Systems: Human factors; D.4.6 Security and Protection: Access controls; H.5.2 User Interfaces: User-centered design

General Terms: Human Factors, Management, Security.

Keywords: Access control, usability, user interfaces.

Validation of Security Policies by the Animation of Z Specifications

Yves Ledru
UJF-Grenoble 1/Grenoble-INP/UPMF-Grenoble2/CNRS
LIG UMR 5217
F-38041, Grenoble, France
Yves.Ledru@imag.fr

Nafees Qamar
INRIA Rhône Alpes &
UJF-Grenoble 1/Grenoble-INP/UPMF-Grenoble2/CNRS
LIG UMR 5217
F-38041, Grenoble, France
mqamar@inrialpes.fr

Akram Idani
UJF-Grenoble 1/Grenoble-INP/UPMF-Grenoble2/CNRS
LIG UMR 5217
F-38041, Grenoble, France
Akram.Idani@imag.fr

Jean-Luc Richier
UJF-Grenoble 1/Grenoble-INP/UPMF-Grenoble2/CNRS
LIG UMR 5217
F-38041, Grenoble, France
Jean-Luc.Richier@imag.fr

Mohamed Amine Labiadh
UJF-Grenoble 1/Grenoble-INP/UPMF-Grenoble2/CNRS
LIG UMR 5217
F-38041, Grenoble, France
labiadh@imag.fr

ABSTRACT

Designing a security policy for an information system is a non-trivial task. In this paper, we consider the design of a security policy based on a variant of the RBAC model, close to SecureUML. This variant includes constraints for the separation of duty, as well as contextual constraints. Contextual constraints use information about the state of the functional model of the application to grant permissions to users. These constraints add flexibility to the security policy, but make its validation more difficult. In this paper, we first review two tools, USE and SecureMOVA, which can be used to analyse and validate a security policy. These tools focus on analyses of static aspects of the secured system. We then propose a new tool, based on the Z formal language, which uses animation of the specification to validate the static as well as dynamic aspects of the security policy, taking into account possible evolutions of the state of the functional model. We discuss how the security policy and the functional application are described to the tool, and what kind of queries and animations can be performed to analyse nominal and malicious behaviours of the system.

Categories and Subject Descriptors

H.2.7 [**Information Systems**]: Database Administration
—*Security, integrity, and protection* ; D.2.1 [**Software Engineering**]: Requirements/Specifications

General Terms

Design, Security

Keywords

Security policy, RBAC, Validation, Animation, Z Formal Specification, SecureUML

1. INTRODUCTION

The design of today's information systems must not only take into account the expected functionalities of the system, but also various kinds of non-functional requirements such as performance, usability or security. Security policies are designed to fulfill non-functional requirements such as confidentiality, integrity and availability. They are usually expressed as abstract rules, independently of target technologies. In the past, various access control models have been proposed to design security policies. In this paper, we focus on role-based access control models (RBAC) [7], including evolutions such as SecureUML [4]. An important feature of such models is the notion of role: permissions are granted to roles which represent a set of users. Moreover users may play several roles with respect to the secure system.

Constraints can be associated to these access control models. They allow to express Separation of Duty properties [5], and other properties on roles (e.g. precedence, see Sect. 3.2). Constraints may also link permissions to contextual information, such as the current state of the information system. This is one of the interesting features of SecureUML which groups UML diagrams of the application with security information describing the access control rules. In the remainder, we will refer to the UML diagrams of the application as the *functional model*. The term *security model* will refer to the access control model. Constraints give flexibility to describe security policies, but result in complex descriptions which need tool support for their verification and validation. Verification checks that the description is consistent. In particular, it must check that constraints are

155

not contradictory, which would result in unsatisfiable policies. Validation checks that the policy corresponds to the user's requirements. Our work focusses on validation.

With such complex models, validation can become a difficult task. The separation between the functional model and the security model is an interesting solution, based on separation of concerns. However, existing works [12, 15] are mainly interested by the security part. They propose techniques to verify the consistency of an access control policy without taking into account the impact of the functional part. Although it is definitely useful to analyse both models in isolation, interactions between these models must also be taken into account. Such interactions result from the fact that constraints expressed in the security model also refer to information of the functional model. Hence, evolutions of the functional state influence the security behaviour. Conversely, security constraints can impact the functional behaviour. For example, it is important to consider both security and functional models in order to check liveness properties on the information system. Indeed, it can be the case that security constraints are too strong and block the system. Only a few tools have been proposed to support validation of RBAC models. They focus on static analyses of the model. In this paper, we propose a toolset which supports both static and dynamic analyses, allowing to study nominal and malicious behaviours of the secure system.

In Sect. 2, we present the meeting scheduler example which will illustrate our work. In Sect. 3, we review the features of two tools, USE and SecureMOVA, which are representative of the current state of the art. In Sect. 4, we discuss the interest of leading dynamic analyses of security policies. Sect. 5 discusses the translation of security and functional diagrams into a Z specification. Sect. 6 details the dynamic analyses that can be performed on our specification. Finally Sect. 7 draws the conclusions of this work.

2. THE MEETING SCHEDULER

To illustrate our work, we consider a meeting scheduler example used by Basin et al to illustrate SecureUML and SecureMOVA [3]. The meeting scheduler helps users plan a "meeting" involving several "persons". Basically, the information system records information about persons, meetings, and the links between these. These links are (a) the owner-

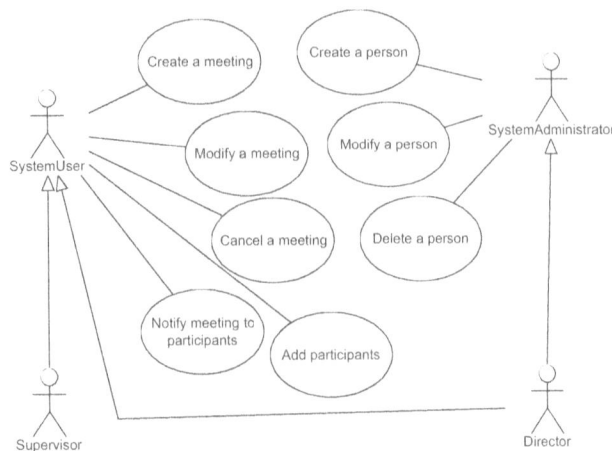

Figure 1: Use cases for the meeting scheduler

ship of a meeting by a person who organizes it, and (b) the participation of a given user in a meeting. Fig. 1 gives the major use cases of this system and the related actors. The major kind of actor is the system user. System users can create and cancel meetings, modify the meeting's information (e.g. change the time or duration of the meeting), add participants to a meeting, and notify the participants about the meeting (which performs some side-effecting operation such as sending a mail to the participants). The system administrator is another actor. Basically, he is responsible of managing information about the persons, i.e. the potential owners of and participants to the meetings.

Fig. 1 gives the basis for access control rules: users are in charge of their meetings and system administrators manage the persons. An important security property is related to the integrity of information about meetings. It is expressed by the following rules: (1) a meeting may only be modified or canceled by its owner, and (2) supervisors have the privilege to modify or cancel meetings they don't own. Supervisors are thus introduced as a specialisation of system users. Another kind of actor is the Director, who is both a user and an administrator.

3. STATE OF THE ART TOOLS

3.1 RBAC and SecureUML

Our security model is based on SecureUML [4, 3], an extension of RBAC (Role-Based Access Control) [7]. In RBAC, access control is expressed by a set of *permissions*. A permission allows to perform a set of *actions* on a set of *resources*. Instead of directly granting permissions to *users*, RBAC abstracts users performing the same duties into *roles*. Permissions are thus granted to roles. When a user wants to access some action on a resource, he starts a *session* and activates one or several roles in this session. Based on the activated roles, he gets the permission to access the resource.

RBAC has been extended with several constraint mechanisms. One of the goals is to achieve separation of duty. Separation of duty aims at forbidding a user to take conflicting roles. In our example, one may consider that roles System Administrator and Supervisor give too much privilege and forbid that a user takes these roles. Dynamic separation of duty (DSD) requires that a given user may not take these conflicting roles simultaneously in the same session. Static separation of duty (SSD) forbids a user to take these conflicting roles even in different sessions.

SecureUML is a UML profile which expresses RBAC rules in a class diagram, using stereotyped elements. The class diagram provides a functional model of the application, and the stereotyped elements define the security model. It includes the concepts or RBAC and the possibility to associate permissions with contextual constraints. These constraints involve elements of both security and functional models and restrict the applicability of the permission to the cases where the constraint is verified. In the meeting scheduler, such a constraint is associated to the permission of system users to modify or cancel a meeting. The constraint restricts this permission to the owner of the meeting. Information about the owner of the meeting will be retrieved from the functional class diagram, while information about the user performing the action is related to the security model.

Contextual constraints give much flexibility to express a security policy, but their validation must take into account both functional and security models. Therefore, they require adequate tools. In the next sections, we briefly review two tools which support the validation of role-based security policies with constraints. In both cases, the constraints are written in OCL [18], a language based on first order logic predicates over the constructs of an UML class diagram.

It must be noted that UMLSec [12] is another attempt to address security in UML, but it focusses on the security model (in particular cryptographic aspects) and does not address its interaction with the functional model.

3.2 USE for the validation of security policies

The USE tool (UML-based Specification Environment) [9] allows to evaluate OCL constraints on a given object diagram. These constraints are usually invariants associated to the classes of the diagram, but can also stand for pre- or post-conditions if the object diagram represents the initial or final state of some operation. The tool also allows to program a random generator for object diagrams, and to program sequences of object diagrams.

Sohr et al [15] have adapted this tool for the analysis of security policies. Their work focusses on the security model, i.e. users, roles, sessions and permissions, constrained by OCL assertions. This allows to express properties such as:

- Cardinality: a given role has at most n users.

- Precedence: u may be assigned to role r_2 only if u is already member of r_1.

- Separation of Duty: roles r_3 and r_4 are conflicting.

- Separation of Duty for Colluding Users, e.g. two brothers may not take conflicting roles.

- Context-dependent permissions, e.g. a meeting may only be modified by its owner.

The last two properties cannot be expressed on a pure security model. It must be augmented with functional information, e.g. some attribute *ownedMeetings* should be added to the users. Another possibility is to explicitly include this information in the constraints, e.g. in [15] all sets of colluding users are listed as OCL rules. Both cases correspond to extensions of the RBAC+constraint model which do not really scale up. Such information definitely belongs to the functional model.

Sohr et al [15] report on two kinds of validation activities. An object diagram can be given to the tool, and the tool will check which constraints are violated. The object diagram can be user-defined, randomly generated, or member of a programmed sequence. This allows to detect unsatisfiable constraints, i.e. constraints which are always false. They have also developed a tool named authorisation editor, which implements the administrative, system and review functions of the RBAC standard. The tool is connected to the API of USE so that the constraints of the security policy are checked after each operation. It detects erroneous dynamic behaviours of the security policy. For example, if two roles are constrained both by a precedence and a conflict relations, it is impossible to find a sequence of RBAC administrative and system operations which leads to create the second role.

3.3 SecureMOVA

In [3], Basin et al report on SecureMOVA, a tool which supports SecureUML+ComponentUML. The tool allows to create a functional diagram, i.e. a class diagram, and to relate it to permission rules. Constraints can be attached to permissions and these constraints may refer to the elements of the functional diagram.

SecureMOVA allows to evaluate queries about the security policy. The tool provides an extensive set of queries over a given model, possibly associated with a given initial state. In [3], Basin et al list the queries that are supported by the tool. A first set of queries explores the relations between roles and actions.

- Given a role, what are the atomic actions that a user in this role can perform?

- Given an atomic action, which roles can perform this action?

- Given a role and an atomic action, under which circumstances can a user in this role perform this action?

Other queries ask more general questions to analyse the security policy. They help identify redundant roles or permissions.

- Are there two roles with the same set of atomic actions?

- Given an atomic action, which roles allow the least set of actions, including the atomic action?

- Do two permissions overlap?

- Are there atomic actions that every role, except the default role, may perform?

With SecureMOVA it is also possible to ask questions about a current state, i.e. a given object diagram. Such queries return the actions authorized for a given role, or to a given user in the current context.

- Given a functional and a security state, can a given user in a given role perform a given action on a given resource?

- Given a user and a state, what are all actions that this user can perform?

- Given a state, which users may perform a given action on a given resource?

- Given a state, which role should take a given user to perform a given action on a given resource?

This extensive set of supported queries is of great help to analyse and validate a security policy. In particular, the last set of queries, which involve a given functional state, can be very useful to study the impact of contextual constraints. Nevertheless, all reported examples [3] are of static nature, i.e. they don't allow to sequence actions (either administrative or functional) and check that a given sequence is permitted by the combination of the security and functional models.

4. THE NEED FOR DYNAMIC ANALYSES

In the sequel, we propose to use animation techniques to further validate security policies. Animation allows to play sequences of actions from a given state. USE and SecureMOVA only report whether the first action of the sequence can be executed from the given state. Animation of sequences of actions is useful to investigate two kinds of behaviours: nominal behaviours, corresponding to the requirements of the system, and malicious behaviours, corresponding to attacks against the secure system.

In both cases, the corresponding behaviour may involve several steps, and it is not sufficient to investigate whether a given action can be performed in a given state. It is also necessary to check that the given state can be reached from the initial state, and when sequences of actions are considered, to compute the resulting state and check that the next action can be performed from this resulting state. Animation tools allow to perform a sequence of actions, starting from an initial state and to compute all intermediate states.

Such dynamic analyses require the availability of executable models. Security policies based on RBAC can easily be made executable, as demonstrated by Sohr in his authorisation editor [15]. Executability of the functional model can be achieved in two ways: either by providing an implementation of the model which can interface with the contextual constraints of the security model, or by providing an executable model. Providing an implementation makes sense in a context where the functional system is designed first, without considering security aspects, and where a security policy must be designed later for this application. It also makes sense during a maintenance phase where a given implemented security policy must evolve. Some prototypes of RBAC can be coupled with an existing implementation. For example, the MotOrBAC tool provides an API between its security engine and the application [2].

Instead of working at the implementation level, our approach favours early validation at the abstract level of a PIM (Platform-Independent Model). The other way is to get an executable functional model. In the case of USE or SecureMOVA, the model is expressed as a class diagram combined with OCL predicates. In order to turn UML methods into executable ones, one need to provide an implementation of the methods. Actually, USE allows to define a body for each method using an imperative language based on OCL. It seems that this feature was not explored in [15] and might be interesting to investigate. Another way is to animate the methods based on their pre- and post-conditions. We don't know of tools which support this approach for OCL, but they exist for formal languages such as Z[10], B[1], or Alloy [11]. In [16], functional and security models are merged into a single UML model which is translated into Alloy. Alloy can then be used to find a state which breaks a given property. The properties described in [16] are mainly of static nature, i.e. they focus on the search for a state which breaks a property, and don't search for sequences of actions leading to such a state. Nevertheless, Alloy can take into account the behaviour of the actions of the model, and we believe it has the potential to perform such dynamic analyses.

In this paper, we adopt the Z language, and the Jaza tool [17] is used to animate the operations of a Z specification.

5. A TOOLSET BASED ON Z

We propose to translate the functional and security models into a Z specification, and then to use the Jaza animator to analyse this specification, using animation and queries. Several attempts have already specified RBAC in Z [8], but these were not aimed to be the input of an animator.

5.1 Input models

Our toolset takes as input: (a) a class diagram of the functional application, possibly annotated in Z, and (b) several security diagrams, including diagrams stating the permissions, and a diagram assigning users to roles. Security diagrams are completed by a description of an action hierarchy linking abstract actions to concrete ones. From these inputs, our toolset computes a Z specification of the system which can be animated with Jaza (see sect. 6).

5.1.1 Functional model

The functional model is described by a class diagram annotated with Z assertions and we use the RoZ tool [6] to complete it and translate it into Z. Given a class diagram, RoZ automatically generates the specification of basic operations (i.e. attribute and association setters). The center of Fig. 2 gives the class diagram for the meeting scheduler. It includes two classes (Meeting and Person) and two associations. A meeting is characterized by its starting date and its duration, a person is simply characterized by his/her name. Most operation specifications have been created automatically. They correspond to operations to create and delete objects, update object attributes, and create links between objects. Three operations are user-defined: notify and cancel are specific to the application, createMeeting creates of an object of class meeting and simultaneously links it to its owner and first participant. This operation is necessary in order to satisfy the arity constraints related to both associations: a meeting has at least one owner and one participant.

From this annotated diagram, RoZ automatically generates a complete Z specification. For example, the specification of operations RemoveMeeting and cancel are as follows:

$$
\begin{array}{|l}
\hline \text{MeetingRemoveMeeting} \underline{\hspace{3cm}} \\
\Delta MeetingExt \\
meeting? : MEETING \\
\hline
Meeting' = Meeting \setminus \{meeting?\} \\
\hline
\end{array}
$$

$$
\begin{array}{|l}
\hline \text{meetingcancel} \underline{\hspace{4cm}} \\
MeetingRemoveMeeting \\
\Xi PersonExt \\
\Delta MeetingOwnerRel \\
\Delta MeetingParticipantsRel \\
\hline
owner' = \{meeting?\} \lhd owner \\
participants' = \{meeting?\} \lhd participants \\
\hline
\end{array}
$$

The first operation takes a meeting as input (denoted by '?') and removes it from the set of existing meetings (Meeting). Operation meetingcancel includes the first operation and extends its scope to access the owner and participant associations. The meeting is also removed from the domains of both associations. The specification of RemoveMeeting was generated automatically by the tool, but the

158

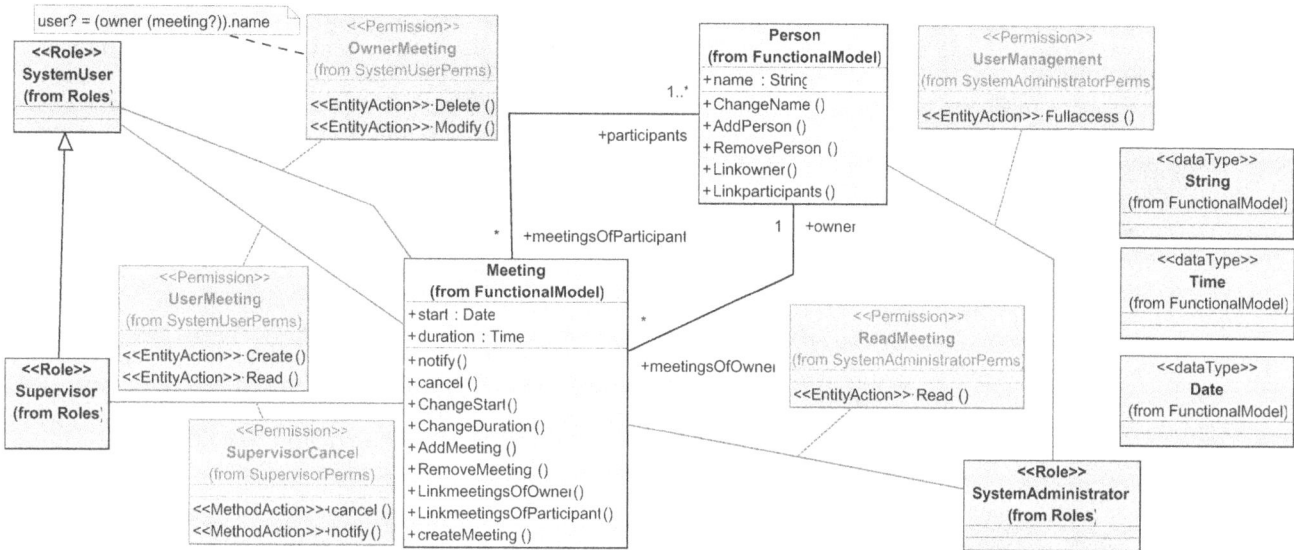

Figure 2: Class diagram and permissions for the meeting scheduler

user had to provide the details of *meetingcancel* as annotations of the corresponding operation in the class diagram.

RoZ generates specifications which can be animated with Jaza [13]. This animation helps to convince the analyst that he has captured the right functional model, and expressed the right specifications for application specific operations.

5.2 Diagrams for the security model

5.2.1 Permissions

The security model involves several diagrams. The main diagram (Fig. 2) expresses the permissions related to each role. In accordance with the use cases of Fig. 1, users may only access meetings. A first permission, UserMeeting, allows them to create and read objects of the class meeting. A second permission, OwnerMeeting, details the rights to update an existing meeting, i.e. to modify it or to delete it. This permission is associated to a constraint, written in the Z language, which states that the user must have the same name as the owner of the meeting.

Similar permissions are expressed for Supervisor and SystemAdministrator. Permission SupervisorCancel grants to supervisors the right to perform operations cancel and notify on any meeting. UserManagement grants to administrators full access to the class Person, and ReadMeeting grants them the right to read class Meeting.

It must be noted that these permissions refer to abstract operations (e.g. Read or Fullaccess) and that a link must be established between these abstract operations and their concrete counterparts. This will be explained in Sect. 5.2.3.

5.2.2 Roles and users

An additional diagram (Fig. 3) declares the roles of the application, and links them to users. In this diagram, the roles correspond to the actors of the use case diagram: SystemUser, Supervisor, SystemAdministrator and Director. Four users are declared and assigned to these roles through UA (User Assignment) links. These user assignments list the roles that a user can take in a session. Yet, the user may

choose to perform the session using a subset of his possible roles. The diagram also declares some separation of duty constraints between roles. Fig. 3 features one static separation of duty (SSD) between Supervisor and Administrator, and one dynamic separation of duty (DSD) between Director and SystemUser. It can be visually checked that the SSD constraint is respected by the user assignments. The DSD constraint, which will be enforced during a session, may only be violated by Mark who may use both roles of the DSD.

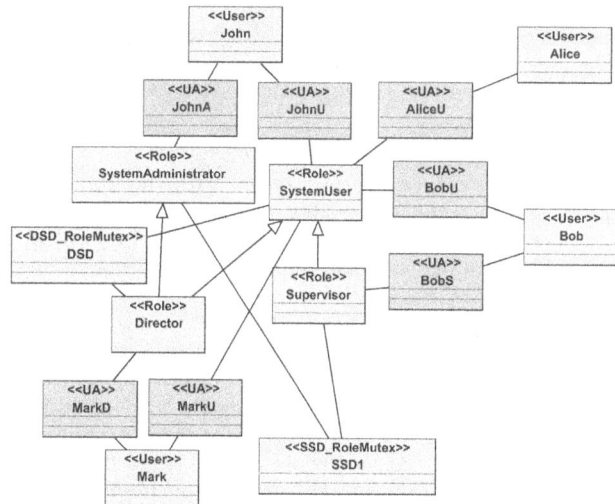

Figure 3: Users, roles and separation of duty for the meeting scheduler

5.2.3 Action hierarchy

As mentioned earlier, the permissions of Fig. 2 refer to abstract actions. A link must be established between these and the actual operations defined in the classes. Currently, our toolset does not provide a graphical notation to express this link. It must be defined directly using the Z syntax. We

159

intend to define a graphical notation for it in a near future. The following table, *action_Relation* expresses how abstract actions are instantiated in each class. For example, action EntityDelete corresponds to Cancel in class Meeting and to RemovePerson in class Person. To avoid name conflicts in the Z specification, operation names are suffixed with "1" and class names with "s".

$$
\begin{aligned}
action\_Relation = \\
\{(EntityDelete \mapsto (Cancel1, Meetings)), \\
(EntityDelete \mapsto (RemovePerson1, Persons)), \\
(EntityRead \mapsto (Notify1, Meetings)), \\
(EntityCreate \mapsto (AddMeeting1, Meetings)), \\
(EntityCreate \mapsto (CreateMeeting1, Meetings)), \\
(EntityCreate \mapsto (AddPerson1, Persons)), \\
(EntityUpdate \mapsto (ChangeStart1, Meetings)), \\
(EntityUpdate \mapsto (ChangeDuration1, Meetings)), \\
(EntityUpdate \mapsto (ChangeName1, Persons)), \\
(AssocEndUpdate \mapsto (Linkowner1, Persons)), \\
(AssocEndUpdate \mapsto (Linkparticipants1, Persons)), \\
(AssocEndUpdate \mapsto \\
\quad (LinkmeetingsOfOwner1, Meetings)), \\
(AssocEndUpdate \mapsto \\
\quad (LinkmeetingsOfParticipant1, Meetings)), \\
(NotifyExecute \mapsto (Notify1, Meetings)), \\
(CancelExecute \mapsto (Cancel1, Meetings)), \}
\end{aligned}
$$

It must be noted that the previous table does not explain what FullAccess stands for. This is because FullAccess corresponds to several abstract operations. This is detailed in *action_Inherits*. The table also defines AssocEndUpdate as a special case of EntityUpdate.

$$
\begin{aligned}
action\_Inherits = \quad &\{(EntityRead \mapsto EntityFullAccess), \\
&(EntityUpdate \mapsto EntityFullAccess), \\
&(EntityCreate \mapsto EntityFullAccess), \\
&(EntityDelete \mapsto EntityFullAccess), \\
&(AssocEndUpdate \mapsto EntityUpdate)\}
\end{aligned}
$$

5.2.4 Z Translation of the security model

The security diagrams are prepared with the TopCased tool[1]. A meta-model and a UML profile have been defined to support the edition of these models. The graphical security models of figures 2 and 3 are translated into Z using Acceleo[2], a MDA based code generator. The original RoZ [6] was designed for the Rational Rose tool[3]; a new version is currently developed for TopCased, which will integrate both security and functional models into the same environment.

The Z specification of the security model is based on the specification of a Z security kernel, independent of a specific application, which specifies the main RBAC data structures (user assignment to roles, role hierarchy, definition of permissions, action hierarchy, session management, Static and Dynamic separation of duty) and computes a table, named *perm_Assignment* which links user ids, users, roles, permissions, actions and resources.

The translation of the security diagrams and the action hierarchy of Sect. 5.2.3 are used to instantiate these data structures, and the associated enumerated types. Using the Jaza animator, we can compute *perm_Assignment* for our

[1]http://www.topcased.org/
[2]http://www.acceleo.org/pages/home/en
[3]http://www.ibm.com/software/rational/

example. Fig. 4 gives a subset of this table. For example, the first line tells us that Alice, whose user id is 001, acting as System User, may cancel a meeting due to permission OwnerMeeting. It also tells us that Bob, acting as a supervisor, has two ways to cancel a meeting, using either permission OwnerMeeting or permission SupervisorCancel. It must be noted that this table does not refer to contextual constraints. Its information is thus partial.

The security kernel defines a generic operation, named *SecureOperation*, which takes as arguments a user, its user id, a role, a session, a permission, an atomic action and a resource and checks that (a) the user is logged in the session with the given role, and (b) that table *perm_Assignment* authorizes this action for the user in the given role. This definition of SecureOperation is actually a precondition that must be satisfied for the action to take place.

$$
\begin{array}{l}
\hline
SecureOperation \\
\hline
\ldots \\
user? : USER \\
userid? : USERID \\
role? : ROLE \\
session? : SESSION \\
permission? : PERMISSION \\
atm\_action? : ATOMIC\_ACTION \\
resource? : RESOURCE \\
\hline
\ldots \\
(session?, user?) \in session\_User \\
(role?, session?) \in session\_Role \\
((userid?, user?, role?), (permission?, atm\_action?, resource?)) \\
\quad \in perm\_Assignment \\
\hline
\end{array}
$$

5.3 Linking both formal models

The last step in the preparation of the Z specification links the Z specifications of both models. First, one must relate the types appearing in both models. Here, the constraint on OwnerMeeting compares the name of the owner to the user performing the cancel operation. This requires that name and user have compatible types. In our example, this is done by redefining type *USER* as a *STRING*.

$$USER == STRING$$

At this point, secure versions of the functional operations can be defined. For example, the secure version of *meetingcancel* includes *SecureOperation* and *meetingcancel* (given in Sect. 5.1.1). What the operation actually does is completely defined in the functional operation (i.e. *meetingcancel*). So the secure operation simply adds several checks to allow the operation to take place. These checks take the form of additional preconditions. These requires the atomic action to be *Cancel1* and the resource to be *Meetings*. They also require that input parameter *meeting?* corresponds to an existing meeting, which allows to retrieve its owner. The last condition includes the contextual constraint (user is owner). Since this constraint only applies for OwnerMeeting and not for SupervisorCancel, it only applies if the role is not Supervisor.

$perm\_Assignment ==$
$\{ (("001", "Alice", SystemUser), ("OwnerMeeting", Cancel1, Meetings)),$
$(("001", "Alice", SystemUser), ("OwnerMeeting", ChangeDuration1, Meetings)),$
$(("001", "Alice", SystemUser), ("OwnerMeeting", ChangeStart1, Meetings)),$
$(("001", "Alice", SystemUser), ("UserMeeting", CreateMeeting1, Meetings)),$
$(("001", "Alice", SystemUser), ("UserMeeting", Notify1, Meetings)),$
$\dots$
$(("002", "Bob", Supervisor), ("OwnerMeeting", Cancel1, Meetings)),$
$(("002", "Bob", Supervisor), ("SupervisorCancel", Cancel1, Meetings)),$
$(("002", "Bob", Supervisor), ("UserMeeting", Notify1, Meetings)),$
$\dots$
$(("003", "John", SystemAdministrator), ("UserManagement", AddPerson1, Persons)),$
$(("003", "John", SystemAdministrator), ("UserManagement", Linkowner1, Persons)),$
$\dots$

Figure 4: A subset of the $perm\_Assignment$ **table**

___Securemeetingcancel_____
$SecureOperation$
$meetingcancel$
─────
$atm\_action? = Cancel1$
$resource? = Meetings$
$meeting? \in Meeting$
$role? \neq Supervisor \Rightarrow (user? = (owner(meeting?)).name)$

$Securemeetingcancel$ has a large number of input parameters. Many of these parameters can be deduced from a subset of the input parameters (here $session?$ and $meeting?$) and the preconditions of the operation. Operation $Securemeetingcancel2$ actually hides the useless parameters. In Z, the hide operation $(\backslash)$ existentially quantifies the hidden variables. This means that the Z animator will have to find a value for each of the hidden parameters.

$Securemeetingcancel2 == Securemeetingcancel \backslash (userid?,$
$\quad user?, atm\_action?, resource?, permission?, role?)$

Currently, secure operations are defined manually. Still this definition is completely systematic and a significant part can be automated, using additional Acceleo transformations of the diagram of Fig. 2.

6. ANIMATION OF THE SPECIFICATION

Based on the resulting Z specification, we can use the Jaza animator [17] to perform static (queries) and dynamic analyses (animations) of the security policy. Jaza is a Z animation tool based on a combination of proof (simplification, rewriting) and search (generate and test) techniques. It covers a wide range of Z constructs and supports some level of non-determinism in the specifications (provided the search space is not too large).

Jaza can execute an operation whose input parameters are fully instantiated. It checks the preconditions, computes the resulting state and checks that the resulting state is in accordance with all postconditions of the operation and with the state invariants. The user may also omit some input parameters, using the hiding operator. In that case, Jaza searches for values which will satisfy the pre-conditions of the operation and chooses one of these. This requires the search space to be finite, and small enough. In the sequel we will exploit both features of Jaza to analyse the Z specification.

6.1 Queries on the security model

We start our analysis by asking some queries, inspired by the ones of SecureMOVA [3](see Sect. 3.3). These queries are mainly based on the $perm\_Assignment$ table (Fig. 4).

- What are the atomic actions associated to a given role?

- Which roles can perform a given atomic action?

For each of these queries, a corresponding Z operation has been defined. Since the queries don't depend on the application, the Z operations are also reusable. For example, let us query which roles may perform the cancel operation. Jaza answers that three roles can perform this action and reports on the associated permissions. A closer look at the diagrams reveals that one of these permissions is associated to a constraint.

$; EvaluateActionsAgainstRoles[atm\_action? := Cancel1]$
$z\_roleAction! ==$
$\{ (Director, ("OwnerMeeting", Cancel1, Meetings)),$
$(Supervisor, ("OwnerMeeting", Cancel1, Meetings)),$
$(Supervisor, ("SupervisorCancel", Cancel1, Meetings)),$
$(SystemUser, ("OwnerMeeting", Cancel1, Meetings))\}$

A second series of queries consider the whole set of rules. They help identify generic flaws in the security policy.

- Are there duplicate roles, i.e. two roles with the same set of atomic actions?

- Do two permissions overlap?

- Is there an atomic action that every role may perform?

- Is there an atomic action that nobody may perform?

For example, the following query reports that Supervisor and SystemUser are duplicate roles. It means that they have the same privileges in table $perm\_Assignment$. Still a closer look at the diagrams shows that a contextual constraint restricts the rights of SystemUser, which justifies the existence of both roles.

$; FindDuplicateRoles$
$z\_role1! == Supervisor, z\_role2! == SystemUser$

The following query looks for operations that are always blocked by the security policy. It reveals that RemoveMeeting is not accessible. Actually, RemoveMeeting is meant to be used as a part of $meetingcancel$. So it is normal that no role has access to this operation.

; $AccessNobody$
$z\_action! == RemoveMeeting1$

It must be noted that the same queries are supported by SecureMOVA, but that it only answers "yes" or "no". We found it useful to provide witnesses when the answer is positive, because it speeds up the debugging process.

6.2 Dynamic analyses : nominal behaviours

The queries of the previous section are of static nature and do not take into account the contextual constraints associated to permissions. So they don't benefit from our integration of the functional and security models. In this section, we will perform dynamic queries, animating sequences of actions which correspond either to nominal behaviours or to possible attacks.

All animations of this section rely on an initial state where some sessions are predefined. Fig. 5 gives information about these sessions.

Session	User	Roles
sess1	Alice	SystemUser
sess2	Bob	Supervisor, SystemUser
sess3	John	SystemAdministrator, SystemUser
sess4	Mark	Director

Figure 5: Sessions with their users and roles

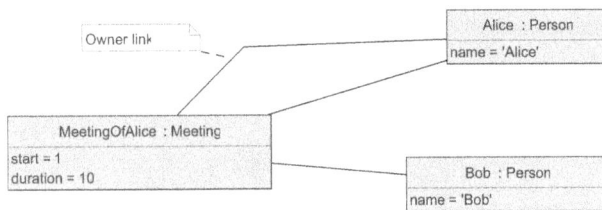

Figure 6: Object diagram for the meeting scheduler

First, we explore nominal behaviours. Our first goal is to find a sequence of actions which will lead us to the functional state depicted in Fig. 6. This requires to create two persons, one meeting, and three links. Persons must be created by the system administrator (i.e. John in session 3), then the meeting and its links will be created by Alice (session 1). This corresponds to the following Jaza animation.

; $SecurePersonAddPerson2[session? := "sess3",$
    $person? := \langle\!\langle\, name == "Alice"\, \rangle\!\rangle]$
; $SecurePersonAddPerson2[session? := "sess3",$
    $person? := \langle\!\langle\, name == "Bob"\, \rangle\!\rangle]$
; $SecuremeetingcreateMeeting2[session? := "sess1",$
    $meeting? := \langle\!\langle\, start == 1, duration == 10\, \rangle\!\rangle,$
    $owner? := \langle\!\langle\, name == "Alice"\, \rangle\!\rangle]$
; $SecuremeetingLinkmeetingsOfParticipant2[$
    $session? := "sess1",$
    $meeting? := \langle\!\langle\, start == 1, duration == 10\, \rangle\!\rangle,$
    $person? := \langle\!\langle\, name == "Bob"\, \rangle\!\rangle]$

This animation proceeds with success. Actually it covers a nominal behaviour which includes several use cases of Fig. 1: create a person, create a meeting, add participants.

We proceed by trying to cancel the meeting. This will validate the contextual constraint. First, we use the session

of John to perform this attempt. Since John is neither supervisor nor the owner of the meeting, this attempt should fail. And this is exactly what happens.

; $Securemeetingcancel2[session? := "sess3",$
    $meeting? := \langle\!\langle\, start == 1, duration == 10\, \rangle\!\rangle]$

No solutions

We then try the same operation, using the session of Alice, the owner of the meeting. This time, the operation succeeds and the set of meetings is empty after the operation.

; $Securemeetingcancel2[session? := "sess1",$
    $meeting? := \langle\!\langle\, start == 1, duration == 10\, \rangle\!\rangle]$
$Meeting' == \{\}, \ldots$

These animations increase our confidence that we expressed the right rule and the right constraint.

Another nominal behaviour is to delete some person. Let us consider that Alice has left the company and that we must delete object Alice, starting from the state of Fig. 6. Only system administrators are allowed to remove a person, so this will be performed by John in session 3.

; $SecurePersonRemovePerson2[session? := "sess3",$
    $person? := \langle\!\langle\, name == "Alice"\, \rangle\!\rangle]$

No solutions

Jaza reports that the operation failed. Actually, this is due to the fact that deleting Alice leads to have a meeting without owner, which is forbidden by the class diagram (every meeting has one and only one owner). So the functional model requires to first cancel Alice's meeting and then remove Alice. Since John is administrator, he has no right to cancel Alice's meeting. Since Alice has left the company, we need the help of a supervisor, here Bob in session 2. Now the following sequence of operations will succeed.

; $Securemeetingcancel2[session? := "sess2",$
    $meeting? := \langle\!\langle\, start == 1, duration == 10\, \rangle\!\rangle]$
; $SecurePersonRemovePerson2[session? := "sess3",$
    $person? := \langle\!\langle\, name == "Alice"\, \rangle\!\rangle]$

This animation convinces us that it was useful to create role Supervisor in our security policy, otherwise, the security rule would make it impossible to remove a user who has left the company. One may wonder whether role Director could be used to cancel the meeting and then remove the person. But the animator reports that the Director, who is neither supervisor nor the meeting owner, may not cancel Alice's meeting. This may suggest to modify the definition of Director and make him inherit from Supervisor (but this will conflict with the SSD constraint).

Other analyses of nominal behaviours can test SSD and DSD constraints. For example, the following animation shows that the SSD constraint works as expected

; $AddRole[user? := "Mark", role? := SystemAdministrator]$
; $AddRole[user? := "Mark", role? := Supervisor]$

No solutions

and the following one gives a similar result for DSD

; $NewSession[session? := "sess5",$
    $user? := "Mark", role? := Director]$
; $AddSessionRole[session? := "sess5",$
    $user? := "Mark", role? := SystemUser]$

No solutions

162

The current tool supports an elementary definition of DSD which forbids simultaneous use of conflicting roles in the same session. More elaborate versions of DSD, which consider non-simultaneous use during the same session or during the life-cycle of an object will be studied in future work.

6.3 Further dynamic analyses

In [3], SecureMOVA is used to evaluate queries which depend on a given context. "Given a state, which role should take a given user to perform a given action on a given resource?" For example, which role should take Bob to cancel Alice's meeting?

This result does not only depend on $perm\_Assignment$, but also on the current state of the data. We can ask a similar query in Z, by defining the following operation.

$$RoleNeededForMeetingCancel == (NewSession \setminus (role?))$$
$$\overset{\circ}{\text{\tiny 9}}(Securemeetingcancel2)$$

$RoleNeededForMeetingCancel$ first creates a new session, then uses this session to cancel the meeting. It hides input parameter $role?$ so that Jaza must find a role which satisfies the preconditions of both operations. When we call this operation, acting as user Bob, it actually leads to a resulting state where the set of meetings is empty. A closer look at the state shows that session 6 was created with Bob as user, and in the role of Supervisor. This answers our question: Bob may cancel Alice's meeting if he logs in as a supervisor.

> $RoleNeededForMeetingCancel[session? := "sess6",$
> $user? := "Bob",$
> $meeting? := (|\ start == 1, duration == 10\ |)]$

$Meeting' == \{\}, \dots$
$session\_Role' == \{\dots, (Supervisor, "sess6")\},$
$session\_User' == \{\dots, ("sess6", "Bob")\},$

6.4 Studying an attack scenario

Integrity of meetings is an important security property we want to enforce on our information system. Let us now focus on user John, who may play the role of SystemAdministrator and SystemUser. For some malicious reason, John wants to cancel the meeting of Alice. Since John may play two different roles, we can ask which role he should use to cancel the meeting (as we did for Bob in the previous section).

> $RoleNeededForMeetingCancel[session? := "sess7",$
> $user? := "John",$
> $meeting? := (|\ start == 1, duration == 10\ |)]$

No solutions

As expected, the system answers that John is not allowed, in any of his roles to perform this action. In Sect. 6.1, we

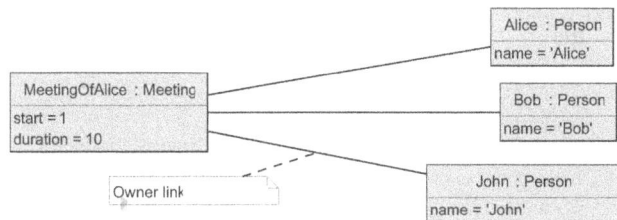

Figure 7: Another Object diagram for the meeting scheduler

already queried which roles allow to perform action Cancel1 (using $EvaluateActionsAgainstRoles$), and found that it requires roles SystemUser, Supervisor, or Director. John may only use role SystemUser to cancel the meeting, but a closer look at Fig. 2 tells us that permission "OwnerMeeting" requires John to be the owner of the meeting. This explains why he is not allowed to cancel the meeting. This also suggests that John may get this permission if he becomes owner of the meeting. This requires a more elaborate attack where John first becomes owner of the meeting and then cancels it. The functional model provides two methods to change the owner of the meeting (see Fig. 2): `LinkmeetingsOfOwner` in class `Meeting` and `Linkowner` in class `Person`.

Let us check which roles may use these operations:

> $EvaluateActionsAgainstRoles[$
> $atm\_action? := LinkmeetingsOfOwner1]$

$z\_roleAction! ==$
$\{\ (Director,$
     $("OwnerMeeting", LinkmeetingsOfOwner1, Meetings)),$
   $(Supervisor,$
     $("OwnerMeeting", LinkmeetingsOfOwner1, Meetings)),$
   $(SystemUser,$
     $("OwnerMeeting", LinkmeetingsOfOwner1, Meetings))\}$

None of these permissions apply for John, because he may only take the role SystemUser in this list, and in that case, he must be the owner of the meeting. Operation `Linkowner` corresponds to the other end of the association. A similar query may be performed.

> $EvaluateActionsAgainstRoles[atm\_action? := Linkowner1]$

$z\_roleAction! ==$
$\{\ (Director, ("UserManagement", Linkowner1, Persons)),$
   $(SystemAdministrator,$
     $("UserManagement", Linkowner1, Persons))\}$

So John may perform action `Linkowner` as SystemAdministrator. This action requires to first create an object of class `Person` corresponding to John. John being system administrator, he may create this object, using session sess3.

> $SecurePersonAddPerson2[session? := "sess3",$
> $person? := (|\ name == "John"\ |)]$
> $SecurepersonLinkowner2[session? := "sess3",$
> $person? := (|\ name == "John"\ |),$
> $meeting? := (|\ start == 1, duration == 10\ |)]$

John is now the owner of the meeting, as shown in Fig. 7. Being the owner, he may now cancel the meeting.

> $Securemeetingcancel2[session? := "sess3",$
> $meeting? := (|\ start == 1, duration == 10\ |)]$

$Meeting' == \{\} \dots$

The attack of John has succeeded! This may be considered as a flaw of the security policy. The meeting scheduler example was discussed in several articles, and defined independently of our research team. To the best of our knowledge, this problem was never reported before. We foresee that similar problems will happen in SecureUML descriptions which use contextual constraints.

The problem is that SystemAdministrator has full access to class `Person`, which includes the right to modify association ends. One solution is to add a SSD constraint between SystemAdministrator and SystemUser. Hence, John will still be able to become owner of the meeting, but will not be able to log in as SystemUser in order to delete it.

Currently, finding out attack scenarios relies on the analyst's skills. Regarding contextual constraints, we believe that this study can become quite systematic using our query tools to review how, and by which role, the functional state can be modified to change the outcome of these constraints.

7. CONCLUSION

This paper has addressed the validation of security policies expressed as RBAC rules with contextual constraints. Such constraints refer to elements of both security and functional models, using the state of the functional model as a context to grant access rights. Separation of concerns suggests to treat the functional and security models in isolation. Unfortunately, when constraints establish a link between these models, validation must take both models into account.

We have presented a toolset based on a variant of SecureUML and the Z specification language. It allows to perform static analyses, as done by the SecureMOVA tool, and dynamic analyses, playing sequences of actions. Such sequences of actions correspond to expected behaviours, and to attacks against the secure system. We presented these tools on a classical example, the meeting scheduler, addressed in the presentation of SecureMOVA. We identified a potential attack against the integrity of the information system that requires a sequence of actions to allow evolutions of the functional state. We believe that it is easier to analyse this sequence of actions with animation tools, than with static analyses only.

Our toolset includes a large number of the queries supported by USE and SecureMOVA; it can be extended to support most of the remaining ones. One feature of SecureMOVA remains difficult to support. SecureMOVA is able to report the text of the conditions that are associated to a permission, due to the reflexive character of the UML model. Our Z specification does not allow such reflexivity mechanisms, and can only evaluate the condition in a given state.

A limited part of our translation from diagrammatic models to Z specifications is currently performed manually (see Sect. 5.3). Still, this manual translation is systematic, and we are confident that it will be soon handled automatically. Our short term goal is to integrate the translation of both security and functional parts into TopCased. Finally, we did not evaluate the capability of our tool to scale up, and only used it on small models, with acceptable response times (a few seconds). Further work is needed to experiment it on real-size models and, if needed, to optimize its calculations.

Animation is not the only way to perform dynamic analysis. Model-checking provides an interesting alternative. In this paper, we showed a sequence of actions which compromises the integrity of the information system. Our tools help identify such sequences, but model-checking could help find a sequence of actions which leads from a given initial state to some unwanted state. Model-checking tools are not available for the Z language, but Pro-B [14] provides such a tool for the B language, which is close to Z. This gives an interesting perspective for future work.

Acknowledgments.
This research is partly supported by the ANR Selkis and TASCCC Projects under grants ANR-08-SEGI-018 and ANR-09-SEGI-014.

8. REFERENCES

[1] J. Abrial. *The B-Book*. Cambridge Univ. Press, 1996.

[2] F. Autrel, F. Cuppens, N. Cuppens-Boulahia, and C. Coma-Brebel. MotOrBAC 2: a security policy tool. In *SARSSI'08 : 3e conf. Sécurité des Architectures Réseaux et des Systèmes d'Information*, 2008.

[3] D. A. Basin, M. Clavel, J. Doser, and M. Egea. Automated analysis of security-design models. *Inf. & Softw. Technology*, 51(5):815–831, 2009.

[4] D. A. Basin, J. Doser, and T. Lodderstedt. Model driven security: From UML models to access control infrastructures. *ACM Trans. Softw. Eng. Methodol.*, 15(1):39–91, 2006.

[5] D. D. Clark and D. R. Wilson. A comparison of commercial and military computer security policies. In *IEEE Symp. on Security and Privacy*, 1987.

[6] S. Dupuy, Y. Ledru, and M. Chabre-Peccoud. An Overview of RoZ: A Tool for Integrating UML and Z Specifications. In *Proc. 12th Conf. on Advanced information Systems Engineering (CAiSE'2000)*, pages 417–430. LNCS, Vol. 1789, Springer, 2000.

[7] D. Ferraiolo, D. Kuhn, and R. Chandramouli. *Role-Based Access Control*. Computer Security Series. Artech House, 2003.

[8] D. F. Ferraiolo, R. S. Sandhu, S. I. Gavrila, D. R. Kuhn, and R. Chandramouli. Proposed NIST standard for Role-based Access Control. In *ACM Transactions on Information and System Security (TISSEC'-01)*, pages 224–274, 2001.

[9] M. Gogolla, F. Büttner, and M. Richters. USE: A UML-based specification environment for validating UML and OCL. *Science of Computer Programming*, 69(1-3):27–34, 2007.

[10] ISO. *Information technology – Z formal specification notation – Syntax, type system and semantics*, 2002.

[11] D. Jackson. *Software Abstractions: logic, language and analysis*. MIT Press, 2006.

[12] J. Jürjens. *Secure Systems Development with UML*. Springer, 2004.

[13] Y. Ledru. Using Jaza to Animate RoZ Specifications of UML Class Diagrams. In *Proc. 30th Annual IEEE/NASA Software Engineering Workshop (SEW-30 2006)*. IEEE CS Press, 2006.

[14] M. Leuschel and M. J. Butler. ProB: an automated analysis toolset for the B method. *Software Tools for Technology Transfer*, 10(2):185–203, 2008.

[15] K. Sohr, M. Drouineaud, G.-J. Ahn, and M. Gogolla. Analyzing and managing role-based access control policies. *IEEE Trans. Knowl. Data Eng.*, 20(7):924–939, 2008.

[16] M. Toahchoodee, I. Ray, K. Anastasakis, G. Georg, and B. Bordbar. Ensuring spatio-temporal access control for real-world applications. In *SACMAT 2009, 14th ACM Symp. on Access Control Models and Technologies*. ACM, 2009.

[17] M. Utting. *Jaza User Manual and Tutorial*, 2005. http://www.cs.waikato.ac.nz/~marku/jaza/.

[18] J. B. Warmer and A. G. Kleppe. *The Object Constraint Language: Precise Modeling With UML*. Addison-Wesley, October 1998.

Anomaly Discovery and Resolution in Web Access Control Policies

Hongxin Hu, Gail-Joon Ahn and Ketan Kulkarni
Arizona State University
Tempe, AZ 85287, USA
{hxhu,gahn,kakulkar}@asu.edu

ABSTRACT

The advent of emerging technologies such as Web services, service-oriented architecture, and cloud computing has enabled us to perform business services more efficiently and effectively. However, we still suffer from unintended security leakages by unauthorized actions in business services while providing more convenient services to Internet users through such a cutting-edge technological growth. Furthermore, designing and managing Web access control policies are often error-prone due to the lack of effective analysis mechanisms and tools. In this paper, we represent an innovative policy anomaly analysis approach for Web access control policies. We focus on XACML (eXtensible Access Control Markup Language) policy since XACML has become the *de facto* standard for specifying and enforcing access control policies for various Web-based applications and services. We introduce a policy-based segmentation technique to accurately identify policy anomalies and derive effective anomaly resolutions. We also discuss a proof-of-concept implementation of our method called XAnalyzer and demonstrate how efficiently our approach can discover and resolve policy anomalies.

Categories and Subject Descriptors

D.4.6 [**Security and Protection**]: Access controls

General Terms

Security, Management

Keywords

Access control policies, XACML, anomaly management

1. INTRODUCTION

With the explosive growth of Web applications and Web services deployed on the Internet, the use of a policy-based approach has received considerable attention to accommodate the security requirements covering large, open, distributed and heterogeneous computing environments. XACML (eXtensible Access Control Markup

Language) [27], which is a general purpose access control policy language standardized by the Organization for the Advancement of Structured Information Standards (OASIS), has been broadly adopted to specify access control policies for various applications [3], especially Web services. In an XACML policy, multiple rules may overlap, which means one access request may match several rules. Moreover, multiple rules within one policy may conflict, implying that those rules not only overlap each other but also yield different decisions. Conflicts in an XACML policy may lead to both safety problem (e.g. allowing unauthorized access) and availability problem (e.g. denying legitimate access).

An intuitive means for resolving policy conflicts by a policy designer is to remove all conflicts by modifying the policies. However, resolving conflicts through changing the policies is remarkably difficult, even impossible, in practice from many aspects. First, the number of conflicts in an XACML policy is potentially large, since an XACML policy may consist of hundreds or thousands of rules. Second, conflicts in XACML policies are probably very complicated, because one rule may conflict with multiple other rules, and one conflict may be associated with several rules. Besides, an XACML policy for a distributed application may be aggregated from multiple parties. Also, an XACML policy may be maintained by more than one administrator. Without a priori knowledge on the original intentions of policy specification, changing a policy may affect the policy's semantics and may not resolve conflicts correctly. Furthermore, in some cases, a policy designer may intentionally introduce certain overlaps in XACML policy components by implicitly reflecting that only the first rule is important. In this case, conflicts are not an error, but intended, which would not be necessary to be changed.

Since the *conflicts* in XACML policies always exist and are hard to be eliminated, XACML defines four different combining algorithms to automatically resolve conflicts [27]: *Deny-Overrides*, *Permit-Overrides*, *First-Applicable* and *Only-One-Applicable*. Unfortunately, XACML currently lacks a systematic mechanism for precisely detecting conflicts. Identifying conflicts in XACML policies is critical for policy designers since the correctness of selecting a combining algorithm for an XACML policy or policy set component heavily relies on the information from conflict diagnosis. Without precise conflict information, the effectiveness of combining algorithms for resolving policy conflicts cannot be guaranteed.

Another critical problem for XACML policy analysis is *redundancy* discovery and removal. A rule in an XACML policy is redundant if every access request that matches the rule also matches other rules with the same effect. As the response time of an access request largely depends on the number of rules to be parsed within a policy, redundancies in a policy may adversely affect the performance of policy evaluation. Therefore, policy redundancy is treated as policy *anomaly* as well. With the significant growth of Web applications deployed on the Internet, XACML policies grow rapidly in size and complexity. Hence, redundancy elimination can be treated as one of effective solutions for optimizing XACML policies and improving the performance of XACML evaluation.

Recently, policy anomaly detection has received a great deal of attention [7, 10, 22, 28], especially, in firewall policy analysis. Corresponding policy analysis tools, such as Firewall Policy Advisor [7] and FIREMAN [28], with the goal of discovering firewall policy anomalies have been developed. However, we cannot directly adopt those prior analysis approaches for XACML due to several reasons. First, most prior approaches mainly have the capability to detect *pairwise* policy anomalies, while a complete anomaly detection should consider all policy components as a whole piece. In other words, prior policy analysis approaches are still needed to be improved [8]. Second, the structure of firewall policies is flat but XACML has a hierarchical structure supporting recursive policy specification. Third, a firewall policy only supports one conflict resolution strategy (*first-match*) to resolve conflicts but XACML has four rule/policy combining algorithms. Last but not the least, a firewall rule is typically specified with fixed fields, while an XACML rule can be multi-valued. Therefore, a new policy analysis mechanism is desirable to cater those requirements from anomaly analysis in XACML policies.

In this paper, we introduce a policy-based segmentation technique, which adopts a binary decision diagram (BDD)-based data structure to perform set operations, for policy anomaly discovery and resolution. Based on this technique, an *authorization space* defined by an XACML policy or policy set component can be divided into a set of disjoint segments. Each segment associated with a unique set of XACML components indicates an overlap relation (either conflicting or redundant) among those components. Accurate anomaly information is crucial to the success of anomaly resolution. For example, conflict diagnosis information provided by a policy analysis tool can be utilized to guide the policy designers in selecting appropriate combining algorithms. Moreover, we observe that current XACML conflict resolution mechanisms are too restrictive by applying only one combining algorithm to resolve all identified conflicts within an XACML policy or policy set component. Also, many other desirable conflict resolution strategies exist [15, 18, 20], but cannot be directly supported by XACML. Thus, we additionally propose a flexible and extensible policy conflict resolution in this paper. Besides, we implement a policy analysis tool XAnalyzer based on our approach. To evaluate the practicality of our tool, our experiments deal with both real-life and synthetic XACML policies.

The rest of this paper is organized as follows. Section 2 overviews the XACML policy and briefly discusses anomalies in XACML policies. We describe the underlying data structure for XACML representation based on binary decision diagrams in Section 3. Section 4 presents our conflict detection and resolution approaches. In Section 5, we address our redundancy discovery and removal approaches. In Section 6, we discuss the implementation of our tool XAnalyzer and the evaluation of our approach. Section 7 overviews the related work and we conclude this paper in Section 8.

2. PRELIMINARIES

2.1 XACML Overview

XACML has become the *de facto* standard for describing access control policies and offers a large set of built-in functions, data types, combining algorithms, and standard profiles for defining application-specific features. At the root of all XACML policies is a *policy* or a *policy set*. A *policy set* is composed of a sequence of *policies* or other *policy sets* along with a *policy combining algorithm* and a *target*. A *policy* represents a single access control policy expressed through a *target*, a set of *rules* and a *rule combining algorithm*. The *target* defines a set of subjects, resources and actions the policy or policy set applies to. For an applicable policy or policy set, the corresponding target should be evaluated to be *true*; otherwise, the policy or policy set is skipped when evaluating an access request. A *rule set* is a sequence of rules. Each *rule* consists of a *target*, a *condition*, and an *effect*. The *target* of a rule decides whether an access request is applicable to the rule and it has a similar structure as the target of a policy or a policy set; the *condition* is a boolean expression to specify restrictions on the attributes in the target and refine the applicability of the rule; and the *effect* is either `permit` or `deny`. If an access request satisfies both the *target* and *condition* of a rule, the response is sent with the decision specified by the *effect* element in the rule. Otherwise, the response yields `NotApplicable` which is typically considered as `deny`.

An XACML policy often has conflicting rules or policies, which are resolved by four different *combining algorithms*: *Deny-Overrides*, *Permit-Overrides*, *First-Applicable* and *Only-One-Applicable* [27]. Figure 1 shows an example XACML policy. The root policy set PS_1 contains two policies, P_1 and P_2, which are combined using *First-Applicable* combining algorithm. The policy P_1 has three rules, r_1, r_2 and r_3, and its rule combining algorithm is *Deny-Overrides*. The policy P_2 includes two rules r_4 and r_5 with *Deny-Overrides* combining algorithm. In this example, there are four subjects: *Manager*, *Designer*, *Developer* and *Tester*; two resources: *Reports* and *Codes*; and two actions: *Read* and *Change*. Note that both r_2 and r_3 define conditions over the *Time* attribute.

2.2 Anomalies in XACML Policies

An XACML policy may contain both policy components and policy set components. Often, a rule anomaly occurs in a policy component, which consists of a sequence of rules. On the other hand, a policy set component consists of a set of policies or other policy sets, thus anomalies may also arise among policies or policy sets. Thus, we address XACML policy anomalies at both policy level and policy set level.

- **Anomalies at Policy Level:** A rule is **conflicting** with other rules, if this rule overlaps with others but defines a different effect. For example, the *deny* rule r_1 is in conflict with the *permit* rule r_2 in Figure 1 because rule r_2 allows the access requests from a designer to change codes in the time interval [8:00, 17:00], which are supposed to be denied by r_1; and a rule is **redundant** if there is other same or more general rules available that have the same effect. For instance, if we change the effect of r_2 to *Deny*, r_3 becomes redundant since r_2 will also deny a designer to change reports or codes in the time interval [12:00, 13:00].

- **Anomalies at Policy Set Level:** Anomalies may also occur across policies or policy sets in an XACML policy. For example, considering two policy components P_1 and P_2 of the policy set PS_1 in Figure 1, P_1 is **conflicting** with P_2, because P_1 permits the access requests that a developer changes reports in the time interval [8:00, 17:00], but which are denied by P_2. On the other hand, P_1 denies the requests allowing a designer to change reports or codes in the time interval [12:00, 13:00], which are permitted by P_2. Supposing the effect of r_2 is changed to *Deny* and the condition of r_2 is removed, r_4 is turned to be **redundant** with respect to r_2, even

```
1<PolicySet PolicySetId="PS₁" PolicyCombiningAlgId="First-Applicable">
2   <Target/>
3   <Policy PolicyId="P₁" RuleCombiningAlgId="Deny-Overrides">
4     <Target/>
5     <Rule RuleId="r₁" Effect="Deny">
6       <Target>
7         <Subjects><Subject>      Designer   </Subject>
8                   <Subject>      Tester     </Subject></Subjects>
9         <Resources><Resource>    Codes      </Resource></Resources>
10        <Actions><Action>        Change     </Action></Actions>
11      </Target>
12    </Rule>
13    <Rule RuleId="r₂" Effect="Permit">
14      <Target>
15        <Subjects><Subject>      Designer   </Subject>
16                  <Subject>      Developer  </Subject></Subjects>
17        <Resources><Resource>    Reports    </Resource>
18                   <Resource>    Codes      </Resource></Resources>
19        <Actions><Action>        Read       </Action>
20                 <Action>        Change     </Action></Actions>
21      </Target>
22      <Condition>      8:00 ≤ Time ≤17:00        </Condition>
23    </Rule>
24    <Rule RuleId="r₃" Effect="Deny">
25      <Target>
26        <Subjects><Subject>      Designer   </Subject></Subjects>
27        <Resources><Resource>    Reports    </Resource>
28                   <Resource>    Codes      </Resource></Resources>
29        <Actions><Action>        Change     </Action></Actions>
30      </Target>
31      <Condition>      12:00 ≤ Time ≤ 13:00     </Condition>
32    </Rule>
33  </Policy>
34  <Policy PolicyId="P₂" RuleCombiningAlgId="Permit-Overrides">
35    <Target/>
36    <Rule RuleId="r₄" Effect="Deny">
37      <Target>
38        <Subjects><Subject>      Developer  </Subject></Subjects>
39        <Resources><Resource>    Reports    </Resource></Resources>
40        <Actions><Action>        Change     </Action></Actions>
41      </Target>
42    </Rule>
43    <Rule RuleId="r₅" Effect="Permit">
44      <Target>
45        <Subjects><Subject>      Manager    </Subject>
46                  <Subject>      Designer   </Subject></Subjects>
47        <Resources><Resource>    Reports    </Resource>
48                   <Resource>    Codes      </Resource></Resources>
49        <Actions><Action>        Change     </Action></Actions>
50      </Target>
51    </Rule>
52  </Policy>
53</PolicySet>
```

Figure 1: An example XACML policy.

though r_2 and r_4 are placed in different policies P_1 and P_2, respectively.

Most prior anomaly detection work only treat a policy anomaly as an inconsistent or redundant relation between *two* rules. However, a policy anomaly may involve in multiple rules. For example, in Figure 1, access requests that a designer changes codes in the time interval [12:00, 13:00] are permitted by r_2, but denied by both r_1 and r_3. Thus, this conflict associates with *three* rules. For another example, suppose the effect of r_3 is changed to *Permit* and the subject of r_3 is replaced by *Manager* and *Developer*. If we only examine *pairwise* redundancies, r_3 is not a redundant rule. However, if we check multiple rules simultaneously, we can identify r_3 is redundant considering r_2 and r_5 together. We observe that precise anomaly diagnosis information is crucial for achieving an effective anomaly resolution. In this paper, we attempt to design a systematic approach and corresponding tool not only for accurate anomaly detection but also for effective anomaly resolution.

3. UNDERLYING DATA STRUCTURE

Our policy-based segmentation technique introduced in subsequent sections requires a well-formed representation of policies for performing a variety of set operations. Binary Decision Diagram (BDD) [13] is a data structure that has been widely used for formal verification and simplification of digital circuits. In this work, we leverage BDD as the underlying data structure to represent XACML policies and facilitate effective policy analysis.

Given an XACML policy, it can be parsed to identify subject, action, resource and condition attributes. Once these attributes are identified, all XACML rules can be transformed into Boolean expressions [9]. Each Boolean expression of a rule is composed of atomic Boolean expressions combined by logical operators $\vee$ and $\wedge$. Atomic Boolean expressions are treated as equality constraints or range constraints on attributes (e.g. $Subject = \text{"student"}$) or on conditions (e.g. $8:00 \leq Time \leq 17:00$).

EXAMPLE 1. *Consider the example XACML policy in Figure 1 in terms of* atomic Boolean expressions. *The Boolean expression for rule r_1 is:*

$$(Subject = \text{"Designer"} \vee Subject = \text{"Tester"}) \wedge$$
$$(Resource = \text{"Codes"}) \wedge (Action = \text{"Change"})$$

The Boolean expression for rule r_2 is:

$$(Subject = \text{"Designer"} \vee Subject = \text{"Tester"}) \wedge$$
$$(Resource = \text{"Reports"} \vee Resource = \text{"Codes"}) \wedge$$
$$(Action = \text{"Read"} \vee Action = \text{"Change"}) \wedge$$
$$(8:00 \leq Time \leq 17:00)$$

Boolean expressions for XACML rules may consist of atomic Boolean expressions with overlapping value ranges. In such cases, those atomic Boolean expressions are needed to be transformed into a sequence of new atomic Boolean expressions with disjoint value ranges. Agrawal et al. [5] have identified different categories of such atomic Boolean expressions and addressed corresponding solutions for those issues. We adopt similar approach to construct our Boolean expressions for XACML rules.

Table 1: Atomic Boolean expressions and corresponding Boolean variables for P_1.

Unique Atomic Boolean Expression	Boolean Variable
$Subject = \text{"Designer"}$	S_1
$Subject = \text{"Tester"}$	S_2
$Subject = \text{"Developer"}$	S_3
$Subject = \text{"Manager"}$	S_4
$Resource = \text{"Reports"}$	R_1
$Resource = \text{"Codes"}$	R_2
$Action = \text{"Read"}$	A_1
$Action = \text{"Change"}$	A_2
$8:00 \leq Time < 12:00$	C_1
$12:00 \leq Time < 13:00$	C_2
$13:00 \leq Time \leq 17:00$	C_3

We encode each of the atomic Boolean expression as a Boolean variable. For example, an atomic Boolean expression $Subject=\text{"Designer"}$ is encoded into a Boolean variable S_1. A complete list of Boolean encoding for the example XACML policy in Figure 1 is shown in Table 1. We then utilize the Boolean encoding to construct Boolean expressions in terms of Boolean variables for XACML rules.

EXAMPLE 2. *Consider the example XACML policy in Figure 1 in terms of* Boolean variables. *The Boolean expression for rule r_1 is:*

$$(S1 \vee S2) \wedge (R2) \wedge (A2)$$

The Boolean expression for rule r_2 is:

$$(S1 \vee S2) \wedge (R1 \vee R2) \wedge (A1 \vee A2) \wedge (C1 \vee C2 \vee C3)$$

BDDs are acyclic directed graphs which represent Boolean expressions compactly. Each nonterminal node in a BDD represents a Boolean variable, and has two edges with binary labels, 0 and 1 for *nonexistent* and *existent*, respectively. Terminal nodes represent Boolean value T (True) or F (False). Figures 2(a) and 2(b) give BDD representations of two rules r_1 and r_2, respectively.

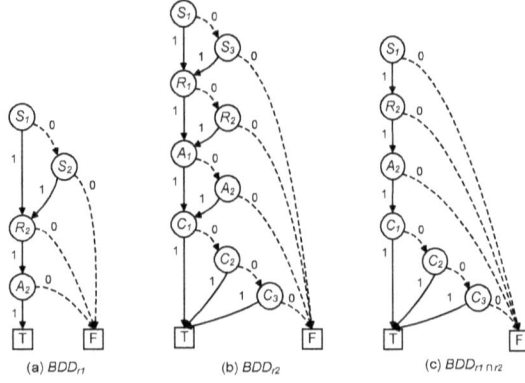

Figure 2: Representing and operating on rules of XACML policy with BDD.

Once the BDDs are constructed for XACML rules, performing set operations, such as unions ($\cup$), intersections ($\cap$) and set differences ($\setminus$), required by our policy-based segmentation algorithms (see Algorithm 1 and Algorithm 2) is efficient as well as straightforward. Figure 2(c) shows an integrated BDD, which is the intersection of BDDs of r_1 and r_2. Note that the resulting BDD from the intersection operation may have *less* number of nodes due to the canonical representation of BDD.

4. CONFLICT DETECTION AND RESOLUTION

We first introduce a concept of *authorization space*, which adopts aforementioned BDD-based policy representation to perform policy anomaly analysis. This concept is defined as follows.

DEFINITION 1. *(Authorization Space).* Let R_x, P_x and PS_x be the set of rules, policies and policy sets, respectively, of an XACML policy x. An authorization space for an XACML policy component $c \in R_x \cup P_x \cup PS_x$ represents a collection of all access requests Q_c to which a policy component c is applicable.

4.1 Conflict Detection Approach

Our conflict detection mechanism examines conflicts at both policy level and policy set level for XACML policies. In order to precisely identify policy conflicts and facilitate an effective conflict resolution, we present a policy-based segmentation technique to partition the entire authorization space of a policy into disjoint authorization space segments. Then, conflicting authorization space segments (called *conflicting segment* in the rest of this paper), which contain policy components with different effects, are identified. Each conflicting segment indicates a policy conflict.

4.1.1 Conflict Detection at Policy Level

A policy component in an XACML policy includes a set of rules. Each rule defines an authorization space with the effect of either permit or deny. We call an authorization space with the effect of permit *permitted space* and an authorization space with the effect of deny *denied space*.

Algorithm 1 shows the pseudocode of generating conflicting segments for a policy component P. An entire authorization space derived from a policy component is first partitioned into a set of disjoint segments. As shown in lines 16-32 in Algorithm 1, a function called Partition() accomplishes this procedure. This function works by adding an authorization space s derived from a rule r to an authorization space set S. A pair of authorization spaces must satisfy one of the following relations: *subset* (line 19), *superset* (line 24), *partial match* (line 27), or *disjoint* (line 31). Therefore, one can utilize set operations to separate the overlapped spaces into disjoint spaces.

Algorithm 1: Identify Disjoint Conflicting Authorization Spaces of Policy P

Input: A policy P with a set of rules.
Output: A set of disjoint conflicting authorization spaces CS for P.
1   /* *Partition the entire authorization space of P into disjoint spaces*/
2   $S.New()$;
3   $S \longleftarrow$ **Partition_P**(P);
4   /* *Identify the conflicting segments* */
5   $CS.New()$;
6   **foreach** $s \in S$ **do**
7   /* *Get all rules associated with a segment s* */
8     $R' \longleftarrow GetRule(s)$;
9   **if** $\exists r_i \in R', r_j \in R', r_i \neq r_j$ and $r_i.Effect \neq r_j.Effect$ **then**
10      $CS.Append(s)$;

11   **Partition_P**(P)
12   $R \longleftarrow GetRule(P)$;
13   **foreach** $r \in R$ **do**
14     $s_r \longleftarrow AuthorizationSpace(r)$;
15     $S \longleftarrow$ **Partition**(S, s_r);
16   **return** S;

17   **Partition**(S, s_r)
18   **foreach** $s \in S$ **do**
19   /* s_r *is a subset of s*/
20   **if** $s_r \subset s$ **then**
21      $S.Append(s \setminus s_r)$;
22      $s \longleftarrow s_r$;
23      $Break$;
24   /* s_r *is a superset of s*/
25   **else if** $s_r \supset s$ **then**
26      $s_r \longleftarrow s_r \setminus s$;
27   /* s_r *partially matches s*/
28   **else if** $s_r \cap s \neq \emptyset$ **then**
29      $S.Append(s \setminus s_r)$;
30      $s \longleftarrow s_r \cap s$;
31      $s_r \longleftarrow s_r \setminus s$;
32   $S.Append(s_r)$;
33   **return** S;

Conflicting segments are identified as shown in lines 6-9 in Algorithm 1. A set of conflicting segments $CS : \{cs_1, cs_2, \ldots, cs_n\}$ from conflicting rules has the following three properties:

1. All conflicting segments are pairwise disjoint:
   $cs_i \cap cs_j = \emptyset, 1 \leq i \neq j \leq n$;

2. Any two different requests q and q' within a single conflicting segment (cs_i) are matched by exact same set of rules:
   $GetRule(q) = GetRule(q'), \forall q \in cs_i, q' \in cs_i, q \neq q'$; and

3. The effects of matched rules in any conflicting segments contain both "Permit" and "Deny."

Figure 3 gives a representation of the segments of authorization space derived from the policy P_1 in the XACML example policy

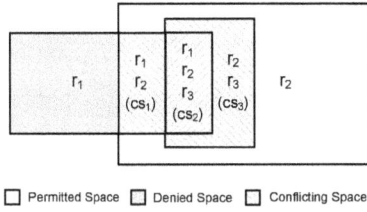

Figure 3: Disjoint segments of authorization space for policy P_1 in the example XACML policy.

shown in Figure 1 [1]. We can notice that five unique disjoint segments are generated. In addition, three conflicting segments cs_1, cs_2 and cs_3 are identified. They represent three policy conflicts, where conflicting segment cs_1 is associated with a rule set consisting of two rules r_1 and r_2, conflicting segment cs_2 is related to a rule set including three rules r_1, r_2 and r_3, and conflicting segment cs_3 is associated with a rule set containing two rules r_2 and r_3.

4.1.2 Conflict Detection at Policy Set Level

There are two major challenges that need to be taken into consideration when we design an approach for XACML analysis at policy set level.

1. XACML supports four rule/policy combining algorithms: *First-Applicable*, *Only-One-Applicable*, *Deny-Overrides*, and *Permit-Overrides*.

2. An XACML policy is specified recursively and therefore has a hierarchical structure. In XACML, a policy set contains a sequence of policies or policy sets, which may further contain other policies or policy sets.

Each authorization space segment also has an effect, which is decided by XACML components covered by this segment. For non-conflicting segments, the effect of a segment equals to the effect of components covered by this segment. Regarding conflicting segments, the effect of a segment depends on the following four cases of combining algorithm ($\mathcal{CA}$), which is used by the owner (a policy or a policy set) of the segment.

1. $\mathcal{CA}$=*First-Applicable*: In this case, the effect of a conflicting segment equals to the effect of the first component covered by the conflicting segment.

2. $\mathcal{CA}$=*Permit-Overrides*: The effect of a conflicting segment is always assigned with "Permit," since there is at least one component with "Permit" effect within this conflicting segment.

3. $\mathcal{CA}$=*Deny-Overrides*: The effect of a conflicting segment always equals to "Deny."

4. $\mathcal{CA}$=*Only-One-Applicable*: The effect of a conflicting segment equals to the effect of only-applicable component.

To support the recursive specifications of XACML policies, we parse and model an XACML policy as a tree structure, where each terminal node represents an individual rule, each nonterminal node whose children are all terminal nodes represents a policy, and each nonterminal node whose children are all nonterminal nodes represents a policy set. At each nonterminal node, we store the target

---

[1] For the purposes of brevity and understandability, we employ a two dimensional geometric representation for each authorization space segment. Note that a rule in an XACML policy typically has multiple fields, thus a complete representation of authorization space should be multi-dimensional.

and combining algorithm. At each terminal node, the target and effect of the corresponding rule are stored.

Algorithm 2 shows the pseudocode of identifying disjoint conflicting authorization spaces for a policy set PS based on the tree structure. In order to partition authorization spaces of all nodes contained in a policy set tree, this algorithm recursively calls the partition functions, `Partition_P()` and `Partition_PS()`, to deal with the policy nodes (lines 16-17) and the policy set nodes (lines 19-20), respectively. Once all children nodes of a policy set are partitioned, we can then represent the authorization space of each child node (E) with two subspaces *permitted subspace* (E^P) and *denied subspace* (E^D) by aggregating all "Permit" segments and "Deny" segments, respectively, as follows:

$$\begin{cases} E^P = \bigcup_{s_i \in S_E} s_i & \text{if } Effect(s_i) = Permit \\ E^D = \bigcup_{s_i \in S_E} s_i & \text{if } Effect(s_i) = Deny \end{cases} \quad (1)$$

where S_E denotes the set of authorization space segments of the child node E.

For example, Figure 4 shows the result of aggregating authorization spaces shown in Figure 3. Two subspaces P_1^P and P_1^D are constructed for the policy P_1, which is a child node of the policy set PS_1 in our example XACML policy.

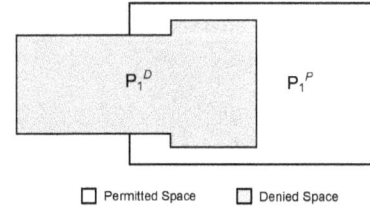

Figure 4: Aggregation of authorization spaces.

In order to generate segments for the policy set PS, we can then leverage two subspaces (E^P and E^D) of each child node (E) to partition existing authorization space set belonging to PS (lines 28-29). Figure 5 represents an example of the segments of authorization space derived from policy set PS_1 in our example policy (Figure 1). We can observe that seven unique disjoint segments are generated, and two of them cs_1 and cs_2 are conflicting segments, where cs_1 is related to P_1^P and P_2^D, and cs_2 is associated with P_1^D and P_2^P. They indicate two conflicts occurring in PS at policy set level.

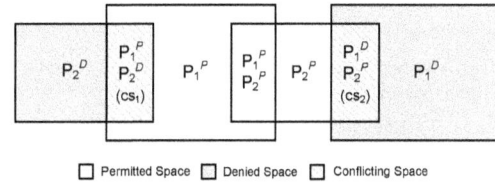

Figure 5: Disjoint segments of authorization space for policy set PS_1 in the example XACML policy.

4.2 Fine-Grained Conflict Resolution

Once conflicts within a policy component or policy set component are identified, a policy designer can choose appropriate conflict resolution strategies to resolve those identified conflicts. However, current XACML conflict resolution mechanisms have limitations in resolving conflicts effectively. First, existing conflict resolution mechanisms in XACML are too restrictive and only allow a policy designer to select one combining algorithm to resolve all

Algorithm 2: Identify Disjoint Conflicting Authorization Spaces of Policy Set PS

Input: A policy set PS with a set of policies or other policy sets.
Output: A set of disjoint conflicting authorization spaces CS for PS.
1 /* Partition the entire authorization space of PS into disjoint spaces*/
2 $S.New()$;
3 $S \longleftarrow$ **Partition_PS**(PS);
4 /* Identify the conflicting segments */
5 $CS.New()$;
6 **foreach** $s \in S$ **do**
7      $E \longleftarrow GetElement(s)$;
8   **if** $\exists e_i \in E, e_j \in E, e_i \neq e_j$ and $e_i.Effect \neq e_j.Effect$ **then**
9          $CS.Append(s)$;

10 **Partition_PS**(PS)
11 $S''.New()$;
12 $C \longleftarrow GetChild(PS)$;
13 **foreach** $c \in C$ **do**
14      $S'.New()$;
15   /* c is a policy*/
16   **if** $IsPolicy(c) = true$ **then**
17          $S' \longleftarrow$ **Partition_P**(c);
18   /* c is a policy set*/
19   **else if** $IsPolicySet(c) = true$ **then**
20          $S' \longleftarrow$ **Partition_PS**(c)
21      $E^P.New()$;
22      $E^D.New()$;
23   **foreach** $s' \in S'$ **do**
24   **if** $Effect(s') = Permit$ **then**
25              $E^P \longleftarrow E^P \cup s'$;
26   **else if** $Effect(s') = Deny$ **then**
27              $E^D \longleftarrow E^D \cup s'$;
28      $S'' \longleftarrow$ **Partition**(S'', E^P);
29      $S'' \longleftarrow$ **Partition**(S'', E^D);

30 **return** S'';

---

identified conflicts within a policy or policy set component. A policy designer may want to adopt different combining algorithms to resolve different conflicts. Second, XACML offers four conflict resolution strategies. However, many conflict resolution strategies exist [15, 18, 20], but cannot be specified in XACML. Thus, it is necessary to seek a comprehensive conflict resolution mechanism for more effective conflict resolution. Towards this end, we introduce a flexible and extensible conflict resolution framework to achieve a fine-grained conflict resolution as shown in Figure 6.

4.2.1 Effect Constraint Generation from Conflict Resolution Strategy

Our conflict resolution framework introduces an *effect constraint* that is assigned to each conflicting segment. An effect constraint for a conflicting segment defines a desired response (either permit or deny) that an XACML policy should take when any access request matches the conflicting segment. The effect constraint is derived from the conflict resolution strategy associated with the conflicting segment. A policy designer chooses an appropriate conflict resolution strategy for each identified conflict by examining the features of conflicting segment and associated conflicting components. In our conflict resolution framework, a policy designer is able to adopt different strategies to resolve conflicts indicated by different conflicting segments. In addition to four standard XACML conflict resolution strategies, user-defined strategies [20], such as *Recency-Overrides*, *Specificity-overrides* and *High-Authority-Overrides*, can be implied in our framework as well.

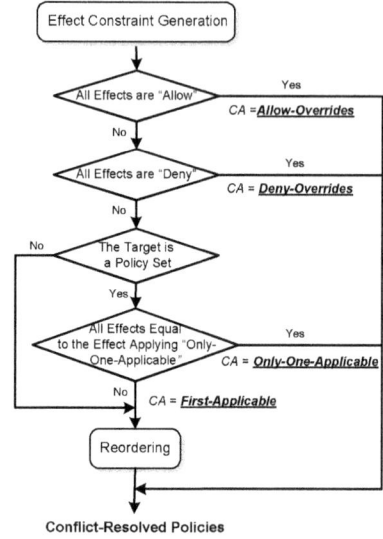

Figure 6: Fine-grained conflict resolution framework.

4.2.2 Conflict Resolution Based on Effect Constraints

A key feature of adopting *effect constraints* in our framework is that other conflict resolution strategies assigned to resolve different conflicts by a policy designer can be *automatically* mapped to standard XACML combining algorithms, without changing the way that current XACML implementations perform. As illustrated in Figure 6, an XACML combining algorithm can be derived for a target component by examining all effect constraints of the conflicting segments. If all effect constraints are "Permit," *Permit-Overrides* is selected for the target component to resolve all conflicts. In case that all effect constraints are "Deny," *Deny-Overrides* is assigned to the target component. Then, if the target component is a policy set and all effect constraints can be satisfied by applying *Only-One-Applicable* combining algorithm, *Only-One-Applicable* is selected as the combining algorithm of the target component. Otherwise, *First-Applicable* is selected as the combining algorithm of the target component. In order to resolve all conflicts within the target component by applying *First-Applicable*, the process of reordering conflicting components is compulsory. Therefore, the first-applicable component in each conflicting segment has the same effect with corresponding effect constraint.

5. REDUNDANCY DISCOVERY AND REMOVAL

Our redundancy discovery and removal mechanism also leverage the policy-based segmentation technique to explore redundancies at both policy level and policy set level. We give a definition of rule redundancy as follows, which serves as a foundation of our redundancy elimination approach.

DEFINITION 2. *(**Rule Redundancy**). A rule r is redundant in an XACML policy p iff the authorization space derived from the resulting policy p' after removing r is equivalent to the authorization space defined by p.*

5.1 Redundancy Elimination at Policy Level

We employ following four steps to identify and eliminate rule redundancies at policy level: authorization space segmentation, property assignment for rule subspaces, rule correlation break, and redundant rule removal.

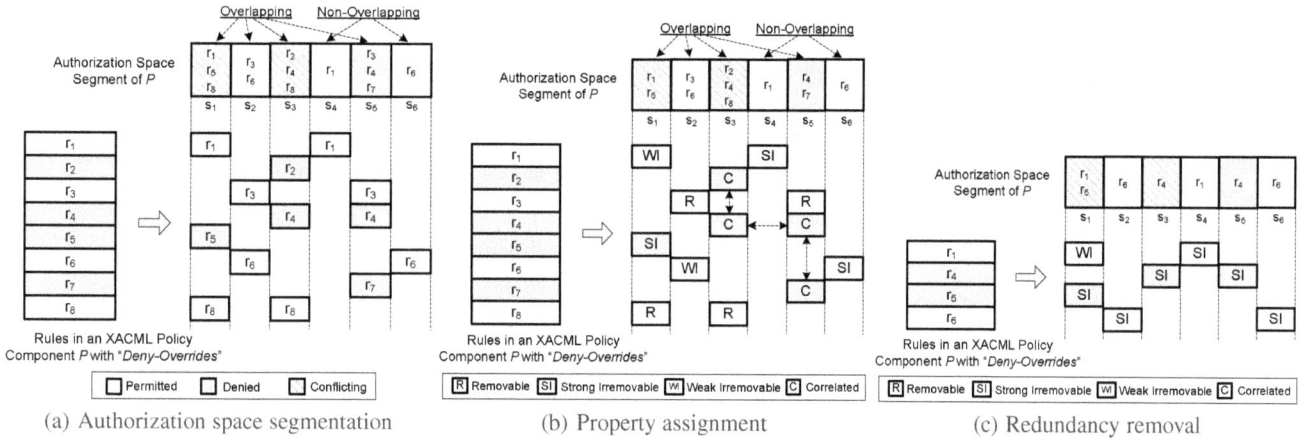

(a) Authorization space segmentation   (b) Property assignment   (c) Redundancy removal

Figure 7: Example of eliminating redundancies at policy level.

5.1.1 Authorization Space Segmentation

We first perform the policy segmentation function `Partition_P()` defined in Algorithm 1 to divide the entire authorization space of a policy into disjoint segments. We classify the policy segments in following categories: *non-overlapping* segment and *overlapping* segment, which is further divided into *conflicting overlapping* segment and *non-conflicting overlapping* segment. Each *non-overlapping* segment associates with one unique rule and each *overlapping* segment is related to a set of rules, which may conflict with each other (*conflicting overlapping* segment) or have the same effect (*non-conflicting overlapping* segment). Figure 7(a) illustrates an authorization space segmentation for a policy with eight rules. In this example, two policy segments s_4 and s_6 are *non-overlapping* segments. Other policy segments are *overlapping* segments, including two *conflicting overlapping* segments s_1 and s_3, and two *non-conflicting overlapping* segments s_2 and s_5.

5.1.2 Property Assignment for Rule Subspaces

In this step, every rule subspace covered by a policy segment is assigned with a property. Four property values, *removable* (R), *strong irremovable* (SI), *weak irremovable* (WI) and *correlated* (C), are defined to reflect different characteristics of rule subspace. *Removable* property is used to indicate that a rule subspace is removable. In other words, removing such a rule subspace does not make any impact on the original authorization space of an associated policy. *Strong irremovable* property means that a rule subspace cannot be removed because the effect of corresponding policy segment can be only decided by this rule. *Weak irremovable* property is assigned to a rule subspace when any subspace belonging to the same rule has *strong irremovable* property. That means a rule subspace becomes irremovable due to the reason that other portions of this rule cannot be removed. *Correlated* property is assigned to multiple rule subspaces covered by a policy segment, if the effect of this policy segment can be determined by any of these rules. We next introduce three processes to perform the property assignments to all of rule subspaces within the segments of a policy, considering different categories of policy segments.

Process1: *Property assignment for the rule subspace covered by a non-overlapping segment.* A non-overlapping segment contains only one rule subspace. Thus, this rule subspace is assigned with *strong irremovable* property. Other rule subspaces associated with the same rule are assigned with *weak irremovable* property, excepting the rule subspaces that already have *strong irremovable* property.

Process2: *Property assignment for rule subspaces covered by a conflicting segment.* We present this property assignment process based on the following three cases of rule combining algorithm ($\mathcal{CA}$).

1. $\mathcal{CA}$=*First-Applicable*: In this case, the first rule subspace covered by the conflicting segment is assigned with *strong irremovable* property. Other rule subspaces in the same segment are assigned with *removable* property. Meanwhile, other rule subspaces associated with the same rule are assigned with *weak irremovable* property except the rule subspaces already having *strong irremovable* property.

2. $\mathcal{CA}$=*Permit-Overrides*: All subspaces of "deny" rules in this conflicting segment are assigned with *removable* property. If there is only one "permit" rule subspace, this case is handled which is similar to the *First-Applicable* case. If any "permit" rule subspace has been assigned with *weak irremovable* property, other rule subspaces without *irremovable* property are assigned with *removable* property. Otherwise, all "permit" rule subspaces are assigned with *correlated* property.

3. $\mathcal{CA}$=*Deny-Overrides*: This case is dealt with as the same as *Permit-Overrides* case.

Process3: *Property assignment for rule subspaces covered by a non-conflicting overlapping segment.* If any rule subspace has been assigned with *weak irremovable* property, other rule subspaces without *irremovable* property are assigned with *removable* property. Otherwise, all subspaces within the segment are assigned with *correlated* property.

Figure 7(b) shows the result of applying our property assignment mechanism, which performs three property assignment processes in sequence, to the example presented in Figure 7(a). We can easily identify that r_3 and r_8 are *removable* rules, where all subspaces are with *removable* property. However, we need to further examine the *correlated* rules r_2, r_4 or r_7, which contain some subspaces with *correlated* property. The extension with correlation break algorithm remains in our future work. Figure 7(c) depicts the result of redundancy removal for the example.

5.2 Redundancy Elimination at Policy Set Level

Similar to the solution of conflict detection at policy set level, we handle the redundancy removal for a policy set based on an

XACML tree structure representation. If the children nodes of the policy set is a policy node in the tree, we perform `RedundancyEliminate_P()` function to eliminate redundancies. Otherwise, `RedundancyEliminate_PS()` function is excused recursively to eliminate redundancy in a policy set component.

After each component of a policy set PS performs redundancy removal, the authorization space of PS can be then partitioned into disjoint segments by performing `Partition()` function. Note that, in the solution for conflict detection at policy set level, we aggregate authorization subspaces of each child node before performing space partition, because we only need to identify conflicts among children nodes to guide the selection of policy combining algorithms for the policy set. However, for redundancy removal at policy set level, both redundancies among children nodes and rule (leaf node) redundancies, which may exist across multiple policies or policy sets, should be discovered. Therefore, we keep the original segments of each child node and leverage those segments to generate the authorization space segments of PS. Figure 8 demonstrates an example of authorization space segmentation of a policy set PS with three children components P_1, P_2 and P_3. The authorization space segments of PS are constructed based on the original segments of each child component. For instance, a segment s_2' of PS covers three policy segments $P_1.s_1$, $P_2.s_1$ and $P_3.s_2$, where $P_i.s_j$ denotes that a segment s_j belongs to a policy P_i.

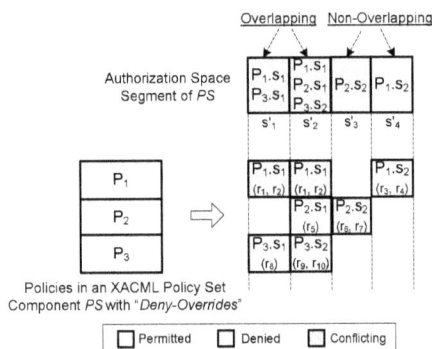

Figure 8: Example of authorization space segmentation at policy set level for redundancy discovery and removal.

The property assignment step at policy set level is similar to the property assignment step at policy level, except that the policy combining algorithm *Only-One-Applicable* needs to be taken into consideration at policy set level. The *Only-One-Applicable* case is handled similar to the *First-Applicable* case. We first check whether the combining algorithm is applicable or not. If the combining algorithm is applicable, the only-applicable subspace is assigned with *strong irremovable* property. Otherwise, all subspaces within the policy set's segment are assigned with *removable* property.

After assigning properties to all segments of children components of PS, we next examine whether any child component is redundant. If a child component is redundant, this child component and all rules contained in the child component are removed from PS. Then, we examine whether there exist any redundant rules. In this process, the properties of all rule subspaces covered by a *removable* segment of a child component of PS needs to be changed to *removable*. Note that when we change the property of a *strong irremovable* rule subspace to *removable*, other subspaces in the same rule with dependent *weak irremovable* property need to be changed to *removable* correspondingly.

6. IMPLEMENTATION AND EVALUATION

We have implemented a policy analysis tool called `XAnalyzer` in Java. Based on our policy anomaly analysis mechanism, it consists of four core components: segmentation module, effect constraint generation module, strategy mapping module, and property assignment module. The segmentation module takes XACML policies as an input and identifies the authorization space segments by partitioning the authorization space into disjoint subspaces. `XAnalyzer` utilizes APIs provided by *Sun* XACML implementation [4] to parse the XACML policies and construct Boolean encoding. JavaBDD [2], which is based on BuDDy package [1], is employed by `XAnalyzer` to support BDD representation and authorization space operations. The effect constraint generation module takes conflicting segments as an input and generates effect constraints for each conflicting segment. Effect constraints are generated based on strategies assigned to each conflicting segment. The strategy mapping module takes conflict correlation groups and effect constraints of conflicting segments as inputs and then maps assigned strategies to standard XACML combining algorithms for examined XACML policy components. The property assignment module automatically assigns corresponding property to each subspace covered by the segments of XACML policy components. The assigned properties are in turn utilized to identify redundancies.

Table 2: XACML policies used for evaluation.

Policy	Rule (#)	Policy (#)	Policy Set (#)
1 (CodeA)	4	2	5
2 (SamplePolicy)	6	2	1
3 (GradeSheet)	13	1	0
4 (Pluto)	22	1	0
5 (SyntheticPolicy-1)	147	30	11
6 (Continue-a)	312	276	111
7 (Continue-b)	336	305	111
8 (SyntheticPolicy-2)	456	65	40
9 (SyntheticPolicy-3)	572	114	75
10 (SyntheticPolicy-4)	685	188	84

We evaluated the efficiency and effectiveness of `XAnalyzer` for policy analysis on both real-life and synthetic XACML policies. Our experiments were performed on Intel Core 2 Duo CPU 3.00 GHz with 3.25 GB RAM running on Windows XP SP2. In our evaluation, we utilized five real-life XACML policies, which were collected from different sources. Three of the policies, *CodeA*, *Continue-a* and *Continue-b* are XACML policies used in [14]; among them, *Continue-a* and *Continue-b* are designed for a real-world Web application supporting a conference management. *GradeSheet* is utilized in [11]. The *Pluto* policy is employed in ARCHON [2] system, which is a digital library that federates the collections of physics with multiple degrees of meta data richness. Since it is hard to get a large volume of real-world policies due to the reason that they are often considered to be highly confidential, we generated four large synthetic policies *SyntheticPolicy-1*, *SyntheticPolicy-2*, *SyntheticPolicy-3* and *SyntheticPolicy-4* for further evaluating the performance and scalability of our tool. We also use *SamplePolicy*, which is the example XACML policy represented in Figure 1, in our experiments. Table 2 summarizes the basic information of each policy including the number of rules, the number of policies, and the number of policy sets.

We conducted two separate sets of experiments for the evaluation of conflict detection approach and the evaluation of redundancy removal approach, respectively. Also, we performed evaluations at both policy level and policy set level. Table 3 summarizes our evaluation results.

[Evaluation of Conflict Detection]: Time required by `XAnalyzer`

---
[2] http://archon.cs.odu.edu/

Table 3: Conflict detection and redundancy removal algorithms evaluation.

Policy	Partitions (#)	BDD Nodes (#)	Conflict Detection			Redundant Removal		
			Policy Level(#)	Policy Set Level(#)	Time (s)	Policy Level(#)	Policy Set Level(#)	Time (s)
1 (CodeA)	6	16	1	1	0.082	1	0	0.087
2 (SamplePolicy)	8	34	0	2	0.090	0	2	0.095
3 (GradeSheet)	18	45	0	4	0.098	0	2	0.113
4 (Pluto)	34	78	0	5	0.136	0	3	0.147
5 (SyntheticPolicy-1)	205	112	8	14	0.329	7	4	0.158
6 (Continue-a)	439	135	9	17	0.583	10	7	0.214
7 (Continue-b)	468	146	10	21	0.635	12	6	0.585
8 (SyntheticPolicy-2)	523	209	29	17	0.896	14	8	0.623
9 (SyntheticPolicy-3)	614	227	39	19	0.948	16	9	0.672
10 (SyntheticPolicy-4)	814	265	56	19	1.123	21	11	0.803

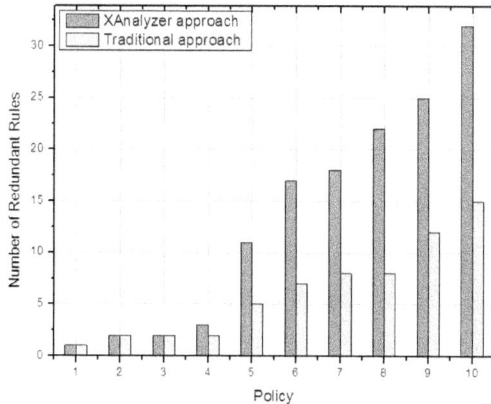

Figure 9: Evaluation of redundancy removal approach.

for conflict detection highly depends upon the number of segments generated for each XACML policy. The increase of the number of segments is proportional to the number of components contained in an XACML policy. From Table 3, we observe that XAnalyzer performs fast enough to handle larger size XACML policies, even for some complex policies with multiple levels of hierarchies along with hundreds of rules, such as two real-life XACML policies *Continue-a* and *Continue-b* and four synthetic XACML policies. The time trends observed from Table 3 are promising, and hence provide the evidence of efficiency of our conflict detection approach.

[**Evaluation of Redundancy Removal**]: In the second set of experiments, we evaluated our redundancy analysis approach based on those experimental XACML policies. The evaluation results shown in Table 3 also indicate the efficiency of our redundancy analysis algorithm. Moreover, we conducted the evaluation of effectiveness by comparing our redundancy analysis approach with *traditional* redundancy analysis approach [7, 22], which can only identify redundancy relations between *two* rules. Figure 9 depicts the results of our comparison experiments. From Figure 9, we observed that XAnalyzer could identify that an average of 6.2% of total rules are redundant. However, *traditional* redundancy analysis approach could only detect an average 3.7% of total rules as redundant rules. Therefore, the enhancement for redundancy elimination was clearly observed by our redundancy analysis approach compared to *traditional* redundancy analysis approach in our experiments.

7. RELATED WORK

Many research efforts have been devoted to XACML. However, most existing research work focus on modeling and verification of XACML policies [6, 12, 17, 14, 19]. None of them dealt with anomaly analysis in XACML policies. We discuss a few of those work here.

In [12], the authors formalized XACML policies using a process algebra known as Communicating Sequential Processes (CSP). This work utilizes a model checker to formally verify properties of policies, and to compare access control policies with each other. Fisler et al. [14] introduced an approach to represent XACML policies with Multi-Terminal Binary Decision Diagrams (MTBDDs). A policy analysis tool called Margrave was developed. Margrave can verify XACML policies against the given properties and perform change-impact analysis based on the semantic differences between the MTBDDs representing the policies. Ahn et al. [6] presented a formalization of XACML using answer set programming (ASP), which is a recent form of declarative programming, and leveraged existing ASP reasoners to conduct policy verification.

Several work presenting policy analysis tools with the goal of detecting policy anomalies in firewall are closely related to our work. Al-Shaer et al. [7] designed a tool called Firewall Policy Advisor which can only detect *pairwise* anomalies in firewall rules. Yuan et al. [28] presented a toolkit, FIREMAN, which can detect anomalies among *multiple* firewall rules by analyzing the relationships between *one* rule and the collections of packet spaces derived from all preceding rules. However, the anomaly detection procedures of FIREMAN are still incomplete [8]. Our tool, XAnalyzer, could conduct a complete examination of policy anomaly and provide more accurate anomaly diagnosis information for policy analysis. On the other hand, as we discussed previously, XACML policy and firewall policy have some significant distinctions. Hence, directly applying prior policy anomaly analysis approaches to XACML are not suitable.

Some XACML policy evaluation engines, such as *Sun* PDP [4] and XEngine [21], have been developed to handle the process of evaluating whether a request satisfies an XACML policy. During the process of policy enforcement, conflicts can be checked if a request matches multiple rules having different effects, and then conflicts are resolved by applying predefined combining algorithms in the policy. In contrast, our tool XAnalyzer focuses on policy analysis at policy *design* time. XAnalyzer can identify all conflicts within a policy and help policy designers select appropriate combining algorithms for conflict resolution prior to the policy enforcement. Additionally, XAnalyzer has the capability of discovering and eliminating policy redundancies that cannot be dealt with by policy evaluation engines.

Some work addressed the general conflict resolution mechanisms for access control including Fundulaki et al. [15], Fisler et al. [14] and Jajodia et al. [18]. Especially, Li et al. [20] proposed a policy combining language PCL, which can be utilized to specify a variety of user-defined combining algorithms for XACML. These conflict resolution mechanisms can be accommodated in our fine-grained conflict resolution framework.

Other related work includes XACML policy integration [24, 25, 26] and XACML policy optimization [21, 23]. Since anomaly discovery and resolution are challenging issues in policy integration and redundancy elimination can contribute in policy optimization, all of those related work are orthogonal to our work.

8. CONCLUSION

We have proposed an innovative mechanism that facilitates systematic detection and resolution of XACML policy anomalies. A policy-based segmentation technique was introduced to achieve the goals of effective and efficient anomaly analysis. In addition, we have described an implementation of a policy anomaly analysis tool called XAnalyzer. Our experimental results showed that a policy designer could easily discover and resolve anomalies in an XACML policy with the help of XAnalyzer. We believe our systematic mechanism and tool will significantly help policy managers support an assurable Web application management service.

As our future work, the coverage of our approach needs to be further extended with respect to obligations and user-defined functions in XACML. In addition, we would like to extend our tool with information visualization techniques [16], providing an intuitive cognitive sense for policy anomaly to facilitate a more effective policy management. Moreover, we would explore how our anomaly analysis mechanism can be applied to other existing access control policy languages.

Acknowledgments

This work was partially supported by the grants from National Science Foundation (NSF-IIS-0900970 and NSF-CNS-0831360) and Department of Energy (DE-SC0004308 and DE-FG02-03ER25565).

9. REFERENCES

[1] Buddy version 2.4. http://sourceforge.net/projects/buddy.

[2] Java BDD. http://javabdd.sourceforge.net.

[3] OASIS eXtensible Access Control Markup Language (XACML) TC. http://www.oasis-open.org/committees/xacml/.

[4] Sun XACML Implementation. http://sunxacml.sourceforge.net.

[5] D. Agrawal, J. Giles, K. Lee, and J. Lobo. Policy ratification. In *Sixth IEEE International Workshop on Policies for Distributed Systems and Networks, 2005*, pages 223–232, 2005.

[6] G. Ahn, H. Hu, J. Lee, and Y. Meng. Representing and Reasoning about Web Access Control Policies. In *34th Annual IEEE Computer Software and Applications Conference*, pages 137–146. IEEE, 2010.

[7] E. Al-Shaer and H. Hamed. Discovery of policy anomalies in distributed firewalls. In *IEEE INFOCOM*, volume 4, pages 2605–2616. Citeseer, 2004.

[8] J. Alfaro, N. Boulahia-Cuppens, and F. Cuppens. Complete analysis of configuration rules to guarantee reliable network security policies. *International Journal of Information Security*, 7(2):103–122, 2008.

[9] A. Anderson. Evaluating xacml as a policy language. In *Technical report*. OASIS, 2003.

[10] F. Baboescu and G. Varghese. Fast and scalable conflict detection for packet classifiers. *Computer Networks*, 42(6):717–735, 2003.

[11] A. Birgisson, M. Dhawan, U. Erlingsson, V. Ganapathy, and L. Iftode. Enforcing authorization policies using transactional memory introspection. In *Proceedings of the 15th ACM conference on Computer and communications security*, pages 223–234. ACM New York, NY, USA, 2008.

[12] J. Bryans. Reasoning about XACML policies using CSP. In *Proceedings of the 2005 workshop on Secure web services*, page 35. ACM, 2005.

[13] R. Bryant. Graph-based algorithms for boolean function manipulation. *IEEE Transactions on computers*, 100(35):677–691, 1986.

[14] K. Fisler, S. Krishnamurthi, L. A. Meyerovich, and M. C. Tschantz. Verification and change-impact analysis of access-control policies. In *ICSE '05: Proceedings of the 27th international conference on Software engineering*, pages 196–205, New York, NY, USA, 2005. ACM.

[15] I. Fundulaki and M. Marx. Specifying access control policies for XML documents with XPath. In *Proceedings of the ninth ACM symposium on Access control models and technologies*, pages 61–69. ACM New York, NY, USA, 2004.

[16] I. Herman, G. Melançon, and M. Marshall. Graph visualization and navigation in information visualization: A survey. *IEEE Transactions on Visualization and Computer Graphics*, pages 24–43, 2000.

[17] G. Hughes and T. Bultan. Automated verification of access control policies. *Computer Science Department, University of California, Santa Barbara, CA*, 93106:2004–22.

[18] S. Jajodia, P. Samarati, and V. S. Subrahmanian. A logical language for expressing authorizations. In *IEEE Symposium on Security and Privacy*, pages 31–42, Oakland, CA, May 1997.

[19] V. Kolovski, J. Hendler, and B. Parsia. Analyzing web access control policies. In *Proceedings of the 16th international conference on World Wide Web*, page 686. ACM, 2007.

[20] N. Li, Q. Wang, W. Qardaji, E. Bertino, P. Rao, J. Lobo, and D. Lin. Access control policy combining: theory meets practice. In *Proceedings of the 14th ACM symposium on Access control models and technologies*, pages 135–144. ACM, 2009.

[21] A. Liu, F. Chen, J. Hwang, and T. Xie. Xengine: A fast and scalable xacml policy evaluation engine. *ACM SIGMETRICS Performance Evaluation Review*, 36(1):265–276, 2008.

[22] E. Lupu and M. Sloman. Conflicts in policy-based distributed systems management. *IEEE Transactions on software engineering*, 25(6):852–869, 1999.

[23] S. Marouf, M. Shehab, A. Squicciarini, and S. Sundareswaran. Statistics & Clustering Based Framework for Efficient XACML Policy Evaluation. In *IEEE International Symposium on Policies for Distributed Systems and Networks*, pages 118–125. IEEE, 2009.

[24] P. Mazzoleni, B. Crispo, S. Sivasubramanian, and E. Bertino. XACML Policy Integration Algorithms. *ACM Transactions on Information and System Security*, 11(1), 2008.

[25] Q. Ni, E. Bertino, and J. Lobo. D-algebra for composing access control policy decisions. In *Proceedings of the 4th International Symposium on Information, Computer, and Communications Security*, pages 298–309. ACM, 2009.

[26] P. Rao, D. Lin, E. Bertino, N. Li, and J. Lobo. An algebra for fine-grained integration of xacml policies. In *Proceedings of the 14th ACM symposium on Access control models and technologies*, pages 63–72. ACM, 2009.

[27] XACML. OASIS eXtensible Access Control Markup Language (XACML) V2.0 Specification Set. http://www.oasis-open.org/committees/xacml/, 2007.

[28] L. Yuan, H. Chen, J. Mai, C. Chuah, Z. Su, P. Mohapatra, and C. Davis. Fireman: A toolkit for firewall modeling and analysis. In *2006 IEEE Symposium on Security and Privacy*, page 15, 2006.

On the Management of User Obligations

Murillo Pontual
The University of Texas at San Antonio
mpontual@cs.utsa.edu

Omar Chowdhury
The University of Texas at San Antonio
ochowdhu@cs.utsa.edu

William H. Winsborough
The University of Texas at San Antonio
wwinsborough@acm.org

Ting Yu
North Carolina State University
tyu@ncsu.edu

Keith Irwin
Winston-Salem State University
irwinke@wssu.edu

ABSTRACT

This paper is part of a project investigating authorization systems that assign obligations to users. We are particularly interested in obligations that require authorization to be performed and that, when performed, may modify the authorization state. In this context, a user may incur an obligation she is unauthorized to perform. Prior work has introduced a property of the authorization system state that ensures users will be authorized to fulfill their obligations. We call this property *accountability* because users that fail to perform authorized obligations are accountable for their non-performance. While a reference monitor can mitigate violations of accountability, it cannot prevent them entirely. This paper presents techniques to be used by obligation system managers to restore accountability. We introduce several notions of dependence among pending obligations that must be considered in this process. We also introduce a novel notion we call *obligation pool slicing*, owing to its similarity to program slicing. An obligation pool slice identifies a set of obligations that the administrator may need to consider when applying strategies proposed here for restoring accountability. The paper also presents the system architecture of an authorization system that incorporates obligations that can require and affect authorizations.

Categories and Subject Descriptors

K.6.5 [**Management of Computing and Information Systems**]: Security and Protection

General Terms

Security, Theory

Keywords

Obligations, RBAC, Policy, Authorization, Accountability

1. INTRODUCTION

Obligations are actions that principals are required to perform, often within a pre-defined time interval. The majority

of previous work focuses on obligations [4, 6] that are to be performed by computer systems instead of users. Relatively few researchers [8, 12, 15] have focused on obligations that are performed by users, where they can affect and depend on the system's authorization state. A correctly functioning system has predictable behavior, while a human does not. This raises complexity in designing and analyzing a user obligation system. In particular, it makes it essential to have deadlines. One such situation arises when a user Alice is assigned an obligation to perform an action in July of the next year, but she currently does not have the proper authorization to perform the action. Unless someone gives Alice the proper authorization beforehand, her request to perform the obligatory action will be denied. The inevitability of this outcome may not be discovered until she attempts that action.

Irwin *et al.* [8] were the first to study user obligations that affect and depend on authorizations. They introduced a property of the authorization state and the obligation pool called *strong accountability* that guarantees each obligatory action will be authorized during the entire time interval associated with the obligation. They present a polynomial time decision procedure for strong accountability. To accomplish this, they made an additional assumption that obligatory actions do not incur further obligations (*cascading of obligations*). In this work, we make the same assumption. This is a strong restriction and it makes our model less expressive. The challenges of deciding accountability in presence of cascading obligations is discussed later (subsection 2.3).

The property's name, accountability, reflects the fact that it is appropriate for an organization to hold accountable those that fail to perform authorized obligations. (A related notion called "weak accountability" was also introduced. However deciding weak accountability is intractable; when we refer to accountability, we mean strong accountability.) To the extent that it can be maintained, accountability is helpful for heightening the benefits derived by assigning user obligations. These benefits include facilitating effective planning, including obtaining early warning when plans are infeasible, as well as transparency and awareness of which users are failing to fulfill their duties and the impact of such failures.

Deciding whether a system state is accountable requires reasoning about future states of the authorization system. It is reasonable to assign to a user an obligation that the user is not currently authorized to perform, provided that other obligations will grant that authorization prior to the time the first obligation must be performed.

As we have discussed elsewhere [8,15], a reference monitor can help maintain accountability by preventing actions that would cause it to be violated. However, even with such a reference monitor in place, accountability is still violated when an obligation is not or will not be performed. For instance, if a user fails to fulfill an obligation, say, to grant Alice the rights she needs next July, the system will become unaccountable, and Alice will be unable to perform her own obligation. Thus, an obligation system manager needs strategies and support tools that she can use to restore accountability. Three of the four present contributions seek to address these needs.

The prior work that has studied accountability [8,9,15,16] focused on several technical problems. However, the architecture of a user obligation management system has never been presented. This is the **first contribution** of this paper. We give a brief overview of each of the components of the framework and discuss their interaction. A central organizing principle of the architecture is that the system should be in an accountable state as much of the time as possible without interfering unnecessarily with usability. We also provide an example illustrating the utility of this goal.

As part of supporting an obligation system manager in restoring accountability, we present three forms of dependency that can exist among obligations within a system's obligation pool. While functional dependencies also exist, here we focus exclusively on dependencies that are based on authorization requirements. The three kinds of authorization dependencies we formalize are positive dependency, negative dependency, and antagonistic dependency. This is our **second contribution**.

Borrowing a term from programming languages, we introduce what we call a *slice* of an obligation pool. A slice of a program is a subset of the statements in a program that define a portion of the program's behavior [20]. In our context, a slice is a subset of the current pool of pending obligations. We introduce two kinds of slice. One is based on positive dependency among obligations. The other is based on all three forms of dependency mentioned above. An obligation system manager who is working on restoring accountability can use a slice of the current obligation pool to identify which obligations she needs to consider modifying. As we shall see, the choice of which kind of slice to use depends on the strategy being applied to the restoration of accountability. This is our **third contribution**.

Our **final contribution** consists of several strategies that an obligation system manager can use for accountability restoration. These strategies can be supported by AI planning techniques [16] and by tools that compute the kinds of obligation pool slice discussed above.

The remainder of this paper is organized as follows. Section 2 provides background necessary to understand our contributions. Section 3 presents our architecture for managing user obligations that depend and affect authorization. Section 4 introduces the notion of authorization dependency between obligations and also the slice properties. In section 5, we present approaches that can be used by an administrator for restoring accountability. Section 6 discusses related work. Section 7 discusses future work and concludes.

2. BACKGROUND

This section reviews the obligation model that we use for studying the interaction between authorizations and obligations that depend upon and affect them. It recalls simplified versions of the RBAC model and the administrative ARBAC model that fulfill our study's need for an authorization system that supports changes in authorization state. It summarizes the notion of accountability, which is a property of the obligation system state that ensures required authorizations are available to enable the fulfillment of obligations under the assumption that users are diligent in attempting to fulfill their obligations. Based on a software development-environment scenario, an example is presented that introduces some aspects of the problem of restoring accountability when it has been violated and preventing its violation ahead of time when doing so is possible. Building on that scenario, we finally show that even the simple approach of reassigning obligations, for instance when a user leaves the company, involves solving a PSPACE-hard problem. We show how some of our prior work will be used to address this aspect as part of a solution to the larger problem that we take it on in later sections.

2.1 An Obligation Model

This section summarizes the essential elements of the obligation system used in our study [8,15]. At any given point in time, the set of users $U \subseteq \mathcal{U}$ in the system is finite, but unbounded (which requires that $\mathcal{U}$, the universe of users, be countably infinite). We denote users by u, possibly with subscripts. Objects follow the same pattern. The set of objects in the system is given by $O \subseteq \mathcal{O}$ and individuals are ranged over by o. To accommodate administrative operations, we require that $\mathcal{U} \subseteq \mathcal{O}$. The set of supported actions is given by $\mathcal{A}$. Each $a \in \mathcal{A}$ is parameterized by the user requesting the action and zero or more objects (denoted by $\vec{o}$) to which the action will be applied. The type of a will be given later. At any given point in time, the state of the system is given by $s = \langle U, O, t, \gamma, B \rangle$, in which $t \in \mathcal{T}$ is the current time, $\gamma \in \Gamma$ is an authorization state (in the current paper we use mini-RBAC as the authorization model, defined just below); B is a pool of *pending* obligations. An obligation has the form $b = \langle u, a, \vec{o}, \text{start}, \text{end} \rangle \in \mathcal{B}$ and $B \subseteq \mathcal{B}$, where $\mathcal{B} = \mathcal{U} \times \mathcal{A} \times \mathcal{O}^* \times \mathcal{T} \times \mathcal{T}$ is the universe of obligations[1]. Times start and end delimit the *interval* during which the obligation must be performed. We use record field-selection notations such as $b.u$ to select the user of b and require that $b.\text{start} < b.\text{end}$. Note that $b.\vec{o}$ is a tuple of objects to which the action $b.a$ must be applied by $b.u$.

At each point in time, an obligation b is in one the following states: pending, fulfilled or violated. We say b is *fulfilled* if the action identified in b has been executed during b's time interval. We say b is *violated* if b was not executed in the proper time and the current time is greater than $b.\text{end}$. Finally, we say b is *pending* if the current time is less than $b.\text{end}$ and b has not yet been executed.

A pending obligation can be in one of the two states, available or unavailable. We say b is *available* if b is pending and all the resources, authorization and users required to fulfill b are available. On the other hand, b is *unavailable* if b is pending and one of the following is not available during b's entire time interval: authorization, user, or resources. Of

---

[1] We use $\mathcal{O}^*$ to represent the Cartesian product of zero or more copies of $\mathcal{O}$.

principal interest to us here is guaranteeing authorization availability. (Ensuring user availability and resource availability are matters for future work.)

2.2 mini-RBAC and mini-ARBAC

The widely studied ARBAC97 model [17] has been simplified by Sasturkar *et al.* for the purpose of studying policy analysis, forming a family of languages called *mini-RBAC* and *mini-ARBAC* [18]. The member of the family that we use, supports administrative actions that modify user-role assignments, but does not consider role hierarchies, sessions, mutual exclusion of roles, changes to permission-role assignments, or role administration operations. As we are combining our model with the mini-RBAC authorization state, some redundancy are shared between the models, more specifically the set of users U is the same for both models.

DEFINITION 1 (MINI-RBAC MODEL). *A mini-RBAC model is a tuple $\gamma = \langle U, R, P, UA, PA \rangle$ in which:*

- *R and P are the finite sets of roles and permissions respectively. While P remains abstract in most RBAC models, for simplicity we assume $P \subseteq \mathcal{A} \times \mathcal{O}^*$.*
- *$UA \subseteq U \times R$ indicates users' role memberships.*
- *$PA \subseteq R \times P$ indicates permissions assigned to each role.*

DEFINITION 2 (MINI-ARBAC POLICY). *A mini-ARBAC policy is a tuple $\psi = \langle CA, CR \rangle$ in which:*

- *$CA \subseteq R \times \mathcal{C} \times R$ is a set of can_assign rules, in which $\mathcal{C}$ is the set of preconditions. A precondition is a conjunction of positive and negative role memberships, denoted by c. Each $\langle r_a, c, r_t \rangle \in CA$ indicates that users in role r_a are authorized to assign a user to the target role r_t, provided the current role memberships of the target user u_t satisfy precondition c. In this case we write $u_t \vDash_\gamma c$. For instance $u_t \vDash_\gamma r_1 \wedge \neg r_2$ if $\langle u_t, r_1 \rangle \in \gamma.UA$ and $\langle u_t, r_2 \rangle \notin \gamma.UA$.*
- *$CR \subseteq R \times \mathcal{C} \times R$ is a set of can_revoke rules. Each $\langle r_a, c, r_t \rangle \in CR$ indicates that a user in role r_a can revoke the role r_t from any target user if her current role memberships satisfy precondition c.*

For examples of mini-RBAC model and mini-ARBAC policy consult the technical report version of this paper [1].

2.3 State Transitions for Obligation Model

User-initiated actions are events from the point of view of our system. We denote the universe of events that correspond to nonobligatory, discretionary actions by $\mathcal{D} = \mathcal{U} \times \mathcal{A} \times \mathcal{O}^*$. We denote the universe of all events, obligatory and discretionary, by $\mathcal{E} = \mathcal{D} \cup \mathcal{B}$.

Obligations are introduced in our system when users perform nonobligatory actions. This is done according to a fixed set of policy rules $\mathcal{P}$. A policy rule $p \in \mathcal{P}$ has the form $p = a(u, \vec{o}) \leftarrow cond(u, \vec{o}, a) : F_{obl}(s, u, \vec{o})$, in which $a \in \mathcal{A}$ (which means $\langle u, a, \vec{o} \rangle \in \mathcal{E}$) and *cond* is a predicate that must be satisfied by $(u, \vec{o}, a)$ (denoted $\gamma \vDash cond(u, \vec{o}, a)$) in the current authorization state γ when the rule is used to authorize the action. F_{obl} is an *obligation function*, which returns a finite set $B \subseteq \mathcal{B}$ of obligations incurred (by u or by others) when the action is performed under this rule. Each action a denotes a curried function of type $(\mathcal{U} \times \mathcal{O}^*) \rightarrow (\mathcal{FP}(\mathcal{U}) \times \mathcal{FP}(\mathcal{O}) \times \Gamma) \rightarrow (\mathcal{FP}(\mathcal{U}) \times \mathcal{FP}(\mathcal{O}) \times \Gamma)^2$.

---

[2]We use $\mathcal{FP}(\mathcal{X}) = \{X \subset \mathcal{X} | X \text{ is finite}\}$ to denote the set of finite subsets of the given set.

So, given a user u and a tuple of objects $\vec{o}$, $a(u, \vec{o})$ is a mapping that, when applied to the user set, object set, and authorization state of the current state, returns the values of these structures in the new system state. We require that $\forall a \in \mathcal{A} \cdot \exists p \in \mathcal{P} \cdot p.a = a$. Here, u and $\vec{o}$ are variables and the objects in $\vec{o}$ are the arguments given in the invocation of a. So, for instance, if read(bookA) is attempted, then a = read and $\vec{o} = \langle bookA \rangle$. We say that a is an administrative action (denoted by $a \in$ administrative) if it has the form $\langle u, grant/revoke, \vec{o} \rangle$, otherwise a is a non-administrative action (denoted by $a \notin$ administrative).

When one obligation leads to another being incurred, we call these *cascading* obligations. The obligation model discussed in this paper prevents cascading by partitioning $\mathcal{A}$ into those actions that can be discretionary and those that can be obligatory, and statically ensuring that policy rules for the latter do not add obligations. Preliminary investigations of allowing cascading suggest that the accountability problem is likely to be computationally expensive and that accountable system states are likely to be uncommon, making systems that maintain the property unusable. More specifically, three issues make supporting cascading difficult and unproductive with our current model. (i) Different policy rules can cause different (disjunctive) obligations to be incurred, making it computationally expensive to reason about the future state of the obligation pool and authorization system. (ii) Cycles can easily be formed that introduce the likelihood of infinite sequences of new obligations being incurred as the result of a single action. (iii) In the current model, the time intervals during which new obligations are to be performed depend on the time at which the action that causes them to be incurred is performed. As obligations are scheduled times further from the current time are considered, the time intervals in which obligatory actions could occur become longer. This makes it increasingly unlikely that these obligations will be authorized throughout the entire interval in which they must be to satisfy accountability.

Clearly, cascading obligations are important in many potential deployment environments. A design meeting this requirement is a matter of future work, in which we plan to alter and/or extend the current model.

Let us now consider the transition from state s to some state s' that occurs when an event e is handled according to policy rule p. The fact that this is the transition taken is denoted by $s \xrightarrow{\langle e, p \rangle} s'$. Letting $e = (u, a, \vec{o})$, we require that $u \in s.U$ and $\vec{o} \in s.O^*$. The action $a(u, \vec{o})$ determines the values $(s'.U, s'.O, s'.\gamma)$ based on $(s.U, s.O, s.\gamma)$. Thus, actions can introduce and remove users and objects and change the authorization state. The condition, $cond(u, \vec{o}, a)$, in the policy rule p must be satisfied for p to be used in the transition; p determines any new obligations added in obtaining $s'.B$ from $s.B$. These points are formalized in definition 4 below.

There are three cases in which a user u is authorized to perform an action a on an object tuple $\vec{o}$. (i) When a is non-administrative, authorization depends on the permissions assigned to u's roles; (ii) when a grants a role, there must be a *can_assign* rule for one of u's roles such that the target user u_t satisfies the precondition; (iii) when a revokes a role, a similar requirement holds on the existence of a *can_revoke* rule. This is formalized in definition 3.

The transition relation presented in definition 4 preserves the invariant over states $s = \langle U, O, t, \gamma, B \rangle$ given by $\forall b \in s.B \cdot (b.u \in s.U) \wedge (b.o^* \subseteq \mathcal{O}^*)$ and $s.U = s.\gamma.U$.

DEFINITION 3. *For all $u \in \mathcal{U}$ and $\vec{o} \in \mathcal{O}^*$, $\gamma \models cond(u, \vec{o}, a)$ if and only if the following holds.*

$$(\exists r).(((u, r) \in \gamma.UA) \wedge$$

(i) $\quad [a \notin \text{administrative} \rightarrow (\langle r, \langle a, \vec{o} \rangle \rangle \in \gamma.PA)] \wedge$

(ii) $\quad (\forall u_t, r_t).[a = grant \wedge \vec{o} = \langle u_t, r_t \rangle \rightarrow$

$$(\exists c).((\langle r, c, r_t \rangle \in \psi.CA) \wedge (u_t \models_\gamma c))] \wedge$$

(iii) $\quad (\forall u_t, r_t).[a = revoke \wedge \vec{o} = \langle u_t, r_t \rangle \rightarrow$

$$(\exists c).((\langle r, c, r_t \rangle \in \psi.CR) \wedge (u_t \models_\gamma c))])$$

DEFINITION 4 (TRANSITION RELATION). *Given any sequence of event/policy-rule pairs, $\langle e, p \rangle_{0..k}$[3], and any sequence of system states $s_{0..k+1}$, the relation $\longrightarrow \subseteq \mathcal{S} \times (\mathcal{E} \times \mathcal{P})^+ \times \mathcal{S}$ is defined inductively on $k \in \mathbb{N}$ as follows:*

(1) $s_k \xrightarrow{\langle e, p \rangle_k} s_{k+1}$ holds if and only if, letting $p_k = a(u, \vec{o}) \leftarrow cond(u, \vec{o}, a) : F_{obl}(s, u, \vec{o})$, we have $s_k.\gamma \models cond(e_k.u, e_k.\vec{o}, e_k.a)$, and $s_{k+1} = \langle U'', O'', t'', \gamma'', B'' \rangle$, in which $\langle U'', O'', \gamma'' \rangle = a(u, \vec{o})(s_k.U, s_k.O, s_k.\gamma)$, $B'' = (s_k.B - \{e\})$ when $e_k \in \mathcal{B}$, and $B'' = s_k.B \cup F_{obl}(s_k, e_k.u, e_k.\vec{o})$ otherwise.

(2) $s_0 \xrightarrow{\langle e, p \rangle_{0..k}} s_{k+1}$ if and only if there exists $s_k \in \mathcal{S}$ such that $s_0 \xrightarrow{\langle e, p \rangle_{0..k-1}} s_k$ and $s_k \xrightarrow{\langle e, p \rangle_k} s_{k+1}$.

Note that a reference monitor in our obligation system is going to require more than simply that a transition is well defined to permit an action to be performed according to a given policy rule. It will further require that performing the action and adding any obligations required by the policy rule leaves the system in an accountable state. The next section specifies the property of accountability.

2.4 Strong Accountability Property

As discussed in the introduction, even though users are capable of failing to fulfill their obligations, it is very helpful to make use of a conditional notion of correctness that says, roughly, assuming the users fulfill their obligations diligently, all users will be authorized to perform their obligations. This section formalizes that notion. This notion is called (strong) accountability [8] [15].[4]

Accountability is defined in terms of hypothetical schedules according to which the given pool of obligations could be executed, starting in a given system state. Under the assumption that each prior obligation has been fulfilled during its specified time interval, accountability requires that each obligation be authorized throughout its entire time interval, no matter when during that interval the other obligations are scheduled, and no matter which policy rules are used to authorize them.

Given a set of obligations B, a *schedule* of B is a sequence $b_{0..n}$ that enumerates B, for $n = |B| - 1$. A schedule of B is *valid* if for all i and j, if $0 \le i < j \le n$, then $b_i.\text{start} \le b_j.\text{end}$. This prevents scheduling b_i before b_j if $b_j.\text{end} < b_i.\text{start}$. Given a system state s_0, and a policy $\mathcal{P}$, a proper prefix $b_{0..j}$

of a schedule $b_{0..n}$ for B is *authorized by* policy-rule sequence $p_{0..j} \subseteq \mathcal{P}^*$ if there exists s_{j+1} such that $s_0 \xrightarrow{\langle b, p \rangle_{0..j}} s_{j+1}$.

DEFINITION 5 (STRONG ACCOUNTABILITY). *Given a state $s_0 \in \mathcal{S}$ and a policy $\mathcal{P}$, we say that s_0 is strongly accountable if for every valid schedule, $b_{0..n}$, every proper prefix of it, $b_{0..k}$, for every policy-rule sequence $p_{0..k} \subseteq \mathcal{P}^*$ and every state s_{k+1} such that $s_0 \xrightarrow{\langle b, p \rangle_{0..k}} s_{k+1}$, there exists a policy rule p_{k+1} and a state s_{k+2} such that $s_{k+1} \xrightarrow{\langle b, p \rangle_{k+1}} s_{k+2}$.*

Please see [1] for an example of strong accountability.

2.5 Illustrations and Utility of Accountability

This section presents three simple examples in a software-development environment that illustrate the use of accountability in detecting that obligatory actions are unauthorized when the obligation is introduced, rather than when the action is attempted. Eve is a project manager. She uses the action *assignProjObl* to assign obligations to team members. The action *assignProjObl* takes as input the values that are placed into the new obligation[5].

Suppose that Alice's only role is that of a developer, which enables her to develop software. In scenario 1, Eve creates an obligation that requires Alice to perform black-box testing. In doing so, Eve makes the state unaccountable, as Alice does not have the requisite roles to perform this action. Thus, a reference monitor that enforces accountability prevents Eve from performing this *assignProjObl*. Without this intervention, the inadequacy of Alice's roles would be discovered only when Alice attempts to perform the testing.

Now suppose Bob has the role blackBoxTester. Assume that the organization uses mandatory vacation to help prevent insiders committing fraud and that Eve is responsible for ensuring her employees adhere to this policy. In scenario 2, Bob is required to take mandatory vacation in July. Eve adds obligations that Joan, in the role securityManager, remove Bob's roles while Bob is on vacation and restore them when he returns. Now, if Paul, another projectManager, tries to assign Bob an obligation to perform black-box testing in July, Paul will be prevented from doing so because Bob will not have the necessary roles that time. Paul discovers this when he tries to assign obligations to Bob rather than when Bob attempts to perform the task or fails to make the attempt due to being out of the office.

In scenario 3, suppose Bob already has an obligation to perform black-box testing of a software component. Should Joan attempt to revoke Bob's blackBoxTester role, she would be prevented because Bob will need it to fulfill his existing obligation. Under normal circumstances, this prevents Joan inadvertently removing a needed role. However, in some situations, such as when Bob leaves the company, Joan must be able to force the role revocation and in this case must remove or reassign Bob's obligations. Either of these courses of action could interact with other obligations

---

[3]Notation: for $j \in \mathbb{N}$, we use $s_{0..j}$ to denote the sequence $s_0, s_1, \ldots, s_j$, and for $\ell \in \mathbb{N}$, $\ell \le j$, $s_{0..\ell}$ denotes the prefix of $s_{0..j}$ and when $\ell < j$ the prefix is *proper*. Similarly, $\langle e, p \rangle_{0..j}$ denotes $\langle e_0, p_0 \rangle, \langle e_1, p_1 \rangle, \ldots, \langle e_j, p_j \rangle$. We use "[" and "]" as an alternate form of parenthesis to aid the eye in recognizing the formula's syntactic structure

[4]A notion of *weak* accountability has also been proposed [8]. However, deciding weak accountability in general is co-NP-complete, so we do not discuss it here, as the current paper focuses on practical issues.

[5]Passing an action's parameter values into obligations that are assigned when the action is performed must be permitted only with care. Specifically, a parameter must not be permitted to define the action part of the new obligation. This is necessary for enforcing the separation of discretionary and obligatory actions and thereby preventing cascading. For example, *assignProjObl* cannot be made obligatory because it is a discretionary action. This means that *assignProjObl* must be authorized by a separate policy rule for each obligatory action that *assignProjObl* can be used to assign.

already in the pool. For instance, there may be no other user to whom Bob's obligation can be assigned. Simply removing the obligation might be unacceptable, either because the action is required in its own right or because some later obligation depends on its having been performed. Sometimes there will be no satisfactory solution, as when a key employee leaves the company. However, to assist Joan in managing the situation when a solution exists, we provide the designs of tools that support finding such a solution. These designs will be presented below in section 5.

2.6 Avoiding Violations of Accountability: Complexity and Planning

In the previous section, scenarios 1 and 2 led to an action being denied, while 3 led to a possible need to reassign obligations to users that may not currently be authorized to perform them. Suppose that Joan wants to give Bob's black-BoxTest obligation to Carl, but Carl does not currently have the roles to perform it. Joan needs to find a sequence of administrative actions that can be performed to enable Carl to complete the test at the appointed time. This entails giving Carl a new role. In the simplest instance, doing so does not conflict with any other obligations already in the pool. So Joan just needs to find a sequence of administrative actions that can be performed by various administrators that results in Carl receiving the necessary role. In this case we assume that there are no administrative actions that will modify Carl's roles between the current time and the time at which the blackBoxTest obligation is to be performed.

The simple class of instances of our problem illustrated here defines a subproblem that is essentially identical to the *role reachability* problem [18]. In this problem, one seeks a sequence of grants and revokes that modifies the current role memberships of a given user to include a given role. Determining whether there is such a sequence that leads to the user having a given role is, in the unrestricted case, PSPACE-complete [18]. This is particularly daunting because RBAC systems used in practice often have hundreds of roles, thousands of users, and millions of objects [5].

The fact that the role reachability problem can be reduced trivially to this subproblem establishes the intractability of one of the techniques that we propose to use for accountability restoration, namely obligation reassignment. For dealing with a generalized variant of the role-reachability problem that arises in this context, we have developed an AI planning tool that is often able to find suitable action sequences (provided the sequences are not too long) [16]. There are several other aspects of our problem for which an administrator attempted to restore accountability will also require tool support. The design and use of such tools is taken up in section 5 below.

3. GENERAL ARCHITECTURE

This section presents our architecture for managing user obligations that can depend on and affect authorization (figure 1). We assume that obligations are triggered by two classes of events: *controllable events* and *uncontrollable events*. Controllable events are originated by actions taken by users of the local system. (*E.g.*, when Alice attends a conference, she may incur an obligation to later present a conference summary to members of her home organization. Presumably attending the conference is a controllable event.) Uncontrollable events are generated by the environment. (*E.g.*, a policy might require that when a court order

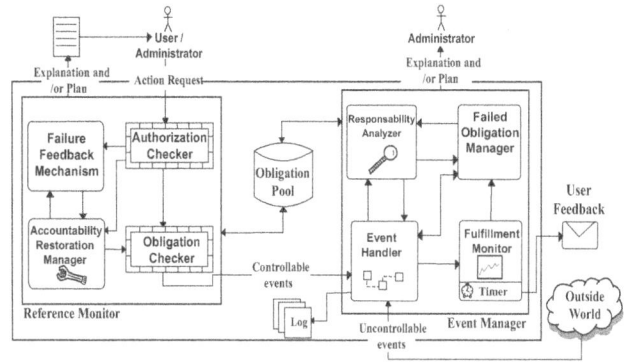

Figure 1: Obligation Architecture

arrives, a company lawyer must review and respond. Receiving a court order is an uncontrollable event.) In figure 1, arrows represent messages that can be exchanged among software components and users. The direction of the arrow indicates the direction of message flow. Let us consider the main components of the architecture.

Reference Monitor. The standard function of a reference monitor is to disallow actions that are not authorized. We augment this requirement so that the reference monitor also disallows controllable actions when the obligations that they cause to be incurred, or the action itself, would violate the accountability property of the system. The Reference Monitor is further divided into four main components.

(a) **Authorization Checker** It checks standard authorization.

(b) **Obligation Checker** It is responsible for denying actions that violate the accountability property of the system. The Obligation Checker can deny an action if one of the following cases occurs. (*i*) The action is administrative and can make an obligated user unable to perform her obligation. (*ii*) The action causes an obligation to be incurred that will not be authorized. (*iii*) The action introduces an administrative obligation that will make an obligated user unable to perform a subsequent obligation.

Denying an action that violates accountability is an attempt to maintain accountability incrementally as often as possible. By providing an algorithm for checking accountability and evaluating it empirically, it has been shown [15] that one can efficiently maintain accountability of a large scale system in practice.

An additional function of this component is to select or help a user to select among the policy rules that can be used to authorized the desired action (see section 2). When multiple rules preserve accountability, the appropriate rule to select may be application dependent. In some cases, it may even be appropriate to let the user requesting the action make the selection. When this is inappropriate, for example, due to performance issues, a range of policy-driven alternatives are possible.

(c) **Failure Feedback** When the Obligation Checker component denies an action because it would violate accountability, the failure feedback component attempts to present the user with an alternate plan of action that will enable her to accomplish her desired actions without violating accountability. The user has the option of accepting the plan, or not . If accepted, the actions in the plan become obligations. The plan can involve actions for the user herself and for others. If the plan contains actions for other users, they must also agree to the plan before the system will convert the plan into user obligations. If no plan is found, the action will be denied and the user will be notified. This problem is called the Action Failure Feedback Problem ($AFFP$). Pontual *et al.* [16] present a formal specification of the $AFFP$, complexity analysis, an AI-based approach that can encode instances of the AFFP problem as an input to a partial order AI planner, and empirical evaluation of the resulting tool.

(d) **Accountability Restoration Manager** When an obligation is violated, unavailable, or some external uncontrollable event results in the violation of the system's accountability, this is detected by the failed obligation manager module (in the event manager) that will be discussed shortly in detail. When the administrator is notified of the violation, he uses the automatic tool support provided by the Accountability Restoration Manager to restore accountability. For that, we consider that the obligation pool is an object that an administrator can edit. Strategies for doing so are discussed in section 5.

Event Manager. The major responsibilities of the event manager are altering authorization state of the system according to administrative events, monitoring obligation status, and recognizing responsible users for obligation violation. The main components of it are presented next.

(a) **Event Handler** It observes controllable and uncontrollable events, and is also responsible for performing administrative events, modifying the authorization state accordingly. It also adds new obligations to the obligation pool, per the policy rule requirements. All the events are also logged by the event handler.

(b) **Fulfillment Monitor** It is responsible for checking whether an observed event constitutes the fulfillment of a pending obligation. It uses a timer to keep track of the obligations that are nearing their deadlines and notifies the appropriate users. Finally, it detects violated obligations and notifies the Failed Obligation Manager.

(c) **Failed Obligation Manager** It is responsible for determining the violated and unavailable obligations. After that, it determines all the obligations that are affected by them. (See section 5.)

(d) **Responsibility Analyzer** It is important for organizational managers to be aware of which employees are diligent and which are not. This component provides this information.

Assuming the system was initially in an accountable state, any single obligation violation is the responsibility of the user charged with fulfilling it. This also holds when multiple obligations are violated concurrently. When an administrative obligation is violated other obligations may inevitably also be violated due to lack of permissions.

This component may not be run immediately each time an obligation goes unfulfilled. Consequently, it is possible that this component is presented with multiple obligations that have been violated, some of which were supposed to be performed by users that had inadequate permissions. In this case, the user that is ultimately responsible for a violation is the one that had the permissions required to perform the administrative obligation to grant the missing permission. This module determines which users are responsible for causing each violation. Identifying users that are ultimately responsible for violations is known as the *blame assignment problem*, which is solved by this module.

Irwin *et al.* [9] provide a general approach for recognizing users responsible for accountability violation. However, they do not provide appropriate treatment to obligations incurred by unavailable users. We present techniques such as, reassignment of obligations, removal of obligations *etc.*, that an administrator can use to manage such obligations.

The architecture presented above is our vision for managing user obligations as part of the system's security policy. As mentioned at various points in the discussion above, several parts of this architecture (Obligation Checker, Failure Feedback, and Responsibility Analyzer) have been designed, implemented, and empirically evaluated elsewhere. The remaining components are subjects of on-going and future work. The current paper focuses on the Accountability Restoration Manager.

Restoring accountability is a complex problem. It requires consideration of characteristics of obligations such as their importance, purpose, and level of urgency. The capabilities of individual users that might be candidates for assuming obligations previously assigned to others must also be considered. Therefore, a fully operational, deployed obligation system must include human actors to handle or help with accountability restoration. Thus the Accountability Restoration Manager includes a human, probably the same human as is generally responsible for obligation system management. It is on the techniques and tools used by this individual to restore accountability that the current paper focuses.

4. OBLIGATION DEPENDENCIES

Our system uses a reference monitor that attempts to maintain accountability by denying action requests that would violate it. Accountability can be violated nevertheless. For instance, suppose that obligations b_1 and b_2 are scheduled so that b_1 happens first and grants necessary permissions for performing b_2. If b_1 is violated, b_2 may no longer be authorized, so the obligation pool ceases to be accountable. A similar situation arises when a manager or administrator learns ahead of time that, if nothing is done to prevent it, b_1 will become violated owing to user or resource unavailability. As the violation is anticipated before it has occurred, in this latter case it may be easier to recover gracefully than in the former. In both cases, however, methods for restoring or preserving accountability are needed.

Ultimately, when accountability is violated, a human obligation system manager will generally have to participate in its restoration. To facilitate her task, we can provide information about dependencies among obligations that are relevant to the various approaches available to her for this purpose. For instance, in the previous example, b_2 cannot be fulfilled if b_1 is violated, as b_1 provides the necessary permissions for b_2. When an obligation is or will be affected by the (eventual) violation of another obligation, we say that the former has a dependency on the latter obligation. Changes in the obligation pool that affect accountability can have their impact on other obligations indirectly. The obligation system manager is best served by being provided an aggregation of dependencies that connect multiple obligations to the source of the disruption of accountability. We call the aggregate we define for this purpose an *obligation-pool slice*. In this section, after discussing each form of dependence, we return to the notion of a slice.

Various forms of dependence arise depending on the strategy one tries to use to restore accountability. In this section,

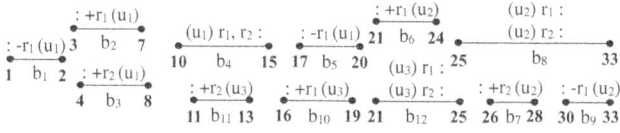

Figure 2: Dependencies among obligations

we identify three different categories of dependencies on this basis. When one plans simply to let an obligation go unfulfilled ("removing" the obligation), then one is concerned only with the impact this will have on later obligations via the authorization state. We call this *positive dependence*. (Positive dependence can also arise when the violated obligation revokes a role if the second obligation is an administrative action that requires the target user not to have the role.) When one plans to reschedule an unfulfilled obligation, it may be necessary also to reschedule later obligations that have a positive dependence on it. When this is done, the second obligation is moved later in time, possible moving it past some other obligation that modifies the authorization state in a way that interferes with the execution of the second obligation. We call this interference *negative dependence*. Finally, when one obligation is rescheduled to occur after an obligation it once preceded, the authorization state in which a third, later obligation must be executed may be different as a result. For instance, if an obligation is moved past another that would reverse a change made by the first to the authorization state, the third obligation would no longer be exposed to an authorization state in which the reversal has been applied. We call this third form of dependence *antagonistic dependence*.

The notions of dependency among obligations presented here are based only on the authorization requirements of the obligations. There could be other notions of dependency, such as functional dependencies that expresses requirements on the temporal ordering of obligations. However, we do not consider this here.

EXAMPLE 6 (OBLIGATIONS). *We use the obligation pool pictured in figure 2 to illustrate the various notions of dependencies. Each obligation has a unique identifier, b_i. The roles r_j that the obligated user requires to perform his obligation are given on the left hand side of the colon, along with the obligated user u_k. In this example u_1 executes b_4, u_2 executes b_8, u_3 executes b_{12}, and u_0 is responsible for the rest. When multiple policy rules enable the obligation, the requirements for each rule are presented in separate annotations, as illustrated by obligation b_8. When one rule requires multiple roles, they are listed in the same annotation, as illustrated by obligation b_4. For economy of space, we have chosen an example that avoids the need to represent negative preconditions. When an obligation performs an administrative action (grant or revoke), the right hand side of the colon indicates the effect of this action. When an obligation grants a role r to a user u, this is indicated by $+r(u)$ on the right hand side of the colon; when it revokes r from user u, this is indicated by $-r(u)$. (E.g., obligation b_1 revokes the role r_1 from the user u_1). In the case of non-administrative obligations, this part of the annotation is empty. The current user role assignment we consider for the example is $\gamma.UA = \{\langle u_0, r_0 \rangle \langle u_1, \varnothing \rangle \langle u_2, r_0 \rangle \langle u_3, \varnothing \rangle\}$.*

DEFINITION 7 (POSITIVE DEPENDENCY). *Given a system state $s = \langle U, O, t, \gamma, B \rangle$, a set of policy rules $\mathcal{P}$, an obli-*

gation $b \in B$ and a set of pending obligations $\hat{B} \subseteq B$, such that $(\forall \hat{b} \in \hat{B} \cdot \hat{b}.end < b.end)$. We say b has a positive dependence on $\hat{B}$, denoted by $\hat{B} \xrightarrow{+} b$, if and only if removing $\hat{B}$ from B yields an obligation pool in which b is not guaranteed to be authorized during its entire time interval and $\hat{B}$ is a minimal set satisfying this property.

The arrow direction signifies that $\hat{B}$ is establishing in the authorization state the necessary permissions required by b.

EXAMPLE 8. *In figure 2 we have the following positive dependencies $\{b_2\} \xrightarrow{+} b_4$, $\{b_3\} \xrightarrow{+} b_4$, $\{b_6\} \xrightarrow{+} b_8$, $\{b_7\} \xrightarrow{+} b_8$ and $\{b_{11}, b_{10}\} \xrightarrow{+} b_{12}$. Here, $\{b_2\} \xrightarrow{+} b_4$ and $\{b_3\} \xrightarrow{+} b_4$, because without b_2 and b_3, b_4 cannot be performed. The same is true in the case of obligation b_8. Note that b_{12} will be authorized if one of b_{10} and b_{11} is absent, but when both of them are absent, b_{12} will be not be authorized. Thus, b_{12} does not have a positive dependence on b_{10} or b_{11} individually, but does have a positive dependence on the set $\{b_{11}, b_{10}\}$.*

DEFINITION 9 (NEGATIVE DEPENDENCY). *Assume we are given a system state $s = \langle U, O, t, \gamma, B \rangle$, a set of policy rules $\mathcal{P}$, an obligation $b \in B$ and a set of pending obligations $\hat{B} \subseteq B$. We say that b has a negative dependence on $\hat{B}$ if $\hat{B}$ is a minimal set satisfying the following property. The start time of b is before that of each element of $\hat{B}$ (i.e., $\forall \hat{b} \in \hat{B} \cdot \hat{b}.start > b.start$) and if b is rescheduled so that it starts after obligation in $\hat{B}$, then b is no longer guaranteed to be authorized throughout its entire time interval. In this case we write $b \xleftarrow{-} \hat{B}$.*

The direction of the arrow indicates that $\hat{B}$ yields an authorization state in which b may not be authorized during its entire time interval.

EXAMPLE 10. *In figure 2, we have $b_4 \xleftarrow{-} \{b_5\}$ due to the fact that if we reschedule b_4 after b_5, it will not be authorized.*

DEFINITION 11 (ANTAGONISTIC DEPENDENCY). *Given a system state $s = \langle U, O, t, \gamma, B \rangle$, a set of policy rules $\mathcal{P}$, and three obligations $b_1, b_2, b_3 \in B$, we say that b_2 has an antagonistic dependence on b_1 via b_3, denoted by $b_2 \xrightarrow{b_3} b_1$, if inverting the order of b_1 and b_2 may result in there being a point during the interval of b_3 at which b_3 is not authorized.*

EXAMPLE 12. *In figure 2, we have the following antagonistic dependencies $(b_1 \xrightarrow{b_4} b_2)$, $(b_6 \xrightarrow{b_8} b_9)$ and $(b_7 \xrightarrow{b_8} b_9)$. b_7 and b_9 have an antagonistic dependency via b_8 although they consider different roles (viz., r_2 and r_1, respectively).*

Having defined the dependence relations of interest, we now consider how to aggregate the dependencies at a higher level where they are more easily applied by the obligation system manager for the purpose to restoring accountability. The aggregation is a structure we call an *obligation-pool slice*, or simply *slice*. A slice is a subset $\hat{B}$ of a given obligation pool B. Intuitively, $\hat{B}$ consists of obligations that interact directly or indirectly with an input set of obligations $B_0 \subseteq B$ via various dependence relations relevant to the authorization requirements of obligations. The slice satisfies $B_0 \subseteq \hat{B} \subseteq B$ and is given by the closure of B_0 under some operation defined in terms of the dependence relation. The formal definition of each specific slice depends on the nature of the dependence relation used in its construction. We next provide these formal definitions, along with theorems that characterize them in terms of accountability, as needed for their use in accountability restoration.

DEFINITION 13 (POSITIVE DEPENDENCY SLICE).
Assume we are given a system state $s = \langle U, O, t, \gamma, B \rangle$, a set of policy rules $\mathcal{P}$, and a set of pending obligations $B_0 \subseteq B$. $PS_B(B_0)$ is the positive dependency slice of B with respect to B_0 if it is given by $PS_B(B_0) = B_p$ in which $B_p \subseteq B$ is the smallest set that satisfies the following requirements:

- $B_0 \subseteq B_p$
- $\forall b \in B \cdot (\exists \check{B} \cdot (\check{B} \subseteq B_p \wedge \check{B} \xrightarrow{+} b) \longrightarrow (b \in B_p))$

Note that this notion of slice would be useful when the administrator is considering removal of pending obligations as (part of) her strategy for restoring accountability. The following theorem shows the utility of this slice with respect the to administrators objective of leaving the obligation pool in an accountable state.

THEOREM 14. *Given an accountable system state $s_0 = \langle U, O, t, \gamma, B \rangle$, a policy $\mathcal{P}$, a set of obligations $B_0 \subseteq B$, and $B_p = PS_B(B_0)$, the state given by $s = \langle U, O, t, \gamma, B \setminus B_p \rangle$ is accountable.*

DEFINITION 15 (FULL DEPENDENCY SLICE). *Assume we are given a system state $s = \langle U, O, t, \gamma, B \rangle$, a set of policy rules $\mathcal{P}$, and a set of obligations $B_0 \subseteq B$. The full dependency slice of B with respect to B_0, denoted by $FDS_B(B_0)$ is given by the smallest set B_f that satisfies the following properties:*

- $B_0 \subseteq B_f$
- $\forall b \in B \cdot (\exists \check{B} \cdot (\check{B} \subseteq B_f \wedge ((\check{B} \xrightarrow{+} b) \vee (b \xleftarrow{-} \check{B}))) \longrightarrow (b \in B_f))$
- $\forall b \in B \cdot (\exists b_1 \in B_f \cdot \exists b_2 \in B \cdot ((b \xrightarrow{b_2} b_1) \vee b_1 \xrightarrow{b} b_2) \longrightarrow (b \in B_f))$

When the administrator is considering rescheduling the violated obligations and all its dependent obligations, this notion of slice would be used.

THEOREM 16. *Given an accountable system state $s_0 = \langle U, O, t, \gamma, B \rangle$, a policy $\mathcal{P}$, a set of obligations $B_0 \subseteq B$, and $B_f = FDS_B(B_0)$, the state given by $s = \langle U, O, t, \gamma, B \setminus B_f \rangle$ is accountable.*

Please consult [1] for detailed proof of theorem 14 and 16.

5. RESTORING ACCOUNTABILITY

In this section, we present several possible techniques by which an administrator can restore accountability. The selection among the techniques is application and system-requirement dependent. In practice, the administrator will use a combination of these techniques. Some obligations will, of course, be too important just to drop. Among these may be user-level obligations that do not change the authorization state. Achieving the intended changes to the authorization state might also influence the administrator's decision whether to drop obligations (including the violated ones), or instead to reschedule or reassign them.

It is important to bear in mind that restoring accountability while preserving all the desired obligations is not always possible. For instance, if an obligation with a hard deadline has been violated, this situation cannot be reversed. Furthermore, even when a solution exists, enabling us to reorganize existing obligations and add new obligations with the result that all desired obligations are fulfilled, it is not always going to be possible to find that solution in practice, as the problem is fundamentally intractable. Thus the support techniques and tools we discuss in section can at best

increase the likelihood of finding a satisfactory solution. In the following we take B_0 to be the set of obligations that either have been violated or are unavailable.

Removal of Obligations: When applying the *removal strategy*, the user removes the entire positive slice $B_p = PS_B(B_0)$ from the obligation pool B. The resulting obligation pool is accountable, as shown by theorem 14. Among the strategies for restoring accountability, this one modifies the fewest obligations, owing to the minimality of the sets in the forward dependency relation. Of course it may often be undesirable, depending on the importance of some of the obligations in the positive slice. However, sometimes there is really no alternative, since some deadlines are hard.

Rescheduling of Obligations: In this approach, we can take advantage of the fact that some pairs of obligations in $B_f = FDS_B(B_0)$ are independent. In particular, B_f can be partitioned into sets such that obligations from different sets are independent on one another. In this case, each partition can be rescheduled independently of one another. We denote each partition of B_f as $B_f^i \subseteq B_f$, $0 \leq i \leq |B_0|$.

EXAMPLE 17 (PARTITIONS OF B_f). *Using the example in figure 2, let the current system time be 15, and that b_4 and b_{11} have been violated. Thus, $B_f = \{b_4, b_{11}, b_5\}$ creates two partitions $B_f^1 = \{b_4, b_5\}$ and $B_f^2 = \{b_{11}\}$.*

For each B_f^i, we find the set of obligations $B_0^i \subseteq B_f^i$ that have already been violated or are unavailable. We assume an obligation $\tilde{b}$ has already been violated if $\tilde{b}.start \leq t_c$ where t_c is the current system time. We use t_s and t_e to denote the earliest start time and the latest end time among all the obligations in B_0^i. Next, we find the obligation b_n with the earliest start time among all the obligations in $B_f^i \setminus B_0^i$. We then check whether it is possible to reschedule the obligations in B_0^i after t_c but before $b_n.start$ $((t_e - t_s) < (b_n.start - t_c))$. If so, we reschedule all the obligations in B_0^i after t_c keeping their original relative distance. If this is not the case, then we add b_n to the set B_0^i, and repeat the steps presented above (*i.e.*, compute t_e, and find a new b_n), until we find a time interval that is large enough to fit all the obligations in the current B_0^i. If no such intervals are found, we shift all the obligations in B_f^i so that the obligation with the earliest start time is scheduled at time $t_c + 1$ and the obligations maintain their original relative positioning. The intuition behind this approach is that all the obligations that can interact with each other will maintain their original relative positions and will be authorized.

EXAMPLE 18 (RESCHEDULING OF OBLIGATIONS). *the current time be 8 and b_2 and b_3 have been violated. If we reschedule b_2 and b_3, we need to reschedule the entire set $B_f = \{b_2, b_3, b_4, b_5\}$. The new time windows for the set could be $b_2 = [21, 25]$, $b_3 = [22, 26]$, $b_4 = [28, 33]$ and $b_5 = [35, 38]$.*

In some cases, it might not be possible to use the above approach. For instance, it may be essential that one of the obligations not be delayed. In such cases, the administrator must keep the time window of this obligation fixed, and attempt reschedule the other dependent obligations around it. However, if this is not possible, then the administrator may consider shrinking the width of some of the dependent obligations' time windows. Note that, every time the administrator tries to shrink the time window of an obligation, the reference monitor needs to check if the system is still accountable. It is up to the administrator to decide which obligations' time windows can be shrunk and by how much.

Reassignment of Obligations: In this strategy, the administrator reassigns new users to the obligations that are unavailable. When an obligation's window has already passed, this approach must be combined with rescheduling. This case is discussed below under "hybrid strategy." Along with the reassigning technique, the administrator may use an AI-planner [16] to check what other actions (*e.g.*, giving required permissions to the new users) are required in order to transfer these obligations to the new users.

Addition of Obligations: In this strategy the administrator adds new obligations in order to make the system accountable. (*E.g.*, let us consider obligation b_x needs a permission given by b_y which is scheduled before b_x. If b_y is violated, then the administrator can restore accountability by adding an obligation before b_x that grants the necessary permissions to it.) Again, the administrator can utilize the AI-planner presented in [16] to identify the new obligations she needs to add to the obligation pool to restore accountability when it has been violated.

Hybrid Strategy: Obligations can be deemed by the administrator to have different levels of importance. It may be reasonable to remove some obligations, while other must be performed according to their original schedule. Moreover, some obligations that have been violated may have had hard deadlines and cannot be rescheduled or reassigned. Thus, the administrator requires the flexibility to apply a mixture of strategies to restore accountability. We propose a *hybrid strategy* for this purpose. In it, the administrator takes an incremental approach to constructing a solution to the accountability violation. The techniques presented above are applied to different violated or unavailable obligations and different portions of their slices.

Suppose the administrator decides to divide B_0 into three subsets: obligations that must be removed (B_0^{Rem}); obligations that must be reassigned (B_0^{Rea}); and obligations that must be rescheduled (B_0^{Res}). Of course, these choices cannot be made independently of one another. For instance, it is not possible to reschedule an obligation that depends on an obligation that will be removed. On the other hand, some obligations can be both rescheduled and reassigned.

The administrator then computes the positive dependency slice of B_0^{Rem}, denoted by B_p^{Rem}, and the full dependency slice for B_0^{Res}, denoted by B_f^{Res}. As discussed in "removal of obligations", if the administrator needs to remove the obligations in B_0^{Rem}, she also has to remove the obligations in B_p^{Rem}. Moreover, for rescheduling obligations in B_0^{Res}, she also has to reschedule obligations in B_f^{Res}. If B_p^{Rem} and B_f^{Res} intersect then removing B_p^{Rem} could yield an authorization state where rescheduling obligations in $B_f^{\mathrm{Res}} \setminus B_p^{\mathrm{Rem}}$ would not yield an accountable system. When B_p^{Rem} either contains any non-administrative obligation that is important or contains any administrative obligation that yields an authorization state necessary for discretionary actions, then she can not also remove the set B_p^{Rem} to yield an accountable system. In such cases, she tries to find a maximal subset of B_0^{Rem}, denoted by $\hat{B}_0^{\mathrm{Rem}}$, so that the positive slice of it has neither any intersection with the full dependency slice of $(B_0^{\mathrm{Rem}} \setminus \hat{B}_0^{\mathrm{Rem}}) \cup B_0^{\mathrm{Res}}$ nor does it contain any obligations that the administrator is unwilling to remove.

If she can find such a maximal subset, she can remove the obligations in the positive slice of of $\hat{B}_0^{\mathrm{Rem}}$. Then, she can reschedule the full dependency slice of $(B_0^{\mathrm{Rem}} \setminus \hat{B}_0^{\mathrm{Rem}}) \cup B_0^{\mathrm{Res}}$.

Finally, for reassigning the obligations in B_0^{Rea} she can use the approach discussed in "reassignment of obligations".

Rescheduling the full dependency slice of $(B_0^{\mathrm{Rem}} \setminus \hat{B}_0^{\mathrm{Rem}}) \cup B_0^{\mathrm{Res}}$ can also introduce incompatibility. For instance, the administrator might not want to reschedule some obligations in the full dependency slice of $(B_0^{\mathrm{Rem}} \setminus \hat{B}_0^{\mathrm{Rem}}) \cup B_0^{\mathrm{Res}}$ because of their urgency. We can address this problem in a manner similar to that discussed under "rescheduling of obligations".

Each time an administrator uses one of the techniques presented above to restore accountability, it is the system's responsibility to ensure that it is still in an accountable state. This can be checked using the algorithm in [15].

6. RELATED WORK

Many obligation models have been proposed, ranging from largely theoretical [4,7,11] to more practical [2,3,6,10,12,19].

Ni *et al.* [12] presented a concrete model for obligations that interact with permissions based on PRBAC [13] that handles repeated obligations, pre and post-obligations and also conditional obligations. They also presented two algorithms to analyze the dominance and infinite obligation cascading properties. In addition, they pointed to other important issues that one needs to consider when implementing a real obligation system, namely, techniques for analyzing unfulfillable obligations, sanctions and reward mechanisms. Their obligation model is more expressive than ours. However, they do not address how to decide accountability in such a model. In the same vein, they also do not investigate the impact of unfulfilled obligations. In this regard, they identify some of the same problems we try to address in this work and in our previous work.

Casassa and Beato [3] provide a formal framework to enforce and specify privacy obligation policies. In their model, they allow user and system obligations. Obligations can be triggered by time or events, and they use a special kind of action called *on violation actions* for restoring the security state of the system when some user obligations are violated. Such actions allow the system to take some counter measures in order to fulfill the missed obligation. By contrast, we give the administrator some tool support in order to handle violated obligations (*e.g.*, finding the responsible user for the missed obligations, finding the obligations that can be affected by the missed obligations, and techniques to restore the accountability of the system).

Katt *et al.* [10] augmented UCON model [14] to support post-obligations. Their system considers two types of obligatory actions *non-trusted obligations* and *trusted obligations*. Trusted obligations are performed by the system, so they consider that they are never violated. Non-trusted obligations however are user obligations and can be violated. They proposed a mechanism that makes decisions based on the status of fulfilment of the non-trusted obligations (*e.g.*, if a client did not pay a bill, the system needs to send a email and a fine to the client). However, they do not consider interaction of authorization systems and obligations.

Hilty *et al.* [7] provide an obligation specification language (OSL) for distributed usage control. They also show how an OSL can be further translated into right expression languages that can be enforced by some existing DRM mechanisms. In contrast to our work, they consider obligations in a data containment mechanism, whereas we consider obligations and their interactions with authorization systems.

7. CONCLUSION

We have presented an architecture for managing user obligations, that affect and depend on authorization, as part of a system's security policy. We suggest to maintain accountability of a system by denying actions violating it. However, there are situations when the accountability property of a system can be violated. For this, we provide some restoration techniques that can be used by the system administrator to restore accountability. We also introduce different notions of authorization dependency among obligations. We also provide formal specification of two different notions of slice that calculates the set of obligations the administrator needs to consider when applying the different restoration techniques given a set of violated obligations.

We considered obligatory actions do not incur obligations and also assumed that the only dependencies obligations can have among them are based only on their authorization requirements. Relaxing these constraints is future work.

8. ACKNOWLEDGEMENT

Ting Yu is partially supported by NSF grant CNS-0716210. William H. Winsborough is partially supported by NSF grants CNS-0716750, CNS-0964710, and THECB ARP 010115-0037-2007. We would like to thank Dr. Lujo Bauer and the anonymous reviewers for their helpful suggestions.

9. REFERENCES

[1] A Framework for Enforcing User Obligations. Technical Report CS-TR-2011-001. The University of Texas at San Antonio.

[2] M. Ali, L. Bussard, and U. Pinsdorf. Obligation Language and Framework to Enable Privacy-Aware SOA. In *Data Privacy Management and Autonomous Spontaneous Security*, volume 5939 of *Lecture Notes in Computer Science*, pages 18–32. Springer Berlin, Heidelberg, 2010.

[3] M. Casassa and F. Beato. On Parametric Obligation Policies: Enabling Privacy-Aware Information Lifecycle Management in Enterprises. In *Policies for Distributed Systems and Networks.*, pages 51 –55, jun. 2007.

[4] D. J. Dougherty, K. Fisler, and S. Krishnamurthi. Obligations and their interaction with programs. In *Proceedings of the 12th European Symposium On Research In Computer Security, Dresden, Germany, September 24-26, Proceedings*, pages 375–389, 2007.

[5] M. P. Gallaher, A. C. Oconnor, and B. Kropp. The Economic Impact of Role-Based Access Control, March 2002. Available at http://www.nist.gov/director/prog-ofc/report02-1.pdf.

[6] P. Gama and P. Ferreira. Obligation policies: An enforcement platform. In *6th IEEE International Workshop on Policies for Distributed Systems and Networks*, Stockholm, Sweden, June 2005. IEEE Computer Society.

[7] M. Hilty, A. Pretschner, D. Basin, C. Schaefer, and T. Walter. A policy language for distributed usage control. In J. Biskup and J. Lopez, editors, *Computer Security - ESORICS 2007*, volume 4734 of *Lecture Notes in Computer Science*, pages 531–546. Springer Berlin, Heidelberg, 2008.

[8] K. Irwin, T. Yu, and W. H. Winsborough. On the modeling and analysis of obligations. In *Proceedings of the 13th ACM conference on Computer and communications security*, pages 134–143, New York, NY, USA, 2006. ACM.

[9] K. Irwin, T. Yu, and W. H. Winsborough. Assigning responsibilities for failed obligations. In *IFIPTM Joined iTrust and PST Conference on Privacy, Trust Management and Security*, pages 327–342. Springer Boston, 2008.

[10] B. Katt, X. Zhang, R. Breu, M. Hafner, and J.-P. Seifert. A general obligation model and continuity: enhanced policy enforcement engine for usage control. In *Proceedings of the 13th ACM symposium on Access control models and technologies*, pages 123–132, New York, NY, USA, 2008. ACM.

[11] N. H. Minsky and A. D. Lockman. Ensuring integrity by adding obligations to privileges. In *Proceedings of the 8th international conference on Software engineering*, pages 92–102, Los Alamitos, CA, USA, 1985. IEEE Computer Society Press.

[12] Q. Ni, E. Bertino, and J. Lobo. An obligation model bridging access control policies and privacy policies. In *Proceedings of the 13th ACM symposium on Access control models and technologies*, pages 133–142, New York, NY, USA, 2008. ACM.

[13] Q. Ni, A. Trombetta, E. Bertino, and J. Lobo. Privacy-aware role based access control. In *Proceedings of the 12th ACM symposium on Access control models and technologies*, pages 41–50, New York, NY, USA, 2007. ACM.

[14] J. Park and R. Sandhu. The uconabc usage control model. *ACM Trans. Inf. Syst. Secur.*, 7(1):128–174, 2004.

[15] M. Pontual, O. Chowdhury, W. Winsborough, T. Yu, and K. Irwin. Toward Practical Authorization Dependent User Obligation Systems. In *Proceedings of the 5th International Symposium on ACM Symposium on Information, Computer and Communications Security*, 2010.

[16] M. Pontual, K. Irwin, O. Chowdhury, W. H. Winsborough, and T. Yu. Failure feedback for user obligation systems. In *The Second IEEE International Conference on Information Privacy, Security, Risk and Trust*, pages 713 –720, 2010.

[17] R. S. Sandhu, V. Bhamidipati, and Q. Munawer. The ARBAC97 model for role-based aministration of roles. *ACM Transactions on Information and Systems Security*, 2(1):105–135, Feb. 1999.

[18] A. Sasturkar, A. Yang, S. D. Stoller, and C. Ramakrishnan. Policy analysis for administrative role based access control. volume 0, pages 124–138, Los Alamitos, CA, USA, 2006. IEEE Computer Society.

[19] V. Swarup, L. Seligman, and A. Rosenthal. A data sharing agreement framework. In *Information Systems Security, Second International Conference, Kolkata, India, December 19-21, Proceedings*, pages 22–36, 2006.

[20] M. Weiser. Program slicing. In *Proceedings of the 5th international conference on Software engineering*, pages 439–449, Piscataway, NJ, USA, 1981. IEEE Press.

Author Index